AMERICAN GOVERNMENT IN ACTION: NATIONAL, STATE, AND LOCAL

AMERICAN GOVERNMENT IN ACTION: NATIONAL, STATE, AND LOCAL

Edited by
KARL M. SCHMIDT
Maxwell Graduate School of Citizenship
and Public Affairs
Syracuse University

DICKENSON PUBLISHING COMPANY, INC., BELMONT, CALIFORNIA

To Paul S. Jacobsen
Inspiring teacher, understanding friend

353
S352a

American Government in Action: National, State, and Local
edited by Karl M. Schmidt

L.C. Cat. Card No.: 67-12286
Printed in the United States of America

PREFACE

Modern democratic government is designed to be the servant, not the master, of the people. Implicit in the concept of government of, by, and for the people is the belief that the people will display the necessary knowledge, understanding and interest in the conduct of their governmental affairs. And yet, increasing complexity seems also to be an inevitable part of modern government. In the United States a rapidly growing population and increasing demands for services are further complicated by a federal system in which national, state, and local governments are more and more intermingled. As one commentator has put it, our triple-layered cake has become increasingly marbleized.

How well do the American people understand and participate in this complex system? Can their understanding be improved? Can their participation be stimulated? These are critical questions for the conduct of American government in action.

Among the more valuable aids to increased understanding of, and greater interest in, government are the incisive, analytical articles that appear regularly in leading periodicals. All too often, however, publication in this format means that the material rapidly vanishes from sight, its lessons hidden away in dusty attics or on inaccessible library shelves. The present volume is the third in a series devoted to making available to the college student and the interested layman a representative selection of such recent articles.

American Government in Action: National, State and Local has been planned for use in college and university courses and in adult-education programs, and is designed for the single-semester course in National, State and Local Government.

This volume developed from an experimental course, Government in Action, which was initiated under a grant from the Fund for Adult Education to University College of Syracuse University and the Carrie Chapman Catt Memorial Fund, affiliated with the League of Women Voters. This grant also permitted a systematic scrutiny of the periodical literature, the selection of articles, and their testing on the adult community leaders who participated in the project. Further trials were subsequently undertaken with the undergraduate students in the American Government and State and Local Government classes at the Maxwell Graduate School, Syracuse University. All these studies indicated that the basic approach was sound; they also suggested that the greatest impact was achieved by using the articles in their entirety, free from editorial cutting.

In selecting the articles, I have sought a range of viewpoints based on a wide spectrum of experience—from that of senators to Supreme Court justices, from Washington correspondents to White House aides, from governors to city managers. The common element in each selection is the insight it provides into the way government actually runs, the dynamics of a govern-

15425

ment in action. My choices may well reveal an editorial bias, the view that government constitutes a most valuable invention of mankind, an institution to be applauded and improved rather than feared and denigrated. It is my further conviction that it is not so much the structure of government as the process that requires better understanding; and that what really matters is less the skeleton of the organization than the flesh and blood of those who staff it. In short, since "government is people," people and the institutions they have created must be the basic subjects of any effective inquiry into government in action.

In the introductions to the chapters, I have briefly examined some common American conceptions and beliefs (many of them erroneous) about the nature of their government. I have then suggested some of the goals and expectations for government commonly shared by Americans. Finally, I have identified some of the significant problems faced in each area. Following this, I have allowed the authors their full, unedited say.

For the encouragement given me in the initial stages of the undertaking, I am deeply indebted to Harlan Cleveland, at that time Dean of the Maxwell School, and to Alexander Charters, then Dean of University College of Syracuse University. For his continuing support in the latter phases, I am grateful to Dean Clifford Winters of University College. But, above all, I must thank both the adult participants and the undergraduate students for their valuable criticism and comments on the materials. To Alfred Cope and Stephen Koff, colleagues who have shared the teaching chores of the program in my absence, my sincere appreciation for their constructive suggestions; and to Mrs. Mary Braundel, who has so capably aided in obtaining the necessary permissions, my warm thanks.

Finally, I am most deeply indebted to the many authors whose insight and understanding constitute the real justification for this book; and I wish to thank their publishers, who have made it possible to share that insight and understanding with the reader. For the selection of the articles and for the introductory passages provided, I, of course, accept sole responsibility.

K.M.S.

CONTENTS

1 THE DEMOCRATIC IDEAL

Before inquiring into the institutions and processes that shape our government in action, it seems appropriate first to examine briefly the democratic ideal— that vague, ill-defined, but nonetheless real set of goals that has governed the thinking of most Americans throughout their history. Although they may possess a varied and sometimes less than accurate understanding of the theory and manner in which their government operates, Americans tend to concur in defining those goals for which it *should* operate. Thus, even extremely hetero- geneous groups agree that, if their ideal of democracy is to be fulfilled in prac- tice, conclusive answers are needed to some half-dozen basic questions.

First, most Americans want to know: "Is the individual the end for which the government has come into being?" Without necessarily ever having heard of the *social compact*—that government is a contract entered into with the consent of the governed—they instinctively suspect those nations where it ap- pears that the individual exists to serve the state and that rule has been imposed against the will of the ruled.

Second, they ask: "Is there equality of opportunity?" Granting that individual differences in ability distinguish people just as much as long and short noses, black, brown, blond, and red hair, their concern is whether the individual may have an equal opportunity to make use of his God-given talents, however abundant or sparse they may be.

Third, they raise the question "Is there freedom of choice?" Although few Americans would argue for any absolute freedom—recognizing that, in the words of the familiar saying, "One's freedom to swing his fist stops where the other fellow's nose begins"—fewer still seem willing to accept more than min- imal limitations on their basic independence.

Fourth, most are concerned with inquiring: "Is there majority rule?" The more sophisticated, concerned with the nationwide hysteria of the McCarthy era and mass displays in such communities as Little Rock, Arkansas, and Ox- ford, Mississippi, add significantly: "In addition to majority rule, are minority rights secure—protected not only in theory but also in practice?" Furthermore, these citizens want to know whether that protected minority accepts the ma- jority decisions—at least until the minority may, by constitutional processes, achieve majority status.

Fifth is the closely related question "Can political differences be peacefully resolved?" Not only on the international level, where the prospect of a hydrogen holocaust may be all too vivid, but on the local scene, where the necessity of day-to-day living with sometimes unpleasant neighbors is all too real, the ma- jority of Americans view *accommodation* as essential. They instinctively recog- nize that the alternatives to coexistence and compromise are but two in number —subjugation or submission. Most Americans automatically reject the latter; and only a few, once they have fully examined the implications, yearn for the former.

Their sixth question deals with their fellow citizens: "Are the people interested and informed, and do they participate in public affairs?" Most Americans agree that in a democracy, the level of government cannot long be sustained at a level above that of the participants. In this respect, Americans look upon themselves and their fellows as both an end and a means to an end. They concede, sometimes reluctantly, that the days are forever vanished when democracy could be absolute ("pure," in the sense of everyone's direct participation), that a representative system has emerged of necessity, and that it is up to the people to select wise and capable leaders. Thus, they are led to inquire: "Are these leaders democratically responsible? Are they willing to guide and inform their followers while remaining responsive to the informed judgments of the rank and file?"

These questions reflect some aspects of the American consensus on the democratic ideal and pinpoint some of the goals and criteria by which governmental performance may be judged. We may keep these questions in mind as we proceed, chapter by chapter, to a more detailed examination of the way American government works in practice. Thus we begin the inquiry into our government in action.

WHAT IS DEMOCRACY?
Walter Lippmann

Walter Lippmann, newspaper columnist and former editor of the *New York World,* is one of America's most distinguished political commentators. He is the author of many books, including *Public Opinion, A Preface to Politics, The Good Society,* and *The Public Philosophy.*

THE UNATTAINABLE IDEAL

A false ideal of democracy can lead only to disillusionment and to meddlesome tyranny. If democracy cannot direct affairs, then a philosophy which expects it to direct them will encourage the people to attempt the impossible. . . .

The private citizen today has come to feel rather like a deaf spectator in the back row, who ought to keep his mind on the mystery off there, but cannot quite manage to keep awake. He knows he is somehow affected by what is going on. Rules and regulations continually, taxes annually and wars occasionally, remind him that he is being swept along by great drifts of circumstance.

Yet these public affairs are . . . for the most part invisible. They are managed, if they are managed at all, at distant centers, from behind the scenes, by

Adapted with permission of The Macmillan Company from *The Phantom Public* by Walter Lippmann. Copyright 1925 by Walter Lippmann. Renewed 1953 by Walter Lippmann.

unnamed powers. As a private person he does not know for certain what is going on, or who is doing it, or where he is being carried. No newspaper reports his environment so that he can grasp it; no school has taught him how to imagine it; his ideals, often, do not fit with it; listening to speeches, uttering opinions and voting do not, he finds, enable him to govern it. He lives in a world which he cannot see, does not understand and is unable to direct. . . .

There is then nothing particularly new in the disenchantment which the private citizen expresses by not voting at all, by voting only for the head of the ticket, by staying away from the primaries, by not reading speeches and documents, by the whole list of sins of omission for which he is denounced. I shall not denounce him further. My sympathies are with him, for I believe that he has been saddled with an impossible task and that he is asked to practice an unattainable ideal. I find it so myself for, although public business is my main interest and I give most of my time to watching it, I cannot find time to do what is expected of me in the theory of democracy; that is, to know what is going on and to have an opinion worth expressing on every question which confronts a self-governing community. And I have not happened to meet anybody, from a President of the United States to a professor of political science, who came anywhere near to embodying the accepted ideal of the sovereign and omnipotent citizen. . . .

The actual governing is made up of a multitude of arrangements on specific questions by particular individuals. These rarely become visible to the private citizen. Government, in the long intervals between elections, is carried on by politicians, officeholders and influential men who make settlements with other politicians, officeholders, and influential men. The mass of people see these settlements, judge them, and affect them only now and then. They are altogether too numerous, too complicated, too obscure in their effects to become the subject of any continuing exercise of public opinion.

Nor in any exact and literal sense are those who conduct the daily business of government accountable after the fact to the great mass of the voters. They are accountable only, except in spectacular cases, to the other politicians, officeholders and influential men directly interested in the particular act. Modern society is not visible to anybody, nor intelligible continuously and as a whole. One section is visible to another section, one series of acts is intelligible to this group and another to that.

Even this degree of responsible understanding is attainable only by the development of fact-finding agencies of great scope and complexity. These agencies give only a remote and incidental assistance to the general public. Their findings are too intricate for the casual reader. They are also almost always too uninteresting. Indeed the popular boredom and contempt for the expert and for statistical measurement are such that the organization of intelligence to administer modern affairs would probably be entirely neglected were it not that departments of government, corporations, trade unions and trade associations are being compelled by their own internal necessities of administration, and by compulsion of other corporate groups, to record their own acts, measure them, publish them and stand accountable for them. . . .

It may be objected at once that an election which turns one set of men out of office and installs another is an expression of public opinion which is neither secondary nor indirect. But what in fact is an election? We call it an expression of the popular will. But is it? We go into a polling booth and mark a cross on a piece of paper for one or two, or perhaps three for four names. Have we expressed our thoughts on the public policy of the United States? Presumably we have a number of thoughts on this and that with many buts and ifs and ors. Surely the cross on a piece of paper does not express them. It would take us hours to express our thoughts, and calling a vote the expression of our mind is an empty fiction.

A vote is a promise of support. It is a way of saying: I am lined up with these men, on this side. I enlist with them. I will follow. . . . The public does not select the candidate, write the platform, outline the policy, any more than it builds the automobile or acts the play. It aligns itself for or against somebody who has offered himself, has made a promise, has produced a play, is selling an automobile. The action of a group as a group is the mobilization of the force it possesses. . . .

I do not wish to labor the argument any further than may be necessary to establish the theory that what the public does is not to express its opinions but to align itself for or against a proposal. If that theory is accepted, we must abandon the notion that democratic government can be the direct expression of the will of the people. We must abandon the notion that the people govern. Instead we must adopt the theory that, by their occasional mobilizations as a majority, people support or oppose the individuals who actually govern. We must say that the popular will does not direct continuously but that it intervenes occasionally. . . .

The attempt has been made to ascribe some intrinsic moral and intellectual virtue to majority rule. It was said often in the 19th Century that there was a deep wisdom in majorities which was the voice of God. Sometimes this flattery was a sincere mysticism, sometimes it was the self-deception which always accompanies the idealization of power. In substance it was nothing but a transfer to the new sovereign of the divine attributes of kings. Yet the inherent absurdity of making virtue and wisdom dependent on 51 percent of any collection of men has always been apparent. The practical realization that the claim was absurd has resulted in a whole code of civil rights to protect minorities and in all sorts of elaborate methods of subsidizing the arts and sciences and other human interests so they might be independent of the operation of majority rule.

The justification of majority rule in politics is not to be found in its ethical superiority. It is to be found in the sheer necessity of finding a place in civilized society for the force which resides in the weight of numbers. I have called voting an act of enlistment, an alignment for or against, a mobilization. These are military metaphors, and rightly so, I think, for an election based on the principle of majority rule is historically and practically a sublimated and denatured civil war, a paper mobilization without physical violence.

Constitutional democrats, in the intervals when they were not idealizing the majority, have acknowledged that a ballot was a civilized substitute for a bullet.

"The French Revolution," says Bernard Shaw, "overthrew one set of rulers and substituted another with different interests and different views. That is what a general election enables the people to do in England every seven years if they choose." . . . Hans Delbruck puts the matter simply when he says that the principle of majority rule is "a purely practical principle. If one wants to avoid a civil war, one lets those rule who in any case would obtain the upper hand if there should be a struggle; and they are the superior numbers." . . .

To suport the Ins when things are going well; to support the Outs when they seem to be going badly, this, in spite of all that has been said about tweedledum and tweedledee, is the essence of popular government. Even the most intelligent large public of which we have any experience must determine finally who shall wield the organized power of the state, its army and its police, by a choice between the Ins and Outs. A community where there is no choice does not have popular government. It is subject to some form of dictatorship or it is ruled by the intrigues of the politicians in the lobbies.

Although it is the custom of partisans to speak as if there were radical differences between the Ins and the Outs, it could be demonstrated, I believe, that in stable and mature societies the differences are necessarily not profound. If they were profound, the defeated minority would be constantly on the verge of rebellion. An election would be catastrophic, whereas the assumption in every election is that the victors will do nothing to make life intolerable to the vanquished and that the vanquished will endure with good humor policies which they do not approve.

In the United States, Great Britain, Canada, Australia and in certain of the Continental countries an election rarely means even a fraction of what the campaigners said it would mean. It means some new faces and perhaps a slightly different general tendency in the management of affairs. The Ins may have had a bias toward collectivism; the Outs will lean toward individualism. The Ins may have been suspicious and non-cooperative in foreign affairs; the Outs will perhaps be more trusting or entertain another set of suspicions. The Ins may have favored certain manufacturing interests; the Outs may favor agricultural interests. But even these differing tendencies are very small as compared with the immense area of agreement, established habit and unavoidable necessity. In fact, one might say that a nation is politically stable when nothing of radical consequence is determined by its elections. . . .

The test of whether the Ins are handling affairs effectively is the presence or absence of disturbing problems. . . . It is my opinion that for the most part the general public cannot back each reformer on each issue. It must choose between the Ins and the Outs on the basis of a cumulative judgment as to whether the problems are being solved or aggravated. The particular reformers must look for their support normally to the ruling insiders.

EDUCATION FOR DEMOCRACY

Education has furnished the thesis of the last chapter of every optimistic book on democracy written for one hundred and fifty years. Even Robert

Michels, stern and unbending antisentimentalist that he is, says in his "final considerations" that "it is the great task of social education to raise the intellectual level of the masses, so that they may be enabled, within the limits of what is possible, to counteract the oligarchical tendencies" of all collective action. . . .

The usual appeal to education as the remedy for the incompetence of democracy is barren. It is, in effect, a proposal that school teachers shall by some magic of their own fit men to have had a free hand in writing the specifications. The reformers do not ask what men can be taught. They say they should be taught whatever may be necessary to fit them to govern the modern world.

The usual appeal to education can bring only disappointment. For the problems of the modern world appear and change faster than any set of teachers can grasp them, much faster than they can convey their substance to a population of children. If the schools attempt to teach children how to solve the problems of the day, they are bound always to be in arrears. The most they can conceivably attempt is the teaching of a pattern of thought and feeling which will enable the citizen to approach a new problem in some useful fashion. But that pattern cannot be invented by the pedagogue. It is the political theorist's business to trace out that pattern. In that task he must not assume that the mass has political genius, but that men, even if they had genius, would give only a little time and attention to public affairs. . . .

At the root of the effort to educate a people for self-government there has, I believe, always been the assumption that the voter should aim to approximate as nearly as he can the knowledge and the point of view of the responsible man. He did not, of course, in the mass, ever approximate it very nearly. But he was supposed to. It was believed that if only he could be taught more facts, if only he would take more interest, if only he would read more and better newspapers, if only he would listen to more lectures and read more reports, he would gradually be trained to direct public affairs. The whole assumption is false. It rests upon a false conception of public opinion and a false conception of the way the public acts. No sound scheme of civic education can come of it. No progress can be made toward this unattainable ideal.

This democratic conception is false because it fails to note the radical difference between the experience of the insider and the outsider; it is fundamentally askew because it asks the outsider to deal as successfully with the substance of a question as the insider. He cannot do it. No scheme of education can equip him in advance for all the problems of mankind; no device of publicity, no machinery of enlightenment, can endow him during a crisis with the antecedent detailed and technical knowledge which is required for executive action. . . .

The fundamental difference which matters is that between insiders and outsiders. Their relations to a problem are radically different. Only the insider can make decisions, not because he is inherently a better man but because he is so placed that he can understand and can act. The outsider is necessarily ignorant, usually irrelevant and often meddlesome, because he is trying to navigate the ship from dry land. That is why excellent automobile manufacturers, literary critics and scientists often talk such nonsense about politics. Their congenital excellence, if it exists, reveals itself only in their own activity. The aristocratic theorists work from the fallacy of supposing that a sufficiently excellent square peg will also fit a round role. In short, like the democratic theorists, they miss the essence of the matter, which is, that competence exists only in relation to function; that men are not good, but good for something; that men cannot be educated, but only educated for something. . . .

Democracy, therefore, has never developed an education for the public. It has merely given it a smattering of the kind of knowledge which the responsible man requires. It has, in fact, aimed not at making good citizens but at making a mass of amateur executives. It has not taught the child how to act as a member of the public. It has merely given him a hasty, incomplete taste of what he might have to know if he meddled in everything. The result is a bewildered public and a mass of insufficiently trained officials. The responsible men have obtained their training not from the courses in "civics" but in the law schools and law offices and in business. The public at large which includes everybody outside the field of his own responsible knowledge, has had no coherent political training of any kind. Our civic education does not even begin to tell the voter how he can reduce the maze of public affairs to some intelligible form. . . .

Education for citizenship, for membership in the public, ought, therefore to be distinct from education for public office. Citizenship involves a radically different relation to affairs, requires different intellectual habits and different methods of action. The force of public opinion is partisan, spasmodic, simpleminded and external. It needs for its direction . . . a new intellectual method which shall provide it with its own usable canons of judgment. . . .

THE ROLE OF THE PUBLIC

If this is the nature of public action, what ideal can be formulated which shall conform to it?

We are bound, I think, to express the ideal in its lowest terms, to state it not as an ideal which might conceivably be realized by exceptional groups now and then or in some distant future but as an ideal which normally might be taught and attained. In estimating the burden which a public can carry, a sound political theory must insist upon the largest factor of safety. It must understate the possibilities of public action. . . .

We cannot, then, think of public opinion as a conserving or creating force directing society to clearly conceived ends, making deliberately toward socialism or away from it, toward nationalism, an empire, a league of nations or any other doctrinal goal. . . .

The work of the world goes on continually without conscious direction from public opinion. At certain junctures problems arise. It is only with the crises of some of these problems that public opinion is concerned. And its object in dealing with a crisis is to help allay that crisis.

I think this conclusion is inescapable. For though we may prefer to believe that the aim of popular action should be to do justice or promote the true, the beautiful and the good, the belief will not maintain itself in the face of plain experience. The public does not know in most crises what specifically is the truth or the justice of the case, and men are not agreed on what is beautiful and good. Nor does the public rouse itself normally at the existence of evil. It is aroused at evil made manifest by the interruption of a habitual process of life. And finally, a problem ceases to occupy attention not when justice, as we happen to define it, has been done but when a workable adjustment that overcomes the crisis has been made. . . .

Thus we strip public opinion of any implied duty to deal with the substance of a problem, to make technical decisions, to attempt justice or impose a moral precept. And instead we say that the ideal of public opinion is to align men during the crisis of a problem in such a way as to favor the action of those individuals who may be able to compose a crisis. The power to discern those individuals is the end of the effort to educate public opinion. The aim of research designed to facilitate public action is the discovery of clear signs by which these individuals may be discerned.

The signs are relevant when they reveal by coarse, simple and objective tests which side in a controversy upholds a workable social rule, or which is attacking an unworkable rule, or which proposes a promising new rule. By following such signs the public might know where to align itself. In such an alignment it does not, let us remember, pass judgment on the intrinsic merits. It merely places its force at the disposal of the side which, according to objective signs, seems to be standing for human adjustments according to a clear rule of behavior and against the side which appears to stand for settlement in accordance with its own unaccountable will.

Public opinion, in this theory, is a reserve of force brought into action during a crisis in public affairs. Though it is itself an irrational force, under favorable institutions, through leadership and decent training the power of public opinion might be placed at the disposal of those who stood for workable law as against brute assertion. In this theory, public opinion does not make the law. But by canceling lawless power it may establish the condition under which law can be made. It does not reason, investigate, invent, persuade, bargain or settle. But, by holding the aggressive party in check, it may liberate intelligence. Public opinion in its highest ideal will defend those who are prepared to act on their reason against the interrupting force of those who merely assert their will. . . .

These in roughest outline are some of the conclusions, as they appear to me, of the attempt to bring the theory of democracy into somewhat truer alignment with the nature of public opinion. I have conceived public opinion to be, not the voice of God, nor the voice of society, but the voice of the interested spectators of action. I have, therefore, supposed that the opinions of the spectators must be essentially different from those of the actors, and that the kind of action they were capable of taking was essentially different too. It has seemed to me that the public had a function and must have methods of its own in controversies, qualitatively different from those of the executive men; that it was a dangerous confusion to believe that private purposes were a mere emanation of some common purpose. . . .

It is a theory which puts its trust chiefly in the individuals directly concerned. They initiate, they administer, they settle. It would subject them to the least possible interference from ignorant and meddlesome outsiders, for in this theory the public intervenes only when there is a crisis of maladjustment, and then not to deal with the substance of the problem but to neutralize the arbitrary force which prevents adjustment. It is a theory which economizes the attention of men as members of the public, and asks them to do as little as possible in matters where they can do nothing very well. It confines the effort of men, when they are a public, to a part they might fulfill, to a part which corresponds to their own greatest interest in any social disturbance; that is, to an intervention which may help to allay the disturbance, and thus allow them to return to their own affairs.

For it is the pursuit of their special affairs that they are most interested in. It is by the private labors of individuals that life is enhanced. I set no great store on what can be done by public opinion and the action of masses.

I have no legislative program to offer, no new institutions to propose. There are, I believe, immense confusions in the current theory of democracy which frustrate and pervert its action. I have attacked certain of the confusions with no conviction except that a false philosophy tends to stereotype thought against the lessons of experience. I do not know what the lessons will be when we have learned to think of public opinion as it is, and not as the fictitious power we have assumed it to be. It is enough if with Bentham we know that "the perplexity of ambiguous discourse . . . distracts and eludes the apprehension, stimulates and inflames the passions."

WHERE THE AMERICAN TRADITION LIVES
Bruce Catton

Bruce Catton received the Pulitzer Prize for History in 1954 for his work *A Silence at Appomattox*. A leading historian of the American Civil War, he is also the author of such books as *War Lords of Washington* and *Glory Road*.

A real national tradition is something that we live by rather than something that we talk about. We seldom try to define it: We feel that we don't have to, tradition—we simply respond to it. We respond to it instinctively, because it is so deeply a part of our lives that it has us in its possession.
because if it is a real, living, moving force—and it is, if it is a genuine national

From *Saturday Review*, July 6, 1957. Reprinted by permission.

The greatest of all American traditions is the simple tradition of freedom. From our earliest days as a people this tradition has provided us with a faith to live by. It has shaped what Americans have done and what they have dreamed. If any one word tells what America really is, it is that one word, Freedom.

This is a word that is eternally growing broader. If any single thing gives us reason to have confidence in this infinite future of the American people it is the fact that this most basic of our traditions is capable of infinite expansion. It does not limit us. On the contrary, it forever invites us to grow—to see beyond the horizon, to look ahead to a fairer and a brighter day, to develop and to strengthen the noble concept of brotherhood by which we live.

I think we can say now that this national tradition is as strong and as healthy as it ever was. Today, as always in the past, its best and strongest defense lies in the reactions which individual Americans make when they find the tradition under attack. The tradition may be a national thing, but it resides finally in the hearts of individual men and women. These men and women do not always bother to work out elaborate rationalizations of their sets of defense. They simply respond instinctively to specific cases. When they encounter a situation which denies the tradition of freedom, an inner force which they do not need to define impels them to go out and do something about it. They move, without thought of what the cost to themselves may be, to put themselves in between the oppressor and the oppressed. They strengthen freedom simply by going ahead and living it.

We find them, quite literally, everywhere. A state legislator in Florida discovers that his stand for school integration makes him a minority of one in his legislature; no matter, he goes on as he had started and attainment of the brotherhood of man comes one step nearer as a result. A Catholic priest in Indiana finds immigrant farm laborers suffering medieval exploitation and injustice; he refuses to walk on the other side of the road but stops to demand that the exploitation and injustice be remedied—and, after months of unremitting effort, finally sees his demand made good; and fifty or sixty human beings move out of peonage into the sunlight of American life. A handful of Protestant ministers risk their careers to stand against bigotry and intolerance in their own Tennessee town—and, after a long struggle see the area in which bigotry and intolerance can operate perceptibly narrowed. A young Oklahoma schoolteacher loses his job in order to make his lone protest against racial discrimination—and, telling why he had done so, gives a noble and eloquent explanation of the spirit that moves Americans who love freedom: "In a thing like this you don't stop to think. You just do what you feel you have to do."

You don't have to stop to think: You just do what you feel you have to do. From the earliest days, the presence of that spirit in the breasts of American men and women has been our most profound national asset. It is where this tradition really lives. Not all the petty malignant forces of reaction—the men who think the people need a guardian and a keeper to guide their way into a blighting conformity; the men who dread freedom unless it be limited to those who think and talk as they themselves do; the men who believe that there should be classes and grades in American citizenship, and dread anything that tends to remove the barriers that set men apart from men—not all of them together, operating in a time of confusion and danger, can summon a simple, instinctive reaction that rises in the breast of the ordinary American when he sees American freedom being cut down.

We seem to have begun, in this country, with a demand for freedom of religious belief—in Plymouth colony and Providence plantation, in William Penn's settlement of Pennsylvania and in the charter for the first colonization of Maryland.

We moved on to see that freedom must also mean freedom from foreign oppression, and fought the American Revolution.

Then we came to see that there must also be freedom from domestic tyranny, and we put together the Constitution of the United States.

We came, as well, to see that freedom has to be unlimited—that it has to apply all across the board, to men of all colors, all races, and all conditions—and we struggled through a terrible Civil War in order to make such an extension of freedom possible.

All of these are not separate freedoms so much as they are varying forms of an undivided whole. For one of the things we have learned in this country is that freedom has to be indivisible. Anything that limits any part of it, for anyone, is a menace to all of us, a threat to the tradition by which we live.

American freedom today is under attack—very often by people who insist that they are trying to defend it. In a short-range view conditions are extremely ominous. Yet I think if we look at our present situation long-range we can see that we have little reason to be afraid. We get waves of reaction in this country, periodically, in times of extreme national stress, and the great national tradition comes under attack—seems, indeed, to be in a fair way to be overwhelmed entirely. But the waves always pass—with however much incidental injustice and oppression for certain individual victims—because the instinct of the American mind and heart which the tradition is based on is, finally, irrepressible.

In the early days of the Republic we had, for instance, the Alien and Sedition Acts. Europe was torn by a great war and by an unpredictable revolutionary movement. America's position seemed insecure; external pressures were becoming all but intolerable, and men hardly knew which way to turn to find national security. Out of this came these almost unbelievably repressive laws. Freedom of the press and freedom of speech were effectively outlawed. It was made a crime to criticize acts of the national administration. Editors who spoke out against these laws were imprisoned. Thomas Jefferson's mail was opened, in the hope that some paragraph or sentence could be found on which he could be arrested. A man who tried to get signatures to a petition to Congress urging repeal of these laws was arrested and sentenced to jail. Lawyers who defended victims of this oppression were denounced by judges as traitors. To all appearances American freedom had been done to death.

All of this lasted two years or more. Then came a change. Jefferson himself, against whom so much of this attack had been directed, became President. The laws expired. The freedom that had been assailed so malevolently was restored —stronger than ever for the very virulence of the onslaught that had been made upon it. Today the men who inspired and supported the Alien and Sedition Laws are remembered only because they have come to symbolize the stupidity and the viciousness of those who tried, briefly and unsuccessfully, to turn backward the mainstream of American life.

Similar things have happened at other times. During the early part of the Civil War a brigadier general in the Union army was called before a Congressional committee and questioned because of suspicion that he had been having traitorous dealings with the Confederates—his real offense being that by following the instructions of his superior, and returning fugitive slaves to their Maryland owners, he had given offense to the powerful and suspicious abolitionists who were rising to dominance in Congress. He was accused of nothing whatever; indeed, he never quite realized that he was even under suspicion; but he was finally removed from command and sent off to prison by a War Department which dared not oppose a powerful Congressional committee, and his career was ruined. He was released, finally—not exactly cleared, because nobody had ever formally accused him of anything, so there was no charge from which he could be cleared—but at least released. And the episode comes down in history as a melancholy illustration of the way in which fear and hysteria, operating together, can lead even a committee of Congress to narrow the area of American freedom and justice.

I have cited two cases out of the past. There are many more that could be cited, some of them, indeed, matters of tolerably recent memory. But the thing to bear in mind is that these spasms to which we are now and then subjected are always of temporary effect. We do come out of them; their authors pass on and are forgotten, surviving only as melancholy footnotes in history; and our great tradition, down the years, grows broader and stronger despite these temporary setbacks.

We are today emerging from the latest of these spasms of terror. We have seen some highly discouraging things in recent years. We have seen an atmosphere in which the mere fact that a man was accused of something was taken as proof of his guilt. We have been reminded of Mark Twain's comment on the reign of terror that prevailed in late medieval times under the Doges of Venice, when a committee on public safety received anonymous accusations against the loyalty of citizens; as Mark Twain remarked, if the committee could find no proof to support an accusation, it usually found the accused guilty on the ground this simply showed how deep and devious and inscrutable the man's villainy really was. We have witnessed an era in which it was widely taken as a crime for an accused person to invoke the Bill of Rights itself in his own defense —as if the provisions of the Bill of Rights were not meant to operate in precisely a time like the present. We have seen times in which no one in authority seemed willing to place the slightest amount of trust in the innate loyalty, good faith, and intelligence of the American people; times which led former Senator Harry

Cain to burst out with the cry: "A whole clique of spies could hardly do as much damage to us as could our failure as a government to have confidence in the people."

We have seen all of this, and we can still see too much of it if we look around carefully. Yet the crest of the wave is passing. It is passing because the American people are responding once more to that deepest and most profound of all of their instincts—the instinct to defend the tradition of freedom when it comes under attack. It is passing because the courts of America have stood firmly in defense of individuals and their liberties. It is passing because many groups and individuals have stood up for the rights of their fellow Americans.

Scientists have made a contribution by their efforts to promote rational discussion of the dangers of too much secrecy about their work. The Congressional committee headed by Representative Moss has thrown much light on the secretive practices of some government agencies. The press, through its reports on the Moss Committee's work and through the efforts of individual newspapermen, has helped to break through some of the official barriers to the free flow of information. The American people are gradually getting the materials for a more factual understanding of Communism in the United States and the world. The events in Hungary have clearly demonstrated the essential falsity of Communist claims to a concern for civil liberties—and have contributed to the decline of the Communists here and in other free countries.

When I say that the crest of the wave is passing I don't mean that no threats to liberty exist. Arbitrary censorship both by private and governmental groups has continued to affect a wide area of American life. Government restrictions on the flow of information are still excessive in some agencies. Much confusion remains in the administration of security measures; some unfair procedures have become institutionalized. The pressures of conformity are still strong in many places. Yet I feel confident that the American tradition will flourish in the future as it has in the past. That tradition, to repeat, is something that lives inside of us. It is not a set of laws; and freedom itself is not simply the absence of restraint. Rather, it is an abiding inner faith that cannot be limited by doubt or by confusion or by fear. It is something built into the American soul, and in the long run it is unconquerable.

The secret of the American tradition is freedom—freedom unabridged and unadulterated, freedom that applies to everybody in the land at all times and places, freedom for those with whom we disagree as well as for those with whom we do agree.

And the secret of freedom, in turn, is—just courage. The kind of courage, welling up instinctively in the breasts of individual citizens, which over and over again leads to the kind of actions that are commemorated in the experiences I have been writing about; the kind of courage which led the poet to cry:

> Yet, freedom, yet, thy banner,
>   torn but flying,
> Stream like the thundercloud
>   *against* the wind—

Freedom rests on courage; and courage, in its turn, rests on faith—on faith in ourselves and faith in our fellows, on faith that the thing which we believe in and which we live by is immortal and everlasting, a fundamental truth of the universe with which we move on toward the future. It is on this faith that our confidence finally rests. For out of this faith come those noble statements which show why this American tradition is in the end invulnerable; statements like that one of the Oklahoma schoolmaster—

"In a thing like this you don't stop to think. You just do what you feel you have to do."

On that spirit, and in that spirit we can go ahead to broaden the great American tradition.

IS DEMOCRACY POSSIBLE?
Robert M. Hutchins

Robert M. Hutchins is President of the Fund for the Republic. A former President of the University of Chicago, he has devoted a lifetime to strengthening the fibers of democracy. He is the author of *Freedom, Education and the Fund: Some Observations on American Education.*

The faith in which I was brought up was as simple and confident as the environment. Democracy was the answer to everything, including the ills of democracy. These ills would be cured by more democracy. The ideal toward which we were moving was the civilization of the dialogue where everybody talked with everybody else about everything; where nobody tried to get his way by force or fraud, where everybody was content to abide by the decision of the majority as long as the dialogue could continue. Democracy meant self-government, and self-government meant primarily participation by the individual, at least through the selection of his representatives, in decisions affecting his life and happiness. Since decisions affecting the citizen's life and happiness were taken not merely by his government, but also by many other institutions, corporations, trade unions, and political parties, for example, the thing to do was to democratize them, as well as the government.

In this view the great crime is to try to prevent other people from speaking up, or to say that there are certain things you won't talk about, or certain people you won't talk to, either at home or abroad. In this view education and communication are of prime importance, because if you can't hear what the

From *Saturday Review*, February 21, 1959. Reprinted by permission.

others are saying, or can't understand it, or if they can't hear or understand you, there can't be any dialogue, and democracy becomes meaningless.

The democratic faith is faith in man, faith in every man, faith that man, if he is well enough educated and well enough informed, can solve the problems raised by his own aggregation.

One advantage of this faith is that it is practically shockproof. Industrialization can sweep the world; nationalism and technology can threaten the extinction of the human race; and population can break out all over. Man can take off from this planet as his ancestors took off from the primordial ooze and try to make other planets from which to shoot. Education can be made trivial beyond belief. The media of communication can be turned into media of entertainment. The dialogue can almost stop because people have nothing to say, or, if they have something to say, no place to say it. And still it is possible to believe that if democracy and the dialogue can continue, if they can be expanded, if they can be improved, freedom, justice, equality, and peace will ultimately be achieved.

Some shocks I have received lately have bothered me a little. The first came when during the excitement of last year I was recommending my democratic panacea as a remedy for the ills of the labor unions to the people on the trade union project of the Fund for the Republic. They informed me that the idea of government by the people had little application to labor unions and that in any event democratic forms in unions were no safeguard against antisocial behavior on their part. In fact, they said, some of the unions in which democratic forms were most conspicuous were the most antisocial.

The second shock came when at the conclusion of my usual tirade against the wild irrationality of our foreign policy I explained to the people on the common defense project of the Fund for the Republic that we should subject that policy to democratic control. My colleagues pointed out to me that in addition to being impossible this was unconstitutional, and had always been regarded as such, and that whatever I might think of the policies followed by the President and the Secretary of State, and however much I might dislike being blown up or suffocated as a result of these policies, the Founding Fathers intended that I should be in precisely this position. At any event, they said, there was no way, particularly in view of the enormous technical problems of modern warfare and international relations, in which the citizens could actually participate in the decisions upon which their lives depended.

The third shock came when I was proposing my usual remedy to the people on the project on political parties, which deals with the political process in a free society. Participation was my watchword. Get out the vote. Or, as the Advertising Council has it, "Vote as You Please, but Please Vote." My associates indicated to me that getting people out to vote when they did not know what they were voting for was not helpful, and might be harmful, to the objects I had in view. Under modern conditions, they said, it might be that responsible political participation and decision by the citizens would prove to be impossible, anyway.

Somewhat shaken, I went to the conference on the Island of Rhodes on Representative Government and Public Liberties in the New States. The basic problem of the conference turned out to be whether government by the people is possible, or even desirable, in the modern world. The sense of relief with which members from the new states welcomed military dictatorships in their countries and with which the Frenchmen present welcomed de Gaulle was a measure of the current disenchantment with democracy. These men saw no way of adjusting democratic institutions to contemporary realities. What they hope for is a period of order in which the most acute problems, like Algeria in France and corruption in Siam, may be solved; after which they may, or may not, try government by the people again.

Eminent European philosophers and political scientists present reassured the members from the new states, three of whose governments turned into military dictatorships while the conference was in session, by telling them that democracy was an illusion in both old and new states, for different reasons. The new states could not expect government by the people because they lacked education, communication, organization, and law. In the old states it had been out of date since the Peloponnesian War, and even then it was not what we mean by democracy now. Pericles, a leader of the Left, struck thousands of voters from the rolls because they could not prove that both their parents were native-born Athenians. Greek democracy was based on a uniformity of ideas and practices appropriate to an extended family group. The kind of government by the people that may be said to have worked in Athens and in the New England town meeting could not possibly work in a large, heterogeneous, industrial, bureaucratic society. The most we could hope for was order, efficiency, and the maintenance of civil liberties, those rights historically carved out against governmental interference with private life. Alexander Pope, whose celebrated lines had always seemed to me as false as they were celebrated, was justified at last:

> For forms of government let fools
>   contest
> Whate'er is best administered is best.

I came away from Rhodes with the foreboding that we might be at the beginning of something new in the last 100 years—a worldwide antidemocratic trend that had little or nothing to do with the intimidations or seductions of the Kremlin. (It was significant that in eight days of discussion no member from any new state said a word about Communism or Russia.) This antidemocratic trend would reverse the aspirations of all men of good will—at least since 1848—for government by the people. It would have alarming connotations for the United States in the realm of foreign policy. It should force us to re-examine the assumption and slogans by which we have lived in the light of the actual operation of our institutions in the new industrialized, polarized, bureaucratic world.

If you ask how my democratic faith is doing

> Whither is fled the visionary gleam,
> Where is it now, the glory and the dream?

I reply that it is still here. Perhaps the gleam is not quite as bright as it used to be, and somewhat more visionary, but it is still here. Yet, even at my age, I cannot long sustain a position to which my reason will not assent. The shocks I have received are recent; and I cannot claim that I have absorbed them or that I know how to repel others in the future. Perhaps what I can do is to communicate the sense of crisis that I feel and to ask others to join in thinking for a moment how that faith can be defended.

The faith rests on the propositions that man is a political animal; that participation in political decisions is necessary to his fulfillment and happiness; that all men can and must be sufficiently educated and informed to take part in making these decisions; that protection against arbitrary power, though indispensable, is insufficient to make either free individuals or a free society, and that such a society must make positive provisions for its development into a community learning together. For this is what political participation, government by consent, and the civilization of the dialogue all add up to.

If we are to become a community learning together, as I insist we can, the first thing we have to do is to make up our minds that we want to learn. We have lived on a note of triumphant philistinism. Here is a characteristically triumphant proclamation made by Carl D. Becker, perhaps the most celebrated American historian of his day, in 1931. He said, "Our supreme object is to measure and master the world, rather than to understand it. . . . Viewed scientifically, it appears as something to be accepted, something to be manipulated and mastered, something to adjust ourselves to with the least possible stress. So long as we can make efficient use of things, we feel no irresistible need to understand them. No doubt it is for this reason chiefly that the modern mind can be so wonderfully at ease in a mysterious universe."

At ease, indeed! Anybody who feels at ease in the world today is a fool. And anybody who would say now that he was content to master and manipulate the environment without bothering to understand how it worked or what to do with it would show first that he did not know what science was, for science is nothing but organized understanding, and second that he had no grasp of the kind of problems we now confront. The great overwhelming problems of our country are how to make democracy a reality, how to survive in the nuclear age, and what to do with ourselves if we do survive. None of these problems is technological, though technology has helped to create all of them, and none of them will yield to the kind of measurement, manipulation, or mastery that Professor Becker had in mind. We may, in fact, reverse his statement of 1931 and come nearer the truth of 1959. Then it would go like this: no doubt it is because we have felt no irresistible need to understand the world that the modern mind can be so wonderfully ill at ease in a mysterious universe.

The next question is, how are we going to learn? History will have trouble with American education in the twentieth century. It will see a people who say they are dedicated to education and who are the richest in the world indifferent to education and unwilling to pay for it. It will see an educational system that delivers less education per dollar than any I can think of, saying that all it needs is more money. The people and the educators are united only in this: They both want education without pain, either intellectual or financial. History will find it hard to explain how a nation that is one, a nation in which the political subdivisions have almost no relation to social or economic life and very little to political life, can entrust its future to these subdivisions by relegating education to them. History will smile sardonically at the spectacle of this great country getting interested, slightly and temporarily, in education only because of the technical achievements of Russia, and then being able to act as a nation only by assimilating education to the Cold War and calling an education bill a defense act.

We might as well make up our minds to it. If our hopes of democracy are to be realized, every citizen of this country is going to have to be educated to the limit of his capacity. And I don't mean trained, amused, exercised, accommodated, or adjusted. I mean that his intellectual power must be developed. A good way to start finding the money that is needed for education would be to kick out of it the subjects, the activities, and the people that make not a contribution to the development of intellectual power. Such an operation would produce just sums. I suggest that two things might be done with this money and with any more that may be needed: first, we should double teachers' salaries, not because all the teachers we have deserve twice as much as they are getting, but because we want to attract the ablest people into the profession; and second, we should establish a national system of scholarships that makes it possible for every citizen of this country to be educated to the limit of his mental capacity, regardless of the financial capacity of his parents.

If life is learning, and I think it is, and if our object is to become a community learning together, education ought to continue throughout life. Here is the great educational opportunity and obligation of the next generation. The education of adults is not only indispensable to the continuation, expansion, and improvement of the dialogue, but it is also an answer to the question of what we are going to do with ourselves if we survive. As automation advances, as new sources of energy are applied in industry, as the hours of labor decline, we have the chance to become truly human by using our new and disturbing leisure to develop our highest human powers to the utmost. Here we can build on the experience of such organizations as the Great Books Foundation, which has succored tens of thousands of refugees from television.

This brings me to the media of mass communications. If our hopes of democracy are to be realized, the media must supply full and accurate information on which the people can base their judgment on public affairs, and they must offer a forum for the discussion of those affairs. I doubt if there are six cities of any size in the United States in which the newspapers come anywhere near meeting these requirements. As for radio and television, with a few distinguished exceptions now and then, they make no attempt to meet them. A dozen years ago the Commission on the Freedom of the Press recommended the establishment of a continuing independent agency, privately financed, to appraise and report periodically on the performance of the media. Everything that has happened since, and especially the use of the most marvelous electronic methods of communication for the communication of the most insignificant material, makes the adoption of this recommendation more urgent every day. If we were well educated and well informed could we make ourselves felt in the realm of political action?

In the Republic as I have described it every act of assent on the part of the governed is a product of learning. Could we learn by doing in politics? Or would the archaic structure of our government and the vast bureaucratic machine that goes creaking on, following the right procedure instead of seeking the right result, prevent us from using our newly won education and information as active, deciding, responsible citizens?

Today the dialogue is impeded by obsolescent practices and institutions from the long ballot to the presidential primary, from the electoral college to the organization of cities, counties, and states. In too frequent elections unknown persons by the hundreds running for insignificant offices, and improper questions, like the dozens submitted at every California election, are presented to the electorate. This is not democracy, but the perversion of it. The political anatomy is full of vermiform appendices, many of them, like Arkansas, inflamed.

Some of these obsolescent practices stop the dialogue in its tracks, like the failure of the FCC and Congress to develop any concept of the public interest, convenience, and necessity. Some of them distort the dialogue by throwing false weights into it, as the electoral college gives a false weight to the large state and the laws on campaign expenditures give money an overwhelmingly false weight in elections. One thing is certain: if our hopes of democracy are to be realized, the next generation is in for a job of institutional remodeling the like of which has not been seen since the Founding Fathers.

Well, suppose we got this remodeling done. Could we then turn ourselves into active, responsible, participating citizens? Wouldn't the bureaucracy, though better, and administering better laws, still have us by the throat? The answer depends partly on our capacity for political invention, which in 1787 was quite large, and partly on what participation means. If we can be equipped for the dialogue and then invent the means by which the bureaucracy can hear it and be made responsive to it, we shall have come a long way from where we are now in relation for example, to the State Department and the Atomic Energy Commission. Then political participation would mean not only what it too often means exclusively now, the ballot, but also participation in the dialogue about the ends and means of the political society. We would be a community learning together, and the bureaucracy would be learning, too.

The notion that the sole concern of a free society is the limitation of governmental authority and that government is best which governs least is certainly archaic. Our object today is not to weaken government in competition with other centers of power, but rather to strengthen it as the agency charged with the responsibility for the common good. That government is best which governs best. Mr. Hoover could see no constitutional way of coping with depression, as Buchanan before him could see no constitutional way of coping with secession. We started out to show in 1932 that our institutions were sufficiently flexible to care for the welfare of all the people. The demonstration was never made. We have got instead the pressure-group state, which cares for the welfare of those who are well enough organized to put on the pressure.

The genealogy of this development is strange. When I was a boy, we knew what stood between us and freedom, justice and equality: It was special privilege. Get rid of special privilege, we said, and the common good will be achieved. In our time pacification has been attained not by getting rid of special privilege, but by extending it, by extending it to those well enough organized to threaten the special privileges under attack.

Is the tariff hurting the farmers? Retain the tariff and subsidize the farmers. Are administered prices hurting labor? Let's have administered wages, too. Is industry demoralized by expense accounts and tax dodges? Let's have featherbedding in labor, too. Is something done by some group antisocial? Let's all of us—all of us who can put on the pressure—be antisocial, too. And if a Federal agency is established to regulate us, never fear, we have the pressure that will shortly make the agency the servant and mouthpiece of the interests it was intended to control. And as we laughingly count our gains at the expense of the public, we can reverently repeat the solemn incantation that helped to make them possible; that government is best which governs best.

The Constitution must protect the citizen against the government. The government must protect him against the pressure groups. The government must protect him against society and the rapacity of organizations in it by seeing to it that these organizations pursue purposes and programs consonant with the common good.

The stresses and strains in our society are obscured for us partly by our preoccupation with Russia, which plays a curious double role in our lives as the devil in our world and as the standard by which we measure our progress. If we weren't getting ahead of Russia, or falling behind her, how could we tell where we were?

Our real problems are also concealed from us by our current remarkable prosperity, which results, in part, from the production of arms that we do not expect to use and in part from our new way of getting rich, which is to buy things from one another that we do not want at prices we cannot pay on terms we cannot meet because of advertising we do not believe.

But beneath these superficial manifestations, fantasies of fear on the one hand and wealth on the other, are moving those great, fundamental, historic forces which will put our institutions and our democratic faith to the test. This is the basic fact of our life as people.

I have never subscribed to the proposition once debated in the Oxford Union, that in the opinion of this House Columbus went too far. Nor can I bring myself to refer to man as he is now referred to in military technology, as a "biomechanical link." If Columbus had not gone so far, man might never have had the chance to become anything more than a biomechanical link. It is still our responsibility, now more than ever, to see to it that government of the people, by the people and for the people does not perish from the earth.

2 POLITICS, POWER, AND PUBLIC PARTICIPATION

Before we can adequately assess the role of politics in the power structure and the decision-making process of democratic government, we must examine the belief systems that determine the attitudes of many Americans toward their political parties.

Underlying most Americans' attitudes is a fundamental contempt for politics; a widespread belief that its practitioners are inevitably corrupt and dishonest. The word *politician* is more often used by them as an epithet than as the name of a profession. Reflecting another basic misunderstanding is the all-too-common statement "Both parties are just the same." On the local level, this misconception frequently takes form in the time-worn saying "There is no Republican, there is no Democratic way to pave a street"; at the polling place, it may be reflected in the conclusion "I'm going to vote for the best man, since the parties are both bad." The individual thus expressing himself often holds an ill-disguised contempt for those who admit to straight-ticket voting. He feels that he is an "independent" and hence possessed of more objective judgment—that he has risen above the level of the political party. To others, the party appears a necessary—or, in some instances, an *unnecessary*—evil. Reinforcing this viewpoint has been the frequency with which political figures blame the other party for all the evil that befalls the nation and claim for their own the credit for all the good. Understandably the public often rejects both sides of the argument and concludes that the parties have no relationship whatsoever to the implementation of public policy—except, perhaps, a negative one. This conclusion has been reflected in the frequent drives to "take politics out of government," to institute nonpartisan elections, and to separate the nomination of candidates from the party process.

Another set of complaints concerns the lack of honesty and the organized graft, fraud, and corruption that are thought by some to be the inevitable concomitants of party operation. These complaints note the regular recurrence of bosses, machines and dictatorial organizations, though frequently without any serious attempt to identify the causal link—a link that would be absent were the parties more democratic.

Still another widely held belief is that political parties are nasty compromisers. *Compromise* is a loaded word on the American scene. For an older generation, it raises visions of Chamberlain, Munich, and umbrellas; for a younger generation, the fear of "giving in to the Communists." Consequently, this view of the party as compromiser is a negative one, suggesting that the party is lacking in principle and concerned only with getting its candidates into office.

Finally, there is the reaction of untold others, who take the ultimate retreat from political responsibility, asking, "What difference does my vote make? After all, I'm only one among millions. Why should I bother?"

In order to establish some firmer ground for our consideration of the readings in this chapter, it seems essential to define as accurately and clearly as possible some of the terms commonly employed by political scientists in the realm of partisan politics. For instance what is a *political party?* Three elements are essential: (a) a *group,* or numbers; (b) some degree of *organization;* and (c) a *common purpose*—certainly the purpose of taking control and accepting responsibility for the conduct of the government. In this definition, the third characteristic distinguishes a political party from a private-interest group. A pressure group may seek to elect candidates and to influence official policy, but it does so without accepting public responsibility.

We frequently hear talk of *principles, issues,* and *policies.* In the partisan context, a *principle* may be defined as a long-held fundamental belief concerning the over-all conduct of government. Thus, one might contend that the Republican Party is a party that holds to a belief in property rights and personal rights, and that the Democratic Party is a party that adheres to a belief in personal rights and property rights. The distinction would lie in the emphasis, or in the order of priority assigned by each. An *issue,* on the other hand, is a specific difference, stemming from a concrete problem that has arisen —a problem for which each party provides a different answer. For example, public housing for low-income groups might constitute a concrete issue, with the Democrats urging a federally subsidized program and the Republicans supporting a state-financed one, or a completely private one. Finally, *policies* are the programs developed by the parties, in line with their fundamental principles, to meet the issues of the day. One example might be a Democratic (or Republican) program to meet the farm problem by providing income supports (or marketing assistance) for small farmers.

Some of these observations may suggest a basic similarity between the two great American political parties. But are the parties as identical as is commonly believed? A certain amount of light may be shed on this question by an examination of the characteristics of the American two-party system. A brief historical survey will serve to focus their many similarities and some of their differences. Both parties accept the Constitution, with its concepts of limited government and popular sovereignty. In this sense, both parties are republican and both are democratic. Neither party strives to overturn the government by extralegal means. Both parties are broad and somewhat lacking in precision. They unquestionably overlap. Nevertheless, year in and year out, there has been a discernible difference in their respective philosophies. This difference has been measurably reflected in their consistently varying approaches to such matters as public housing, farm policy, fiscal policy, aid to education, taxation, social security, unemployment compensation, and—through many an earlier day—the tariff.

Yet often the lines have seemed blurred, particularly since party discipline has seldom proved strong enough to array the partisan troops in orderly, opposed lines. Moreover, there has been a notable looseness attached to party membership; for the most part, the individual voter has remained free to come and go at will. Despite this fluidity, however, there has been a persistence of party adherence, loyalty, and devotion on the part of a substantial majority—indeed, some studies suggest that as many as three out of four partisans never deviate from their paternally inherited political affiliation.

Throughout our nation's life, the alignment of opposing party interests has remained basically the same. Thus, the direct descendants of the early Federalists became Whigs and, later, Republicans. The Jeffersonian Republicans and Republican-Democrats continue in a straight line of succession through the Jacksonian Democrats to become the modern Democratic Party. The Federalist-Republican succession has reflected an ongoing community of interest among the relatively well-to-do and affluent of the society—the businessman and the industrialist, later joined by the farm owner and the craft unionist. The Jeffersonian-Democratic succession has evidenced a general orientation toward the "common man"—at least in the dominant, New Deal wing of the party. The Civil War produced a major shift in the previous homogeneity, preventing the erstwhile Whigs of the reconstructed South from rejoining their Northern colleagues under the Republican banner, and driving them instead into the ranks of a Democratic Party that ever since has been uneasy with their presence.

Finally, a careful evaluation of congressional voting patterns demonstrates the existence of a substantial difference in the "center of gravity" between the two major parties. This legislative record shows that the preponderant voting strength of the more liberal Democratic Party is identifiably to the left of center, that of the more conservative Republicans well to the right.

With some of these background factors in mind, we are now in a position to raise some of the questions that the articles in this chapter discuss. First, what functions are served by the political parties in our governmental system? Numerous observers have suggested that our Constitution—with its separation of powers, its checks and balances, and its varied attempts to insure individual freedom—has set up an essentially unworkable mechanism. They point to the requirement of an electoral-college majority to elect a president, the single-member-district method of congressional election, and the federal system itself; and conclude that these technicalities have created a governing system admirably suited to the slower tempo of the eighteenth century but inadequate to the demands for action of the twentieth. Only the parties, they claim, have provided a bridgework for surmounting these structural barriers. By their nominating devices, the parties provide a limited number of candidates among whom to choose. By their selection, emphasis, and discussion, they stimulate an awareness and knowledge of the issues upon which to base our decisions. Once the election verdict has been rendered, they organize a government to effectuate the mandate, and an opposition to criticize and suggest alternatives.

Second, what are the problems and deficiencies of existing party organization, operation, and behavior? Analysis suggests that many problems arise from a lack of party responsibility—a lack created partly by the imprecision of ideological alignment and partly by the absence of effective discipline in each party. Other problems result from a want of citizen participation in policy making, organizational work, and financial support. Thus, by default, party control often gravitates to the bosses and "fat cats"—the people with time, money, and interest. Finally, it is suggested that the failure of the two parties to centralize in pace with the increasing federalization of our formal government has left political power highly diffuse—in the hands of some three thousand county chairmen for each party.

What are some of the more promising proposals for improving the political parties? Party realignment, with all the liberals in one party and the all conservatives in the other, as has often been suggested? Increased "responsibility," as proposed in the 1950 report of the American Political Science Association? Better integration, greater resistance to pressures, greater internal cohesion? Or does the only solution lie in increased public participation; and, if so, how is that participation to be achieved? There is no dearth of answers to these questions. Perhaps some of the divergent views presented in this chapter may shed light on them—as well as provide an answer to that most important question: "Does party make a difference in our government in action?"

THE VOTER AND THE PARTY
Joseph C. Harsch

Joseph C. Harsch, news correspondent, commentator, and foreign-affairs columnist, has been with the *Christian Science Monitor* since 1952. He is the author of *Patterns of Conquest* and *The Curtain Isn't Iron*.

The relationship of the individual voter to the American political party is undergoing a transition.

We have witnessed a growth of the "independent" class of voters.

The party label tends increasingly to be worn in the open by those engaged in active work, less frequently by the mere voter, the customer in the American system as it is operating in mid-twentieth century.

This is not necessarily a good or a desirable thing.

Those who take pride in being "independent" miss out in the selection process for candidates and thus fail to participate in efforts to raise the level of candidate quality. Their seclusion in an ivory tower above party can contribute to concentration of party control in the hands of an oligarchy or machine. And sometimes machines get together and form what becomes a political monopoly in fact, although it may still retain the outward form of the two-party system.

Also when independence becomes apathy such machines are allowed to

From *The Role of Political Parties U.S.A.* (pamphlet), 1955. Reprinted by permission of the League of Women Voters Education Fund.

continue, thus depriving all voters of a bona fide choice on election day. A monopoly machine may govern well or poorly, but it governs arbitrarily, and it is free from the useful restraint of the competitive system.

Add that the *active* party worker tends to be a livelier and more experienced voter.

However, in actual practice two sets of reasons impel a minority of American voters into active party work and leave the majority in a state of "independence."

One group goes into party work to obtain a political career, to get a job, to seek advancement for a special interest. These are the most influential reasons and account for the work of the most active party workers.

Others go in to preserve the two-party system, or to raise the quality of the preferred party.

In both parties there are patriotic men and women who seek to promote the public welfare and to carry out their citizen responsibility through active party work.

For better or worse, the majority of American voters have become shoppers from one party store to the other, and back again. The flow of their inclination between the parties has become the principal stimulus to good deeds and proper behavior by the parties.

The American party itself is a business corporation, not an ideological vehicle. Its accepted task is not to further the special interest of some single group in the population, but to arrive by theory and practice at the given formula which at any given time will best serve the general welfare of the whole community. It is the trial-and-error method, if you like, but this is safer for us than a party governed by a rigid dogma which attempts to govern by some ideological book of rules. The Soviet Union has tried that and it is fairly clear by now, even to some orthodox communists, that the ideas of Karl Marx evolved in mid-nineteenth-century Europe are not ideally suited to all the needs of today. As *Harper's* magazine brightly pointed out, Karl Marx was a city boy and didn't know anything about farming. The attempt of the Russians to solve their farm problems out of Marx became the most open and dangerous failure of the communist system. Government out of a book doesn't work. The man who wrote the book, no matter how wise, couldn't foresee everything. Pragmatism is the only safe way of meeting the problems of tomorrow.

The average American has long since come to express his group interest not in his political party, but in his trade association, labor union, church or chamber of commerce. Each such organization has group interests which it promotes, but by indirect rather than direct, political action. These organizations have learned by long experience that they do better for themselves by the indirect method.

If, for example, business men formed a political party and sought to win the White House they would probably fail. Then, because they had alienated themselves from the winning coalition they could expect little consideration from the winner. But if they remain independent of party they can make the best case they have to both parties. If business men did succeed as business men in winning an election the country would be divided on sharp economic lines. The country would be split vertically instead of horizontally, and we would have a condition which at the very least would not resemble our present and reasonably workable system. Such divisions lead to civil war.

As it is in our country, the great issues between groups of citizens are fought to a decision inside the two parties, rather than in open political action between the parties. True, there was a tendency during the New Deal period for the parties to begin to divide by social and economic groups. Labor moved significantly although never totally into the Democratic party, and business and the professions moved towards the Republican party. We came uncomfortably close in those days to dividing by economic class. The bitterness and intensity of the period was a reminder of how dangerous such a division could become.

When World War II ended and the two parties had time to reconsider their attitudes on domestic matters it was quickly evident that they preferred to avoid plunging back into the New Deal strife. Harry Truman made immediate gestures towards a reconciliation of Democrats with business and industry, suffered a relapse during the 1948 campaign, but promptly thereafter sent his Secretary of Commerce, Charles Sawyer, on an extended new mission among the "heathen." Republicans, on their part, developed a vocal new-dealish wing which went about the land urging what their more orthodox brethren called "me-too-ism." Henry Cabot Lodge, Jr., and Phillip Willkie broke into the "slick" magazines with arguments for the new Republican "modernism" and a crop of post-war young Republican Governors, like Driscoll in New Jersey, stole the reforming lead from local Democratic machines.

This trend of the two parties towards the center became pronounced with the Republican election of Dwight D. Eisenhower in 1952 followed by the Democratic capture of Congress two years later. Mr. Eisenhower achieved more harmony with a Democratic Congress than most Presidents had been able to enjoy with Congresses of their own party persuasion. The Eisenhower-Democratic coalition government of 1954–55 produced the nearest thing to political harmony in Washington since the nostalgic days of "normalcy" under Calvin Coolidge.

So changed was the relationship of the parties in 1955 from what it had been in the New Deal period that Republican party strategists had to consider what they would do if the Democrats were suddenly to swing right by nominating a deeply conservative candidate. If such a thing were to happen Republicans could find themselves outflanked on the right with a possibly profitable opportunity for a leftward move of their own. To persons mentally conditioned by the New Deal battles it seems incredible that such a shift of relative positions could ever happen. Yet it is a fact that over the span of American political history since 1860 the Republicans have been the radical or left wing party about as much of the time as they have been the conservative or right wing party.

There is nothing inherent in the political system which prevents such a thing from happening again, for there is no firm and abiding commitment by either party to right or to left. There is a ceaseless search for opportunities to profit from the mistakes of the other, and such opportunities can occur on either right or left.

In this situation the average American seeks the furtherance of his personal economic or social ends by working through his economic group organization. A farmer has the Grange or the Farm Bureau or the Farmers' Union. If he is a big industrialist, the National Association of Manufacturers is looking out for his interests. If he is a businessman he will probably be a member of the U.S. Chamber of Commerce. Every labor union has its architectural palace in Washington from which it projects the strongest influence it can upon Congress and the White House. The latest of these almost literally casts its shadow on the White House from just across Lafayette Park, and just around the corner from the classic marble facade of the U.S. Chamber of Commerce.

The group and class interests of the individual American are well tended, nourished and nurtured by these vast, wealthy and powerful institutions which are ever vigilant in presenting their views to Presidents, legislators and the respective National Committees of the two parties. In fact, the staffs of the two committees reflect in their composition the kaleidoscope of group or "lobby" interests in Washington.

Come Presidential election year, each party produces a campaign "platform" which reflects its best judgment at the time of the most expedient, and vote winning, blend of the views of the "pressure" organizations. The tendency, of course, is for the platforms to express a substantial degree of similarity whenever they deal with promises for the future. They manage to conceal this largely by devoting long passages to ingenious and zestful accounts of each other's real or imagined misdeeds of the past.

But the substantial, and usually transparent, element of genial fraud in all of this does not detract from the fact that year by year, through this process, the voter directs and controls the evolution of the two major parties in a direction which serves his political needs. True, he does this less by being impressed by campaign promises than by his ability to reject the party in power. It is frequently, and truthfully, said that the voter seldom votes "for," he votes "against." After twenty years of Democrats in Washington, he voted "against" another tour of duty for Democrats. He wanted to try something else for a change.

But by rejecting a party in power the voter induces both the loser and the winner to revise its policies and plans in order to avoid the condition which brought the governing party down. There is a constant, gradual assimilation of new ideas and new approaches. The voter checks or encourages the new trend by selecting the party which, in any given year, is ahead or behind on the particular issue.

The plain voter reaches his moment of greatest influence through the simple process of putting his ballot in a box on election day. At other times, he influences the direction of a party more by outside activity than by participating in the renewal of the faith at party gatherings.

Active party membership and a system of party dues are characteristic of continental European parties, which are more nearly like the American trade associations and labor unions, and lay church societies. The American voter is a customer, not a communicant. His vote provides the acid test of the validity of a party's policies and performances. His tastes determine the style and horsepower of next year's model in politics, precisely as in the automobile industry.

But, to do this we must have a choice between two parties.

THE PARTIES AND RESPONSIBLE POWER
Stephen K. Bailey

Stephen K. Bailey is Dean of the Maxwell School of Citizenship and Public Affairs. Formerly a Professor of Political Science, he has had an active political career, including a term as Mayor of Middletown, Connecticut. He is the author of *Roosevelt and His New Deal, Congress Makes a Law,* and *The New Congress.*

The American government today suffers from three weaknesses:

1. Its difficulty in developing a flow of imaginative, informed, consistent, and power-related responses to pressing national and world issues.

2. Its difficulty in generating sustained political power.

3. Its difficulty in making policy truly accountable to a national popular majority.

These are serious defects, not only because they interfere with wise and coherent governing in these dangerous days, but because they undermine the faith of the citizen in the reality or even the possibility of responsible representative government.

The temptation to blame all this on the President, the 22nd Amendment, the split election of 1956, or the present Democratic majorities in Congress is easy—and perhaps partly justified. But the defects are not new. Occasionally, in the past, they have been masked by brilliant presidential leadership in times of crisis or by the virtuosity of congressional leaders in times of presidential ineptitude. But the underlying defects have not disappeared. Nor, in spite of the hopes of a few recent writers, are they going to be overcome by countervailing pressure groups or by the expertness, decency, and continuity in office of civilian and military career officials, important as these factors are in the conduct of free and effective government.

V. O. Key sounds not a hopeful but an ominous note when he writes:

From *The Condition of Our National Political Parties* (Fund for the Republic, 1959). Reprinted by permission of the author.

Representative bodies, the institutional embodiment of democratic ideology, have by the compelling force of events lost both power and prestige. Their role in the initiation of public policy has been diminished by losses to pressure groups and administrative agencies; their authority to decide many issues has, of necessity, been delegated to the administrative services. They have been driven towards a role of futile and uninformed criticism, at its worst motivated either by partisan or picayune considerations.

Even if we assume that the work of modern government is so technical and complex that enormous discretion must be lodged in the hands of experts, their capacity to act steadily in the public interest depends upon the effectiveness of the very institutions whose influence is threatened by the expert mind. This dilemma will continue until we recognize that our representative institutions invite disuse and denigration because their structure is inadequate to perform the functions required of them. It is increasingly obvious that there are innovative, integrative, and perhaps sacrificial tasks ahead for which our government is not institutionally equipped.

IS LEADERSHIP THE BASIC ISSUE?

To say that we need a new kind of political leadership may be true, but it begs the question. Where and how does political leadership arise in the United States? How can the process of selection be improved? How can leadership be sustained? How can first-class political executives be found to run our great public departments? Why is their present tenure so ephemeral? By what means can presidential and congressional purposes be brought into working relationship? And why cannot leadership be held more fully accountable to the desires of popular majorities?

All these questions are related to the structural handicaps under which the American government now operates. At first glance, the problem seems to be constitutional—and in part it is. But the only two structural faults of the Constitution which really get in the way of responsible power in the national government are the 22nd Amendment, which limits the President to two terms, and the provisions for staggered elections. The only two constitutional reforms that this paper will suggest are the repeal of the 22nd Amendment and changes in the term of Member of the House from two to four years and of United States Senators from six to eight years (half the Senate coming up every four years at the same time as the presidential elections). The real problem is *political*. If our *political* institutions can be modernized by certain changes in statutory law and in political party rules, the old problems associated with separation of powers, checks and balances, and federalism would, it seems probable, largely disappear.

The root of the weakness is that while the two national parties for years have genuinely competed for the Presidency they have not made a similar effort in the election of United States Senators and Members of the House of Representatives. Nor have they been of sufficient help to the President and the

Congress in providing candidates of high quality for the grand patronage of departmental and agency direction. So long as we lack strong national parties operating as catalysts in the Congress, the executive branch, and the national government as a whole, and between the national government and state and local governments, power will continue to be dangerously diffused or, perhaps what is worse, will whip-saw between diffusion and presidential dictatorship.

THE NATURAL PARTY DISTINCTIONS

Contrary to the view of many writers, the parties do not need to be strongly ideological or even strongly programmatic—that is, beholden to comprehensive and distinct sets of policies—in order to accomplish the kind of re-alignment of the party system that would stabilize the national power and help to make it responsible. There are vast areas of overlap in the rather vague programmatic shadows that our two great parties cast over the nation—and this is as it should be if consensus is to continue in the making of public policy and in the administration of foreign policy.

But the centers of gravity of the two parties are quite distinct. The Democratic party basically is a party of innovation, with a "pro-government" bias. The Republican party is an essentially "consolidating" party with a limited-government bias. The distinction has become blurred in the last two generations, largely because of the extreme economic and social conservatism of one-party areas in the South—a conservatism which has been reflected in the Congress through its seniority rules and some other carefully contrived rules and myths. But now, the peculiar condition which has smudged party images for so long is on its way out. The economic base of the solid South has shifted monumentally in the past fifteen years: one-party areas across the land are on the wane; the northern migration of the Negro is having vast political consequences.

Political reform does not include making the parties any more ideological than they are now. It does include making them competitive across the nation, allowing them to appeal to the natural ideological divisions within the population and within us as individuals. The stumbling block in this task is that neither party has a sufficiently unified structure to enable it to dramatize its program around its ideology: neither has the power, even if it had the right structure, to carry out the program; neither has sufficiently clear and unambiguous lines of political accountability running to the voters.

THE RESULTS OF PARTY DIFFUSION

The structural limitations of the parties have grave consequences. First, they virtually insure a government by fits-and-starts. Some historians claim that the United States was wise in having rejected the League of Nations; but few would claim that the *process* by which the League was rejected was a rational way of arriving at a major foreign policy decision. In more recent times presidential requests for an adequate United States Information Agency budget have been listened to one year and ignored the next by the House Appropriations Committee. As a result, cultural officers abroad have had to spend much of their time hiring and firing—inflating and deflating programs like an accordion. This has made us look ridiculous as a nation, and has also made it extremely difficult for a coherent information program to develop as a vital element in our foreign policy. The same has been true of foreign economic aid.

Spasms in domestic policy have been equally obvious and equally unsettling. The executive department and the Congress have been unable to agree on any coordinated methods of applying the kind of devices needed to stabilize the economy and promote the goals of the Employment Act of 1946. Similar fits and starts have been noticeable in defense policy, atomic energy policy, welfare policy, and conservation policy. They have been quite as apparent when the Presidency and both Houses of Congress have been in one party as when the control of the government has been divided.

The second consequence of the structural limitations of the parties has been the lack of rationality and consistency in the substance of much public policy. In Paul Appleby's phrase, in this day and age someone or something has to "make a mesh of things." In a world in which, for example, the indiscriminate dumping of rice on the world market in order to erase a temporary glut in Louisiana could cost the friendship of Burma, there are huge dangers in having unlinked centers of power making their own policy for the nation. And yet, parochial groups in the Congress (often in league with sections of the executive branch and with outside pressure groups) still carry an inordinate amount of power.

The third consequence of the absence of coherent party machinery truly responsive to popular majorities is that congressional compromise tends to fall with considerable regularity on the side of minority rather than majority interests. Committee chairmen from "safe" and often sparsely populated, one-party states and districts; the minority-weighted bipartisan rules committee; and the myths, rules, and influence structure which enable congressional leaders to ignore demands for greater majority representation in policy decisions—all these combine to inflate the power of minority interests at the expense of the national popular majority. The pages of the *Congressional Record* or the *Congressional Quarterly Almanac* in any year since the war offer substantiating evidence. The bills and policies introduced or supported by Senators and Congressmen from the areas of greatest popular concentration in America have almost without exception been substantially watered down according to the predilections and petitions of powerful minority interests in and out of the Congress.

This is government by tollgate. It leads directly to consequence four; the increasing danger of public cynicism and apathy toward the Congress, partly because its power is too diffused, too subtle to comprehend; partly because when the power is clearly identifiable it seems to work more consistently for minorities than for the majority.

The last and by no means the least important consequence stemming from the absence of unified party structure is that desperately needed criticism of both domestic and foreign policy is dissipated and discouraged. There is no effective vehicle for responsible opposition criticism of programs; there is no machinery for anticipating the implications of social changes and their effects on policy. With the help of a huge and in part brilliant staff, members of Congress may fill the air and the *Congressional Record* with daring solutions to our dilemmas. But without some sort of party sanction, these ideas are worth little more than an inch or two in *The New York Times*.

In sum, the absence of effective party machinery in each House, and in the government generally, means that policy is fragmentally developed by an infinitely intricate system of barter and legerdemain.

Some defenders of America's traditional disorder have discounted the dangers to policy-making of these intermittencies and irresponsibilities. They argue that our survival suggests that presidential leadership and a congressional desire to cooperate during periods of crisis can save us in the future as they have in the past; that the thermidor between crises allows the divergences in our society to have their day without being subject to the tyranny of a transient numerical majority; and that the accepted American tradition of government by extraordinary or "concurrent" majority has not stopped innovation or social criticism, it has only slowed change, and in the process has insured a healthy unity behind public policy.

In relation to the past, these may be strong arguments. But are they addressed to a world of big bureaucracies, sustained cold wars, and chronic international periods between crises? As long as the frontier was open and the spirit of laissez faire encouraged political parties to be barriers against government action, anarchy in program and uncontrolled shifts in power within the national government were of little consequence. For many years the parties were anti-governmental vehicles, so to speak, minimizing public policy and fencing off large sections of the population and of the domain for private exploitation and private dreams. But we are now in a very different world. As E. E. Schattschneider has pointed out:

> The revolution in communications, the dissolution of nationality blocs, the impact of the labor movement, urbanization, the revolution in public policy, the expansion of the practising electorate in recent years, and the new world position of the United States are only a few of the influences likely to give impetus to political reorganization in the present generation. It is obvious that the purposes of political organization are not what they once were. There was a time when it might have been said that the purpose of the party system, or large parts of it, was obstruction. In an era of perpetual crisis, political organization is reasonably certain to reflect the anxieties that now dominate all public life.

THE PROPHETS

For three quarters of a century America has heard warnings from a variety of distinguished political prophets about its governmental weaknesses. Whether their solution has been constitutional revision or political revision, they have

Woodrow Wilson, Henry Jones Ford, and A. Lawrence Lowell, and continuing through William MacDonald, William Y. Elliott, E. E. Schattschneider, Henry Hazlitt, Thomas K. Finletter, James M. Burns, and Paul T. David, criticism has been directed at a single issue; the difficulties of achieving sustained and responsible political power adequate to contemporary necessities.

All seem to accept one proposition: Such power can be achieved though a greater synthesis is impossible without broad constitutional revisions along the lines of the British parliamentary system, including provision for the executive dissolution of the legislature in case of loggerheads and provisions for concurrent terms for President and Congress. Others believe that the catalytic effect of a reformed party system, together with certain changes in congressional organization and procedure, will make drastic constitutional reform as unnecessary as they believe it to be impossible.

all argued about the limitations of our governing instruments. Starting with
Two statements—one from Woodrow Wilson and one from Thomas K. Finletter—sum up seventy-five years of prophetic writing on this subject. In the 1880's, Wilson wrote:

> The Constitution is not honored by blind worship. The more open-eyed we become as a nation, to its defects, and the prompter we grow in applying with the unhesitating courage of conviction all thoroughly-tested or well considered expedients necessary to make self-government among us a straight-forward thing of simple method, single, unstinted power, and clear responsibility, the nearer will we approach to the sound sense and practical genius of the great and honorable statesmen of 1787.

Two generations later, Thomas Finletter wrote:

> The question thus is whether means, that is the procedures of our government, are adequate in relation to its objectives, or its ends. The usual pattern has been long periods of negative government interlarded with short periods of strong action . . . The irregular flow of power endangers representative government in the United States . . . You cannot have a government capable of handling the most difficult problems that peace-time democracy has ever faced with the two main parts of it at each other's throats . . . A government of fits and starts is no longer good enough for our purposes.

In 1950, a Committee on Political Parties of the American Political Science Association brought out a report which was in the direct line of this earlier prophetic writing. Called "Towards a More Responsible Two-Party System," the APSA report discounted the possibility of drastic constitutional change, but put forward a series of suggestions for political reform designed to create a party system capable of enabling the national government to cope effectively and responsibly with the great national and international issues of the twentieth century.

Nearly a decade has elapsed since the publication of the Committee's report.

Nothing has happened in that time to suggest that the basic issues raised have dwindled in significance. The report itself has been subject to academic debate. Some of its recommendations have been misunderstood or misinterpreted by its critics: other recommendations and assumptions have been justly criticized.

What is increasingly apparent is that the authors of the report were closer than its critics to the spirit and necessities of the age. And inexorable forces, only dimly observable when the report was being written, are now clearly at work preparing the soil for a crop of politics far different from what we have known in the past century.

It is time for a stringent look at the national politics we have had, the kind of national politics we want, and the reasons for believing that our traditional party system, like a vast glacier may now have reached the edge of the sea.

WANT TO BE ELECTED?
Martin Abramson

> Martin Abramson is a magazine writer who has contributed many articles dealing with social and civic problems to leading national publications. He also writes for the United Features Syndicate and contributes to the *London Express*. He is a former New York newspaperman and a one-time writer of "We the People," a TV show. Together with his wife, Mr. Abramson has helped manage and publicize the campaigns of a number of "good government" candidates.

One evening about two years ago a tall, dark-haired, community-minded young mother named Marie Santagata got a telephone call from a group of home owners who called themselves the Efficiency party of Westbury, Long Island. Would Marie care to run for trustee of the village of Westbury? Marie ordinarily commands an impressive arsenal of words but this time she reacted like the shy maiden of the melodramas who gets an unexpected proposal and can't think of anything to say—except, of course, "This is so sudden."

Once the element of surprise wore off and Marie regained her usual self-possession, she decided she'd indeed like to run. The political sages of West-bury greeted this decision with a loud and meaningful yawn. The village had been under the control of one political group for eons and, as a candidate of a "rump" party, Mrs. Santagata was at a decided disadvantage.

Besides, she was a woman, and no female representative had ever been elected to legislative office in Westbury. Like most of the suburban communities in the New York metropolitan area, Westbury had always considered females un-

From *New York Herald Tribune Magazine, Today's Living,* July 2, 1961. Reprinted by permission.

desirable (or ineligible) for public stewardship. Therefore, this woman's race was classed as nothing more than spirited exercise.

To the astonishment of almost everyone in town—including, probably, the Efficiency party itself—Marie not only won her election but rolled up a margin large enough to cause the surprised *Westbury Times* to headline the event with two giant words—"Oh Marie!" To prove this was no fluke, Marie ran for re-election with fellow Efficiency candidate Tom Johnson and amassed another large plurality. Her male compatriots on the village board were so impressed that they broke another precedent and gave the woman trustee the extra chore of serving as commissioner of police and public safety—probably the only such post in the country held by a female.

Until recently the mere act of running under the Republican emblem in villages that have the elephant-donkey political setup, or being chosen as candidate of the "old settlers" group in other communities, was all that was necessary to get elected to local office. But the floods that have washed new populations into Suburbia and that have created the headaches of helter-skelter growth and high taxes have also done violence to established political mores. More and more fresh faces are replacing in office the familiar personalities who used to get elected by force of habit.

"After the scandals investigations of recent years here, people became a lot more mature politically," says James E. Jarvis, chairman of the Fusion Economy party of Huntington, Long Island. "We're getting more discerning people to the polls in suburban communities these days, and they aren't interested so much in party as they are in individuals who, they feel, can give them the best government at the lowest cost per tax dollar."

"We tell the members of our organization that they have to go out and prove their value to the community before they can be considered for nomination to office," says John R. Dunne, president of the Republican Recruits of Nassau County, New York. "Just being a party worker isn't, in my opinion, enough to warrant a nomination anymore—let alone an election."

"The day of the cut-and-dried local election is past," says Mrs. Helene Rosenberg, vice chairman of the town of Eastchester Democratic Committee in Westchester County, New York. "We've elected Democrats in some staunchly Republican villages when we were able to show that they could provide better government than the incumbents."

Could *you* get elected to local public office? On the basis of conversations with local officials, political leaders, civic leaders and the League of Women Voters in Westchester, Long Island, New Jersey and Connecticut, we're ready to say that you can—provided you have or can develop certain personality traits and are willing to follow a specific program of action. "We desperately need new blood in many of our local offices," says a League of Women Voters official in Bergen County, New Jersey. "And the blood should be not only new but also capable." . . .

The attributes are these:

1. An outgoing manner.

2. An affinity for liking and getting along with people.

3. A forceful voice that carries and a habit of expressing decisive opinions. "Voters don't want a shilly-shallier in office; they want someone who represents leadership," a Westport, Connecticut, selectman points out.

4. An ability to listen patiently to others and give their remarks thoughtful appraisal.

5. Plenty of free time and an understanding spouse who doesn't mind your spending that time on public business.

"My wife *does* mind the time but I've appeased her by turning over to her my stipend as mayor the minute I get it," says Sidney Haber, commuter-mayor of Cedarhurst, Long Island.

"My wife objects too but my job doesn't pay anything, so I've just cultivated the habit of not listening to her," says Joseph Dalfonso, mayor of Mamaroneck, New York. "I guess I'm an exception," he adds.

6. A full pocketbook, or friends with full pocketbooks, or a talent for coaxing strangers with full pocketbooks to contribute to your campaign cause. "Inflation has come to local politics," says Eli Wager, former president of the Hempstead, Long Island, town civic council. "Today it costs thousands of dollars to run for the school board or even, in many cases, for sanitary commissioner. I know of a candidate who ran uncontested for the school board and yet spent $2,500 to advertise himself. He was afraid of a write-in opposition."

7. A thick skin. Traditionally, village, school and local district elections have been considered Alphonse-and-Gaston affairs but the winds of change have made that too an obsolete concept. "It now takes more courage to run for a local office, in which you get very little for your public efforts, than for a well paid state or federal office," a Fairfield County, Connecticut, civic leader says.

"The local officeholder is the only remaining public official who'll sooner or later meet his critics face to face in the town hall," maintains Marie Santagata.

"The mud that's thrown in a local election is the hardest to take because it comes from your own people, not from outsiders," says Frank Bear, a veteran of Long Island school board service.

"A local election here is about as mild as a battle between a cobra and a mongoose," says a League of Women Voters worker in Stamford, Connecticut.

"It takes a particular brand of courage to run for office in a small town," says Matthew Feldman, mayor of Teaneck, New Jersey. "The pressures exerted on local officials are considerable. New York City residents write or wire their complaints to the mayor but suburbanites simply pick up the telephone. They rightfully feel that the officials should be responsive to their needs, so we hear on the phone about sewers backing up, about stray dogs, about a skunk having been run over, about unplowed streets. Nevertheless, one Bergen County, New Jersey, mayor, who'd announced his decision not to run again because of hundreds of calls he received in the wake of a February snowstorm, changed his mind and was re-elected in May." ...

A former school board trustee in suburban New Jersey, who describes himself as a Republican, an Episcopalian and a fifth-generation American, heard himself called a "damned Red," an atheist and a "damned foreigner" when he advocated a hike in school expenditures during a bitterly fought school election. "I never ran for office again after that experience and you can bet your life I never will," he says.

"When election time gets close, there'll be whispers that you drink heavily, chase redheads, are in trouble with the Internal Revenue Service, or intend to use public office for your personal gain," says Jerry Kremer, assistant corporation counsel of Long Beach, Long Island, and an official of the Long Beach Young Democratic Club. "How do you fight these things? You don't spend your time going around denying the whispers, that's sure. Instead, you brush them off and paint a positive picture of yourself so that people will forget the rumors."

This is your course of action:

Become a member, become active, become a leader of local organizations. "It's important to work in charity groups, in service organizations such as Kiwanis and Rotary, and in educational groups," says John Dunne. "But the most important field of activity for anyone interested in public life is the civic association. These associations get involved directly in problems of zoning, taxes, recreation, public improvement projects and the like, and experience in these areas is the right preparation."

See that your activities are publicized in the local press by sending out news releases. "It's important that *all* the people in the community, not just the members of your civic or charity group, get to know your name and what you're doing," says Eastchester's Mrs. Rosenberg.

Become affiliated with a church or synagogue as a worshipper and a worker. "People feel that their officials should be identified with an organized religious group," says Mayor Haber.

Once you've become established as a civic personality, a local political organization may tap you as good candidate material. If it doesn't, you'll have to become active in the organization to earn your nomination. If you're out of sympathy with the party or parties dominant in your community, form your own. In most areas only three people are required to form a political party legally.

"We formed the Independent party in Norwalk several years ago because we felt that neither the Democrats nor the Republicans were doing a job," says Peter Leavitt, a Norwalk, Connecticut, community leader. "That was the time of the teachers' strike—when our whole educational system was in danger. I'd been outspoken in public meetings about the failure of our local government to deal properly with education, to correct an inequitable tax system and to do a lot of things they should have been doing. So, when we started our own party, I was asked to run for councilman. I didn't think I had a chance; I ran as a token candidate—merely to present our case to the public. But we were able to convince the people that the status quo simply had to be changed and I ended up being elected and then re-elected several times." . . .

Put color into your campaign. "If you can get volunteer help from somebody in publicity or advertising to dramatize your activities, it will help you considerably," says Julian Kane, an official of the Levittown, Long Island, Property Owners Association. "Too many of the brochures that are sent out in local campaigns are as dry as dust. Political literature that has an artistic presentation will get read instead of being dropped into the garbage. Anything that stimulates public interest and also gets across an important point can be used to advance a good cause. A restaging of the Boston Tea Party by candidates in Nassau County, who were protesting inequitable representation, got a lot of attention and something similar was done in Westchester. In Suffolk County, New York, candidates who were demanding a cleanup of corrupt government made their point by having housewives parade in front of town hall with brooms."

Present a specific program. "Too many outs who want to get in base their whole campaign on the argument that the ins are no good and should be out," a White Plains, New York, Republican leader notes. "People in local communities don't fall for that. They want specifics; they want to be told just what the outs can do that the ins haven't done."

"The candidate we backed for supervisor—Bob Flynn—had plenty to say about the boss-ridden political machine he was fighting; but, more important, he had a program of action that the voters liked," says Huntington's James Jarvis. "Flynn said he was going to cut political padding and waste out of the government, adopt the first code of ethics for a township government in New York State, cut taxes, set up a new recreation program and institute planning studies to deal with the impact on the township of the sudden population growth. As supervisor he's done what he promised, which is the best way I know of for a man to get re-elected."

It should be noted here that the things you should not do when running for public office are as important to your political hopes as the things you should do. Suburban politicos of all stripes agree, for example, that you should not dwell on the problems of the Congo, Castro's Cuba, or unemployment in West Virginia's depressed areas when campaigning for local office.

"We had one candidate who was wonderfully eloquent when it came to discussing foreign affairs, but he acted as if he felt that garbage disposal and building codes were much too mundane for him; so when the election results came in he was trounced," a Rockland County, New York, political leader recalls.

It's important, too, when you're working in civic organizations with an eye toward a political future, that you don't give your civic associates the idea that you're exploiting them for personal gain.

"There's nothing wrong with having political ambition. But if you don't do your civic and charity work sincerely and you adopt the cynical approach— 'This is all right for today but, thank God, I'll be done with it tomorrow'—the people you expect to have working for you later will instead mark you as a bad apple," says Dr. Jacob Fried of Woodmere, Long Island, professor of political science at the New School for Social Research.

Westbury's Marie Santagata recommends, surprisingly, that you *don't* ring doorbells. "It may be all right for the party workers, but not for the candidate himself," she says. "When I rang my first doorbell, the door opened and the cry of a young child, awakened from his nap by my ring, greeted me. When I rang my next bell, the door opened and out ran a dog with its mistress in hot pursuit. Having lost two votes, I decided to stop ringing and start meeting people instead at prearranged coffee parties, small house meetings, neighborhood socials and the like—and also by asking for invitations to speak or debate before any and every local organization that would have me."

One final warning: If you finally win election to local office, don't expect caviar and cream. Garden City's Mayor William J. Maslanka devotes every night and most weekends to his village duties. In order to attend special luncheons or consult with county officials who work during the day, he'll sometimes leave his office in Manhattan (where he works as a production executive), take a midday train to Garden City, do whatever he has to do there, rush back to Manhattan, stay late at the office to catch up, take a late train home, bolt his supper, and then hurry to a night meeting.

Maslanka used to enjoy family outings with his wife and four children on weekends but since he became a mayor his outings, picnics and fishing dates with the youngsters have fallen by the wayside. Also public offices in local communities carry salaries ranging from zero to about $2,750 a year; Maslanka is in the zero category and pays all his own expenses.

Then why should anybody want such a job?

"Primarily because it gives you a chance to perform a public service on behalf of all your neighbors and friends," says Maslanka. "If you don't care about public service, you shouldn't get involved in local politics.

"Of course," he adds, "there's the factor of ego, too. When somebody comes up to me and says, 'Good morning, Mr. Mayor,' it makes me feel very good, very proud. After all, I'm only human."

3 DECISION MAKING IN A DEMOCRACY—THE VOTERS

Although the debate over party realignment goes on, and the inquiry into the possibility of "more responsible" parties continues along the lines suggested in the preceding chapter, certain political questions may be answered only by examining the behavior of the voters, the participating members of the democracy themselves. Therefore, we must ask two significant questions about the voters. First, what factors determine the voting patterns and behavior of the individual in the polling place? Second, since much evidence suggests that party affiliation is one of these determining factors, what factors determine party affiliation?

With respect to the latter question, studies indicate that people seem to be swayed far less by party principles and party issues than by environmental factors and institutional surroundings, such as family influence, traditional geographical patterns, national origins, religious affiliation, economic status, social environment, friends, education, and, perhaps to a lesser extent, age. In short, party preferences are seldom based on purely intellectual or cold-bloodedly rational lines.

In the area of voting behavior, regular or traditional party adherence seems to be the primary determinant for an overwhelming majority of voters. For such citizens, voting is much more an affair of the heart (an emotional reaction) than of the head (a rational decision based on the issues). A second major factor affecting electoral decisions seems to be an economic one—the pocketbook. Indeed, if the pocketbook has been hurt enough, the voter's reaction may overcome his underlying traditional motive. When the voter's decision is more or less reasoned, or based on issues, negative influences usually rate high, as reflected in the broad tendency of people to "vote against"—to voice their discontent with programs that have failed, rather than to rally in support of proposed alternatives.

Do party platforms serve as guides to issues-oriented voting? The widespread disregard for party platforms among the voters suggests that the public views them—not without some perspicacity—more as devices for getting elected than as guidelines to prospective action. In the absence of more systematic surveys and data, we can conclude only that voting behavior seems little affected by the issues so laboriously spelled out in formal party programs.

If issues do not determine the voting, is it "the man"? What about the candidates? What moves people to vote *for* one candidate, or *against* another? Is it some aspect, revealed or hidden, of personality? Is it press coverage—favorable or unfavorable treatment at reportorial hands? Or is it "image"—that carefully contrived but seemingly spontaneous build-up of a candidate's reputation? Is it physical appearance, the capacity to project a photogenic or videogenic impression? Is it speaking ability or appearance of sincerity? Or is it some factor half-hidden in inheritance or history—ethnic or racial ties, religious affiliation, or marital status? Limited inquiry suggests that all these items may be far more important than the basic intelligence of a candidate, his stand on the issues, or the record he has made in public life. Once again, we are faced with a lack of sufficient studies in depth, of final evidence on which to base our conclusion. Nonetheless, even a brief inquiry into some of these factors may help us to understand better the decision-making processes of the voters who shape our government in action.

THE HEAD, THE HEART, OR THE POCKETBOOK?
Louis Bean

Louis Bean, a career civil servant and statistician in the Department of Agriculture, is the author of *How to Predict Elections*. He was also the only major prognosticator to forecast the victory of Harry S. Truman in 1948. In 1952, however, he predicted that Adlai Stevenson would win the election.

Why do people vote as they do? This is as complex a question as any in the whole field of politics. There is no single answer nor is there a simple classification of the thousand and one reasons influencing voters. If you want to visualize the extremes within which the answers may lie, think first of the traditional solid Republican or the solid Democrat who votes as he does because his father and grandfather voted that way. Then think of the kind-hearted Republican lady, ready to vote for Dewey in 1948 but so affected by the public opinion polls showing Dewey far in the lead that she voted for Truman, not wanting at all to elect him but unwilling to see the President so crushingly defeated.

Apparently people vote as they do for reasons that may go back as far as grandfather's genes or no farther back than the emotional response to the breakfast headlines just before going to the polls.

People vote as they do for reasons related to every facet of human behavior. Education, occupation, income status, sex, age, race, nationality, religion, even regional differences are some of the standard items of classification against which the political scientist tests the issues of an election. Issues, in turn, may be grouped "anatomically" as pertaining to:

(1) The head, applying to voters who try to reason things out, to evaluate issues and candidates, and also to those who vote on the basis of their prejudices, acquired or hereditary.

(2) The heart, for those voters who respond emotionally.

(3) The pocketbook, whether full, empty or squeezed.

From *The New York Times Magazine*, October 31, 1954. © 1954 by The New York Times Company. Reprinted by permission.

If you scan the political fever chart of the United States over the last 100 years you are forced to two broad conclusions: One, that there is a general tendency for people to vote along traditional lines which hold election results within certain percentage bounds; the other, that the greatest variations in voting behavior, the greatest shifts from one party to the other, are associated with pocketbook issues.

The general magnitude of traditional voting is suggested by the fact that each party, judging from past experience, can expect to receive a minimum of about 35 to 40 percent of the votes cast. The Democratic bloc of traditional voters is centered in the Southern states. The Republican bloc is more widely distributed throughout the Northern states, particularly in the rural areas. This means that there is usually an in-between group, the so-called independent group of 20 to 30 percent of the voters, which in reality determines the outcome of the national elections.

But even this independent group is not entirely uninfluenced by tradition; it is not, perhaps, as independent as is supposed. Public opinion tests have shown that most of the independent voters voting Republican come from Republican backgrounds whereas those independents voting for Democratic candidates for the most part come from Democratic backgrounds.

Just as we cannot draw a firm line between Democrats and independents and between independents and Republicans so we are unable to draw exact lines between head, heart and pocketbook reasons for voter behavior. Voters are human beings and human beings are mechanisms in which intellect and emotion operate in complex relationship, a relationship further complicated when you attach a pocketbook to that mechanism. The pocketbook issues which I find creating the greatest amount of variation in political behavior should therefore not be taken as entirely unrelated to the head and heart reactions; nor should the head and heart issues that I point out be taken as entirely unrelated to the pocketbook reactions.

The 100-year record of political tides from 1854 to 1954 is clear on this point. Unemployment, financial crisis and collapse, industrial and agricultural depressions—these, in combination, have been the basic reasons for major shifts in control of the Federal Government.

The Republicans were thrown out by the Democrats with the aid of the great depression set off by the financial and industrial collapse of 1873. Twenty years later the Democrats, in turn, were ousted by the Republicans with the aid of the financial and industrial collapse of 1893. The Democrats were returned to control in Congress in 1910 and in the White House as well in 1912, aided by a delayed reaction to the sharp but brief industrial depression of 1907–08 and the economic reform movements that culminated in the election of Woodrow Wilson.

The depression of 1914 whittled down Wilson's support in Congress and the post-war deflation of 1920 and the onset of the 1920–21 depression completed the downturn in the Democratic political tide with the Democratic defeat in 1920. Then in 1929 came the peak of the greatest boom ever erected during any previous Republican era, or Democratic for that matter, to be followed by the greatest collapse and worst industrial and agricultural depression this country had ever experienced.

Empty dinner pails, envelopes with little take-home pay, abundant farm products sold dirt cheap, empty brokerage houses in the financial and commodity markets and idle money in the lending houses have marked every one of our abrupt, conclusive political upheavals and justify the conclusion that the pocketbook issues have been prime factors in voting alternately for Democratic or Republican control of the Federal Government.

But doesn't recent experience go contrary to this generalization? Didn't the Republicans take over in 1946 and again in 1952 when this country was enjoying economic prosperity? Every rule must have its exceptions or there would be no place in the dictionary for the word "uncertainty."

It is true that in 1946, as in several other mid-term election years, the party in power lost control of the legislature but the 1946 episode was not devoid of the pocketbook issue. In fact it may have been dominated by it.

There was much dissatisfaction in 1946 with the way the Democrats were helping the country to shift from war to peacetime activity and much confusion in matters of foreign as well as domestic policy, but the Republican campaign took full advantage of the sharp rise in prices that squeezed the pocketbooks of consumers. The Republican gains were in the urban centers, not among the farmers who benefited by the high prices.

The 1952 exception to this pocketbook rule must be credited to the power of hero worship. Without Eisenhower's extraordinary popularity among Democrats as well as among Republicans, the Republicans, in my estimation, could not have capitalized so effectively as they did on the various issues that filled the air in 1952, particularly the issues of Korea and corruption and communism in Government, or the catchy line "it's time for a change." But the pocketbook issue was there nevertheless, even if less dominant, in the form of the desire of businessmen to have businessmen run the Government, and the universal desire to lower taxes, to lower living costs and to "take Government out of business."

The heart and the head issues are, of course, present in all elections but, unlike the pocketbook issues that sweep one party out and the other in, these tend to set up conflicting tendencies among voters. Given a general depression, which means a nationwide depression all groups, all regions are affected. Bankers, industrialists, farmers, workers, professors, ministers, men, women, Catholics, Protestants, Jews, Easterners, Southerners, Northerners, Westerners, all were, in 1932, for example, swept by a common economic disaster into the Roosevelt-Democratic tide. The usual reasons for voting Republican gave way under the impact of the need for economic security. Under more nearly normal business conditions voters respond to head and heart issues and it is here that the differences among voters create counteracting cross-currents that tend to give stability to election results.

Scanning the national elections for issues of the head and heart I find several outstanding cases. I bypass the silver and other economic or pocketbook elections of the Eighteen Nineties and early Nineteen Hundreds and come to the election of 1916. On the eve of our entry into World War I, the re-election of

Woodrow Wilson in 1916 was a close affair, made so by the fact that the international issues of that campaign did not sway voters uniformly. The nationality factor, whether you classify this under head or heart, was perhaps the most important feature in the voting behavior of 1916.

Wilson received relatively more support in the Eastern and Far Western states, where voters are more positively interested in issues of an international character, less support in the Midwestern states, the so-called isolationist states, where there were and are many voters of German origin or with other German ties. The nationality issue also cost Roosevelt some support in certain Italian-American communities because of his "stab in the back" remark in referring to Mussolini's declaration of war on France and Great Britain in 1940.

Religion is another strong heart or emotional reason. For the most part, religion is of only local significance, though there have been occasions when national elections were clearly shaped by cleavages along religious lines. The Al Smith election campaign is the prize example. Many Southern Protestant voters turned against him because of his Catholic religion and put a sharp dent in the otherwise solid Democratic record of the Southern states. Just the opposite reaction showed up in the Northern and other states where Catholics constitute large segments of the voting population. Those two opposite responses tended to offset each other.

We skip the Democratic defeat in 1920, having already indicated that it was a pocketbook defeat, though I must recognize that most political scientists attribute it to the League of Nations issue—chiefly a head and heart issue—and move to the 1940 campaign.

The 1940 Roosevelt election was a close parallel to the 1916 Wilson election. In this campaign, too, the nationality cleavage showed up. Roosevelt's strength increased in the internationally minded Eastern and Pacific states but sagged decidedly in the Middle states where Willkie gained substantially among the German-American communities and the isolationist groups.

Another recent instance where voting behavior touches religious affiliation is the 1950 mid-term election. The McCarthy efforts against Senator Tydings in Maryland were more consistently effective in predominantly Catholic communities and the same observation may be made regarding the 1950 Senatorial results in such states as Pennsylvania, Illinois, Utah and California. Politicians of both parties consider this factor as important in 1952 also. Republicans hope and Democrats fear that it may play some part again in this year's results.

For a combination of all kinds of issues, head, heart and pocketbook, the 1952 election is our best example. Voters' fears were played upon by means of the Communists-in-Government issue. Voters' emotions were played upon by the publication of shocking war pictures in some of the most widely read national magazines. Voters' hatreds were played upon in Southern states and focused against Truman, therefore against Stevenson. Voters' intelligence was influenced by the logical sounding argument that twenty years of one party is too long, that in a two-party country the Republicans should be given a chance at control and responsibility.

Voters in general were approached by Republicans through mass-media advertising devices that have proved effective in selling commodities to consumers. Above all, the young, the old, the educated, the uneducated, the rich, the poor were all influenced by idol worship, by the power of the well-known name of the general who had led the troops to victory in the greatest of all wars.

In this brief review, what more can be said for the standard classifications of voter behavior? Can we put them into categories of education, occupation, income, status, sex, age, race, region, religion and nationality and expect to find them behaving according to a common pattern in any election? Obviously not, although there may be greater stability in some categories than in others.

You can expect the South to be dominantly Democratic just as you can expect Maine, Vermont, Nebraska and the Dakotas to go Republican. You can expect women to vote about as men do. You can expect farmers, outside the South, to be predominantly Republican while the majority of workers will be found on the side of the party in power. Businessmen for the most part still think that there is more profit to be gained under a Republican than under a Democratic Administration.

Religious and nationality groupings will be predominantly in one political column or the other depending on the election and its dominant issues. Age groups, especially the voters in the younger brackets, do not stay put. Youth in 1932 favored the New Deal. Youth in 1952, not having lived through the experience of the Nineteen Thirties, was inclined to hero worship and in recognition of that fact the Republicans have proposed lowering the voter age level.

Local issues may not be as significant generally as people think. A survey conducted by Elmo Wilson's International Research Associates in eleven states, from Massachusetts to California and from Minnesota to New Mexico, on issues and other problems in this election indicates, among other interesting things, that the results are more likely to be determined by voters' opinions of the attitude of the two parties in matters of human welfare and enterprise.

While the 1954 campaign was tailored to the localities in recognition of the importance of local issues and personalities, the survey, in September, revealed the astonishing fact that about 80 per cent of those questioned could name neither their Democratic nor Republican Congressional candidates and nearly 75 per cent were unable even to name their Senatorial candidates. Such popular figures as Gillette in Iowa, Humphrey in Minnesota and Anderson in New Mexico are exceptions.

The survey also showed that, among the reasons for their preferences, party affiliation counts most heavily. About 80 per cent of the Democrats chose on a party and personality basis, whereas among Republicans party and personality reasons add up to about 85 per cent. Recommendations of a candidate by family or friends are relatively minor factors both among Republicans and Democrats.

The real difference shows up in two other sets of reasons given: among Democrats the fact that the party of the candidate favors "underdog" groups has an importance of 15 per cent, but only 2 per cent among Republican voters.

On the other hand, among Republican voters association with Eisenhower rates about 6 per cent, the need for a Republican Congress to support Eisenhower 4 per cent. This is a total for the Republican Eisenhower factor of 10 per cent in contrast with Democratic concern with issues affecting "underdog" groups of 15 per cent.

This leads me to the conclusion that the 1954 election is essentially a pocketbook election, even though a strong effort has been made through emotional appeal to convert a mid-term election favoring the Democrats into the equivalent of a Presidential, Eisenhower election. There is some unemployment, concentrated chiefly in the northeastern quarter of the country, where many of the marginal seats are located. There is farmer dissatisfaction with lowered farm income. The basic underlying fact is that more people consider the Democratic party the party of the "underdog" groups and the Republican party the party of business groups. This essentially pocketbook cleavage constitutes a basic reason for people voting as they have—and as they will.

IS IT THE MAN OR IS IT THE ISSUE?
Henry Steele Commager

Henry Steele Commager is one of America's most distinguished historians and the author of many studies, including *The American Mind* and *Living Ideas in America*. After many years on the faculty of Columbia University, he now is Professor of American History at Amherst.

The framers of our Constitution gave more, and more elaborate, consideration to the executive office than to any other feature of our Federal Government. Yet we look in vain through all the prolonged debates in the Convention, and through the eleven Federalist papers on the executive, for any suggestion that there is any relation between the election of a President and political principles or issues.

The framers were not political innocents; they were hardheaded realists. But they hoped, nevertheless, to create a Chief Executive who would be above party and above faction, who would decide on issues impartially and dispassionately. They thought that they had contrived an ingenious method of selection of the executive which would guarantee such impartiality, and would guarantee a lofty eminence as well.

As long as Washington was willing to serve as Chief Executive, these expectations were not disappointed. But no sooner was Washington out of the reckoning than the whole machinery so carefully provided by the framers fell

From *The New York Times Magazine,* October 15, 1952. © 1952 by The New York Times Company. Reprinted by permission.

apart. Parties came in to take over the job of selecting a candidate; electors—who were supposed to exercise independent judgment—came to be morally committed to the party choice. Presidential nominees were selected first by caucuses, then by popular conventions, and the careful arrangements of the framers were frustrated.

Thus for well over a century now our Presidential elections have been characterized by what Winston Churchill calls two grand climacterics: first the choice of candidates of the major parties, second the choice between them. From beginning to end it is the candidates who dominate the political scene —or who fail to do so at their peril. Does this mean that Americans are more interested in candidates than in issues, and that their votes are given to men rather than to parties or principles? Superficially it does, but only superficially.

After all, it is relevant to note that the choice of candidates itself is dictated, in large part, by the outcome of intraparty contests over issues. Thus the selection of Alton B. Parker instead of Bryan, in 1904, was a public confession that the conservative Democracy was back in the saddle. Eight years later, the victory of Woodrow Wilson, over the party war-horse, Champ Clark, was proclamation of the triumph of the progressive wing of the party. To take an example fresher in our minds, the nomination of General Eisenhower was not a personal tribute only, but a verdict on the struggle between internationalism and isolationism inside the Republican party.

The issues that candidates choose to talk about, the manner in which they discuss them, the attitudes they reveal, consciously or unconsciously, the interests they come to represent—all these are important in the elections themselves—and may be decisive. Thus it may be argued that the ability of McKinley—or of Mark Hanna—to dramatize the issue of "sound money" was largely responsible for Republican victory in 1896; thus the position, or the supposed position, of the two opposing candidates of 1916 on the question of war or peace proved decisive in a very close election.

Parties may not have firm principles but they do sometimes have firm reputations. The vague feeling that the Democratic party is liberal and the Republican party conservative, that the Democratic party represents the interests of the forgotten man and the Republican of the man who could never be forgotten —these feelings are none the less effective for their vagueness or even for their error.

And there is usually a long psychological lag before opinion catches up with reality. It took half a century for the Democratic party to overcome the onus of slavery and the Civil War; only now is the Republican party recovering from the embarrassment of the Depression.

But before we discuss further the question whether Americans vote for men or for issues, we must face the fact that we still do not know why people vote or fail to vote, and we do not know why they vote as they do.

It is indeed a bit embarrassing how little we actually know about voting or non-voting. Although every party in power during a major depression has been swept out or repudiated at subsequent elections, we do not really know the effect of economic conditions on voting. Even prosperity is no automatic guarantee of victory; thus, 1884, 1912, and even 1920 fell in periods of general prosperity, but in each case the election went against the party in office. Although war is supposed to be unpopular, no party or Administration has been thrown out during a war. The political pendulum swings so erratically that it is next to impossible to draw a reliable pattern.

What, after all, influences or controls voting? Is it party loyalty, hereditary or acquired? Is it habit? Is it geography? Is it class or group interest? Is it argument and propaganda? It is doubtless some or all of these considerations with various people at various times. Surely something explains our voting patterns. If Vermont or Westchester County invariably vote Republican and South Carolina or Jersey City invariably vote Democratic, we may be allowed to suspect that something besides rational arguments are operating. If four-fifths of the newspapers of this country support the Republican ticket, year after year, through thick and thin, we may wonder whether it is always because the Republican candidates have an intellectual appeal not vouchsafed the Democrats or whether the Republican platform is invariably more logical and more eloquent.

It is doubtless true that long before the nominations and campaigns a substantial proportion of all voters have committed themselves to one party or another as certainly as they have to one church or another, and are no more likely to be weaned from party than from church allegiance. It is equally true that these fixed voting habits seem to run in certain patterns which persist from election to election, and that it is possible to predict these patterns with considerable accuracy.

Thus, regardless of candidates, it has been true for some time that big cities tend to vote Democratic and small towns Republican; that skilled and semi-skilled workers vote Democratic and professional men and women Republican; that Negroes tend to vote Democratic and that voters under 25 are more likely to be found in the Democratic than in the Republican ranks.

Nor is this tendency to vote along lines of real or supposed economic or social interests confined—as some campaign orators would have us believe— to the ranks of labor and of farmers, who are somehow unpatriotic for consulting their interests in voting. After all there is little doubt about the way Westchester and Nassau Counties are going to go in any election; the medical profession is probably more of a unit in voting than, let us say, the railroad unions, and John Hersey's statistics on the class of '36 suggests that there is more uniformity of voting in graduates of Yale than in graduates of any Midwestern secretarial school.

Yet granted all this, it still cannot be said that any major group, except perhaps in the Deep South, is committed in advance to party or to candidate. There is not, in the United States, such a thing as a labor vote, a farm vote, a Negro vote, a Protestant or a Catholic or a Jewish vote, an Irish or a Polish vote, a teacher vote—or be it noted—a civil servant vote, or a Social Security vote.

While it is no doubt true that the groups indicated by these terms *tend* to vote in one way rather than another, the groupings are overlapping and blurred and unreliable. Any careful study of, for example, the farm vote would have to analyze it county by county and almost farm by farm, and would quickly discover that politically there was no such thing as the "farmer" but that there were instead Connecticut Valley tobacco farmers and Maine potato farmers and Georgia cotton farmers and Minnesota wheat farmers and Long Island truck farmers and California fruit farmers.

Furthermore, the various factors that condition party allegiance and voting are important but they are not decisive. They are not decisive for two reasons: first, because they cannot be counted on with certainty—witness the vast swings of the popular vote from 1916 to 1920 and from 1928 to 1932 for example. And second, because in so large and diversified a nation as ours most of these special interests cancel out. What these two qualifications mean is that within each group, class, section, or interest there is always a substantial number of independent votes, and that these along with the traditionally independent vote can be decisive.

What then decides the large floating vote? What decides the marginal independent vote within each supposedly committed group—Texas Democrats, for example, or Iowa corn farmers or New York Negroes—and the broad floating vote that is never wholly committed? What determines—parties or principles, men or issues, or a combination of them all?

Now the first thing that strikes the observer who looks objectively at the American political scene is that the American voter is rarely confronted with real issues—with issues that take on the dignity of principles. And the second thing that must impress him is that only very rarely do parties actually divide on issues or on principles; that even when—as this year, for instance—there are genuine issues, they are not such as to divide the major parties ideologically.

A third consideration at once qualifies these two. It is that Americans commonly think that they are confronted with great questions of principle and that the division between the parties is profound.

This elementary fact that the division between parties is more notorious than real pains most of our European friends, and astonishes a good many Americans who ought, by now, to have got over their astonishment. It is, however, not only an elementary but a wholesome fact. For it is the essential character of our major parties that they are the great common denominators of the American people, embracing within their hospitable folds men and women of all classes, faiths, interests and sentiments. And it is the historical function of parties, in normal times at least, to be all things to all men. It is this, indeed, which enables our two-party system to function at all.

History furnishes us innumerable examples of this party parallelism, as does, for that matter, the contemporary scene. Thus outraged Federalists insisted, correctly enough, that Jefferson had out-Federalized them, and, in revenge, they themselves adopted a good many former Republican principles. Thus, a century later, cartoonists displayed T. R. stealing the clothes of Bryan, off swimming in the Democratic pond. And thus in our own day Governor Stevenson can observe, somewhat wistfully, that he would be glad to stand on the Fair Deal platform if only General Eisenhower would move over and make a little room.

There are, of course, important exceptions to all this. Once in a while—fortunately not too often—the country is called upon for decisions on real issues. There was a real issue in 1892—an issue of Bank versus Government and of nationalism versus states' rights. In 1856 the people were confronted with very real issues in Kansas and the Fugitive Slave Law—issues so real that they destroyed the Whigs and largely destroyed the new American or Know Nothing Party. By 1860, people and parties were divided on the tragically real issue of the maintenance of the Union.

Then in 1896 Americans appeared to be confronted with real issues, and on these the parties divided: free silver or the gold standard. In 1912, too, there was a division, at least between the right and left wings of the Republican party—and again in 1916, although the division of that year was canceled by the swift events in the next few months.

It is worth noting that on most of these occasions parties broke into fragments—in 1856, 1860, 1896, and 1912. For just as our parties manage to hold together their varied and often conflicting elements by the calculated avoidance of vital issues, so the necessity of embracing such issues tends to divide and to destroy them.

In recent years we have witnessed a division on issues and on personalities as well—in 1932 and in 1936. If we look to party platforms, or to what candidates and parties are actually prepared to do rather than merely to say, it is difficult to find any genuine division after 1936.

To those who remember clearly the heat and excitement and acrimoniousness of the three campaigns of the Forties, this statement may arouse astonishment. But we have only to compare the party platforms of these years, or to recall the practical proposals of the candidates—as distinguished from their rhetoric—to realize that the statement is essentially true. We have only to ask ourselves what important features of the New Deal the opposition would have repealed or modified if it had won office, or what essentials of foreign policy it would have reversed.

But while it is probably true that parties are not really divided on principle, and that there are but few genuine issues in a normal campaign, it is equally true that a great many people, including the candidates themselves, persuade themselves that there are genuine issues and that parties are divided on matters of principle.

The human mind—and not least the American—yearns for simplification, loves the dramatic, and prefers its issues painted in black and white. Our political oratory, our campaign literature, often our very conversation, falls into stereotypes of issues and principles. . . . How much more dignified, after all, and how much more heroic to contend for great principles than merely for office! How dramatic to stand at Armageddon and battle for the Lord!

And what of the candidates? So Americans normally vote, then, for men? Again no generalization is possible. This much can be said: the vast majority of Americans know more about the candidates than about the issues; a powerful candidate can rise superior to party and ignore issues; candidates are most effective when they appear as symbols for some great principle, and it is only in third or minor parties (and not always there) that principles pretty consistently overshadow the personality and character of the candidate.

History, again, affords abundant illustration for those rather broad observations. Jefferson all but created his party and as long as he cared to, he dominated it. Jackson, one feels, could have run on any ticket and won—Jackson who in the beginning did not rightly know what his political convictions really were. Clay was as much Mr. Whig as Senator Taft is Mr. Republican, but the former dominated his party as no twentieth century politician has dominated the Republican party, commanding the allegiance of his followers for almost forty years. Bryan, too—perhaps the most neglected major figure in our political history—captured not only the Democratic party but the hearts and imaginations of his devoted following; alone among political candidates he survived three sharp defeats and remained a figure to reckon with.

The first Roosevelt dominated the whole political scene, not by virtue of his principles but by force of personality, by energy, vigor and excitement. Franklin Roosevelt overshadowed his party as had Jefferson and Jackson and —as with these predecessors—passed his power on to a successor.

Some of these men, so powerful, so dazzling, in their own right, were significant, too, as symbols. Thus Jackson came to be a symbol of democracy and Lincoln of the Union. Clay came to be a symbol of compromise. Bryan, too, and F.D.R. were not only spokesmen but symbols of great popular movements, of revolt and reform. General Grant had no known political convictions, but when Robert Ingersoll declaimed,

> When asked what state he hails from
> Our sole reply shall be
> That he comes from Appomattox
> And its famous apple tree,

Grant was irresistible. McKinley—not a strong character—was a persuasive symbol of prosperity and respectability, as Coolidge came later to seem a symbol of frugality and security.

When we come to symbols, we are in the realm of the intangible. No one who studies the American political past or observes the contemporary scene can doubt that the intangibles are important and may be decisive.

One final observation is, perhaps, relevant. At least, three of our Presidents who clearly stood for principles failed to win either contemporary popularity or historical acclaim for their courage. John Quincy Adams was very much a man of principle, of such firm principles, indeed, as all but disqualified him for the rough and tumble of American politics. After an unhappy Presidency he was defeated by a man who had yet to learn what he believed about public questions. James K. Polk was another man of principle—a man who boldly announced a program and carried it through, item by item: Oregon, Texas, bank reform, tariff reform. He, too, was allowed to retire after a single term. Andrew Johnson was most certainly a man of principle, a man who endured every indignity that a reckless Congress could heap upon him rather than surrender. Probably a fourth name should be added to this brief list—that of Herbert Hoover. Few will deny that he was a man of principle, as candidate, as President and as party mentor.

What emerges from all this? We do not know what men vote for, but we may conclude that they rarely vote for a candidate alone, or for issues alone. To be successful a candidate must have more than charm and eloquence and magnetism, important as these are. He must have more than principles and popular issues, important as these are. He must persuade the voters that he understands the vital issues, that he has a practical program, that his program is based not alone on immediate needs but on eternal verities, and that he can carry through the program and vindicate the principles.

THE CHANGING U. S. ELECTORATE
Samuel Lubell

Samuel Lubell is a political analyst who has spent a career in newspaper reporting and free-lance writing. He is a columnist for the United Features Syndicate and the author of *The Future of American Politics, Revolt of the Moderates, and White and Black: Test of a Nation.*

To many Republicans, 1964 seems hardly worthwhile. Often during recent months I have been told, "This isn't a Republican year" or "What difference does it make whom we nominate?" This sense of depression has been only deepened by the fact that the bitterly fought series of primaries in New Hampshire, Oregon, and California produced three different winners. To their distress, the Republicans must go into their convention this month with the sharp policy disagreements among themselves painfully exposed and a leading candidate for the nomination who is more popular with the delegates than with the Republican voters.

This sense of Republican futility about 1964 is unjustified for two reasons. First, an election is never settled until it is over. No one can predict the turn of events over the next months, and President Johnson's recent remark ("I hope that they feel in November as they do in April") was a pertinent one. Second, the feeling of helplessness overlooked the true significance of the

Reprinted from the July 1964 issue of *Fortune* magazine by special permission; © 1964 by Time Inc.

election. Every Presidential election has an importance beyond mere victory or defeat. Each election is inescapably a step in the growth of both political parties—in the emergence from the past into the future or both parties and the nation.

In these terms, 1964 is a crucial year for the Republicans. Its import arises less from the remote chance of a stunning upset in November than from changes taking place in the electorate itself. The challenge to the Republicans is to recognize and adapt to these changes, some of which are working to their long-term advantage and against the Democrats.

These changes can be summed up by saying that both parties are in the process of being restructured. The South, long a one-party citadel, is in transition toward having two competing parties. Simultaneously, through the whole nation all sorts of nonpolitical changes are making the country more homogeneous. But this breakdown of traditional barriers does not mean that the American electorate is now huddled together in one great mass of unanimity. Far from it. The steady drift toward a managed economy ("mismanaged" if you don't like what is going on) is rearranging our politics into new divisions and patterns, largely reflecting group—rather than individualistic—economic interest. The political test of the future revolves around the skill with which both parties adjust to these nationalizing forces.

To continue as the majority party, the Democrats must keep their followers happy and committed. But keeping the party glued together is becoming more and more difficult, and only President Johnson's personal popularity makes it look easy this year. The danger to the Democrats—and the opportunity for the Republicans—can be discerned in the three great running conflicts of our era: economic policy, race, and foreign affairs.

On economic issues many voters find themselves torn and divided. Our affluent electorate is marked by a basic conservatism, in the sense that the citizens want to preserve what they believe has helped them in their economic climb. They identify approvingly with some government actions—like social security and minimum-wage laws. But they also are impatient with government spending when carried too far, with inflation that cuts into their purchasing power, with taxes that take money they would like to spend on other needs and wants. When a Democratic Administration proposes, as has Johnson's, to expand welfare programs, some Democrats will applaud—but many would prefer a cut in federal spending.

The racial issue also threatens wholesale defections from the Democrats in the years ahead, not just in the South but in the North as well. The heavy vote for Governor George Wallace of Alabama in the Maryland, Wisconsin, and Indiana primaries shows the increasing political explosiveness of racial feeling outside the Deep South. Some of this "white blacklash" is strongly anti-Negro, but more of it reflects divided emotions—a recognition that Negroes deserve equal treatment wars in the minds of most voters with the tensions stirred by Negro pressures to gain these rights.

In foreign policy many voters are subject to a conflict of hopes and fears, which poses distinct problems for both parties. The electorate wants to see war avoided and is willing to go along with efforts to negotiate better relations with Russia. But at the same time people are wary of strengthening Russia and, even more so, Communist China. Asked on what basis we should trade with Russia, most voters say, "Sell them food or consumer goods but not machinery that will help them in war." The public generally doubts that the Russians can be trusted to keep any agreement they sign. The Democrats seem committed to seek a basis for relaxing tensions with the Russians. Most voters are going along with this effort—with fingers crossed. Relaxation of international tensions will have political value for the Democrats only so long as it seems to work.

The Democratic party's travail, postponed though it appears to be by Johnson's wide appeal, should give Republicans hope for the future growth of their party. A minority party draws unto itself, whether it wants them or not, the voters who dislike the policies of the majority. But the Republican opportunity in the years ahead is far wider than merely harvesting disaffected Democrats. The Republicans have a chance to transform themselves into a truly national party, breaking down the old one-party South and encompassing a wide range of viewpoints of different interest groups.

My surveys indicate that this opportunity has not been fully exploited by the Republican leaders. The shaping of the G.O.P. into an effective national party will have to be done mainly in the areas of the conflicts over economic policy, race, and foreign affairs. But before discussing these in detail it may be helpful to examine the changing social patterns reflected in today's electorate.

A HARVEST OF SOCIAL CLIMBERS

As I see it, the orbit of political conflict that binds both parties has been shaped by a historic migration. For seventy years after the Civil War the Republicans were in the majority. But immigrants were pouring into the country from Europe during this period, filling the tenements of the great urban slums. Joining them were the native American migrants—people leaving the land and seeking opportunity in city factories. With the depression and the New Deal, these slum dwellers, their children, and grandchildren swung over into the Democratic party. The old Republican role as the majority party in the nation was taken over by the Democrats, who have held it ever since.

Even after these onetime minorities came together as the new majority, they did not stop migrating. They continued marching and climbing toward middle-class blessedness, first inside the cities and then into the suburbs. This migration, as important in its latter-day way as that which pushed back the nation's frontiers, could be scoffed at as social climbing of a sort. But social climbing is the great Americanizing institution, the necessary process by which the country has assimilated its different elements.

As the migration of these urban masses proceeded, their economic and political interests changed. In 1936, the year of the greatest Roosevelt sweep, hardly a Democrat paid taxes. Today these Democratic families are affluent or in debt, or both—and strongly tax-conscious. Their gains of recent years have set up a conflict with old underdog attitudes. They still tend to distrust Republicans, whom they thought of as the "haves" in the bad old days when they were "have-nots," but this new middle class no longer buys, sight unseen, all the New Deal slogans. Their values have changed with their net worth. The change was helped along by the Eisenhower years. Two terms of a Republican President without a depression virtually erased the memory link that had tied the Republican party to Hoover and the great depression in the minds of many Democrats.

The memories and interests of these prospering Democrats no longer entirely jibe. They really are voters in transition. Some, if they advance far enough in their economic climb (or if they identify with management), may make a deliberate decision to go over to the Republicans. Most of these in-transition voters, however, just stay in the middle, voting Democratic if their political habits are undisturbed, but ready to shift politically if troubled sufficiently. In 1952 anger over the stalemate in Korea brought a landslide break from old loyalties. One can point to a long roster of Democratic governors who were defeated in recent years largely because of a revolt against the taxes that had been levied to pay for the services demanded by their citizens.

The existence of these restless Democrats has shaped the dominant G.O.P. strategy in the North, a strategy calling for the blurring of party differences. Nelson Rockefeller in New York and William Scranton in Pennsylvania are only two examples of Republicans who have won with this strategy. During these gubernatorial campaigns I interviewed a cross section of the electorate. Repeatedly, Democratic voters who said they intended to vote Republican would explain that they did not feel this meant any change in basic party loyalty. A Democrat did not have to renounce his party and become a Republican for all time to vote for Rockefeller or Scranton.

Some Republican politicians in the North have insisted on sharpening rather than blurring the sense of party difference. This has brought some disastrous Republican defeats, as happened in 1958 when Senator John Bricker was toppled in Ohio and Senator William Knowland in California. Both men were beaten largely because of the bitter resentments kicked up by efforts to push through "right-to-work" laws in those states.

The great right-to-work fiasco of 1958 reflected a misunderstanding of voter attitudes toward labor unions. In my interviews with union members over the years I have found that they draw a distinction in their own minds between the union, which they will fight to preserve, and their leaders, whom they often dislike or disagree with. Frequently union members will protest against what their union proposes—as, for example, with union demands that many members feel may intensify inflation. When a political issue involving unions is presented as a "reform"—a step in a new direction—it will gain the support of many union members. But if the issue is posed as it was in 1958—as an effort to destroy the union—the membership solidifies in opposition. I remember a bakery driver's wife in Carrollton, Ohio, saying: "Sure, our union leaders are crooks. But we need our union and we'll keep it, crooks and all." So deep were the emotions stirred that even workers who had been lifelong Republicans broke and voted Democratic in 1958.

In most northern states, one must remember, there are sizable numbers of voters who are Republican primarily because of inherited family tradition rather than any sense of current economic interest. When the lines of economic conflict tend to be drawn more sharply, as happened during the recession of 1958 and in the farm-belt reaction to Ezra Benson's economic ideas, some of these Republicans-by-tradition are likely to break with their traditional loyalties.

In the South the pattern is almost exactly the reverse. There the Republicans need to sharpen economic issues to free lukewarm Democrats of party tradition. The south's political insurgency is primarily economic in motivation and traces back to the region's awakening to the rewards and excitement of industrial progress. To win over the new middle-class elements in the South, the Republicans need to sharpen their differences on economic issues with the Democrats.

This divergence between the northern and southern political strategies could prove as embarrassing to the Republicans as a similar conflict has proved to the Democrats in the past. In their search for maneuverability, the Republicans may need to develop the equivalent of the "border states" Democrats, who have served as "brokers" to bridge Democratic extremes, both economic and racial. Both Alben Barkley and Harry S. Truman kept open the lines of communication between the anti-Negro South and the big-city machines, to which the Negro vote was important. For the Republicans, Minority Leader Everett Dirksen appears to be filling such a role on the civil-rights bill, partly because of his position in the Senate but also because Illinois is a state with a large Negro vote. Probably the chief need for Republican "brokers" lies in the economic area.

THE BIG SPENDING MACHINE

Today it is the economy that does most to shape the basic party allegiance of the average voter throughout the nation. Not too many years ago, high-income southern precincts were almost as Democratic as low-income precincts. The historic significance of Dwight D. Eisenhower's victories was that they extended into the South this pattern of economic voting. In the last three presidential elections in every southern city the precincts at comparable income levels have shown much the same Republican vote as in the North. The higher up on the economic scale the more Republican the precinct has been. This economic voting pattern now seems so strongly rooted in the South that I don't believe it can be entirely wiped out by Lyndon Johnson's "local boy" appeal or by a continuance of Johnson's success in pleasing many members of upper-income groups, North and South. The relative showing of the Republicans in the South this year will constitute one measure of the G.O.P.'s progress toward becoming a national party.

In a context broader than the South, the key factor determining how people feel about economic issues has become their relation to the big spending machine that is now the federal government. Over the years one of my standard questions has been, "What is the biggest difference between the two parties?" In pre-Eisenhower days the answers nearly always ran: "The Republicans will bring another depression," or "The Republicans are the party of business, while the Democrats are for the workingman" (or "little people," or "middle class," depending on how the person interviewed saw himself).

But today most voters respond to the question with comments on spending, taxes, and inflation. Opposition to increased government spending may be more vocal among Republicans than Democrats, but it exists among all groups. A strange kind of balance prevails on this issue. Most people want to keep spending up to a level that will assure prosperity (though they may be confused on cause and effect), but will oppose spending that increases taxes or prices. Both the Kennedy and Johnson administrations seem to have tailored their economic programs to this public sentiment. Income taxes have been cut; and some effort has been directed toward keeping a lid on price increases, even while new welfare programs have been instituted to benefit specific voting segments.

Opposition to spending, however, does not signify universal disillusionment with government programs. The citizenry has come to prize the economic stabilizers instituted by the New Deal, and each economic group tends to want to hold onto the program that subsidizes it, even while grumbling against spending generally. Continuing these programs does not seem radical or even liberal to many voters, but conservative.

This attitude showed up as early as 1948. Many voters I talked with that year told me they voted for Harry Truman because they considered Thomas E. Dewey "too risky" a candidate. Overconfident of victory, Dewey failed to spell out what parts of the New Deal he proposed to keep and what he would scrap or change. Today I continue to find that to many voters "conservatism" means holding on to much of the legislation begun by the New Deal, retaining the gains they have made in recent years.

It was this personalized definition of "conservative" that hurt Senator Goldwater so badly in the New Hampshire primary. Nothing cut into his support there more than his statement that the social-security system should be made voluntary. Those who favor a voluntary system argue that young people should be free to do anything they want to do with their savings. But this appeal is countered by a double argument raised by many Republicans. One was that without forced savings of this sort, most people would do no savings at all, and the welfare burden would be even heavier than it is now. The other was that loss of the social-security system after all these years would penalize the prudent more than the imprudent.

In Dover, New Hampshire, I recall one old couple's telling me, "If we didn't have social security, we'd have to sell our home and go on relief." Republicans who voiced conservative views by almost any standard were appalled by Senator Goldwater's suggestion. Men and women who said staunchly, "We don't want any more of this welfare state" would still come to the defense of the social-security system. "We've lived with this for twenty-five years," said one storekeeper in Pittsfield. "You can't just drop it."

In contrast, Senator Goldwater's ideas are much more attractive in areas of rapid economic growth, such as southern California and parts of the Southwest. There people find it easier to make money, to start a new enterprise, to sell a piece of property at a profit, to strike it rich by tapping the population rise. These entrepreneurs are ambitious, active types. They really do not want to turn the clock back, but are seeking to hold a larger share in the returns from their activities. This desire encourages them to a more militant resistance to government policies which skim off so large a part of the profits that can be earned in this region.

These contrasting examples from New Hampshire and California point the need for Republican leaders to view primary campaigns not as "disruptive" but as a means of arriving at a unifying definition of what the party is to stand for. As a result of New Hampshire, I am sure the Goldwater forces learned to respect the electoral sentiment that attaches a high value to preserving the social-security system. From the voting in southern California anti-Goldwater forces should learn that these self-styled "conservatives" cannot be dismissed as merely "crackpots" or "backward looking."

A GAIN ON RACE

The second of the great policy conflicts in our present society—over race—poses perhaps the most pressing political danger to the Democrats, not only in the South but in the North and West as well. In such a situation some Republican strategists seem to be tempted to adopt a hands-off policy calculated to let the white South do as it pleases racially. To yield to this temptation would be unwise politically because the nation is looking for political leadership on the racial issue. Indeed, the chief defect of the Democratic party's recent record is its failure to unify the nation on policy questions arising from relations between the races. Deadlocked on race, the Democrats have bought time—and wasted the time that was bought, spreading the cancer of racial strife ever wider. The ultimate challenge before the Republicans is whether they can succeed where the Democrats failed in achieving a unifying national policy toward race problems.

Unification cannot be achieved on the basis of so-called "states' rights." That approach has already been tried and proved utterly inadequate. The inescapable fact is that civil rights has long been a national issue, requiring national policy. My own study of this tangled problem suggests that the course of unification lies in a quickening of the pace of desegregation, even while pursuing a gradualistic, moderate course. The emphasis must be on action. "Gradualism," if it is to be effective, cannot be used as a cloak for doing nothing. On this issue, in short, the Republicans should stand for real progress through moderate action, not for inaction under the guise of "states' rights."

The Republican need is to think beyond the temptations of the next election and aim at the failure of the Democrats as a unifying force. If insurgencies develop because of the enforcement of integration decrees or other racial tensions, the political reaction will need to champion a course of racial progress that avoids extremism on either flank, moving desegregation forward at a unifying pace. The ground that makes unification possible is where the Republicans should take their stand.

The last of the three great political conflicts in our society is over foreign policy. At this writing, my voter interviews show no single foreign-policy issue that is so tied to people's emotions as to endanger Lyndon Johnson's election. Vietnam seems far away to the average voter, despite the years of our involvement there. Republican campaign orators may hope to fan a Korea-type resentment over this struggle, but so far voters remain more uneasy and puzzled than emotionally aroused about Vietnam.

Cuba sparks more emotional interest. Republicans and Democrats alike nurse anger over a Communist base "only ninety miles off our shores." But President Kennedy's firm stand on Soviet missiles in Cuba in 1962 erased much of the political stain of the Bay of Pigs fiasco, while Johnson has been in office too short a time to absorb any blame for anything about Cuba. Most voters, when asked about Cuba, say, "We should have gone in earlier, but now it's too late." A new threat or provocation from Castro's Cuba might spur new demand for U.S. action. But, at this stage, Cuba is no political burden on Johnson. Voters feel that he didn't make our foreign-policy bed; he's just sleeping there. Every honeymoon ends, however, and Johnson—or at least the Democratic party—will in time be called to account for his stewardship of our foreign policy.

In this, as in other arenas, the Republican party will attract those who disagree with the majority party's policy. Because Roosevelt was President when the U.S. started lend-lease prior to entering World War II, those who disagreed with his actions—the so-called isolationists—automatically moved into the Republican party. Memories of Roosevelt's foreign policy have remained a basic divider between Republicans and Democrats ever since. Although Eisenhower was internationalist in his outlook, and was "imaged" as such by his speech writers, his greatest voter gains in 1952 came among Democrats with an isolationist tradition. The more international-minded Democrats stuck with Adlai Stevenson. Ike won the people who were disillusioned by Democratic foreign policy—many saw Korea as an extension of Roosevelt's policy—and who felt they wanted a change in it.

Too many politicians act as if in each new election people were voting for the first time. Actually, all elections begin as a projection of the past. Because of its past appeal the Republican party will continue to be a haven for those who are distrustful of the U.S. course abroad. This remains true even though the internationalist aspect of that policy was left relatively untouched in the Eisenhower Administration. Recently, for example, I conducted a survey on

Red China. Republicans were more opposed to admitting Peking to the United Nations than Democrats (though a majority of Democrats also opposed its admittance). Even more interesting were the responses to the question "Which is the bigger threat to the U.S., Russia or Red China?" Democrats tended to pick China while Republicans tended to see Russia as the bigger threat and to be less hopeful of the prospects of attaining a genuine relaxation of tensions between the U.S. and the Soviet Union.

One major difficulty the Republicans face is how to campaign for a stiffer foreign policy without seeming to be warlike. In California more adverse criticism was voiced against Senator Goldwater on this point than on any other aspect of his views. Goldwater's proposal to send the Marines in to turn on the water at Guantanamo Bay was recalled by many voters with the comment, "He'd rush us into war." Justly or unfairly, they concluded: "He doesn't talk like a President. He shoots off his mouth without thinking."

In an age of nuclear weapons and missiles, belligerent political partisans— whether Republican or Democratic—defeat their own purposes when they pound the table. The need of the nation is for an opposition party that can point out the risks and weaknesses in Administration policy without sounding as if it were issuing a call for war. The American voter will respect differences of opinion on foreign-policy issues when supported by reasonable arguments. It is worth noting that Senator Goldwater lost no public support by his vote against the nuclear-test-ban treaty. Many voters were as doubtful of its wisdom as he was, even when they resolved their doubts by being ready to take a chance on the treaty. A number of voters told me: "I can see how anybody could be suspicious of that test ban."

WHAT IS POVERTY?

Not just on foreign policy but on all the great issues of our time there is a pressing need for genuine cause-and-effect study of the problems facing the nation. On the Democratic side too much energy is devoted to keeping in line the party faithful and too often there is a tendency to deal with problems in quick headlines and New Deal imagery. The Republicans, on the other hand, in their efforts to chip away Democratic support, tend to react too often in terms of quick opposition to whatever Democratic leaders propose. In place of quick appeals and quick opposition, the nation needs to get down to fundamentals on many questions.

The opportunity to do so is perhaps greater for the Republicans, since Democratic thinking has hardened almost into dogma. There is scarcely a problem for which the Democratic strategists do not trot out the same solution—spend more money. The tax cut was presented as a way of ensuring "full employment" by priming more spending, with little real attention given to the many varied causes of unemployment.

Last year I did an exhaustive survey of unemployed workers to determine why we had so high a jobless rate in a booming economy. I concluded that the unemployment figures on which both Democrats and Republicans rely are no longer an accurate measure of our economic performance. Largely because of labor unions and corporate economic strength, we have turned most of our economy into a protected fortress. The worker with enough seniority to be within the fortress gets the high wages and fine fringe benefits of our modern society. Those who are outside the fortress bear the brunt of the unemployment.

The same people get thrown out of work repeatedly because they are low in seniority. With any downturn in the economy, they are the first to go. If inflation pushes up labor costs, those without seniority are most vulnerable when efforts to cut costs are made. I have interviewed young people of thirty and thirty-five who have never held a steady job in their lives. They have been laid off time and time again. Many live mainly for the time when they will finally build up enough seniority to be assured of working steadily. Waiting for seniority has become part of the pattern of industrial living. Often the wives of those without seniority must go to work to supplement the family income.

This unemployment survey emphasized the need for examining the different kinds of unemployment on a cause-and-effect basis. Neither party has yet given the unemployment problem the kind of study that is needed.

The "war on poverty" is another example of a headline in search of analysis. The statistics being used of the people who are supposed to be living in poverty are not good figures at all. Some professor-politicians set up arbitrary statistical dividers and say, "This is poverty." Their proposed solution is not soundly based because it is not derived from a diagnosis of poverty, of the many different causes of "poverty," of why particular people are poor. One should also question whether poverty is what the government says it is. I remember interviewing one Iowa couple who had moved from fertile Story County to southern Iowa, where the land is poor and eroded. When I asked why they had left good land for poor, the wife replied, "Up in Story County people had dollar signs for eyes; all they thought about was money." This couple was willing to accept a lower standard of material comforts in order to escape competitive pressures. Is that true "poverty?" I told this couple, "Some people in government think that you should not be farming such poor land, that you ought to be retrained for other work." The husband replied stiffly, "I don't want to be retrained. We're doing all right."

What is called "poverty" involves more situations than can be dealt with under one statistical headline. Instead of having just a label, we need more digging to determine the numerous kinds and causes of poverty. Then our corrective efforts should be addressed to those causes.

WHO CAN DO BETTER?

To sum up, I believe the nation needs a change in the terms of party competition. Ordinarily, the majority party is in the better position to set the terms of party competition, with the minority party left to wait for sizable segments of the majority to fall out among themselves. But the trend toward a managed economy, the spreading racial strife, the dangers of both nuclear and submarine war require a party competition that will be more sensitively attuned to the emerging problems of the future rather than the lingering quarrels of the past.

This is why, as a nonpartisan student of politics, I feel the interests of the whole country will be advanced by a strengthening of the Republican party so it can be an effective national party. The nation's interests would be advanced even further if either party were to change the terms of party competition by framing policy proposals that go to the heart of the difficulties we face in economic affairs, foreign relations, and the racial conflict.

This, it seems to me, is the real challenge to the Republican party in 1964. My interviews with voters in every part of the country show this need to move the party competition closer to realistic solution of national problems. It is a challenge that the G.O.P. may find easier to pick up, if only because the Democrats, with their deadlocked majority, may not be capable of much more than a holding action for some years ahead. American history suggests that political power ultimately goes to the party of unification in the nation. The Democrats, despite a masterful blurring of differences by Lyndon Johnson, seem to have lost this unifying power, at least temporarily. One way of looking at 1964—and beyond—is to ask: can the Republicans transform themselves into the party of national unification?

The importance of public opinion in a democracy can scarcely be over-stressed. As the famed pollster George Gallup has pointed out, "What we don't know *can* hurt us." The need for an enlightened people has been recognized throughout American history by virtually every leader identified with the advancement of democratic principles. From Thomas Jefferson through Abraham Lincoln and Woodrow Wilson down to Dwight D. Eisenhower, John F. Kennedy, and Lyndon B. Johnson, all have agreed on the significance of participation by an informed public—if enlightened decisions are to be reached, errors are to be corrected, and wise leadership is to be selected.

Analysis of public opinion suggests the existence of a threefold relationship between government and its citizens in a democracy. First, there is the problem of determining what public opinion is; second, there is the task of reflecting that opinion; and third, there is the creation of opinion, a task of leadership even in a democracy.

In its First Amendment, the American Constitution undertakes to guarantee that there shall be a broad and unrestricted realm for the development of public opinion—with freedom of speech, freedom of the press, and freedom of assembly. Most state constitutions repeat these guarantees. But how do these protections emerge in actual practice?

The attempt to determine public opinion leads first to the question "What public?"—for, indeed, there seem to be many. Apparently, a crisscross network exists, in which one segment of the public may believe one thing and another segment the opposite. But frequently there is no precise way of determining the outlook of a mathematical majority. Furthermore, opinions may be held with varying degrees of intensity, with virtual indifference at one extreme and strong, emotionally held points of view at the other. Then, too, many degrees of knowledge and understanding may underlie the opinion—in short, the basis of opinion may be rational and enlightened or just the reverse. Moreover, public opinion may be latent rather than crystallized and clearly formulated; it may be more a subconscious feeling than a well-defined credo.

The measurement of public opinion—still far from an exact science—has come a long way from that day in 1936 when the *Literary Digest* so confidently predicted, on the basis of a sample drawn from its own subscription list and the telephone directory, a triumph for Landon over Roosevelt. Even today, as the more recent experience of 1948 suggests, polls are not yet completely accurate barometers. Nonetheless, they have their place—together with the more subjective personal-interview surveys (of the Samuel Lubell type), press samplings of editorial comment, and letters from constituents—in estimating the public pulse.

But how should opinion, even if susceptible to increasingly precise measurement, be reflected in public policy? This remains one of the most perplexing questions facing the public servant, whether he is a ward politician or chief executive, an administrator or legislator, or any combination thereof. Phrased perhaps oversimply, is it the duty of the representative in a democracy to follow, as accurately as polling techniques will permit and as slavishly as individual conscience will allow, the voice of the people? Or does he have an obligation to pursue a stronger and more forthright position than the statesman in the possibly apocryphal story, who admits, "There go my people. I must follow them for I am their leader"?

Certainly, if he chooses a more independent course, today's leader has many powerful weapons at his disposal. For public opinion, it is well recognized, is amenable to many types of manipulation—covert as well as open, subliminal as well as visible; for better or worse, it may be created or destroyed, used or abused.

The institutions that shape public opinion may be divided into two distinct categories—the *unconscious* and the *conscious* movers. In the first group is the over-all pattern of cultural heritage and of social institutions: home, school, and church, and the personal environment, including friends and family, associates, neighbors, and co-workers. In the second are the activities of advertisers and editorialists, press agents and pamphleteers, panacea peddlers and politicians, news reporters and news "managers."

It is the latter group that has been the subject of most the recent public concern. In the light of this group's reputed ability to mold public thinking, such attention is well merited. But perhaps in the long run the subconscious influences—the more basic and less publicized—are the more important, in that they are responsible for the very definition of the society—the society whose underlying attitudes shape our government in action.

WHAT WE DON'T KNOW *CAN* HURT US
George Gallup

George Gallup, America's best-known pollster, founded the American Institute of Public Opinion. He is the author of *The Pulse of Democracy, Guide to Public Opinion Polls,* and other publications.

The most disturbing fact about the present American scene is the ignorance on the part of a large segment of our population regarding issues vital to their very existence. Like the poor, the ignorant are always with us. Normally, lack of information on the part of some of the voters has little effect upon national policy. But when this same lack of knowledge is widespread, the consequences can be dangerous.

From *The New York Times Magazine,* November 4, 1951. © 1951 by The New York Times Company. Reprinted by permission.

Today for the first time I must confess that I am concerned lest lack of information lead the American people to decisions which they will regret. When the public is reasonably well informed on any issue, it generally comes to the right conclusion. Today, however, poll takers daily bring to light misconceptions and ignorance which I think should be corrected. I have listed five of the most important of these "areas of ignorance" which affect the thinking of large segments of the population.

The first area of ignorance concerns foreign affairs.

What is the state of knowledge regarding some of the problems of combating Communist aggression which face us in the Orient and Europe? To get some idea of how well informed the voters of this country are we devised a very simple set of questions which our interviewers put to a cross-section of the adult population in a . . . survey.

These are the questions which we asked of this cross-section: (1) Will you tell me where Manchuria is? (2) Will you tell me where Formosa is? (3) Will you tell me what is meant when people refer to the 38th Parallel? (4) Will you tell me what is meant by the term "Atlantic Pact?" (5) Will you tell me who Chiang Kai-shek is? (6) Will you tell me who Marshal Tito is?

Certainly there is no question here that should stump any citizen. Yet only 12 percent of all adults we questioned could answer all six correctly. A higher percentage—19—could not answer a single one. The amazing thing is that virtually all of these people read a newspaper and listen to their radio daily. . . .

When the Iranian situation was boiling to a crisis, only four Americans in ten knew where Iran was, and only three in ten knew what the trouble in Iran was all about.

Keystone of our European foreign policy is the Marshall plan. Yet after the plan had been in effect for more than two years, one-third of the American voting population either knew nothing at all about the Marshall plan or had mistaken ideas concerning it.

Ignorance of domestic affairs is likewise alarming.

It was shocking to learn . . . that 34 per cent of the American people could not correctly identify Dean Acheson [when he had been] Secretary of State . . . for two years. One third didn't know who Senator Joseph McCarthy is either.

Six out of every ten [didn't] know what the Reconstruction Finance Corporation (R.F.C.) is, despite all the publicity over questionable R.F.C. loans. Fewer than one-third of the adult population has followed any of the discussions about the Brannan plan. In one survey the public was asked to state approximately how much the Federal debt is. The average guess was $150 billion short of the mark.

It is little wonder that the Herbert Hoover Commission reports on reorganizing the executive branch of the Government to save money and increase efficiency are largely Greek to the great majority of Americans. Only about four voters in every ten (44 per cent) have ever heard of the Hoover Reports, and only 24 per cent know what they recommend.

Another misconception has to do with the destructiveness of the atom bomb.

Some six years ago the world witnessed the collapse of Japan shortly after we had dropped atom bombs on two of her cities. I am not competent to say just what part these bombs played in the surrender of Japan.

However, it is easy to see how this success in the war against Japan could give many persons the fantastic idea that all we have to do to bring Red China and Red Russia to their knees is "drop an atom bomb" on their cities.

Further questioning of these same individuals reveals the extent of their misinformation about the bomb. They do not seem to realize that its effectiveness is a matter of a few miles. In their minds, just a few A-bombs are capable of destroying virtually a whole nation.

I am not an authority on the A-bomb. But I do believe it is a threat to this country to permit so many persons to have an exaggerated idea of its destructive power.

The fourth major area of ignorance is the inability of many Americans to envisage the awesome effect of another world war on our present civilization.

Polls show that only a fraction of the population has any conception of the staggering cost of war in money alone, to say nothing of blood. Only 13 per cent of Americans polled were able to make even a rough guess as to the amount—approximately $57 billion—being spent on defense in 1951–52.

Moreover, most Americans really cannot conceive of our not winning any war we undertake. The delusion is that we can fight World War III, get home quickly, and live happily ever after. Consequently, many voters tell our poll interviewers: "War with Russia is inevitable. So let's get it over with, so we can stop worrying."

The only proper rejoinder to this is that death, too, is inevitable; so let's all go out and jump in the river and have done with this waiting and worrying.

The confidence in our ability to win a war is encouraging evidence of our national morale and patriotism. But it fails to take into account that even the victor in the next war is likely to suffer more than the losers of past wars.

Europeans, whose lives are more directly affected than ours ever were even at the height of World War II, do not share the sanguine belief that everything would return to normal if the Soviets were defeated in World War III.

Lastly, few Americans seem to understand or take much interest in the possible alternatives to a shooting war.

Our polls show that 77 percent have never even heard of the Point Four program and only 5 per cent understand what it is trying to accomplish.

A surprisingly large number—more than half—don't know what the "Voice of America" is or what it does.

Our national lack of appreciation of the importance of ideological warfare is particularly disturbing in view of the fact that we are going to have to live in the same world with the Communists for a good long time to come. We not only have to outsmart the Communists in the struggle for men's minds, we have to understand what's going on in the minds of men all over the world, rather than expect them to think as we do. As a nation, we're still largely ignorant of the impact of ideas on other nations. Witness the sudden dismay of many Americans at starving India's acceptance of Russian grain.

Only our failure to see what is going on in the world and to face up to the realities of the struggle we are engaged in keeps us from doing the things which we need to do to win the war of ideas.

Who is to blame for our ignorance about current world problems?
First, I think, the chief blame lies with the people themselves.

We have become so bent on entertainment that anything which doesn't fit easily and unconsciously into this groove tends to be ignored. The old-fashioned idea that everyone should "keep abreast of the times" apparently has lost much of its early appeal. Either this must be true or that admonition has become corrupted to mean keeping abreast of winning football teams or the latest bulletins on Hollywood marital affairs.

Next, let's look at our educational system. It is my conviction that educators have succeeded admirably in making learning dull and lifeless in this era of universal education. The conception that the ultimate goal of education is to inspire students to carry on the process of learning throughout their lives, to give them an unquenchable thirst for knowledge, seems to be lost in the struggle to equip students to capitalize on what they have been taught in the classroom.

What about the role of the newspaper in this situation? The historical function of the newspaper has been to keep the public informed about issues of the day. It is, in a very real sense, "the schoolmaster of the people." But have the newspapers of the country lost a sense of mission in this respect? Have they begun to worry too much about having the most popular comic strips and the most complete sports pages and too little about keeping their readers interested in, and informed about, the important problems of the day?

I recently conducted a small survey among working newspaper men actively engaged in processing the daily flow of reporting—copy desk chiefs—asking them to rate on a scale of 100 the quality of the job being done today by daily newspapers in treating news of world events and issues in such a way as to interest the maximum number of newspaper readers.

Interestingly, the copy desk chiefs rated this aspect of today's journalism *lower* than any other practice. They gave it a score of only 36. In other words, their combined judgment is that the press today is doing a pretty poor job in presenting national and foreign news to readers. Or put in a more encouraging way, there is tremendous room for improvement in this department.

An important part of the job of a public opinion polltaker, as I see it, is to keep uncovering and reporting the more serious "areas of ignorance." What people know has an important bearing upon what they think. And what they think almost invariably influences the course of action taken by government.

That is why it is so vital today to see that decisions which the government makes aren't influenced by lack of information on the part of voters. Our very lives are at stake.

Perhaps we should revise the old statement, "What you don't know won't hurt you," to read: "What you don't know may destroy you."

GOVERNMENT BY PUBLICITY
Douglass Cater

Douglass Cater, Special Assistant to President Lyndon B. Johnson, was formerly Washington Editor of *The Reporter* magazine. He is the author of *The Fourth Branch of Government,* and *Power in Washington.*

More than in any other capital in the world or any other city in the United States, there is prestige and privilege belonging to the lowly reporter in Washington. Even those who have graduated to the higher callings of columnist or bureau chief still take a modest pride in identifying themselves by the lesser title. Within the press corps, faint derision attaches to one who prefers anything more pretentious.

The Washington correspondent clings to the image of the reporter as the supreme individual in the age of the organization man. His prestige symbols encourage him in this notion. The Pulitzer Prizes, the Heywood Broun and Raymond Clapper Awards handed out each year, all go to the individual who has beaten the system and gotten the "scoop." Even the hoary myth of the swashbuckling, free-wheeling, heavy-drinking reporter who pursues news with a hunch and a hangover dies hard. It is desperately nourished in the literature of the profession and in the tall tales swapped around the Press Club bar.

The reality is a bit different. The Washington correspondent's business, like most big businesses, has become specialized, compartmentalized, channelized, even routinized to a degree that would shock his predecessor of a few decades ago.

The backbone of the business and, to a certain extent, its central nervous system are the giant wire services with a labor force large enough to monitor every major news outlet in the capital and to maintain a steady outgoing flow of words. The wire-service employee scarcely conforms to old-fashioned notions of the reporter who each twenty-four hours dictates a first draft of history. He is rather the bucket boy for a never-ceasing stream of news that may be scooped up at any hour of day or night and poured into print by the far-flung distributors.

There are the Washington bureaus of the big-city dailies and the chain papers—highly varied operations ranging from the twenty-three man princely state maintained by the *New York Times* to the one- and two-man outposts of

the Denver *Post* and the Providence *Journal*. These reporters are the most direct spiritual heirs of the ancient tradition of the Washington correspondent.
They range widely in their purpose. For some it is an unending search for
scandal and expose. Some consider their function to be the more leisurely
digestion of the raw meat of the headlines. Another sizable contingent of the
Washington press corps is composed of the "localizers" of the news. They bear
daily testimony to the fact that the United States has become a world power
whose interests are still heavily provincial. These reporters view Washington
through the eyes of Dubuque, or Kalamazoo, or Nashville.

Other reporters view the Washington scene from other perspectives. Reporters for the news weeklies—artisans on a different type of assembly line from
the wire services—dig out the primary components necessary to give a factual
shape and color to the week's events. Other components—style, polish, "meaning"—are added further along the assembly line, in the skyscraper workshops
of New York. Reporters for radio and television scan the horizon with restless
radarscopes in search of news in shapes than can be heard and seen. And syn-
dicated columnists, the most independent of the news merchants, batter the
barricades for their "inside news" purveyed three times or more weekly and
ranging in content from foreign policy to freight rates.

The reporter is the recorder of government, but he is also a participant. He
operates in a system in which power is divided. He as much as anyone—and
more than a great many—helps to shape the course of government. He is the
indispensable broker and middleman among the subgovernments of Washington. He can choose from among the myriad events that seethe beneath the surface of government which to describe, which to ignore. He can illumine policy
and notably assist in giving it sharpness and clarity; just as easily, he can pre-
maturely expose policy and, as with undeveloped film cause its destruction. At
his worst, operating with arbitrary and faulty standards, he can be an agent of
disorder and confusion. At his best, he can exert a creative influence on Washington politics.

In no other major capital does the reporter have quite this political role.
Patrick O'Donovan, correspondent for the London *Observer,* has commented:
"Most strangers are astonished by the power of the American and, more par-
ticularly, the Washington press. It fulfills an almost constitutional function.
And it works with a seriousness and responsibility which—even though it may
lack the luxuries of style—cannot be matched in Britain today."

During the latter years of the Truman administration, the widely publicized
Congressional challenge to Presidential leadership aroused deep concern among
those anxious about America's role in the free-world alliance. Yet, viewed with
the hind-sight of a very few years, it appears a curious sort of challenge. It is
doubtful whether a single prerogative of the Presidency was actually diminished.
What had in fact happened was simply that *the focus of public attention shifted
from the White House to the committee rooms of Congress*. Prior to 1950, the
major events of government that attracted public attention included the Tru-

man Doctrine, the Marshall Plan, Point Four, the Berlin airlift, and the North Atlantic Treaty Organization with its accompanying Military Defense Assistance Program—all Executive-inspired and carried out with the "advice and consent" of Congress. From 1950 to 1953, in any newsman's book the major Washington stories would include the Tydings investigation of the McCarthy charges, the MacArthur dismissal inquiry, the McCarran hearings, and McCarthy's continuing warfare against the State Department. Congress, not the President, became the principal source of news, explanation, and opinion.

The investigations themselves were singularly barren of conclusions. Despite all the furor, they did not result in drastic legislative reforms or even in substantial defeats to the administration's foreign-policy program. Yet it would be idle to claim that this shift in public attention had not affected the workings of the American government. It served to diminish the usefulness of a great many of the President's chief lieutenants and to elevate into positions of commanding importance hitherto obscure members of Congress. It enabled one comparatively junior senator lacking the conventional trappings of seniority and prestige to sustain for a considerable time a threat to the President's control over the Executive branch. It created serious doubts at home and abroad whether the President did in truth stand at the helm of government during a critical time in world affairs. This era, in brief, illustrates the degree to which the reporting of events can itself be a major political event.

Publicity is a force that has become uniquely essential to the American system of government, in which "public opinion" is called on daily to arbitrate between two competing branches of government that are supposedly separate and co-ordinate to what Woodrow Wilson called the "literary theory" of our Constitution.

In recent years, U.S. government has, in fact, experienced a curious turnabout in the exercise of powers from what was envisaged in Constitutional doctrine. The President, aided by a growing staff of experts, has become the prime formulator of legislative programs and the chief budget maker. Congress, on the other hand, with the proliferation of its investigative committees, ever attempts to serve as board of review and veto over the ordinary administration of the Executive departments. Each, in testing the undefined limits of these new claimed prerogatives, must resort unceasingly to public explanation to sustain the logic of its claims.

Within the Executive branch itself, grown large and infinitely compartmentalized, the publicity competition often takes on the character of a life-and-death struggle. Inside the Pentagon, where a sizable chunk of the Federal budget is divided up, the highest classifications of military secrecy often go out the window in the rivalry among the three services. When an Army colonel was court-martialed in 1957 for leaking to the press information about the Army missile Jupiter, Dr. Wernher von Braun, head of the Army Missile Program, testified in his defense: "Jupiter involves several million dollars of the taxpayers' money. One hundred per cent security would mean no information for the public, no money for the Army, no Jupiter. . . . The Army has got to play the same game as the Air Force and the Navy."

The reporter in Washington has witnessed on numerous occasions how the journalistic mask of a public figure can take possession of the man himself. More than witnessed—he has often played an active role in the transformation. A leading correspondent who prefers to remain anonymous has provided a revealing illustration of this creative function of journalism in a letter to a friend: "I have had one very important experience in this town. I knew Arthur Vandenberg when I thought he was the most pompous and prejudiced man in the United States Senate. I saw him change partly by the processes of mellowing old age, but mainly by accident and particularly as a result of public reaction to his famous speech of January 10, 1945. I happen to know that that speech, or rather the main parts of it, were largely accidental. I can say to you privately that I was, myself, quite by chance responsible for that change in the speech. But my point is that what changed Vandenberg was not the speech itself, but the press of public reaction to the speech, and from then on, as you know, he played an important role in winning bipartisan support for the concept of collective security."

What the writer failed to add was that the "public reaction" was in large part stimulated by the tremendous fanfare that leading newspapers gave to Vandenberg's speech—a build-up that took the senator quite by surprise, as he confessed in his private papers, published posthumously. It was not the first time—nor will it be the last—that the Washington journalist has hailed the policy declaration that he himself had a hand in ghosting.

This tendency for the development of news to influence reactively the development of events is a force that cannot be precisely charted. The interaction can be a result of pure chance. It can, as modern practitioners of the art of public relations appreciate, be made the object of manipulation. It can even be a product of conscious co-operation, or lack of it, between the politician and the press.

News standards go to the very core of policy formulation by high officials. At a gathering of newsmen to pay honor to him for his famous plan, General George C. Marshall described the publicity problems of putting the plan across. And Paul G. Hoffman, at the same gathering, paid glowing tribute to certain members of the Washington press corps. "We would have never gotten the dollars," said Hoffman, "if it hadn't been for the support of the reporters of the Overseas Writers' Club." The tribute was duly and modestly accepted by those present.

Yet there is a basic conflict of interest between the government and the press that creates continuing unrest in Washington. On Dean Acheson's last day in office as Secretary of State, he was paid a visit by James Reston, Washington correspondent for the *New York Times*. The purpose of Reston's call was to ask quite bluntly why the Secretary and he had not enjoyed better working relations. Underlying his question was the unhappy conviction that Acheson, who brought unusually high talents to the office, had been unwittingly caught in the riptides of publicity. His effectiveness had been gradually eroded by failures of communication.

Secretary Acheson answered with equal bluntness that better relations would have been impossible, since there was a basic conflict of purpose between the two of them. A Secretary of State, Acheson said, had to germinate new policies and to nurse them along until they have reached the stage of development when they can withstand the battering assaults of the political arena. The reporter's primary purpose, on the other hand, is to get news for his paper, no matter what the effect on policy.

Reston stoutly denies that the conflict can be defined in quite these terms. He admits that it is the duty of the reporter to get at the news while it is still news. In government today, when so many policy decisions are made in the closed precincts of the Executive departments, the press would be abdicating its function if it were to sit by until these decisions are formally announced. But Reston argues that Secretary Acheson failed to understand and make use of the creative power of the press to muster public support for sound policy and, alternatively, to gauge the full extent of public reaction to unsound or unrealistic policy.

This dialogue between the Secretary and the reporter—both able and earnest men, both anxious that democratic government also be effective government— reveals a dilemma of government and the press. It is more recognizable in the American system than in those parliamentary democracies where the press does not play nearly so intimate a role.

The American fourth estate today operates as a *de facto* quasi-official fourth branch of government, its institutions no less important because they have been developed informally and, indeed, haphazardly. Twelve hundred or so members of the Washington press corps, bearing no authority other than accreditation by a newspaper, wire service, or network, are part of the privileged officialdom in the nation's capital. The power they exercise is continuing and substantive.

Yet the interaction of the government and the press needs to be examined to discover how much or how little it contributes to a continuing disorder in American democracy when government fails to explain itself clearly and candidly to the citizens. It is equally a failure when the press fails to communicate intelligibly the news of government or when that news becomes an instrument in the hands of self-seeking interests.

"THANK YOU, MR. PRESIDENT"

No monarch in history has had a retinue like that which gathers about the American President and calls itself the White House press corps. The reporters hang about his antechamber with the self-assurance of privileged courtiers at some federal court, keeping under constant surveillance and interrogation those who pass in and out—governors, cabinet members, senators, ambassadors. They dog the President's every step and turn his most casual conversation into a mass meeting. Their special plane takes off after the one carrying the President and alights just in advance of it. Thus even the contingency of a fatal crackup has been calculated so as not to interrupt the flow of prompt and plentiful publicity about our President.

Just to the right of the entrance to the White House's west wing where the President has his office, a special room has been set aside for the press, its typewriters, its telephones, its poker table. There the twenty to thirty White House "regulars"—reporters whose sole assignment is to cover this tiny beat—spend much of their day. Directly across the entrance hall, the Press Secretary has offices connected by private corridor to the President's own office. Two and three times daily the Press Secretary meets with the regulars and any other reporters who may wander in. And throughout the day the reporters are in constant touch with the Press Secretary and his assistants, checking leads, listening for tips, or simply killing time.

But the chief event of the week is when the reporters, one hundred and fifty to two hundred strong, file into the ornate little room in the old State Department Building once used for signing treaties. They pack themselves into row on row of tightly spaced steel folding chairs and overflow onto the rococo balcony up near the ceiling. Along the back of the room a solid bank of floodlights and cameras adds to the congestion. In the heat of Washington summer it is almost unbearable. At the appointed hour the doors are closed against the laggards, and the nation's leading citizen hurries in from a side entrance to meet the press. His assistants march in behind him to listen, but seldom to intercede. There may be a few prepared words, and then, with a barely perceptible Presidential nod, it begins. Reporters rise and vie for recognition. For the next half hour, the President's gaze scans the assemblage and the President's nod designates who shall be his interrogators. His choice is generally a random one and as a consequence the interchange of question and answer is apt to be quite haphazard. The ceremony is not very solemn, but the underlying solemnity of the occasion can never be entirely forgotten. For a time the President of the United States stands alone, unshielded by the layers of officialdom that lie between him and the American public.

The conference may follow a smooth and gentle course. Or it may explode with unabashed savagery, the reporters probing relentlessly into a touchy subject and the President lashing back angrily at question and questioner. Then, at a signal from the press itself, it is all over. The grand finale is a scene of frenzy. Turning their backs on the still standing President, reporters from the wire services and networks who occupy the frontmost seats charge down the center aisle in a pushing, shoving race to reach telephone booths just outside the door.

Foreign visitors to the President's press conference depart from this undisciplined ritual with a feeling of awe, consternation, or outright disgust. But they rarely fail to be impressed by its importance as a central act in the high drama of American government.

Why such mutual fascination between the President and the press? What prompts the editor and publisher to devote so much money and space to the Presidential press conference? And what, in turn, causes the President to put up with the incessant inroads on his privacy? The answer lies in the very nature of modern American government. Proper relations with the press are as essential to its orderly functioning as the power to levy taxes and pass laws.

The Press Beats the Measure

Any President who may lightly consider abolishing the press conference, as Eisenhower reportedly did during the hectic months before his inauguration, must come to recognize its value as a device for keeping public attention focused on himself as the single most important person in the United States and, for that matter, the free world. By having the floodlights thus fixed, the President can give his words and gestures subtle gradations of meaning, and avoid the stark black-and-white they would acquire in a formal announcement. He can, if he chooses, address words of intercession or exhortation to Congress that would not be altogether effective for him to speak in his weekly conferences with Congressional leaders of his party. He can, with a casual word at his press conference, break an administrative log jam in the vast Federal Bureaucracy spread out beneath him. Finally, he can speak to the foreign governments, for which his slightest nuance may have considerable meaning.

All this the press conference can do for the President. Yet the blunt fact remains that to a large extent, its ritual has been shaped by the specialized needs of the press rather than by his needs. While the President and his aides must give considerable thought to anticipating the questions that will be directed to him, he can never be altogether certain that one will not come hurtling his way to catch him completely unawares. The press, not he, regulates the pattern, the flow, and to some extent the mood of the conference. The press even controls, within limits, its duration. It is the prerogative of the senior wire-service man to call out "Thank you, Mr. President" in order to terminate it. There have been times when the conference was terminated well ahead of the usual half hour because, in the judgment of the senior wire-service man, there was news enough.

During his press conference, the President is exposed. He knows his moment of truth as clearly as any matador. Of course he can refuse, he can evade, or he can angrily rebuff an impetuous questioner. But he must do it before curious eyes. Frequently what he does not say may prove just as newsworthy as what he does say. He must endure the stupid question and maintain his composure. He must be prepared to leap from a penetrating query about a most delicate policy matter to one about the appointment to a district judgeship, and then leap back again without growing rattled. His questioner may serve him false or misleading information on which to comment. He may suddenly find himself confronted with a diplomatic question from a foreign correspondent who is really an agent of his government.

Almost as irritating to the President are the questions never asked for which he has prepared an answer. After one of Eisenhower's conferences, a White House aide listed for me six major questions involving events, policies, and programs that had gone unasked at that week's conference, despite their prominence in the news. One time Eisenhower commented wryly as the reporters trooped out of the conference room, "No one gives me an opportunity to talk about defense."

Misadventures

The Presidential press conference can result in startling fiascoes. The most celebrated, which occurred in November 1950, resulted in news stories all over the world that President Truman was considering use of the atom bomb in Korea. It brought Prime Minister Attlee flying to America for consultation, and indirectly hastened the death of the President's Press Secretary, Charles G. Ross. John Hersey has provided a masterful account of this ill-fated conference. Having been present in the White House at the time to gather research material for a *New Yorker* profile of Truman, Hersey was able to describe in detail the development of what was a major failure in communication.

The Chinese Communists had just entered the Korean War and the situation was admittedly grave. Several days before the conference, a number of top United States policy planners had worked to prepare a statement which the President dutifully read at the beginning of his press conference. At no time, according to Hersey, had there been any mention of using the atom bomb. But Truman's prepared statement, expressing general determination to remain steadfast in the face of the new peril, was not particularly newsworthy and the reporters probed for "hard" news. They got it when, in response to a question, the President affirmed that the use of the atom bomb was "always under consideration." The headlines that resulted dropped the "always" and played heavily upon the "under consideration."

Hersey's analysis, which tends to place all the blame on the reporters, could be criticized as the work of someone who was not accustomed to the routine of the press conference. The reporters could legitimately argue that there was no way for them to know what had gone on in the minds of those who had planned the President's statement. They could only assume, in the light of the President's vague intimations, that he deliberately intended to raise the specter of the atom bomb at that critical time. By their recurrent questions—there had been five or six—they had sought to alert him to the significance of his utterances. A final definite warning had been sounded by Anthony Leviero of the *New York Times* when he asked if the President's remarks could be quoted directly. The President refused but made no effort to clarify his remarks until after the conference, when the first wire-service bulletins had already begun to spread the alarming story.

But regardless of any specific finding of guilt, Hersey's documentary was in fact a damning indictment of the slipshodness of the press conference as an institution for conveying vital information. It gave meaning to the judgment of Charles A. Beard, who declared "no President should be encouraged or forced to speak offhand on any grave question of national policy." On the press's side, it illustrated the unspeakable folly of measuring the President's utterances with the same yardstick of "newsworthiness" as that used on a minor news event. It bordered on complete irresponsibility to take his words and edit them for the sensational headline and the startling lead paragraph, which was the way Mr. Truman's atom-bomb remarks were handled. All the qualifying details were left out of the early bulletins. The President's statement was given shape by the inexorable pattern of "the news."

Whereas Mr. Truman was the backwoods Baptist laying down a personal testament of God and Mammon to the congregated reporters, President Eisenhower has preferred to be the high priest, whose utterances contain less fire, more theology. Matured in the practice of conducting military briefings for the politicians, he is a master at the art of saying little while talking a great deal.

President Eisenhower has had his rough moments with the press. One such occasion was in late 1953, when reporters took him to task for Attorney General Brownell's speech accusing ex-President Truman of knowingly promoting a Communist spy in his government. From abroad Harold Callender of the *New York Times* cabled an account of the astounded European reaction: "Few would believe that the reporters would dare address the President with the challenging questions asked or that their editors published the questions and answers."

Once, in response to persistent queries about the McCarthy forays against his administration, Eisenhower stalked angrily from the conference room. On a number of occasions, he has flushed deep red when prodded about a sensitive subject and rejected the questioner abruptly. But in the main he has achieved a gentleness in his conferences that contrasts strangely with the flamboyant Truman ones. Questions involving high policy matters are asked with the broadest kind of hook, on which the president can hang any answer he likes. There are dark suspicions that the partisan preferences of newspaper publishers have caused this. Certainly a more direct cause has been the fact that these are the kinds of questions the President will answer.

Eisenhower's use of the press conference has not furthered it as an instrument of lucid communication. His penchant for the vague generality as well as his willingness to comment volubly on almost any subject has tended to debase the currency value of his words. After one notable conference, a reporter observed that if the President's remarks that morning were to be taken as policy, it could be assumed (1) that he was in conflict with his own administration on the right and duty of public officials to state opinions on Supreme Court decisions; (2) that United States commanders in the field might or might not have authority to use atomic weapons in defense of their commands—he was not sure; (3) and that the United States might or might not wait to be attacked in a major war. There have been a number of times when the reporter would have devoutly preferred a terse "no comment" to the President's rambling soliloquy in which they could find neither sense nor syntax no matter how they searched.

For both the two latest Presidents, the press conference has been in a deeper sense a failure. For Truman it produced an impression of Presidential arrogance and obstinacy that worsened his working relations with Congress. Eisenhower, on the other hand, has conveyed through it an impression of irresolution. He has maintained the image of the President who reigns, but there has been a blurring in the eyes of the world of the image of the President who rules, of the leader who stands for specific issues and against specific issues, who likes certain people and, yes, detests certain people.

It can be argued that in both Truman's and Eisenhower's cases the failure of the press conference has been merely symptomatic of more fundamental failures of leadership. Most observers, however, would concede that it has tended to aggravate their problems. It has compounded the difficulty of leadership for the President in an era when he grapples with issues incapable of easy or quick solutions.

The President's press conferences have not contributed the way they should to the formation of a truly enlightened public opinion. As Zechariah Chafee has noted, "They tempt a President to blurt out anything that boils up in his emotions and do his thinking out loud in public." There are times when the thoughtful onlooker is dumbfounded by the offhand manner in which unmatured convictions on critically grave issues are voiced by the nation's chief executive. The difficulties provoked by this practice are not lessened now that the President's every word becomes a part of historic record.

The Interpellative Branch

Quite a few people have critically examined the shortcomings of the President's press conference. By and large they fall into two groups: the abolitionists and the reformers. The abolitionists claim that the conference is one of the worst abuses in a capital where publicity has become a policy in itself, rather than a product of policy. But a telling riposte to the abolitionists was voiced by one veteran Washington correspondent: "O.K., cut out the President's press conferences—better cut out the Secretary of State's and the other cabinet officers' while you're at it. Then let the administration's enemies on the Hill dominate the headlines." His answer reveals the extent to which the need for publicity must be a dominating concern among those responsible for Executive leadership in America.

Those who would reform the President's press conference have suggested such changes as more systematic preparatory briefing; active participation by the President's advisers, especially when they sense something going wrong; a brief post-conference session conducted by the Press Secretary to clear up possible misunderstandings; and a delayed release time on publication of conference news. Most practicing newspapermen are strongly opposed to a return to the requirement of submitting written questions in advance—a practice that evokes memories of the stuffy days of Harding and Hoover. Instead, many support James Reston when he suggests that to certain difficult questions the President might promise to provide studied answers in writing, later in the week. With a newspaperman's shrewdness, he points out that this practice would lighten the burden imposed on understaffed Washington news bureaus, which can hardly do justice in a single day to the great variety of questions and answers presently evoked at the press conference. The President would thus reap the benefit of providing "more front page copy on more days of the week."

It is noteworthy that all of these reforms would in effect give formal recognition to the Fourth Estate as the interpellative branch of the American government. It would, however, be less a Constitutional revolution than the admission that such a revolution has already taken place, and that the time has come to set our new house in order.

MAKING NEWS ON THE HILL

The member of Congress is uniquely both a creator and creature of publicity. By the very nature of his job, with its relative insecurity of tenure, he is concerned with the processes by which the public attention is attracted. He lives in a state of intimacy with the newspaperman that outsiders mistake for pure cronyism. He employs his highest-paid assistant to diagnose and fill the prescriptive needs of the press.

The individual publicity drive of any particular congressman may seem a minor and even ludicrous phenomenon. But collectively, reinforced by the publicity-making mechanisms of Congressional committees, it gives a distinct Congressional bias to the news, and creates certain advantages for the Legislative branch of government in its continuing power struggle with the Executive. It contributes at times to a Constitutional imbalance that seems to be a recurrent disorder of American government.

The press is omnipresent on the Hill. Room for its ever-expanding needs has been carved out of every strange nook and cranny of the ancient Capitol. Just over the presiding officer's desk in each House hovers the press gallery, its occupants constantly monitoring the proceedings and frequently outnumbering the legislators present on the floor below. For the wire services there are special muted telephones within the chamber itself, ready for the instant communique about a critical Congressional action. Behind swinging doors, off the gallery, the press has its quarters for work and relaxation. Teletypes stand ready to relay copy to the central offices of the wire services. The walls are lined with typewriters and telephone booths. Great leather couches offer all-night accommodation should the legislative session drag on. In nearby studios the reporters for radio and television can originate their broadcasts.

Favor for Favor

The reporter's access to individual legislators is frequent and intimate. Near each chamber there are private rooms to which members of Congress are summoned, in a never-ending file, for communion with the press. They come, obediently and willingly. During a lively session, the President's Room just off the Senate Lobby is continuously crowded with little clusters of solons and scribes, two by two, exchanging earnest confidences. Special doormen stand ready at the request of reporters to call still others away from the debate. At times this little anteroom contains more senators than the Senate Chamber. The creation of the public image of the debate is more engrossing to most of them than the actual debate itself.

Across the Capitol, a similar drama is being enacted in the House of Representatives. There, even the members' lobby is open to the prowling correspondent. The senior reporters assigned to the Hill share an intimacy with Congressional leaders far beyond that possessed by lesser members of Congress. At least once daily the wire-service representatives are invited in for sessions with the Speaker of the House and the Senate majority leader. On countless occasions the reporter may attend informal convocations at which down-to-earth matters of politics are explored. He may find himself a direct witness to, even a participant in, the drafting of laws.

At times the raw competition by congressmen to serve the press takes on bizarre proportions. The following account appeared in a "Footnote to the News" column of the *Washington Post and Times Herald:*

> A freshman Senator outslicked his veteran colleagues to pick off his easiest publicity plum available last week. He was Clifford P. Case (R.-N.J.) whose reaction comment to the President's decision (to veto the natural-gas bill) was the first to hit the Senate press gallery. His prize was a prominent play in the afternoon newspapers.
>
> Behind his speed was the quick thinking and faster legs of Sam Zagoria, Case's administrative assistant and former *Washington Post and Times Herald* reporter.
>
> Zagoria had run off several copies of the Senator's "isn't-it-grand" statement early Wednesday morning. He then parked himself by the Associated Press teletype in the Senate lobby. When the flash came through, he hightailed it back to the press gallery, one floor above, where eager reporters were waiting to write reaction accounts. Zagoria beat a runner for Senator William A. Purtell (R.-Conn.) by one minute flat.

For the reporter, it is more than easy access that makes Congress a primary news source. The business of Congress is the stuff of which good news reporting is made. Congress is a continuing scene of drama, conflict, and intrigue. Its battles can be described in terms of colorful personalities rather than amorphous and complicated issues that may confound the copy desk and confuse the reader. It is therefore perhaps inevitable that there should be this "Congressional bias" to the news. But some of the results need to be examined.

Powerful pressures dissuade the reporter from being as zealous a prober of Congress as he is of the Executive departments. His obtaining of news "exclusives" depends upon the preservation of a chummy relationship with members of Congress. A great amount of news is dispensed to him as a favor, and must be regarded as such. Furthermore, retaliation for unfavorable publicity can be swift and vengeful. It is by no means unusual for a member, enraged by something appearing in print, to take to the floor in a violent attack against the offending reporter. And such is the clublike atmosphere of the two houses that no member is likely to come to the reporter's defense.

Thus, on April 10, 1950, Senator Harry Cain rose on the Senate floor to answer an assertion by *Time* magazine that he was among the Senate's "expendables." For the better part of the afternoon he centered an attack on *Time's* Congressional correspondent. "If ever I sat with a human being who was smug, arrogant, self-centered, vain and frustrated . . . This ulcer-burdened young American who could neither vote nor fight . . . The agent *Time* magazine has today was a 4-F in war . . . (He) has undoubtedly encouraged other men to die, but he has never . . . watched them die." Not one senator raised a protest against this stream of abuse.

There are countless instances when Congressmen demand special privileges which go unpublicized but which would provoke a furor if made by an administration official. Members of the press often apply a deliberate censorship to a legislator's unwise public utterances. One neophyte reporter who unwittingly quoted a rash remark revealing bigotry on the part of a leading congressman was afterward chastised by his press colleagues for this indiscretion.

Women correspondents covering Capitol Hill circulate among themselves a list of those members of Congress with whom it is unsafe to be alone. One or two solons have been known to be outrageous sex reprobates. But no word of their misdemeanors ever reaches the reading public. Senators have been seen to stagger drunkenly onto the Senate floor and deliver unintelligible harangues without creating a ripple in the press.

Amid the publicity drives of Congress, the investigating committee exerts the most powerful thrust. It is geared to the production of headlines on a daily and even twice-daily basis. It is able to create the news story that lingers week after week on the front pages to form an indelible impression on the public mind. No institution of the Executive branch is capable of such sustained and well-manipulated publicity.

The most notable committee investigations are seldom in point of fact "investigations" once the public hearings commence. They are planned deliberately to move from a preconceived idea to a predetermined conclusion. The skill and resourcefulness of the chairman and a sizable staff are pitted against any effort to alter its destined course. Whatever investigating takes place is done well in advance. The hearing is the final act in the drama. Its intent, by the staging of a spectacle, is to attract public attention, to alarm or to allay, to enlighten or sometimes to obscure.

How to Run a Hearing

In 1943, the counsel of a House committee investigating the Federal Communications Commission distributed a confidential memorandum to committee members that fell into the hands of outsiders. It had been prepared for the committee by a reporter for International News Service, whose talents later carried him high in the employ of the Republican National Committee. Its seven points remain a classic disquisition on the publicity requirements for an investigation:

1. Decide what you want the newspapers to hit hardest and then shape each hearing so that the main point becomes the vortex of the testimony. Once that vortex is reached, adjourn.
2. In handling press releases, first put a release date on them, reading something like this: 'For release at 10:00 a.m., EST July 6,' etc. If you do this, you can give releases out as much as 24 hours in advance, thus enabling reporters to study them and write better stories.
3. Limit the number of people authorized to speak for the committee, to give out press releases or to provide the press with information to the fewest number possible. It plugs leaks and helps preserve the concentration of purpose.
4. Do not permit distractions to occur, such as extraneous fusses with would-be witnesses, which might provide news that would bury the testimony which you want featured.
5. Do not space hearings more than 24 or 48 hours apart when on a controversial subject. This gives the opposition too much opportunity to make all kinds of countercharges and replies by issuing statements to the newspapers.
6. Don't ever be afraid to recess a hearing even for five minutes so that you keep the proceedings completely in control so far as creating news is concerned.
7. And this is most important: don't let the hearings or the evidence ever descend to the plane of a personal fight between the Committee Chairman and the head of the agency being investigated. The high plane of a duly-authorized Committee of the House of Representatives examining the operations of an Agency of the Executive Branch for constructive purposes should be maintained at all costs.

The allusion in point 5 to "the opposition" simply means those who are being investigated. It is a rare investigation, and certainly a poorly publicized one which has not passed judgment on the "opposition" long before the hearings commence.

The Uses of Laughter

The proliferation of publicity-inspired investigations has taken us in the direction of what might be called "government by concurrent publicity." Decisions tend to be taken not in an orderly, procedural way but on the basis of what is instantly explainable to the public through the mass media.

The investigated, too, have turned to publicity as a weapon. Last year, there was a fantastic case study when the House Special Subcommittee on Legislative Oversight began to probe the affairs of the New England tycoon Bernard Goldfine and particularly his dealings with the Assistant to the President, Sherman Adams. Goldfine, accompanied by a retinue of lawyers and publicity agents, set up headquarters in a Washington hotel, staged press and television conferences day and night, timed releases to compete with committee-inspired headlines, and pursued a calculated public-relations policy to make himself appear, as one aide put it, "a simple, innocent, underdog type being persecuted by a powerful congressional committee."

Philip Deane of the London *Observer* cabled home a graphic account of his visit to the Goldfine publicity headquarters:

> We were shushed into silence while the television news was switched on. One of the well-known commentators was speaking of the latest developments in the Goldfine case. When mentioning Goldfine himself, the television star lost control and an Homeric laugh spread across his distinguished face. . . .
>
> "Great! Great!" said Mr. Jack Lotto, Public Relations Counselor to the Goldfine interests. "That's what we want; we want people to laugh."
>
> "Please!" said a European journalist. "Did you say you wanted people to laugh at your employer?" . . .
>
> "It's like this," explained a fellow journalist. "When McCarthy attacked Senator Millard Tydings, of Maryland, Tydings tried to defend himself with dignity and failed miserably. His Public Relations firm made a fascinating study of this and decided that the only way to fight an attack by Congressional investigation is to raise more noise than your opponent, make the whole thing into a farce."
>
> "People don't think of you as a villain when they are laughing at you," said Williamson thoughtfully.
>
> "Doesn't Goldfine mind being made a clown?" asked the European.
>
> "You're thinking in terms of your own country. People here are different," said the American journalist. "Actually, there's a good deal of sympathy for Goldfine. He has done less than most business men do. He gives vicuna coats. Others give mistresses to married men. Have you seen salesmen entertaining buyers at Las Vegas?"
>
> This is sad because Goldfine is cute and he is not such a bad example of the great American dream—poor immigrant boy makes good. Lotto here is applying the conclusions of the Tydings case, defending the Goldfine integrity by destroying the Goldfine dignity while incidentally, the whole United States Administration goes down gloriously in a cloud of fudge.

The net effect of this and similar publicity brouhahas has been to divert the public's attention from the underlying ills in government that need legislative attention. Amid the aimless airing of charges, the quest reduces itself to a confused chase after individual villains rather than a purposeful inquiry to get at the root causes and to devise lasting solutions.

A NEW KIND OF DEMAGOGUE

The American politician has always been something of a dramatist in search of an audience, more flamboyant, a greater individualist than his European counterpart. Recently, however, there has begun to emerge in the halls of Congress a new type of politician conditioned to the age of mass media and more keenly aware of the uses of publicity. He is not apt to be a member of what William S. White calls the "Inner Club," where emphasis is still put on seniority and skill in negotiation. He need not be in the forefront among those who uphold the ancient traditions of eloquence in Congressional debate. Nor need he be assiduous in preparing legislation and attending to the thousand and one chores of pushing it through to enactment. Rather he is a man versed in the subtleties of appealing beyond Congress directly to the mass audience. He knows the formula of the news release, the timing, the spoon-feeding necessities of the publicity campaign. He assesses with canny shrewdness the areas of enterprise that will best lend themselves to a sustained publicity build-up. He is a master at shadow play, creating the illusion of magnificent drama from a reality that may be quite mundane. Usually he lacks direct influence among his colleagues, but he acquires a special standing commensurate with his reflected power as a "nationally known" figure.

To a greater or lesser degree, every politician who makes his way in Congress today must have something of this new sense. But it is possible to isolate advanced specimens of this *genus politicus* for which publicity has been a more durable stock in trade than seniority or legislative prestige. Among these, one would have to include Richard Nixon, Republican, who was catapulted to national prominence and power—from newly elected congressman to Vice-President—in the brief span of six years without having his name tied to a single notable achievement except the exposure of Alger Hiss.

Also to be included high on this list of the new politician is Senator Estes Kefauver, Democrat, who has been regularly rejected by his more powerful colleagues from membership in the Inner Club but stands as the symbol of senator for countless Americans. A quiet-spoken, not particularly eloquent man, he scarcely fits the picture of the new-type politician. But as reporters who have worked closely with him can testify, he shows an uncanny knack for lifting an idea or an issue out of the slough of neglect and placing it squarely on page 1. On one occasion during the Dixon-Yates controversy, Kefauver exposed with resounding headline clatter the name of a Budget Bureau official who was reputedly guilty of attempting to sabotage the Tennessee Valley Authority. It turned out that the same man had been named months earlier by Senator Lister Hill, a more traditional politician without the flair for publicity. No one had noticed.

McCarthy and the Press

The career of Senator Joseph McCarthy is, of course, by now a classic case. Whereas the traditional demagogue could be measured by how skillfully he sized up and played on fears and prejudices existing in a region or within a social group, McCarthy's skill lay primarily in his capacity to "stage" a single issue so as to dominate the channels of communication and to distract a national audience. Huey Long or Tom Heflin knew how to sway the crowd, stirring its emotions, playing on its vanities. McCarthy was never terribly good before a large crowd. But he knew how to rule the headlines.

In February 1950, brandishing stage-prop documents that he never let anyone examine, McCarthy showed his talents for the first time. As Richard Rovere has pointed out, *Senator charges communist influence in state department* might have produced a two-inch story on page 15 of the local newspaper. *Over two hundred with communist ties* would have done slightly better. But *205 card carrying communists* was something else. It was as if the press yearned for the really big lie.

Responsible newspapers tried hard to live up to the American Society of Newspaper Editors' ethical rule entitled "Fair Play"; "A newspaper should not publish unofficial charges affecting reputation or moral character without opportunity given to the accused to be heard." But in practice it worked like this: Late one afternoon Senator McCarthy might name a person, more likely a series of them. All through the evening the accused's telephone kept ringing. He was told briefly the nature of the charge made against him—let us say, "top Soviet agent"—and asked for a brief reply. McCarthy's charge was controversial and unexpected—a news count of two. The denial was controversial and completely expected—a news count of one. Both were equally lacking in proof. Nobody, after all, carries the credentials on his person to prove that he is not the "top Soviet agent."

By such means, McCarthy held the headlines. Day after day, several times a day, in time for the morning, afternoon, the seven o'clock, and late evening editions, he served up the scabrous material that he was attempting to make the national folklore. He knew the ingredients for the "lead," the "overnight," and the "sidebar." He could evoke the most publicity bounce from the ounce. Not one of the succession of department and agency heads who came up against him was able to find an effective defense. Neither of the two Presidents who had to reckon with him ever discovered a truly satisfactory counter-publicity weapon. He threw great governmental establishments like the State Department and the Army into confusion and provoked precipitate decisions on policy and personnel resulting in untold damage.

Unlike certain senior members of Congress, McCarthy lacked the capacity to insert a crippling rider into legislation or to tamper with an appropriations bill in committee as a way of blackmailing the Executive. He never had the physical means, as his apologists frequently point out, to intimidate or to punish those who aroused his ire. There was no violence, in the ordinary sense of that word, during the reign of McCarthyism. All McCarthy could do was to carry his vendettas into the public headlines. That was enough. It produced unparalleled fear and pusillanimity in Washington.

Few of the reporters who regularly covered McCarthy believed him. Most came to despise and fear him as a cynical liar who was willing to wreak untold havoc to satisfy his own power drive. But though they feared him, it was not intimidation that caused the press to serve as the instrument for McCarthy's rise. Rather it was the inherent vulnerabilities—the frozen patterns of the press—which McCarthy discovered and played upon with unerring skill. "Straight" news, the absolute commandment of most mass journalism, had become a strait jacket to crush the initiative and the independence of the reporter.

McCarthyism was an unparalleled demonstration of the Congressional publicity system gone wild, feeding on the body politic like a cancerous growth. It demonstrated that public opinion when incessantly nagged by the instantaneous communications of the mass media and prodded by the pollsters is not capable of rendering sure verdicts on matters of great complexity. It showed that the publicity-generating power of Congress can be a dangerous force when it is not subject to check and review by higher bodies in or out of Congress.

McCarthyism sought to provide a vocabulary for our fears that had no relevance to the world we actually live in. Responsible men, talking to each other in this synthetic language, for a time lost contact with reality. McCarthyism's greatest threat was not to individual liberty or even to the orderly conduct of government. It corrupted the power to communicate which is indispensable to men living in a civilized society.

As a group, the reporters have made Washington the most thoroughly covered and most heavily reported capital in the world. Well over a hundred thousand words daily, the volume of a good-sized novel, pour out over wire, radio, and television. In periods of peak stress, the sheer productive capacity of this industry defies the imagination.

Ever since the arrival of the New Deal, the press corps has forsaken its old simple ways just as government has. The old-fashioned general-assignment reporter in Washington, who nibbles at news wherever he can find it, still survives but in reduced circumstances. In his place, Washington reporting has discovered new methods of organization, new ways of packaging news in response to the newly felt needs and the newly developed media of communication.

Reporting has moved to keep up with the changing times. Yet it would be preposterous to argue that the press has met the enormous challenge confronting it. For the dimension of the challenge goes beyond the requirements of speed, specialization, and clever new ways of packaging news. It is, rather, to be measured by how well our system of government, which is dependent on publicity to ensure its orderly functioning, is actually being reported. Viewing the problem in these terms, the reporter in Washington has cause for sober and troubled reflection.

The McCarthy era came as a deeply unsettling experience to many Washington correspondents. The demagogue has been defined as the undetected liar. Yet all the elaborate reporting mechanisms of the press seemed unable to detect McCarthy's lies and to communicate the basic fact that he *was* lying. As McCarthyism mushroomed in the nation's capital, the public dialogue grew strangely distorted. Serious reporters understood that the press was adding to the distortion rather than helping bring things into focus.

HOW STRAIGHT IS STRAIGHT NEWS?

"The job of the straight reporter," a wire-service editor once defined for me, "is to take the place of the spectator who is unable to be present. Like the spectator, he does not delve into motives or other side issues except as they become a part of the public record." Unfortunately, the spectator is a casual witness, usually bewildered by any unexpected event. The reporter who limits himself to this role often becomes an unwitting agent of confusion. The trouble with "straight" reporting is that it attempts to deny the creative role the reporter in fact plays in government. It is myth that even the most passionately objective reporter can be truly "straight" in translating the multiple events he covers into the staccato of the teletype. He must constantly make decisions—for good or bad.

Even the purely technical aspects of news production raise their own problems so far as objectivity is concerned. Let us examine the candid account of a typical working day described for me by an able wire-service reporter whose beat has been Capitol Hill:

A central fact of life for the wire-service reporter in Washington is that there are a great many more afternoon than morning papers in the United States. This creates a problem because the early afternoon paper on the East Coast goes to press between 10 and 10:30 A.M.—before the "news development" of the day. It means the wire-service reporter must engage in the basically phony operation of writing the "overnight"—a story composed the previous evening but giving the impression when it appears the next afternoon that it covers that day's events.

Let's take as an example the day the Austrian treaty came up in the Senate. The evening before, I prepared a story of which three-quarters was mere "background" concerning the treaty. In the progressive developments that followed, this part of the story remained untouched. But I had to have a "lead" on my overnight, so I called on Senator Walter George, chairman of the Foreign Relations Committee, and tried out an "angle" on him. Would there be any U.S. military aid for the Austrian army? George said, "No money. Only long-term credits." That became my lead. I had fulfilled the necessary function of having a story that seemed to be part of the next day's news.

Next day, when the treaty came up for debate in the Senate, it was my job to get some "top" on this story. Senator Sparkman led off for the supporters of the treaty. He had in his speech a couple of newsy items though nothing worthy of filing as a "bulletin." So I dictated a new lead and picked up the main body of the story from my overnight. I threw away the George lead because it was a phony one.

After Sparkman came Senator Jenner. He was vitriolic against the treaty. It was close to 2:30, which meant the deadline for the late afternoon papers. Was he worth a lead? I thought "No" because he represented such a minute minority in the Senate. But that was where a matter of judgment entered.

Suddenly, Jenner made a nasty crack about Eisenhower which was certainly newsier than anything Sparkman had said. How should I handle it? In deciding problems like this, I always have to consider what the other wire-service reporters covering the same story may be doing. I decided not to lead with Jenner, but instead to move his section of the story into the office as an insert. (All my decisions are reviewable in the office, where the editors may make a decision based on factors I know nothing about.) But the Jenner paragraph moved as an insert, which meant that there was a slug on the A-wire: "Insert—"Austrian Treaty paragraph after 'It was said . . .' "

A little after 3:30 P.M. the treaty was adopted. That automatically constituted a bulletin to be sent out immediately on the A-wire even though Senate passage had been accepted by everybody as a foregone conclusion. So I wrote a third lead for that particular story and then it was time to write a completely new story for next day's A.M. papers.

But my job had not finished. The treaty-adoption bulletin had gone out too late to get into most of the East Coast afternoon papers except for the big-city ones like the Philadelphia *Evening Bulletin,* which has seven editions. I had to find a new angle for an overnight to be carried next day by those P.M.s which failed to conclude the treaty story.

They don't want to carry simply a day-old account of the debate. They want a "top" to the news. So, to put it quite bluntly, I went and got Senator Thye to say that Jenner by his actions was weakening the President's authority. Actually, the Thye charge was more lively news than the passage of the Austrian treaty itself. It revealed conflict among the Senate Republicans. But the story had developed out of my need for a new peg for the news. It was not spontaneous on Thye's part. I had called seven other senators before I could get someone to make a statement on Jenner. There is a fair criticism, I recognize, to be made of this practice. These senators didn't call me; I called them. I, in a sense, generated the news. The reporter's imagination brought the senator's thinking to bear on alternatives that he might not have thought of by himself.

This can be a very pervasive practice. One wire-service reporter hounded Senator George daily on the foreign-trade question until he finally got George to make the suggestion that Japan should trade with Red China as an alternative to dumping its textiles on the American market. Then the reporter went straight-way to Senator Knowland to get him to knock down the suggestion. It made a good story, and it also stimulated a minor policy debate that might not have got started otherwise. The "overnight" is the greatest single field for exploratory reporting for the wire services. It is what might be called "milking the news."

The point of this description is to indicate just how complex the business of reporting really is. The phantasmagoria of "straight" news can itself produce a departure from true "objectivity." Within the routines that govern the straight reporter, there is abundant room for bias to enter. Unless he makes reasonable choices, difficult and long-drawn-out issues become progressively more distorted. He finds himself granting the forces of confusion greater access to the loudspeaker system of the press than the forces of clarity. McCarthy proved how pliant such "objectivity" can be in the hands of the skilled manipulator.

GOVERNMENT BY LEAK

By conservative estimate, ninety per cent of the conflicts arising between government and the press in Washington lie in that shadowy no man's land of news that is ahead of the public event. This quest for what is variously called "background reporting," the "news behind the news," and "inside dope" engages the highest talent of the less restricted Washington correspondents. It is frequently a source of bafflement to the public official. Senator Robert Taft used to complain bitterly that reporters in Washington were so busy trying to find out what was going to happen that they didn't provide a decent account of what had already happened.

In Washington it is always embarrassing when the lid blows off a background story that was meant to be strictly "not for attribution." Like the small-town gambler who gets word from the police department that the heat is on, the reporter knows that for some time there are going to be slim pickings in that particular vicinity. For the government official, it is no less embarrassing. Not only have policies got caught and perhaps irredeemably mangled in the machinery of publicity; the official himself has been exposed in a practice that officialdom can never admit goes on. In all the formal literature on the functioning of the American government, there is not one word on what has been variously called the "leak" or "cloaked news."

For the average citizen, who can be expected to bring only so much sophistication to the business of reading his newspaper, the problem is also serious. Unattributed news can be a highly confusing matter. Take, for example, what happened during the spring of 1955 when there was one of those recurrent crises over the islands in the Formosa Strait. On Saturday, March 26, the reader found a three-column thirty-six-point headline in the upper right-hand corner on page 1 in the *New York Times:* "U.S. Expects Chinese Reds to Attack Isles in April; Weighs All Out Defense." Three days later, the reader found another headline in the same position, same type: "Eisenhower Sees No War Now over Chinese Isles."

If the reader studied the two stories closely, he noted one similarity. Neither had a single word to indicate who had presumed to speak in the first instance for the United States or in the second for President Eisenhower. The reader was obliged to take the word of the reporters—in these two instances highly reliable men—that these contradictory stories had some basis in fact. Actually, the source of the first story was Chief of Naval Operations Robert B. Carney, speaking to a select group of reporters at a background dinner. The second was none other than the White House Press Secretary, James Hagerty, who attended a hastily called second background conference in order to repudiate the stories arising out of the first.

The newspaper reader is obliged to accept a sizable quantity of news in this fashion. He has been given lengthy and varying descriptions of the timing, the extent, and the conditions of potential war—frequently without being told who was making these life-and-death judgments. A newspaperman once catalogued five basic contradictions in "authoritative" reports about American policy in the Far East during a single crisis. It was truly a period of the background story gone wild. But it was by no means a unique period. Cloaked news has become an institution in the conduct of modern government in Washington, part of the regular intercourse between government and the press. During periods of high tension when more formal channels of communication—such as the President's and the Secretary of State's press conferences—are cut off, it often becomes the major means by which important news is transmitted. As one reporter described a critical period, "At a time when any word out of Washington was considered of international significance, what had developed, it appeared, was government by leak."

Compulsory Plagiarism

The ritual of the formal leak is fairly uniform. On a specified evening, a dozen or so correspondents gather in one of the private dining rooms in the Metropolitan Club or in a nearby downtown hotel. They are joined by the guest of honor, usually a high government official. It is not always clear who has initiated the meeting. Usually, the official has graciously "responded" to a standing invitation to meet with the reporters. He may or may not wish to admit that he has something to disclose. Drinks are served and all sit down to dinner. Until the meal is completed, the conversation follows an aimless pattern. No one likes to appear eager. Then chairs are pushed back, the presiding correspondent raps on his glass, reminds his colleagues of the rules, and the session begins.

Usually the official makes no formal remarks. He exposes himself to questions from the correspondents. If he knows his business, he can always manage to steer things in the direction he wishes to move. Frequently he does not openly admit that he is outlining a new government program or a drastic new approach to policy. He is merely "talking over" with the reporters some of the problems that confront him. He relies on them to have sense enough to grasp his meaning without having it spelled out for them. This studied casualness, at times, can breed misunderstanding and produce woeful consequences. The session sometimes goes on till quite late. Afterward, the chairman reminds everyone of the rules and each goes his separate way.

As background briefings grew more frequent, the rules of the game also began to multiply and become more complex. Partly because the matters discussed at the conferences were not so delicate as during wartime, partly because the newsmen chafed at information given purely for self-edification, there was an inevitable trend toward relaxing the strictures against publication. Now, conferences may range from "deep" background to a variety of lighter hues, depending on the secretiveness of the informant. In the main, the so-called Lindley Rule, first developed by Ernest K. Lindley of *Newsweek,* governs the proceedings. It requires what has been called compulsory plagiarism. The journalist may use what he has learned, but strictly on his own authority. Sometimes there are variations permitting him to quote "informed circles" or "a high government spokesman."

Usually there is at least one day's moratorium on the news coming out of such background briefings. If the news is especially hot, it may be arranged that nothing will be printed until the informant gets out of town so that he can establish a convenient alibi. But nothing is hard and fast about the arrangements. Misunderstandings are frequent, increasing in direct ratio to the importance of the news.

The postwar uses of the background session have been varied. It has been a means of alerting the press to the gravity of a situation being overlooked in the news. Dean Acheson, while still Under Secretary of State, once called in a small group of reporters and gave them the "background" on current Soviet demands against the Turks. It helped focus world attention on a situation that might have grown much worse.

The background conference is also used to play down the gravity of a situation. A dubious instance occurred when George Kennan, then chairman of the Policy Planning Board of the State Department, arranged a briefing at the time of President Truman's announcement of Russia's first atomic explosion. Contrary to the facts, Kennan assured reporters that the timing of the Soviet feat did not come as a surprise to American policy planners. He was deliberately trying to minimize the news value of the story in an effort to avert a strong public reaction.

Most frequently, the leak is symptomatic of rivalry in the higher echelons of government itself. Harold E. Stassen, once Special Assistant to the President on the disarmament question, would hold a background conference to discuss his thoughts on modifying U.S. proposals for arms controls. Promptly, Secretary of State Dulles would hold his own background conference to "clarify" the news coming out of the Stassen conference. Both conferences resulted in "news" about American policy. Unfortunately, the sum total of "news" on this crucial subject was and continues to be highly confusing.

The leak is traditionally used as a method of promoting a new program before it is formally unveiled before Congress. In Great Britain, where the cabinet has an obligation to report initially to the House of Commons, such use of the press to launch legislative programs would be unthinkable. In Washington it is habitual. Prior to the announcement of the so-called Eisenhower doctrine for the Middle East, Mr. Dulles engaged in three days of systematic leakage to reporters of the details of the new policy. By the third day, when Congressional leaders were themselves briefed on the proposal, a news dispatch in the *New York Times* noted that they ". . . were cautious in their reaction . . . but the Administration's plan had been so widely publicized before the leaders reached the White House that . . . they can do little more than adopt the new policy as presented."

The Cloak of Semi-Anonymity

The often sorely pressed Washington official sees numerous advantages in this system. It gives him a semi-anonymous voice in the cavernous echo chambers of the nation's capital. By keeping members of the press informed the official can engage in preventive action against the thousand and one stories that crop up from nowhere and do damage to sound policy. In addition, it permits greater flexibility in taking policy initiatives. Without risking either his own . . . or his department's reputation, he has an opportunity to take the measure of public and—more immediately important—Congressional opinion. If it is hostile, he can always fall back on what has been called "the technique of denying the truth without actually lying."

This latter technique works as follows: Secretary Dulles, in 1953 held a background conference in which he revealed to reporters that he had been doing some tentative thinking about a Korean boundary settlement along the line of the narrow waist of the peninsula. The news stories that emerged provoked criticism on Capitol Hill, particularly from Senator Knowland. Forthwith, the White House issued a denial, drafted by none other than Dulles himself, which stated that "the Administration has never reached any conclusion that a permanent division of Korea is desirable or feasible or consistent with the decisions of the United Nations." The pertinent words of course were "conclusion" and "permanent." The White House statement was not, in fact, what it seemed—a clear repudiation of what Mr. Dulles had told the reporters and what they had written, perforce on their own authority.

Despite its ambiguities, cloaked news has at times played a creative part during the malleable period of policy formation. Historian Bruce Catton has concluded that "our particular form of government wouldn't work without it." The critics—and there are a lonely few among the newsmen who stubbornly refuse to attend any news conference that is not on the record—make a number of arguments. They decry the informality that curses the whole practice. Mixing business and pleasure at the background dinner, with usually a goodly number of drinks thrown in, serves to befuddle the newsmen as well as the official. The reporter usually does not take notes while the official is present. (This might cramp the official's style.) There is a painful reconstruction afterward of what exactly was said. No one ever seems to be quite sure what the rules are. Moreover, because the reporter cannot quote a source, he finds it almost impossible to convey in his story the subtle gradations of meaning that good reporting requires. The background briefing provides a field day for those who prefer to present the news in stark, dramatic terms.

Agent or Tool?

Inevitably, the case against cloaked news gets down to fundamental concepts of reporting. What is the reporter's responsibility? Is he an intelligence agent for his paper and, ultimately, for the American public? Or is he to be made a tool of the government's counterintelligence operations? Arthur Schlesinger, Jr., once put the problem this way: "Washington newspapermen today hardly know whether to believe the Secretary of State, because they do not know if he is speaking to them as reporters or seeking to use them as instruments of psychological warfare. . . . What is the responsibility of a newspaperman when he discovers that some rumored development of policy is really only a psychological warfare trick? Should he print the truth at the risk of wrecking the plans of the Secretary of State? Or should he suppress the truth, betray himself, and deceive the American people?"

In this, as in much that concerns reporting in Washington, the absolutist position has little relevance to the reporter's workaday world. He cannot narrowly demarcate his sphere of operations. He is caught and intimately involved in the ceaseless battle of intelligence versus counterintelligence in Washington.

He can remove himself from the battlefield only at the risk of negating his role as a reporter.

A more fruitful inquiry may be directed into the conditions that should be imposed on cloaked news as a technique of communication. On the government's part, there needs to be a clearer recognition of the limits to which this practice can go. No matter how compelling the exigencies, the press in a free society should not be turned into the government's propaganda instrument. A fine line has to be drawn between the diplomatic and the deceitful. Secretary Dulles went over that line when, during the Quemoy-Matsu crisis of August, 1958, he issued a public statement of official policy, then immediately afterward made more sweeping pronouncements to reporters on a not-for-attribution basis. He was transferring an unfair burden to the reporter.

The main responsibility in guarding against the misuse of counterintelligence, however, lies not with the government but with the press. Just as government must take initiative in safeguarding its essential secrets, so the reporter must in the first instance decide what is proper and what is improper practice in the handling of the leak.

There are grounds for thoughtful review in this field. In his eagerness to get at the inside news, even the good reporter frequently loses the keen discrimination as shows in his more open reporting. As William S. White has written:

> Often reporters handle a leaked story with a solemn uncriticalness. The documents, or whatever, are ceremoniously produced for the public— which at times must scratch its head in perplexity as to what the devil they are all about. The motivation for the leak usually is not mentioned, although that may be the most significant part of the story.

The reporter himself is often guilty of deceit in the business of cloaking the news. He refers vaguely to "informed circles," implying a plurality of opinion when in fact he may be quoting the views of one person. He also plays up leaks with an importance they would not deserve if their sources were made known.

There is no reason why the rules for cloaked news cannot be made to fit more adequately the needs of honest reporting. For example, when anything of a highly controversial nature comes forth at a background session, the moratorium should be extended long enough to enable the reporter to check other sources. Few instances occur when anonymity needs be carried to the point that the reporter must deliberately confuse his reader about what is being related. The reporter's first obligation is to present a clear and balanced story.

No matter what improvements are made, however, this war of intelligence and counterintelligence is likely to remain one of the perplexing phenomena of the Washington scene. Though limits may be imposed on its excesses, there is no possibility of ever declaring a permanent truce. The conditions that give rise to it are basic to the American system of government and the free condition of American society. For the reporter, few hard and fast rules can be laid down to serve him as a permanent code of conduct. Instead, he must be governed in his daily work by his best judgments. It is one more measure of the creative role he has to play in the political life of Washington.

"MANAGED" NEWS

When James Reston appeared before the Moss Committee investigating "Availability of Information from Federal Departments and Agencies," he voiced an uneasiness felt by many:

> Most of my colleagues have been talking primarily about the suppression of news. I would like to direct the committee, if I may, to an equally important aspect of this problem which I think is the growing tendency to manage the news. Let me see if I can illustrate what I mean:
> I think there was a conscious effort to give the news at the Geneva Conference (in 1955) an optimistic flavor. I think there was a conscious effort there, decided upon even perhaps ahead of time, for spokesmen to emphasize all the optimistic facts coming out of that conference and to minimize all of the quarrels at that conference. . . .
> After the Geneva Conference a decision was taken in the government that perhaps this was having a bad effect, that the people in the western countries were letting down their guard, and therefore a decision was made, primarily upon the appeal of Chancellor Adenauer of Germany, that the government should strike another note. So that after the Geneva smiling, the new word went out that it might be a good idea now to frown a little bit, so the President made a speech at Philadelphia, taking quite a different light about the Geneva Conference. That is what I mean by managing the news. And I would urge your committee to look into that a bit, because, while it is bad to suppress a bit of information, it would seem to me to be even worse if all of the news-making powers of the Federal government were to blanket the newspaper situation with the theme which perhaps they did not believe was quite true, but might be an instrument of their thought.

Ethics in Action

From time to time the reporter in Washington becomes uneasily aware of a developing technique among the politicians for giving shape and direction to the news. In 1953, for example, there were telltale signs to indicate that Attorney General Herbert Brownell's attack on former President Truman for "knowingly" promoting "a Communist spy," i.e., Harry Dexter White, was part of a carefully planned operation calculated to garner maximum publicity. Shortly before Brownell made the attack, the Republican National Committee had ordered fifty thousand reprints of a Senate Internal Security Committee report on "Interlocking Subversion" in which White's name was prominently mentioned. The timing of the attack itself was most delicate. Brownell made it in a speech before the Chicago Executives Club at approximately 12:30 P.M. Chicago time (1:30 in Washington). Advance texts of two other speeches he gave that day had been distributed to the press the preceding afternoon, but this one, ironically entitled "Ethics in Government," was held up until an hour before Brownell spoke. As a result there was no chance for reporters to alert Truman until the story began to move on the press wires and out over radio and television. When frantic calls reached him in Missouri, Mr. Truman had to answer fast if he wanted to get his statement into the afternoon papers along with Brownell's charges. Inevitably, he reacted too quickly. He said that he did not remember any FBI memorandum on White and that he had gotten rid of him when he found that White was "wrong." By four o'clock that afternoon (Washington time), Press Secretary Hagerty had called in reporters and made public the text of a Truman letter in 1947 accepting Harry Dexter White's "resignation" and praising him for his services. Hagerty did not bother to explain how a six-year-old letter had been dug out of the files so quickly—in plenty of time for the evening papers and newscasts.

The G.O.P. publicity director gave this reporter an account of what went on at the Republican National Committee that same afternoon: "We put four men on the telephone to alert members of Congress. Three placed simultaneous calls to Velde, Jenner, and McCarthy." Those three gentlemen, of course, were chairmen of the investigating committees and could be counted on to pick up the publicity ball and carry it for an indefinite period. A secret FBI memorandum on White and others was leaked to reporter Richard Wilson of the Cowles publications. Wilson reported its contents in a series of stories. (For this piece of enterprise, Wilson was later awarded a Pulitzer Prize.)

Despite the careful publicity planning, the White affair took a strange turnabout when Senator McCarthy demanded and got free time on a nation-wide radio and television hookup to answer a televised reply Truman had made to Brownell. Instead of answering Truman, however, McCarthy launched a biting attack on the Eisenhower administration for not being sufficiently tough on Communists. The whole episode with its farcical climax was a distasteful case study in the misuse of publicity.

The Washington correspondent does not always know how to handle the "managed" news event, which he is expected to report while pretending to be blind to the props and staging devices. Too often, he tamely falls in with the purpose of the publicists. For a prolonged period, administration spokesmen were able to carry on a fantastic game of juggling the numbers of "security risk" dismissals in such a way as to create the impression that a wholesale cleanup of "subversives" in the government was taking place. Diligent reporters compiled documentary proof that the mounting totals furnished to them included a loose accumulation of resignations and dismissals on grounds other than security. But it was a complicated story, and most reporters were content to play it just the way the government spokesmen wished.

Manipulated news can also be used as an instrument against an administration. In 1954, Democratic National Chairman Stephen Mitchell suddenly accused Eisenhower's friend Bobby Jones of having conspired with the President on the golf course to destroy the Tennessee Valley Authority. Jones was supposedly an agent for a private power combine, Dixon-Yates, seeking to invade TVA. The particular charge was utterly without foundation. Yet because it was so sensational it succeeded in returning the Dixon-Yates story to the front pages and, as a direct consequence, revived interest in a lagging Congressional investigation. Once again an unsubstantiated attack served to trigger the publicity mechanisms and yield calculated results. The press was used as a vehicle for the transmission of managed news. A complex and important issue was reduced to an absurdity.

Mr. Hagerty at Work

A more subtle case study in the management of news is provided by the recent career of James Hagerty, who, in the opinion of an admiring critic, *Time* magazine, has been "by every standard the best—and most powerful—White House press secretary in U.S. history . . . Day in, day out, year in, year out, between Presidential speeches and press conferences, during Eisenhower's vacations and Eisenhower illnesses, Hagerty is the authentic voice of the White House and, to an extent rarely recognized, of the whole Administration."

With Washington reporters, and especially the group who are assigned on a continuous basis to the White House, Hagerty has proved thoroughly skilled and obliging in meeting the vexing demands of their business. He knows particularly well their nagging need to produce a steady flow of news. Twice a day and sometimes more he holds informal press conferences in a diligent effort to meet this need.

Hagerty has shown shrewd and farsighted judgment on occasion. When the President was stricken with his heart attack in 1955, passing along the word "Tell Jim to take over," the Press Secretary instituted a publicity operation remarkably candid in view of the grave situation. On the other hand, Hagerty is capable of rather subtle judgments in this business of public relations. Less than a year later, when Eisenhower was again hospitalized for the ileitis operation, the Press Secretary was not nearly so obliging to the press. "A Presidential heart attack is the property of the people," he explained afterward. "But we did not consider the ileitis something that endangered the President's life."

All these qualities may be considered virtues in the public-relations business. But an underlying suspicion that has disturbed a number of correspondents in Washington has been that Hagerty has carried these virtues too far. He has made of public relations an end in itself rather than a means to an end.

This was most apparent during the prolonged periods when the President has been ill or on vacations. As *Time* has since reported:

> Hagerty struggled valiantly and, to a point, successfully, in stressing work over play. He took with him on trips briefcases full of executive orders, appointments, etc. and parceled them out daily to make news under the Augusta or Gettysburg dateline. He encouraged feature stories on the Army Signal Corps' elaborate setup to keep Ike in close touch with Washington. He produced Cabinet members in wholesale lots (Does Hagerty

really call for Cabinet members? Says he: "Maybe sometimes I do"). He did anything and everything, in short, to keep the subjects of golf and fishing far down in the daily stories about the President.

Hagerty has not been above hocus-pocus. Once, during an Eisenhower illness, he handed a visiting cabinet member a statement to read to reporters about how well the President was looking. The man had not yet been in to see the President.

The trouble is that Hagerty has so arranged the lights and shadows that he has distorted the public image of the President and, more importantly, of the Presidency itself. For prolonged periods, he has attracted public attention away from compelling problems of leadership with a succession of makeshift and inconsequential diversions. His skill has been so great that the editors of at least one major United States newspaper felt obliged to cut down the number of frontpage stories coming out of the White House because they judged they were causing a false public impression of the President's activities.

The Hagerty-type operation, despite its technical proficiency, cannot substitute for having a responsible source of explanation at the highest level of government. In his management of news, Hagerty has in fact discouraged such explanation. He has rebuffed the reporter's attempts to approach other White House sources for briefings on important questions. The office of the President has become a no man's land for the reporter seeking guidance on major policies in flux.

THE NEWS AND THE TRUTH

When, on rare occasions, he takes time to review his many mandates, the reporter in Washington is apt to be overwhelmed. His preparation of the news cannot help but be conditioned by the audiences for whom he writes. Amid competitive, ofttimes contradictory pressures he must somehow achieve equilibrium. And he must do it, usually in a hurry, while the waiting presses set the one unyielding pressure.

There is the audience composed of his sources, the various protagonists in the Washington arena, who read his copy with great care and sensitivity. The correspondent who intends to survive must be ever mindful of them. Even the most powerful reporter learns to ration his enemies. Too open an approach to the news can mean too many closed doors.

There is the audience of his bosses. Their cupidity and their influence have been berated and at times overrated. It varies, of course, from boss to boss. But a more continuous and compelling pressure upon the Washington correspondent comes from basic economic trends in the communications industry. News is big business. News is a commodity that must be purveyed to an ever-expanding audience by increasingly monopolistic distributors.

There is the audience of his readers—a frenetic group who, he is told, spend eighteen and a half minutes a day reading five columns of news, of which only one-eighth is international. The reader, it has been said, is the median man, destined, like Orphan Annie, never to grow an inch. To hold his attention, the reporter feels a gnawing compulsion to devise ever more resourceful ways of perfecting the "leads" and "angles" of his stories.

When he is in a philosophical frame of mind, the Washington reporter asks himself whether news was ever meant to serve as the vehicle for communicating the "Truth" about government. Many years ago, Walter Lippmann, while still a comparative newcomer to journalism, examined the proposition and reached a pessimistic conclusion. "If we assume . . . that news and truth are two words for the same thing, we shall, I believe, arrive nowhere," he wrote. The function of news, Lippmann pointed out, is "to signalize an event," whereas the function of truth is "to bring to light the hidden facts, to set them into relation with each other, and make a picture of reality on which men can act." Lippmann ridiculed the notion that the press, by acting upon everybody for a few minutes each twenty-four hours, "can create a mystical force called Public Opinion that will take up the slack in public institutions."

Yet this is precisely the job that the Washington correspondent has been called upon to attempt. As the business of government has become more complicated, responsible reporters have felt a driving urge to expose the "hidden facts," to relate them, and to furnish a realistic picture of what is happening. It is a job that has to be done if the American system of government is to function properly.

The reporter knows that he has done his job well at times. On occasion, he has stimulated public controversy when even members of the opposition party have maintained a discreet silence. He has broken up petty conspiracies among politicians too long vested with arbitrary power. He has exposed the corruption that desire for power and, conversely, the careless use of power breeds. On the positive side, he has served as middleman and broker for important new ideas and policies. He, as much as anyone, has helped to keep Washington in healthy ferment.

Still, it comes as a shock to realize just how precarious is the base from which the responsible reporters in Washington operate. The constituency to which they communicate about the state of the nation is pitifully small compared. say, to the constituency of the television comedian or the comic-strip artist. Outside of Washington they are not big guys. Most are aware that they are allowed to operate not because of economic benefits they bring in but because their bosses believe that their work is in the public interest. They are aware, too, that concepts of the public interest can change radically.

Finally, the reporter in Washington has had to consider the subject matter with which he deals daily. He has watched politics—the stuff of his trade—explode like the now familiar mushroom cloud, engulfing economics, military strategy, and at last the worlds of nuclear and space science. He suspects darkly that somewhere along the way the essentials of a reporter's knowledge moved into a new order of magnitude. He looks back nostalgically to the time when the subjects government dealt with did not seem so alien or formidable to the gifted amateur.

This fantastic role the reporters play in Washington must be in large part self-directed. Yet they lack even a set of guiding principles commonly imposed within the press corps to satisfy the ethical exigencies. "Shyster lawyers can be disbarred, quack doctors can have their licenses revoked, and unworthy ministers can be unfrocked, but the newspaper profession had no method of dealing with black sheep," wrote a disgruntled critic about an earlier period in Washington. The profession has no such method even today.

But the good reporters are linked by a sense of the importance of what they are doing that compensates for all the low pay, long working hours, high tensions, and unending dilemmas of the business. "Above all reporting offers the sense of being "engagé" in the political process of one's own time," the brothers Alsop have remarked. It is only the very bad and unsuccessful reporter in Washington who does not share this sense.

WHO DECIDES WHAT'S FIT TO PRINT?
T. S. Matthews

T. S. Matthews is a career journalist and author who joined the staff of the *New Republic* in 1925 and then moved to *Time* Magazine in 1929, where he was managing editor and editor from 1943 to 1953. He is the author of *The Sugar Pill*.

The main business of the press, supposedly, is news, as the main business of banks is money. It may surprise the public to discover how incurious many bankers are about the real nature of money, and how unclear they are about it. In just the same way, and perhaps to a greater extent, many journalists are incurious about the real nature of news and just as unclear about it. This particular question has been begged for so long that it now seems either self-evident or insoluble. Ask a journalist "What is news?" and you'll get one of a number of answers, ranging from "It's what interests *me*" (meaning "the paper I work on") to "how should I know?" (meaning "I just work here").

Perhaps the neatest as well as the most generally accepted definition of news is "what happened yesterday." I remember once totting up the front-page news stories (the news of the day considered most important) in a good provincial newspaper, in America. Of the eleven stories on the page, seven had not happened at all—in the sense of man biting dog, or even of dog biting man. Some of the speculations about the future—and there were many —might have come true, but so far they were just speculations. If news is

From *Saturday Review,* January 24, 1959. © Copyright 1958 by T. S. Matthews, *The Sugar Pill.*

what happened yesterday, the newspapers print an awful lot of phony news. But we have seen how the practical definition of news varies from paper to paper. Journalists never have been very keen on defining news theoretically, except in a parlorgame spirit. Someone whose faith in the news was simple, like C. P. Scott, the famed editor of the *Manchester Guardian,* took news for granted; news was the sacred facts. An equally inexact but more inclusive description might be, "News is what the press produces." It isn't only physics that's getting more complicated: we now know the facts, like the atom, can be split.

I mustn't push the analogy with banks too far, but there is one striking similarity between banks and the press. Both, to a great extent, manufacture their product, though they are not popularly supposed to. By far the greatest part of the world's "money" is issued by banks in the form of credit. Most of the world's "news" is manufactured by the press itself: Interviews with important men; reports on grave situations; press conferences; press investigation; political surveys; "informed speculation," etc., etc. Most "hard news" falls into the press's lap like the meteorites or manna from heaven: murder and suicide, rape, war, pestilence, famine, catastrophes of all kinds. This bad news is the best news to the press—it's not only exciting to read but it comes ready-made. Mongers of sensational news, like *The London Daily Mirror,* admitting that the supply of this sort of news is unsteady, meet the daily demand for sensation in two ways; by dressing up small news to look big, and by ballyhooing daily features. There is no essential difference between the inevitable screaming front-page headline of the *Mirror* and the "running story" from a wire service of a diplomatic conference. Both are manufactured news. They are said to have happened big; actually, they either didn't happen at all, or they only happened a little.

Some of the more exacting followers of C. P. Scott still insist that their paper deals in sacredly regarded facts. That is probably true in spots, although they conveniently overlook the other spots in the paper that are profanely opinionated rather than sacredly factual. A large part of the press has, in effect, abandoned the pretense of dealing exclusively with facts, or the pretense that their source is invariably as pure as the Pierian spring. A great many newspapers, for example, make no bones about printing gossip. They still, officially at least, exclude rumor (except from the gossip columns, or unless it can be attributed to a "hitherto unimpeachable source," when it rises from "rumor" to "speculation" or "inside information").

The only journalists who are consistently successful in keeping rumor and gossip out of the news are the Communists. The Communists' press, an avowed instrument of government, is dedicated to the proposition that facts equal propaganda equals truth. The facts are chosen, the propaganda ordered, and the truth announced. It's much simpler than with us. And the Russians have a great contempt for the confusions of the Western press, which all stem from this inadmissible search for news. "News" in Russia is issued as a valuable, State-controlled ration.

When Ilya Ehrenburg, one of the dark stars of Communist journalism, visited the United States a few years ago, he was much bothered by reporters who pried into what he considered irrelevant personal questions—the one that moved him to most sardonic mirth was whether a suit he was having made at a New York tailor was to have trousers with buttons or a zipper. There, he said triumphantly, you have a picture of the Western press, which concerns itself with gossip; buttons or zipper, that is all they care to know about. In the doctrinaire Communist view, our free press makes too little distinction between public news (which is the press's only business) and private news (which is none of its business). Moreover, say the Communists, nobody but they know what news is fit to publish, or what news really is.

One defense to this is apt to be: "The truth shall make you free"—by which we mean that if everybody talks continuously at the top of his lungs, somebody from time to time will probably say something true, somebody else may hear it, and it may have some good effect, by and large. Nevertheless, we have an uneasy suspicion that there should be some distinction between public and private news, and that the press doesn't make the distinction clear—no doubt because of the general confusion about what news really is. Public or private, the news must affect our individual lives, it must be translatable into our personal terms, before we will pay attention to it. Even the news in Russian papers can be so translated, I should imagine. Everything *Pravda* or *Izvestia* publishes means some action or threat of action by the Government; the trick is to see: "How is that going to affect *me?*" We read the newspapers that way in time of war, when all governments are gray. In peace-time, public news for most of us is just something to quack about, and it rolls off our backs; the news that really concerns us comes by word of mouth or by mail. The opening door, the doctor's verdict, the expected letter, the telegram that says "death" or "life"; this is the kind of news that comes home to us. Perhaps it is the only real news there is.

Nevertheless, we feel that there should be bigger news than this, and the press continually assures us that indeed there is. The press keeps on telling it, in big headlines; big good news and big bad news. The big good news is mainly manufactured, not so much because the press is sanguine by nature as that it is committed to the encouraging notion of progress. The big bad news is what has actually happened. When our candidate is elected or the war ends, we may call the news both big and good; but what will it be called by the people who voted for the other man, or who lost the war? No, real good news, in the public sense, is either incredible or beyond our understanding. And yet we crave it, its absence seems wrong, we want it to be. The press, which is as human as the rest of us, shares this craving and gropes for big news—however incredible or beyond our understanding. When the *New York Times* printed the text of Einstein's theory, it was in this mystical and groping spirit. The hope was that Einstein had found a large piece of truth—even if nobody, or almost nobody, could understand it; and in that hope the *Times'* editor was willing to bow his uncomprehending head, and take the whole congregation of the *Times* to their knees with him.

In less than two generations science has become untranslatable, and its speculations about the world come to us more and more faintly, like the dwindling shouts of a search-party that have disappeared into an enormous maze. The news they succeed in sending back to us (with the press as messenger) often seems contradictory of earlier bulletins; the gist of it comes across as a progressive disillusionment with accepted facts and an immense widening and deepening of the unknowable. But this is depressing and therefore unacceptable to our optimistic habit of mind—as if, with all our advantages, we were just catching up with Socrates, and as it were from behind! So the press continues to hail scientific "discoveries" (the substitution of a new theory for an abandoned one) as if they were real news, big news and good news. And the public, official view of science's search for knowledge is one of untiring hope and faith. In private, however, there is skepticism and doubt, and not just among illiterate peasants either.

The only big news, private and public, that human beings are really concerned about is news of life and death. There has been no new news on either subject for some time—nearly 2,000 years, in fact. The Resurrection was tremendous good news, if true; the best news ever reported. But though it has been told wherever Christian missionaries have gone and a large proportion of the earth's population must have heard it, it is still widely disbelieved or believed only in a poetic or mystical sense, as "an honorable thought" or an incomprehensible symbol. Even those Christians who believe that the Resurrection was an event that actually happened and a demonstration that individual human beings are literally immortal would nowadays hesitate to apply it without qualification to their own personal lives and deaths. As for agnostics and unbelievers, they have accepted and spread the persistent rumor that the news of the Resurrection was exaggerated or false.

The press is only a reflection of the world it reports, and like the world it reports, is quite unable to recognize or accept really good news—a saint for the ages, a hero both immediate and lasting, a revelation of permanent truth; it can only exaggerate or minimize, ignore, misreport, or doubt, just like the rest of us. Big bad news it can't miss; big good news it never sees—though it pretends a lot of little good news is big, and manufactures all the big good news it can. What keeps the press going is mainly snippets; some news, much gossip, loads of rumors—not to speak of all the features, extras, special acts and entertaining etceteras.

The biggest piece of clap-trap about the press is that it deals almost exclusively, or even mainly, with news.

And the next-biggest piece of clap-trap is that the press has enormous power. This delusion is persistent and widespread. It is taken for granted by the public-at-large, who are apt to be impressed by anything that is said three times; it is continually advertised by the press itself; and it is cherished by press lords, some of whom, at least, should know better. The Hutchins Commission of the Freedom of the Press, which represented a more-than-usually-intelligent public-at-large in the United States, not only took the power of the press at the Press's own valuation, but thought it very alarming:

We have the impression that the American people do not realize what has happened to them. They are not aware that the communications revolution has occurred. They do not appreciate the tremendous power which the new instruments and the new organization of the press place in the hands of a few men.

In what way is the press supposed to be so powerful? The general notion is that the press can form, control or at least strongly influence public opinion. Can it really do any of these things? Hugh Cudlipp, editorial director of *The London Daily Mirror,* and a man who should know something about the effect of newspapers on public opinion, doesn't share this general notion about their power. He thinks newspapers can echo and stimulate a wave of popular feeling, but that's all. "A newspaper may successfully accelerate but never reverse the popular attitude that common-sense has commended to the public." In short, it can jump aboard the bandwagon, once the bandwagon's under way, and exhort others to jump aboard too; but it can't start the bandwagon rolling, or change its direction after it's started.

Like other habit-forming pills, the press can stimulate or depress, but it cannot cure. It can fan fear and hatred of another nation (when the fear and hatred are there, waiting to be fanned) but it cannot make peace. As more and more people have painful reason to know, the press has a nasty kind of power—the same kind of power a bully has, of hurting somebody smaller and weaker than himself. An individual's only defense against the press is the law of libel, but considerable harm and much pain can be caused without going as far as to commit an actionable libel. Journalists themselves generally have a horror of being interviewed, "written up" or even noticed by the press—they know too well from their own experience how inept and cruel a distortion the result is likely to be. Nine times out of ten, as they know, ineptness is to blame rather than conscious cruelty; but there is always that tenth case. And a blundering friendly fist. The press is often like a clumsy giant who gives you a pat on the back and knocks the wind out of you, if he doesn't cause internal injuries. I remember once coming upon an elderly professor of my university who had just been "written up" by the paper I worked on. When he saw me, tears came into his eyes, and he said, "What have I done to them? What have I done to deserve this?" He was deeply wounded by the article, and regarded it as an extremely unkind caricature. Knowing that it had been written by one of his former students who liked and admired the professor, I tried to reassure him that it was at least kindly meant; I don't think I succeeded.

The press has a negative power—to titillate, alarm, enrage, amuse, humiliate, annoy, even to drive a person out of his community or his job. But of the positive power to which it pretends, and of which the press lords dream—to make and break governments, to swing an election, to stop a war or start a revolution—there is no tangible evidence. Its vaunted might is a gigantic spoof. Professor David Mitrany, speaking in 1932 on "The Press and International Relations," put the case with delicate irony: "There is no need to spend time in an attempt to show how great is the influence of the press. It is greater in certain fields than in others. It is greater, one could say, in any field in which the knowledge and interest of the man in the street is lesser. For in that case the reading public is apt to think that the press speaks with the voice of authority; while the authorities are apt to assume that the press is speaking the voice of the people . . ."

Everyone has heard of the "power of the press"; no one has seen it. The greatest believers in this exaggerated "power" and the loudest promoters of it are, naturally, the press lords themselves. One of the most deluded of these, not even excepting Northcliffe or Beaverbrook, was Robert McCormick, Publisher of the *Chicago Tribune* (still emblazoned with his modest motto: "The world's greatest newspaper"). McCormick, and of course his paper, were always in bitter opposition to the Roosevelt Democrats, as well as to the liberal element in his own Republican Party. A story used to be told about the *Tribune*—no doubt apocryphal but in essence true—that one of the janitors in the Tribune building always bet against any political candidate the paper supported, and gave odds to boot; and that he found this sideline so profitable that he was able to buy two sizable blocks of flats.

The people in Chicago who bought the *Tribune* didn't buy it to find out how to cast their votes: they bought it in spite of its advice and its bias, because on the whole they liked its personality and found it entertaining. Does this seem to argue a too shrewd, calm and sensible attitude on the part of the ordinary newspaper reader? The press is generally appreciated by the public for what it is rather than for what it pretends to be. They don't feel it as a power in their lives, but as a working-day prerequisite.

5   GOVERNMENT UNDER PRESSURE

In recent years, Americans have become increasingly aware of the existence of pressure groups in their society. They have heard tales of the not quite reputable operations by which Big Business, Big Labor, Big Agriculture, and others seek to influence the legislative process. They have read about the subterranean workings of wily lobbyists and the assorted blandishments with which legislators are reputedly plied. All these tales are a part of the popular folklore; and yet the real world of pressure politics, where the administrator is often a more important target than the lawmaker, and where the lobbyist openly provides invaluable services for the harried official, is not well understood. Indeed, the simple identification of pressure groups inevitably omits one of the very largest—the military-industrial complex spotlighted by President Eisenhower in his farewell message of January 1961. Other top interest groups frequently go unrecognized—the many foreign governments, large and small, that seek to reinforce their American favor, and the federal government itself, its administrators often linked to formally organized clients in a binding community of interest.

It is not easy to determine the magnitude of pressure operations. The best "hard" figures available date back more than a decade, to the days before court decisions revealed the loopholes, which lobbyists have since taken advantage of, in the Lobbyist Registration Act of 1946. In 1950, we learned that some two thousand registered lobbyists spent an annual $10,-000,000 to influence the work of the Congress alone. Congressman Frank Buchanan of Pennsylvania, who had conducted one of the most searching inquiries into the subject, used the analogy of the iceberg to estimate the total expenditure at some six or seven times the visible portion. Today, lobbying—even when defined in a limited sense, as direct attempts at legislative influence—is probably a $100,000,000-a-year business. Direct congressional lobbying, however, represents only a portion of the total outlay in a nation where the creation of "image" and the building of "grass-roots" attitudes annually involve the expenditure of corporate and organizational millions in so-called "institutional advertising."

The techniques of lobbying are as varied as their practitioners, and attempt to influence not only the legislator and administrator but even the courts—particularly those on the state and local level—as well as influential citizens and community leaders, the molders of local opinion. Although illicit methods of influence, such as bribery and corruption, are still occasionally uncovered, they have generally given way to more honorable and more effective techniques. The lobbyist today may do research for the administrator, draft bills for the legislator, or direct community-improvement projects to create a favorable climate of opinion.

Pressure groups provide a valuable reflection of economic and social interests in a pluralistic society whose formal representation is geographically based. Consequently, pressure activity has at least two dimensions: (a) it provides certain desirable services; and (b) it creates certain significant problems. A series of questions may suggest some of the difficulties involved. Since not all pressure groups are balanced by "countervailing power," one may well ask: "Who speaks for the consumer, the nonveteran, the atheist, the agnostic, or for the nonunion worker?" "To what extent do the interest-group leaders reflect the views of the rank and file?" "Are American Legionnaires as reactionary as some of their Commanders' views would indicate?" "Is there dissenting opinion within the monolithic facade of the American Medical Association?" "How many businessmen share the progressive economic ideas of their colleagues in the Committee for Economic Development?"

These are some of the queries, perhaps unanswerable, that we should keep in mind as we examine the workings of the special interests in and on the American society. And yet, as we explore the problems, and the reforms suggested by some, we should bear in mind the wise guarantee of the First Amendment—the right to petition for a redress of grievances. For it seems not only inevitable but, indeed, a necessity that there be pressure—democratic pressure—if our government in action is to serve the needs of all its people.

HOW PRESSURE GROUPS OPERATE
Henry A. Turner

Henry A. Turner is Associate Professor of Political Science at the University of California, Santa Barbara. His articles have been published in a number of professional journals. He is the editor of *Politics in the United States* and co-author of *The Government and Politics of California* and *American Government in World Perspective*.

Pressure groups have participated actively in politics from the establishment of the first governments in America and must, therefore, be considered as an intrinsic element of our political system.

The manner in which pressure groups operate in the United States today is determined basically by the political environment: the federal form of government; separation of powers; electoral system; political parties; technological development; and the economic, social, ethnic, and religious composition of the population. Individual interest groups generally function in

From *The Annals of the American Academy of Political and Social Science,* September 1958. Reprinted by permission.

a pragmatic and opportunistic fashion, using any method or technique which they believe will serve their purpose effectively. Undoubtedly dictating most pressure group activity is the criterion: what action will produce the maximum desired result with the minimum expenditure of time and resources. The techniques and tactics which any particular group employs will be determined largely by such factors as size and geographic distribution of the membership, cohesion of membership, financial resources, prestige position of the organization, quality of leadership and staff, and relations with the political parties and other organized groups.

Where are pressures applied? Depending on the aims and characteristics of the individual organization, an interest group may attempt to influence its own membership; other pressure groups; the electoral process; the legislative, executive, and judicial branches of the government; and public opinion.

INFLUENCING THE MEMBERSHIP

One characteristic of virtually every large organization is the tendency for a few individuals to gain effective control of the group. In some associations the officers may enjoy near permanent tenure, and in others they may be selected from a relatively small elite. These officers and the paid bureaucracy in many instances literally run the organization. Hence, from the standpoint of origination of policy, they become the organization.

In some organized groups, a considerable portion of the time and energy of the staff may be expanded to influence the members of the group and potential members. Most associations wish to retain and enlarge their membership—if for no other reason—in order to increase the political strength of the group. In group meetings, publications, and direct communications, to the membership, efforts are also directed toward producing greater group cohesion, to "educating" the membership to accept and support the policies of the organization, and to inducing the members to engage in desired political activity. Types of activity urged on group members include: registering and voting; working in political campaigns and making financial contributions; and communicating via personal conversations, letters, telegrams, and telephone calls to public officials and those who control the media of mass communication.

CO-OPERATION BETWEEN GROUPS

In a sense, pressure groups lobby other pressure groups. Organized interest groups seek the active support of their allies or potential allies, the endorsement of groups less directly interested, and the neutralization of their opponents. Such co-operation may be achieved by one group merely activating another, by promising future assistance, or by making concessions or compromises. In some cases co-operating groups develop only informal working arrangements, but there are instances in which organizations have signed formal agreements to pool their political efforts in working for a program. Examples may also be cited of groups co-operating through inter-locking directorates.

In 1950, a Congressional committee investigating lobbying found that interest groups co-operate not only "within so obvious a functional area as an industry," but also on an ideological basis, for "there is a growing joint effort in lobbying by groups whose unity is philosophical rather than func-tional in character." The Committee added, "The general theme of combi-nation rather than conflict grows bolder and more insistent every year."

A particular type of pressure organization, the catalytic pressure group, has been developed to promote joint action by interest groups. Catalytic groups usually consist of representatives of several pressure organizations, but an established pressure group may itself serve as a catalytic organization. Some catalytic groups have been established on an *ad hoc* basis for the purpose of stimulating and coordinating the activities of several organiza-tions to secure the adoption of a specific policy; and once the policy has been effected, the catalytic group has been disbanded. An example of such a group is the Citizens Committee to Repeal Chinese Exclusion. Other catalytic groups such as the National Tax Equality Association have been established on a permanent basis.

PRESSURE ON THE ELECTORAL PROCESS

By definition, pressure groups are nonpartisan organizations which at-tempt to influence some phase of public policy. They do not, themselves, draft party platforms or nominate candidates for public office. Pressure associations do, however, appear before the resolutions committees of the political parties to urge the endorsement of their programs as planks in the parties' platforms. They often attempt to secure the endorsement of both major parties and thus remove their program from the area of partisan controversy. Many groups are also active in the nomination and election of party members to political offices.

Most interest groups which are active in election campaigns will support a candidate of either party if his general outlook is similar to that of the group. Thus organized labor has followed the policy, first prescribed by Samuel Gompers, of "rewarding friends and punishing enemies" by support or opposition in campaigns and at the polls. Apparently, however, some labor, business, farm, professional, and other organizations have found most of their "friends" in one party and most of their "enemies" in the other, for they have tended to align themselves with one or the other of the two major parties.

The most common method of aiding in a campaign is through financial contribution. Labor unions and corporations are prohibited by law from making "a contribution or expenditure in connection with any election" at which a member of Congress or the President and Vice-President are selected; but they have devised means for evading the spirit, if not the letter, of the law.

Testimony before the Senate subcommittee investigating the 1956 election campaign revealed that both labor unions and corporations pay salaries to officers and employees working full time for a party or candidate, publish political arguments in their house organs, and purchase television and radio time and newspaper space to present political views. In addition, the subcommittee was informed that corporations make political contributions by permitting party officials or candidates to use offices and equipment without charge and pay bonuses and permit expense accounts to be padded with the understanding that political contributions will be made from the bonuses and padded accounts.

Influencing Legislators

A century ago pressure groups concentrated most of their efforts on promoting and opposing legislative proposals. During recent decades, their activities have been expanded into other areas; yet even today, the methods employed to influence legislative decisions are the most obvious actions of pressure groups.

The major organized interests maintain permanent staffs of professional lobbyists, research personnel, press agents, and secretaries in Washington throughout the year and have similar but smaller staffs in most state capitols during legislative sessions. Associations which have only an incidental interest in legislative proposals customarily do not have a full-time lobby staff, but may employ a lobbyist to represent them on occasions when legislative issues of interest to their members arise.

Some interest groups have "stables" of legislators who will work closely with them either because they owe their election largely to those groups or because they are themselves members of those groups. Pressure organizations with like-minded spokesmen in the legislature, or "inside lobbyists," naturally have an advantage over other groups.

Available information indicates that pressure associations originate a large percentage of the bills introduced in Congress and the state legislatures. Many organizations have their staff members read all bills introduced to determine which they wish to support, which to oppose, and which to attempt to have amended. As would be expected, lobbyists customarily watch the bills which they have sponsored to help expedite their movement through the various stages of the legislative process to enactment.

Committee hearings on bills provide the various organizations with opportunities to present their information and arguments and also to show how strongly the members of the group favor or oppose a given proposal. Officers of the association, their lobbyists, or lay members will testify before committees, often with charts and graphs to show statistical data. Sizable delegations may be organized to attend committee hearings. At crucial times—such as when a committee is considering a bill or when the measure is being debated by one of the houses of the legislature—pressure associations often have their members write, telegraph, or call their legislators. Some groups attempt to flood the legislators with messages, while others concentrate on having communications sent by the principal supporters of each legislator and other key persons in each district.

Basically, lobbying consists of communicating with the legislators. Organized groups utilize every available opportunity to inform legislators of their wishes; to provide them with facts, information, and arguments; and to impress upon them the ability of the organization to reward or punish the legislator by giving or withholding support at the polls, campaign contributions, or gifts and items of value to the legislator. In spite of the pressures brought upon them, most legislators agree that private groups perform a valuable function in presenting information regarding a multitude of bills— many of them of a highly technical nature—introduced in each legislative session.

Any survey of pressure group operations would be incomplete that omitted reference to the social lobby and the use of unethical or illegal methods. There is widespread agreement that both types of practices still exist, but that they are of much less importance than in the days of the "old lobby." It should also be noted that these methods are undoubtedly employed as much today to influence administrators as legislators. Although the social lobby, minor favors, and practices of a distinctly corrupt nature may influence some public officials, their total impact on the political process is probably not great today.

Pressure on the Executive Branch

One of the most noteworthy changes in pressure-group activity during this century is the increased effort to influence the executive branch of the government. Pressures are applied on executive and administrative personnel who are in the position to render decisions or take action of interest to organized groups. As in earlier years, after a bill has been passed by the legislature, interest groups may inundate the Chief Executive with statements, letters, telegrams, and memorials; and they may appeal to him personally to veto or sign the measure. Well aware of the importance of the Chief Executive's recommendations regarding legislative policies and budgetary matters, organized interests urge the President or governors to incorporate or omit specific proposals from their legislative programs and to increase or decrease budgetary requests for particular administrative departments or agencies.

The vast expansion of governmental regulation of economic life and the tendency of the legislatures to grant administrative officials broad discretionary powers have caused pressure associations to evince more interest than in the past in the selection of administrative personnel. Moreover, it is apparent to most groups that administrators may forcibly execute a statute or virtually nullify it. For these reasons it is not uncommon for groups to seek the appointment of their members or of individuals friendly to their group to administrative posts of particular interest to them. Pressure organizations with friends in top administrative positions have found that they have advantages not available to other groups in securing permits, licenses, contracts, subsidies, favorable adjustments of tax problems and antitrust suits, and various other types of privileges and favors.

Administrative agencies which have been granted quasi-legislative powers find that representatives of interest groups commonly appear before them to oppose or support rules and regulations. On the national level, the Administrative Procedure Act requires most administrative agencies to hold public hearings on proposed rules and permits interested individuals to request the issuance, repeal, or amendment of rules. Pressure associations have availed themselves of these rights and lobby the administrators in much the same fashion as they lobby Congress or the state legislatures.

Interest groups may importune the legislature to amend the statutes under which an agency operates and to increase or decrease its appropriation in order to expand or curtail its operations. In some instances, organized interests have been able to get legislators to investigate administrative agencies in an effort to punish administrators for uncooperative or unfriendly action. It is incorrect, however, to assume that the relationship between private associations and governmental agencies is typically one of antagonism. On the contrary, it is not uncommon to find pressure organizations, legislators, and administrative agencies working together harmoniously for their mutual benefit.

Pressure Groups and the Judiciary

Although pressure organizations expend considerably less energy and time attempting to influence the judicial branch of the government than either the executive or legislative branch, reference should be included of their efforts to influence the courts. Whether judges are elected or appointed, organized interests often participate in their selection.

Occasionally groups seek to advance the cause of their members by initiating litigation to test the constitutionality of legislation or the action of public officials. For a number of years the National Association for the Advancement of Colored People has relied on litigation as a principal means for upholding Negro rights. Some organizations also file briefs as friends of the court to support other groups involved in litigation, or they have articles prepared for publication in law reviews with the expectation that they will be used as briefs or may be read by judges and possibly influence their decisions.

Pressure Groups and Public Opinion

The continual increase in the efforts of interest groups to win support for their organizations and programs by using the mass media of communication to influence public attitudes is perhaps the most significant recent development in pressure-group activity. Among factors contributing to this development are the increasing awareness on the part of interest-group leaders that public opinion is an entity which must be considered; the development and refinement of new propaganda techniques and devices; and the revolutionary changes in communication media which make it possible for literally millions of Americans to be reached daily via television, radio, the motion pictures, newspapers, and periodicals.

The rise of the public-relations counsel has occurred concomitantly with the growth of pressure groups and the extraordinary development of the communication media. To advise their highest officials on public relations and to direct propaganda programs many business organizations, labor unions, farm groups, professional associations, government agencies, and other organizations now employ public-relations counsels—some on a full-time basis in the top-echelon-planning and strategy group; others only occasionally to direct specific campaigns.

PROPAGANDA

Although the term propaganda is not new, there is general agreement that propaganda as employed today is a "new thing." The distinctive feature of modern propaganda is that it is disseminated principally through the media of mass communications by pressure groups who employ public-relations experts to develop their propaganda themes and techniques.

Pressure groups use propaganda both as a tactical means of accomplishing specific short-term goals and as a part of their long-range political strategy. From a tactical standpoint, a well-organized public-relations campaign may have either of two results. It may give the impression that there is such broad public support for a proposal that the campaign itself will result in the effectuation of the desired policy. Or, the campaign may activate the citizenry to the extent that they will demand through letters, telegrams, and other means that the officials make the decision wished by the organized group. In either event, the basic aim is to make the program of the group appear synonymous with the general welfare.

The strategic or long-term goal of a public-relations campaign tends to be ideological. Groups employing propaganda for strategic purposes often have as their aim selling the public a particular philosophy of government. In effect, they wish to condition the attitudes of the people so that a state of public opinion will be created in which the public will almost auto-matically respond with favor toward programs desired by the group and reject programs opposed by the group. The National Association of Manu-facturers has referred to their strategic concept of public relations as the "bank account theory." In one of their publications they explain: "It neces-sitates making regular and frequent deposits in the Bank of Public Good-Will so that valid checks can be drawn on this account when it is de-sirable. . . ."

Virtually all major interest groups attempt to influence public attitudes, but business organizations tend to exert more effort and to enjoy more success than most. Business groups usually have the financial resources with which to employ public-relations personnel and to purchase advertising space and time; they often have the added advantage of being able to compute these expenditures as normal operating expenses for taxation pur-poses. The fact that American culture is basically a business culture and that such traditional American values as low taxes and limited government are among the propaganda themes of organized business has undoubtedly contributed to the success of their campaigns.

As V. O. Key has noted, an organization's public-relations program may increase the prestige of the group and its leaders. Indeed, an organization may elevate itself in the esteem of the public by using proper publicity in a manner not dissimilar to that by which movie stars, athletes, and presi-dential contenders are made national celebrities. Definite political advan-tages accrue to the group with status: their views are heard with more respect and given greater weight than those of lower prestige groups, and their members may be appointed to important advisory committees or influential governmental positions.

Propaganda Campaigns

Pressure organizations usually direct their propaganda campaigns at spe-cific target groups. For example, Richard Gable notes that the public-relations programs of the National Association of Manufacturers—which he describes as "the most intensive, comprehensive, and expensive means by which it attempts to influence the formation of public policy"—are directed toward particular groups of individuals. He states:

> The NAM's public relations and propaganda programs can be classified according to the audience as external, indirect, and internal. The audience of the external appeal is the general public. The indirect approach covers educators, churchmen, women's club leaders, agricultural leaders, and sim-ilar community leaders who in turn mold specific publics. Internal pro-grams are directed at state and local associations affiliated through the National Industrial Council as well as the NAM membership. Their pur-pose is to induce and assist members and affiliates to conduct community public relations programs using manuals and materials supplied by the Association.

Nationwide propaganda campaigns directed by public-relations experts often are organized and executed with the care for detailed planning and proper timing characteristic of highly successful military campaigns. One notable example was the American Medical Association campaign, directed by the Whitaker and Baxter firm, Campaigns, Inc., against the Truman national health insurance program. The total cost of the three-and-a-half year campaign was $4,678,000, of which approximately $775,000 was spent for propaganda skills. In this campaign, as in most others of this scope, virtually every conceivable communication medium was utilized. Physicians and laymen were enlisted to deliver to various clubs speeches prepared by the Whitaker and Baxter staff. In 1949 aone, 54,233,915 leaflets, pamphlets, booklets, and other pieces of literature were distributed. Radio, television, newspaper, and periodical advertising was purchased. Physicians placed literature in their waiting rooms, discussed the issue while treating their patients, wrote letters to patients, and placed enclosures in bills mailed to patients. One physician even dropped 50,000 leaflets from his airplane on a community.

Of the various methods of disseminating propaganda, the distribution of press releases, clipsheets, and prepared editorials apparently is one of the more effective. If used, such material gives the impression of straight reporting or editorials conceived and written by the staff of the local press. Through its public-relations department, the National Association of Home Builders has supplied its local associations with such items.

Pressure organizations in their efforts to influence public attitudes have not overlooked the educational system. The National Association of Manufacturers and other groups have prepared and distributed to the public schools posters, booklets, books, radio skits, film strips, and other "teaching aids." In 1957 the NAM announced that it distributed "at least two million booklets" free to the schools every year. The gas and electric public utilities during the 1920's surveyed textbooks and suggested changes in the presentation of materials regarding public utilities. Approximately three decades later an official of the National Association of Real Estate Boards told a Congressional committee that his organization had stimulated the writing of textbooks that were used "in 127 colleges and universities in teaching . . . the economics of real estate."

Institutional Advertising

Institutional advertising, which may be defined as the use of paid space or time in the communication media to promote or oppose ideas, has been used extensively to shape public sentiment since the early part of World War II. In 1954 the editors of the *Saturday Review* wrote: "one of the extraordinary things about American business is that it feels a responsibility to communicate with the American people about the ideas and philosophy that animate business and govern its multiple relations with society." And the Senatorial committee investigating the 1956 election reported finding "numerous instances of institutional advertising, either clearly political in nature or with definite political implications." Thus another recently developed activity of pressure groups is their use of institutional advertising to establish a climate of opinion which will promote their political objectives.

COMMITTEES, FOUNDATIONS, COUNCILS, AND INSTITUTES

The dynamic nature of interest-group activity may perhaps be seen most vividly by noting a new type of pressure organization, the oldest of which was established slightly over two decades ago. These organizations have as their primary purpose the publication and dissemination of leaflets, pamphlets, and books which present a particular viewpoint on current political and economic problems. Some of the more active of these groups are: The Committee for Constitutional Government, the Foundation for Economic Education, the National Economic Council, the Constitution and Free Enterprise Foundation, and the Public Affairs Institute. Of these five groups, the first four have been financed primarily by donations from large corporations and wealthy individuals, the Public Affairs Institute, on the other hand, has been supported in part by contributions from labor unions. All of these organizations receive some income from the sale of their publications.

The Committee on Lobbying Activities noted that to these organizations "the dissemination of literature is both the reason for the group's existence and a primary means by which it exists." Much of the success of these organizations in raising funds may be due to the fact that they have succeeded in getting the United States Treasury Department to classify them as educational foundations with contributions to them deductible for income-tax purposes. A Senatorial committee recently commented that "such foundations may be used as a device to avoid controls upon political expenditures and to provide tax benefits for political contributors."

The efforts of organized interests to propagandize the public have caused some concern regarding the future of the American democratic system. The very fact, however, that pressure groups believe it necessary to make extraordinary expenditures of time and resources to shape public attitudes may be evidence of the fundamental strength of American democracy; although interest groups can on occasion manage public sentiment, they are aware that they court defeat if they flout it.

American democracy is based on the premise that the people if provided sufficient information can be trusted to make correct decisions. The general public is not well informed regarding pressure groups. The basic problem, then in controlling pressure-group activity is how to give the people more adequate information about organized interests, their methods of operation, and their aims for "an informed and vigilant public is the only lasting guarantee that pressure groups will operate in an open and aboveboard manner."

THE FOREIGN LEGION OF
U.S. PUBLIC RELATIONS
Douglass Cater and Walter Pincus

Walter Pincus, Washington correspondent for *News Focus,* has been the recipient of several awards for distinguished journalism.

Douglass Cater, formerly Washington editor of *The Reporter,* has served since 1964 as Special Assistant to President Lyndon B. Johnson.

The article presented below gained for its authors the Page One Award of the American Newspaper Guild, New York.

On January 30, 1959, the president of the Mutual Broadcasting System, Alexander L. Guterma, accompanied by the chairman of Mutual's board of directors, Hal Roach, Jr., and several other associates, flew to Ciudad Trujillo, Capital of the Dominican Republic. There he entered into an unusual agreement with representatives of dictator Rafael Trujillo. For a consideration of $750,000, paid in advance, Guterma agreed that for an eighteen-month period Mutual would broadcast a "monthly minimum of 425 minutes of news and commentary regarding the Dominican Republic." Trujillo's government would serve as its own news agency, supplying Mutual with items of news interest "by telegrams, air-mail dispatches, or telephonic beeper calls." Guterma also gave the Dominicans power of censorship by guaranteeing not to broadcast news inconsistent with their country's best interests, "in your sole and exclusive judgment."

Subsequently, a series of legal actions proceeded out of this deal—a hearing under the Bankruptcy Act involving Mutual, a civil action filed by the Dominicans to get their money back, and a Justice Department case against Guterma for failing to register as a foreign agent. From these proceedings, a fairly detailed account of what happened can be pieced together.

The origins of the agreement Guterma made in Ciudad Trujillo may be traced back to several earlier encounters between Saul S. Nevins, an attorney seeking capital for Guterma, and Porfirio Rubirosa, the celebrated international bridegroom who at the time was serving as Dominican ambassador to Cuba. During one meeting, Rubirosa complained about the unfavorable press coverage his government was getting in the United States. Nevins had earlier shown how Mutual could do something about it. Nevins had phoned in a story from Ciudad Trujillo about anti-Batista sentiment in the Dominican Republic that subsequently was broadcast twice from Washington, with Nevins identified as Mutual correspondent in the Dominican Republic. Mutual's Washington news director testified later that the practice of taking such information was not unusual. "We get a good deal of our news from people (who are not) newsmen. These can be fire chiefs, senators, congressmen."

Evidently the idea that such news coverage could be a salable commodity did not take long to develop. When Guterma's group met with Otto Vega, special assistant to Generalissimo Trujillo, they came right to the point. "They said they were in a position to secure . . . in the United States an outlet for our news," Vega testified later. Guterma produced a map of the Mutual Network and pointed out the number of stations that would be involved.

BROKER RUBIROSA

Guterma also provided another quick demonstration of the product he was prepared to sell. According to Vega's testimony: "He said, 'Give me an idea, some piece of news you would like to broadcast.' I said that I did not have anything. He said, 'Well, since we have Mr. Rubirosa here and Mr. Roach here, why not say Mr. Rubirosa is going to make a picture for Hal Roach in the Dominican Republic and they are negotiating that.' " The very next day, returning to New York in Guterma's private plane, the group heard Walter Winchell recite their make-believe news item over the Mutual Network.

During that same flight, Guterma showed Nevins a draft copy of the specific terms he was prepared to offer the Dominicans. The lawyer later professed amazement at their boldness. It amounted to nearly fifteen minutes daily to be "carried by the entire network . . . in a normal course of our broadcasting day." There was only one restriction: "We will not carry any news extolling the Communist cause but agree that the primary purpose is to exemplify the stability and tranquillity of the Dominican Republic and its unequivocal position and stand against Communism."

Nevins was fearful that the contract might run afoul of the law requiring agents of foreign governments to register with the Justice Department. To get around this requirement, he arranged to draw up papers creating for Guterma a new corporation, Radio News Service, which could claim exemption from the act on the grounds that it was a bona fide news-gathering agency.

The terms were acceptable to both sides, and on February 5, the negotiators having returned to Ciudad Trujillo, Vega brought to Guterma's suite at the El Embajador Hotel a cloth sack containing the $750,000, mostly in thousand-dollar bills. Not all of it, however, went to Guterma. Later, in trying to account for it, he claimed that he had been obliged to pay "brokerage fees" of $50,000 to Rubirosa, $25,000 to Vega (Vega denied receiving it), $37,500 to Nevins, and $57,500 to his other associates.

What remained was evidently insufficient to meet Guterma's pressing financial needs. In mid-February, 1959, he lost control of F. L. Jacobs, the holding company in which he combined his various enterprises, and was forced to resign as president of Mutual. Not long afterward, he was indicted for stock fraud in connection with his F. L. Jacobs dealings and he is now serving a five-year prison term. When that is completed an additional eight- to twenty-four-month sentence awaits him for failing to register as a Dominican agent.

How seriously did Guterma ever intend to live up to the terms of this agreement with Trujillo? The Dominican government, in filing suit for the return of its money, now claims that the contract was "not performed, was incapable of performance and was entered into by claimant on the basis of mistake in law and fact."

Because Guterma pleaded *nolo contendere* to the illegal-agent charges filed by the Justice Department, there was only fragmentary evidence of the extent to which Guterma managed to turn Mutual into a propaganda outlet of the Dominicans. Robert Hurleigh testified that as Mutual vice-president, he once received a call at his Washington office from Guterma in Ciudad Trujillo. He "said he had a congressman there who had . . . made a speech before the Legislature, or whatever the name is, and he thought this would be a good broadcast, so we took the Congressman in on a beeper . . ." Tapes of the visiting congressman, Gardner Withrow (R., Wisconsin), were used on newscasts during the day. On another occasion Hurleigh sent Guterma a note calling his attention to a "Capitol Cloakroom" interview with Senator Allen Ellender (D., Louisiana) on the Caribbean situation. Guterma promptly forwarded tapes of the two network broadcasts to Vega as proof the contract was being fulfilled.

Apparently Hurleigh, who succeeded Guterma as president of Mutual was unaware at the time of what lay beneath this sudden interest in the Dominicans. The first he learned of it, according to his testimony, was in May, 1959, when he and a Mutual reporter visited Ciudad Trujillo on a press junket arranged by the Dominicans. Hurleigh was shocked when Vega made inquiries about the contract. To stave off further involvement in this embarrassing affair, the Dominican government was paid $12,500, and it returned the eleven hundred shares of Mutual stock that Guterma had turned over to Vega as "good faith" collateral.

In becoming a publicity agent for a foreign government, Guterma was going into a business that has been expanding rapidly in this country during the last few years. Several hundred agents of foreign governments are duly registered at the Justice Department (as Guterma was not), and the number is constantly increasing. Many of these foreign agents are simply promoting tourism, while others are lawyers carrying on the various legal and lobbying activities in Washington that are considered necessary to backstop diplomatic missions. As the files at Justice indicate, a good many—comparative newcomers but more numerous all the time—are professional public-relations experts engaged in the business of influencing American opinion.

In the main, of course, this expansion of P.R. in the United States on behalf of foreign governments is no more surprising or sinister than the growth of the domestic variety as an adjunct to private or public business. They are, in fact, parallel efforts to meet the same basic need. The systematic cultivation of public opinion is frequently more fruitful than more direct attempts to influence government officials. But the ways of communicating with the public are intricate indeed. As Harold Oram, Inc., put it in a memorandum soliciting the P.R. account of the government of Ghana: "The services of a professional public relations firm are . . . becoming more of a necessity than ever before. The vast and complex network of media outlets, both mass and specialized, require, for effective utilization, long years of experience and understanding . . ."

UNLABELED COMMERCIALS

In seeking this "effective utilization" of the "media outlets," not every P.R. agent of a foreign government has done its work as openly and candidly as the Oram firm. A great temptation for many of them lies in the fact that the press and the other media have proved to be peculiarly vulnerable to the infiltration of blatant propaganda.

For example, in 1954 the government of Guatemala, then headed by Carlos Castillo Armas, hired John A. Clements Associates at a fee of $8,000 a month to engage in a public-relations campaign on its behalf. This job, according to the Justice Department registration, was to be handled by Clements and Patrick McMahon, who were at the same time serving as editor and Washington editor, respectively, of the *American Mercury*. As a further coincidence, that magazine published a number of articles on Guatemala during the period, three of them of a political nature. While on the Guatemala payroll, McMahon also acted as consultant to the House committee which investigated Communism in Guatemala and, according to his statement to the Justice Department, "prepared (its) report and helped edit the hearings . . ."

Or take the special case of the Nationalist Chinese government, which has long displayed an anxious regard for its public image in this country:

Item: Early in 1959, the North American Newspaper Alliance carried a series of stories written from Formosa by Don Frifield. The reader was not informed that NANA's correspondent was also employed by Hamilton Wright, the U.S. public-relations firm handling the Nationalist China account. Frifield has received $19,700 during the past two years for "editorial services."

Item: In June, 1958, during one of the periodic crises over the offshore islands of Quemoy and Matsu, there was shown at Radio City Music Hall in New York a documentary film entitled "Fortress Formosa," which had been "produced" by Twentieth Century-Fox. It was subsequently distributed to movie theaters all over the country. In the screen billings, a credit line indicated that it had been "Arranged by Hamilton Wright," but the viewer had no way of knowing that Hamilton Wright serves as Nationalist China's registered agent. The film, in Technicolor and CinemaScope, had actually been shot by the P.R. firm's camera crews and then turned over without cost to Twentieth Century-Fox.

Item: Last October 14, the morning after the third "Great Debate," in which the presidential candidates tangled over Quemoy and Matsu, NBC's "Today" carried on its news roundup a report of Chiang Kai-shek's angry rejection of Kennedy's position on those islands. While the television viewer heard Chiang quoted as voicing firm determination to resist the surrender of the islands, he watched a film clip depicting Nationalist Chinese troops and tanks parading in full battle array. This film was another production of Hamilton Wright supplied gratis to the NBC film library and used without credit.

Item: Since 1957, the *Saturday Evening Post* has carried a series of signed editorials by Geraldine Fitch in which she has defended Chiang's policies and criticized others for their lack of sympathy with those policies. The *Post* has identified Mrs. Fitch as an author who "spent many years in China and now lives in Formosa." But it has made no mention of the fact that she is also employed in Taipei as "consultant editor" of the Government Information Office, Republic of China.

Item: In a catalogue of free programs offered to independent television stations, Radiant Films of 358 West 44th Street, New York, includes a half-hour documentary, "Miracle in Free China" ("... where Madame and Generalissimo Chiang Kai-shek and their ten million followers are marking time for the return to the mainland!") and "Face of Free China" ("How American defense in the Pacific is tied into the general defense of the free world through the U.S. Alliance with the Republic of China"). The only hint of who produced and paid for this entertainment is the cryptic mention that it was "Filmed by the world-renowned Hamilton Wright Organization." Neither Hamilton Wright nor Radiant Films, which is not registered as a foreign agent, has supplied the Justice Department with information about the distribution of these films, which were paid for by the government of Nationalist China.

Item: On a number of occasions in recent years, the *New York Times* has published letters to the editor, supporting the Chinese Nationalist stands, from Harold Riegelman, a New York attorney who has been both the city's acting postmaster and the Republican candidate for mayor. Though Mr. Riegelman is registered as a foreign agent of Nationalist China, he has not felt an obligation to label his communications under the Foreign Agents Registration Act. Neither the *Times's* editors nor its readers could be expected to know from his letters of Mr. Riegelman's connections with the Nationalist Chinese.

PRIVATE VS. PUBLIC P.R.

Foreign governments have provided Americans with information about themselves for a good many years. The British, starting with a modest library shortly after the First World War, have expanded the British Information Services in the United States into an efficient operation that now spends $1 million a year, with publishing and film facilities in New York and a B.I.S. representative stationed in Washington's National Press Building, where he is an accessible companion and counselor to the capital's reporters. Thirty-five other countries have established more or less similar information facilities, and have reported expenditures in 1959 totaling nearly $7 million. We do the same thing on a large scale in our U.S. Information Service missions around the world.

But the use of private P.R. firms in the United States on behalf of foreign governments dates largely from the end of the Second World War. Sometimes it was a matter of special necessity. The Roy Bernard Company of New York, which works for West Germany, took the account when its government was not entitled to send an official information mission to this country. A number of firms quickly moved into what was fast becoming a highly profitable field of enterprise. In addition to Nationalist China, Hamilton Wright's clients include Italy and Mexico. Hill & Knowlton, Inc., handles Japan; Harold L. Oram, Inc., has South Vietnam; Curtis J. Hoxter, Inc., works for Austria, Guatemala, and Brazil; Max Rogel, Inc., which formerly had the South Korean account, also takes care of Nicaragua.

During the past two or three years there has been a scramble among American P.R. firms to sign up the emerging African nations. When Vice-President Nixon visited Africa in 1957, one enterprising P.R. man got himself included in the entourage and tried to sell his services along the way.

The size of a foreign government's P.R. operation in the United States is by no means related to the country's size or relative power. The Dominican Republic, for example, has spent during the past five years more than $2,500,000 for assorted P.R. projects here. In 1946, the Dominicans hired Harry Klemfuss of New York to set up a Dominican Republic Information Center at $1,500 monthly. In 1952, a Miami *Herald* columnist, Jack Kofoed, was paid $2,300 monthly, which included $800 for expenses, to prepare a book on Trujillo and to write magazine and newspaper stories about the Dominican Republic. ("General Trujillo isn't as well known to the American people as he could be," ran one of several Kofoed columns that year dealing with the Dominicans. "Even his enemies can't deny that Trujillo has, single handed, lifted his country from the lowest state it could reach to the place it occupies now.") In 1957, A. Tyler Hull, a maker of documentary films, was paid $35,000 to prepare a thirty-minute color film and a twenty-six-minute black-and-white film for television, guaranteeing in his contract "a minimum of 300 television broadcasts in the United States to an estimated audience of more than 15 million viewers within a period of twenty-four months."

During that same year, Trujillo hired Sydney Baron, Inc., to combat adverse publicity arising from the mysterious disappearance in New York City of Dr. Jesús de Galindez, an outspoken opponent of the Dominican dictatorship. Baron listed receipts for 1957 and 1958 amounting to $562,-855, of which more than $200,000 went to the well-known attorney Morris Ernst, who was retained "to undertake an investigation of the so-called Galindez affair in so far as it touches upon implications and accusations against . . . the government of the Dominican Republic and persons holding high office in that government." In 1959, even as Guterma was making his deal with the Dominicans, By-Line Newsreel Productions was hired to produce a fifteen-minute sound movie each month for the purpose of "making increasingly known the progress achieved in the Dominican Republic." The agreement specified that these newsreels, which cost $3,000 apiece, would be shown in nine hundred movie houses throughout the United States.

As any reporter can testify, much of foreign P.R. performs a useful service in keeping the press informed about facts they need to know. Taken as a whole, it is no more mysterious or unscrupulous than P.R. work done for domestic clients. It varies, of course, from firm to firm and client to client, since in this unlicensed and unlimited profession the practitioners are pretty much able to devise their own rules and ethics as they go along. But in one respect the work done for a foreign government does differ from that performed in behalf of, say, an American manufacturer. For one thing, the American public's familiarity with the domestic client's product is apt to exert some check on the activities of those who promote it. But such restraints do not apply so rigorously to a foreign client, particularly if it happens to be the government of a country not visited by many American tourists, congressmen, and journalists who may snoop around a little during their travels.

Obviously in our days, nearly all nations are engaged in some sort of direct or indirect public-relations activities abroad. The United States, it is hoped, operates constantly and efficiently in this field. But the activities and the policies of a large country are always the object of scrutiny and debate. The same does not apply to small countries, or rather to their governments—all too often when the very survival of those governments depends to a large extent on the assistance they receive from us. The facts we need to know are often concealed, or get to us too late. All of a sudden there may be a blow-up in a country with which we have been deeply involved. When that happens, it not only upsets the best-laid plans of the P.R. men but greatly harms America's prestige.

'HOW MUCH WOULD IT COST?'

A foreign government's assumptions about how to handle press relations in the United States are heavily conditioned by the way it treats the press back home. Generalissimo Trujillo had no reason to doubt that he could buy the services of a radio network. When General Batista was still boss in Cuba in 1958, he approached a New York P.R. firm with a query about how much it would cost to get favorable stories in the *New York Times* (Batista felt sure that Herbert Matthews of the *Times* was in the pay of Castro).

False expectations, it must be added, have sometimes been encouraged by overzealous P.R. firms. On file at the Justice Department is a copy of a prospectus prepared by Max Rogel, Inc., soliciting the Nicaraguan account. It makes this claim: "We now have a comprehensive news service that makes it possible to flash a story or a photograph to every major daily newspaper in the United States. This story will come across the wire into the offices of these newspapers. It will be treated as a news story and will be received as such. . . . This is an operation that is very similar to the workings of the two major news services in the United States. It is, in actuality, a service extended to us by one of these two news services on an exclusive basis." What the prospectus apparently referred to was the PR Newswire in New York, which transmits releases around the city and which, of course, has no official connection with either AP or UPI.

A similar impression of accessibility to the heartbeat of the news system was contained in the Rogel proposal to the Korean government that the first step in its operations would be "to secure a newspaper person who could act as our leg man or stringer in Seoul. . . . This individual will be someone who is known in Seoul and approved by your government. He will be attached to one of the wire services." In a recent interview, Rogel's executive vice-president, Clyde Matthews, has stated that his firm never obtained such a wire-service stringer in Korea. But he pointed out that it is not out of keeping with P.R. practice. In Nicaragua, according to the firm's filings with the Justice Department, payments were made to one Leonardo Lacayo, who also serves as a UPI stringer in Managua as well as editor of the pro-government newspaper *Novedades*. Matthews estimates that half of the news stories that come out of Nicaragua are in one way or another the products of the firm's initiative.

SWEETNESS AND LIGHT

Naturally those who are in the business of creating favorable impressions about their clients are not apt to underestimate their own accomplishments. Many of the reputed feats of the P.R. men prove after investigation to be pretty trivial stuff, a conspicuous waste of a foreign government's money.

But it would be a mistake to think that P.R.'s foreign legion is ineffective. Perhaps the most dramatic example of what it can accomplish occurred in 1955, when the Cubans were faced with the imminent threat that their quota of sugar exports to the United States would be slashed in order to favor domestic producers. Forty-nine senators had gone on record for revising the Sugar Act ahead of its scheduled expiration at the end of 1956. In desperation, the Cuban sugar industry hired Samuel E. Stavisky, a Washington newspaperman turned public-relations counsel.

Stavisky, who has described what ensued in a document entitled "The Sweetest Story Ever Sold," launched a campaign that was responsible in large measure for thwarting Congressional action in 1955 and led the next year to a new and highly favorable quota for Cuban sugar that lasted until Castro upset everything. Stavisky estimates that "Effective public relations helped the Cuban sugar industry gain an extra million tons of sugar quota in the American market." It was, according to Stavisky, a P.R. job with a $100 million payoff for his client.

The operation was directed more at the press than at the politicians. Stavisky reasoned that he had a good but complex story to get across on a subject about which most reporters were notably ignorant. Liked and respected by his former colleagues, he gathered small groups of them for lunch at Washington's Colony Restaurant and discussed the political ramifications of sugar with an old newsman's sense for the interesting "story angle." With the help of a liberal expense account, he "encouraged" reporters to visit Cuba. Some were provided with travel subsidies when they couldn't make it on their own. One correspondent even charged off his gambling losses.

More important, Stavisky soon worked out a news angle that made the fate of Cuban sugar important local news all over the United States. Using an IBM punch-card breakdown of shipping invoices, he traced the origin of the more than $400 million in U.S. exports to Cuba the previous year by state, city, Congressional district, product, industry, and company. Soon a steady flow of stories began to appear in local papers around the country about the importance of the Cuban market to Texas oil, California beans, Arkansas rice, and Ohio lard. In the western tier of the North Central States, whose congressmen were generally hostile to sugar imports, it was discovered that 708 manufacturers had sold Cuba more than $22 million in 1953. This was considered news throughout that region.

A newsman's intimate connections on Capitol Hill served Stavisky in good stead. In early 1955, Stavisky relates, when Vice-President Nixon visited Cuba during a Caribbean tour he was briefed with a Stavisky memo and the Havana reporters were loaded with Stavisky-inspired questions for Nixon.

Publicity counterattacks against the domestic sugar interests were also part of the Stavisky operation. When Senator Ellender took two "experts" representing those interests into a closed Senate committee session, the fact was soon published in a Drew Pearson column that proclaimed, "Ellender Works for Sugar Lobby."

Stavisky measured his impact on newspapers in column-inches. His scrapbook is crammed with clippings from newspapers all over the country, many bearing a word-for-word identity with his press releases. Frequently they have omitted any mention of their origin.

WHO PICKS UP THE TAB?

In assessing the abuses that crop up, those involved in public relations often pass the blame to the press. One veteran P.R. man for a Central American client estimates that his firm "places" between a hundred and two hundred stories a week in the newspapers, often used verbatim and sometimes with a prominent reporter's by-line added. He finds that it is getting easier all the time to do the newsman's job for him. "From my point of view as a P.R. man, this is good," he remarks, "but from journalism's point of view it is not good. The number of reporters with time to dig beyond the surface facts seems to be getting smaller and smaller. We fill a vacuum in the flow of news."

He ascribes this condition in part to the economics of U.S. news coverage. Despite the hordes of reporters who congregate in Washington or accompany the President on his good-will missions, the ranks of American journalists covering the rest of the world are remarkably thin. By his estimate, nine-tenths of our news from the smaller foreign countries is handled by stringers who piece out their income with other jobs. The Associated Press claims that it services eighty countries, maintaining regular correspondents in more than fifty of them. In many places, at least until events reach a crisis point, news coverage is very much a hit-or-miss proposition.

In Cuba, for example, it turned out after the Castro revolution that the AP stringer at the Presidential Palace had been on Batista's payroll. The Dominican Republic long controlled stringers working for U.S. publications by its control over all domestic papers.

To get coverage for the countries they represent, both great and small, P.R. agencies frequently provide travel subsidies for the press. But many feel that the practice has been increasingly getting out of hand and has dubious benefits. Curtis Hoxter says he receives as many as ten calls a week from reporters looking for junkets. Among a dozen or so P.R. firms we interviewed, none had failed to get requests for travel subsidy or other gifts, ranging from a case of liquor on up, as incentives to do a "good" story.

Among reporters, whose income averages far less than that of their P.R. counterparts, there are no generally agreed-upon ethics about these practices. Free-lancers particularly, having no guarantee that their articles will be bought, accept it as part of the game. The Society of Magazine Writers does not include in its Code of Ethics and Good Practices anything on the subject of accepting or labeling such financial assistance. James Doyle, who wrote a story for North American Newspaper Alliance after a week's trip to Nicaragua last August, paid for by the P.R. firm of Max Rogel, argues: "You are not deceiving editors. They know somebody pays your way. But no good reporter is going to be seduced by room, board, or an airplane ride." Doyle claims that for "marginal" stories like Nicaragua, its government must pay the freight or nobody will go. "After all, who gives a damn about Nicaragua?"

Neither Doyle nor John McBride, Latin-American columnist for the New York *Mirror,* who also went on the Nicaraguan junket, believes it would be appropriate to state who paid for such trips in published copy. "When you do something like that," McBride says, "it takes away from your writing no matter what you say. It would hurt if readers knew the paper wouldn't send you down but the Nicaraguan government would."

Economics plays an even bigger role in the newsreel business. Placing films seems to be a nearly sure-shot proposition for the knowledgeable P.R. man. The firm of Hamilton Wright, for example, has some of the finest camera crews and equipment in the business. One of its typical contracts, drawn up with the government of Chile, provides that newsreels with commentary will be prepared and delivered free of charge to Fox Movietone, MGM Newsreel, Paramount, Warner Pathé, and Universal International: "This organization guarantees that five or more of the above newsreels shall be accepted and shown by at least one of the above-mentioned companies throughout its entire chain of theaters in the United States." Much the same guarantee has been made to Nationalist China.

According to Hamilton Wright, Jr., such a guarantee is "based on past experience." The normal procedure in placing a newsreel for a client is to prepare seven hundred feet on a subject and supply an informational sheet that will permit the editors to edit it for themselves. Last spring for example, the firm offered footage on the Formosan elections that Fox Movietone used in its regular newsreels.

The documentary "Fortress Formosa" was turned over to Twentieth Century-Fox with a grant of full ownership rights for a five-year period. But Wright minimizes the propaganda value of these efforts. "For theatrical distribution, they must be subtle," he declared. "They cannot have much political content."

He was seconded on this point by John Kuhne, a veteran documentary producer for Twentieth Century-Fox, who claims that he turns down most film submissions even though they are free. The ones he accepts, like "Fortress Formosa," are picked solely for their entertainment value. He rejects the suggestion that the source of such films might be clearly labeled: "It would look like a direct propaganda bit." He points out that Twentieth Century-Fox does not label the Defense Department films that are supplied regularly to all major distributors.

Jerome Kahn, assistant news editor of Twentieth Century-Fox, has said he will incorporate P.R. film in his newsreels only when it contains a legitimate news story. There have been times, he claims, when Hamilton Wright has had the only footage of areas Chiang bars to regular photographers. He doesn't object to having a P.R. outfit handle the Dominican Republic because this is the only way to get films. The newsreel company simply can't afford to send its own crew.

Among P.R. firms, there is general agreement that the theater newsreel is in a declining state and pretty well forced to live on handouts. Even those who do this handing out sometimes feel the pinch. An executive at Harold Oram, Inc., which handles the account of South Vietnam for an annual fee of a mere $38,000, has said, "You never see a film on Vietnam in your theaters because we don't have the money to make it."

Television networks generally keep a sharp eye out for attempts at infiltration by P.R. operators. "They try to use us," said Piers Anderton of NBC News, who handles the Huntley-Brinkley newscasts, "but we use them." He will accept footage but not the accompanying scripts. In reference to the film clip of Chiang's forces that was shown on "Today" right after the Nixon-Kennedy debate over Quemoy, Bill Fitzgerald, news director for the program, points out that it was only a brief sequence and that it had been stored for some time in the NBC film library. He does not feel that the network was under any obligation to identify those who originally provided the film. "They are satisfied with the exposure. There is no prerequisite to mention their name." What about responsibility to the public? "I don't think the public is too interested in knowing," Fitzgerald said.

By far the most fertile field for the planting of P.R. film has been in direct submission to independent television stations. It has, in fact, become such an active market that there are now a number of middlemen who specialize in distributing free films being offered for television use. These distributors are paid for each showing, not by the station but by the supplier of the film.

One of the biggest of these distributors, Sterling Movies U.S.A., Inc., puts out quarterly a fat catalogue of offerings that have been prepared to fill half- and quarter-hour time slots in a TV station's schedule. The catalogue usually makes no mention of who has paid for the production of these films. It is obvious that many are veiled advertisements for tourist resorts or industrial sponsors. In its foreign listings, the Spring 1960 catalogue listed eight films on Algeria ("The background story on this critical area in world affairs. . . . Enlightening information on the movement toward nationalism"), four on the Sahara, two on Morocco, three on Tunisia, one of Turkey, and six on South Africa "Points up similarities between U.S. and South African history"). On investigation, it turned out that several of the Algerian films had actually been paid for by the French government, which then hired New York producers to edit them, dub in English voices, and pay for the distribution. Essentially the same procedure is known to have been followed by South Africa and governments of several of the other countries involved.

"Public advocacy" by a foreign country's diplomats, argues the Ghana memorandum prepared by Harold L. Oram, Inc., is generally regarded as "improper interference in the internal affairs of the United States" and "a highly ineffective method to convert or persuade the American public . . ." Therefore, the memorandum goes on, "One of the cardinal rules of effective public relations, particularly in the political sphere, is to remove the source of the ideas (in this case the Government of Ghana or its representatives) as far as possible from the advocates (whether they be private individuals, organizations or media)."

THE DIM SPOTLIGHT

Oram may be right. But one trouble with his argument is that it does not entirely square with the terms of the Foreign Agents Registration Act of 1938, amended in 1942, which specify that a public-relations agent employed by a foreign government is required, after registering with the Justice Department, to make full disclosure of activities and expenditures and to label all communications intended to influence "any section of the public . . . with reference to the political or public interests, policies, or relations of a government of a foreign country . . ." The act grew out of Congressional concern over Nazi propaganda agents in this country. "Resting on the fundamental Constitutional principle," according to an interpretation by Justice Hugo Black, "that our people adequately informed may be trusted to distinguish between the true and the false, the bill is intended to label information of foreign origin so the hearers and readers may not be deceived by the belief that the information comes from a disinterested source." The chairman of the House Judiciary Committee, Representative Emanuel Celler, who helped draft the law, counted on fighting fire with fire by using "the spotlight of pitiless publicity" to expose foreign propaganda.

But the law has had a hard time keeping up with expanding P.R. activities in the postwar period. Nathan B. Lenvin, chief of the Justice Department's registration section, is quite confident "that the vast majority who come within the purview of the statute have registered." Over its twenty-two-year history, there have been twenty-three prosecutions for failure to do so and twenty-one convictions.

But the spotlight in which Congress placed its trust has certainly been less than pitiless. Few people come to look at the files in Lenvin's outer office, and few of the documents give the kind of details that Congress ordered. Many of the reports filed there make only the barest statement about expenditure or activities in behalf of foreign clients. Some P.R. agents who submitted fuller details in former years have dropped the practice. (One, who admits that his reports are not very lengthy, says frankly that he has no intention of telling his competitors what he is doing.)

The act's most neglected provision has been the requirement to label the source of political information. Time and again in our investigations we came across what appeared to be clear violations. But the Justice Department has never brought a test case in this area. No one is certain, for example, how precisely a distributor or a television station is supposed to identify films prepared by foreign agents. The Federal Communications Commission has also failed to explore this field despite its regulation that "a station disclose to its audience exactly who is paying for or furnishing the broadcast material . . . (on) political matters or controversial issues of public importance."

The FCC's own precedents governing domestic P.R. would seem to be pertinent. In 1958, the commission censured Westinghouse Broadcasting for failing to label film used on a news program that had been provided free of charge by the National Association of Manufacturers. Such a practice, the FCC held, required "the highest degree of diligence on the part of the licensee . . . in ascertaining . . . the actual source . . . and identifying this source plainly to the viewing audience."

Perhaps the law is too cumbersome to cope with the way some news finds its path to the public nowadays; foreign agent to producer to distributor to middlemen to media representative. Frequently, it is a difficult matter to determine the origin of something that finally appears in print or on the screen. And it could quickly become a rather absurd pursuit if the Justice Department were to try to monitor all the stages of this very broad enterprise. Too much that passes for high-powered P.R. work is too picayune to matter.

In the long run, the responsibility for keeping the communications channels open and working properly must be borne primarily by those engaged in the business of communication. It is up to those who control the spotlight of publicity to see that it is bright enough and properly focused. The press and other media surely ought not to pass along cheap propaganda simply because they haven't the time or the cash to check stories for themselves. Ultimately, it is not just a matter of economics but even more one of ethics.

There are no cut-and-dried rules to be laid down in this game. A reporter or a broadcaster would be a fool to chuck pertinent information in the wastebasket simply because it came to him from a P.R. source. Foreign P.R., as practiced by reputable private firms as well as official government information agencies, has done a great deal to break down the barriers of isolation and lack of interest that once kept our public opinion aloof and ill informed.

But the press must apply its criteria of selection very carefully in an area of communication that vitally affects our understanding of what is going on in the rest of the world—and of what we are asked to do about it.

A SENATOR LOOKS AT THE LOBBIES
Eugene J. McCarthy

Eugene J. McCarthy has served as Democratic Senator from Minnesota since 1959. He is the author of *Frontiers of American Democracy*.

The word "lobbying" has a derogatory ring. This is not surprising for good or bad lobbying occurs in the processes of democracy at the point of rough transition where interests conflict and judicial processes fall short. Lobbying is a test—sometimes a raw test—of the judgment and integrity of political officeholders, both elected and appointed.

Who are the lobbyists? What do they do in order to affect the course of government? How effective are they? Is lobbying a threat to democracy? Do government officials need more protection from lobbyists? What can or should be done about lobbying? It is important that these questions be asked and that an attempt be made to answer them.

This has been a most active year for lobbyists in Washington. They were drawn especially by the tax bill, the Trade Expansion Act, the medical insurance program and by the Sugar Act.

The activities of lobbyists on the Sugar Act, which involves foreign countries, have moved the Senate Foreign Relations Committee to make a special study of lobbying—or, as the committee described it, of "non-diplomatic activities of representatives of foreign governments or their agents in promoting the interests of those governments." Investigation or inquiry into the operation of lobbyists in other fields has been suggested by some members of Congress.

By statute, the lobbyist today is any person who solicits money or anything of value to be used principally to secure or influence the passage or defeat of any legislation by the Congress of the United States.

Lobbying has a long history. The word "lobby" appeared first in the English language about the middle of the sixteenth century. It was derived from the medieval Latin word *lobium,* a monastic walk or cloister.

Three hundred years later the word was in politics. It was used both to identify a hall or corridor in the British House of Commons and as a collective noun applied to all those who frequented these lobbies. It covered those who sought to influence men in office as well as newspaper men and others looking for news and gossip.

Today the word "lobbyist" is used both in its narrow legal sense and, more broadly, as a description of all attempts to influence not only the legislators, but also any agency or officer of government. Registered lobbyists in

Washington number approximately 1,100, but the number of persons and agencies involved in efforts to influence the Government is much greater.

Some lobbyists represent big interests and well organized groups. The Chamber of Commerce and the National Association of Manufacturers have registered lobbyists along with the A.F.L.-C.I.O.; so do the American Petroleum Institute, the Association of American Railroads, and nearly all major industrial and financial interests. The so-called "little people" and the unorganized or less organized also have lobbyists. For example, the American Committee for Flags of Necessity, the Hualapai Reservation, and the Arthritis and Rheumatism Foundation are among those groups or organizations represented by lobbyists.

Some lobbyists are well paid; some get little more than expense money. Some operate directly on government officials, others primarily by indirection through appeals to constituents or voters. Some are professional, others amateur. Some lobbyists represent only one position or program, while others are available as free lancers on an issue-by-issue or client-by-client basis.

Some lobbyists are quite open—they seek their own gain, the protection of an economic advantage, or the elimination or reduction of advantages held by their competitors. These cry more often for equity than they do for justice. Others speak for the arts, for morality, for aid to the sick and for the oppressed among the family of man.

What do lobbyists do in order to affect government decisions?

The methods used by the lobbyists are almost as varied as their causes. Some appeal on a purely personal basis, as friend to friend. Some undoubtedly use monetary or material appeals, but there is little evidence of direct pay-off in lobbying activities affecting the Congress. In some fourteen years of membership in the Congress, I know of no case in which a member was moved to support or to oppose a position in response to any kind of direct financial or material reward. The indirect influence of campaign contributions is more difficult to assess but it is, I believe, more important.

The most common method of lobbying is that of simply appearing before a committee of Congress or speaking to individual members in an attempt to bring them to understand one's position or to influence them to support that position.

How effective are the lobbyists?

Some are wholly ineffective but take credit for what happens without, in fact, having in any way influenced events.

Among the regular lobbies, the postal employes' organizations are usually very active and, whenever postal pay legislation is before Congress, they are listed at or near the top in terms of total expenditures. In order to raise wages or to change working conditions significantly, the spokesmen for the postal workers of the country must influence either the Congress or the Administration—or both—for Government employe unions are not recognized and dealt with in the same way as other labor unions are by private employers. There is little doubt that the existence of this Washington lobby has influenced the Congress and successive Administrations to raise salaries and to improve working conditions not only for postal employes, but for all Government workers.

The major farm organizations in the country maintain regular lobbies in Washington. The American Farm Bureau Federation and the National Farmers Union usually take opposite sides on farm legislation. The apparent success of the two organizations parallels closely the success of the two major political parties. The Farmers Union position is favored when the Democrats are in power, and the Farm Bureau position when the Republicans are in power.

One of the most interesting and continuing lobbying efforts of recent years has been that in support of a bill which is known as H.R. 10. This bill proposes to change existing income tax laws to allow members of professions and other self-employed persons a limited income tax credit on money invested in private pension or retirement programs. Starting almost from scratch, the supporters of this legislation have secured the approval of the House of Representatives and of the Senate Finance Committee. Victory in this case—if it comes—must be credited in great measure to the efforts of a lobby registered as the American Thrift Assembly, a kind of holding company or organizing lobby, which was supported in testimony by the U. S. Chamber of Commerce, the National Association of Manufacturers, the Farm Bureau, the American Medical Association and others.

In this session of Congress, lobbies have been most active in four major areas: taxes, trade and tariffs, medical aid for the aged and extension of the Sugar Act. Undoubtedly the lobbyists did have or will have some effect on action in each of these areas.

Any significant change in tax laws attracts the attention of those who may be affected. The changes being considered this year were significant and controversial and the lobbying effort extensive.

THE BIG ONES

As reported, according to law, to the Clerk of the House of Representatives and the Secretary of the Senate, the ten biggest-spending lobbies in Washington in 1961 were:

American Medical Association	$163,405
A.F.L.-C.I.O.	139,919
American Farm Bureau Federation	111,364
American Legion	103,566
U.S. Savings and Loan League	101,801
National Committee for Insurance Taxation	90,058
National Farmers Union	88,273
National Housing Conference	88,141
American Trucking Associations, Inc.	84,986
International Brotherhood of Teamsters	81,918

Industries likely to be affected by trade and tariff policies are always well represented in Washington. Whenever an issue even remotely bearing upon trade is brought up for consideration, the representatives of these industries seek permission to testify. The hearings on the President's new tariff and trade program have attracted them in great numbers. Members of the House Ways and Means Committee and the Senate Finance Committee, which ordinarily hold trade and tariff hearings, are generally familiar with the testimony of these witnesses. They have been described as somewhat like professional soldiers who regularly go to battle, seldom win wars and suffer few casualties.

One of the most active Washington lobbies this year, and through the years, is that of the American Medical Association—better known in Washington for what it is against than for what it is for. The spokesmen for the A.M.A. have effectively opposed the inclusion of doctors in the Social Security retirement program. They were strongly opposed to amending the Social Security Law to provide for the payment of Social Security pensions to people who are permanently or totally disabled after they pass the age of 50. And in the present session of Congress, the A.M.A. lobby led the opposition to the establishment of a medical insurance program for the aged as a part of the Social Security program. Action in this Congressional session has been a real test of the power of the A.M.A. lobby.

Lobbying activities with reference to the Sugar Act revision this year involved lobbyists in greater numbers than ever in the past, and the lobbying activities were more intensive. At least twenty-two lobbyists testified before Congressional committees in behalf of the countries they represented. The list of lobbyists included former members of both the Eisenhower and Truman Administrations, Washington lawyers, and public relations men. Their agreements with their principals varied from flat fees to contingency agreements, depending upon the action taken by Congress.

The massive lobbying activity this year arose from the fact that the Administration recommended that the Cuban sugar quota of some three million tons, withdrawn from Cuba because of Castro, be purchased in the world market at something like 2.8 cents a pound rather than on a quota basis from designated countries at traditional premium prices. At the premium price the supplying country would receive approximately $54 a ton more than it would receive at world prices. The Administration's counterproposal was an open, almost demanding invitation to every sugar-producing country interested in getting a share of the premium market to seek representation. Most of them did.

We now come to the basic question: Is lobbying a threat to democracy?

The effects of lobbying can be good or bad, helpful or harmful to democracy, depending upon two things: the purposes or objectives of the lobbying effort, and the methods or devices by which the lobby seeks to accomplish its objectives.

There are some who take the extreme view that lobbies are by their very nature power blocs and therefore inconsistent with democratic government:

that since lobbies represent special or limited interests, their objectives are of necessity not directed to the general welfare and, therefore, they should be abolished.

There are some who see nothing wrong with lobbies except when they represent economic interests.

There are some who hold that the dangers in lobbying arise from secrecy and behind-the-scenes operations and from the amount of money that may be spent by lobbyists.

There are regular demands that more publicity be given to lobbying activities, that lobbying be more closely regulated, and that the amount of money which can be spent by a lobbyist or lobbying groups be limited and fully reported.

Positively, the activity of lobbyists is often very helpful. Lobbyists can help maintain a balance between Congress and the Executive Branch of the Government. The Executive Branch has a prepared case, usually sustained by expert witnesses. The Congress can offer in opposition the knowledge and experience of its own members and that of the Committee staff or Congressional assistants. Often this is an unfair contest. The expert testimony of lobbyists or witnesses from outside may help to bring the contest closer to balance.

Congress, of course, does not depend entirely upon lobbyists for its information. It is the usual practice to call upon governmental experts and also on independent experts drawn from groups directly affected by the legislation under consideration or from related fields and from the academic profession.

For example, in special hearings on unemployment in 1959, invitations to testify were sent to these organizations: the National Association of Manufacturers, the U. S. Chamber of Commerce, the National Coal Policy Conference, the A.F.L.-C.I.O., the United Mine Workers, the National Small Businessmen's Association, the Railway Labor Executives Association and others. Representatives of the U. S. Departments of Labor, Commerce, and Defense were called. Leading labor economists were asked to submit papers, to testify, and to meet with the members of the committee. Hearings were also held in the field. These hearings were open to the testimony of anyone who wished to speak on the subject.

Apart from laws and regulations, there are some built-in protections against the power and influence of lobbyists. One safeguard is that usually there are organized lobbies on both sides of controversial issues: protectionists on the one hand versus free-traders on the other; the A.F.L.-C.I.O. opposed by the National Association of Manufacturers; growers' associations against those seeking to improve working conditions of migratory farm workers; anti-vivisectionists against those who favor medical experimentation with animals.

Sometimes the opposition is not direct but involves competition for a larger share of a quota or a subsidy, or for greater participation in advantageous tax concessions.

Political party positions and programs, too, tend to eliminate large areas of political action from the influence of lobbyists. The political campaign in the United States is a rather severe testing. Most of the important national issues are raised during political campaigns, and most men who are elected to office have made firm commitments on most issues.

The President of the United States is called to account and judged by the people every four years; members of the United States Senate must run for re-election every six years, members of the House of Representatives every two years.

The activities of members of Congress are watched closely by colleagues, particularly by those of the opposite party. They are watched by newspaper men whose reputations in many cases are based upon their ability to ferret out and report any action and conduct unbecoming Government officials.

In addition, of course, everyone who holds office must assume that there are at least two or three people—perhaps in his own party and certainly in the opposition party—who are quite willing to replace him and consequently are likely to give more than ordinary attention to his conduct in public office.

What can or should be done about lobbying?

Members of Congress cannot be fully protected from lobbyists by regulation. They cannot be expected to keep a check list of registered lobbyists or demand proof of registration or defense of non-registration before responding to a request for conversation or for a conference. Yet, members of Congress and other Government officials can be given some protection by law.

The present lobbying registration act should be fully enforced, and financial reporting should be checked carefully. Fees contingent on successful lobbying should be outlawed. Care should be taken to remove from direct legislative determination those questions which should be settled by other branches of government: by the President, by special commissions, by departments and agencies of government or by international agreement.

Much of the agitation over the Sugar Act could have been prevented if the Administration, acting directly or possibly in cooperation with the Organization of American States or the signatories to the International Sugar Agreement had determined the way in which the Cuban sugar quota was to be allocated. There would have been some Congressional protest, since in a broad way Congress has determined sugar allocations since the Sugar Act was passed in 1934. But the protest would have been limited and the compromises so minor that extensive lobbying activities, brought on when the whole question of re-allocation was left open by the Administration, would have been discouraged.

Better salaries for Government officials and sounder methods of financing campaigns would also lessen the likelihood of undue financial influence on public officials by lobbyists and others.

There is always the risk that public officials may be unduly subject to outside influence. But it is hard to imagine a meeting of a national legislature today that could or should be insulated from public pressure or demand. The practice of some primitive tribes, in which the wise men or elders withdrew from society periodically to consider laws and practices, is not likely to be revived.

The whole concept that lobbying opposes the majority, that it seeks to manipulate and subvert the majority will and the public interest, is unrealistic. Lobbyists seldom manufacture a problem. They call attention to an existing problem and try to guide the course of events. Action in Washington sometimes supports the judgment of J. B. S. Hardman, the philosopher and intellectual mentor of industrial trade unionism in America: "Majorities never rule, they merely give credentials to contending minorities."

Although lobbying does not usually involve a physical assembly—such as the 1932 veterans bonus march on Washington or current picketing of the White House—it does involve organization, a bringing together of citizens seeking a common objective. Thus, the act of lobbying is basically an exercise of the right to petition the Government—a right set forth in the Constitution. Lobbying also involves, in a way, the exercise of the right of assembly.

In a democratic society there must be a point at which influences, both good and bad, are brought to bear upon government. The point at which these influences meet finally is in the elected and appointed officials of the country. They are supposed to be men skilled and experienced in politics and possessing the character to withstand improper pressures and improper demands.

Until a clear case can be made against the lobbyist, his voice should be heard in Washington. But his voice must be identified and, insofar as possible, restricted to that influence which is justified by the facts and the conclusions to be drawn from those facts.

What are the attitudes of most Americans toward their national legislative body?

For the most part, popular attitudes reflect the negative, hostile treatment of the Congress by the press, which has tended to emphasize the errors, shortcomings, and wrongdoings and to ignore the positive accomplishments. Many Americans view their congressmen and senators as little more than "party hacks," "errand boys on missions of trivia," or compromisers who are all too willing to jettison principles for the sake of political expediency. They often think of their representatives as wasters—wasters of time, in such fruitless activities as filibustering, or as wasters of money on "junkets" that are invariably reported as heading for Hawaii in the winter or Alaska in the summer. In another vein, no less hostile, the public has viewed its representatives, through the eyes of the press, as lacking in leadership, deficient in initiative, unrepresentative of the popular will (whatever that may be), mere rubber stamps for presidential legislation, and far too responsive to pressure groups.

In order to make a fair appraisal of the Congress, however, we must establish more definite criteria than these popular impressions afford. Several questions are pertinent. For example: Is the Congress truly representative? Is it responsible? Is it democratic? Does it operate in the public interest? That is, does it understand that "what's good for General Motors" may *not* necessarily be good for the United States? Is it constructively critical?

These questions suggest a conclusion that has become increasingly apparent to observers of the Washington scene—namely, that we expect far more of Congress than mere legislating. Thus, it is necessary to clarify the functions of Congress before we may pass judgment on the way Congress performs.

Two of its four leading functions have involved substantial changes since the Constitution was written; the other two have evolved more nearly as planned. First, in enacting legislation, Congress now has a *screening* rather than an originating role; it regularly reviews, but it seldom creates major public policy.

Second, the function of *popular representation* has also undergone a subtle mutation: congressmen today, in a very real sense, *must* be the errand boys for the American public, since some public body must provide popular checks on an administration grown so necessarily large. How else may bureaucracy be kept responsive to the desires of the people that it serves?

A third valuable function of Congress is *compromise*. Despite its negative aspects, compromise is a vital part of the democratic process; for its alternatives, suppression or surrender, are generally unacceptable to thoughtful persons everywhere.

Finally, the Congress has the major task of *informing and educating* the American public. Not only is it charged with reflecting public opinion; it must lead and create that opinion, as well as discover what public opinion is.

With these functions in mind, what elements are essential to an understanding of our Senate and our House of Representatives? First is the changing nature of the American representative system. Contrary to the expectations of the Founding Fathers, the Senate has emerged as the voice of the nation—despite its states'-rights intonations and its occasional southern accents. On the other hand, the House, created as the popular spokesman, has emerged as a more provincial body, far more subject than the Senate to the importunings of local pressures.

The second essential element, the lack of strong party leadership, reflects the shortcomings of our national political organizations. While the nation has been centralizing its federal system for more than 175 years, the political parties have remained much as they were a century and a half ago—county-oriented groups far more interested in getting their henchmen elected to local offices than in the subtleties of national policies. Lacking in discipline and more concerned with candidates than with issues, the parties have frequently been irresponsible in their behavior, and since the Civil War they have been guilty of mislabeling—with Northern liberals retained for nearly a century in a predominantly conservative G.O.P., and with Whig-type Southern conservatives still to be found among progressive Democratic ranks.

The third element is personality—the personality of the House Speaker, the personality of the Senate Majority Leader, and the personalities of the key committee chairmen. Here one encounters the seniority system, with its negative impact on party legislative programs. One finds the House Rules Committee—that "traffic cop of legislation," which, for the Democratic Party at least, has proved more of a road block than a traffic regulator, seldom signaling a green light without exacting an undue toll of concessions. There are other committees: the standing committees, with virtual life-or-death powers over proposed legislation; and the conference committees, those "third houses" of the Congress with powers to mold the final shapes of laws. These are some of the elements at work in the nation's Capitol—elements which, despite extensive press coverage, are too little understood by the public as it views the legislative branch of our government in action.

PORTRAIT OF A "TYPICAL" CONGRESSMAN
David S. Broder

David S. Broder, a member of *The New York Times* Washington bureau, regularly observes congressmen at work on and off Capitol Hill.

From *The New York Times Magazine*, October 7, 1962. © 1962 by The New York Times Company. Reprinted by permission.

If Congress is, as its critics say, a sickly institution, then those who run for Congress presumably have no objections to catching some sort of Capitol fever. About 900 of our fellow citizens are seeking the 435 House and 39 Senate seats available this November—a record number. And for what? For the honor of serving in a body whose reputation with its critics has rarely been lower?

In order to know what lures these men and women to Congressional service—why an institution that has been pronounced a failure by its critics should exert such magnetism across the land—we must understand the nature of the office itself.

What is a Congressman, really? Is he legislator or errand boy, an ambassador from his state or district or an officer of the national Government? By what standards should he be judged? The chances are these questions will be raised in few of the current campaigns. And yet one cannot shake the suspicion that they are overdue for discussion.

The burden of this article is that the Congressman is a most misunderstood creature. He is not one man, as the critics would have it, but three. He is a legislator for the nation; he is a mediator between his district and the central Government; and he is a teacher of his people. His performance in his three roles varies. In the first, he is adequate; in the second, excellent, and in the third, deficient.

But before pulling him apart this way, let us see him whole, as he is in life.

The typical Congressman is an unbashful, churchgoing fellow of 52, a veteran and a college graduate. He has made his living as a lawyer or businessman and has learned something of the management of human affairs. He also has behind him some years in public office—as a prosecutor perhaps, or as a mayor or a state assemblyman. He is, in all likelihood, a man of above-average sensitivity, stamina, ambition and acumen.

This bears importantly on the Congressman's performance in his first role, as a national legislator. The critics of Congress sometimes talk as though ignorance, indifference and inertia are so inbred in Senators and Representatives that they are literally incapable of writing good legislation.

The contrary seems closer to the truth. Most Congressmen are far ahead of their constituencies, both in sensing national problems as they arise and in understanding the strengths and weaknesses of proposed solutions. It is not just accident that the average Congressman is better informed than almost any of his voters. He has to be, for in the Washington arena knowledge is power, whether the struggle concerns the tax code, the merits of rival weapons systems or the mechanisms of the farm program.

Because he is a decision maker, the Congressman is the beneficiary of a constant flow of information and instruction from committee staff members, from his colleagues, from the Administration and from representatives of interest groups. Even the dullest Senator or Representative cannot fail to learn something from this process and most of them learn a great deal more than a little.

Is the problem, then, that the mechanism of Congress will not enable its members to put their knowledge to work? Lately, it has become fashionable to suggest that this is the answer. The seniority system must be abolished, it is said. Committees must be curbed, or perhaps strengthened. Debate must be curtailed, or perhaps extended. The leadership must be broadened, or made more responsive, or something.

The pertinent point about these criticisms is not that they are irrelevant but that they are not new. The conflict-of-interest problem, so much discussed recently, was not unfamiliar to Daniel Webster. The struggle between the party leadership in each house and the committee chairmen is routine, not novel. Congress operates now very much as it has throughout its history.

What has changed is the amount of time, energy and brains Congressmen can devote to the tasks of devising legislation and overcoming the built-in obstacles to its enactment. The main reason, I suggest, that Congress does not legislate better is simply that most Congressmen can no longer afford to regard legislation as the most important part of their jobs.

Indeed, many of them find it very difficult to sandwich legislative work into the busy schedule of what they describe—correctly—as their more important functions. These functions relate to their second role, as mediators between their districts and the central Government, and we will examine in a moment why the burdens they carry in this area have increased so in recent years.

But first it is important to understand that the conflict between the Congressman as national legislator and the Congressman as agent for his district is not just a theoretical struggle.

The practical problem the Congressman faces is well described by Representative Clem Miller, a California Democrat, in his revealing little book about the realities of Congressional life, just published under the title, "Member of the House."

In one of the letters comprising the volume, he explains to his friends at home that most of the vital decisions on the floor of the House are made on teller votes, with the opponents and supporters of the bill or amendment passing up the aisle between counters to indicate their stand. Mr. Miller reports, accurately, that "at least 150 members can be counted on to be absent from any teller vote."

"What is it that happens to these members of Congress?" he asks. "Presumably they were elected for this very task above all others: to be in the chamber, to vote.

"The fact is that this objective is blurred with time and circumstance. . . . What is of overriding significance gives way to what is immediate. The competing interests, the endless details of Congressional routine, take hold.

"Members are called to the floor . . . as the afternoon's debate begins . . . Most stay for a while listening and chatting. Then, inevitably, the drift begins. Pages hurry up and down the aisles with sheaves of messages . . .

"Gradually . . . (the Congressman) is caught up in the inescapable workaday world of Congress. Almost without volition, he finds himself back in his office, trying to keep up with the mail, interviewing and being interviewed by streams of callers. Now he is too far away to get back to the floor for a teller vote.

"Once away from the chamber, he is far away. The urgency, the insistence, is gone. A million words of testimony, the results of a thousand patient meetings may be going down the drain. But it is another world from the Congressional office."

The conflict between these two worlds has another dimension, because it is also a conflict between pleasure and duty. Most Congressmen find the pleasures of their work lie mainly in the legislative world, in the personal relationships between competitors and cohorts in the Insiders' World of Washington Influentials, a world where strength and shrewdness, wit and will are savored as much as wealth in Dallas.

But pleasurable as his life in the Insiders' World may be for the Congressman, his job security and his political future depend chiefly on how well he serves the residents of the Outsiders' World—the people of his state or district. Cultivating his relationship with them must be given first priority, no matter what his personal tastes dictate and no matter what the critics of Congress may think.

The plain fact is that a man's legislative work is commonly a matter of indifference—if not outright suspicion—for his constituents. What can hurt politically is the charge that he has failed to look after his district. Neglect of correspondence, of constituent services or of vital local needs lies behind the defeat of a vast majority of those few in Congress who fail of re-election.

No wonder, then, that the first move of distinguished chairman of the Senate Foreign Relations Committee, Senator J. W. Fulbright, made in preparation for his current campaign in Arkansas was to turn over leadership of his committee for the year to the next-senior Democrat, Senator John Sparkman of Alabama (whose term does not expire until 1967). Rice, cotton and flood control projects are safer concerns for a man seeking re-election than U.N. bonds or foreign aid.

There is no sense mourning the fact that the Congressman's constituent-service role is interfering ever increasingly with his work as a legislator. It is the inevitable result of the changes that have taken place in our society and Government in the past 175 years.

The Founding Fathers knew the conflict would exist, but they misjudged the dimensions of the problem. In Federalist Paper No. 56, Madison recognized that the Congressman "ought to be acquainted with the interests and circumstances of his constituents." But in a simple society under a government of limited powers, this requirement, he believed, could easily be met.

"This principle," he argued, "can extend no farther than to those circumstances and interests to which the authority and care of the Representative relate. An ignorance of a variety of minute and particular objects, which do not lie within the compass of legislation, is consistent with every attribute necessary to a due performance of the legislative trust."

The increase in our population, the growing complexity of our economy and the proliferation of government functions have made it far more burdensome than Madison ever dreamed for the Congressman to define and defend "the interests and circumstances of his constituents"—to serve as a mediator between them and their Government. This function is consistently undervalued by critics of Congress, particularly those who are Washington-based, who fail to comprehend the gulf between the constituencies and the capital.

To the average citizen preoccupied with his own affairs, the central Government is a remote colossus, incomprehensible, almost unapproachable, but not safely ignored. His link—his sole link—with it is his Congressman.

The Congressman must protect his district and its people from the mischance and mischief that almost inevitably accompany bureaucracy's rather rigid way of doing its work. He *must* do it, for his people have no one else to look to. Because the work is essential and unavoidable, most Congressmen have become very proficient at the task. And that is the main reason why, in recent elections, less than one incumbent in ten seeking re-election has been denied another term.

But the Congressman's position as the middleman between his district and the central Government imposes another duty on him—one which he meets less adequately. I refer now to his third major role—not as legislator, not as a broker, but as a teacher, an educator and a shaper of opinion back home.

To some it will seem strange to charge the Congressman with this responsibility. It has become customary to say that the President has the job of telling the people where the country stands and what it needs to do. He does. President Kennedy has been criticized for failing to do this sufficiently, and so were his predecessors. The inescapable fact is that all our Presidents for the last quarter-century have been preoccupied with foreign affairs. Most of their speeches have sought public understanding of our responsibilities in that area.

Domestic affairs have been left largely to Congress. If domestic needs are unmet—as many believe—the blame must rest on the Congressmen for failing to bring their people to an understanding of the programs required.

How can Congress do this job? One of the most effective devices is the public hearing. Look, for example, at the way in which the 1959–60 revision of the labor law came about. A Senate committee held a series of hearings that gave the public dramatic evidence of the extent of criminal infiltration into labor unions. Another committee drafted remedial legislation. The topic was discussed in the districts by virtually every member of Congress. Only in the final stages of the debate did the President join the dialogue, and then his intervention was a marginal influence. It was a Congressional project.

"The job of a Congressman," Representative Miller says in his book, "in major degree is communicating—making our political world understandable."

Congressmen communicate through their newsletters and radio and television reports to their districts; through the frequent speeches they make to civic and political groups at home; and through their innumerable conversations with individual constituents.

But how well do they communicate? Too often, I am afraid, the same Congressman who will tell a bureaucrat bluntly and honestly how a proposed policy would affect his constituents will equivocate and hesitate before giving his constituents the blunt truth about what can and cannot be done in the national interest.

Nothing is more important to our democracy than the kind of information our Congressmen spread. The operations of the representative system enable the vast majority of these men to stay in office as long as they wish. Do they use their time preparing their constituents to cope with the world as it is, or do they conceal the world from them? That is the crucial question about this year's election, as about every Congressional election.

Will the Midwestern conservative who is certain to be back for another term give his constituents the old line about balancing the budget first and then cutting taxes? Or will he help them try to understand that our present tax structure is keeping us from balancing the budget and achieving a lot of other economic goals as well?

Will the Eastern liberal from a safely gerrymandered district go back to his voters with the same shopworn promise about passing a massive aid-to-education bill? Or will he tell them what he knows to be true: that those sincerely interested in helping education must define the goals and limit the scope of the program much more strictly than they have in the past in order to meet the legitimate objections of those who, for a variety of reasons, fear the impact of massive Federal aid?

Too frequently in Washington one hears a Congressman say, "I understand the need for this, but my people back home don't, so I won't vote for it." That may be acceptable as an excuse on that particular day, but it ought to oblige that Congressman to spend a good many days helping his people grasp the situation as well as he does.

By way of summary, then, our scorecard on Congress looks something like this:

As the agent for his constituents in protecting their interests in Washington, the average Congressman does an excellent job. The role is a vital one from his district's point of view and, if the critics of Congress want to be fair, they should give him high marks for the quality of his performance in this field.

As a national legislator, the Congressman is at least adequate. Men will disagree on how many desirable bills are left unpassed, on how many bad ones become law, and on what provisions any particular measure should contain. But it seems fair to say that most of the bills Congress does approve are well-designed for their purpose, are drawn with some attention to the technical, legal and political niceties of the problem and generally emerge in a more satisfactory form than they began.

As a teacher of his people, the average Congressman leaves much to be desired. The gap between the reality of the situation the nation faces and the public's understanding of it seems to be growing, not shrinking. This trend must be reversed if our Government is going to remain both representative and effective.

By now it must be obvious why so many men and women this fall are seeking to gain or retain membership in Congress.

The power and the pleasures of a Congressman's job are unique in the structure of American public offices. He is a key member of the small world of Washington Influentials, sharing in the secrets and the satisfactions that attend the management of the world's most powerful nation.

He is also the protector of his people in their dealings with the central Government and, frequently, the dispensing angel through whom that Government lavishes its gifts upon the land. He is able, in other words, to perform a great many services of great importance for people who are of personal concern to him.

Finally, he is, or can be if he wishes, a great source of wisdom to his people—an influence upon their thinking and upon their lives.

Because he is all of these things, he is also a very busy man—so busy, often, that he cannot do any of these jobs as well as he would like.

The second-commonest remark on Capitol Hill is, "I don't know why I put up with this rat race." But the commonest is, "I don't know anything I would rather be doing."

THE SENATE ESTABLISHMENT
James McCartney

James McCartney is in the Washington Bureau of the *Chicago Daily News*.

Early this month, Senator Joseph Clark, the studious, liberal Democrat from Pennsylvania, astonished his fellow Senators by opening a speech with these words: "Mr. President, I desire to address the Senate on the subject of the Senate Establishment and how it operates." For, of course, the one subject that by unspoken rule is taboo in this most exclusive club in the world is the power structure of the club itself, or the impugning, no matter how indirectly, of the motivations of any of its members.

Senator Clark's remarkable speech deserves the closest attention of all those who tend to confuse the *forms* and the *substance* of democratic gov-

From *The Nation,* March 15, 1963. Reprinted by permission.

ernment. In sum, Clark charged that the Senate as a whole was a virtual prisoner of about twelve of its members—eight Democrats and four Republicans—who, by virtue of seniority and their alliances with essentially conservative interests, can direct legislation by rigging committees and by the control they can exert over the destinies of individual Senators. These dozen men constitute, in Senator Clark's phrase, the "Senate Establishment"— and its power became dramatically evident even as the Senator was attacking it.

A few days earlier, it had become apparent that the Establishment had seen fit to deprive a raft of liberal Senators of important committee assignments to which they were clearly entitled. Yet so great was the victims' fear of further punishment that not one of them had dared to complain publicly. Nor, with two exceptions, was this silence broken when Clark made his speech: only William Proxmire (D., Wis.) and Paul Douglas (D., Ill.) had the temerity to agree openly with their colleague from Pennsylvania.

Clark elaborated his thesis for three days, off and on. At no time did he attempt to list completely the members of the Establishment by name and rank. But some of his research aides, together with aides of other liberal Senators, have pieced together a reasonable version of the membership and made a number of illuminating points concerning this *ex-officio* "in-group."

For example, they say that Senate Majority Leader Mike Mansfield, theoretically the most powerful figure in the Senate, may not be a member, although he is often a spokesman for it. On the other hand, the Minority Leader, Everett Dirksen of Illinois, is definitely a member, even though he has only half as many Republicans to "lead" as Mansfield has Democrats. Moreover, two men who are not even Senators and who are almost unknown outside of Washington, are considered by some observers to be members: Robert Baker, secretary to the Democratic majority, and Mark Trice, who holds the comparable job for the Republicans.

Mr. Clark's description of the Senate Establishment at work began with a general summary of its significance and *modus operandi:*

> The Senate Establishment is almost the antithesis of democracy. It is not selected by any democratic process. It appears to be quite unresponsive to the caucuses of the two parties, be they Republican or Democratic.
>
> It is what might be called a self-perpetuating oligarchy with mild, but only mild, overtones of plutocracy. The way it operates is something like this:
>
> There are a number of states, most of them Democratic, but one or two of them Republican, which inevitably and always return to the U.S. Senate members of one party, and under a custom which has grown up over the years of following the rule of seniority in making committee assignments, and in connection with the distribution of other perquisites of Senate tenure, the result has been that those who have been here longest have become chairmen of committees.
>
> As such, they have exercised virtual control over the distribution of

favors, includings committee assignments and other perquisites of office in the Senate and largely . . . determine who shall be selected to posts of leadership in this body.

The point is hardly new that conservatives, most of them Southerners with seniority, dominate the Senate, but Clark brought the mathematics of their power up to date. Of the Senate's hundred members, 67 today are Democrats and 33 are Republicans. Of the Democrats, 23 are from the South (the 11 states of the old confederacy plus Oklahoma and Arkansas). The hardcore Southerners, in other words, make up 34 per cent of the Democratic bloc. But on the vital Appropriations Committee, for example, they hold 50 per cent of the Democratic seats; on the Armed Services Committee, 42 per cent; of the important Foreign Relations Committee, 42 per cent; on the Democratic Steering Committee (which selects other committee members), 47 per cent.

In this session of Congress especially, no body is more important than the Senate Finance Committee, which will handle President Kennedy's top-priority legislative items—his tax-cut program as well as medicare. Thus a battle has been waged over the committee's composition, and the winners are now more than clear: the Southerners wind up with 6 out of the 11 Democratic members for a representation of 55 per cent.

Senator Clark had sought to get the committee enlarged in order to give the President's programs a better chance. The justification for his attempt was mathematical. There have been 11 Democrats and 6 Republicans on the committee and, according to Clark's theory, the Democrats—outnumbering the Republicans in the Senate by 2 to 1—should be entitled to at least a 2 to 1 ratio on the committee. He proposed that the ratio be 12 to 6 or 14 to 7, or any one of several other combinations which would have reflected the party balance of the Senate as a whole. But it was not to be. The Establishment was able not only to maintain the present inequitable ratio, but to deliver another blow at the liberals by appointing to the committee Senator Dirksen to replace the late Senator Robert Kerr (D., Okla.), oil man and frequent spokesman for business interests.

Senator Mansfield supported Clark's proposal. But by his own admission on the Senate floor, the Majority Leader could line up only 40 to 42 votes in favor. The point was that neither the Republicans nor the Southerners would "buy" the proposal, and Mansfield must have help from one group or the other or he gets nowhere, clearly exposing the deficiencies of the official and formal Democratic leadership's position.

Clark emphasized that a key instrument of the Establishment is the Democratic Steering Committee. In a careful analysis, he showed that 9 of its 15 members are Southerners and conservatives and only 6 might be called liberals, in spite of the fact that Democratic liberals actually outnumber conservatives in the Senate. Stated the Senator:

I suggest in all candor that the Steering Committee does not fairly represent either the geography or the ideology of the Democratic members of the Senate. . . . Whom does the Steering Committee of the Democratic Party represent? It represents the Democratic side of the Establishment.

And how does the Steering Committee wield its power? Clark produced an analysis of committee appointments in an effort to indicate possible motivations, although he refrained from drawing conclusions. His analysis suggested a relationship between votes by nonfreshman Senators on the filibuster issue and the degree to which the Democratic Senators received their requested committee assignments from the Steering Committee. Six of eight Senators who voted with the South on the issue got their first choice of committee; only one who voted against the South got his first choice—and that was the Majority Leader, who traditionally can go to any committee he wants.

The role of the Republicans in the Establishment should not be overlooked.

> The senior ranking members of the minority party are a part of the Establishment (said Clark) and they, in conference—usually informal, always friendly—with their colleagues on the other side of the aisle pretty well decide who is going to do what to whom. That is what is happening in the Senate today.

Who are the actual members of the Establishment? There is a considerable amount of friendly disagreement among Senate liberals on just how powerful a number of individuals are, but there is wide agreement on the key figures. The following list of eight Democrats and four Republicans is based largely on the judgment of Clark and his aides.

The most powerful figure of all is Senator Richard Russell (D., Ga.). Among the Democrats, the number two man is probably Senator Lister Hill, of Alabama. Other Democratic members are Senators George Smathers of Florida, the close personal friend of President Kennedy; Carl Hayden of Arizona, John McClellan of Arkansas, Allen Ellender of Louisiana, John Stennis of Mississippi, and, perhaps, Harry Byrd of Virginia (although his influence has declined with his advancing years).

Heading the GOP membership is Dirksen, whom Clark terms "the champion of the Republican Establishment." The other Republicans are Bourke Hickenlooper of Iowa, Norris Cotton of New Hampshire and, perhaps, Carl Curtis of Nebraska.

The significance of all this, as far as Clark is concerned, is what the Establishment has been doing to President Kennedy's programs. A large majority of Congressmen supported the Democratic platform adopted at the Los Angeles Convention in 1960—the platform on which President Kennedy won office. Then Clark added:

> We now stand at the beginning of the third session of what might be called a Kennedy Congress, but actually it is not a Kennedy Congress. . . . The principal reason . . . so far as the Senate is concerned, is, in my opinion, that we are operating under archaic, obsolete rules, customs, manners, procedures and traditions—and because the operation under those obsolete

and archaic setups is controlled by this oligarchical Senate Establishment, a major part of the members of which, by and large, are opposed to the program of the President. . . .

The two-thirds majority of the Democratic Senators who are Kennedy men, and therefore liberals, and therefore want to get the country moving again, and therefore believe in the inevitability of change, are represented sparsely, if at all, in the Senate Establishment.

Senator Paul Douglas noted:

> The Democratic Party wins its Presidential elections by the votes of the great industrial states. It wins those elections on platforms which are believed in by the voters and which pledge to carry out legislative programs which will be in the interest of the great masses of the American people; namely, the wage earners, the small farmers, the white-collar workers, the small businessmen, the housewives and the consumers.
>
> That is how we win our Presidential elections. Then the Congress convenes, and we are not able to pass any considerable portion of the program upon which we have gone to the country.
>
> We find that the machinery of the Senate, and I think largely of the House, is in the hands of those who fundamentally do not believe in the program by which the Presidential election was won and for which the great mass of voters in the country cast their ballots.

One may well ask: Why did Clark, after seven years of relative silence on the subject, decide that 1963 was the time to start talking publicly about the Establishment? The answer offers some encouragement to liberals, if not for this year, then for the future. For Clark's underlying motivation was the belief that the time is coming when the Establishment can be overthrown.

Clark's message to the liberals, in other words, is one of hope, in spite of many disappointments and disillusionments—some of them with the Kennedy Administration itself—in recent years. His theory is that the voters, beginning especially in the off-year Congressional elections of 1958, clearly expressed themselves as supporting an essentially liberal approach to legislation. Conservatives, however, by controlling Senate machinery, have seen to it that the wishes of the voters haven't been turned into legislation. Now, Clark believes, the conservative Establishment that runs the Senate is on the ropes, or at least close to it. The Establishment has already lost control of some committees and, inevitably, in the years to come, will lose control of more as the number of liberally inclined votes grows.

Watching the Senate in operation now, one hardly gets the impression that the liberals are about ready to take over. Liberals like Clark, Douglas, Proxmire, Albert Gore of Tennessee, Estes Kefauver of Tennessee, Wayne Morse of Oregon and Phil Hart of Michigan are clearly not members of the Establishment. Douglas, for example, in spite of the fact that there is a Democrat in the White House, clearly has less influence in the Senate than his fellow Senator from Illinois, Dirksen—even though Dirksen represents the party out of power. The White House recognized this all but formally last year when, over Douglas' strong objections, it gave a friend of Dirksen's an Illinois federal judgeship.

The fact is that some of the pragmatic operators on the White House staff —who have a tendency to value pure political muscle over principle—privately joke about some of the fruitless efforts of the liberals in Congress.

The White House group, for example, had a vast respect for the late Senator Kerr, a thoroughgoing pragmatist. And the White House tends to admire the work of such as the secretary to the majority, Robert Baker, a friend of Lyndon Johnson's. Asked why the White House seemed to like to deal with Baker more than with some of the Senate liberals, one Presidential aide put it bluntly: "He can count." The statement meant that Baker respected votes in the Senate—respected practical possibilities. The liberals, in the view of the White House, often waste their time tilting at windmills.

The underlying question posed by Senator Clark, then, is one that the White House itself might ponder. Clark is saying that the liberals actually have political muscle at the polls—where it counts in Presidential elections. They just haven't been able to defeat the powers of the Establishment in the Senate to put that muscle to work.

> We are playing (as Clark put it) with a stacked deck. The deck is stacked against the President of the United States and I want to shuffle that deck so that in the end the President of the United States will have his fair share of trumps and we can play the game with an honest deck of cards.

TO MOVE CONGRESS OUT OF ITS RUTS
Hubert H. Humphrey

Hubert H. Humphrey, Vice President of the United States, was formerly Democratic Senator from Minnesota. In addition to his role as majority whip, he served on four committees, including one on reorganization of government.

Sixteen years ago, the United States held a monopoly of atomic weapons. Jet aircraft were barely operational. The Space Age could be found only in science fiction magazines. Television was an eight-inch infant in electronics laboratories. The nation's elementary schools had classrooms to spare. The cold war could be seen on the horizon only by a handful of political wise men. Europe was near economic collapse, Africa was still a continent of colonies and Chiang Kai-shek still ruled the Chinese mainland. Cuba, to most Americans, was a plush and pleasant vacation spot. And Fidel Castro was a teenager.

It was 16 years ago when the United States Congress last turned to the tedious task of self-criticism and produced a major legislative reform. Since the Legislative Reorganization Act of 1946, Congress has changed little. The structure is the same. The committee lineups are almost identical. The traditions are preserved. And the basic attitudes of Congress toward its own prerogatives and centers of power are still tuned to 1946 or the more distant past.

But the needs of the nation and the demands of Congress have multiplied.

Since 1946 the nation's population has increased 33 per cent, its government has grown to include many more services and duties, its problems are infinitely more complex, and its involvement in world affairs is no longer fractional and irregular but rather total and constant.

The essential problem of Congress today is simply that there is more to do but only the same number of men to do it. The members of Congress have to find enough time to fulfill their thousands of obligations and to develop a Congressional system in which they can use their time most effectively.

The most pressing day-to-day demands for the time of Senators and Congressmen are not directly linked to legislative tasks. They come from constituents. And the constituency of a member of Congress is not limited to his home state or district. He gives priority attention to the people "back home," but as a United States Senator or Representative, his constituency is the whole nation.

The image of a member of Congress engaged in debate of issues or in study and reflection on the problems of the nation and freedom is accurate for only a fraction of his time. At any point in his workday, the Congressman is more likely to be talking about a housing development with municipal officials, or phoning an executive agency for an answer to a constituent complaint, or dictating a letter to a citizen who wants some information for his son's term paper for a school civics class.

Speedy air travel, the low cost of telegrams or long-distance telephone calls and campaigns to encourage citizens to "write your Congressman" have turned most Congressional offices into operations resembling a complex of train station, post office, airline terminal and communications center. My own experience may or may not be typical, but it is significant of the increased personal workload for members of Congress.

In 1949, I moved into an office of four rooms. My staff and I had the use of two telephone lines. An average of 50 letters a day were received. Thirty telephone calls a day were considered heavy. A personal visit to the office by a constituent on any day was a special event.

In 1962, my office had doubled to eight rooms. Now, 12 telephone lines funnel an average of 500 calls into the office each day, and I keep two private lines just to be sure I will be able to get through the crowded switchboard to reach my staff. One hundred and twenty personal visitors—not counting large groups of students or tourists—come into the office each day, about half of them constituents from my home state.

How does the member of Congress handle this workload? He has a staff to help, and he and his assistants work long hours at a fast pace. Any citizen who doubts that he is getting "an honest day of work" for the salary he pays his Congressman need only walk by the Senate or House office buildings late at night or on weekends. Most of the lights are burning through the evening hours, and many still shine after midnight on any night of the week.

Congressmen do not complain about the demands on their time for service to constituents. They perform that service because it is their job, because it is vital for their political survival, and because they know that the individual citizens with a need, complaint or idea cannot even hope to dent the surface of big government unless he works through his elected representative.

But members of Congress do complain often that they have little time to perform their duties as legislators. This is perhaps the central, general problem and defect of Congress today: the inability of Congressmen to find the time to inform themselves of the issues they face, to give their best talents to committee assignments, and to legislate responsibility.

The day is long gone when a member of Congress could be satisfied with mastery over two or three limited, precise subjects and follow a policy of voting the party line on other issues. Today, the Senator or Congressman is expected to be thoroughly informed on hundreds of different subjects and issues—from agricultural economics in Minnesota to the administration of foreign aid in Bolivia, from federal housing needs in New York to Soviet strategy in the Middle East, from a flood control project in California to the merits of a "man on the moon" spaceship project.

The complexities and variety of issues which members of Congress must master will continue to increase in an age of nuclear power, scientific advances, fast-changing social patterns and international involvement and leadership by the United States.

The pattern is already evident: At the time of the last Legislative Reorganization Act, the 79th Congress (1945 and 1946) initiated 12,656 bills or resolutions. The 87th Congress (1961 and 1962) initiated 20,316 bills or resolutions—a 60 per cent increase in the Congressional workload.

Most of these measures were relatively routine, but each took some time from Congress in general and individual members in particular.

There has been a comparable increase in the flow of major, controversial and thus time-consuming legislative proposals. Traditionally, the average Congressional session has seriously considered and attempted to hammer out one major new program or reform in a single year. The second session of the 87th Congress last year made a serious effort on many major legislative programs, including the trade bill, tax reform, Social Security financing of health insurance, authorization to purchase United Nations Bonds and the Communications Satellite Act.

A realistic accounting by the White House concluded that the 87th Congress approved, and the President signed into law, 73 major legislative proposals. The 83rd Congress, representing the first two years of the Eisenhower Administration, approved 29 major legislative proposals. The 87th Congress of 1961 and 1962 approved a total of more than 1,000 public bills. The 83rd Congress of 1953 and 1954 approved about half that number.

These figures are not mentioned to play a sort of partisan numbers game, but rather to emphasize the increased legislative workload of Congress and its members.

The result of that heavy workload, in 1962, was one of the longest peacetime sessions of Congress in history. Congress met continually from early January to mid-October. In the final months, a few old-timers on Capitol Hill grew frustrated enough to look back fondly on the year 1923, when Warren Harding was President and the Congress convened in March just long enough to recess until December.

But even nine or ten-month Congressional sessions do not solve the problem of the individual Senator or Congressman who must find the time to inform himself about the legislative issues he faces.

Most members of Congress are dedicated and conscientious legislators and public servants, aware of the power they hold over the dollars and destiny of the American people and so many others throughout the world. If they are given extra time—or rather freed from unnecessarily time-consuming duties—they will spend most of it tackling the huge task of informing themselves.

Several steps can be taken to give them that extra time. These are not the final answers to the time problem of members of Congress, but they would help.

First, more joint meetings of Congressional committees. A legislative question involving disarmament and arms control, for example, normally requires consideration by the Foreign Relations and Armed Services Committees of the Senate and the House and the Joint Committee on Atomic Energy. Joint meetings would save the time of members serving on more than one of these committees.

Second, more standing joint committees including members of both the House and the Senate. Such committees would save time, particularly toward the end of each Congressional session, by paving the way to speedier conference agreements between the Senate and the House on controversial issues.

Third, more efficient scheduling of the work days of Congress. Certain days could be scheduled specifically for floor debate and action by the full House or Senate. Other days could be restricted exclusively for hearings and action by the Congressional committees.

In the early months of the session, the full House or Senate would meet only a few days each week. As committees completed their action in the later months of the session, the Senate and House would meet more often.

This pattern would save time for members, and end the absurd necessity of members literally running from committee room to Senate or House chamber when issues in which they are involved are up for action at different places at the same time.

Fourth, modification of the "Morning Hour" in the Senate, in which members read miscellaneous speeches of marginal or undated importance and insert various articles into the Congressional Record. Instead, members would be permitted to send their "morning hour" speeches and articles to the clerk for insertion in the Record, without taking their own time and the time of other Senators to read them word-for-word.

Fifth, a requirement in the Senate that members restrict their remarks to the issue formally listed as the business of the Senate. In a debate over agricultural programs, for example, a Senator would not be able to spend an hour discussing a totally unrelated subject. This "Rule of Germaneness" now applies only to debate in the House of Representatives.

Sixth, a summer recess of Congress of at least three weeks. This would take time away from legislative duties, but ultimately, I am convinced, would save time. The immediate value would be the opportunity for members of Congress to spend some time with families and constituents in a period (June or July) when schools are closed and citizens are not tied at home because of weather.

The indirect value would be the change of pace and rest such a recess would give to each member. He would return for the final busy weeks of the session refreshed for more efficient performance of his legislative duties. Congressmen are human beings; they get tired and their nerves can become frayed from long months of pressure and hard work. A summer recess would probably reduce the inevitable tensions and bickering so common in the final weeks of Congressional sessions.

Seventh, modification and adoption of the British "Question Period," in which Administration leaders would report on and answer questions of general importance before the full Senate and House. This would save time, help to keep members of Congress better informed on Administration programs and policy and sustain the necessary frequent contact between the Executive and Legislative branches of government.

This final suggestion—and some of the others—would have a valuable side-effect; it would save the time of high Administration leaders who have their own crucial problems of too many duties for too few hours.

It is not unusual for the Secretary of State and the Secretary of Defense and other Cabinet officers to give basically the same testimony and answer basically the same questions for several different congressional committees. The Secretary of State, for example, might be called early in the session to outline the foreign aid program—including military aid—to the Senate Committee on Foreign Relations. He will then repeat the same testimony to the Senate Armed Services Committee, and again to the House Armed Services Committee.

The result, I believe, is an excessive demand on the time of these officials. Secretary of State Dean Rusk made 54 personal appearances before Congressional committees during the 87th Congress—29 in 1961 and 25 in 1962. Secretary of Defense Robert McNamara spent a total of 203 hours before Congressional Committees during the 87th Congress—88.75 in 1961 and 114.23 in 1962.

Standing Joint Committees, more joint meetings of committees and a "Question Period" for the full House or Senate would save the time of Congressmen and these high officials—and serve to inform all members of Congress more thoroughly.

Another Congressional defect which tends to waste time—and to cause confusion and occasional conflict between members—rests with the lineup of Senate and House Committees. New problems and programs created by a world transformed by nuclear power and the space age are being handled by a Congressional committee system which has changed little in 50 years.

There were two weeks of confusion following introduction of my bill in 1961 to establish a United States Arms Control and Disarmament Agency. This measure was first assigned to the Foreign Relations Committee, then switched to the Government Operations Committee, then back to the Foreign Relations Committee. At one point, it almost went to the Armed Services Committee. (The bill finally remained with Foreign Relations, was approved and signed into law.)

The Communications Satellite Act bounced from committee to committee before it was finally processed and sent to the floor last year. At one time or another, this bill involved the Interstate and Foreign Commerce Committee, the Foreign Relations Committee, the Government Operations Committee, the Space and Astronautics Committee and, of course, the Appropriations Committee.

Is a more up-to-date committee lineup, responsive to modern problems and modern opportunities, needed? I believe it is, and that a thorough review of the present committee and sub-committee lineups and jurisdictions is necessary.

That review would be one of the prime responsibilities of a "Joint Committee on the Organization of Congress," which would be established by a resolution sponsored by Senator Joseph S. Clark (D., Pa.) and 31 other Senators representing both parties. A companion measure in the House agrees that this committee of seven Senators and seven Representatives should conduct a complete review—the first since 1946—of Congress and produce recommendations for its improvement.

I expect this "Joint Committee on the Organization of Congress" to be established. Its work will be one of the most significant efforts of the 88th Congress. And its task will be difficult, because there is little popular interest or direct political advantage in the tedious effort for procedural reform within Congress.

But the American people want good government, and sense that the legislative branch has not been performing its functions with the order and effectiveness the nation deserves. The waning weeks of the 87th Congress included fights over such petty issues as what room the Appropriations Conference Committee should meet in, and long delays over minor details of legislation.

Displays of bickering and pettiness tend to obscure the real record of achievement written by recent Congresses and to diminish the respect and confidence of the people in their own representative government. Perhaps the greatest need in Congress today is not so much for studies, procedural changes and committee modernization. It may rather be a more thoroughly responsive attitude by members of Congress, who need to realize that the rules and traditions of Capitol Hill are not sacred, and that the national interest and public service are more important than individual or committee powers and prerogatives.

7   THE PRESIDENCY

The American presidency has been called the most powerful democratically filled office on earth. But just what is the presidency? In a timeworn yet descriptive phrase, it is an empty vessel waiting to be filled—filled to the brim by strong presidents or in much shorter measure by the less willing or less able. Constitutionally, the incumbent is free to fill the job much as he wishes; although he will discover maximum limits to his power, he is unlikely to find minimal requirements for his performance.

There is no training, either formal or informal, that can begin to match the twentieth-century demands of the job. Forged by various craftsmen with varying designs for over 175 years, the presidency has emerged as an alloy of four main elements—executive leadership, legislative leadership, party leadership, and popular leadership.

Executive leadership incorporates two significant aspects. A president is both chief executive and chief administrator. He is charged with law enforcement—a straightforward task which, nonetheless, may vary from the overstrict application of a McCarran-Walter immigration law under a Truman to the virtual cessation of enforcement of a Volstead Act (Prohibition) under a Hoover. The president alone possesses the responsibility for administrative leadership, including decision making, policy determination, and departmental coordination. Although he may delegate a portion of this task to his subordinates, he finds, in the motto that adorned the desk of Harry S. Truman, that "The Buck Stops Here." He possesses a full power of appointment and removal of subordinates, subject only to those limits imposed by the workings of "senatorial courtesy" [1] and the Humphrey decision.[2] He is commander-in-chief, possessed of significant powers at home, as witnessed in the Little Rock incident of Eisenhower's time, the Pullman strike of Cleveland's day, and the Whiskey Rebellion put down by Washington; and abroad, as displayed by such strong presidents as the two Roosevelts and by only slightly less powerful incumbents, including Polk and Truman.

The total power of the White House in foreign affairs is clearly superior to that of the Congress, despite constitutional limits. For example, the president may bypass the treaty-ratification requirement with an executive agree-

---

[1] According to the workings of "senatorial courtesy," the Senate of the United States will refuse to confirm the president's appointment of an individual to a federal post, such as judge or marshal, within a state, if the appointee is "personally distasteful" to the senior senator, of the president's own party, from that state.

[2] In the case of Federal Trade Commissioner Humphrey (*Rathbun v. U.S.*), the Supreme Court ruled that the presidential removal power was constitutionally limited, in the instance of those independent commissions to which the Congress has delegated "quasi-legislative" powers, by those conditions, such as removal only "for cause," set by the Congress itself.

ment, and he may grant recognition or withdraw diplomatic representation—
thus establishing or severing our international relations—without any action
on the part of the House or Senate. He alone receives communications
from foreign nations, passing them on to the Congress or the public at his
discretion. (A notable instance is McKinley's failure to inform the public
that he had received a virtual surrender by cable the night before he asked
Congress for a declaration of war against Spain.) He may make all kinds
of commitments, open or secret, which the nation must then fulfill. Franklin
D. Roosevelt summed up these tremendous executive powers in a single
sentence, penned to Winston Churchill November 9, 1941: "I do not have
the power to declare war, I may only *make* war."

The president is clearly the nation's legislative leader, primarily because
the parochial nature of our national legislature does not provide or promote
leadership in public policy. Unlike the state or local representative, the
president (with administrative experts to advise him, and with the public
support he can command through television, radio, and the press) is in a
strong position to initiate policy, to prevent conflicting policy through the
use of the veto, and to exercise financial leadership through the executive
budget.

In addition, the president is the leader of his party—he has the high-level
contacts, the power of patronage, and the prestige of his office, if he is inclined to use these weapons to enforce his party command. If he fails to
take the helm, his party can only drift.

At home and abroad, the president is considered the leader of the free
world. Domestically, he is the representative of all the people—a father
image and royal head combined. Overseas he is the symbol of American
prestige. Representing the power of democracy and freedom, he is a tower
of strength, or a crumbling pillar, as viewed by the people of the world.

For all the respect the president commands, however, he is not possessed
of power without limit. The resident of the house that Harry Truman called
"the great white jail" at 1600 Pennsylvania Avenue finds certain bounds
beyond which he cannot move with impunity. There is the sheer magnitude
of the job—an overwhelming task for some, because of the multiple skills
required. There is the inertia of bureaucracy, the separate empires, the
status quo within the departments—departments that exist presumably to
carry out the president's will but that so often delight in frustrating it. There
are the special interests with their constant importuning, their many friends
in high places. There is the public itself, whose ultimate support must be
retained—the public with its sometimes fickle responses to actions conse-
quential and minute alike. The ability to keep these conflicting interests
satisfied is essential to a favorable "public image." A president ignores them
only at the risk of rejection at the polls.

A further problem is the political opposition a president encounters—
frequently more bitter from within his own party than from without. He
must be ever wary of the "nine old men"—the Supreme Court, with its

power of judicial review. In recent years, the president has come to know the force of the congressional inquiry—whether designed for self-seeking, witch-hunting, or more constructive purposes. And finally, the president, like any lesser man, is frequently the captive of events—events not only in the United States but throughout the world. Over these he may have little control, but they may make him a hero or a goat (perhaps both) in short order.

These, then, are some of the aspects of the presidency that we shall keep in mind as we analyze the decision-making process that revolves around our chief executive, and as we review the changes the American presidency has undergone throughout our history. For the president in the twentieth century is clearly the focal point of our national government in action.

THE U.S. PRESIDENCY
Gerald W. Johnson

Gerald W. Johnson is one of America's most respected political journalists and historians. A former editor of the *Baltimore Sun,* he is the author of *American Heroes and Hero Worship, The Lunatic Fringe,* and *A History for Peter.*

The Presidency of the United States has come down from George Washington to Dwight D. Eisenhower in a succession uninterrupted for nearly 175 years by any exterior force save that of human mortality. The contingency of death was foreseen, and the succession provided by law. Even when there was no clear election by the people, as in 1800 and 1824 when no candidate received an electoral majority, and in 1876 when the apparent majority was challenged, those crises were successfully met by legal devices without resort to force.

This gives the Presidency an appearance of great stability. It is probable that the typical American, if questioned, would confidently assert that no political office in the world is more solidly established, or has been less affected by the sweeping changes that have transformed almost everything else since the establishment of the republic. But the appearance is deceptive. The real characteristic of the office has been and is now a malleability that amounts almost to fluidity. Under no two men has the Presidency been exactly the same, and even its constitutional significance has altered until it is, in important respects, the opposite of what it was in Washington's time.

The impact of personality upon the office has been too conspicuous to

From *Saturday Evening Post,* June 11, 1960. Reprinted by permission.

pass unnoticed by the most superficial observer; but the changes forced by events are more important, although subtler and hard to perceive except in historical perspective. Everyone knows that the Presidency changed radically when Abraham Lincoln succeeded James Buchanan, and the facile explanation that Lincoln was a war President is inadequate. The country was at peace when Theodore Roosevelt succeeded William McKinley, yet the change in the Presidency in 1901 was, if anything, more spectacular than the change in 1861. Far more important than the effects of individual temperament, although less readily observed, are such changes as that between the time when Jefferson established the rule that the President receives, but makes no social calls, and the time when Eisenhower set out on his 1959 odyssey across the world.

Temperament has nothing to do with these changes. All men know that as far as his personal desires were concerned, the last thing Mr. Eisenhower wished was to undertake that physically and mentally arduous journey; he went because he deemed it his duty, not his pleasure, to go. It was the same motive that impelled President Washington to make his even more taxing trips through the country. The difference is that the first President could halt at the national boundary, while the thirty-fourth must cover the world. But nobody planned it so; it is the effect of the trend of events, not of human volition.

Washington did not expect this kind of development. The "Farewell Address" is full of foreboding, but the changes he foresaw and dreaded were to be effected by ambition, not by necessity. "In the most solemn manner" he warned us "against the baneful effects of the Spirit of Party . . . a fire not to be quenched; it demands a uniform vigilance to prevent its bursting into a flame, lest, instead of warming, it should consume." The Spirit of Party, he thought, must in the end "incline the minds of men to see security and repose in the absolute power of an individual; and sooner or later the chief of some prevailing faction, more able or more fortunate than his competitors, turns this disposition to the purposes of his own elevation, on the ruins of Public Liberty."

A dismal prospect indeed, but severely logical in view of the information available to Washington. The power of the presidential office has increased, not steadily, but by fits and starts, speeded up by strong Presidents, slowed down by weak ones, but never reversing its general trend; until today it vastly exceeds anything dreamed of at the beginning of the nineteenth century.

Yet the calamitous results foretold in the "Farewell Address" have not yet come upon us. They may be impending, for it would be fatuous to deny that the Presidency contains the seeds of dictatorship; but they are not here yet, and an inquiry into why the seeds have not sprouted, flourished and borne their deadly fruit ought to be suggestive, at least, of means by which we may hope to keep them latent indefinitely.

Washington's anxiety was based upon the assumption that any additional powers accruing to the Presidency must of necessity be subtracted from those of one or both of the other branches of government. It was his belief that the "system of checks and balances" in the Constitution had separated the powers of government and distributed them all; he and his contemporaries accepted the theory that the powers of Government consist of the legislative, the executive and the judicial, and that once these were lodged in different and independent hands, government would be completely organized. The problem thenceforth would be to keep any one from encroaching on the authority of the others.

What the men of 1787 did not suspect—and is, indeed, but imperfectly realized by our own generation—is that there is a fourth power of government difficult to define legally and not disposed of by the Constitution, yet as important in a democracy as the executive, legislative or judicial. This is the power of the initiative, which we commonly term leadership. The history of the Presidency is a story of the slow accretion of this power in the hands of the man in the White House.

To understand why this factor was overlooked by statesmen as farsighted as those who dominated the Constitutional Convention, one must remember that they were theorists, guided by reason, not by experience. The only form of government under which any of them had lived was monarchial; parliamentary government was indeed taking shape in England, but it was not yet clearly defined, and parliament was far from being a representative democracy, such as our Constitution envisaged. Thus the Americans had no pattern to follow; for the direct, not representative, democracies of ancient times were horrible examples rather than models, since all of them had failed. The Greek city-states, for example, where each man entered the assembly representing himself alone and, therefore, usually voted in his own interest alone, oscillated between tyranny and anarchy, never establishing an enduring balance of public and private interests. Nor were other democracies able long to escape either domestic autocracy or foreign domination.

But if the founding fathers lacked a reliable guide, they did have a stern warning. The centuries old, not then terminated, struggle for power between the king and parliament had taught them that in such a contest the rights of the people are pretty sure to be trampled by both contestants; and the logical means of protection against that was the system of checks and balances.

Some of them—Hamilton, for a conspicuous example—did understand that such a system, if brought to perfection, would result in impotence, a government hung on dead center, unable to move in any direction. They had an example in the Polish monarchy of the seventeenth century, so effectively checked and balanced by the requirement of a unanimous vote of the nobles that it was brought to ruin by sheer inertia. But the highly practical Americans were aware that their own system was by no means so delicately adjusted, since even the veto of the President could be overridden, and they assumed correctly that its very imperfections would prevent a complete deadlock.

What they did not take into account, or did not give sufficient weight in their accounting, was the possibility that in making absolute power unattainable, they had checked ambition, especially in the legislative branch, severely enough to discourage the development of effective leadership there. This was a contingency extremely remote in a government of undivided powers. Leadership originally vested in the monarch, could not be wrested from him except by leadership developed elsewhere—in a court favorite, perhaps, or in the legislative or even in the judiciary. The complete disappearance of the fourth power of government was one danger against which the Americans did not prepare, presumably because they did not envisage it.

It can be plausibly argued, nevertheless, that this country has suffered more, very much more, from excessively static than from excessively dynamic government. The example customarily cited is the inertia of James Buchanan as the danger of secession was visibly mounting; but the monumental uselessness of Buchanan was merely a continuation of a condition that had afflicted the Presidency ever since the administration of James K. Polk. The Pennsylvanian's misfortune was merely that he happened to be in office at the time when the lack of effective leadership produced its logical result. Buchanan is its spectacular example, but the condition has been characteristic of the Presidency more often than not.

Evidence to support this assertion is not far to seek. How many Americans can name offhand eighteen of the individuals who have held the office? Everyone remembers Washington, Jefferson, Jackson, Lincoln, Wilson and the second Roosevelt because great significance attaches to their names. Perhaps most of us recall also the first Roosevelt, John Adams, Monroe (on account of the Doctrine), possibly Cleveland; but beyond that the typical American grows vague. The reason is that none of the others exercised the power of the initiative in any memorable way. Hoover, Truman and Eisenhower are excluded from this account because all three are still living as these lines are written.

The half dozen first named, pretty generally regarded as the Big Six, are a remarkably varied assortment as regards their intellectual and cultural endowments, but they are alike in one respect—Washington established the Presidency and each of the other five added materially to its power. Each was, in Washington's words, "the chief of some prevailing faction," but that any turned the situation "to the purposes of his own elevation, on the ruins of Public Liberty," as the "Farewell Address" grimly predicted, will be asserted only of Franklin Roosevelt, and of him only by blind and bitter partisanship. To the vast majority of Americans they were great Presidents, the greatest in the list.

Here, then, is what at first glance seems to be a mystery, a cause not followed by its logical effect: the vast accretion of power that Washington apprehended has come to the Presidency, but the calamitous results that he feared have not followed. This odd circumstance can be explained only on the theory that the President has added to his power by occupation, but not by usurpation; that is to say, the addition to the Presidency has not been a subtraction from either of the other two branches. They retain unimpaired to this day all the powers delegated to them in 1789. If the Presidency has advanced relatively, it is by assuming the power of the initiative, never clearly envisaged by the Constitution makers, and, if it had been, probably incapable of legal definition.

Some years before he entered the White House Woodrow Wilson noted the fact. In *Constitutional Government,* published in 1908, he observed that "the President is at liberty, both in law and in conscience, to be as big a man as he can. His capacity will set the limit; and if Congress be overborne by him, it will be no fault of the makers of the Constitution—it will be from no lack of constitutional powers on its part, but only because the President has the nation behind him and Congress has not. He has no means of compelling Congress except through public opinion."

What a tremendous exception that is, probably Wilson did not fully realize in 1908, although he had the example of Theodore Roosevelt before his eyes. But Wilson himself demonstrated it during his first two years in the White House, and the overwhelming proof was furnished by the second Roosevelt in his first Hundred Days. A President who can seize the initiative at all is assured of some success; and one whose first few moves receive popular approbation is irresistible.

The recourse of Congress is to seize the initiative itself, and occasionally—as, for instance, in the case of Andrew Johnson—it has done so. Congress, too, is at liberty, both in law and in conscience, to be the biggest thing in the nation if it can. But the historical record of congressional efforts to assume leadership makes depressing reading. Certainly the most brilliant, and perhaps the most honorable, of those men who have seized leadership outside the White House were Alexander Hamilton and Henry Clay; but Hamilton succeeded only in hobbling—and infuriating—John Adams, while Clay was a millstone hung around the neck of every President of his own party. In later days the Reconstruction policy imposed upon the country by Thaddeus Stevens brought upon his memory an odium that still persists; and if the almost equally powerful legislative leaders, Thomas B. Reed and Joseph G. Cannon, are remembered more favorably it is because of their more amiable personalities rather than for their triumphs of statecraft.

The member of Congress, senator or representative, is not in a favorable position to exercise national leadership. One of its essentials, and one that is increasingly important as government becomes more complex, is the capacity for swift and decisive action. In this respect the President enjoys an inestimable advantage in that his close associates are his subordinates, whereas those of a member of Congress are his equals. The President can order, where the congressman can only argue. For this reason a weak President can contend on better than equal terms with a legislator immeasurably his intellectual superior—a John Tyler can frustrate a Henry Clay.

The first genius to appreciate this situation to the full and to exploit it was Andrew Jackson. The magnitude of his achievement is evidenced by the fact that the tradition still persists that Old Hickory was a simple soul, rough, but transparent. In fact, Jefferson himself was not more complex and devious.

Jackson was the first to understand the implications, for the President, of the fact that the votes are cast by individuals, although the country does not consist exclusively of individuals. The country includes territory, wealth, land and water, forest and field, mountain and plain, ecological variations that are wide and highly important. Individuals are, however, one constant in this giant aggregate of variables. Since the President is the sole elected official chosen by the whole country—for who ever voted for or against a Vice President?—he alone can afford to neglect the variables and devote his whole attention to the constant.

A senator from Texas, for example, must represent the Texans, of course, but he must represent oil also, as a senator from Montana must represent copper and one from Oregon, lumber. Not long ago the late Senator Neuberger acknowledged that publicly, and said that if any senator had failed to represent the dominant economic interest of his state, the fact had escaped Mr. Neuberger's notice.

Jackson's triumphant career was based on his success in convincing men and women that he represented people in a special way that no other official could. But he did more. He persuaded them that the President is, and of right ought to be, the people's man, speaking for them and for no local or nonhuman interest whatsoever. Jackson, more than any other President, established the claim of the Presidency to the power of the initiative. Incidentally, he also furnished at least one glaring illustration of its dangers. "John Marshall has made his decision; now let him enforce it," may not have been his exact words, but they certainly portray his attitude in the Indian lands case. By withholding the comity due from one branch of the government to another he, in effect, vacated a ruling of the Supreme Court— as clear a usurpation of the power of the judiciary as can be imagined. But there can be no shadow of doubt that it asserted the leadership of the Presidency in the nation at large, not merely in the executive branch.

Nearly a hundred years passed, however, before the claim was formalized by Wilson in his public announcement that he proposed to be head of his party, as well as head of the state. Even then the opposition professed to regard Wilson's statement as scandalous, although every strong President since Jackson had held leadership of the party; and to this day there is some dispute as to where the power of the initiative should lie.

Curiously enough, opposition to Wilson's position has included some of the Presidents themselves. Harding is the obvious example, but it may be argued that he was incapable of leadership in any circumstances; McKinley and Benjamin Harrison are better illustrations. Their distaste for the Wilsonian doctrine is understandable, if not particularly creditable, for it imposes upon the President formidable responsibility. If he is to lead the country successfully he must be resourceful, energetic and resolute, all to a high degree. This is hard labor, not to be undertaken willingly by a man who approaches the office in the spirit of the remark attributed, doubtfully, to Giovanni de'Medici, "Since God has given us the Papacy, let us enjoy it."

But evidence is already abundant and increases daily that the Presidency is the right location for the power of initiative. Since 1914 the tempo of events has accelerated to such an extent that crises tread upon one another's heels, and capacity for rapid and decisive action may soon be, if it is not already, the price of national survival. The Korean affair is an instance still vividly in mind; President Truman's course may not have been the ideal one, but his action was swift; and in politics as in military operations it is better to do any intelligent thing than to lose time searching for the perfect move.

In a world as tense as that of the twentieth century, speed in seizing the initiative seems likely to increase, rather than to diminish in importance; which suggests that the dominance of the Presidency in that respect is more likely to be strengthened and extended than to be reduced. Hitler, being only human, could not always be wrong, and he hit upon a great truth in his assertion of "the leadership principle" as essential to successful government in the modern world. Certainly a huge democracy, such as the United States, stands in as grave danger from lack of leadership as from usurpation of power.

It is not that usurpation is inconceivable in this country. Jackson's case was not the only one. Lincoln in suspending the writ of habeas corpus where the courts were still open, unquestionably infringed the prerogative of the judiciary, and Theodore Roosevelt, in ordering the motto, "In God We Trust," left off the coins, invaded Congress' exclusive right to coin money. Jefferson was inclined to think that he usurped powers of both legislative and judiciary in making the Louisiana Purchase. But the usurpations thus far have been either pardonable, as conducing to the general welfare, or unsuccessful, or so trifling as to come under the rule *de minimis.* . . .

This is, however, no guarantee that they will retain that character; and a generation that has been appalled by such apparitions as Mussolini, Hitler and Stalin knows only too well what horrors may rise from a perversion of leadership. The Twenty-second Amendment, forbidding any man to hold the Presidency more than ten years, is evidence of our extreme sensitiveness to the remotest possibility of the rise of dictatorship here. Our immediate peril, in fact, is probably much less the risk of submitting to tyranny than the risk of hobbling necessary leadership by hysterical efforts to ward off tyranny.

At the same time every thoughtful American must regard the development of the Presidency with something less than ebullient enthusiasm. It is clearly necessary to lodge the power of the initiative somewhere, and the hands of the President seem to be its logical repository, because he alone can exercise it effectively. It is clearly necessary, also, to insist that he shall exercise it, and to avoid electing any man incapable of doing so. In prudence as well as in equity it is clearly necessary to support the President strongly in the legitimate exercise of this power.

But it is not to be denied that this course, however necessary, involves a calculated risk, and it is always possible to miscalculate. This possibility must be taken into account in any extrapolation of the historical development of the Presidency. The tricky factor is the enormous potential of the force that we call public opinion. Against it, neither legislative, executive, judiciary, nor even the Constitution itself can stand. It has hitherto been the constructive power in erecting the political fabric of the republic; but a power capable of so gigantic a feat obviously could be terrifically destructive were it channeled in that direction.

To put this power absolutely in the hands of one man would be suicidal. We have had a grisly demonstration of that in the case of the German people, when the potent majority of them committed their minds and consciences to Hitler and blindly followed him to destruction.

That the American people will go to any such extreme seems highly improbable. Our historical experience, our educational methods, even to some extent our prejudices and superstitions militate against it. Artemus Ward's complacent proclamation, "I am not a politician, and my other habits are good," was something more than a jape. It reflects a skepticism of Whitman's "elected persons" that is deeply embedded in the American character —a prejudice perhaps touched with superstition, but one that operates against any attempt at the deification of Caesar.

It would be unrealistic, however, to deny that there are forces in the modern world that operate in the other direction; nor are they confined to the ideologies of Marx, Lenin or Mao. We seem, indeed, relatively immune to ideologies. In no large country has the Communist Party had less success in recruiting the masses, and even the Socialists have never polled as many as 1,000,000 votes. But there are conditions, not theories, that are subjecting the traditional American system to a considerable strain.

Some of these conditions are technological, others political. Communication, for instance, has been perfected to the point at which one man may speak to the entire nation; and with the aid of television he may bring to bear upon an audience of many millions all the resources of dramaturgy— not rhetoric and euphony only, but gesture also, as well as "wanton Wiles, Nods and Becks and wreathed Smiles," and if you think these are ineffective, remember that David Garrick, the actor, once said that he would give 100 guineas to be able to say "ah" as the Rev. George Whitefield, the evangelist, could say it.

The assistance of technology is available equally to statesmen and to demagogues. The statesman may employ it to inspire the nation to great deeds; but the demagogue may use it to foment all the evils inherent in hard psychology. Since demagogues as a rule outnumber statesmen, it is evident that the mass media of communication, especially the newer ones, radio and television, must subject the common sense of the American electorate to a severe test.

The political organization of the modern world also is a condition and not a theory. American military and economic power is now the chief defense of political liberty abroad as well as at home. When the Constitution assigned to the President the conduct of foreign relations, the work consisted almost exclusively of safeguarding American interest; its expansion to cover the whole free world obviously has put the President in a different position. His power has been greatly increased, but so has his vulnerability; the President in self-defense is being forced more and more to act as his own Secretary of State. Even Mr. Eisenhower, who disliked and distrusted this development, was finally forced to accept it.

A President of a different temperament, however, might find it very much to his taste. Think what Theodore Roosevelt, for example, might have done with the leadership of the free nations! That idea is in a sense a test of the division in American political philosophy—one school holding that so dynamic a character given Eisenhower's opportunity would have ruined us, the other holding that lack of dynamism in the Presidency is the cause of at least half our present difficulties.

The mocking devil of it is that both schools seem to be right. A generation that has witnessed the passing of Mussolini, Hitler and Stalin must shudder at the idea of leadership concentrated in an individual; at the same time, a generation numbed by fifteen years of cold war must be appalled by the possibility of a total paralysis of leadership.

The rather dismal conclusion of the whole matter would seem to be that the American who seeks to peer into the future, no matter what his philosophy, has reason to shudder.

But was it ever otherwise? Our Constitution, said Justice Holmes, is an experiment, but only, he added, as all life is an experiment. It is unrealistic to ignore the fact that it is dangerous to be free, but it is equally unrealistic to ignore the fact that this nation has lived dangerously yet has survived for nearly 200 years. In that period the Presidency has gradually acquired powers that would have staggered the writers of the Constitution, and the prospect, at least for the years immediately ahead, is that the welfare of the nation and the world will necessitate entrusting greater, not diminished, authority to the office.

This may be the road to dictatorship, but it is the road we have been following because we could find no other. And there are optimists who do not believe that it leads inevitably to tyranny. Unreasonably, perhaps, they see the history of the United States as the aged Jefferson described it in that famous letter to the still-older Adams: "Laboring always at the same oar, with some wave ever ahead threatening to overwhelm us and yet passing harmless under our bank, we knew not how, we rode through the storm with heart and hand, and made a happy port . . . and so we have gone on, and so we shall go on, puzzled and prospering beyond example in the history of man."

THE JOHNSON WAY WITH CONGRESS
Tom Wicker

Tom Wicker, chief Washington correspondent for *The New York Times* and head of their Washington bureau, has regularly reported White House news.

"For 32 years," said Lyndon B. Johnson in his first Presidential address to Congress, "Capitol Hill has been my home. I have shared many moments of pride with you—pride in the ability of the Congress of the United States to act, to meet any crisis, to distill from our differences strong programs of national action . . . I firmly believe in the independence and integrity of the legislative branch. And I promise you that I shall always respect this. It is deep in the marrow of my bones."

Probably no part of Mr. Johnson's speech was more heartfelt. The ninth President of the United States to have served in both Houses of Congress, the fourth Senator to have reached the White House in this century, one of the most effective floor leaders ever to serve in the Senate, Mr. Johnson has made it plain since November 22 that he is one of the most thoroughgoing Congressional men ever to become Chief Executive.

That can be said of him not just because he has applied himself with skill and assiduity to the problems of achieving legislation that had seemed lost or stalled; Mr. Johnson also has brought the legislative branch—or at least its leadership—closer than it has been in years to the arena of action, to that area of ultimate power where, decisions are taken, policies made, directions set. The latter case, if sustained, may yet prove the most important result of the President's ardent wooing of Capitol Hill.

It has been no pallid hothouse courtship but a many-splendored thing. Senator Harry F. Byrd of Virginia, for instance, is empowered to tell the press that the President will show him the Federal Government's budget before submitting it to Congress or to anyone else. Senator Richard Russell of Georgia and others are asked to vote informally on an important policy decision concerning Panama. Well-known members of Congress are whisked off from parties to the White House, there to swap ideas until midnight or beyond with a President who seems genuinely interested in what they think.

From *The New York Times Magazine*, March 8, 1964. Copyright © 1964 by The New York Times Company. Reprinted by permission of Paul R. Reynolds, Inc., 599 Fifth Avenue, New York 17, N.Y.

When Robert Kennedy returns from his mission to Indonesia and Malaysia, he is dismayed to find himself in the White House delivering not a privileged communication to the Chief Executive but a general report to Mr. Johnson and a flanking group of members of the legislative branch—including J. W. Fulbright of Arkansas and Hubert Humphrey of Minnesota.

Members of Congress get treatment at the White House of a cordiality unmatched in their memories: their wives danced with by the President and taken on a tour of the residential quarters by the First Lady, themselves briefed on world affairs by Secretary of Defense McNamara and Secretary of State Rusk. When Mr. Johnson nominates Carl Rowan to head the U.S. Information Agency, he provides Mr. Rowan with precise and knowing advice about which Senators to call on and what to say to them in order to make his nomination more popular.

A Senator like Olin D. Johnston of South Carolina gets Presidential congratulations via the telephone for a document he has caused to be printed in the Congressional Record. An obscure House member finds himself in the White House spotlight, receiving a ceremonial handshake and fountain pen from the President in return for his minor part in getting a bill passed.

When the extended foreign-aid fight keeps Congressmen in town almost until Christmas Eve—and on the surface seems to threaten an all-out struggle between Congress and President—a White House holiday reception is hastily organized for friend and foe alike, Charlie Halleck as well as Carl Albert. And it is Lyndon Johnson who at the party's height pulls an elegant White House chair into the middle of the state dining room, climbs on its damask seat and pours the following oil:

"We're Americans first . . . we're proud of our ancestry and hopeful for our posterity . . ." The President goes on to say that he hopes he and the Congressmen can "disagree without being too disagreeable." He reminds them that "you only have one President, you only have one Congress, and you only have one judiciary and your country is no stronger than your Government."

That is just the kind of medicine members of Congress like—pain-killing and not too hard to swallow.

This extended form of the celebrated "Johnson Treatment" has a palpable effect on Congress. Republicans, of course, in an election year have been getting in their usual oratorical licks, but compared with the criticism John Kennedy used to get, that directed at Mr. Johnson has been no more forceful (to borrow a phrase from Everett Dirksen) "than a snowflake on the bosom of the Potomac." And the Republican-Democratic coalition that put over the civil rights bill for the White House stayed notably glued together under the greatest of strains.

Southern Democrats—those honey-voiced avengers of Appomattox and the Brown Decision, thorns in the flesh of every Democratic President since F.D.R.—have turned finger-lickin' good in the presence of a Chief Executive from south of Mason-Dixon. "Judge" Howard Smith of Virginia, to cite a striking example, concedes on national television that where Barry Goldwater might have carried the South against John Kennedy, he will run like a dry creek against Mr. Johnson. Southerners in the house conduct their none too fierce fight against the Kennedy-Johnson civil rights bill on the plane of a law school course in constitutional theory. It is obvious by now that the Southerners want Mr. Johnson to succeed. Whom else can they get who will be as sympathetic?

More important, Congress as a legislative body gives the impression that it is coming alive. Where it had seemed bogged down in ineptitude and sloth, defiant of Kennedy, disregardful of editorial contempt and ignorant of the national interest, it now seems to be responding with bill after bill to a President who knows how to arouse it, and what makes it tick.

It is a classically romantic drama—unsung new President makes good; rags to riches. Unfortunately, like most such dramas, it is a little larger than life. Mr. Johnson has not really passed a miracle on Capitol Hill. His achievement in Congress has been substantial, not magical.

For instance, skeptics find no trace of magic in Mr. Johnson's handling of the perennially defiant Representative Otto L. Passman of Louisiana. Mr. Passman, the scourge of foreign aid, once was summoned to the White House by John Kennedy for a showdown. When the smoke cleared, Kennedy told his aides with a shudder: "Don't ever bring that man here again."

When Mr. Johnson in his turn called Mr. Passman in for another showdown, there must have been the greatest display of jawbone since Samson slew that horde, for the Texan and the Louisianan rank as two of the most voluble politicians of our time. But in the end, what did Mr. Johnson get for his pains? "He got zero," an Administration official reports.

Nor has Mr. Johnson converted Representative Clarence Cannon of Missouri into a spender. In pursuit of his war against outgo, the wizened Chairman of the House Appropriations Committee has summarily abolished a subcommittee that used to deal with the annual supplementary appropriations requests. Now such requests must be broken down by departmental totals, each separate total to be handled by the departmental subcommittees, and considered together with the next year's regular budget. The net effect is to put off until May 15, for example, a full committee hearing on a supplemental space appropriations request that was submitted early this year. A President would need to be a real magician to do anything about it because in that kind of infighting Clarence Cannon has got the power.

A more important retort is often made, however, to those who claim that Lyndon Johnson singlehandedly got Congress moving again. It is that nothing much has been done on Capitol Hill since November 22 that would not have been done—perhaps a little more slowly—had Kennedy lived.

One fact not widely credited was that, at Kennedy's death, the record of the 88th Congress was by no means so horrendous as some editorial writers contended. The Senate had ratified the test-ban treaty; the House had passed the tax bill, and Congress had approved a precedent-breaking measure that helped head off a national railroad strike (ordinarily, any Congressman would rather break a metatarsal than a precedent). Moreover, two major education bills were on the verge of passage. Each was in a Senate-House conference, having been approved in both Houses.

When Mr. Johnson took over, the most important objectives were to move the civil rights bill through the House Rules Committee and the House itself; and to move the tax-reduction bill through the Senate Finance Committee and the Senate itself. Here is a brief accounting, as objective as possible, of Mr. Johnson's contribution to the achievement of both objectives.

Tax Reduction: The President's reduction of the budget below the level of that submitted by Mr. Kennedy last year undoubtedly pleased Senator Byrd and other fiscal conservatives and improved the climate for tax reduction. A number of informed sources, however, doubt that it produced the votes for passage. There never was much doubt, they say, that the bill would pass the Senate, or even the Finance Committee. The real question was when.

Lyndon Johnson disagrees emphatically. "That tax bill never would have been gotten out of the Finance Committee unless the budget had been cut below $100 billion," he declares.

Those who disagree say the Johnson budget-cutting and the President's considerable rapport with Senator Byrd certainly helped speed the bill through the Finance Committee, but not by any great number of days. They concede that these factors probably kept the Senator from trying to hamstring the bill with amendments and limitations—although they are not sure that he would have tried to do so in any case.

They also concede that Mr. Johnson talked Senator Dirksen of Illinois out of an attempt to put off final passage until March. But they contend that it was before Mr. Johnson came into office that the most crucial time was lost. As a result of exhaustive hearings in both the House Ways and Means Committee and the Senate Finance Committee, it became impossible to get passage before Christmas.

On one score, however, no one questions Mr. Johnson's effectiveness. It is agreed that he contributed directly to the fight to preserve excise-tax revenues in the bill. With personal telephone calls, he laid the groundwork (and Presidential assistant Lawrence F. O'Brien followed through in person) for switching two votes and producing a 9–8 victory on this issue in the Finance Committee.

And when the committee finally had approved the bill, Mr. Johnson was on the phone almost immediately—not to a Senator but to Elizabeth Springer, its staff director.

"This is the President," he said (according to one version). "How soon can you have the tax bill report going to the printer?"

"Four P.M.," Mrs. Springer replied.

"Well, let's push it up all we can," Mr. Johnson said.

Then he called James Harrison, the head of the Government Printing

Office. "I want you to have that report out in the morning," he told Mr. Harrison. (This was characteristic. As a young legislative assistant 30 years ago, Lyndon Johnson was known for his ability to figure out what low-level official actually was responsible for a given piece of work, and to deal effectively with that official.)

Civil Rights: Here again, Mr. Johnson's contributions were valuable but not necessarily in the sense of producing needed votes that might not otherwise have been had. Sources in a position to know report that the existence of a petition that would have taken the bill out of the hands of the House Rules Committee was the major factor in forcing Chairman Smith of Virginia to permit the measure to go to the House by the end of January.

There never were enough signatures on the petition actually to make it effective. But there were enough to threaten Judge Smith's position and there were enough to force a number of members of the House into an uncomfortable position. They had refused to sign the discharge petition on the ostensible grounds that they believed the Rules Committee would act on its own sooner or later. The favorable response to the petition forced them to bring pressure on the chairman to make good their own promises that he would act.

President Johnson has confided to acquaintances, however, that the discharge petition was a stratagem he disliked, no doubt "in the marrow of the bones." No Congressional man is sanguine about such an undermining of the power of the Establishment.

Nevertheless, the President swallowed his objections and used his influence to get 10 Texas Representatives to sign the petition—no mean achievement, since only four of these same Texans actually voted for the civil-rights bill when it came to a final vote.

The bipartisan coalition that passed the bill had been put together by John Kennedy and Republican leader Charles Halleck of Indiana—but it had to be held together under the tense conditions of House debate. The bill's supporters in both parties give Mr. Johnson ample credit for maintaining a strict and necessary bipartisanship during those crucial days in February. They also credit him with an effective job, in the weeks before the debate, of keeping public pressure on Congress. The fact that he was a Southerner, they think, accounts in part for the lack of bitterness in the Southern opposition. But Mr. Johnson took no part at all—having no need to—in the tactical battle of the House floor.

But the President's decisions, phone calls and pressures form only half the story. Perhaps more significant than any of these positive actions is the fact that, coming in such tragic circumstances into his heavy responsibilities, Mr. Johnson avoided the numerous pitfalls into which a less surefooted leader might have stumbled.

No one will argue that tax reduction went through the Senate and the civil rights bill through the house *more slowly* because John Kennedy was dead. Yet, it could easily have happened that way. One or both bills could have been lost and Congress could have overrun a hesitant leader—just as it tried unsuccessfully to do when House Republicans sought to put restrictions on the executive branch's ability to work out a sale of wheat to the Soviet Union.

Now the greatest of Mr. Johnson's challenges is before him—the filibuster in the Senate against the most significant civil rights bill in history. He is doubtful the Senate will vote to end the filibuster, owing to the historic reluctance of small-state Senators to strike down unlimited debate—their last weapon, as many of them see it, against the big urban centers.

To illustrate the difficulty of cutting off a civil rights filibuster, one Administration strategist estimates that in order to attract the necessary Republican support, the move would have to be supported by three key Senators—Dirksen of Illinois, Bourke B. Hickenlooper of Iowa and George Aiken of Vermont. Those three represent almost all shades of Republican opinion, all sizes of Republican states, and both East and West.

Nor does Mr. Johnson have much room for maneuver and compromise— the weapons by which, as Majority Leader, he wriggled the 1957 and 1960 civil rights bills through the Senate. The Southerners' main target is the public accommodations section, but it is precisely this section that Mr. Johnson believes he must keep in the bill at all costs. It is a political necessity for him to do so because the section has become symbolic of the Negro's whole effort to win his rights legally and politically. If it fails, or is compromised into banality, the Negro may turn to more direct methods.

To bring such men as Aiken, Dirksen and Hickenlooper into some sort of unity with the disparate individuals of his own party, to find some politically feasible compromise formula—these are legislative problems that will challenge to the utmost a leadership that, on the record of Mr. Johnson's years in the Senate and his months in the White House, seems to rest, first, on an ability to find common ground on which men can stand; second, on a sort of relentless persuasiveness, and third, on decisiveness—approaching ruthlessness—in pursuing a course once determined upon.

Ever since the rights bill passed the House, there has been talk in Washington that Mr. Johnson was seeking a compromise formula to present to the filibustering Southern Senators. If so, it would be in his established *modus operandi*. An Administration official, wise in the ways of Congress, offers this assessment of one part of that method: "Kennedy came too late to many of his problems in Congress. He would hold back, let things develop, come in at the top of the crisis. Johnson likes to stay ahead and anticipate what will happen and how to meet it."

But beyond the fates of even such major legislation as tax reduction and civil rights, Mr. Johnson's affinity for Congress—the feeling "in the marrow of his bones"—offers him at once a greater opportunity and a greater peril.

The danger arises from the fact that a President cannot always act as his own Majority Leader and Congress cannot always be his main reliance in matters large and small. If Mr. Johnson involves himself too readily in the minutiae of Congressional procedure and politics, if he expends his prestige and power too rapidly on matters of secondary importance, the whole scope and course of his magistracy will be affected and not for the better.

And while no President can proceed far at home or abroad without substantial backing from Congress, there comes the inevitable time when he must push ahead either without it or without as much of it has he would like. Moreover, Congressional leaders—products of a system based on local districts and states and their interests—are not always the most far-seeing and disinterested advisers.

Mr. Johnson is reported to have been disillusioned by the vote he once called for when he had gathered Congressional and Administration leaders together to discuss Panama. He wound up with no majority for anything and had to make his own decision anyway. When later crises arose in Cyprus and over the Guantanamo water supply, the Congressional leaders were much less in evidence at the White House.

Mr. Johnson's opportunity, if realized, could be of importance beyond any conceivable single bill. It is somehow to achieve, not just on one measure or in one session, but in the broadest sense, a new atmosphere of mutual respect and mutual confidence in which Congress and President can work together effectively—coequal branches in fact as well as in theory.

One speaks for the national interest; the other for the vast diversity of local interests. Seldom in American history have they functioned in real harmony. Lyndon Johnson and the 88th Congress seem more willing than most to work together, and that fact may yet prove the first step toward a real "miracle" on Capitol Hill.

THE PRESIDENCY AND THE PEACE
McGeorge Bundy

McGeorge Bundy heads the Ford Foundation. He was Special Assistant for National Security Affairs to Presidents Kennedy and Johnson. A graduate of Yale University (1940), Bundy was a Lecturer and Associate Professor of Government at Harvard University before becoming Dean of Harvard's Faculty of Arts and Sciences in 1953, the job he relinquished to join the White House staff.

It is with some sense of temerity that a member of the White House staff undertakes to comment on the large topic of the Presidency and the Peace.

Reprinted by special permission from *Foreign Affairs*, April 1964. Copyright by the Council on Foreign Relations, Inc.

Loyalty and affection are so normal in such service that detachment is difficult.

Nevertheless, the importance of the topic and the enforced familiarity of close experience with the presidential task may justify a set of comments whose underlying motive is to express a conviction that is as obvious as the daylight, in general, and as fresh as every sunrise, in particular: a conviction that the American Presidency, for better, not for worse, has now become the world's best hope of preventing the unexampled catastrophe of general nuclear war.

Moreover, both charity and sorrow can be good lenses for perception, and it may therefore be possible to consider the subject without impropriety by focusing upon the years of John F. Kennedy.

The tragedy which has moved his Administration from politics to history may allow to his critics and excuse in his friends some generosity in the assessment of his three years. His death revealed his greatness, and the grief of the world was less for his tragedy than for its own—in that he had shown his spreading grasp of his duty to mankind as Chief Executive for Peace.

THE PURPOSE IS PEACE

To focus on the Kennedy years is not to forget those before, and still less the firm continuation after November 22. The Presidents of the nuclear age before Mr. Kennedy also made the service of peace the first of their purposes, and the determined commitment of President Johnson to this same end, matured in decades of direct knowledge of our nuclear world, has been made plain in his own words and actions already. Indeed one purpose of a retrospective assessment is to clarify purposes which are as important to the President today as to the President last year.

A President in search of peace has many powers, but none is more relevant or more effective than his power as Commander-in-Chief. The President is keeping the peace as long as he keeps his own nuclear power in check, and with it the nuclear power of others. The most obvious of his powers, apparently so simple and so negative, can be used for peace in a number of ways.

POWER PREREQUISITE

The prerequisite, of course, is that this power should exist, and that there should be confidence in its future as well as its present effectiveness. Nothing is more dangerous to the peace than weakness in the ultimate deterrent strength of the United States. In the quarter century that man has known the atom could be split, each American decision to enlarge its powers has been the President's alone. More subtly, but with just as great importance, the choices of methods of delivery and their rate of development have also been presidential.

As important as having strength is being known to have it; and here, if anything, the presidential authority and responsibility are still more clear. This is the lesson of Sputnik, and of the "missile gap" which was forecast and feared by responsible and well-informed men both in and out of government between 1957 and 1961.

There was ground for doubt and need for rapid action; the ground and the need were recognized, and important steps were taken, but an appearance of complacency led to an appearance of weakness, with considerable costs abroad. These costs would surely have been greater had it not been for the remarkable personal standing of President Eisenhower.

HONEST SURPRISE

At the beginning of the Kennedy Administration there was need both for further action and for a re-establishment of confidence. The new President himself had feared the missile gap and had pressed his concern in the campaign.

It was with honest surprise and relief that in 1961 he found the situation much less dangerous than the best evidence available to the Senate had indicated the year before. His Administration moved at once to correct the public impression, and thereafter, throughout his term, he encouraged and supported policies of action and of exposition which aimed to insure not merely that American strategic power was sufficient but that its sufficiency was recognized.

The adequacy of American strategic strength is a matter of such transcendent importance that it must always be a legitimate topic of political debate.

"How much is enough?" is a question on which honest men will differ, and interested parties will find room and reason for their claims. Thus, it is natural that in the present political year we have ranging shots already from the fringes, some saying that our strength is too little and others that it is too great.

Just as it is the responsibility of the Commander-in-Chief to insure the adequacy of our strength, so it is his task, either directly or through his principal defense officers, to meet and overcome such criticism.

The present Administration will not be lax in the exposition of the real situation, and no one who has closely examined the present and prospective balance of strategic strength can doubt that this year any assertion that we are weak will be found wanting to the point of irresponsibility.

EQUAL OBLIGATION

There is an equal obligation to meet the arguments of those who think we are too strong. When these arguments grow out of fundamentally different views on the purpose and meaning of effective strategic strength, it may be necessary to agree to disagree.

"Unilateral disarmament" is a tainted term, but it does embody something of what is desired by most of those who criticize our present strength as gravely excessive.

The Presidents of the nuclear age have recognized that the law of diminishing returns applies to strategic missiles as to all other commodities; they have also agreed with President Johnson's comment that our nuclear defense expenditures can never be justified as WPA for selected towns or states.

But they have all rejected the gamble of limiting our strategic strength in terms of any absolute concept of what is enough.

They have measured our strength against that of the Soviet Union and have aimed at strategic superiority; that superiority has had different meanings at different stages, but seen from the White House its value for peace has never been small.

Yet even in this rejection of the underlying arguments which move so many of those who find our strength excessive, a President who cares for peace will respect their general concern. It is entirely true that nuclear strength can be provocative, that it is full of the hazard of accident or misuse and that it imposes upon its commander, in his own interest as in that of mankind, a passion for prudence.

All the Presidents of the nuclear age have understood this responsibility and have sought to meet it by insisting on disciplined and responsible control of this power.

In the case of President Kennedy, the pressing need was that as the number and variety of weapons systems increase, there should be ever more searching attention to effective command and control. To him, this was a better answer to the dangers of accident than some arbitrary limitation of numbers; a thousand well-controlled and safely designed missiles could be less dangerous than a hundred of lower quality, as well as more effective in deterrence.

POWERFUL AVERSION

A related point was the President's powerful aversion to those nuclear weapons which could be used effectively only in a first strike. In 1961 and 1962 he faced a series of judgments on major systems; he always preferred the system which could survive an attack as against the system which might provoke one.

In the same way and for related reasons, he preferred the system which was on the high seas or at home to that which required a base abroad and evoked a real or pretended charge of encirclement from Moscow.

The Commander-in-Chief must be strong, then, but also restrained. And as his strength must be recognized, so must his restraint. The doctrine of "massive retaliation" was never as absolute as Secretary Dulles at first made it seem, and its real weakness lay not in the undoubted fact that against certain kinds of aggression a nuclear response would be necessary, but in the appearance of a bomb-rattling menace which it created.

The Presidency does well to avoid this appearance; in the Kennedy Administration the rule was that statements of strength and will should be made as calmly as possible. The President himself watched constantly to prevent the appearance of belligerence, and when the White House watch nodded—as in one magazine account in which a single phrase out of context was seized upon by Soviet propaganda—he made his dissatisfaction plain.

A similar discipline was enforced throughout the Administration upon both civil and military officials. Those who have read speech drafts for clearance know how seldom there is need for major change and how often divergence between presidential purposes and a speaker's draft can be corrected by revision which reconciles the real purposes of both.

And again it is not only the act of coordination but the appearance of it which is helpful. The nuclear age multiplies the mistrust that peaceable men must feel toward military men who appear not to be under effective control, and nothing adds more to a President's reputation abroad than recognition that he is Commander-in-Chief in fact as well as in name.

PRESIDENTIAL CONTROL

Yet the Kennedy years show again, as the terms of strong Presidents have shown before, that harmony, not conflict, is the normal relation between the armed services and the Presidency.

The maintenance of clear presidential control over military policy and over public statements gave rise to some criticism, and intermittently there were assertions that this or that military need was being overridden, this or that viewpoint silenced.

Energy and strength in the office of the Secretary of Defense produced similar worries, and challenges to cherished privileges were not unresisted.

But the center of emphasis belongs on the fact that the Presidency has these powers in this country; a President who uses them firmly, with a defensible concept of the national security, can count on the support of the officers and men of the armed forces. The American tradition of civilian control is strong and the tradition of loyalty among professional officers high; the services are eager for a strong and active Commander-in-Chief. The armed strength of the United States, if handled with firmness and prudence, is a great force for peace.

ROOSEVELT'S WEAKNESS

The President who seeks peace must have a clear view of the Soviet Union. The one great weakness of Franklin Roosevelt was that he did not; he had not the advantage of living, as all his successors have, through the realities of the years after 1945. Nothing is gained for peace by forgetting Czechoslovakia or Hungary or the recurrent menace to Berlin, or Korea or Southeast Asia or any of the dozens of times and places where Communists with help from Moscow have sought to put an end to liberty.

Mr. Kennedy had this clear view. He had it before he became President; he confirmed it in his first state papers; he understood not only the unrelenting ambition and the ruthlessness of communism, but also the weakness and disarray of much of the non-Communist world. And for almost two of his three years—from the very beginning until the offensive weapons were gone from Cuba—he had an exposure to Communist pressure in Berlin, in Laos and in the Caribbean which could only confirm the somber estimate with which he entered office.

Against these pressures he was firm, and to meet them more effectively he greatly strengthened the defenses of the United States—not merely in strategic weapons for basic deterrence but also in forces designed more precisely to meet the hazards of each point of pressure.

The reserves who were called up for Berlin never fired a shot in anger, but military service by Americans has seldom made a more effective contribution to the defense of freedom and the keeping of peace.

The new kinds of strength deployed to South Viet-Nam have not finished that hard job, but they have prevented an otherwise certain defeat and kept the door open for a victory which in the end can be won only by the Vietnamese themselves.

And never in any country did President Kennedy leave it in doubt that Communist subversion is always the enemy of freedom, and of freedom's friends, the Americans.

Yet always—and again from the beginning—he put equal emphasis on the readiness of the United States to reach honorable settlement of all differences, the respect of the United States for the reality of Soviet strength and the insistence of the United States that both sides accept and meet their joint responsibility for peace.

He rejected the stale rhetoric of the cold war; he insisted not on the innate wickedness of communism but on its evil effects. The Communist world was seldom if ever "the enemy." Characteristically, as in his Inaugural Address, the President used a circumlocution whose unaccustomed clumsiness was proof that it was carefully chosen: "those nations who would make themselves our adversary." Characteristically, too, what he there offered them was a request "to begin anew the quest for peace."

And he pressed in this same direction himself. In Laos, in Berlin, and most persistently of all in the search for a test ban, the President's powers, from beginning to end, were used toward the goal of agreement. Agreement must never be surrender; that would be no service to peace. The firmness of the United States under pressure was made plain both in Berlin and in Southeast Asia. But firmness was a means to honorable settlement, not an end in itself.

Harboring no illusion about the difficulty of success, the President nevertheless persevered. He was convinced that at the least it was essential to leave no doubt, in all these issues, of the good will and peaceful purpose of the United States.

If there were to be a continued arms race, or a test of strength it must be plain where the responsibility lay. But the larger truth, as he saw it, was that in these areas of difference there was real advantage to both sides in reliable agreement—if only the other side could be brought to see its own real interests, free of ambition that would be resisted and of fear that was unjustified.

THIN RESPONSE

In 1961 and 1962 the invitation to seek peace together met a thin response. True, the threat to Berlin, so noisy in 1961 and so sharpened by the confession of Communist bankruptcy which was the Wall, seemed slightly milder in 1962. And an agreement was reached on Laos, imperfect in its terms and in its execution but much better than no agreement at all. It was in Laos above all that one could see the advantage to both sides of even the most incomplete disengagement as against a tightening and sharpening of confrontation.

But no agreement at all had come in the field nearest the President's heart—that of limiting the nuclear danger. On the contrary, Soviet tests had led inexorably to American tests. It was somehow a measure of the Kennedy temper and purpose that of all the Soviet provocations of these two years it was the resumption of testing that disappointed him most.

The Cuban missile crisis was the most important single event of the Kennedy Presidency. As the President himself pointed out afterward, it was the first direct test between the Soviet Union and the United States in which nuclear weapons were the issue.

Although vast amounts have been written about the crisis, we still have no solid account of one half of it—the Soviet side. What is not known of one side limits our ability to assess action on the other, and this limitation should warn us against judgments that this act more than that, or one advantage more than another, was decisive. It does not prevent a more general judgment of the main elements contributing to success.

What is at once astonishing and wholly natural is the degree to which the clear components of this success are precisely those to which the Presidency had been bent and not only in the Kennedy Administration; strength, restraint and respect for the opinions of mankind.

That strength counted we cannot doubt—though it is typical of the uncertainties of assessment that the partisans of specific kinds of strength remained persuaded, afterward as before, of the peculiar value of their preferred weapons.

Believers in nuclear dissuasion as an all-purpose strategy asserted the predominant role of strategic superiority; believers in the need for conventional strength, while not usually denying the role of SAC in the success, were convinced that what mattered most was usable non-nuclear strength at the point of contest.

Interesting as this argument may be, it can have no certain conclusion. Prudence argues for a judgment that all kinds of military strength were relevant. The existence of adequate and rapidly deployable strength, at all levels, was the direct result of the reinforcement of balanced defenses begun in 1961.

A further element of strength in this crisis was the firmness and clarity of the presidential decision to insist on the withdrawal of the missiles. This was not merely a matter of one speech or even of one decision from a week of heavy argument. It was a position clearly stated, and internationally understood, well before the crisis broke. It was reinforced in its power, and the Communist position correspondingly weakened, by the repeated Soviet assertions that no such weapons were or would be placed in Cuba.

The strength of this position, like the strength of the available military force, was reinforced by its disciplined relation to a policy of restraint. That nuclear weapons should not be strewn around as counters in a contest for face was a proposition commanding wide support. Any impulse to discount or disregard the direct threat to the United States, as a problem for the Americans to solve, was deeply undercut by awareness of the difference between American and Soviet standards of nuclear responsibility as revealed in this moment of danger.

More broadly, the strength and restraint of the American position in October stood in striking contrast to the position in which others found themselves.

As a first consequence, and to a degree that exceeded predictions, the allies of the United States both in this hemisphere and in Europe were clear in their support, though in public comment, especially in the United Kingdom, there was evidence of the difficulties we should have faced if we had been less clearly strong, restrained, and right.

It can be argued, of course, that in this crisis the opinions even of close allies were not crucial, and it does seem probable that such critical decisions as the turnaround of armsbearing ships and the announcement that the missiles would be removed were not determined by OAS votes or by world opinion. This particular crisis might have been successfully resolved even in the face of doubt and division among allies whose immediate power at the point of contest was negligible.

But so narrow a judgment neglects two great hazards. Immediately, a serious division among the allies might have provoked action elsewhere, most dangerously at Berlin (and indeed in all the postwar annals of the bravery of West Berlin there is no moment in which the courage and strength of the Berliners—and indeed of all free Germans—have been more important in discouraging adventure).

And even if no such adventure had been attempted, the position after the crisis would not have been one in which "the quest for peace" could easily be led from Washington. It was and is the central meaning of this affair that a major threat to peace and freedom was removed by means which strengthened the prospects of both.

The October crisis came out better than President Kennedy or any of his associates had expected. The analysis suggested above would not have been compelling in the discussions of the week of October 15, and the predominant reaction in Washington on October 28 was one of simple and enormous relief.

In the weeks after the crisis, attention was diverted, first by backstairs gossip over who gave what advice and then by a renewal of political debate over Cuba, a problem of another order of meaning than the missile crisis and one which had rightly been left essentially as it was while the major threat was removed.

And finally, it was far from clear, in the immediate aftermath, that "those who had made themselves our adversary" in such a sudden and shocking way would now be ready for a different relation.

But what is important for our present purposes is that what shaped American action in this crisis—what set and sustained the tempered response, both to danger and to success, was the President. And while the man in the office was Kennedy, with a taste and style of his own, I think it is right to claim that the office as well as the man was embodied in the resolution, restraint and responsibility that governed in these weeks.

As the great disappointment of 1961 was the renewal of testing, so the great satisfaction of 1963 was the limited test-ban treaty.

The withdrawal of missiles from Cuba did more than end a specific crisis of great gravity. It also signaled an acceptance by the Soviet government, for the present at least, of the existing nuclear balance. In that balance there is American superiority, as we have seen, but it is a superiority that does not permit any lack of respect for the strength of the Soviet Union. No safer balance appears possible at present. No overwhelmingly one-sided margin is open to either side, and it was one lesson of the Cuban affair—as of many others since 1945—that it was well for peace that Communist strength should be matched with a margin.

But the purpose of this margin must still be peace, and the aim of policy must still be to get beyond conflicting interests to the great common need for safer prospect of survival. This is the meaning of the limited test-ban treaty.

If the missile crisis was the proof of American strength in conflict, the test-ban treaty was the proof of American readiness to work for this common purpose. And whatever the moving forces on the Soviet side, in the non-Communist world the Presidency was the necessary center of action.

A special and distinguished role was played by the British Prime Minister, but Macmillan would be the first to recognize that it was mainly through his close relation to two Presidents that he was able to make the British contribution effective.

POWER WITH ENERGY

It is only the American President who can carry the American Senate and the American people in any agreement on arms control, and it is only with American participation that any such agreement can have meaning for the Soviet government.

Unless a President uses these powers with energy, arms control agreements are improbable. The momentum of the arms race—the power at work to keep it going almost without conscious new decision—is enormous. Military men in all countries find it hard to approve any arms control proposal which is not either safely improbable or clearly unbalanced in their own favor.

In the United States, only a strong Commander-in-Chief with a strong Secretary of Defense is in a position to press steadily for recognition that the arms race itself is now a threat to national security.

Only the President can insure that good proposals are kept alive even after a first rejection, and that new possibilities are constantly considered—so that there may always be as many proposals as possible on the table waiting for the moment of Soviet readiness. The readiness to meet all threats must be matched by a demonstrated readiness to reach agreement.

In the case of the limited test-ban, it was President Kennedy himself who reached the conclusion in the spring of 1963 that the United States would not be the first to make further atmospheric tests. That quite personal decision, recognized at the time as fully within the presidential power and announced in an address on peace whose power and conviction were immediately recognized, was as likely an immediate cause as any for the announcement, less than a month later, that the Soviet government would now be willing to sign an agreement which had been open for two years.

There followed a period of negotiation and then a debate on ratification, and in these again the Presidency was central. The test-ban treaty, as we have all told each other a hundred times, is only one step, and President Johnson has made clear his determination to seek further steps with all the energy and imagination the Government can command.

Meanwhile, the lesson of the test-ban is that no step at all can be taken in this field unless the President himself works for it. A President indifferent to arms control, or easily discouraged by Soviet intransigence or irresponsibility or inclined to a narrow military view of the arms race, would be a guarantee against agreed limitation of armaments.

Conversely, where there is zeal in the search for agreement, refusal to accept initial disappointment as final, a cool and balanced assessment of the risks of agreement against the risks of unlimited competition and a firm use of the powers of the office, the Presidency can become—as in this case—an instrument of hope for all men everywhere.

In concentrating attention upon the great requirements of strength and a love for peace, and in using as examples of such very large matters as the missile crisis and the test-ban treaty, I do not pretend to have exhausted the connections between the Presidency and the Peace, even as they showed themselves in the short Kennedy years.

There is more in the Presidency that the special powers of the Commander-in-Chief or the special responsibility for pressing the hard cause of disarmament. There is more, too, than a need for understanding of Soviet realities.

The Presidency is a powerful element in the strength or weakness of the United Nations, as every Secretary General has known. The Presidency remains the headquarters of the Great Alliance, as even the most separated of national leaders has recognized.

The Presidency is an indispensable stimulus to progress in the Americas. The Presidency must make the hard choices of commitment that have brought both honor and difficulty, as in Korea in 1950 or in South Viet-Nam in 1954.

The White House visit and the White House photograph are elements of democratic electioneering not just in the United States but wherever the name of the American President can bring a cheer.

The death of a President men loved has shown how wide this larger constituency is. Allies, neutrals and even adversaries attend to the Presidency.

When the American President shows that he can understand and respect the opinions and hopes of distant nations, when he proves able to present the interests of his own people without neglecting the interests of others, when in his own person he represents decency, hope, and freedom—then he is strengthened in his duty to be the leader of man's quest for peace and in the age of nuclear weapons. And this strength will be at least as important in meeting danger as in pursuing hope.

NEW PROBLEMS

The administration in Washington, led now by President Johnson, will face new problems and make new decisions, and as time passes the new imprint of a strong mind and heart will be felt increasingly—in the presidency, in the Government and in the world.

President Kennedy would have been the last to suppose that the purely personal characteristics of any President, however loved and mourned, could or should continue to determine the work of the Presidency after his death.

President Johnson will conduct the office in his own way. Yet the short space of three months is enough to show plainly that the pursuit of peace remains his central concern, while the effective transfer from one administration to the next has reflected the fact that loyalty to President Kennedy and loyalty to President Johnson are not merely naturally compatible but logically necessary as a part of a larger loyalty to their common purpose.

And as we remember John Kennedy, let us separate the essential from the complementary. The youth, the grace and the wit were wonderful, but they were not the center. There lay courage, vision, humanity and strength, tested on the path to the office and tempered by the office itself. It is these qualities, applied to the greatest issues, that belong not only to the man but to the job.

It is my own conviction that this kind of President and this kind of Presidency reflect the general will of Americans. Temperate use of strength, respect for honest difference, sympathy for those in need and a readiness to go our share of the distance—these qualities, which I have described in phrases borrowed from our new President, are qualities of the American people.

They have their opposites in our character, too, but these are what we honor; these we expect of our Presidents.

In the terrible shock of President Kennedy's death there were so many— perhaps too many—who saw the foul deeds of a few days in Dallas, and not the dead President himself, as the embodiment of the real America. They were wrong.

As a man, as a President, as a servant of the peace, he was what we are, and his achievement belongs to us all. Strengthened by his service, the Presidency continues, and so does the quest for peace.

Many Americans—Republicans and Democrats alike—have displayed a long-standing, if less than reasoned, suspicion of "Big Government." They tend to view bureaucracy as a necessary evil at best and to regard civil servants as generally inadequate and inefficient. "Unbusinesslike" is the damning phrase frequently applied to the civil-service system and "bureaucrat" is the individual condemnation. Yet, despite the popular saying "Those who can, do; those who cannot, go into the public service," many Americans fear the public servant's power—his supposed ability to regulate lives, his alleged tendency to build empires. Even the sophisticated have fallen prey to certain questionable beliefs—for example, that policy and execution should be kept separate, and that the quick solution to administrative problems lies in a neat, symmetrical government structure outlined by simplified flow charts and hierarchical diagrams.

Before attempting an analysis of such stereotyped thinking, however, let us isolate some of the possible goals that may prove acceptable to Americans of all political persuasions. First, what do we expect of our public executives—our "bureaucrats"? In the broadest sense, we expect them to facilitate social achievements, whether in meeting the progressive challenges of "new frontiers" or in consolidating the rewards of an "enlightened conservatism." More than mere governmental efficiency is involved in this expectation, since we also expect our civil servants to assure governmental stability through periods of social development and change. It is their task to make things come out as planned, and to provide the greatest amount of government service for the least possible cost.

What kind of public servant, then, do we want, and what are the tasks we assign him? If he is to meet fully the demands we make upon him, he must combine the qualities of responsibility, leadership, and initiative. Furthermore, he must understand fully the nature of democracy, and possess a strong sense of public service—a sense of mission. Above all, he must possess that all-too-rare ability to distinguish goals from techniques; the tax collector, for instance, must never succumb to the delusion that revenue raising is one of the ends of government.

We must consider some of the problems faced by the public executive before we can understand his role. Perhaps his most important problem is the magnitude of his task—a magnitude completely unknown to his counterpart in even the largest corporate entity, such as General Motors or General Electric. Moreover, his is a complex of responsibilities that the business executive finds bewildering. He is not only held to account by the press, with its speedy public disclosures; by the Congress with its appropriation power; and by the courts, with their prerogative of review. He must answer, even as his business counterpart must answer, to his chief executive and to his immediate agency superiors. In all his dealings, he must be a paragon of propriety, keeping a wary eye out for ethical temptations unknown to the business world and maintaining a moral posture beyond reproach. "Conflict of interest" is his ever present shadow.

What are his rewards for such demanding service? In addition to the accidental public distortions of his labors, deliberate attempts to disparage and discredit him are often his lot—not only on the part of political attackers but on the part of well-equipped pressure groups and, sometimes, elements of the press itself. In the face of all this verbal abuse, the public executive must, nonetheless, not only continue to operate the vast machinery of administration but carry out the delicate process best described as "the engineering of consent." He finds, even on the highest levels, that his authority is diffuse and that decisions are made by groups rather than individuals even though departmental shortcomings are all too frequently attributed to individuals—especially to those presumably in charge. His primary role is often one of coordination—of compromise rather than command—as he is called up to persuade the unyielding, to cajole his organization, and to better his "public relations." A generalist, he supervises specialists who are technically far more knowledgeable than he, but who are often hesitant to act, because of the myopia of their own expertness. In short, the task of the American public executive, as Harlan Cleveland has put it so well, is to "make a mesh of things," though his efforts may bring accusations of responsibility for the "mess in Washington."

We shall now examine the role that public-executive leadership plays in our government in action.

THE POLICYMAKER AND THE INTELLECTUAL
Henry A. Kissinger

Henry A. Kissinger, who served as one of President Kennedy's top foreign-policy advisers, is Associate Director of the Harvard Center for International Affairs. An educator, lecturer, and government specialist, he is the author of *Nuclear Weapons and Foreign Policy, A World Restored: Castlereagh, Metternich and the Restoration of Peace, The Necessity for Choice: Prospects of American Foreign Policy,* and many other books.

Any observer of the American scene must be struck by the tentative quality of our policy both foreign and domestic. Major parts of the world are undergoing revolutionary upheaval; but we seem hardly aware that peo-

From *The Reporter,* March 5, 1959. Copyright 1959 by The Reporter Magazine Company. Reprinted by permission.

ples abroad find increasingly little in America with which to identify themselves. Beyond any disagreement or dissatisfaction over specific policies there exists an evergrowing distrust or at least incomprehension of America's purposes.

It would be comforting to believe that this state of affairs is due to particular mistakes of policy that can be reversed more or less easily. Unfortunately the problem is more deep-seated. Our policymakers' lack of vigor is matched by that of many of their critics. It has been a long time since there has been a real debate on policy issues beyond a bland competition for slogans such as coexistence or flexibility.

The stagnation is often ascribed to the fact that our best people are not attracted into government service. But it may be pertinent to inquire how qualified our eminent men are for the task of policymaking in a revolutionary period. Others trace the cause of our difficulties to the lack of respect shown the intellectual by our society. However, a case could be made for the proposition that in some respects the intellectual has never been more in demand; that he makes such a relatively small contribution not because he is rejected but because his function is misunderstood. He is sought after enthusiastically but for the wrong reasons and in pursuit of the wrong purposes.

ADMINISTRATIVE STAGNATION

One of the paradoxes of an increasingly specialized, bureaucratized society is that the qualities rewarded in the rise to eminence are less and less the qualities required once eminence is reached. Specialization encourages administrative and technical skills, which are not necessarily related to the vision and creativity needed for leadership. The essence of good administration is co-ordination among the specialized functions of a bureaucracy. The task of the executive is to infuse and occasionally to transcend routine with purpose.

Yet while the head of an organization requires a different outlook from that of his administrative subordinates, he must generally be recruited from their ranks. Eminence thus is often reached for reasons and according to criteria which are irrelevant to the tasks which must be performed in the highest positions. Despite all personnel procedures and perhaps because of them, superior performance at the apex of an organization is frequently in the deepest sense accidental.

This problem, serious enough in the private sector, is even more complicated in government. In a society that has prided itself on its free-enterprise character, it is inevitable that the qualities which are most esteemed in civilian pursuits should also be generally rewarded by high public office. But very little in the experience that forms American leadership groups produces the combination of political acumen, conceptual skill, persuasive power, and administrative ability required for the highest positions of government.

Our executives are shaped by a style of life that inhibits reflectiveness. For one of the characteristics of a society based on specialization is the enormous work load of its top personnel. The smooth functioning of the administrative apparatus absorbs more energies than the definition of criteria on which decision is to be based. Issues are reduced to their simplest terms. Decision making is increasingly turned into a group effort. The executive's task is conceived as choosing among administrative proposals in the formulation of which he has no part and with the substance of which he is often unfamiliar. A premium is placed on "presentations" which take the least effort to grasp and which in practice usually mean oral "briefings." (This accounts for the emergence of the specialist in "briefings" who prepares charts, one-page summaries, etc.) In our society the policymaker is dependent to an increasing extent on his subordinates' conception of the essential elements of a problem.

The bureaucratization of our society reflects not only its inevitable specialization but also certain deepseated philosophical attitudes all the more persuasive for rarely being made explicit. Two generations of Americans have been shaped by the pragmatic conviction that inadequate performance is somehow the result of a failure to properly understand an "objective" environment and that group effort is valuable in itself. The interaction of several minds is supposed to broaden the range of "experience" believed to be the ultimate source of knowledge.

Pragmatism, at least in its generally accepted forms, produces a tendency to identify a policy issue with the search for empirical data. It sees in consensus a test of validity; it distrusts individual effort or at least individual certitude and it tends to suppress personal judgment as "subjective."

The low valuation of personal views produces a greater concern with the collection of facts than with an interpretation of their significance; therefore the myth in our government that intelligence does not advise, it only reports. It leads to a multiplication of advisory staffs and a great reliance on study groups of all types. Each difficulty calls into being new panels which frequently act as if nothing had ever been done before, partly, at least, because the very existence of a problem is taken as an indication of the inadequacy of the previous advice.

The situation is compounded by the personal humility that is one of the most attractive American traits. Most Americans are convinced that no one is ever entirely "right," or, as the saying goes, that if there is disagreement each party is probably a little in error. The fear of dogmatism pervades the American scene. But the corollary of the tentativeness of most views is an incurable inward insecurity. Even very eminent people are reluctant to stand alone, and they see in concurrence one of their chief tests of validity.

Philosophical conviction and psychological bias thus combine to produce in and out of government a penchant for policymaking by committee. The obvious insurance against the possibility of error is to obtain as many opinions as possible. And unanimity is important, in that its absence is a standing reminder of the tentativeness of the course adopted. The committee approach to decision making is often less an organizational device than a spiritual necessity.

In this manner, policy is fragmented into a series of *ad hoc* decisions which make it difficult to achieve a sense of direction or even to profit from experience. Substantive problems are transformed into administrative ones. Innovation is subjected to "objective" tests which deprive it of spontaneity. "Policy planning" becomes the projection of familiar problems into the future. Momentum is confused with purpose. There is greater concern with how things are than with which things matter. The illusion is created that we can avoid recourse to personal judgment and responsibility as the final determinant of policy.

The debilitating tendency of this approach is often obscured in the private sector of our society because the goals of our economic effort are relatively limited. They involve less the creation of a policy framework than successfully operating within one—itself a conciliatory procedure. But when the same method is applied to national policy, its limitations become dramatically apparent. Many of our policymakers begin their governmental careers with only superficial acquaintance with the problems of their office. This is partly because the rise to eminence has often absorbed most of their energies, partly because civic consciousness, where it exists, most often finds its outlet on the local level. Whatever the reason, few of our executives (or lawyers with business background) can benefit in government from the strong will which is often their outstanding trait and which gained them success. Consciously or not, our top policymakers often lack the assurance and the conceptual framework to impose a pattern on events or to impart a sense of direction to their administrative staffs. Their unfamiliarity with their subject matter reinforces their already strong tendency to identify a policy problem with an administrative breakdown and a policy solution with an aggregate of administrative proposals.

The impact on national policy is pernicious. Even our highest policy bodies such as the National Security Council, are less concerned with developing overall measures in terms of a well-understood national purpose than with adjusting the varying approaches of semi-autonomous departments. The elaborateness of the process is compounded by the tendency of advisers to advise; for silence may be taken to mean not that the idea under discussion is good but that the adviser is inadequate. The committee system is more concerned with co-ordination and adjustment than with purpose.

A policy dilemma is produced because the advantages and disadvantages of alternative measures appear fairly evenly balanced; otherwise there would be no need for discussion. (This leaves aside the question to what extent the committee procedure encourages a neutral personality to which the pros and cons of almost any course of action always seem fairly even and which therefore creates artificial dilemmas.) But in assessing these alternatives the risks always seem more certain than the opportunities. No one can ever prove that an opportunity existed, but failure to foresee a danger involves swift retribution. As a result, much of the committee procedure is designed to permit each participant or agency to register objections, and the system stresses avoidance of risk rather than boldness of conception.

Our method of arriving at decisions and the attitudes of our officials distort the essence of policy. Effective policy depends not only on the skill of individual moves but even more importantly on their relationship to each other. It requires a sense of proportion; a sense of style provides it with inner discipline. All these intangibles are negated where problems become isolated cases each of which is disposed of on its merits by experts in the special difficulties it involves. It is as if in commissioning a painting, a patron would ask one artist to draw the face, another the body, another the hands, and still another the feet, simply because each artist is particularly good in one category. Such a procedure in stressing the components would lose the meaning of the whole.

The result is a paradox: the more intense the search for certainty by means of administrative devices, the greater is the inward insecurity of the participants. The more they seek "objectivity," the more diffuse their efforts become. The insecurity of many of our policymakers sometimes leads to almost compulsive traits. Officials—and other executives as well—tend to work to the point of exhaustion as one indication that they have done all that could be asked. The insecurity of many of our policymakers sometimes is also shown by the fact that almost in direct proportion as advisory staffs multiply they are distrusted by those at the top. Officials increasingly feel the need for "outside"—and therefore unbiased—advice. Memoranda that are produced within the bureaucracy are taken less seriously than similar papers that are available to the general public. Crucial policy advice is increasingly requested from *ad hoc* committees of outside experts. (See, e.g., the Gaither Committee on national defense or the Draper Committee on economic assistance.)

These committees are often extraordinarily useful. They provide a fresh point of view. They can focus public discussion. They make possible the tapping of talent that would otherwise be unavailable, particularly in the scientific field. (A good case in point is James Killian's method of operation as science adviser to the President.) They may even galvanize the bureaucracy. Nevertheless they suffer from serious drawbacks. Whatever the previous experience of the members, they require extensive "briefing." This places an additional strain on the bureaucracy, while the members of the committee are frequently ready to make their best contribution at the point when the group is disbanded. Then again, the committee is inevitably drawn from the same segment of society as the top officials. Its members have therefore also been victims of the prevailing administrative pace. And the committee process, with its trend toward the fragmentation of policy and its bias toward simplified approaches, is almost as pervasive in *ad hoc* groups as in regular governmental committees.

In some respects *ad hoc* groups can even be said to represent an important diversion of talent. The number of outstanding individuals with experience in a given field is severely limited. As a result the same group is called again and again on related tasks. Its discussions soon become predictable and sometimes even stereotyped. The ideal situation would be a "leap-frogging" process in which the current high officials expend their intellectual capital while others, usually outside government, develop new concepts and approaches. But constant membership on committees causes many of their members to stagnate and freezes them at the level of the experience or effort that gained them their reputation.

Moreover, outside groups are handicapped by the fact that unless they constitute themselves into a pressure group seeking to mold public opinion— a function beyond their scope and usually contrary to their purpose—they can be effective only if they convince the bureaucracy. If they are too far in advance of existing thinking, they are ignored. If they only confirm what has already been considered within the government, they are unnecessary. *Ad hoc* committees generally can be effective only in a narrowly circumscribed area which may be somewhat ahead of official views but which rarely touches the essence of the problem: to challenge the existing assumptions or to define a new sense of direction.

The committee system not only has a tendency to ask the wrong questions, it also puts a premium on the wrong qualities. The committee process is geared to the pace of conversation. Even where the agenda is composed of memoranda, these are prepared primarily as a background for discussion, and they stand and fall on the skill with which they are presented. Hence quickness of comprehension is more important than reflectiveness, fluency more useful than creativeness. The ideal "committee man" does not make his associates uncomfortable; he does not operate with ideas too far outside of what is generally accepted. Thus the thrust of committees is toward a standard of average performance. Since a complicated idea cannot be easily absorbed by ear—particularly when it is new—committees lean toward what fits in with the most familiar experience of their members. They therefore produce great pressure in favor of the *status quo*. Committees are consumers and sometimes sterilizers of ideas, rarely creators of them.

For all their cumbersome procedure and their striving for "objectivity," there is something approaching frivolity about many committees. Ideas are accepted because no one can think of an objection fast enough; or they are rejected because they cannot readily be grasped. Unfortunately, not everything that sounds plausible is important and many important ideas do not seem plausible, at least at first glance, the only glance permitted by most committees. Rapidity of comprehension is not always equivalent to responsible assessment; it may even be contrary to it. The result is a vicious circle: in the absence of well-understood goals each problem becomes a special case. But the more fragmented our approach to policy, the more difficult it becomes to act consistently and purposefully. The typical pattern of our governmental process is therefore endless debate about whether a given set of circumstances is in fact a problem, until a crisis removes all doubts but also the possibility of effective action. The committee system, which is an attempt to reduce the inward insecurity of our top personnel, leads to the paradoxical consequence of institutionalizing it.

The result is that American policy displays a combination of abstractness and rigidity. Our method of arriving at decisions and the qualities it reflects and rewards place a greater premium on form than on substance. Thus on any given issue some paper will be produced for almost any eventuality. But because policy results from what are in effect adversary proceedings, proposals by the various departments or agencies are often overstated to permit compromise, or phrased vaguely to allow freedom of interpretation. In any case, what is considered policy is usually the embodiment of a consensus in a paper. The very qualities which make the consensus possible tend to inhibit sustained and subtle effort: for the statement is frequently so general that it must be renegotiated when the situation to which it applies arises.

The rigidity of American policy is therefore a sympton of the psychological burden placed on our policymakers. Policies developed with great inward doubt become almost sacrosanct as soon as they are finally officially adopted. The reason is psychological. The *status quo* has at least the advantage of familiarity. An attempt to change course involves the prospect that the whole searing process of arriving at a decision will have to be repeated. By the same token, most of our initiatives tend to occur during crisis periods. When frustration becomes too great or a crisis brooks no further evasion, there arises the demand for innovation almost for its own sake. Yet innovation cannot be achieved by fiat. Crisis conditions do not encourage calm consideration; they rarely permit anything except defense moves.

The combination of unreflectiveness produced by the style of life of our most eminent people in and out of government, faith in administrative processes, and the conversational approach to policy accounts for much of the uncertainty of our policy. It leads to an enormous waste of intellectual resources. The price we pay for the absence of a sense of direction is that we appear to the rest of the world as vacillating, confused, and, what is most worrisome, increasingly irrelevant.

THE DEMAND FOR INTELLECTUALS

In a revolutionary period, then, it is precisely the practical man who is most apt to become a prisoner of events. It is most frequently the administrator who is unable to transcend the requirements of the moment. Are there any groups in our society who can overcome this impasse? How about those who are not engaged in administrative tasks nor part of large organizations; the individuals who devote themselves to furthering or disseminating knowledge—the intellectuals?

Any survey of the contemporary American scene reveals, however, that the problem is more complicated than our refusal or inability to utilize this source of talent. Many organizations, governmental or private, rely on panels of experts. Political leaders have intellectuals as advisers. Throughout our society, policy-planning bodies proliferate. Research organizations multiply. The need for talent is a theme of countless reports. What then is the difficulty?

One problem is the demand for expertise itself. Every problem which our society becomes concerned about—leaving aside the question whether these are always the most significant—calls into being panels, committees, or study groups supported by either private or governmental funds. Many organizations constantly call on intellectuals. As a result, intellectuals with a reputation soon find themselves so burdened that their pace of life hardly differs from that of the executives whom they advise. They cannot supply perspective because they are as harassed as the policymakers. In his desire to be helpful, the intellectual is too frequently compelled to sacrifice what should be his greatest contribution to society: his creativity.

Moreover, the pressure is not only produced by the organizations that ask for advice: some of it is generated by the self-image of the intellectual. In a pragmatic society, it is almost inevitable not only that the pursuit of knowledge for its own sake should be lightly regarded by the community but also that it should engender feelings of insecurity or even guilt among some of those who have dedicated themselves to it. There are many who believe that their ultimate contribution as intellectuals depends on the degree of their participation in what is considered the active life. It is not a long step from the willingness to give advice to having one's self-esteem gratified by a consulting relationship with a large organization. And since individuals who challenge the presuppositions of the bureaucracy, governmental or private, rarely can keep their positions as advisers, great pressures are created to elaborate on familiar themes rather than risk new departures that may both fail and prove unacceptable.

The great valuation our society places on expertise may be even more inimical to innovation than indifference. Since the American intellectual is so strongly committed to the same pragmatic values as the rest of society, it produces a tremendous overspecialization. This in turn makes it difficult for the intellectual to introduce a general perspective even from the vantage point of his own calling. Panels of experts are deliberately assembled to contain representatives of particular approaches: a committee on military policy will have spokesmen for the "all-out war" as well as for the "limited war" concept. A committee on foreign policy will have proponents for the "uncommitted areas" as well as specialists for Europe. These are then expected to adjust their differences by analogy with the committee procedure of the bureaucracy. Not surprisingly, the result is more often a common denominator than a well-rounded point of view.

This tendency is compounded by the conception of the intellectual held by the officials or organizations that call on him. The specialization of functions of a bureaucratized society delimits tasks and establishes categories of expectations. A person is considered suitable for assignments within certain classifications. But the classification of the intellectual is determined by the premium our society places on administrative skill. The intellectual is rarely found at the level where decisions are made; his role is commonly advisory. He is called in as a "specialist" in ideas whose advice is compounded with that of others from different fields of endeavor on the assumption that the policymaker is able to choose the correct amalgam between "theoretical" and "practice" advice. And even in this capacity the intellectual is not a free agent. It is the executive who determines in the first place whether he needs advice. He and the bureaucracy frame the question to be answered. The policymaker determines the standard of relevance. He decides who is consulted and thereby the definition of "expertness."

The fact that the need for excellence is constantly invoked is no guarantee that its nature will be understood. Excellence is more often thought to consist in the ability to perform the familiar as well as possible than in pushing back the frontiers of knowledge or insight. The search for talent consists more frequently in seeking personnel for well-understood tasks than in an effort to bring about an environment that constantly produces new and not yet imagined types of performance. The "expert" not uncommonly is the person who elaborates the existing framework most ably, rather than the individual charting new paths.

The contribution of the intellectual to policy is therefore in terms of criteria that he has played a minor role in establishing. He is rarely given the opportunity to point out that a query delimits a range of possible solutions or that an issue is posed in irrelevant terms. He is asked to solve problems, not to contribute to the definition of goals. Where decisions are arrived at by negotiation, the intellectual—particularly if he is not himself part of the bureaucracy—is a useful weight in the scale. He can serve as a means to filter ideas to the top outside of organization channels or as a legitimizer for the viewpoint of contending factions within and among departments. This is why many organizations build up batteries of outside experts or create semi-independent research groups, and why articles or books become tools in the bureaucratic struggle. In short, all too often what the policymaker wants from the intellectual is not ideas but endorsement.

This is not to say that the motivation of the policymaker toward the intellectual is cynical. The policymaker sincerely wants help. His problem is that he does not know the nature of the help he requires. And he generally does not become aware of a need until the problem is already critical. He is subject to the misconception that he can make an effective choice among conflicting advisers on the basis of administrative rules of thumb and without being fully familiar with the subject matter. Of necessity the bureaucracy gears the intellectual effort to its own requirements and its own pace: the deadlines are inevitably those of the policymaker, and all too often they demand a premature disclosure of ideas which are then dissected before they are fully developed. The administrative approach to intellectual effort tends to destroy the environment from which innovation grows. Its insistence on "results" discourages the intellectual climate that might produce important ideas whether or not the bureaucracy feels it needs them.

For these reasons, research institutes set up by governmental agencies have sometimes reflected the views of their sponsor even when they were financially independent. As long as the sponsoring agency retains the right to define the tasks of its research agency—or even the majority of these tasks—it will also determine the point of view of the product. The uniformity of the administrative approach is after all primarily the result less of fiscal control than of all the intangibles of fellowship and concern produced by association with a particular group and constant concentration on the same range of issues. It is not overcome if the "outside" research institute has no greater possibility for applying a wider perspective than its sponsoring agency has.

Thus though the intellectual participates in policymaking to an almost unprecedented degree, the result has not necessarily been salutary for him or of full benefit for the organization using him. In fact, the two have sometimes compounded each other's weaknesses. Nor has the present manner of utilizing outside experts and research institutes done more than reduce somewhat the dilemmas of the policymakers. The production of so much research often simply adds another burden to already overworked officials. It tends to divert attention from the act of judgment on which policy ultimately depends to the assembly of facts—which is relatively the easiest step in policy formation. Few if any of the recent crises of U.S. policy have been caused by the unavailability of data. Our policymakers do not lack advice; they are in many respects overwhelmed by it. They do lack criteria on which to base judgments. In the absence of commonly understood and meaningful standards, all advice tends to become equivalent. In seeking to help the bureaucracy out of this maze, the intellectual too frequently becomes an extension of the administrative machine, accepting its criteria and elaborating its problems. While this too is a necessary task and sometimes even an important one, it does not touch the heart of the problem: that purpose must dominate the mechanism if we are to avoid disaster. The dilemma of our policy is not so much that it cannot act on what it has defined as useful—though this too happens occasionally—but that the standards of utility are in need of redefinition. Neither the intellectual nor the policymaker performs his full responsibility if he shies away from this essential task.

RECHARGING THE BATTERIES

This is not a call for the intellectual to remain aloof from policymaking. Nor have intellectuals who have chosen withdrawal necessarily helped the situation. There are intellectuals outside the bureaucracy who are not part of the maelstrom of committees and study groups but who have nevertheless contributed to the existing stagnation through a perfectionism that paralyzes action by posing unreal alternatives. (If we have the choice between rebuilding our cities or launching a satellite, we must choose the former.) There are intellectuals with the bureaucracy who have avoided the administrative approach but who must share the responsibility for the prevailing confusion because they refuse to recognize the inevitable element of conjecture in policymaking. (How can we be *sure* about Soviet motives? How can we be *certain* that in say thirty years the Soviet system will not be like ours?) The intellectuals of other countries in the free world where the influence of pragmatism is less pronounced and the demands of the bureaucracies less insatiable have not made a more significant contribution. The spiritual malaise described here may have other symptoms elsewhere. The fact remains that the entire free world suffers not only from administrative myopia but also from self-righteousness and the lack of a sense of direction.

One reason why intellectuals outside the administrative machines have not made a greater contribution is that for them protest has too often become an end in itself. Whether they have withdrawn by choice or because of the nature of their society, many intellectuals have confused the issues by simplifying them too greatly. They have refused to recognize that policymaking involves not only the clear conception of ideas but also the management of men. In the process analysis has been too often identified with policymaking.

But the equivalence is not absolute, particularly if analysis is conceived too rigidly. Effective policy fits its measures to circumstances. Analysis strives to eliminate the accidental; it seeks principles of general validity. The policymaker is faced with situations where at some point discussion will be overtaken by events, where to delay for the sake of refinement of thought may invite disaster. Analysis, by contrast, can and must always sacrifice time to clarity; it is not completed until all avenues of research have been explored. The difference between the mode of policy and the mode of analysis is therefore one of perspective. Policy looks toward the future; its pace is dictated by the need for decision in a finite time. Analysis assumes an accomplished act or a given set of factors; its pace is the pace of reflection.

The difficulty arises not from the analytic method but from the failure to relate it to the problems of the policymaker. The quest for certainty, essential for analysis, may be paralyzing when pushed to extremes with respect to policy. The search for universality, which has produced so much of the greatest intellectual effort, may lead to something close to dogmatism in national affairs. The result can be a tendency to recoil before the act of choosing among alternatives which is inseparable from policymaking, and to ignore the tragic aspect of policymaking which lies precisely in its unavoidable component of conjecture. There can come about a temptation to seek to combine the advantage of every course of action; to delay commitment until "all the facts are in," until, that is, the future has been reduced to an aspect of the past.

As a consequence, on many issues the short-run and manipulative approach of the bureaucracy and its adjuncts is opposed, if at all, by an abstract, dogmatic moralism that all too often cannot be related to the problem at hand. The technicians who act as if the cold war were its own purpose are confronted by others who sometimes talk as if the cold war could be ended by redefining the term. The Machiavellianism of short-term expedients much too frequently has as its sole antagonist a Utopianism that seems more concerned with registering a dissent than with contributing a sense of direction. The self-righteousness that sees in conscientious co-ordinating procedures a sufficient gauge of valid policy is little affected by a perfectionism that segments policy into cycles of domestic and foreign concerns (do we have the moral right to act abroad as long as there is a Little Rock?); or by a fastidiousness that spends more energy on establishing a moral equivalence between our attitudes and those of Communism than on defining the moral content of what we stand for. (Since we and the Communists distrust each other, an attempt on our part to claim superior morality is the most certain means to prevent a lasting peace.)

Thus if the intellectual is to deepen national policy he faces a delicate task. He must steer between the Scylla of letting the bureaucracy prescribe what is relevant or useful and the Charybdis of defining these criteria too abstractly. If he inclines too much toward the former, he will turn into a promoter of technical remedies; if he chooses the latter, he will run the risks of confusing dogmatism with morality and of courting martyrdom—of becoming, in short, as wrapped up in a cult of rejection as the activist is in a cult of success.

Where to draw the line between excessive commitment to the bureaucracy and paralyzing aloofness depends on so many intangibles of circumstance and personality that it is difficult to generalize. Perhaps the matter can be stated as follows: one of the challenges of the contemporary situation is to demonstrate the overwhelming importance of purpose over technique. The intellectual should therefore not refuse to participate in policymaking, for to do so would confirm the administrative stagnation. But in co-operating, the intellectual has two loyalties: to the organization that employs him as well as to values which transcend the bureaucratic framework and which provide his basic motivation. It is important for him to remember that one of his contributions to the administrative process is his independence, and that one of his tasks is to seek to prevent unthinking routine from becoming an end in itself.

The intellectual must therefore decide not only whether to participate in the administrative process but also in what capacity: whether as an intellectual or as an administrator. If he assumes the former role, it is essential for him to retain the freedom to deal with the policymaker from a position of independence, and to reserve the right to assess the policymaker's demands in terms of his own standards. Paradoxically, this may turn out to be also most helpful to the policymaker. For the greater the bureaucratization and the more eminent the policymaker, the more difficult it is to obtain advice in which substantive considerations are not submerged by or at least identified with organizational requirements.

Such an attitude requires an occasional separation from administration. In all humility, the intellectual must guard his distinctive and in this particular context most crucial qualities: the pursuit of knowledge rather than of administrative ends, the perspective supplied by a nontechnical vantage point. It is therefore essential for him to return from time to time to his library or his laboratory to "recharge his batteries." If he fails to do this he will turn into an administrator, distinguished from some of his colleagues only by having been recruited from the intellectual community. Such a relationship does not preclude a major contribution. But it will then have to be in terms of the organization's criteria, which can be changed from within only by those in the most pre-eminent positions.

THE HIGHEST OF STAKES

Ultimately the problem is not the intellectual's alone or even primarily. There is no substitute for greater insight on the part of our executives, in or out of government. Advice cannot replace knowledge. Neither Churchill nor Lincoln nor Roosevelt was the product of a staff. As long as our executives conceive their special skill to be a kind of intuitive ability to choose among conflicting advice and as long as they see this skill largely in administrative or psychological but not substantive terms, their relationship with the intellectual will produce frustration as often as mutual support. The executive, while making a ritual of consulting the intellectual, will consider him hopelessly abstract or judge him by his suitability in achieving short-term ends. And the intellectual, while participating in the policymaking process, will always have the feeling that he never had a chance to present the most important considerations. The executives' lack of understanding of the process of reflection and the fragmented nature of their approach to policy causes them to place a premium on qualities in intellectuals which they can most easily duplicate in their own organization. It leads them to apply administrative criteria to the problems of creativity, thereby making it difficult to transcend the standards of the moment. The intellectuals' unfamiliarity with the management of men makes them overlook the difficulty in the application of their maxims.

The solution is not to turn philosophers into kings or kings into philosophers. But it is essential that our leadership groups overcome the approach to national issues as an extracurricular activity that does not touch the core of their concerns. The future course of our society is not a matter to be charted administratively. The specialization of functions turns into a caricature when decision making and the pursuit of knowledge on which it is based are treated as completely separate activities, by either executives or intellectuals. Our society requires above all to overcome its current lassitude, to risk itself on new approaches in a situation different from our historical expectation. This sense of purpose cannot come from a bureaucracy, and it will not come from our present leadership groups if they continue to see the challenge primarily as a succession of technical problems.

It is true that many of the difficulties described here are due to qualities which also account for the strength and vitality of our society. Against the background of our sudden projection into world affairs we have undoubtedly performed creditably. Unfortunately, our period offers no prizes for having done reasonably well; it does not permit us to rest on historical comparison. Our sole measure is our ability to contribute a sense of direction in a world in turmoil.

The stakes could hardly be higher. The deepest cause of the inhumanity of our time is probably the pedantic application of administrative norms. Its symbol may well be the "commissar," the ideal type of bureaucrat, who condemns thousands without love and without hatred simply in pursuance of an abstract duty. But we would do ourselves an injustice if we ignored that the commissar is not just a Soviet but a universal phenomenon—the Soviet system has simply encouraged it in its most extreme form. He is the administrator whose world is defined by regulations in whose making he had no part, and whose substance does not concern him, to whom reality is exhausted by the organization in which he finds himself. Our challenge is to rescue the individual from this process; to escape from the pretentiousness and stultifying quality of an atmosphere in which all sense of reverence for the unique is lost in the quest for reducing everything to manipulable quantities. The way we face this challenge will be the ultimate test of our long-proclaimed belief in the dignity of the individual.

POWER AND ADMINISTRATION
Norton Long

Norton Long is a Professor of Political Science at Brandeis University. A career educator, he formerly served as Director of the Education and Transportation Center at Northwestern University.

There is no more forlorn spectacle in the administrative world than an agency and a program possessed of statutory life, armed with executive orders, sustained in the courts, yet stricken with paralysis and deprived of power. An object of contempt to its enemies and of despair to its friends.

Reprinted from the *Public Administration Review*, the journal of the American Society for Public Administration, Autumn 1949, by permission of the publisher.

The lifeblood of administration is power. Its attainment, maintenance, increase, dissipation, and loss are subjects the practitioner and student can ill afford to neglect. Loss of realism and failure are almost certain consequences. This is not to deny that important parts of public administration are so deeply entrenched in the habits of the community, so firmly supported by the public, or so clearly necessary as to be able to take their power base for granted and concentrate on the purely professional side of their problems. But even these islands of the blessed are not immune from the plague of politics, as witness the fate of the hapless Bureau of Labor Statistics and the perennial menace of the blind 5 per cent across-the-board budget cut. Perhaps Carlyle's aphorism holds here, "The healthy know not of their health but only the sick." To stay healthy one needs to recognize that health is a fruit, not a birthright. Power is not only of the considerations that must be weighed in administration, but of all it is the most overlooked in theory and the most dangerous to overlook in practice.

The power resources of an administrator or an agency are not disclosed by a legal search of titles and court decisions or by examining appropriations or budgetary allotments. Legal authority and a treasury balance are necessary but politically insufficient bases of administration. Administrative rationality requires a critical evaluation of the whole range of complex and shifting forces on whose support, acquiescence, or temporary impotence the power to act depends.

Analysis of the sources from which power is derived and the limitations they impose is as much a dictate of prudent administration as sound budgetary procedure. The bankruptcy that comes from an unbalanced power budget has consequences far more disastrous than the necessity of seeking a deficiency appropriation. The budgeting of power is a basic subject matter of a realistic science of administration.

It may be urged that for all but the top hierarchy of the administrative structure the question of power is irrelevant. Legislative authority and administrative orders suffice. Power adequate to the function to be performed flows down the chain of command. Neither statute nor executive order, however, confers more than legal authority to act. Whether Congress or President can impart the substance of power as well as the form depends upon the line-up of forces in the particular case. A price control law wrung from a reluctant Congress by an amorphous and unstable combination of consumer and labor groups is formally the same as a law enacting a support price program for agriculture backed by the disciplined organizations of farmers and their congressmen. The differences for the scope and effectiveness of administration are obvious. The Presidency, like Congress, responds to and translates the pressures that play upon it. The real mandate contained in an Executive order varies with the political strength of the group demand embodied in it, and in the context of other group demands.

Both Congress and President do focus the general political energies of the community and so are considerably more than mere means for transmitting organized pressures. Yet power is not concentrated by the structure of government or politics into the hands of a leadership with a capacity to budget it among a diverse set of administrative activities. A picture of the Presidency as a reservoir of authority from which the lower echelons of administration draw life and vigor is an idealized distortion of reality.

A similar criticism applies to any like claim for an agency head in his agency. Only in varying degrees can the powers of subordinate officials be explained as resulting from the chain of command. Rarely is such an explanation a satisfactory account of the sources of power.

To deny that power is derived exclusively from superiors in the hierarchy is to assert that subordinates stand in a feudal relation in which to a degree they fend for themselves and acquire support peculiarly their own. A structure of interests friendly or hostile, vague and general or compact and well-defined, encloses each significant center of administrative discretion. This structure is an important determinant of the scope of possible action. As a source of power and authority it is a competitor of the formal hierarchy.

Not only does political power flow in from the sides of an organization, as it were; it also flows up the organization to the center from the constituent parts. When the staff of the Office of War Mobilization and Reconversion advised a hard-pressed agency to go out and get itself some popular support so that the President could afford to support it, their action reflected the realities of power rather than political cynicism.

It is clear that the American system of politics does not generate enough power at any focal point of leadership to provide the conditions for an even partially successful divorce of politics from administration. Subordinates cannot depend on the formal chain of command to deliver enough political power to permit them to do their jobs. Accordingly they must supplement the resources available through the hierarchy with those they can muster on their own, or accept the consequences in frustration—a course itself not without danger. Administrative rationality demands that objectives be determined and sights set in conformity with a realistic appraisal of power position and potential.

The theory of administration has neglected the problem of the sources and adequacy of power, in all probability because of a distaste for the disorderliness of American political life and a belief that this disorderliness is transitory. An idealized picture of the British parliamentary system as a Platonic form to be realized or approximated has exerted a baneful fascination in the field. The majority party with a mandate at the polls and a firmly seated leadership in the cabinet seems to solve adequately the problem of the supply of power necessary to permit administration to concentrate on the fulfillment of accepted objectives. It is a commonplace that the American party system provides neither a mandate for a platform nor a mandate for a leadership.

Accordingly, the election over, its political meaning must be explored by the diverse leaders in the executive and legislative branches. Since the parties have failed to discuss issues, mobilize majorities in their terms, and create a working political consensus on measures to be carried out, the task is left for others—most prominently the agencies concerned. Legislation passed and powers granted are frequently politically premature. Thus the Council of Economic Advisers was given legislative birth before political acceptance of its functions existed. The agencies to which tasks are assigned must devote themselves to the creation of an adequate consensus to permit administration. The mandate that the parties do not supply must be attained through public relations and the mobilization of group support. Pendleton Herring and others have shown just how vital this support is for agency action.

The theory that agencies should confine themselves to communicating policy suggestions to executive and legislature, and refrain from appealing to their clientele and the public, neglects the failure of the parties to provide either a clear-cut decision as to what they should do or an adequately mobilized political support for a course of action. The bureaucracy under the American political system has a large share of responsibility for the public promotion of policy and even more in organizing the political basis for its survival and growth. It is generally recognized that the agencies have a special competence in the technical aspects of their fields which of necessity gives them a rightful policy initiative. In addition, they have or develop a shrewd understanding of the politically feasible in the group structure within which they work. Above all, in the eyes of their supporters and their enemies they represent the institutionalized embodiment of policy, an enduring organization actually or potentially capable of mobilizing power behind policy. The survival interests and creative drives of administrative organizations combine with clientele pressures to compel such mobilization. The party system provides no enduring institutional representation for group interest at all comparable to that of the bureaus of the Department of Agriculture. Even the subject matter committees of Congress function in the shadow of agency permanency.

The bureaucracy is recognized by all interested groups as a major channel of representation to such an extent that Congress rightly feels the competition of a rival. The weakness in party structure both permits and makes necessary the present dimensions of the political activities of the administrative branch—permits because it fails to protect administration from pressures and fails to provide adequate direction and support, makes necessary because it fails to develop a consensus on a leadership and a program that makes possible administration on the basis of accepted decisional premises.

Agencies and bureaus more or less perforce are in the business of building, maintaining, and increasing their political support. They lead and in large part are led by the diverse groups whose influence sustains them. Frequently they lead and are themselves led in conflicting directions. This is not due to a dull-witted incapacity to see the contradictions in their behavior but is an almost inevitable result of the contradictory nature of their support.

Herbert Simon has shown that administrative rationality depends on the establishment of uniform value premises in the decisional centers or organization. Unfortunately, the value premises of those forming vital elements of political support are often far from uniform. These elements are in Barnard's and Simon's sense "customers" of the organization and therefore parts of the organization whose wishes are clothed with a very real authority. A major and most time-consuming aspect of administration consists of the wide range of activities designed to secure enough "customer" acceptance to survive and, if fortunate, develop a consensus adequate to program formulation and execution.

To varying degrees, dependent on the breadth of acceptance of their programs, officials at every level of significant discretion must make their estimates of the situation, take stock of their resources, and plan accordingly. A keen appreciation of the real components of their organization is the beginning of wisdom. These components will be found to stretch far beyond the government payroll. Within the government they will encompass Congress, congressmen, committees, courts, other agencies, presidential advisers, and the President. The Aristotelian analysis of constitutions is equally applicable and equally necessary to an understanding of administrative organization.

The broad alliance of conflicting groups that makes up presidential majorities scarcely coheres about any definite pattern of objectives, nor has it by the alchemy of the party system had its collective power concentrated in an accepted leadership with a personal mandate. The conciliation and maintenance of this support is a necessary condition of the attainment and retention of office involving, as Madison so well saw, "the spirit of party and faction in the necessary and ordinary operations of government." The President must in large part be, if not all things to all men, at least many things to many men. As a consequence, the contradictions in his power base invade administration. The often criticized apparent cross-purposes of the Roosevelt regime cannot be put down to inept administration until the political facts are weighed. Were these apparently self-defeating measures reasonably related to the general maintenance of the composite majority of the Administration? The first objective—ultimate patriotism apart—of the administrator is the attainment and retention of the power on which his tenure of office depends. This is the necessary pre-condition for the accomplishment of all other objectives.

The same ambiguities that arouse the scorn of the naive in the electoral campaigns of the parties are equally inevitable in administration and for the same reasons. Victory at the polls does not yield either a clear-cut grant of power or a unified majority support for a coherent program. The task of the Presidency lies in feeling out the alternatives of policy which are consistent with the retention and increase of the group support on which the Administration rests. The lack of a budgetary theory (so frequently deplored) is not due to any incapacity to apply rational analysis to the comparative contribution of the various activities of government to a determinate hierarchy of purposes. It more probably stems from a fastidious distaste for the frank recognition of the budget as a politically expedient allocation of resources. Appraisal in terms of their political contribution to the Administration provides almost a sole common denominator between the Forest Service and the Bureau of Engraving.

Integration of the administrative structure through an over-all purpose in terms of which tasks and priorities can be established is an emergency phenomenon. Its realization, only partial at best, has been limited to war and the extremity of depression. Even in wartime the Farm Bureau Federation, the American Federation of Labor, the Congress of Industrial Organizations, the National Association of Manufacturers, the Chamber of Commerce, and a host of lesser interests resisted coordination of themselves and the agencies concerned with their interests. A Presidency temporarily empowered by intense mass popular support acting in behalf of a generally accepted and simplified purpose can, with great difficulty, bribe, cajole, and coerce a real measure of joint action. The long-drawn-out battle for conversion and the debacle of orderly reconversion underline the difficulty of attaining, and the transitory nature of, popularly based emergency power. Only in crises are the powers of the Executive nearly adequate to impose a common plan of action on the executive branch, let alone the economy.

In ordinary times the manifold pressures of our pluralistic society work themselves out in accordance with the balance of force prevailing in Congress and the agencies. Only to a limited degree is the process subject to responsible direction or review by President or party leadership.

The program of the President cannot be a Gosplan for the government precisely because the nature of his institutional and group support gives him insufficient power. The personal unity of the Presidency cannot perform the function of Hobbes' sovereign since his office lacks the authority of Hobbes' contract. Single headedness in the executive gives no assurance of singleness of purpose. It only insures that the significant pressures in a society will be brought to bear on one office. Monarchy solves the problem of giving one plan to a multitude only when the plenitude of its authority approaches dictatorship. Impatient social theorists in all ages have turned to the philosopher king as a substitute for consensus. Whatever else he may become, it is difficult to conceive of the American president ruling as a philosopher king, even with the advice of the Executive Office. The monarchical solution to the administrative problems posed by the lack of a disciplined party system capable of giving firm leadership and a program to the legislature is a modern variant of the dreams of the eighteenth century savants and well nigh equally divorced from a realistic appraisal of social realities.

Much of the administrative thought, when it does not assume the value of coordination for coordination's sake, operates on the assumption that there must be something akin to Rousseau's *volonte generale* in administration to which the errant *volonte de tous* of the bureaus can and should be made to conform. This will-o'-the-wisp was made the object of an illuminating search by Pendleton Herring in his *Public Administration and the Public Interest*. The answer for Rousseau was enlightened dictatorship or counting the votes. The administrative equivalent to the latter is the resultant of the relevant pressures, as Herring shows. The first alternative seems to require at least the potency of the British Labour party and elsewhere has needed the disciplined organization of a fascist, nazi, or communist party to provide the power and consensus necessary to coordinate the manifold activities of government to a common plan.

Dictatorship, as Sigmund Neumann has observed, is a substitute for institutions which is required to fill the vacuum when traditional institutions break down. Force supplies the compulsion and guide to action in place of the normal routines of unconscious habit. Administrative organizations, however much they may appear the creations of art, are institutions produced in history and woven in the web of social relationships that gives them life and being. They present the same refractory material to the hand of the political artist as the rest of society of which they form a part.

Just as the economists have attempted to escape the complexities of institutional reality by taking refuge in the frictionless realm of theory, so some students of administration, following their lead, have seen in the application of the doctrine of opportunity costs a clue to a science of administration. Valuable as this may be in a restricted way, Marx has more light to throw on the study of institutions. It is in the dynamics and interrelations of institutions that we have most hope of describing and therefore learning to control administrative behavior.

The difficulty of coordinating government agencies lies not only in the fact that bureaucratic organizations are institutions having survival interests which may conflict with their rational adaptation to over-all purpose, but even more in their having roots in society. Coordination of the varied activities of a modern government almost of necessity involves a substantial degree of coordination of the economy. Coordination of government agencies involves far more than changing the behavior and offices of officials in Washington and the field. It involves the publics that are implicated in their normal functioning. To coordinate fiscal policy, agricultural policy, labor policy, foreign policy, and military policy, to name a few major areas, moves beyond the range of government charts and the habitat of the bureaucrats to the market place and to where the people live and work. This suggests that the reason why government reorganization is so difficult is that far more than government in the formal sense is involved in reorganization. One could overlook this in the limited government of the nineteenth century but the multi-billion dollar government of the mid-twentieth permits no facile dichotomy between government and economy. Economy and efficiency are the two objectives a laissez faire society can prescribe in peacetime as over-all government objectives. Their inadequacy either as motivation or standards has long been obvious. A planned economy clearly requires a planned government. But, if one can afford an unplanned economy, apart from gross extravagance, there seems no compelling and therefore, perhaps, no sufficiently powerful reason for a planned government.

Basic to the problem of administrative rationality is that of organizational identification and point of view. To whom is one loyal—unit, section, branch, division, bureau, department, administration, government, country, people, world history, or what? Administrative analysis frequently assumes that organizational identification should occur in such a way as to merge primary organization loyalty in a larger synthesis. The good of the part is to give way to the reasoned good of the whole. This is most frequently illustrated in the rationalizations used to counter self-centered demands of primary groups for funds and personnel. Actually the competition between governmental power centers, rather than the rationalizations, is the effective instrument of coordination.

Where there is a clear common product on whose successful production the sub-groups depend for the attainment of their own satisfaction, it is possible to demonstrate to almost all participants the desirability of cooperation. The shoe factory produces shoes, or else, for all concerned. But the government as a whole and many of its component parts have no such identifiable common product on which all depend. Like the proverbial Heinz, there are fifty-seven or more varieties unified, if at all, by a common political profit and loss account.

Administration is faced by somewhat the same dilemma as economics. There are propositions about the behavior patterns conducive to full employment—welfare economics. On the other hand, there are propositions about the economics of the individual firm—the counsel of the business schools. It is possible to show with considerable persuasiveness that sound considerations for the individual firm may lead to a depression if generally adopted, a result desired by none of the participants. However, no single firm can afford by itself to adopt the source of collective wisdom; in the absence of a common power capable of enforcing decisions premised on the supremacy of the collective interest, *sauve qui peut* is common sense.

The position of administrative organizations is not unlike the position of particular firms. Just as the decisions of the firms could be coordinated by the imposition of a planned economy so could those of the component parts of the government. But just as it is possible to operate a formally unplanned economy by the loose coordination of the market, in the same fashion it is possible to operate a government by the loose coordination of the play of political forces through its institutions.

The unseen hand of Adam Smith may be little in evidence in either case. One need not believe in a doctrine of social or administrative harmony to believe that formal centralized planning—while perhaps desirable and in some cases necessary—is not a must. The complicated logistics of supplying the city of New York runs smoothly down the grooves of millions of well adapted habits projected from a distant past. It seems naive on the one hand to believe in the possibility of a vast, intricate, and delicate economy operating with a minimum of formal over-all direction, and on the other to doubt that a relatively simple mechanism such as the government can be controlled largely by the same play of forces.

Doubtless the real reasons for seeking coordination in the government are the same that prompt a desire for economic planning. In fact, apart from waging war with its demand for rapid change, economic planning would seem to be the only objective sufficiently compelling and extensive to require a drastic change in our system of political laissez faire. Harold Smith, testifying before the Senate Banking and Currency Committee on the Employment Act of 1946, showed how extensive a range of hitherto unrelated activities could be brought to bear on a common purpose—the maintenance of maximum employment and purchasing power. In the flush of the war experience and with prophecies of reconversion unemployment, a reluctant Congress passed a pious declaration of policy. Senator Flanders has recorded the meager showing to date.

Nevertheless, war and depression apart, the Employment Act of 1946 for the first time provides at least a partial basis for the rational budgeting of government activities. The older concept of economy and efficiency as autonomous standards still lingers in Congress, but elsewhere their validity as ends in themselves is treated with skepticism.

If the advent of Keynesian economics and the erosion of laissez faire have created the intellectual conditions requisite for the formulation of over-all government policy, they do not by any means guarantee the political conditions necessary for its implementation. We can see quite clearly that the development of an integrated administration requires an integrating purpose. The ideals of Locke, Smith, Spencer, and their American disciples deny the need for such a purpose save for economy and efficiency's sake. Marx, Keynes, and their followers by denying the validity of the self-regulating economy have endowed the state with an over-arching responsibility in terms of which broad coordination, however, has run well ahead of the public's perception of it and of the development of a political channeling of power adequate to its administrative implementation.

Most students of administration are planners of some sort. Most congressmen would fly the label like the plague. Most bureaucrats, whatever their private faith, live under two jealous gods, their particular clientele and the loyalty check. Such a condition might, if it exists as described, cast doubt on whether even the intellectual conditions for rational administrative coordination exist. Be that as it may, the transition from a government organized in clientele departments and bureaus, each responding to the massive feudal power of organized business, organized agriculture, and organized labor, to a government integrated about a paramount national purpose will require a political power at least as great as that which tamed the earlier feudalism.

It takes a sharp eye or a tinted glass to see such an organized power on the American scene. Without it, administrative organization for over-all coordination has the academic air of South American constitution making. One is reminded of the remark attributed to the Austrian economist Mises; on being told that the facts did not agree with his theory, he replied *"desto schlechter fur die Tatsache."*

It is highly appropriate to consider how administrators should behave to meet the test of efficiency in a planned polity; but in the absence of such a polity and while, if we like, struggling to get it, a realistic science of administration will teach administrative behavior appropriate to the existing political system.

A close examination of the presidential system may well bring one to conclude that administrative rationality in it is a different matter from that applicable to the British ideal. The American Presidency is an office that has significant monarchical characteristics despite its limited term and elective nature. The literature on court and palace has many an insight applicable to the White House. Access to the President, reigning favorites, even the court jester, are topics that show the continuity of institutions. The maxims of LaRochefoucauld and the memoirs of the Duc de Saint Simon have a refreshing realism for the operator on the Potomac.

The problem of rival factions in the President's family is as old as the famous struggle between Jefferson and Hamilton, as fresh and modern as the latest cabal against John Snyder. Experience seems to show that this personal and factional struggle for the President's favor is a vital part of the process of representation. The vanity, personal ambition, or patriotism of the contestants soon clothes itself in the generalities of principle and the clique aligns itself with groups beyond the capital. Subordinate rivalry is tolerated if not encouraged by so many able executives that it can scarcely be attributed to administrative ineptitude. The wrangling tests opinion, uncovers information that would otherwise never rise to the top, and provides effective opportunity for decision rather than mere ratification of pre-arranged plans. Like most judges, the Executive needs to hear argument for his own instruction. The alternatives presented by subordinates in large part determine the freedom and the creative opportunity of their superiors. The danger of becoming a Merovingian is a powerful incentive to the maintenance of fluidity in the structure of power.

The fixed character of presidential tenure makes it necessary that subordinates be politically expendable. The President's men must be willing to accept the blame for failures not their own. Machiavelli's teaching on how princes must keep the faith bears re-reading. Collective responsibility is incompatible with a fixed term of office. As it tests the currents of public opinion, the situation on the Hill, and the varying strength of the organized pressures, the White House alters and adapts the complexion of the Administration. Loyalties to programs or to groups and personal pride and interest frequently conflict with whole-souled devotion to the Presidency. In fact, since such devotion is not made mandatory by custom, institutions, or the facts of power, the problem is perpetually perplexing to those who must choose.

The balance of power between executive and legislature is constantly subject to the shifts of public and group support. The latent tendency of the American Congress is to follow the age-old parliamentary precedents and to try to reduce the President to the role of constitutional monarch. Against this threat and to secure his own initiative, the President's resources are primarily demagogic, with the weaknesses and strengths that dependence on mass popular appeal implies. The unanswered question of American government—"who is boss?"—constantly plagues administration. The disruption of unity of command is not just the problem of Taylor's functional foreman, but goes to the stability and uniformity of basic decisional premises essential to consequent administration.

It is interesting to speculate on the consequences for administration of the full development of congressional or presidential government. A leadership in Congress that could control the timetable of the House and Senate would scarcely content itself short of reducing the President's Cabinet to what in all probability it was first intended to be, a modified version of the present Swiss executive. Such leadership could scarcely arise without centrally organized, disciplined, national parties far different from our present shambling alliances of state and local machines.

A Presidency backed by a disciplined party controlling a majority in Congress would probably assimilate itself to a premiership by association of legislative leadership in the formulation of policy and administration. In either line of development the crucial matter is party organization. For the spirit of the party system determines the character of the government.

That the American party system will develop toward the British ideal is by no means a foregone conclusion. The present oscillation between a strong demagogic Presidency and a defensively powerful congressional oligarchy may well prove a continuing pattern of American politics, as it was of Roman. In the absence of a party system providing an institutionalized centripetal force in our affairs, it is natural to look to the Presidency as Goldsmith's weary traveler looked to the throne.

The Presidency of the United States, however, is no such throne as the pre-World War I *Kaiserreich* that provided the moral and political basis for the Prussian bureaucracy. Lacking neutrality and mystique, it does not even perform the function of the British monarchy in providing a psychological foundation for the permanent civil service. A leaderless and irresponsible Congress frequently makes it appear the strong point of the republic. The Bonapartist experience in France, the Weimar Republic, and South American examples nearer home, despite important social differences, are relevant to any thoughtful consideration of building a solution to legislative anarchy on the unity of the executive.

The present course of American party development gives little ground for optimism that a responsible two party system capable of uniting Congress and Executive in a coherent program will emerge. The increasingly critical importance of the federal budget for the national economy and the inevitable impact of world power status on the conduct of foreign affairs make inescapable the problem of stable leadership in the American system. Unfortunately they by no means insure a happy or indeed any solution.

Attempts to solve administrative problems in isolation from the structure of power and purpose in the polity are bound to prove illusory. The reorganization of Congress to create responsibility in advance of the development of party responsibility was an act of piety to principle, of educational value; but as a practical matter it raised a structure without foundation. In the same way, reorganization of the executive branch to centralize administrative power in the Presidency while political power remains dispersed and divided may effect improvement, but in a larger sense it must fail. The basic prerequisite to the administration of the textbooks is a responsible two party system. The means to its attainment are a number one problem for students of administration. What Schattschneider calls the struggle for party government may sometime yield us the responsible parliamentary two party system needed to underpin our present administrative theory. Until that happy time, exploration of the needs and necessities of our present system is a high priority task of responsible scholarship.

THE EXECUTIVE AND THE PUBLIC INTEREST
Harlan Cleveland

Now American ambassador to NATO, Harlan Cleveland was Assistant Secretary of State for International Organization Affairs under Presidents Kennedy and Johnson. Prior to that he served as Dean of the Maxwell Graduate School of Citizenship and Public Affairs at Syracuse University. He is a former editor of *The Reporter* magazine.

About eleven years ago, I was sitting against the wall of a Senate committee room, watching two political executives sell a lend-lease appropriation to the greatest, or at least the most deliberative, body in the world. My capacity on this occasion was as a briefcase carrier—one of those anonymous civil servants who sit behind government witnesses at these affairs, handing them scribbled calculations and bits of advice on bits of paper. The witnesses were Leo Crowley, the Wisconsin politician who headed the Foreign Economic Administration, and his deputy Oscar Cox, who as one of the New Deal's brightest lawyers had drafted that extraordinary piece of legislation, the Lend-Lease Act.

From *The Annals of the American Academy of Political and Social Science,* September 1956. Reprinted by permission.

The scene was a study in contrast. Crowley seemed more senatorial than the Senators, a languid, paunchy man with a mane of white hair, a florid complexion, and a deceptively benign expression. Cox was thin and efficient, his jerky gestures matching his crisp and factual eloquence. He was easy to carry a briefcase for: he already knew its contents by heart.

Most of the questions were taken by Cox. Before a Senator had finished asking his question, Cox was way ahead of him, guessing what was on his mind and starting to reply in impressive, uncompromising detail. Crowley leaned back, utterly relaxed, sometimes putting in a comment or telling a joke to keep things moving. Finally a Senator asked Crowley a question about one of the most intricate features of the lend-lease program, and I learned an important lesson.

"Well, I'll tell you, Senator," Crowley said in his Middle-Western accent, "I've always wondered how that works too. Let's see if Oscar can explain it to us."

Soon the hearing was over, the lesson complete. Two or three of the Senators were clapping Crowley on the back, saying what a fine presentation he had made. Cox, who had made it, was alone at the other end of the room, stuffing his papers back into his efficient-looking briefcase.

ADMINISTRATION AND POLITICS

A discussion of that political animal, the government executive, should start with some picture of the jungle in which he lives and works and, if he is fit enough, survives. From the requirements of survival in this jungle, the talents needed by the top political executives can readily be deduced. Beyond this we need to consider the civil servant as a political executive.

Let us start with the proposition that government is a mixture of politics and administration, accommodation and logic, consent and decisions—a blend, in short, of Crowley and Cox.

We instinctively demand that our Presidents be "double firsts"—that they be great politicians and great administrators too. Of course they usually do not succeed on both counts. Franklin Roosevelt, who is possibly unsurpassed in this century as a builder of consent in war and peace, was as casual an administrator as ever hit Washington. Harry Truman, whose reputation and training were in politics, proved himself an able and orderly administrator, but when it came to building consent for a government program he can hardly be rated better than fair. President Eisenhower, whose forte was military administration, has combined a remarkable talent for evoking consent with an equally remarkable tendency to appoint as administrators of his policies men who disagree with them.

Yet if we seldom or never get quite the perfect Presidential blend, we continue to pine for that rare amalgam—the man who can run the executive branch and still get along with most of the other Americans, in and out of Congress, who think they are anointed to run the government too.

What is not so clear in much of the literature of public administration is the fact that every official of the executive branch must in some measure combine the two qualities we look for in a President, the ability to manage and the talent to build political support for what is managed. In my own limited experience and observation, I have yet to encounter a government official with any responsibility at all who did not have this dual function. Mark this proposition well: it is bedrock to everything I have to say on this subject. Government is a mixture of administration and politics all the way up and down the line, not merely at something called the political level where people called political executives get jobs by a process called political appointment. As Peter Odegard puts it, "Policy and administration are the Siamese twins of politics and are associated at virtually all levels of the administrative structure." Or, as Paul Appleby wrote back in 1945, "So long as the people vote and have unrestrained the right to complain, the whole process of administration is in a sense political on every level."

Does this seem obvious? Does it go without saying that, in a free society, government is politics? I shall be glad if you agree so quickly. But I should give fair warning: if you take seriously what I have just said, you will, I think, have to disagree with much of what the second Hoover Commission on Organization of the Executive Branch of the Government has said in its 1955 Report on Personnel and Civil Service.

THE DIFFUSION OF POWERS

What is it about our government that makes it so political a jungle? The standard explanation is the constitutional separation of powers, the built-in checks and balances, the fact that everybody is in every act but nobody seems to be in charge of the performance.

Woodrow Wilson called this "administration by semi-independent executive agents who obey the dictation of a legislature to which they are not responsible." He was sure that Congress ran the show, described legislation as "the originating force," and complained that the "blind processes" resulting from the division of power made that power irresponsible. But Wilson was too pessimistic about the ability of the government to function in spite of this division of power and purposes—or better, perhaps, because of it.

He was certainly overimpressed with the power of the legislature in his academic days, though as President he later underestimated its veto power when it came to getting the League of Nations ratified. The legislature is powerful and can do a massive wrecking job, as we know from our own recent history. But the men who wrote our Constitution were clear about the "dangers from legislative usurpations." "One hundred and seventy-three despots would surely be as oppressive as one," Madison said in one of the Federalist papers; ". . . an elective despotism was not the government we fought for."

Despite the periodic flurries of legislative usurpation, we do not have an elective despotism. But we do have a Congress that participates with appalling vigor in the task of running the executive branch of the government. We have, indeed, a system that not only separates the general constitutional powers but diffuses the power of decision on quite specific matters. One of the very first things I ever had to do in Washington, as an "intern" in the office of Senator "Young Bob" LaFollette, was to stand in for the Senator at a hearing in the Veterans Administration on a compensation case. I recall being struck at the time by the distortion of functions thus dramatized: here I was, a legislative bureaucrat horning in on the efforts of executive bureaucrats to perform a judicial function.

Each official in each branch of the government has a chance to exercise two (and occasionally even three) of the constitutional powers at once; and by the same token, each of the three branches sooner or later gets a crack at nearly every major public issue.

The result of this diffusion of power is not merely, as Peter Odegard says, that "Congress has ... found ways and means for interposing itself between the President and his executive subordinates and thus confusing the clear line of bureaucratic responsibility." Each executive official, whether politically appointed or not, has to spend an unconscionable amount of his time and energy telling Congress what he is doing, and why. In my last year with the Mutual Security Agency, I spent the equivalent of six months out of the twelve preparing and presenting on Capitol Hill the detailed exposition of the program I was supposed to be helping "administer."

CONGRESSIONAL COALITIONS

Nor is it enough for an administrator to defend a program from political attack. He finds himself actively promoting a political coalition in its support. For our Congress, which I have heard described to a group of visiting Frenchmen as a model of party discipline, is of course as choice an example of coalition government as the notorious French Assembly.

If there is any doubt that Congress is managed by complex, *ad hoc* coalitions which shift with every issue, look for a moment at the record of the Eighty-third Congress. In this supposedly Republican Congress, the fluctuating balance of power swung against the administration on foreign aid and public housing, but supported the President on farm price supports and (by one vote) the Bricker Amendment. A coalition majority could be put together for confirming the New Deal, reducing taxes, hitting slightly the funds for defense, continuing the 1950 version of United States foreign policy, and allowing some of its committees to trample on Executive toes. On hardly any of these issues could one party get its way solely with the votes it could deliver from its own side of the aisle.

We see the same pattern operating in the Eighty-fourth Congress, which is theoretically led by the Democrats. There was an excellent example in the Senate last spring, when thirty-one Republicans and twenty-two Democrats beat twenty-four Democrats and fourteen Republicans and sent the natural gas bill to Thomasville, Georgia, to be vetoed by a Republican President.

Because Congress is the way it is, every executive must help splice together the particular coalition that will pass his appropriation and protect his program and his reputation from damage. (His coalition may be very different from another one being fashioned for a different purpose by a colleague in the next office.) If every executive has congressional relations as an important segment of his duties—even though he may not himself carry a bulging briefcase up Pennsylvania Avenue to the "Hill"—every executive has to have some of the instincts of a politician. In this sense, the "political executives" in the government are not just the holders of those seven to eight hundred "noncareer executive" posts to which the Hoover Commission Report refers. The number of officials who are involved in this kind of politics is actually well up in the thousands. Under our constitutional diffusion of powers, the federal government would hardly operate at all if they were fewer.

THE INSIDE TRACK

Many distinguished writers have pondered whether the American Congress adequately represents the American people, but this is an academic question about which I have never been able to get excited. For the American people do not limit their representation in Washington to electing half a thousand Congressmen. The people are directly represented in the executive branch, too.

When I say "the people," I mean what David Riesman intends by the phrase "veto groups." In *The Lonely Crowd,* Riesman observed that political leadership has passed from businessmen as a class to . . . a series of groups, each of which has struggled for and finally attained a power to stop things conceivably inimical to its interests and, within far narrower limits, to start things. . . . Among the veto groups competition is monopolistic; rules of fairness and fellowship dictate how far one can go.

The tidelands group refrained from going too far; the natural-gas lobby, consisting of some of the same people, so outraged the public conscience that a President thought to be favorable to its objectives had to turn against the natural-gas bill. The farm group's effective power is enormous; the smaller effectiveness of the labor group may be traced, at least in part, to the fact that it overplayed its hand during the New Deal.

What Riesman did not mention is the fact that the power of these new-style lobbies can be roughly measured by the strength of their surrogates within the executive branch of the government. The Department of Agriculture has long been regarded, by both the farm organizations and the rest of the government, as a farmers' defense league inside the federal bureaucracy. Organized labor, particularly the Congress of Industrial Organizations, substantially controlled the National Labor Relations Board during the period (in the 1930's) when the Board was clearing the way for the rapid expansion of the CIO. The housing program, created by the New Deal for the purpose of getting houses built, placed itself in the hands of the speculative builders and the savings and loan associations to such an extent that moral corruption shaded over into pecuniary corruption. The organized veterans have their own preserve in the Veterans Administration. The Commerce Department has for some years had a Business Advisory Council whose function, in effect, is to bring to bear on internal government decisions an organized business opinion. Defense contracts are habitually given out by men recruited from the businesses that are getting the business, and regulations are drafted by surrogates of the industries to which they apply. The National Recovery Act was declared unconstitutional early in the New Deal, but "self-government of industry" is an established practice with a venerable tradition behind it.

During the Korean War, John Corson has said, ". . . the Office of Price Stabilization official in charge of price regulations for the apparel industry (in 1951) was borrowed from a leading firm in this industry. His aide, who specializes in women's woven underwear, is "on loan" from Barbizon, one of the principal competing manufacturers in this field. A succession of five or more chiefs of the Iron and Steel Division in the National Production Authority have been loaned by their companies, the major companies in the steel industry. The acting director of the Equipment and Materials Division of the Defense Transport Administration for most of 1951 was on loan from the American Car and Foundry Company. He actively promoted, for the Defense Transport Administrator, a plea that the NPA make available sufficient steel to build ten thousand freight cars a quarter; his firm meanwhile is engaged in the production of freight cars.

From time to time this sort of thing gets out of bounds, as in the recent cases of Air Force Secretary Talbott and Chairman Hugh Cross of the Interstate Commerce Commission, both of whom admitted error in using their official positions to advance their private interests. Much more often, there is no formal "conflict of interest." It is considered normal and natural for a steel man to lubricate with government contracts the growth of steel production; for a housing man to get more housing built by having the government absorb a good part of the risk; for a farmers' representative to promote aid for farmers from inside the Department of Agriculture; for a labor organizer temporarily in the government to promote the right of labor to organize. We have institutionalized the inside track.

OUTSIDE INTERESTS AND THE PUBLIC INTEREST

The political executive consequently has to do more than run his shop and deal with Congress. He has to maintain a complex network of horizontal relations with the veto groups whose interests his actions may affect, with others who think their interests might be affected, and with the surrogates of these groups in both the executive and legislative branches of the government.

I am trying hard not to pass any moral judgment on this system, but merely to describe how it seems to work. Given the nature of our society, it is almost bound to work this way. The government is, after all, the least bureaucratic of the major interest groups with which it has to deal. Turnover of government personnel is high, especially at the top. Even if this were not true for other reasons, we make sure of it by having reasonably frequent elections. The same is not true of the major aggregations of veto power outside: in business, labor, agriculture, and a good many other categories, elections are merely a facade for maintaining the same leadership from year to year and even from decade to decade. If you do not like the President of the United States, you can vote against him every four years. If you do not like the President of General Motors or the head of a labor union, you can only wait for him to die.

The difference in tenure between government and outside interest groups is critical. If the outside leaders know more about the subject than their opposite numbers inside the government, if they are providing key experts, advisers, and sometimes even the political executives themselves, the views of the regulated are likely to be pretty influential with the regulators. In the United States, the road to the riskless society that Europeans call socialism is paved with the incestuous intention of nearly every major economic interest to bring the government into its affairs as the risk-taking partner.

Where, in this picture, does the "public interest" appear? Not, certainly, through the organized political parties, which inflate like balloons at election time and are of small consequence in governmental decision making the rest of the time. No, the defense of the public interest rests in the hands of the people as a whole, who cannot do anything much about it, and of the President they elect, who can.

THE BUCK PASSES UP

Whether, under our system, the government ultimately serves the public interest or merely obliges the private and sectional Trojan horses encamped inside the walls of the federal bureaucracy, depends on the President to an extraordinary and alarming degree. He is the chief mediator among the veto groups, the one political executive whose whole job is to consider the situation as a whole. He is the one remaining safety man available to stop a specialized interest which breaks through the normal line of checks and balances and threatens to gain too much yardage at the expense of other groups.

In a revealing passage of his autobiography, Mr. Truman regarded it as quite natural that nobody should consider the public interest but the President:

> I was always aware of the fact that not all my advisers looked at the problem in the same manner I did. This was nothing unusual, of course. It is

the job of the military planners to consider all matters first and always in the light of military considerations. The diplomat's approach is—or in any case should be—determined by considerations of our relations to other nations. The Secretary of the Treasury thinks in terms of budget and taxes. Except for the members of his personal staff, each Presidential adviser has and should have a departmental outlook.

Though we sometimes make gods or supermen of our Presidents, they have not generally been more moral than most of us. The difference is that in the White House they are compelled to stand a little higher on the mountain than anybody else, and they consequently see farther at the horizon. It is this unique and lonely vantage point that lends grandeur to the American Presidency.

Not More Decisions

Yet the President's high rank does not necessarily mean that he makes more "decisions" than other political executives below. Indeed it is arguable that in our government the higher one's rank the fewer decisions one makes. The man who buys paper clips makes a number of unreviewed decisions without consultation—what size and shape of paper clip, from whom to buy, at what price. As you go up the ladder of authority each official is beset with more committees, more horizontal clearances, more veto groups and political personalities whose views must be reconciled or discounted before the "final decision" is reached.

I once tried to get this important idea across to a very bright businessman who had just been appointed a division director and had promptly started to operate as if he were solely responsible for the program co-ordinated by that division. One day, months after he had taken office, I knew he would survive the transition to becoming a public servant, for he came to me and said: "I'm director of this program, but that doesn't mean I direct anybody, does it? I mean I don't make any decisions. I'm really a sort of broker, I guess."

The President's role as chief broker makes possible a certain order in the bureaucratic jungle. It is no accident that matters which frequently get to the White House are so often better handled than matters that do not. The Housing Agency worked off in a corner by itself for years, dealing direct with the housing industry and hardly ever creating a crisis requiring Presidential attention. As a result corrupt practices like "mortgaging out" under Section 608 came to be regarded by some as the natural order of things until Congress finally made a political scandal of it. The foreign aid program, on the other hand, has spent more than fifty billion dollars since World War II, with hardly a trace of scandal. Why? Could it be because so many departments and agencies were always fighting for the right to manage foreign aid that the program was a matter of monthly, even weekly, concern to the President himself?

The saving grace of our executive bureaucracy, then, is that nearly every-body in it works for the President. To be sure, each political executive is also responsible horizontally to four or five congressional committees; he has to deal with several outside interest groups whose leaders feel the execu-tive is answerable to them; and within the executive branch he is constantly evading his own responsibility by burying it in collective decisions by inter-departmental committees. But when the chips are down on any one issue, all political executives are accountable to the President—which is another way of saying that if they get into a tight spot, they can generally pass the buck to him.

The King Can Do No Wrong

The buck passes up: many of the most serious crises in our govern-ment's operations come from temporary lapses in following the first law of the jungle. Many elements of the present federal security system—a major subject in itself when it comes to considering why it is so hard to get and keep good political executives—are a travesty of this principle. For the system legitimizes the downward passing of the buck, and even prepares ahead of time an endless file of scapegoats for administrative error and sacrificial lambs for periodic congressional slaughter. It encourages a rever-sion to the old English principle that the King can do no wrong: if the government errs, it must be some spy in the ointment. One lesson of our recent madness is clear—legislative usurpation generally takes the form of trying to find the disloyal official down the line on whom the blame for bad policy can be laid. The depth of the Army-McCarthy crisis was revealed when it became clear that Secretary Stevens, Counsel John Adams, and General Zwicker were to be left standing out in the rain without the um-brella of Presidential backing. The natural-law reply to that insistent ques-tion, "Who promoted Peress?" was always plain: "The President did. Want to make something of it?"

Perhaps the Hoover Commission Task Force had this in mind when it declared: "Public servants who are unfairly attacked deserve to be de-fended, and the public interest also requires it. . . . Defense is the corollary of discipline. Both are essential." Government is politics, but the executive branch has to be run by executives. And in government as in other hier-archies, the buck can travel in one direction only—up.

QUALITIES OF LEADERSHIP

The habitat of both political executive and civil servant is thus a political government. To be successful every government official needs to be aware of outside considerations, available to the concerned committees of the Con-gress, willing to work in a goldfish bowl, earnest in cultivating his public relations—because his personal public relations are the relations between the people and their government. He must be adept—increasingly so as he rises in rank and responsibility—in helping to build the coalition of outside forces which will provide a "political base" for the program in his charge. He must therefore not be afraid to advocate new policies if he thinks the old ones are worn out, nor can he flinch from becoming identified with the administration of which he is a part and defending his program in public. Since every government executive is something of a political executive, these are to some extent the conditions of work for bureaucrats at every level. They are the main conditions of work for an executive near the top of the heap, whether he is appointed from the outside or lifted out of the civil service from within.

In this jungle of close decisions, openly arrived at, the political executive must have certain natural talents and certain acquired tastes. Everybody who has given any thought to public administration has his pet list of these qualities. Here is mine.

Imbued with the Public Interest

First, he must be imbued with the public interest.

When I was a child, I was told to ask myself three questions before opening my mouth to say anything: "Is it kind? Is it true? Is it necessary?" If I had remembered this advice very often, silence would nearly always have overtaken speech.

Whenever a political executive says, does, or decides anything, he also needs to ask himself a question: Where does the public interest lie? The public interest cannot of course be defined in general. But in our society we have a pretty fair index ready at hand, if we approach each action or decision with the following query, in mind: Would this decision—and the procedure by which it was made—stand the test of detailed public scrutiny?

Asking this question must be second nature, automatic, instinctive. It was not all, in many a famous political scandal. In our own time General Vaughan did not have it on his mind during the deep-freeze affair. The men who tried to slip Dixon-Yates in through the back door (when they could have carried out the Eisenhower power policy by less circuitous and more durable means) must surely have forgotten to ask themselves what would happen if somebody wanted to know what was going on.

There are, of course, a few public officials who never do get the word, even when forcibly reminded. Several days after resigning as Secretary of the Air Force under a conflict-of-interest cloud, Harold Talbott turned up at a Southampton, Long Island, hotel in an Air Force vehicle and was helped in with his baggage by two or three Air Force officers. The action raised the question whether Mr. Talbott had any idea at all what had hit him in Washington.

General Matthew B. Ridgway, in a recent article in the *Saturday Evening Post,* revealed a different kind of fuzziness.

> As Chief of Staff (he wrote) I quickly learned that though my own recommendations were made on a purely military basis, the decision of the Defense Department were based on considerations other than clear-cut military needs. They were based on budgetary considerations, political considerations, on the advantage to be gained in the field of domestic politics by a drastic reduction in military expenditures . . .

How does one get to be a four-star general without learning that at the government level there is no such thing as a decision which is "purely military" or purely anything else, whether the public official making the decision is in or out of uniform?

The retort of President Eisenhower, who had one more star and a little civilian experience to guide him, was right to the point:

> His responsibility for national defense is, you might say, a special one, or, in a sense, parochial. He does not have the over-all responsibility that is borne by the Commander in Chief, and by him alone, when it comes down to making the recommendations to the Congress.

Leader of Men

Second, the political executive must be a leader of men, with a "sense of action." The very size of the government, and the complexity of the horizontal clearances, required to make anything happen, create the temptation to assume that somebody else has the initiative, that it is the other fellow's move. For the effective bureaucrat, it is always his own move.

Chester Barnard has written that a leader needs five qualities: vitality and endurance, decisiveness, persuasiveness, a sense of responsibility, and intellectual capacity—in that order of importance. He points out that only the last, intellectual capacity, can be increased by training. For the rest, . . . there is no substitute for the experience of recognizing and seizing opportunities, or for making one's own place unaided and against interference and obstacles; for these kinds of ability are precisely those that followers expect in leaders.

I suspect that Mr. Barnard would agree that for the political executive intellectual capacity should rank higher on his list than last place. A political executive, unlike a business executive, cannot possibly delegate his thinking to a vice-president for ideas. It is a condition of survival in the jungle that he do his own homework and be in intellectual command of the subject matter of the program for which he is responsible. When a congressional committee or an important "veto group" wants to know the story and asks embarrassing questions, no understudy with a mimeographed statement will fill the bill.

His Own Public Relations Man

Third, it is obvious from our earlier survey of the jungle that the political executive must be his own public relations man. One reason businessmen get into trouble in government is that many of them are accustomed to delegating to others the task of dealing with the public. In January 1953, toward the end of two long days of senatorial hearings on his General Motors stock holdings, Charles E. Wilson revealed how much he had learned about public relations at the age of sixty-two.

> The thing that perhaps I overlooked myself (he mused) was that not only did I have to operate honestly and fairly without prejudice, but all the people should also think that that was the way I was operating, and that part of it I did not quite appraise.

Where had he been? Presumably producing cars and trucks while somebody else worried about what the public would think.

The contrasting case is of course that of Paul Hoffman. By handling his own public relations from the start, he sold the Marshall Plan and himself in the same package: to millions of people in the early days of that singular project, he was the Marshall Plan. And his ideas about public relations permeated the organization he built to administer the European recovery program. I remember his telling us once in a staff meeting that we should answer every letter the day it came in, even if all we could say was that we would reply in detail later on. "When I ran a filling station," he went on, "I found that a man wouldn't wait for gas more than two or three minutes if nobody paid any attention to him. But if you gave him a big hello and explained that there were several cars ahead of him, he would sit there quite happily for a quarter of an hour!"

A Mixed Career

Fourth, the political executive should, preferably, have a mixed career. It has often been a mistake to bring into the government, especially in very high posts, men who have never before worked with or in a public bureaucracy, who have never had to live with the "public interest" from day to day. But it is also true that a lifetime public servant lacks something if he never leaves the bureaucracy; he loses track of the concerns which most of the people think about most of the time. Indeed, the very experience of dealing, year in and year out, with matters of great scale and moment can be a narrowing one; I am sure I am not the only ex-government person to whom the thousands looked like millions for a few months after leaving Washington.

It is beyond my scope in this paper—and probably beyond my powers anyway—to set forth a neat procedure to make sure that prospective political executives in the civil service get some private experience and budding

Assistant Secretaries now in private business or universities or foundations try the bureaucracy for a while. But I would be willing to bet that an objective study of political executives over the last generation would reveal that men with mixed careers behind them had been more effective and lasted longer in their jobs than those less favored by variety in their lives.

A Rare Combination

That is the list. Our political executive must be imbued with the public interest; he must be a leader of men; he must do his own thinking and be his own public relations man; and he should preferably have had some public and some private experience. As the Hoover Commission's Task Force noted:

> The combination of abilities is relatively rare. . . . His foresight must equal the hindsight of a host of critics, both amateur and professional, who are free to be as narrow in their point of view and time perspective as they care to be. The rules of the game of national politics allow no margin for error . . . To lead the life of a political executive of high rank amidst the asperities of American politics is a test of toughness, of intelligence, and of devotion to the public interest.

"Such talents," the Task Force concluded with classic understatement, "are valuable to the Nation but hard to find."

"DRAWING A LINE"

How far down from the President should political appointment and political expendability be the rule? On this, the perennial question in discussions of civil service reform, the Hoover Commission and its Task Force were very clear: A sharp line must be drawn between political and administrative functions. And when they draw it, what a curious boundary it turns out to be.

The second Hoover Commission must be seen as a recession in the seventy-year drive to have civil servants take over the government. From Wilson's professorial days until a few years ago, the general idea has been to reduce to a minimum the number of jobs with a tinge of politics. Wilson himself was not sure, when he published *Congressional Government* in 1885, whether the Secretaries in the Cabinet should be regarded as political or nonpolitical officers. The idea of a strong civil service has been so powerful in this country—even if the prestige of the actual civil service has not—that as late as December 1952 a National Planning Association report seriously suggested that most or all of the President's own staff should be drawn from the career service.

But the reformers overshot their mark. More and more people, especially those who had to run the executive branch of the government, became concerned about the short supply of political executives good enough and knowledgeable enough to manage the government of our big democracy. The second Hoover Commission therefore kept its enthusiasm for civil service reform within bounds, and sought to enlarge the number of political executives, now about seven or eight hundred by Hoover Commission count —though it prudently did not say how many more political executives there should be. Then it added a proposal for a senior civil service of 1,500 to 3,000 individuals, a special tribe of career men and women who have demonstrated their ability to survive and advance in the bureaucracy and are rewarded with personal rank and the permission to serve in any agency that will hire them.

Task Force Definitions

The Task Force wisely abandoned the traditional idea that you can distinguish between two kinds of people, those who determine policies and those who carry them out. But firm in their resolve to separate the political transients from the permanent boarders, the experts laid out a more complicated boundary line, more appropriate to the uneven terrain. Political executives should, they said, be appointed to:

> a) All positions filled by Presidential appointment, with or without confirmation by the Senate;
> b) All positions having vested in them statutory authority or executive delegations of authority requiring the incumbents to make final decisions in the establishment of governing policies, programs, objectives, and in the enunciation of principles which will control the action of subordinates in the implementation of the foregoing;
> c) All positions, the duties of which require the incumbents to act publicly in advocating new policies and in justifying or defending the governing policies or the basic principles or philosophy which controls their department or agency policies. Such duties would include direct participation with, or representation of noncareer executives in public debate, evaluate discussions, and justifications of departmental policies, programs, or activities.
> d) Most positions of a personal and confidential nature, such as personal aides, confidential secretaries, and personal chauffeurs. . . .

Article of Faith

I confess that all this enthusiasm for drawing a sharp line between politicos and careerists leaves me very cold. It is, I know, an article of passionate faith that pervades the literature on this subject. Hardly a month goes by without a scholarly admonition about the "rigid protection of bureau chiefs from political connections and duties"; or a civil service advocate making the misleading analogy between a lawyer's advice to his client and a civil servant's advice to his politically appointed boss; or an expert viewing with alarm the fact that government, the product of politics, is political. In a recent book, Dr. Leonard D. White argues the point so vigorously that in one passage about the making of decisions he draws a rather unattractive picture of a civil servant:

> At the highest levels, only the confidence that comes from an inner conviction of the "rightness" of a course of action and the moral support that comes from the representative capacity of the man who must act can sustain the strength to decide. The career service does not normally breed this type. Its decisions are based primarily on the logic of efficiency rather than on the calculated risks of an uncertain future.

How Government Works

Of course a line does have to be drawn, in the sense that you have to distinguish which jobs are going to be filled by political appointment and vacated by political action, and which jobs are going to be filled by civil servants and vacated under Civil Service safeguards. For this purpose the Hoover boundary is as good as any. What I object to is the Commission's quite unrealistic picture of what will be going on below that line: the image of an executive branch with a few political chiefs making policy and publicly defending it, while the drones below are carefully screened off from the ugly realities of the world of politics. But is this truly the way the government works, or the way a government under our Constitution can possibly work?

The Hoover group draws its line between "departmental management" and "bureau management." Thus in the New Deal Department of Agriculture, the heads of the Agricultural Adjustment Administration, the Farm Security Administration, and the policy-making Bureau of Agricultural Economics, all of whom ran highly controversial programs, would have been career men. Could Congress be kept from summoning such men as witnesses to explain their actions? Should such men as these be protected from the effort to explain to farm groups and business groups and labor groups and the press why they think their innovations are in the public interest? If a ranking bureaucrat cannot help build public support for the segment of the government's work for which he is responsible, is he even the right man for the job? Is there really this clear distinction between "factual material" and the policies which rest on them, between diagnosis and prescription, between "government" and "politics"?

SOURCES OF CONFUSION

The Commission's vision of how the government should work "below the line" strikes me as so exotic that I have tried very hard to think how this dreamworld came into being. There are, I think, three sources of confusion. One may be a misreading of British experience. Another source of confusion is the idea that the erection of defenses against the spoils system is still the cardinal item on the good-government agenda. And a third derangement stems from a concept of "political neutrality" which confuses party politics with the politics of national policy. We might look briefly at each of these confusions in turn.

The False British Analogy

It is easy for a student of American government to be dazzled by the eminence and prestige of British civil servants compared to the low opinion generally expressed about our own bureaucrats in Washington. It is, none the less, faintly ridiculous to make the British model our own. In Britain the Civil Service has an aristocratic tradition; it was the preserve of an upper class. Moreover, the political character of Cabinet Ministers and their immediate staffs was clearer from the outset; since they had to be politicians to get into the House of Commons to begin with, no British scholar is recorded as having asked, as Wilson did about American Cabinet officers, "Are the Secretaries political or non-political officers?"

Apart from their class origin, from what comes the prestige of a British permanent under secretary? Surely not from any system that divorces him from formulating policy or becoming identified with a policy in the public mind. The reverse is true. Indeed, I would suggest that nowadays British civil servants derive much of their prestige from the general knowledge that the civil servants run the government and the political Ministers are left with little room for political deviation from the "nonpolitical" advice they get from their permanent staffs. In many Ministries an independent study would I think reveal that almost the only function performed by the political Minister is the rather specialized task of explaining to his fellow parliamentarians what the civil servants are doing in his Ministry, and why they say they are doing it.

When Hugh Gaitskell gave way to R. A. Butler as Chancellor of the Exchequer several years ago, I was privileged to watch the civil servants in the Treasury put on a routine demonstration of their power. Shortly after the Conservatives took over, Mr. Butler went to a North Atlantic Treaty Organization Council meeting and publicly agreed with the American Secretary of the Treasury, John Snyder, about the need for early convertibility of sterling—a policy which his predecessor Mr. Gaitskell had been resisting with the enthusiastic backing of the .Treasury staff. I was in London not long afterwards, and I vividly remember the quiet strength with which the Treasury civil servants assured me, "Don't worry about it, the Minister will be taking a different line in a few months, after he learns the facts." And indeed, after he learned the facts which the civil servants gave him to learn, nothing more was heard from the Chancellor's office about making sterling convertible with the dollar as soon as possible.

It is, in fact, not convertible yet. Either the facts or the civil servants—or possibly both—have produced an impressive continuity of policy.

The British model is not for us. Our Constitution does not exactly encourage the legislature to lie down and be walked on by an executive of its choice, an oversimplified but not too inaccurate description of British politics. Congress does not choose our President, and it therefore is not beholden to him and cannot be bullied by him. The separation of powers forces us to have the open government which is natural for our open society. With us, civil servants have to be not only responsible to the public interest but responsive to Congress, a myriad of popular organizations, and the press. In our political government there is no room for a bureaucratic manager who is "above politics."

Civil Service: Stifled by Reformers?

Because every program has a political origin, and every public manager must also be something of a politician, the spoils system seemed the natural way to run our national government a hundred years ago. A yard fight has long since reversed Senator William L. Marcy's famous dictum, "To the victors belong the spoils of the enemy." Yet the descendants of the original civil service reformers are still fighting the battle to protect and enlarge the place of the civil service in the scheme of things. In the process they may stifle the growth of the service itself.

Why do I say this? Because I think back to the days when I first joined the government, fresh out of school. In those days there were a good many examples of "government people" reaching high positions in the government. Daniel Bell, a civil servant who became Under Secretary of the Treasury, was held up to us as a model. Joseph Grew, a senior Ambassador and an Under Secretary of State, similarly has served as a symbol of the summit for young Foreign Service Officers. Now, sixteen years later, I find the Hoover Commission telling me that civil servants should not aspire to any post in which they make final decisions, enunciate principles, publicly advocate new policies, justify or defend existing policies, basic principles, or philosophy, or participate in something called "evaluative discussions." That sounds to me like retrogression in the kind of top position a junior civil servant can aspire to.

For purposes of comparison, consider the State Department. Of its ten statutory Assistant Secretaries today, seven are for practical purposes career men who also served under Democrats. There are 75 Chiefs of Mission (72 Ambassadors, 3 Ministers); of these posts 43 are held by career and 32 by non-career people. Of the most important ambassadorial posts, four—Moscow, Tokyo, Buenos Aires, and Rio de Janeiro—are held by career Ministers. A Foreign Service Officer or departmental official can, therefore, get to be an Assistant Secretary and an Ambassador—perhaps a Chief of Mission in several different countries in turn—before he completes a distinguished career.

The best civil servants should be able to look forward to comparable rewards of rank and prestige. They cannot do so today, by and large, and they will never be able to aspire beyond the Bureau level if the Hoover Commission prevails.

But, it will be said, let them become political executives and you make them expendable. This may not necessarily be so; it does not always work that way even in the State Department, which is surely as politically sensitive an agency as we are ever likely to have in the United States government. But even if it be true that the road to glory is strewn with turnover statistics, all is not lost. At this level a senior government official can often find an equally useful job outside the government; it is my impression that the political executives had nothing like the difficulty getting relocated that civil servants had in the 1953 exodus from Washington.

To get the best young people into the civil service, civil servants need to be encouraged to cap their career by becoming political executives, with the glory as well as the risks that choice entails. I see no other course that will enable the government to compete successfully for the very best talent coming out of college.

Party Politics and Policy Politics

The Hoover Commission's passion to separate politics from administration takes its most extraordinary form when the Commission gets to talking about "political neutrality." When I first read the Commission's report I could not believe that a body predominantly composed of practicing politicians could possibly have meant what the Report said. For the Commission has built into its remarks on this subject an appalling confusion between party politics and policy politics.

Most of the policy questions which come up in the executive branch of the government, of course, have little to do with party politics. They are nevertheless highly political. As we have seen, each high administrator uses up a good part of his time and energy building and maintaining a political base to support the program for which he is responsible. In the early days of the Marshall Plan, Paul Hoffman spent nearly all of his time successfully promoting the plan, in the United States and in Europe as well. Douglas McKay, until recently Secretary of the Interior, spent a good part of his time defending the Eisenhower administration's electric power and conservation policies, and the defense of his farm views seems to be almost a full-time job for Secretary of Agriculture Ezra Taft Benson. The higher one goes in the executive hierarchy, the less time there is for outside groups (including other agencies of the government) to support the segment of the government for which one is responsible.

Policy politics of this kind is not at all the same thing as party politics, though there is of course some overlap. The party in office has to run generally on the issue of what it thinks and what it is doing. But the campaign oratory generally has to do with what may be done rather than what is being done. And sometimes, as in the case of Secretary Benson at this moment, the demands of policy politics may run counter to the shortrun interests of party politics. Chairman Leonard Hall of the Republican National Committee would probably settle for a little less rigorous honesty in looking at the farmer's plight; certainly the Democrats, veterans of their own many confusions between party and policy, are making the most of this one.

A "Neutralist" Service?

Bearing in mind this distinction between the two meanings of the word "political," I invite your attention to the Hoover Commission's description of the neutrality required of senior civil servants:

> They should keep clear of all political activity, preserve their neutrality in matters of politics ... This means that they must avoid such emotional attachment to the policies of any administration that they cannot accept change and work in harmony with new leaders. Senior civil servants would necessarily refrain from all political activities that would affect adversely their ability to perform their official duties fairly, or that would tend to identify them personally with a political party or its policies. ...
>
> The senior civil servant should make no public or private statements to the press except of a purely factual nature. He should make no public speeches of a political or controversial character. . . .

The civil servants described in these quotations unquestionably exist. But few of them reach, and none of them should reach, the seniority and rank which would otherwise qualify them for membership in the Hoover Commission's senior civil service.

How can a senior government official, whose touchstone is the public interest, be expected to be "neutral" in dealing with a Senator who is plugging for some private interest that happens to be important in his state? Reading the Hoover Commission Report, I tried to picture myself, during the time when I was presenting the Mutual Security program to the Congress, being "neutral" about the reactions of Congressman John Taber, or about whether the bipartisan coalition which always wanted to cut foreign aid would have its way that year. Far from being "neutral" and avoiding emotional attachment, a bureaucrat in that position has the responsibility— not just the obligation to his administrative superiors but the duty to his own concept of the public interest—to be very active in the effort to build a congressional coalition in support of his program.

Avoid Emotional Attachment?

And how on earth can a senior government official "avoid emotional attachment to the policies of any administration"? To begin with he has to help make them. Correction: he "provides facts and background data." But by a curious coincidence he usually provides just those facts and background data that support the adoption of what becomes the administration's policy.

Even if he had nothing to do with establishing the policy, the Hoover Commission wants him to be "neutral" and to "avoid emotional attachment" on such questions as these:

Whether the federal government or the Idaho Power Company should pre-empt the Hell's Canyon power site.

Whether the federal government should aid schools in states that have not complied with the Supreme Court's desegregation decision.

Whether the federal government has any responsibility to assure a supply of polio vaccine for every child.

Whether the farmers need more subsidies or more competition.

Whether accused subordinates should be allowed to face their accusers and know the charges against them.

Whether we should or should not aid the Nationalist Chinese on Formosa.

Whether we need to be ahead of the Russians in the production of guided missiles.

Whether, in a particular situation, we should or should not go to war.

In the case of each of these issues, and dozens more, there are political executives and senior civil servants working side by side to develop the policy and sell it to the Congress and the public at large. For grown men working on matters like these, the avoidance of emotional attachment is nonsense.

Certainly a man who is protected in his job should avoid party work. There are plenty of examples even of top political executives who have operated on that basis. Republicans Robert A. Lovett and William C. Foster ran the Defense Department without getting into politics in the party sense of the word, and General George Marshall, who stayed clear of party politics in spite of extreme provocation, furnishes another notable example. But the Hoover Commission's ban on controversy and emotion goes far beyond party politics into the politics of national policy.

A senior civil service that took literally what the Hoover Commission has said about "political neutrality" would be a pool of eunuchs, a special breed of Americans who stay out of trouble by staying out of sight. No political executive in his right mind would want one of them assigned to his office. A government staffed with people who "avoided emotional attachment" would be like a hospital full of doctors and nurses who did not care whether their patients lived or died, just so the proper professional procedures were followed.

As anyone knows who has worked in Washington, it is not "neutrality" but vigorous advocacy that overcomes inertia in our big bureaucracy. Too much emphasis on neutrality would shift the whole government into neutral.

No branch of American government has come under more violent attack in recent years than the judiciary. Justices of the Supreme Court have been vitriolically assailed and, in some cases, even their impeachment has been urged.

Since the 1930s, the Court has been embroiled in emotionally charged issues of great historical import—first in the economic realm, more recently in the many areas of personal freedom. Criticism of the Court in these decades has come from many ideological quadrants. In the early 1930s, liberals sharply criticized the "nine old men" for repudiating much of the New Deal. In recent years, white-supremacists in the South have defied the Court's long-overdue rejection of the "separate-but-equal" doctrine, while religious zealots in the North have sought to circumvent judicial reaffirmation of the traditional separation of church and state. Meanwhile, defenders of states' rights, allying themselves with archconservatives of all regions, have assailed the Court's involvement in the "political" arena of state legislative malapportionment.

This motley array of complaints has shared but one common view—the belief that the Court has been guilty of usurping legislative and even administrative prerogatives. In the words of one recent right-wing commentator, the court has been "power hungry and tyrannical."

In order to make a reasoned judgment, it seems desirable to suggest some criteria by which a judiciary may appropriately be judged in a democracy. High on the list must come the question of whether the system serves to protect the individual—if necessary, against public officials and government itself. A corollary question is whether impartiality exists—equality of treatment and of access for all, regardless of wealth, power, privilege, and prestige. In the engraved words above the marble columns of the Supreme Court itself, is there "Equal Justice Under Law"? Second, are the courts independent—are they truly free to arrive at judgments that, no matter how controversial, reflect the studied opinions of mature, competent, and diligent men of good will? Or do the courts yield to the pressures all around them, reflecting now the "vested interests"—be they racial, religious, or economic —and now the majoritarian hysteria of the moment, directed against a currently detested minority? This latter point suggests perhaps the most important question of all—Is justice the concern of the entire community? For without ultimate public support or acceptance of its views, no judicial system, no matter how strong, can long continue as the protector of a waning set of freedoms.

Traditionally the courts have occupied a powerful, if not always hallowed, place in the American system of government. Judicial review, that power of the Supreme Court to pass final judgment upon the constitutionality of state and federal legislation, as well as upon the decisions of the lower courts, has been a keystone of that system. Indeed, judicial review has been accurately described as one of the few uniquely American contributions to the science and art of democratic government. Popular acceptance of this "check and balance" in our system has guaranteed the judiciary an equal role among the three branches of government. It also means that judges and courts must inevitably be involved in functions that are, at least in part, legislative or even administrative. Thus, if the judiciary is to remain independent, the people, and the other branches of government, must accept possible (and even likely) court vetoes over statutes (progressive and otherwise), judicial "legislation" that interprets and sometimes modifies the "will of Congress," and judicial "administration" that sets the pace for desegregation and shapes the boundaries of legislative districts.

In a democracy, the public must ultimately support and obey all decisions of the court—not only those of which it approves but those that it thoroughly deplores. For only if there is public willingness to be guided by a rule of law can the judiciary continue to play its important independent-balance-wheel function in our complex government in action.

THE ROLE OF THE COURTS:
CONSCIENCE OF A SOVEREIGN PEOPLE
J. Skelly Wright

Born and raised in Louisiana, Federal Judge J. Skelly Wright now sits on the United States Court of Appeals in Washington, D.C., where his voice continues to strike a "note of conscience in the breast of America."

There is abroad in this country a major debate concerning the role of the courts in expanding individual freedom and in increasing respect for human rights.

One school of thought, known as the advocates of judicial restraint, has advised the judges to move cautiously. Judges cannot give the people more freedom than the people themselves want or deserve, they tell us. And whatever freedom the people want or deserve cannot be kept from them by the judges. So from this point of view, it is useless for the judges to concern themselves with expanding the sphere of human freedom. It may be worse than useless, for judicial protection of individual rights may well encroach on the powers and prerogatives of other branches of our government, thereby upsetting our Constitutional system of checks and balances. Thus, it is said, it is to state legislatures and to Congress, rather than to the courts, that the people must look for the protection of their rights. Moreover, if the judges take the burden of defending and expanding freedom upon their own shoulders, then the people may grow lazy and less vigilant, and neglect their own duties in protecting freedom. It is the efforts of the people themselves, expressed through the election of their chosen representatives, which underlie whatever freedom exists in our nation. Or so the advocates of judicial restraint would have it.

But the rival school of thought, derisively called the judicial activists, has taken quite a different view. For them, it is the duty of the courts to do all in their power to protect those freedoms which our Constitution grants. The courts will not be able to do all that is necessary by themselves. The courts have no army like the President, nor can the judiciary declare war as Congress can. But the courts can act as the collective conscience of a sovereign people—just as once nations had chancellors to act as conscience to the king. With courts performing their duty of proclaiming the eternal rights and liberties of the people, the people will not be slow to defend the banners raised by the courts. And the President and Congress will fall in line. This judges must do, according to the judicial activist, in deciding the cases and controversies involving the rights of human beings.

Moreover, freedom under our Constitution is not subject to any elections, state or Federal. The fundamental freedoms announced in the Bill of Rights are inalienable, and the protection of those rights, by the Constitution itself, is consigned to the courts. With the late Justice Robert H. Jackson the activists say:

> The very purpose of a Bill of Rights was to withdraw certain subjects from the vicissitudes of political controversy, to place them beyond the reach of majorities and officials and to establish them as legal principles to be applied by the courts. One's right to life, liberty, and property, to free speech, a free press, freedom of worship and assembly, and other fundamental rights may not be submitted to vote; they depend on the outcome of no elections.

WITNESSES AND THE FLAG

Perhaps the most dramatic demonstration of the difference between these two schools of thought occurred during the Second World War, when the Jehovah's Witnesses experienced a wave of persecution in our country because of their unusual religious beliefs and practices. Matters reached a climax when a number of local school boards required that schoolchildren—including Jehovah's Witnesses—give a daily pledge of allegiance to the flag. The Jehovah's Witnesses refused to do this, for they felt that such an act was contrary to the Bible's command "Thou shalt have no other gods before me." As a consequence of this refusal, Jehovah's Witnesses across the country faced the prospect of having their children expelled from school, arrested as truants, taken from their parents, and sent to reform schools.

Eventually this problem arrived at our highest tribunal; the Supreme Court announced that it would not interfere with the requirement of the pledge of allegiance. It recognized a major conflict between the freedom of belief of the individual child and his parents versus the power of the state to command allegiance. But, said the court, the reconciliation of that conflict must be left to the people and their elected representatives—this could not be done for them by judges. If the responsibility for protecting the freedom of the individual were left to the people, said the court, the people would rise to that responsibility.

But without guidance from the Supreme Court, the people misread their responsibilities. From the standpoint of religious freedom and respect for human rights, the effect of that Supreme Court decision in the first flag-salute case was disastrous. School board after school board adopted new requirements commanding the flag salute, on pain of expulsion or other penalties. And often the school boards would quote the very words of the Supreme Court opinion in justification of their action. In many cases the salute to the flag was used simply as a device to expel the unpopular Jehovah's Witnesses. The words of the Supreme Court, that the protection of freedom could best be left the responsibility of local authorities, were perverted and used as an excuse for what was in effect religious persecution by the local school boards.

At the same time, and worse than the official action against the Jehovah's Witnesses, was the nation-wide wave of mob violence, attempts at lynching, and physical brutality against the Witnesses—all in the name of patriotism and support for the Supreme Court's opinion. Conditions were such that within three years after the first flag-salute case was decided, a second one reached the Supreme Court. In a dramatic reversal, the court ruled that no authority, state or Federal, could dictate the religious beliefs of any citizen. Schoolchildren could not be coerced into reciting pledges of allegiance when to do so would violate their freedom of religion. Specifically, the children of Jehovah's Witnesses could not be expelled from school because their religious beliefs prevented them from giving the flag salute.

The Supreme Court decision was honored by the local boards. Much of the official persecution of the Jehovah's Witnesses diminished. The new Civil Rights Section of the Department of Justice—founded by the former Attorney General, later Mr. Justice Frank Murphy—helped communicate the Supreme Court ruling to local authorities, and to the people, explaining that the freedom of belief of the Witnesses was protected by law. The rest is history. The Jehovah's Witnesses have been let alone. At least they have been allowed to practice their religion.

Thus, in the very midst of the Second World War, a court defended—

indeed expanded upon—Constitutional freedoms. It did so despite the opposition of political authorities. It did so in behalf of one of the most unpopular of freedoms—especially in wartime—the freedom *not* to salute the flag.

The Supreme Court's defense of freedom of religion did not cease with the war. The school-prayer cases of the very recent past demonstrate once again that the court is alert to even minor abridgments of fundamental freedoms. Once again the apostles of judicial restraint have been critical. But religious freedom in this country is safer today because the Supreme Court has shown the people why even a minor inroad on religious freedom cannot be tolerated.

PROTECTION FOR THE POOR

The courts have also been expanding the sphere of human freedom in the field of criminal law. It has often been said that "History will judge the quality of a civilization by the manner in which it enforces its criminal laws." The Supreme Court has taken the lead in ensuring that our enforcement of criminal law receives the approbation of history. In decision after decision it has sought to upgrade and civilize the manner in which our criminal laws, state and Federal, have been enforced.

The court has demonstrated a determination to diminish the part that poverty plays in the administration of criminal justice—the type of trial a man gets must not depend on whether he is rich or poor. Following this thesis, the court has recognized the right to counsel in both Federal and state criminal trials and has required the state and the national governments to supply a lawyer for the indigent person. More than this, the Supreme Court has required the state and Federal governments to provide a proper appeal for indigents by paying the costs thereof, including a transcript of the testimony taken at the trial. Thus the court has sought to remove the handicap of poverty so that the indigent, too, may receive a fair trial under our law.

Coerced confessions have also received the condemnation of the current court. Under the Anglo-Saxon system of criminal justice, as distinguished from the Continental system, a defendant has a right to remain silent, not only at the time of trial but, most importantly, after his arrest before trial. The Supreme Court has been at pains to condemn, as uncivilized and as a reproach to our system of criminal justice, not only physical pressure, but psychological pressure as well, designed to force an accused to confess.

Perhaps the keynote case on the subject of coerced confessions and third degree is Chambers v. Florida. There a young Negro was accused of committing a heinous crime that had excited a large number of the white citizens of Florida. Without access to a lawyer or even to members of his family, young Chambers was questioned by the police for days on end while a mob bent on his destruction roamed outside the jail. Under these circumstances, it was said that he confessed to the crime. After his conviction in the state courts of Florida, the Supreme Court heard the case. In reversing that conviction and in denouncing the conditions under which a confession was extracted from Chambers, Mr. Justice Hugo L. Black sounded what has come to be the new creed for the court:

> Under our constitutional system, courts stand against any winds that blow as havens of refuge for those who might otherwise suffer because they are helpless, weak, outnumbered, or because they are non-conforming victims of prejudice and public excitement. . . . No higher duty, no more solemn responsibility, rests upon this Court, than that of translating into living law and maintaining this constitutional shield deliberately planned and inscribed for the benefit of every human being subject to our Constitution—of whatever race, creed or persuasion.

The Supreme Court has not satisfied itself with merely outlawing confessions that are demonstrably involuntary. Taking cognizance of the fact that most confessions are obtained while the accused is alone in police custody immediately after arrest and before being transferred to judicial custody by a committing magistrate, the court has held that where there is unnecessary delay in bringing the accused before the committing magistrate, any confession made during this period of unnecessary delay shall not be received in evidence. Thus the court has sought to outlaw not only coerced confessions but also confessions obtained under circumstances presumptively coercive.

In the protection of rights under the Fourth Amendment against unreasonable searches and seizures, the Supreme Court has also been active. The midnight knock on the door, the hallmark of the totalitarian police, does not pass muster in this country. The court not only has outlawed evidence obtained from unreasonable searches and illegal arrests. By an application of the so-called fruit-of-the-poisoned-tree doctrine, it has ordered excluded from trial of a criminal case all evidence derived from the evidence illegally obtained. "Knowledge gained by the government's own wrong cannot be used by it," says the court.

Through its decisions in criminal law, the court has given rich meaning to our ideal of equal justice under law. Persons accused of crime, as a class, have little claim to sympathy with the public or to influence with political authorities. It would be easy, even popular, to constrict the rights of those who stand at the bar of justice. But the courts have reminded us that the rights of all citizens are safe only to the extent that the rights of each accused person are protected. The phrase "It's his Constitutional right" has entered the common language as a link between the ideals of our civilization and the recognition of the rights of the lowliest offender.

Of course, these civilizing advances in the manner of enforcing criminal justice have also been the subject of criticism. The court itself has been condemned for recognizing the rights of "criminals." What the detractors fail to recognize, of course, is that the Bill of Rights outlined in the first eight Amendments to the United States Constitution are the rights of all citizens of the United States, and until an accused is proved guilty beyond a reasonable doubt after a fair trial, he also, as a citizen, is entitled to those rights.

EQUAL VOTES

The reapportionment cases mark another important area in which the Supreme Court has affected our freedom. When we say "This is a free country," one of the things we mean is that we are a free people who govern ourselves. In order for us to govern ourselves, we require fair apportionment. If, for practical purposes, it were primarily the farmers and small-town residents who voted, and the votes of city people hardly counted at all, then to that extent we would be less a free country.

Reapportionment cases highlight the debate on the role of judges in preserving freedom. And these cases point out the importance of general acceptance, of popular support, of aid from executive and legislature, and of reaffirmation by the national conscience. For many years, judges would not decide reapportionment cases—no matter how unfair the reapportionment, no matter what laws or Constitutional provisions were violated, no matter how many people were denied an effective right to vote. Judges would not decide such cases because, as some of them saw it, a court decision about legislative apportionment could have no effect unless the legislature and the people accepted the decision. And no one could count on, or predict, whether there would be legislative or popular support. And so, though as a matter of law the courts had the power to decide apportionment cases, as a matter of judicial wisdom they generally abstained from these issues. Reapportionment was held to be a political issue that addressed itself to the people.

But the Supreme Court has now declared that such cases are proper for judicial decision. The court has now found that in many areas the political system restrained the people from acting, that there was developing in this country a condition in some respects similar to the rotten-borough system that disgraced England two centuries ago. So the court, in effect, authorized the courts in each state to hear apportionment cases as they came up and to apply to voting the principle of equal protection our Constitution ordains. Some people would resist to the end the court's efforts in this field, and that the nation's refusal to accept the challenge and rise to the responsibility given them by the courts would become a national disgrace. But the results have been quite different, and the response to the judicial spark has been broader and stronger than anyone could have predicted. In state after state, citizens' groups have stepped forward, swiftly and effectively, to demand enforcement of the Constitutional principles of equality of which the Supreme Court had reminded them. Soon local courts took up the matter of reapportionment. And in some states, even before the question came before the local courts, legislators and governors have supported reapportionment proposals of their own. Now, by and large, citizens generally—from the man in the street to newspapers and preachers—have said "at long last" to the principle that a state's apportionment must conform to the standards of equality required by our Constitution.

MAKING A TRUISM TRUE

Of the areas in which courts, particularly the Supreme Court, have been active in promoting the freedom of us all, the one of first concern to us today is racial justice. The Supreme Court decisions in the field of racial equality have attempted to secure an actual freedom for the Negro from the bonds of discrimination and bigotry—and a freedom for the white from having to live in a society where such injustices occur. That these freedoms belong to the white and to the Negro is solid Constitutional law—nothing could be more clear than that the Thirteenth, Fourteenth, and Fifteenth Amendments to the Constitution were adopted exactly for the purpose of raising the former slave to the level of first-class citizen. The court decisions of our day are but long-delayed steps forward in giving actual effect to that Constitutional law.

The question remains, Will these decisions receive the support of the people, or will they remain only words in the mouths of the judges? Will the other branches of the Federal government, the Executive and Congress —and the state and local governments—respond to the challenge of these Supreme Court decisions and make a reality today the promise of a hundred years ago?

In pleading for passage of the Civil Rights Act of 1963, the Attorney General of the United States began his remarks to the Congress with this statement:

"For generations, Americans have prided themselves on being a people with democratic ideals—a people who pay no attention to a man's race, creed, or color. This very phrase has become a truism. But it is a truism with a fundamental defect: it has not been true." Is there an honest person in this country today who will deny this statement? Are there enough people in this country today so depraved that the Supreme Court's efforts in behalf of racial justice shall be in vain?

In answering these questions, we should first take notice that the landmark 1954 school-desegregation case has received both more support and more opposition than any other case in our century. The support it has received is tremendous. Organizations sprang up to implement its philosophy, people who had been apathetic to all things public suddenly took a new interest in the commonwealth, a wave of idealism swept the country—especially among college youth—to see the old Constitutional principle of equal justice given effect in the problems of the day. Even foreign nations looked at us with new respect as we began to practice what for so long we had merely preached.

But the civil-rights cases also provoked opposition. Men whose positions had been entrenched upon the foundation of old injustices resisted the righting of wrongs. Unthinking men, men used to old customs and old thoughts, refused to alter their ways. And many others were fearful; being unused to change, they were not ready to accept what was for them a revolution in their lives.

And so these court decisions that have inspired such enthusiasm from many of our citizens stand in need of even further support. The voices of the judges have struck a note of conscience in the breast of America, and America has been stirred to new efforts in behalf of an old idealism. But so entrenched an evil is not so easily overcome. The rock of selfishness, the hard core of racial injustice, is not so easily dissolved. Idealism alone is not enough. There must be a recognition by all our people that we have been wrong, morally wrong, in our treatment of the Negro. There must be a day of repentance. There must be a determination to redress the injustice of the past and a firm resolve by all branches of the government, and by the people, that the long suffering of the Negro shall not have been in vain.

Thus we see that in the areas of religious freedom, criminal law, reapportionment, and racial justice the courts have indeed played a leading role in expanding human freedom in our time. And for this they, particularly the Supreme Court, have been subjected to a barrage of calumny and vilification in some parts of our country. Even some thinking men, men of good will whose roots in the fight for human freedom go very deep, deplore the leadership the current Supreme Court has given in the fight for social and political justice. They say they fear the rule of judges. I say their fears are foolish fancies. In expanding human freedom, the judges have nothing to enforce their rule but the conscience of America. And as long as we are ruled by the informed and challenged conscience of America, we have nothing to fear.

INSIDE VIEW OF THE HIGH COURT
William J. Brennan, Jr.

William J. Brennan, Jr., has served as Associate Justice on the Supreme Court since 1956. This article was adapted from an address he gave at Maxwell Air Force Base in Alabama in 1963.

Throughout its history the Supreme Court has been called upon to face many of the dominant social, political, economic and even philosophical issues that confront the nation. But Solicitor General Cox only recently re-

From *The New York Times Magazine*, October 6, 1963. © 1963 by The New York Times Company. Reprinted by permission.

minded us that this does not mean that the Court is charged with making social, political, economic or philosophical decisions. Quite the contrary. The Court is not a council of Platonic guardians for deciding our most difficult, and emotional questions according to the Justices' own notions of what is just or wise or politic. To the extent that this is a governmental function at all, it is the function of the people's elected representatives.

The Justices are charged with deciding according to law. Because the issues arise in the framework of concrete litigation they must be decided on facts embalmed in a record made by some lower court or administrative agency. And while the Justices may and do consult history and the other disciplines as aids to constitutional decision, the text of the Constitution and relevant precedents dealing with that text are their primary tools.

It is indeed true, as Judge Learned Hand once said, that the judge's authority "depends upon the assumption that he speaks with the mouth of others: the momentum of his utterances must be greater than any which his personal reputation and character can command; if it is to do the work assigned to it—if it is to stand against the passionate resentments arising out of the interests he must frustrate—he must preserve his authority by cloaking himself in the majesty of an overshadowing past, but he must discover some composition with the dominant trends of his times."

However, we must keep in mind that, while the words of the Constitution are binding, their application to specific problems is not often easy. The Founding Fathers knew better than to pin down their descendants too closely. Enduring principles rather than petty details were what they sought. Thus the Constitution does not take the form of a litany of specifics. There are, therefore, very few cases where the constitutional answers are clear, all one way or all the other, and this is also true of the current cases raising conflicts between the individual and governmental power—an area increasingly requiring the Court's attention.

Ultimately of course, the Court must resolve the conflicts of competing interests in these cases, but all Americans should keep in mind how intense and troubling these conflicts can be. Where one man claims a right to speak and the other man claims the right to be protected from abusive or dangerously provocative remarks the conflict is inescapable. Where the police have ample external evidence of a man's guilt, but to be sure of their case put into evidence a confession obtained through coercion, the conflict arises between his right to a fair prosecution and society's rights to protection against his depravity. Where the orthodox Jew wishes to open his shop and do business on the day which non-Jews have chosen, and the Legislature has sanctioned, as a day of rest, the Court cannot escape a difficult problem of reconciling opposed interests. Finally, the claims of the Negro citizen, to borrow Solicitor General Cox's words, present a "conflict between the ideal of liberty and equality expressed in the Declaration of Independence, on the one hand, and, on the other hand, a way of life rooted in the customs of many of our people."

If all segments of our society can be made to appreciate that there are

such conflicts, and that cases which involve constitutional rights often require difficult choices, if this alone is accomplished, we will have immeasurably enriched our common understanding of the meaning and significance
of our freedoms. And we will have a better appreciation of the Court's function and its difficulties.

How conflicts such as these ought to be resolved constantly troubles our
whole society. There should be no surprise, then, that how properly to
resolve them often produces sharp division within the Court itself. When
problems are so fundamental, the claims of the competing interests are often
nicely balanced, and close divisions are almost inevitable.

Supreme Court cases are usually one of three kinds: the "original" action
brought directly in the Court by one state against another state or states, or
between a state or states and the Federal Government. Only a handful of
such cases arise each year, but they are an important handful. A recent
example was the contest between Arizona and California over the waters of
the lower basin of the Colorado River. Another was the contest between the
Federal Government and the newest state of Hawaii over the ownership of
lands in Hawaii.

The second kind of case seeks review of the decisions of a Federal Court
of Appeals—there are 11 such courts—or of a decision of a Federal District
Court—there is a Federal District Court in each of the 50 states.

The third kind of case comes from a state court—the Court may review
a state court judgment by the highest court of any of the 50 states, if the
judgment rests on the decision of a Federal question.

When I came to the Court seven years ago the aggregate of the cases in
the three classes was 1,600. In the term just completed there were 2,800,
an increase of 75 per cent in seven years. Obviously, the volume will have
doubled before I complete 10 years of service. How is it possible to manage
such a huge volume of cases? The answer is that we have the authority to
screen them and select for argument and decision only those which, in our
judgment, guided by pertinent criteria, raise the most important and far-
reaching questions. By that device we select annually around 6 per cent—
between 150 and 170 cases—for decision. That screening process works
like this: When nine Justices sit, it takes five to decide a case on the merits.
But it takes only the votes of four of the nine to put a case on the argument
calendar for argument and decision. Those four votes are hard to come by—
only an exceptional case raising a significant Federal question commands
them.

Each application for a review is usually in the form of a short petition,
attached to which are any opinions of the lower courts in the case. The
adversary may file a response—also, in practice, usually short. Both the
petition and response identify the Federal questions allegedly involved, argue
their substantiality, and whether they were properly raised in the lower
courts. Each Justice receives copies of the petition and response and such
parts of the record as the parties may submit. Each Justice then, without

any consultation at this stage with the others, reaches his own tentative conclusion whether the application should be granted or denied.

The first consultation about the case comes at the Court conference at which the case is listed on the agenda for discussion. We sit in conference almost every Friday during the term. Conferences begin at 10 in the morning and often continue until 6, except for a half-hour recess for lunch. Only the Justices are present. There are no law clerks, no stenographers, no secretaries, no pages—just the nine of us. The junior Justice acts as guardian of the door, receiving and delivering any messages that come in or go from the conference.

The conference room is a beautifully oak-paneled chamber with one side lined with books from floor to ceiling. Over the mantel of the exquisite marble fireplace at one end hangs the only adornment in the chamber—a portrait of Chief Justice John Marshall. In the middle of the room stands a rectangular table, not too large but large enough for the nine of us comfortably to gather around it. The Chief Justice sits at the south end and Mr. Justice Black, the senior Associate Justice, at the north end. Along the side to the left of the Chief Justice sit Justices Stewart, Goldberg, White and Harlan. On the right side sit Justice Clark, myself and Justice Douglas in that order.

We are summoned to conference by a buzzer which rings in our several chambers five minutes before the hour. Upon entering the conference room each of us shakes hands with his colleagues. The handshake tradition originated when Chief Justice Fuller presided many decades ago. It is a symbol that harmony of aims if not of views is the Court's guiding principle.

Each of us has his copy of the agenda of the day's cases before him. The agenda lists the cases applying for review. Each of us before coming to the conference has noted on his copy his tentative view whether or not review should be granted in each case.

The Chief Justice begins the discussion of each case. He then yields to the senior Associate Justice and discussion proceeds down the line in order of seniority until each Justice has spoken. Voting goes the other way. The junior Justice votes first and voting then proceeds up the line to the Chief Justice who votes last. Each of us has a docket containing a sheet for each case with appropriate places for recording the votes. When any case receives four votes for review, that case is transferred to the oral argument list. Applications in which none of us sees merit may be passed over without discussion.

Now how do we process the decisions we agree to review? There are rare occasions when the question is so clearly controlled by an earlier decision of the Court that a reversal of the lower court judgment is inevitable. In these rare instances we may summarily reverse without oral argument. The case must very clearly justify summary disposition, however, because our ordinary practice is not to reverse a decision without oral argument. Indeed, oral argument of cases taken for review, whether from the state or Federal courts, is the usual practice. We rarely accept submissions of cases on briefs.

Oral argument ordinarily occurs about four months after the application for review is granted. Each party is usually allowed one hour, but in recent years we have limited oral argument to a half-hour in cases thought to involve issues not requiring longer argument. Counsel submit their briefs and record in sufficient time for the distribution of one set to each Justice two or three weeks before the oral argument. Most of the members of the present Court follow the practice of reading the briefs before the argument. Some of us often have a bench memorandum prepared before the argument. This memorandum digests the facts and the arguments of both sides, highlighting the matters about which we may want to question counsel at the argument. Often I have independent research done in advance of argument and incorporate the results in the bench memorandum.

We follow a schedule of two weeks of argument from Monday through Thursday, followed by two weeks of recess for opinion writing and the study of petitions for review. The argued cases are listed on the conference agenda on the Friday following argument. Conference discussion follows the same procedure I have described for the discussion of certiorari petitions. Of course, it is much more extended. Not infrequently discussion of particular cases may be spread over two or more conferences.

Not until the discussion is completed and a vote taken is the opinion assigned. The assignment is not made at the conference but formally in writing some few days after the conference. The Chief Justice assigns the opinions in those cases in which he has voted with the majority. The senior Associate Justice voting with the majority assigns the opinions in the other cases. The dissenters agree among themselves who shall write the dissenting opinion. Of course, each Justice is free to write his own opinion, concurring or dissenting.

The writing of an opinion always takes weeks and sometimes months. The most painstaking research and care are involved. Research, of course, concentrates on relevant legal materials—precedents particularly. But Supreme Court cases often require some familiarity with history, economics, the social and other sciences, and authorities in these areas, too, are consulted when necessary.

When the author of an opinion feels he has an unanswerable document he sends it to a print shop, which we maintain in our building. The printed draft may be revised several times before his proposed opinion is circulated among the other Justices. Copies are sent to each member of the Court, those in the dissent as well as those in the majority.

Now the author often discovers that his work has only begun. He receives a return, ordinarily in writing, from each Justice who voted with him and sometimes also from the Justices who voted the other way. He learns who will write the dissent if one is to be written. But his particular concern is whether those who voted with him are still of his view and what they have to say about his proposed opinion. Often some who voted with him at conference will advise that they reserve final judgment pending the circulation of the dissent. It is a common experience that dissents change votes, even enough votes to become the majority. I have had to convert more than one of my proposed majority opinions into a dissent before the final decision was announced. I have also, however, had the more satisfying experience of rewriting a dissent as a majority opinion for the Court.

Before everyone has finally made up his mind a constant interchange by memoranda, by telephone, at the lunch table, continues while we hammer out the final form of the opinion. I had one case during the past term in which I circulated 10 printed drafts before one was approved as the Court opinion.

The point of this procedure is that each Justice, unless he disqualifies himself in a particular case, passes on every piece of business coming to the Court. The Court does not function by means of committees or panels. Each Justice passes on each petition, each item, no matter how drawn, in long-hand, by typewriter, or on a press. Our Constitution vests the judicial power in only one Supreme Court. This does not permit Supreme Court action by committees, panels, or sections.

The method that the Justices use in meeting an enormous caseload varies. There is one uniform rule: Judging is not delegated. Each Justice studies each case in sufficient detail to resolve the question for himself. In a very real sense, each decision is an individual decision of every Justice. The process can be a lonely, troubling experience for fallible human beings conscious that their best may not be adequate to the challenge. "We are not unaware," the late Justice Jackson said, "that we are not final because we are infallible; we know that we are infallible only because we are final." One does not forget how much may depend on his decision. He knows that usually more than the litigants may be affected, that the course of vital social, economic and political currents may be directed.

This then is the decisional process in the Supreme Court. It is not without its tensions, of course—indeed, quite agonizing tensions at times. I would particularly emphasize that, unlike the case of a Congressional or White House decision, Americans demand of their Supreme Court judges that they produce a written opinion, the collective expression of the judges subscribing to it, setting forth the reasons which led them to the decision. These opinions are the exposition, not just to lawyers, legal scholars and other judges, but to our whole society, of the bases upon which a particular result rests— why a problem, looked at as disinterestedly and dispassionately as nine human beings trained in a tradition of the disinterested and dispassionate approach can look at it, is answered as it is.

It is inevitable, however, that Supreme Court decisions—and the Justices themselves—should be caught up in public debate and be the subjects of bitter controversy. An editorial in *The Washington Post* did not miss the mark by much in saying that this was so because "one of the primary functions of the Supreme Court is to keep the people of the country from doing

what they would like to do—at times when what they would like to do runs
counter to the Constitution. . . . The function of the Supreme Court is not
to count constituents; it is to interpret a fundamental charter which imposes
restraints on constituents. Independence and integrity, not popularity, must
be its standards."

Certainly controversy over its work has attended the Court throughout
its history. As Professor Paul A. Freund of Harvard remarked, this has been
true almost since the Court's first decision:

> When the Court held, in 1793, that the State of Georgia could be sued
> on a contract in the Federal courts, the outraged Assembly of that state
> passed a bill declaring that any Federal marshal who should try to collect
> the judgment would be guilty of a felony and would suffer death, without
> benefit of clergy, by being hanged. When the Court decided that state
> criminal convictions could be reviewed in the Supreme Court, Chief
> Justice Roane of Virginia exploded, calling it a "most monstrous and
> unexampled decision. It can only be accounted for by that love of power
> which history informs us infects and corrupts all who possess it, and from
> which even the eminent and upright judges are not exempt."

But public understanding has not always been lacking in the past. Perhaps
it exists today. But surely a more informed knowledge of the decisional
process should aid a better understanding.

It is not agreement with the Court's decisions that I urge. Our law is the
richer and the wiser because academic and informed lay criticism is part of
the stream of development. It is only a greater awareness of the nature and
limits of the Supreme Court's function that I seek. I agree fully with the
Solicitor General: It is essential, just because the public questions which
the Court faces are pressing and divisive, that they be thoroughly canvassed
in public, each step at a time, while the Court is evolving new principles.
The ultimate resolution of questions fundamental to the whole community
must be based on a common consensus of understanding of the unique
responsibility assigned to the Supreme Court in our society.

The lack of that understanding led Mr. Justice Holmes to say 50 years ago:

> We are very quiet there, but it is the quiet of a storm center, as we
> all know. Science has taught the world skepticism and has made it legit-
> imate to put everything to the test of proof. Many beautiful and noble
> reverences are impaired, but in these days no one can complain if any
> institution, system, or belief is called on to justify its continuance in life.
> Of course we are not excepted and have not escaped. Doubts are expressed
> that go to our very being. Not only are we told that when Marshall pro-
> nounced an Act of Congress unconstitutional he usurped a power that
> the Constitution did not give, but we are told that we are the representa-
> tives of a class—a tool of the money power. I get letters, not always anon-
> ymous, intimating that we are corrupt. Well, gentlemen, I admit that it
> makes my heart ache. It is very painful, when one spends all the energies
> of one's soul in trying to do good work, with no thought but that of solving
> a problem according to the rules by which one is bound, to know that

many see sinister motives and would be glad of evidence that one was consciously bad. But we must take such things philosophically and try to see what we can learn from hatred and distrust and whether behind them there may not be a germ of inarticulate truth.

The attacks upon the Court are merely an expression of the unrest that seems to wonder vaguely whether law and order pay. When the ignorant are taught to doubt they do not know what they safely may believe. And it seems to me that at this time we need education in the obvious more than investigation of the obscure.

ALSO ON THE BENCH: "DOMINANT OPINION"
Alan F. Westin

Alan F. Westin is Associate Professor of Law and Government at Columbia University, and is the author of *The Supreme Court: Views from Inside.*

During the past six months, hardly a day has gone by without some influential figure in American public life denouncing the United States Supreme Court. Twenty-five United States Senators and 75 Representatives in this period have delivered speeches in Congress attacking the Court's constitutional outlook. Hostile editorials have appeared in over 150 newspapers. Arthur Krock of *The New York Times* has complained that the Court's "big brother" attitude constitutes a clear case of "judicial usurpation." Police officials and state judges have attacked the justices for "handcuffing" law enforcement.

The American Bar Association has heard its outgoing president lash the Court for gravely undermining "property rights," "internal security," "good citizenship," and other key values of our system. Many Catholic and Protestant church leaders have criticized the justices for rulings allegedly "secularizing" national life and "protecting immorality" from prosecution, and a shudder of apprehension greeted the Court's recent announcement that it would review two cases involving Bible reading and Lord's Prayer recitation in public schools. When asked recently what businessmen thought of the Court, the general counsel of one major corporation replied: "Well, it pays to be a Negro or a Communist if you want justice from the Warren Court. Business doesn't get it."

Is this criticism only a continuation of the protests that Southerners, conservatives and fundamentalist religious leaders have been aiming at the

Court since the middle nineteen-fifties? Does the recent increase in their volume point to another Court-curbing debate in 1963, comparable to the fight over the Jenner-Butler Bills in 1958? Most important of all, how is the public responding to the Court's disputed rulings of the nineteen-sixties, and does the Court respond in turn to the public?

Any discussion of Supreme Court criticism must start with the recognition that the justices are subject to many direct and indirect controls under our constitutional system. Constitutional amendments and Congressional legislation can reverse unpopular rulings. The Constitution specifically gives Congress control over the Court's appellate jurisdiction and this can be used to cut off the Court's review of specific areas of controversy. Presidents are usually able to appoint new justices and can deliberately seek to change the voting balances within the Court through these appointments. State and Federal officials can mount embarrassingly effective resistance to the Court's orders, ranging from subtle inaction to open defiance, since the justices must usually look to elected officials to enforce their orders. The bar and bench can raise influential protests against the Court's legal arguments and its professional competence. And every Supreme Court, finally, is acutely sensitive to any continuous, widespread mistrust of its decisions by the general public.

Reflecting these realities, no Supreme Court in American history has ever defied for long the sustained will of "dominant opinion" in the nation. When the Court has met the determined will of these dominant forces—as it faced the Radical Republicans in 1866–68 or the New Deal in 1936–37—the existing Court majority has always modified its disputed doctrines to uphold the measure insisted upon by dominant opinion. As Reed Powell said, the Court knows how to execute the "switch in time that saves nine."

The troublesome question in these political-judicial crises, of course, is how to define and measure "dominant opinion." Clearly, the justices do not have to consult public opinion polls about their decisions, or party platforms or even the results of specific elections in which the voters hear debate over issues being considered by the Court. By "dominant opinion," we mean the active consensus of an era as represented in the "passionate truths" held by the majority of elected state and Federal officials; the leaders of the most influential economic, civic and religious groups, and those mass media trusted by the politically active public.

When wholesale criticism of its doctrines begins to dominate these key sectors, the Court must reconsider its checks on dominant opinion or else risk reprisals on charges of being "arrogant, unrepresentative and willful."

But the justices must also decide whether any given flood of attacks really represents dominant opinion or something less than that. If opinion in the nation is broadly divided over the Court's disputed doctrines, or if the Court is really the target of critics who are in dissent from the dominant opinion of their era, then the Court is not in ultimate crisis and the justices can pursue their views of the Constitution in the normal traditions of judicial independence and defense of "unpopular" constitutional rights.

Finally, it must also be realized that the storms that rage over the Court involve only a few of its rulings. Of the 250–275 cases it decides on their merits each year, fewer than a dozen normally make up the "constitutionally sensitive" cases that stir fundamental debate. Yet all the skill and wisdom displayed in the vast majority of its rulings will not alter the fact that it is by these sensitive cases that the Supreme Court will be judged, in its day and by history.

With these factors in mind, the constitutionally sensitive decisions of the present Court which have aroused so much criticism in the nineteen-sixties can be considered under four major headings: the continued application of earlier, disputed constitutional rulings; the Court's extension of existing doctrines beyond their previous boundaries; the entry of the Court into new fields of controversy, and its performance in the wide range of cases involving issues of internal security.

The first set of decisions under debate involves constitutional positions laid down by Court majorities before 1960. The present Court has simply been applying these. In segregation cases during 1960–62, for example, the Court struck down state racial discrimination practices at about the same pace as between 1954–59—drawing a similar volume of protest from Southern segregationists and their "hard conservative" allies like William Buckley Jr., who jointly deplore judicial interference with Southern "gradualism" in race relations. New issues, such as the sit-in demonstrations, have not yet been reached.

In cases involving Federal powers of taxation, spending and regulation of industry, the Court has continued to uphold Congressional measures despite the protests of corporate spokesmen that many of these activities are constitutionally forbidden to the national government. In the area of labor-management relations, the Court has continued to uphold Federal and state power over collective bargaining relationships—Federal pre-eminence—again despite complaints from business and conservatives that these are either private or local matters.

On each of these issues, it seems clear that the present Court is moving in lockstep with the active consensus of this era. Public opinion and national political majorities support judicial activism in behalf of Negro civil rights and judicial self-restraint in matters of industrial relations and welfare programs. On these questions, the South, business and "hard conservatives" are the voice of pre-1929 and pre-World War II America. History has simply outrun their constitutional positions.

The second group of rulings under attack is made up of decisions in which the present Court has been extending significantly constitutional positions first adopted by earlier Court majorities. In the field of church-state relations, for example, the Court's ruling in 1961 that an oath of belief in God could not be required for holding state office, and the 1962 decision striking down a nondenominational prayer composed by the Regents in New York for the public schools, carried judicial review of public religious practices on to new ground.

The same is true with respect to state police methods and trial rules.

While the Court has grappled with the meaning of "due process" for decades, a major step was taken in 1961 with its ruling that all evidence obtained illegally by police must be excluded from state criminal trials. Again, in dealing with government censorship of books and films, the Court of the nineteen-sixties has broadened considerably the area of constitutionally-protected expression.

These increased "interferences" with the action of elected officials account for much of the recent rise in Court criticism. The school prayer case set off more denunciation of the justices than any ruling since the segregation cases rallied Southern officialdom against the Court. When Congressman Glenn Cunningham of Nebraska commented this year that the Court's motto seemed to be "Obscenity, yes; prayer, no," he expressed the level of bitterness that many critics feel.

In matters of religion, censorship and law enforcement, national opinion and civic groups are deeply divided. This means that the Court has not received anything like the mandate from dominant opinion that it had had in the field of segregation or Federal regulation of industry. If anything, I think the balance of opinion probably tips to the side of the critics. It may be in instinctive recognition of this, therefore, that the Court has actually adopted quite guarded and flexible positions in these areas and has consciously refused to accept the absolute doctrines urged by Justices Black, Douglas, Brennan and Warren.

Thus the Court majority has *not* held that movies must be free from all censorship, or that every religious expression in public schools violates the Constitution, or that state criminal procedure must conform exactly to Federal practice. The majority has chosen to advance more slowly, probing to see how fast and how far civil libertarian positions, previously rejected by local political majorities, can now be installed and obeyed because the Supreme Court says they should be.

The third main area in dispute involves the Court's wholly new departure in the state legislative apportionment case of 1962. Over the sharp protests of Justices Frankfurter and Harlan that the Court had deliberately avoided this "political thicket" for many years and should keep out of it still, six members of the Court voted that the citizen denied equal protection of the laws by discriminatory districting was entitled to judicial relief.

With the prospect that Federal judges will now oversee the constitutional fairness of apportionment in 50 states, critics have charged that this is an unprecedented invasion of States Rights and an improper intrusion by judges into the elective politics of the nation. Since the ruling threatens the present rural-conservative advantages in districting and promises to strengthen the representation of urban-suburban areas, the first public response divided largely along that line. Yet the significant thing is how much public support at the grassroots level the Court's ruling seems to be gathering day by day.

Before the decision, only liberal stalwarts were seriously pressing for judicial intervention in this area. Many students of American politics had seemed resigned to gross gerrymandering as a permanent blemish on our democracy. But once the Court stepped in and unclogged the political process, a heavy flow of editorial and public support has developed for making districts fair—preferably by the states themselves but under minimum standards set by the courts. The alarmed cries of conservative critics seem to be falling on unappreciative ears.

The fourth and final group of decisions under attack is in the charged area of internal security, where critics contend that the justices have been steadily "hamstringing" the nation's fight against subversion. Last May, for example, the Chairman of the Senate Judiciary Committee, Senator James Eastland of Mississippi, stated that between 1953 and 1962, the Court had "sustained the position advocated by the Communists" in 46 out of 70 cases involving "Communist or subversive activities." By such decisions, the Senator said, the justices are "lending aid and comfort to the conspiracy" seeking to destroy this nation. Similar charges are heard often from some bar associations, civic groups, and law-enforcement officers, and, of course, as the constant theme of the Radical Right.

Apart from their outrageous premise that judicial protection of constitutional rights is adopting a "Communist position," these attacks have a distinctly ironic character. During the Court-curb debates of 1958, internal-security stalwarts roundly denounced the Court for a dozen or more rapid-fire rulings in 1956-57 that upset Government anti-subversive prosecutions. The Court had questioned the scope of investigations by the House Committee on Un-American Activities, state investigations of "subversion" unconnected with state employees, state loyalty criteria for admission to the practice of law, Federal authority to withhold statements made to the Government by witnesses now testifying in Federal trials, the scope of Federal prosecutions of Communists under the Smith Act and dismissals of state employes for claiming the Fifth Amendment.

Civil libertarians greeted these decisions with cheers and many read them as high constitutional roadblocks against official "McCarthyism." But a storm of protest arose from conservatives. Congress swiftly passed a statute limiting the breadth of the ruling giving defendants access to witness's statements in Government files. Hostile Congressional investigations were held on several other rulings and a sharp Court-curb bill was defeated in the Senate by a 41–40 vote. As late as 1962, Congressional forces were still working to "undo" the Court's "mischief" of 1957; this spring saw the passage of an act reversing the Court's 1957 definition of a key Smith Act term.

By 1962, the Court majority had reacted by distinguishing or diluting virtually all of the bold and assertive rhetoric of the 1957 rulings. While the Court majority did not overrule earlier decisions, it permitted the House Un-American Activities Committee, Federal Smith Act prosecutors, state legislative investigators, state employment officials and state bar admission committees to do almost exactly what the 1957 rulings had seemed to forbid.

The Court's shift came not through the appointment of new justices but through a change in emphasis by Justices Frankfurter and Harlan. In 1956–

57, they had voted with Chief Justice Warren and Justices Black, Douglas and Brennan to provide a majority for striking down extreme Government internal security measures. After 1957, however, Justices Frankfurter and Harlan voted with Justices Clark, Whittaker and Stewart to form a majority that upheld Government power in cases paralleling those of 1956–57.

What prompted this shift? The 1956–57 cases had reviewed internal security actions taken during the hysterical peak of the early nineteen-fifties. In 1957, anti-McCarthy sentiment was strong in the nation and the moment seemed ripe for judicial intervention against anti-Communist measures that were "popular" but, in the mind of the Court's majority, cut dangerously and unnecessarily into American civil liberties. So the Court freed some convicted people, wrote stirring opinions reaffirming our libertarian heritage, and warned Government to take more care in the future.

But when many officials of the states and nation responded by deliberately repeating their anti-Communist programs, when the public did not make such conduct politically unprofitable and when Court curb measures gained ominous momentum, the showdown was at hand. Should the Court transform the warnings of 1956–57 into flat commands outlawing those Government measures? And could the Court make such rulings stick?

To many Americans, and to Warren, Black, Douglas and Brennan, the answer was clear—of course, the Court should strike down "unconstitutional action," or else what are courts and the Constitution for? But for some of the justices, this answer was not enough. The insulation and isolation of the judiciary from elective responsibility, the need to encourage respect for the Constitution within the political process itself and the presence of sustained support for measures the justices might think desperately unwise but Constitutionally on the border lines—these considerations are often paramount in moments of political-judicial crisis. Such factors were probably in the minds of Frankfurter and Harlan, leading them to follow the course of judicial self-restraint and to limit rather than extend the scope of the 1956–57 doctrines.

Could the Supreme Court have held fast to the larger implications of its 1956–57 rulings? The Court *did* remain firm on some sharply criticized rulings, such as those involving passport procedures, Federal loyalty-security programs and state sedition laws. Could it have maintained more? Given the ambiguous, if not hostile, position of the Eisenhower Administration toward the libertarian rulings of 1957 and given the strength of the Court's critics in Congress, an assertion of the full Warren-Black-Douglas-Brennan position would probably have produced swift reversals and even broad Court-curbs. Yet, though post-war generalship is easy, it is hard to believe that as complete a retreat as the Court carried out after 1957 was inescapable.

The Court could have asserted itself more, and even if some of its libertarian rulings had been reversed by Congress or by amendment, the debates stirred by this action would have turned the attention of the public to civil liberties in the cold war in a more systematic and educative way than has been achieved by the mere re-assertion of anti-Communist crusades by some elected officials.

Looking over the present Court's performance in these four major areas under dispute, many people may deny that any justices have been affected by dominant opinion in this way—for if they had, it would have to be considered either as timidity on their part or as a betrayal of the independent status given to the Court by the Founding Fathers for the protection of the Constitution. These people would explain that constitutional cases must be decided as a matter of right and wrong, with the law-trained Justices "finding" the meaning of the Constitution through use of constitutional records, prior decisions and basic canons of construction. These "findings" should be announced in utter disregard of dominant opinion.

Such an approach confuses the usual function of the justices as the nation's highest law court with its more complicated, more vital but less regular role as keeper of our constitutional checks and balances. In this latter capacity, the justices must function as constitutional statesmen, applying the brilliant but ambiguous phrases of 1789 or 1868 to economic, military, political, social and inter-group conditions then undreamed of. The Court must also try to apply to modern circumstances those continuing conflicts that the framers of the Constitution knowingly locked into our political system—conflicts between majority rule and minority rights, Federal authority and local control, the private domain and the public sector. In these areas, it should be remembered, the terms of the Constitution involve such highly elastic concepts as "due process of law" and "establishment of religion."

As constitutional statesmen, the justices must arrive at some ultimate accommodation with dominant opinion. The imperatives of democracy and the need for broad confidence in the Court require this. But the justices must seek to influence dominant opinion as well. The creative challenge is to find exactly the right combination of judicial command, creative suggestion and respectful non-interference that will lead those entrusted with political power in the states and nation to live by the expanding ideals of the American Constitution.

When the Supreme Court opened its 1962–63 term, Justice Frankfurter was already in retirement. Justices Byron White and Arthur Goldberg took their seats at the two opposite ends of the bench, symbolizing by their physical location that the Court's doctrinal boundaries, for the moment, are as undetermined as the constitutional philosophies of the new Kennedy appointees. These two men now hold the Court's balance of power, and with their votes could come important changes in the direction or emphasis of the Court's rulings on sensitive issues.

In this situation, both supporters and critics of the Court can be sure that their efforts to mold dominant opinion in the nation on the great constitutional questions will have a profound impact on the Court of the nineteen-sixties. The justices are listening, and is this not as it should be in a constitutional democracy?

The Bill of Rights and Individual Freedom

The Bill of Rights and Individual Freedom

The Bill of Rights and Individual Freedom

Recent years have witnessed a new and dangerous interpretation, on the part of many Americans, of the rights so bloodily attained by their revolutionary forebears. Despite its national heritage, a substantial segment of the public has been all too willing to accept the un-American doctrines embodied in the phrases "Fifth-Amendment Communist," "Where there's smoke there must be fire" (a saying that ignores the fact that the vilifier himself may have lit the smudge pot), and "There is no right to government employment." In the midst of all these slogans lies the suspicion that the Supreme Court has been "too soft"—too soft in permitting, even perhaps abetting, the escape of Communists and criminals from the clutches of the law.

Such widespread attitudes as these create a doubt whether the Bill of Rights, if introduced today, could be adopted. But what are the rights involved? Where did they originate? Where are they set forth? Whom do they protect against whom?

The "civil rights" stemming from our historical heritage are far broader than the highly publicized racial protections. They include such Anglo-Saxon common-law doctrines as the presumption of the innocence of the accused, the individuality of guilt, the right to confront one's accusers, and the right to know the nature of the charges on which one is held in custody. In addition to these guarantees, common to all our states but one (Louisiana, where Roman code law served as historical foundation), there are the protections afforded in the body of the Constitution itself—prohibitions against the enactment, by Congress or state legislatures, of bills of attainder or *ex post facto* laws, and a strict and limiting definition of treason.

More important than such prohibitions, however, are the many protections incorporated within the Bill of Rights—the first ten amendments. These protections are more specifically found in the substantive guarantees of the First Amendment, and in the procedural guarantees of the Fourth, Fifth, and Sixth. The First Amendment incorporates the five great freedoms—freedom of speech, of the press, of assembly, of religion, and of the vital right to petition. (In some recent decisions, the Supreme Court seems to have been tending toward the protection of such unwritten supplements as a right to travel and a right to read.) Since such abstract substantive rights are of little worth without their implementation, the Fourth, Fifth, and Sixth Amendments provide certain procedural safeguards, including those against self-incrimination, double jeopardy, cruel and unusual punishments, and excessive bail. In addition, these amendments guarantee the accused a speedy and public trial, trial by jury, indictment by grand jury in the event of a major crime, and adequate representation by counsel.

The Bill of Rights was originally drawn up to protect the individual against the central government alone. Today its guarantees have come, by that court doctrine known technically as "substantive due process," to be applied largely (but not yet in their entirety) against the states. Nonetheless, the Constitution applies these many protections only against government in all its forms; it has afforded few protections for the individual against the encroachments of his fellow citizens. The notable exception to this rule has stemmed from the judicial finding that the Thirteenth Amendment, prohibiting slavery, makes illegal the enforcement of contractual obligations that create virtual conditions of peonage or serfdom. The Constitution is a dynamic document, however, and the Fourteenth Amendment in particular contains clauses, including the guarantee of "equal protection of the laws," that may in the future be interpreted to expand this area of individual freedom.

As a further protection against government—against the possible abuses and excesses of bureaucratic procedures and decisions—another major doctrine has been developed. It is the doctrine of "administrative due process." In a series of decisions, judges have ruled, among other things, that hearings before administrative tribunals must be fair and impartial, and that the accused, individuals and corporations alike, must be afforded advance notice and a full opportunity to present evidence in their behalf. In addition, there are rules of federal-court procedure, built up through "case law" and based on a high regard for the due-process clause of the Constitution. According to these strictures, wiretap evidence has been ruled inadmissible in federal courts, and federal enforcement officers have been held to high standards of procedural conduct.

Although these constitutional guarantees have effectively armored the individual against possible persecution by the federal government, a similar degree of protection for the accused has not yet been fully applied against the states. In the American federal system, the police power—that most dangerous of all government weapons—has been reserved to the states. And it is in the state exercise of this power that observers have noted the most significant current infringements of individual liberty.

These are the fundamentals of the American protective system; but, as the late Chief Justice Charles Evans Hughes so pungently put it, "The Constitution is the Supreme Law of the Land, but the Constitution is what the judges say it is." If we are to understand the rights of the individual in our society, we must examine in some detail the processes of the judiciary and of law enforcement, with their all-too-frequent local encroachments on protected rights as well as their abridgment through social pressure and economic sanction. Since human freedom is indivisible, all are equally important in the task of "securing these rights" in a government in action.

THE BLACK SILENCE OF FEAR
William O. Douglas

> William O. Douglas, Associate Justice of the United States Supreme
> Court, has consistently supported the cause of individual freedom from
> his place on the bench. An avid hiker and explorer, he is the author of
> *Strange Lands, Friendly People, Of Men and Mountains,* and many
> other books.

There is an ominous trend in this nation. We are developing tolerance
only for the orthodox point of view on world affairs, intolerance for new or
different approaches. Orthodoxy normally has stood in the path of change.
Orthodoxy was always the stronghold of the status quo, the enemy of new
ideas—at least new ideas that were disturbing. He who was wedded to the
orthodox view was isolated from the challenge of new facts.

The democratic way of life rejects standardized thought. It rejects orthodoxy. It wants the fullest and freest discussion, within peaceful limits, of all
public issues. It encourages constant search for truth at thé periphery of
knowledge.

We as a people have probably never lived up to that standard in any of
our communities. But it has been an ideal toward which most of our communities have strived. We have over the years swung from tolerance to
intolerance and back again. There have been areas of intolerance when the
views of minorities have been suppressed. But there probably has not been
a period of greater intolerance than we witness today.

To understand this, I think one has to leave the country, go into the back
regions of the world, lose himself there, and become absorbed in the problems of the peoples of different civilizations. When he returns to America
after a few months he probably will be shocked. He will be shocked not at
the intentions or purposes or ideals of the American people. He will be
shocked at the arrogance and intolerance of great segments of the American
press, at the arrogance and intolerance of many leaders in public office, at
the arrogance and intolerance reflected in many of our attitudes toward
Asia. He will find that thought is being standardized, that the permissible
area for calm discussion is being narrowed, that the range of ideas is being
limited, that many minds are closed to the receipt of any ideas from Asia.

This is alarming to one who loves his country. It means that the philosophy of strength through free speech is being forsaken for the philosophy of
fear through repression.

That choice in Russia is conscious. Under Lenin the ministers and officials
were encouraged to debate, to advance new ideas and criticisms. Once the

debate was over, however, no dissension or disagreement was permitted. But even that small degree of tolerance for free discussion that Lenin permitted disappeared under Stalin. Stalin maintains a tight system of control, permitting no free speech, no real clash in ideas, even in the inner circle. We are, of course, not emulating either Lenin or Stalin. But we are drifting in the direction of repression, drifting dangerously fast.

What is the cause of this drift? What are the forces behind it? It is only a drift, for certainly everything in our tradition would make the great majority of us reject that course as a conscious choice.

The drift goes back, I think, to the fact that we carried over to days of peace the military approach to world affairs. Diplomacy, certainly in our relations with Asia, took a back seat. The military approach conditioned our thinking and our planning. The military, in fact, determined our approach to the Asians and their problems. That has been a great tragedy in Asia. And the tragedy to us at home has been about as great.

Military thinking continued to play a dominant role in our domestic affairs. The conspiratorial role of Soviet communism in the world scene was apparent to all who could read. This conspiratorial role of Soviet communism was, of course, backed by Russia's military strength. We, therefore, had to be strong in a military sense to hold off Russia. But we soon accepted the military role as the dominant one. We thought of Asia in terms of military bases, not in terms of peoples and their aspirations. We wanted the starving people of Asia to choose sides, to make up their minds whether they were for us or against us, to cast their lot with us and against Russia.

We did not realize that to millions of these people the difference between Soviet dictatorship and the dictatorship under which they presently live is not very great. We did not realize that in some regions of Asia it is the Communist party that has identified itself with the so-called reform program, the other parties being mere instruments for keeping a ruling class in power. We did not realize that the choice between democracy and communism is not, in the eyes of millions of illiterates, the critical choice it is for us.

We forgot that democracy in many lands is an empty word: that the appeal is hollow when made to illiterate people living at the subsistence level. We asked them to furnish staging grounds for a military operation whose outcome, in their eyes, had no perceptible relation to their own welfare. Those who rejected our overtures must be Communists, we said. Those who did not fall in with our military plans must be secretly aligning with Russia, we thought. This was the result of our military thinking, of our absorption in military affairs. In Asia it has brought us the lowest prestige in our existence.

The military effort has been involving more and more of our sons, more and more of our budget, more and more of our thinking. The military policy has so completely absorbed our thoughts that we have mostly forgotten that our greatest strength, our enduring power is not in guns, but in ideas. Today in Asia we are identified not with ideas of freedom, but with guns. Today at home we are thinking less and less in terms of defeating communism with ideas, more and more in terms of defeating communism with military might. The concentration on military means has helped to breed fear. It has bred fear and insecurity partly because of the horror of atomic war. But the real reason strikes deeper. In spite of our enormous expenditures, we see that Soviet imperialism continues to expand and that the expansion proceeds without the Soviets firing a shot. The free world continues to contract without a battle for its survival having been fought. It becomes apparent, as country after country falls to Soviet imperialistic ambitions, that military policy alone is a weak one; that military policy alone will end in political bankruptcy and futility. Thus fear mounts.

Fear has many manifestations. The Communist threat inside the country has been magnified and exalted far beyond its realities. Irresponsible talk by irresponsible people has fanned the flames of fear. Accusations have been loosely made. Character assassinations have become common. Suspicion has taken the place of good-will. Once we could debate with impunity along a wide range of inquiry. Once we could safely explore to the edges of a problem, challenge orthodoxy without qualms, and run the gamut of ideas in search of solutions to perplexing problems. Once we had confidence in each other. Now there is suspicion. Innocent acts become tell-tale marks of disloyalty. The coincidence that an idea parallels Soviet Russia's policy for a moment of time settles an aura of suspicion around a person.

Suspicion grows until only the orthodox idea is the safe one. Suspicion grows until only the person who loudly proclaims that orthodox view, or who, once having been a Communist, has been converted, is trustworthy. Competition for embracing the new orthodoxy increases. Those who are unorthodox are suspect. Everyone who does not follow the military policy-makers is suspect. Everyone who voices opposition to the trend away from diplomacy and away from political tactics takes a chance. Some who are opposed are indeed "subversive." Therefore, the thundering edict commands that all who are opposed are "subversive." Fear is fanned to a fury. Good and honest men are pilloried. Character is assassinated. Fear runs rampant.

Fear even strikes at lawyers and the bar. Those accused of illegal Communist activity—all presumed innocent, of course, until found guilty—have difficulty getting reputable lawyers to defend them. Lawyers have talked with me about it. Many are worried. Some could not volunteer their services, for if they did they would lose clients and their firms would suffer. Others could not volunteer because if they did they would be dubbed "subversive" by their community and put in the same category as those they would defend. This is a dark tragedy.

Fear has driven more and more men and women in all walks of life either to silence or to the folds of the orthodox. Fear has mounted—fear of losing one's job, fear of being investigated, fear of being pilloried. This fear has stereotyped our thinking, narrowed the range of free public discussion, and driven many thoughtful people to despair. This fear has even entered universities, great citadels of our spiritual strength, and corrupted them. We have the spectacle of university officials lending themselves to one of the worst witch hunts we have seen since early days.

This fear has affected the youngsters. Youth has played a very important role in our national affairs. It has usually been the oncoming generation—full of enthusiasm, full of idealism, full of energy—that has challenged its elders and the status quo. It is from this young group that the country has received much of its moral power. They have always been prone to question the stewardship of their fathers, to doubt the wisdom of traditional practices, to explode cliches, to quarrel with the management of public affairs.

Youth—like the opposition party in a parliamentary system—has served a powerful role. It has cast doubts on our policies, challenged our inarticulate major premises, put the light on our prejudices, and exposed our inconsistencies. Youth has made each generation indulge in self-examination.

But a great change has taken place. Youth is still rebellious; but it is largely holding its tongue. There is the fear of being labeled a "subversive" if one departs from the orthodox party line. That charge—if leveled against a young man or young woman—may have profound effects. It may ruin a youngster's business or professional career. No one wants a Communist in his organization nor anyone who is suspect.

And so the lips of the younger generation have become more and more sealed. Repression of ideas has taken the place of debate. There may not be a swelling crowd of converts to the orthodox, military view. But the voice of the opposition is more and more stilled; and youth, the mainstay in early days of the revolt against orthodoxy, is largely immobilized.

This pattern of orthodoxy that is shaping our thinking has dangerous implications. No one man, no one group can have the answer to the many perplexing problems that today confront the management of world affairs. The scene is a troubled and complicated one. The problems require the pooling of many ideas, the exposure of different points of view, the hammering out in public discussions of the pros and cons of this policy or of that.

There are few who know first hand the conditions in the villages of Asia, the South Pacific, South America, and Africa. There are few who really know the powerful forces operating from the grass roots in those areas—forces that are reflected in the attitudes of the men who head up the Governments in those countries. But unless we know those attitudes, we cannot manage intelligently. Unless we know, we will waste our energies and our resources. Unless we know, we are not in position to win even political alliances of an enduring nature. Unless we are eager to know, unless we invite a flood of information on these problems, unless we encourage every avenue of approach to them, we will live and act in ignorance. There are those who think that our present policy toward Asia will lead to disaster—for us. There are those who believe that in Asia we are fast becoming the symbol of what the people of Asia fear and hate. There are those who believe that the most effective bases we can get in Asia are bases in the hearts of

Asia's millions, not bases on their lands. There are those who believe that we must substitute a political for a military strategy in Asia; that when there is a cease-fire in Korea, we must make a political settlement with Red China; that if we apply to China the attitude we are now brilliantly exploiting in Yugoslavia, we can manage to make Soviet imperialism crumble.

There are those who are deeply opposed, many of whom put the issue beyond the pale of discussion. There are even some who make the crucial test of one's loyalty or sanity his acceptance or rejection of our present policy toward Asia.

The question of our Asian policy illustrates the need for a wide range of free public discussion. Asia poses probably the most critical issues of the day. Certain it is that if Asia, like China, is swept into the political orbit of Soviet Russia, the Soviets will then command or be able to mobilize (a) the bulk of the people of the world, (b) the bulk of the wealth of the world.

If that happens, it is doubtful if we, with all our atomic bombs, could even win a war.

The great danger of this period is not inflation, nor the national debt, nor atomic warfare. The great, the critical danger is that we will so limit or narrow the range of permissible discussion and permissible thought that we will become victims of the orthodox school. If we do, we will lose flexibility. We will lose the capacity for expert management. We will then become wedded to a few techniques, to a few devices. They will define our policy and at the same time limit our ability to alter or modify it. Once we narrow the range of thought and discussion, we will surrender a great deal of our power. We will become like the man on the toboggan who can ride it but who can neither steer it nor stop it.

The mind of man must always be free. The strong society is one that sanctions and encourages freedom of thought and expression. When there is that freedom, a nation has resiliency and adaptability. When freedom of expression is supreme, a nation will keep its balance and stability.

Our real power is our spiritual strength, and that spiritual strength stems from our civil liberties. If we are true to our traditions, if we are tolerant of a whole market place of ideas, we will always be strong. Our weakness grows when we become intolerant of opposing ideas, depart from our standards of civil liberties, and borrow the policeman's philosophy from the enemy we detest.

This has been the direction of our drift. It is dangerous to the morale of our people; it is destructive to the influence and prestige of our country that is losing its human resiliency, and much of our inventive genius. The demands of orthodoxy already have begun to sap our strength—and to deprive us of power. One sees it from far-off Asia. From Asia one sees an America that is losing its humanity, its idealism, and its Christian character. From Asia one sees an America that is strong and rich and powerful, and yet crippled and ineffective because of its limited vision.

When we view this problem full face we are following the American tradition. The times demand a renaissance in freedom of thought and freedom of expression, a renaissance that will end the orthodoxy that threatens to devitalize us.

THE FIFTH AMENDMENT
Erwin N. Griswold

Erwin N. Griswold is Dean of the Harvard Law School. An educator who has held many public posts, he is the author of *Spend-Thrift Trusts, Cases on Federal Taxation,* and other books.

Old friends are good friends. Yet even with the best of friends problems sometimes arise. I have the feeling that this is in a sense the situation we find ourselves in with respect to the Fifth Amendment. It has been with us a long time. It is rather comforting to have around. Yet in the past few years it has come to our consciousness as it rarely has before, and it has been troublesome to many members of the public. It has seemed to me worth while, therefore, to undertake a review of the Fifth Amendment with the thought that ordinarily the better we understand something in human experience, the less fearsome it becomes.

Before going further it may be well to introduce our old friend itself. The Fifth Amendment contains a number of provisions which are commonplace. It is the source of our constitutional rule that serious criminal charges must be made by indictment of a grand jury. It provides against double jeopardy, against the taking of property without due process of law and against the taking of private property for public use without just compensation.

Along with these other provisions is the phrase which has currently come to the fore: "No person . . . shall be compelled in any criminal case to be a witness against himself." In this connection, it is well to mention the fact that the Massachusetts Constitution has a corresponding provision, which antedates that in the Federal Constitution. Article XII of the Bill of Rights in the Massachusetts Constitution, adopted in 1780, provides that "No subject shall . . . be compelled to accuse, or furnish evidence against himself." We are not dealing with either an alien or a novel doctrine. . . .

DESIGNED TO PROTECT THE INNOCENT

I am going to offer my own attempt to express the reason for the Fifth

From *The Christian Science Monitor,* February 15, 1954; also in the book *The Fifth Amendment Today* (Cambridge, Mass.: Harvard University Press, 1955), by Erwin N. Griswold. Reprinted by permission of the author.

Amendment, and why I think it is a sound provision of our basic laws, both federal and state.

I would like to venture the suggestion that the privilege against self-incrimination is one of the great landmarks in man's struggle to make himself civilized. As I have already pointed out, the establishment of the privilege is closely linked historically with the abolition of torture. Now we look upon torture with abhorrence. But torture was once used by honest and conscientious public servants as a means of obtaining information about crimes which could not otherwise be disclosed. We want none of that today, I am sure. For a very similar reason, we do not make even the most hardened criminal sign his own death warrant, or dig his own grave, or pull the lever that springs the trap on which he stands. We have through the course of history developed a considerable feeling of the dignity and intrinsic importance of the individual man. Even the evil man is a human being.

If a man has done wrong, he should be punished. But the evidence against him should be produced and evaluated by a proper court in a fair trial. Neither torture nor an oath nor the threat of punishment such as imprisonment for contempt should be used to compel him to provide the evidence to accuse or to convict himself. If his crime is a serious one careful and often laborious police work may be required to prove it by other evidence. Sometimes no other evidence can be found. But for about three centuries in the Anglo-American legal system, we have accepted the standard that even then we do not compel the accused to provide that evidence. I believe that is a good standard and that it is an expression of one of the fundamental decencies in the relation we have developed between government and man.

As said by that old tartar, Mr. Justice Stephen J. Field, who was reared in western Massachusetts, "The essential and inherent cruelty of compelling a man to expose his own guilt is obvious to everyone, and needs no illustration." And in words which he approved, it is the "result of the long struggle between the opposing forces of the spirit of individual liberty on the one hand and the collective power of the state on the other." *Brown* v. *Walker,* 161 U.S. 591, 637 (1896).

Where matters of a man's belief or opinions or political views are essential elements in the charge, it may be most difficult to get evidence from sources other than the suspected or accused person himself. Hence, the significance of the privilege over the years has perhaps been greatest in connection with resistance to prosecution for such offenses as heresy or political crimes. In these areas the privilege against self-incrimination has been a protection for freedom of thought, and a hindrance to any government which might wish to prosecute for thoughts and opinions alone.

But the privilege is broader than that. It is applicable to any sort of crime, even the most sordid. Don't we go too far in giving this protection to criminals? Isn't the claim of the privilege the clearest sort of proof that the person who claims it is guilty of a crime? This has been asserted by high authority, but I do not believe it is true.

Apart from its expression of our view of civilized governmental conduct, another purpose of the Fifth Amendment is to protect the innocent. But how can a man claim the privilege if he is innocent? How can a man fear he will incriminate himself if he knows he has committed no crime? Judge Magruder of our own First Circuit Court of Appeals has recently given some illustrations of this in his illuminating opinion in the Maffia case, decided last month.

There is, for example, the case of the man who has killed another in self-defense, or by accident, without design or fault. He has committed no crime, yet his answer to the question whether he killed the man may well incriminate him. At the very least it will in effect shift the burden of proof to him so that he will have to prove his own innocence. Indeed, the privilege against self-incrimination may well be thought of as a companion of our established rule that a man is innocent until he has been proved guilty.

In this connection let me quote from a Supreme Court decision written long before our present troubles. In *Burdick* v. *United States,* 236 U.S. 79 (1915), Mr. Justice McKenna wrote, "If it be objected that (Burdick's) refusal to answer was an implication of crime, we answer, not necessarily in fact, not at all in theory of law."

TWO HYPOTHETICAL CASES

Now let us turn to an area which is closer to that which has recently been of concern. I am going to ask you to assume two sets of facts. You may think that both of the sets of facts are unlikely, and that they do not correspond with any case you have ever heard of. All I ask is that you assume the facts. I am simply putting a hypothetical case; and the facts are not the facts of any specific case.

Here is Case 1. A man is a college teacher. He is an idealist and perhaps slow to recognize realities as idealists sometimes are. He has a great urge for what he regards as social reform. He is native born, went to American schools, and loves his country despite what he regards as its imperfections. You may not agree with his ideas but you would respect his honesty and sincerity. He believes himself thoroughly attached to the country and the Constitution, and he abhors anything involving force and violence. He is a good teacher and works hard on his subjects. He has always believed that as a good citizen he should be interested in politics. Neither of the established political parties provided what he wanted.

In the relatively calm period of the past middle 1930's, on the solicitation of a friend, he went to a Communist meeting and soon joined the Communist Party. At that time the Communist Party was perfectly legal, and regularly appeared on our ballot. He thought he was simply joining a political party. One of the reasons that led him to join was because he regarded fascism as highly immoral and a great danger to the world, and he felt that the Communists were fighting fascism in Spain at this time. His interest was not merely in protecting Spain, but because he thought that fighting fascism there was an important means of guarding against such a danger here.

Now you may say that this is all very unlikely. To this I reply that I am, for the moment, only assuming a hypothetical case I want. So these are the facts I put before you. You may feel that such a man must have been very naive or lacking in intelligence. To that I would make two replies: First, to say that involves the use of a large amount of hindsight. A man's actions at any time should be evaluated on the basis of the facts then available to him, and the state of his own mind on the basis of what he actually knew, and not by facts we learn later that were not known to him. And my second reply would be that the man may have been naive or obtuse. I would say that he was at least misguided and unwise. But I would point out that being obtuse or naive is a very different thing from being a traitor or a spy.

Let me add a few more facts, assumed by me as before. Our teacher was in a Communist cell, with other teachers. The Communists had great plans for this group. They wanted to use it to infiltrate American education. However, the Communist command was canny. They knew that many or all of the members of this cell of teachers were politically innocent, and that they would recoil quickly from any proposals for sabotage or the use of force and violence. So they treated this group with great care. The group was never subjected to the rigors of Communist discipline. It was a study group, and its discussions were kept on a high intellectual plane. The more sordid features of the Marxist doctrine were kept thoroughly in the background. Our teacher never engaged in espionage or sabotage or anything like that, and never saw or heard of any such activities by any member of his group. He would have been horrified by any such actions.

WHAT HAPPENS TO INDIVIDUALS?

Nevertheless, there were things from time to time which he did not like. He rationalized them in various ways—nothing can be perfect; the thing to do is to stay inside and work against excesses; and so on. Besides he was a stubborn fellow. Once having started out on something he thought was good, he did not give it up lightly. But he became troubled; and after the war he slowly drifted away from the group. He never formally resigned. He just turned away. By the time of the Korean invasion in 1950, he was thoroughly disgusted and saw that he had been used as a dupe. But he was also convinced in his own heart of the rectitude of his actions, if not of their wisdom; and he did not doubt that many of the people who had been associated with him in the venture were just as innocent of wrong-doing as he was sure he was.

Remember I am doing the assuming. You may feel that these facts do not fit an actual case. But I am not trying to state an actual case. I am just assuming a hypothetical case, which is one of the ancient rights of any law teacher.

Now let me turn to Case 2. This man is also a college teacher. He never joined the Communist Party. He never thought of joining the Communist Party. He knew a good deal about the realities of communism, and he was thoroughly opposed to it. He was, however, a man who was interested in causes. His father had been a minister who had dedicated his life to helping people. He himself had a great urge to participate in activities which he felt would help to alleviate suffering or contribute to social progress. In fact he was a sucker for almost any kind of an appeal. He contributed modest amounts to China Relief. He had always had a warm feeling for the Chinese. Sometimes he found himself on some of the letterheads of some of these organizations as a sponsor. He was not sure that he remembered giving permission to use his name this way; but the cause, as indicated by the attractive name of the organization, was one that appealed to him, and he did not bother himself much about it.

After a while he heard some rumblings that there might be some Communist influence in these organizations, but he was slow to believe that that could be true. In some of the organizations, he had been on committees with thoroughly respectable fellow citizens. He did not want to pull out, because he felt that this would let his friends down. Eventually, he heard that some of these organizations had been ruled to be subversive by the attorney general. But, he too, was a stubborn fellow. He believed in the stated objectives of these organizations. He was also a freeborn American, proud of his country's great traditions, and he allowed his name to be used by some of these organizations, as had been said in a recent article, "as a gesture of opposition to the procedure of prescribing organizations without giving them the right to be heard."

Well, that is the end of my assuming. Let us see what happens to these two individuals. Remember that both of these individuals feel that they are innocent of any wrongdoing. Each one is pure in heart, and perhaps a little too certain of his own rectitude. Each one may now regret some of the things he did, but he does not think that they were wrong. Each one is certain that he is morally innocent of any crime.

We will consider Case 1 first. He is the man who was a member of the Communist Party. He is summoned to appear before a congressional committee, and is asked whether he is a Communist. He answers truthfully: "no." Then he is asked whether he ever was a Communist. He is now surely subjected to a substantial risk, even though he honestly believes that he has committed no crime. He knows that a number of Communists have been convicted under the Smith Act of 1940, and more have been indicted. Our teacher perhaps magnifies his own predicament. He sees the jail doors opening up if he gives himself the evidence that he was once a Communist.

Interestingly enough, Section 4 (f) of the Internal Security Act of 1950 (commonly known as the McCarran Act) provides specifically that "Neither the holding of office nor membership in any Communist organization by any person shall constitute per se a violation of . . . this section or of any other criminal statute." But this was enacted after his period of party membership. It has been declared to be a crime to be a Communist in Massachusetts since 1951, but there may be some possible room to question the effectiveness of this statute in view of the provision of the federal act. That the federal statutes may displace state action is indicated by a decision of the Supreme Court of Pennsylvania just last week.

EXAMINER CHANGES TACK

After much internal torment, the witness finally decides to claim the privilege of the Fifth Amendment with respect to the question of his past membership in the Communist Party. Putting aside the question of his wisdom in doing this, can there be any doubt that the claim is legally proper? Past membership in the Communist Party is not a crime in itself; but admitting such membership may well be a link in a chain of proof of a criminal charge against him. Persons have been prosecuted under the Smith Act for membership in the Communist Party plus something else; if he supplies the proof of his own membership in the party, he does not know what other evidence may then be brought against him to show that he has committed a crime. Thus, an answer to the question will definitely incriminate him, that is, provide evidence which could be used in a prosecution against him. Yet, remember that he thoroughly believes that he is not guilty of any crime; and on the facts I have given he is not guilty of a crime.

There are other factors that influence his conclusion. His own experience is an ordeal. He does not want his friends to be subjected to it. He believes in their innocence of any crime. If he thought that they had committed crimes, he would promptly tell the proper officers of the government. By claiming the privilege against self-incrimination, he can refrain from naming any of his associates. He feels a strong sense of loyalty to them. He feels a strong sense of loyalty to his country, too; but since he is convinced that neither he nor his associates have in fact done anything wrong, his desire to protect them from having to experience his own predicament seems to him to have prevailing weight in the actual circumstances.

He claims the privilege. He cannot be prosecuted on the basis of any evidence he has provided. There can be no doubt, I believe, that his claim of privilege is legally justified. Yet, note that on the facts I have assumed he is not guilty of any crime. Of course his claim of privilege as to his membership in the Communist Party means that he must also claim the privilege as to all other questions which relate in any way to what he did, or to his associates in the activity. For if he answers any of those questions, it will clearly connote his own Communist activity. . . .

Let us turn to Case 2, which we can dispose of briefly; you will remember that that was the man who had lent his name to causes, and had contributed money; and the causes have now turned out to be Communist fronts, although they were attractively named, and many good Americans were, at one time or another, associated with them. But he was never a member of the Communist Party.

This man likewise is summoned before a congressional investigating committee. The mere fact that he is summoned shows that he is suspected of something rather serious, and he is badly worried. He is asked whether he is now a member of the Communist Party; and he answers "No." Then he is asked whether he ever was in the past. The answer is in fact "no," as we have seen. But he is now in great fear. If he says "No," then he may be subjecting himself to a real risk of prosecution for perjury. He may rightly fear that proof of the fact of his joining and contributing to so many agencies which have turned out to be front organizations might lead a jury to believe that he actually was a Communist.

Now it is probably true that fear of a prosecution for perjury for an answer given to a question is not a proper basis for a claim of the privilege. If it was, almost any witness could claim the privilege as to any question. But our man is in a somewhat different situation. If he says "no," to the question of the Communist membership, then in his own interest he may have to undertake to state and explain his membership and activities in the various front organizations. The net result may be that he will have to give much evidence which could be used against him in an attempt to prove that he was a member of the Communist conspiracy. It would appear, therefore, that he can properly claim the privilege even though his answer to the question as to Communist Party membership at any time would honestly and rightly be "No."

In both of the cases I have put, the privilege may be claimed although the individual was guilty of no crime. In the second case it may be claimed although the person was never a member of the Communist Party. In each case, the inference which would be taken from the claim of the privilege would in fact be unwarranted. The claim of the privilege is surely a serious business, but it is equally surely not the equivalent of an admission of criminal conduct . . .

OTHER REASONS WEIGHED

A witness lost in fear and confusion might turn to the privilege as a means of sanctuary from a situation which he feels himself incompetent to handle. Consider also how much the chance of a witness losing his calm and collected demeanor is enhanced by such things as television, radio microphones, movie cameras, flashing flash bulbs, and procedures which may not seem to him to be based upon the finest spirit of fairness. In connection with this I might mention the recent decision of the United States Court of Appeals for the Sixth Circuit in *Aiuppa* v. *United States,* 201 F.2d 287, 300 (1952), where we find the following language in the opinion:

> But, in concluding, we think it may not be amiss to say that, notwithstanding the pronouncements of the committee chairman as to intended fairness, the courts of the United States could not emulate the committee's example and maintain even a semblance of fair and dispassionate conduct of trials in criminal cases.
> Despite the enjoyment by millions of spectators and auditors of the

exhibition by television of the confusion and writhings of widely known malefactors and criminals, when sharply questioned as to their nefarious activities, we are unable to give judicial sanction, in the teeth of the Fifth Amendment, to the employment of a committee of the United States Senate of methods of examination of witnesses constituting a triple threat; answer truly and you have given evidence leading to your conviction for a violation of federal law; answer falsely and you will be convicted of perjury; refuse to answer and you will be found guilty of criminal contempt and punished by fine and imprisonment. In our humble judgment, to place a person not even on trial for a specified crime in such predicament is not only not a manifestation of fair play, but is in direct violation of the Fifth Amendment to our national Constitution.

Ordinarily when the privilege of the Fifth Amendment is exercised, it is in a criminal trial. There a specific charge has been made and the prosecution has by evidence established a prima facie case of guilt of the particular crime charged in the complaint or indictment. Under such circumstances there is much more than the mere claim of the privilege on which to rest an inference of guilt.

In investigations, however, there are no carefully formulated charges. Evidence to support such charges has not been introduced and made known to the witness before he is called upon to answer. He has no opportunity for cross-examination of other witnesses, and often little or no opportunity to make explanations which might have a material bearing on the whole situation. In the setting of an investigation, therefore, the basis for the inference from a claim of privilege against self-incrimination is much less than it is when the privilege is exercised in an ordinary criminal trial.

There are two more matters to which I should like to make brief reference. The first of these is the rather technical legal doctrine known as waiver of the privilege. A clear instance of waiver occurs when a defendant in a criminal case voluntarily takes the stand. He then becomes subject to cross-examination, and must answer relevant questions. So far as witnesses at investigations are concerned, our current learning on this is based largely on the Supreme Court's decision in *Rogers* v. *United States,* 340 U.S. 367 (1951). . . .

This doctrine of waiver is, I believe, the true explanation of the refusal of some witnesses to answer such questions as "Have you ever taught Communist doctrine in your classroom?" or "Have you ever solicited students to join the Communist Party?" These refusals have been deeply disturbing to the public. Yet, answers to these questions may be "No"; but the witness nevertheless fears that he cannot give that answer without its being said that he has waived the privilege as to questions about the other sorts of Communist activity. Here again we have a situation where the obvious inference from the refusal to answer the question may be completely unwarranted.

Finally, I would like to make reference to one more problem which is collateral to that of the Fifth Amendment. Suppose a witness is summoned before an investigating committee. He does not claim a privilege against self-incrimination, and talks freely about himself, answering all questions about his own activity. He takes the position, however, that he will not answer questions about others. Or suppose a person first refuses to answer virtually all questions, claiming the Fifth Amendment privilege, but he later decides to waive the privilege as to himself. However, he refuses as a matter which he regards as one of principle to identify other people. What should be the situation with respect to such a person?

There have been a number of people who have been summoned before investigating committees and taken this position from the outset. They have answered all questions about themselves, and have refused to identify others. As far as I know, no academic person who has done this has been cited for contempt; nor has any such person lost his job. Should it be any different where the witness has first relied on the Fifth Amendment, but has later changed his position, waiving the privilege as to himself, but still refusing to answer as to others?

The problem is undeniably a difficult one. So long as the witness was claiming the privilege, it could be argued that he had done no wrong. If he had committed any crime, the evidence should be brought forth in the proper way and tried out in court. His refusal to answer was not evidence of any crime. This argument, however, is not available where he waives the privilege by refusing to answer questions relating to other persons. Then his Fifth Amendment privilege is wholly gone, and his situation presents new and rather different problems.

Whether he has committed a crime by his refusal to testify may be extremely difficult to tell. Even if he is cited by the legislative body, it will still be for the grand jury to decide whether to indict; it will remain to the courts to decide such questions as whether the committee was properly constituted, and whether the question asked was relevant to the inquiry. We should not forget that a prosecution for contempt was set aside within the past year by the Supreme Court on the ground that the questions asked the witness—as to the identity of his contributors—were not relevant to the particular inquiry. *United States* v. *Rumeley,* 345 U.S. 41 (1953).

However such questions go, though, would it not seem that such a person is at least in no worse a position morally than he was when he stood on the Fifth Amendment? He should not be worse off for being willing to speak fully and frankly about himself than he was when he would not talk at all. His refusal to tell on his friends may be both contrary to valid law and unwise. Nevertheless, it may be based on strong grounds of conscience.

UNIVERSITIES DEFENDED

Let me do a little more assuming; let us assume that the witness feels positive in his own mind that the persons with whom he was associated did no wrong to their country. They did not engage in espionage or sabotage or anything like that. They were merely hopeful but misguided people, as he was. Let us assume, too, that this is all far in the past. The persons in question are in other work. They have families to support. If their names are disclosed, they will surely lose their jobs. He must then resolve for himself the question whether he will give their names and subject them to the same sort of ordeal he has been through in order to save himself from further difficulty and possible prosecution. He may be wrong if he decides that he would not protect himself by sacrificing them. I recognize the legal obligation to testify as to others, and the general importance of this both in trials and in investigations. But can it be said clearly that his action is always immoral?

Of course he may be wrong in his judgment of these other people. They may be worse than he thinks they are. But we all have to use judgment on such things. A man may honestly feel that he cannot bring suffering to others in order to save himself. To a considerable extent such questions can only be resolved in a man's own conscience. We are a society which has long depended on and applauded the virtues of the rugged individualist.

I do not justify the past or present conduct of anyone. I seek only to explain. Because of claims of privilege under the Fifth Amendment, and refusal to answer questions, many members of the general public have come to have fear of our educational institutions, and general mistrust of academic people. I firmly believe that these fears are unwarranted. I have tried tonight to show how some of the things that have happened could have happened without there being anything rotten in the universities. It may be a serious error of judgment for an academic person to claim the privilege of the Fifth Amendment, or to refuse to answer questions; but the conduct, regrettable as it is, does not show the existence of treason, espionage, sabotage, or any other serious crime.

The great misfortune from all this, I believe, is that charges are made against our universities and other educational institutions, and more or less believed by some segments of our people. I think that it is easy to overestimate the extent of that belief, but it cannot be denied that there is disagreement, uneasiness, and even fear in some quarters. As I have said, I think these fears are not soundly based.

This is my 20th year as a faculty member at Harvard University, and I am thoroughly convinced that the university has acquitted itself well, and that it has been of great value to the country during that time. It is an injustice not only to the faculty members but to the country to allow any conclusion to stand that they are not good Americans or that they do not serve their country well. I think that the Harvard Law School with which I am intimately connected, is a great asset to the country and to the commonwealth and, in essence, one of the great conservative influences in our land. If there are any who think otherwise, let them examine the facts, carefully and thoughtfully.

And so I come back where I started. The privilege against self-incrimination embodied in the Fifth Amendment and in the commonwealth's Bill of

Rights has been a long time with us. It is, I believe, a good friend as well
as an old friend. It embodies a sound value which we should preserve. As
we increase our understanding of it, and the part it has long played in protecting the individual against the collective power of the state, we will have
better appreciation of some of the basic problems of our time.

THE CURBING OF THE MILITANT MAJORITY
John P. Roche

John P. Roche is Morris Hilquit Professor of Labor and Social
Thought and Chairman of the Department of Politics at Brandeis University. He has written a number of studies of the history of civil liberty
in the United States, including *The Quest for the Dream*. Long active
in the American Civil Liberties Union, he has also served as national
chairman of Americans for Democratic Action.

For some curious reason, historians and political scientists have largely
by-passed the history of civil liberties in the United States before the First
World War. The consequence of this neglect has been the prevalence of an
amazing set of cliches about the character of contemporary American society and the historic position of civil liberty in the American political
tradition.

Once upon a time, so the story runs, the United States was a land of militant, inner-directed non-conformists, men who were as sensitive to the rights
of others as they were fierce in the defense of their own autonomy. Then
slowly over this green and pleasant land crept the miasma of orthodoxy, an
enervating spirit of conformity which left in its wake an atomized population
of other-directed status seekers gibbering the slogans of the moment, terrified
of the FBI, and finding ultimate consolation only in the narcosis of mass
culture. A nation of Thoreaus has in some subtle fashion been transformed
into an atomic mass of dying salesmen.

Underlying all this nonsense, of course, is the myth of bucolic virtue which
Richard Hofstadter so sensitively limned in *The Age of Reform:* the notion,
profoundly Jeffersonian, that the rural yeoman is the paradigmatic Democratic Citizen and that cities are a source of civic degeneracy, a malignant
cancer on the body politic. With this agrarian nostalgia is combined a heavy
dose of sociological paranoia: a self-anointed intellectual elite has simply
lost patience with a mass society that persists in spending its new-found
leisure bowling or watching TV rather than reading Kafka, a society where
the masses refuse to genuflect to their Cultural Betters. So the critics talk

Reprinted from *The Reporter,* July 18, 1963. Copyright 1963 by The Reporter
Magazine Company.

morosely of "the eclipse of community" and "the lonely crowd," conveniently forgetting that a mere half century ago it was precisely the firmly integrated rural community and the accompanying "idiocy of rural life" that set off the mad rush to urban anonymity.

Few historians, political scientists, or sociologists seem to love cities; the medieval German aphorism *"Stadt Luft macht frei"*—city air nourishes freedom—has seldom been echoed by American students of the process of urbanization. Suffice it here to note my conviction that it has been a major factor in the growth of liberty in the United States by bringing about the collapse of that "natural community" which brings nostalgic tears to the eyes of sociological critics of contemporary American culture. Within the cities the breakdown of ethnic ghettos—"natural communities" *par excellence*—has paralleled the demise of a rurally based, authoritarian social structure.

There is a singular durability in the myth that at some undesignated time in the past there was in the United States a golden age of individual freedom. Vernon L. Parrington (*Main Currents in American Thought*) and his followers probably established this tradition so far as modern American historians are concerned, although it should be added that the filio-patristic nationalistic writers, for their own reasons, assigned extraordinary virtue to the founders of the Republic. Parrington was quite explicit: American liberty hit its apogee with the Declaration of Independence and has been on the decline ever since. Jefferson is the folk hero of this tradition, and the basic analytic proposition on which the whole Parringtonian superstructure rests is that the centralized state is the enemy of freedom. The Hamiltonians thus become the sappers under the fortress of liberty, and it follows (quite properly in logical terms) that the increase in the power of the state has automatically led to a decline in the rights of the individual. The better to preserve the pristine ideal, Parringtonians regularly overlook the inconvenient facts that Jefferson opposed both John Adams's Sedition Law and Hamilton's mercantilism on *states'-rights* grounds. Here, for example, is Jefferson's Second Inaugural Address on the subject of religious freedom:

"In matters of religion I have considered that its free exercise is placed by the Constitution independent of the powers of the General Government. I have therefore undertaken on no occasion to prescribe the religious exercises suited to it, but have left them, as the Constitution found them, under the direction and discipline of the church *or state* authorities acknowledged by the several religious societies." (Italics added.) A few paragraphs later, he made the same differentiation between state and national *vires* in connection with the handling of seditious libels.

How can we account for this curious refusal to confront historical reality on its own terms? A generation that ruthlessly suppressed Tory speech and Tory press (not merely "overt" Tory acts), confiscated Tory property with a zeal and efficiency a Bolshevik could admire, and populated the wilds of Canada with its opposition, has somehow been acclaimed as "conservative."

A generation that employed loyalty oaths and disclaimer affidavits in a fashion that would bring joy to the heart of a Joseph R. McCarthy has similarly been credited with establishing civil liberties in the United States. The forty-second and latest *Annual Report* of the American Civil Liberties Union, for example, gives a stirring quotation from Jefferson and bemoans "our twentieth century resurrection of official orthodoxy," with the clear implication that "official orthodoxy" was a foreign product that Jefferson and his fellow libertarians barred from these shores.

STILL FIGHTING THE KING

If there was one thing on which John Adams and Thomas Jefferson always agreed, it was with respect to what has been called the doctrine of "American exceptionalism," the view that the truths of the Old world were not necessarily applicable to the realities of the New. It seems to me that, oddly enough, the source of historical confusion about civil rights has largely arisen from a refusal to recognize the validity of this insight. To put the point precisely, a set of analytic categories devised in Europe to cope with European development has been unthinkingly applied to the American scene. Thus because the political leaders of the American Revolution were not "Jacobins," they must have been "conservatives." Similarly the often terrifying realities of a savage, brawling frontier society and the brutal confrontations in the great Civil War and the lesser civil wars (between labor and management, white and Negro, Mormon and "gentile," Irish and nativist) have been converted into exercises in consensual group therapy because they refuse to fit the standards of European social theory.

What this means in concrete terms is that the European liberal doctrine that the centralized state is the natural enemy of freedom was simply transplanted to the American scene—where, I submit, it was essentially irrelevant. The centralized state, that "Mortal God" which in Europe emerged triumphant over the centrifugal tendencies of feudalism and the religious wars and in the process destroyed the "liberties" of the subject, of the town, and of the province or shire alike, never developed on this side of the water. To the European liberals, Thomas Hobbes was the enemy incarnate, and bravely they fought to put chains on Leviathan, to curb the power of a centralized bureaucracy, to mobilize the power of the community against the artificial "engines of tyranny" created at Paris or Westminster. But the "engines of oppression" were not successfully exported to the American colonies; British efforts to establish centralized colonial administration foundered—as young John Adams pointed out to a Boston discussion group almost two centuries ago—on the stubborn realities of local sovereignty. (And, it should be added, on British inefficiency.)

The American Revolution was—as Adams also pointed out—fought to retain *de facto* local sovereignty against British efforts to establish Leviathan on an international basis. It was fought to maintain the civil liberties of

Americans, i.e., the right of Americans to define their rights for themselves. No one ever suggested that a Tory could assert his rights against his patriot neighbors, and there was certainly no operating concept of "vested individual rights" against the community. John Locke was interpreted, as indeed he had been in his own day, as the theoretician of majority rule, as the tribune of the community, in its resistance to arbitrary, capricious, and above all unrepresentative governmental institutions. There was no appeal to "natural law" against the responsible decision of the society: for Locke and the Americans who set to work building their own governments, it was simply taken for granted that civil law defined natural law in any truly representative system. Bills of rights were thus designed to protect the citizen from the possible usurpations of the government, not from the decisions of his neighbors.

The Federal Bill of Rights, from this viewpoint, was not designed to preserve the liberty of the individual but to guarantee that *local* definitions of liberty would prevail. If one reads carefully the Amendments dealing with criminal procedure (IV through VII), he will appreciate the institutional sagacity of their sponsors: literally enforced, they would make impossible the development in the United States of a Tudor judiciary, that marvelous mechanism of centralization where the royal judge became in effect a local viceroy. (Those who noted the failure of the Federal government to indict former Major General Edwin Walker for incitement to riot against national authority in the wake of the Mississippi crisis last year will admire the effectiveness of the authors of the Fifth Amendment: a Mississippi grand jury refused to turn in a true bill and the United States government was helpless).

The community, then, is charged with protecting civil liberties from any perversion by the state. But, returning to the concept of American exceptionalism, has this curbing of the Federal government ever really been the problem in the United States? It is my contention that since the seventeenth century the basic civil-liberties problem has been not the arbitrary exercise of centralized power but the despotism of the militant majority. Thus while the growth of bureaucracy, particularly of the national government, and the expansion of national law proves to the Parringtonians that liberty is in decline, I look upon the same set of historical developments and find a growing tradition of impersonal bureaucratized justice and a withering away of decentralized authoritarianism. Moreover, I am prepared to argue that something "impossible" has happened, impossible that is in terms of the premises of European liberalism: the national government has become an instrument for protecting individual freedom.

AN INVISIBLE TERROR

Since this involves some drastic shifts in definition, let me set forth in more detail what I mean by the despotism of the militant majority. Until roughly the First World War, excluding the Sedition Act of 1798, it is impossible to find any national laws penalizing dissenting *opinion*. And until the great epidemic of criminal anarchy laws touched off by the assassination of President McKinley, the states had little legislation on the subject. It would, however, be a drastic error to draw from this absence of legislation the conclusion that freedom of opinion was universally respected. Or, if one wishes to quibble with this generalization, we can concede that freedom of opinion was everywhere respected—with the right to define *opinion* reserved to local juries. There was nothing "individualistic" about the common law, and in most states the old common-law remedies for non-conformity were adequate to the needs of the time. Thus a citizen who advocated birth control would find himself in court charged with "lewd behavior" and "breach of the peace" and, unless he could convince stalwart jurymen of the virtue of his cause, would wind up in the workhouse for six months. His opinions were not at issue; it was his "lewd behavior" that got him into trouble—and no one, anywhere, has a constitutional right to behave lewdly. If his opinions were the source of his behavior, that was his problem; his objective actions alone were involved in the trial. He might think whatever he wanted, but he might not behave lewdly.

Let us take another area—freedom of conscience, which most bills of rights guaranteed absolutely. Here we have a classic example of the legal assault on the Church of Jesus Christ, Latter Day Saints, by which the Mormons were savagely persecuted in Missouri and Illinois and eventually besieged and beaten in their Utah fortress. The Mormons, claiming divine inspiration, incorporated as part of their creed the doctrine of "celestial marriage," i.e., polygamy. Their neighbors, suffering perhaps from prurient envy, denounced them as bigamists and the majesty of the law was invoked. To their claim of freedom of religion, the judges and juries uniformly replied that bigamy was a crime, not an exercise of freedom of conscience. Freedom of religion stopped at the outer limits of the criminal code. (In Utah and Idaho, however, the jury system failed in its obligations: Mormon jurors acquitted Mormons. The consequence was that Congress, which had refused to act in defense of Southern Negroes who had been returned to virtual slavery by a militant majority, their white neighbors, passed a bill barring "bigamists," "polygamists," and "any person cohabiting with more than one woman" from voting or serving on juries and thus got the local majority back in sound hands!) A Mormon in jail for bigamy could hardly claim that his religious freedom had been violated; by definition (of twelve good men, well-chosen and true), religious freedom had been held not to include the right to be a bigamist.

To abbreviate a long story, I have been searching for some years for an early (say pre-1900) case in which a state court overruled a decision of a lower court on civil-rights grounds, that is, invoked a provision of a state bill of rights as a bar to prosecution. There are cases that conform to the Parringtonian ideal—where state courts have thrown out *statutes* as violative of a state bill of rights—but I have yet to find an instance in which an appellate state tribunal threw out the decision of a local jury on libertarian grounds. There must be some cases in this category somewhere, but they are fairly well concealed. Perhaps elected judges took a dim view of reversing and remanding the decisions of their constituents.

One of the marvels of the common law in this contest was (and is) its invisibility. No centralized state apparatus had been mobilized; the sheriff or chief of police handled the burden of prosecution; no statute was normally invoked; and the defendant was never put away for sedition but simply for "unlawful assembly" or "breach of the peace"—legal rubrics that are still, as recent Freedom Rider and sit-in litigation demonstrates, extremely difficult to handle at the appellate level. For technical reasons that need not concern us here, appellate courts have always been limited in their ability to go "behind" the record—to investigate *de novo* the facts in a case—so that to this day it is extraordinary to find an instance where sufficient legal sophistication is employed at the trial level to make possible an appellate reversal of a conviction for "breach of the peace." (The NAACP has been infuriating Southern prosecutors by providing precisely this expertise, carefully introducing into the trial record material that opens up the possibility of broad appeal.)

Although one can condemn the consequences of this system as "undemocratic," the system itself seems to have reflected the "will of the people." This pluralism of decentralized authoritarianism made it possible, of course, for a wide range of views to exist, each in its own haven of orthodoxy. "Law and order" in this milieu clearly meant what the local majority defined as such. A sheriff elected on a clean-up program in Nevada gave this position its finest expression: anyone who rejected the principles of "law and order," he proclaimed, would be "summarily hanged."

Now all of this—like the local campaign of extermination in the antebellum South against the Abolitionists—took place below the threshold of classic liberal sensitivity. Civil rights in the United States were secure, an Albert Jay Nock or William Graham Sumner would argue, adducing the absence of centralized, bureaucratized despotism. Also below their threshold were the exercises of sovereign power by economic feudalities, the great private governments of the last quarter of the nineteenth century and the first three decades of the twentieth. While the New York Central Railroad or the United States Steel Corporation, *inter alia,* fulfilled every definition of sovereignty except issuing postage stamps, the restrictions they imposed on their subjects were not violations of individual liberty. On the contrary, from this vantage point they were merely contractual obligations freely accepted as a precondition for making a living. A man might receive the economic equivalent of the death sentence—dismissal and blacklisting—for joining a union, and a union organizer might be forbidden even to discuss the merits of organization with workers who had signed "yellow dog" contracts (a limitation on freedom of speech which the Supreme Court accepted on the grounds that such a speech constituted incitement to breach of contract!), but none of the classic civil-rights issues were involved.

Indeed, civil-rights issues did not arise in this area unless the state attempted to intervene on behalf of the workers—by, say, banning the yellow dog contract, or requiring payment in coin of the realm rather than scrip, or limiting the work-week. The minute the state was sighted on the horizon, classical civil libertarians marshaled their forces for Armageddon.

MOB RULE AND THE LAW

To summarize an elaborate argument, if we examine the "state of civil liberties" in 1900 from the classical liberal viewpoint, we find that the United States was clearly the freest nation in the world (the otherwise sound British had a bad habit of passing Factory Acts and other invasions of Freedom of Contract). There was no centralized bureaucracy, no national police, no income tax, no national control of state and local government—the nation was a libertarian paradise. Yet, if one analyzed the same data from another angle, he might contend that the United States was a nation where the workers were at the mercy of their employers, Negroes were living in serfdom, religious and ethnic minorities were subjected to blatant discrimination, and the "rights of the individual" were those specified by a militant majority of his neighbors.

Patently it is a question of what "model" one employs. In the United States there existed both a weak and decentralized governmental apparatus *and* a fundamental absence of individual freedom for those to whom it was important: those who differed on basic issues with the rural, white, predominantly Anglo-Saxon Protestant majority. The majority was free—it held views approved by the majority, or by those local majorities which characterized a country still strongly regional in emphasis. Community authoritarianism also permeated those subcultures that were under attack by the great society: Brooklyn Jews who sponsored a Yom Kippur ball to demonstrate their liberation from the "superstitions" of the Orthodox were mobbed by their neighbors in the ghetto, and a hard-rock miner in Colorado who refused to respond to the bugle of the Western Federation of Miners could expect little sympathy on his painful ride out of town.

One final example may illuminate the shadowy place in my argument. On April 26, 1913, a tragic sequence of events began in Atlanta, Georgia, when Mary Phagan was found raped and murdered in the basement of Moses Frank's pencil factory, managed by his nephew Leo. Leo Frank was accused of the crime, indicted, tried, and convicted of murder. The evidence was flimsy and wholly circumstantial; the prosecution's key witness, Jim Conley, was certainly himself the murderer. But in no real sense was Frank on trial: the Jews were in the cage. "Our little girl—*ours* by the eternal God!" bellowed Tom Watson, the agrarian demagogue who was to be elected to the Senate in 1920 on a program that mixed equal parts of anti-war Populism, anti-Semitism, and anti-Catholicism, "has been pursued to a hideous death and bloody grave by *this filthy perverted Jew of New York.*"

Frank's lawyer was told bluntly, "If they don't hang that Jew, we'll hang you." In this atmosphere Frank was sentenced to hang (Watson editorially licked his chops at the prospect of vengeance on this "lascivious Jew"); eventually after successive appeals the United States Supreme Court rejected Frank's contention that the state of Georgia had denied him due process of law. Oliver Wendell Holmes, Jr., joined by Charles Evans Hughes, dissented brutally from the seven-justice majority which implicitly ruled (technically they declined jurisdiction) that Frank had been granted his full legal remedies under the Constitution. "Mob rule," said Holmes, expounding a position taken for granted by today's court, "does not become due process of law by securing the assent of a terrorized jury . . . it is our duty [to declare] lynch law as little valid when practiced by a regularly drawn jury as when administered. . . . by a mob intent on death."

It appears that by this time the Georgia judges were well aware of Frank's innocence. Conley had confessed to his lawyer, who, bound by the lawyer-client relationship, could not reveal the information. Finally, incapable of standing silent while Frank was railroaded to the gallows, the counsel confided the matter to Judge Arthur Powell, who was his intimate friend. The latter apparently passed the information on to Governor John Slaton, though still under the seal of secrecy. But with Watson on the war path, no one wished to assume responsibility for letting "the Jew" go free, or even for ordering a new trial. Finally with Frank about to hang, Governor Slaton risked his own neck and commuted the sentence to life imprisonment. Frank, secretly removed from Atlanta to Milledgeville Prison Farm, was immediately knifed by a fellow convict and was soon seized by a mob and lynched. "We regard the hanging of Leo Frank as an act of law-abiding citizens," observed the Marietta *Journal,* and Tom Watson chortled, "Jew libertines take notice!"

Back at the statehouse in Atlanta, only the intervention of armed troops prevented a frenzied mob from hanging Governor Slaton and dynamiting his home. When Slaton left office, and Georgia, three days after commuting Frank's sentence, his once promising political career was over. And when Tom Watson died in 1922, Eugene V. Debs sent his widow a letter praising this "heroic soul who fought the power of evil his whole life long." More appropriately the Ku Klux Klan sent a huge floral cross.

THE SOURCES OF FREEDOM

This was the militant majority in action, and one can find other episodes that equally demonstrate the unfettered passion of mob rule operating under the procedural formulas of "due process of law"—the extirpation of opposition during the First World War presents the interested student with an endless accumulation of relevant data. But the classical liberal would theoretically remain unmoved: the centralized state, that evil abstraction, played a minor role or none. (A. Mitchell Palmer's brutal raids in the immediate postwar period were the first nationally directed sedition hunt on a large scale since 1798, but Harding's victory put an end to any national concern with ideas—"good" or "bad.") The absence of a star chamber has been taken as proof of the existence of freedom of opinion, the lack of an FBI or a "security program" as evidence of unfettered individual freedom.

Actually, in the transformation of American life from the condign direct democracy of the "old order" to the regularized tradition of due process of law, enforced by national courts, a major share of the credit for converting civil liberties from privileges a community granted to its members to rights which can be defended against a militant local majority must be accorded to the intervention of the centralized state. The passage of the Wagner Act, for example, was one of the greatest acts of liberation in American history; decisions of the Supreme Court in school segregation, reapportionment, search and seizure, right to counsel, and other cases have played a notable part in the expansion of individual freedom; and one should not overlook in this context the work of the national Executive, such as President Truman's desegregation orders for the Federal administration and the armed forces and President Kennedy's housing order. The same pattern of governmental action has been instituted in many states.

And yet this state action for *individual* freedom—not group freedom, not majority freedom—still arouses the wrath of classical liberals; and contemporary liberals, who hold no general brief against the state, often seem hypnotized by the litany. Last December, for instance, the Center for the Study of Democratic Institutions held a potlatch in New York where speaker after speaker, mostly from civil-liberties circles, echoed the mordant warning that American liberty was in unprecedented jeopardy. No sane man will deny that the *potential* threats to American freedom from possible state action are far greater in 1963 than they were in 1833 or 1913. The great apparatus of Federal power *could* be employed for evil ends as well as good ones, and the real possibility of resistance to centralized power has vanished. But what indications are there that our modern Leviathan is driven by totalitarian compulsions? One hundred and nine once jailed Communists, many now busy lecturing to liberal-arts colleges? Without suggesting that one can adopt a quantitative scale in matters of this sort, I would submit that any sober evaluation of the contribution of the national government to the improvement or the decline of civil liberty must conclude on the basis of the evidence to date with a decision in favor of Federal intervention.

Anyone who cherishes the ideals of individual freedom and justice can never relax his efforts to push forward the frontiers of liberty. But the historian of civil liberty in the United States (though himself a civil libertarian who realizes that history can grant no absolution) has the obligation to assert the relative proposition that the contemporary American, despite the existence of a huge centralized state, is today free to enjoy a range of personal liberty unknown to his ancestors.

11   PERSPECTIVE ON INTERGOVERNMENTAL RELATIONS

"The federal government is taking over everywhere; the states are doomed." "With the state governments assuming more and more responsibilities, local self-government is becoming more and more a cipher."

Such statements as these reflect a common American view of federal-state-local relations. This viewpoint is fostered not only by those who view it with alarm ideologically, but also by those who, while defending the trend, share some of the mistaken notions about these governmental relationships. Before embarking on a study of state and local government in action, it is essential that the student understand clearly both the theoretical underpinnings and the practical modifications of the American system of intergovernmental relations.

Theoretically, the American national-state relationship is clear, based as it is upon the first federal system in world history. Two elements are essential to any federal system of government; both are present in America. The first, a clear allocation of the powers of government to two separate and distinct levels, is contained in the "delegated and reserved powers" system by which, in the words of the Tenth Amendment to the Constitution, "The powers not delegated to the United States by the Constitution, nor prohibited by it to the States, are reserved to the States respectively, or to the people."

The second element, just as essential, though not always recognized, was implicit in the New Jersey Plan of union presented to the 1787 Constitutional Convention even though it was never specifically stated. This element involves the ability of both levels of government to operate directly upon the individual citizen. Whereas, in the days of the Articles of Confederation, the Continental Congress had to request the states to raise money or troops for its use, today's Congress can levy taxes directly and induct young men into its armed forces. However, the states have not yielded their power to act directly on the citizen in enforcing their own laws or in raising their own revenue.

In *practice,* however, the relationship between the national and state levels of American government has emerged in a much different fashion. There is little doubt that the federal government has come to exert the powers of a senior member in the federal-state partnership. This process, the centralization of federalism, has come about gradually, sometimes imperceptibly, in the 175 years of national existence, by at least five different methods.

(1) *Court Interpretation* has spelled out the meaning of the Constitution. The Supreme Court has consistently held that the commerce clause provides federal power to regulate "all intercourse" among the states, and hence to regulate interstate businesses of all kinds, from insurance to labor unions and even such nefarious enterprises as white slavery, car theft, and kidnap-

ping—so long as the crime involves interstate transportation. In the "due process" clause of the Fourteenth Amendment, the Court has found the authority to apply the substantive as well as procedural protections of the Bill of Rights against the states, requiring them to afford their citizens such freedoms as speech, press, religion, assembly and petition—all explicitly protected only against Congressional infringement. In the "equal protection of the laws" clause, also in the Fourteenth Amendment, the Court has recently discovered grounds for requiring state legislative reapportionment.

(2) Evidence that this centralizing trend has the implied consent of the American people is to be found in the *formal amendments* to the Constitution adopted since the Bill of Rights. In each instance save one (the Twenty-first, or Prohibition Repeal Amendment), every formal amendment of the nineteenth and twentieth centuries which has affected federal-state relations has tended to limit the states or grant additional powers to the Federal government. Thus the power of the states to restrict the franchise because of race or sex has been abolished, the power of the federal government to impose an income tax confirmed, and so on.

(3) In defining and spelling out the terms of the Constitution, Congress itself has utilized the powerful device of *statutory amplification* to expand the powers of the central government. It has used the grant-in-aid as a financial "carrot" to lure the states into many kinds of administrative and policy compliance that could not be coerced under the Constitution. It has employed the "matching dollar" device (one federal-to-one state) in a wide range of areas, from hospital construction to slum clearance. In the interstate highway program it has made refusal almost impossible by offering *nine* national dollars for every state dollar.

(4) *Executive amplification* has been the method by which presidents of the United States have contributed to the expansion of federal power. From Washington to Johnson, presidents have used their authority as Commander-in-Chief of the Armed Forces for such actions as suppressing a tax rebellion in Pennsylvania, engaging in strike-breaking in Chicago, and putting down racial disorders in Little Rock, Arkansas, and Oxford, Mississippi. Employing his treaty-making powers (with Senatorial consent), one president provided, in an agreement with Canada, the means for policing wild-fowl hunters in Missouri. Bypassing the Senate in an executive agreement with the same nation for the St. Lawrence Seaway, another president, Franklin D. Roosevelt, put near-irresistible pressure on New York State to engage in the generation of electric power.

(5) Finally, *custom and usage,* the product of time honored tradition and public expectation, have served to limit the power of the states, and to contribute further to the expansion of the federal domain. Thus the public has sanctioned the emergence of the FBI as a quasi-national police force, even though the police power in our system is nominally reserved to the states. In many other areas the public has been unwilling to accept a state's impotence in dealing with complex interstate problems and has demanded federal intervention.

In the relations of states to local governments of all kinds—cities and villages, counties and towns, school districts and other special districts—it is theoretically established that the latter are the "creatures of the state." In the words of the long-time Mayor of New York, Robert F. Wagner, the city "holds no powers to tax, even to exist as a governmental unit, which the state does not control." The conclusion seems inescapable that there is no firm theoretical foundation for any direct federal-local relationship—that the national government should operate through state intermediaries in dealing with the cities, just as the United Nations would proceed through the British government in any negotiations involving Wales or Scotland.

The principal development in the field of state-local relations has been the evolution of a *quasi-federalism,* a working relationship in which the local governments are far more than mere "creatures of the state," to be called into existence or abolished at state whim. The "home rule" movement of the twentieth century has brought strong trends toward local self-determination of government form, with local drafting of city, village, and county charters. Similarly, well-recognized—if extra-constitutional—jurisdictional bounds have been established between state and local governments; the property tax is left for the most part to local governments, and state police are often restricted from involvement in urban law enforcement activities. While prosecutions are still traditionally brought in the name of the "People of the State vs. John Doe," the arrest actually results from local police activity, with subsequent trial (barring appeal) in a local court which is only nominally part of a state system.

Finally, in spite of the theoretically non-existent relationship between the federal and local governments, the states have in fact been bypassed in such areas as urban renewal. With only a few states able or willing to assume the financial burdens of city-rebuilding, it seemed logical for the federal government to step in. Since many rural-dominated state legislatures showed marked hostility to, or lack of interest in metropolitan problems, it seemed practical for federal authorities to work directly with the cities. The resultant relations, while far from perfect, have proven highly satisfactory to large city mayors of both political parties. Federal funds for airport construction, for urban highways, and for the war on poverty have similarly led to increasing direct federal-local contact.

To summarize, there has been a quiet revolution in federal-state-local relationships in America. This has been not the result of ideological change nor constitutional violation, but rather the work of pragmatic leaders of both political parties who have found in our system the flexibility to adapt to modern needs. Moreover, the change has come about in response to citizen pressures that "something be done about" immediate and specific problems. The man in the street, by and large, has viewed with equanimity the assumption by federal and state governments of an increasing share of the over-all government burden. In so doing he has accepted two concepts: the greater equity of the tax systems employed by the larger jurisdictions, particularly the broad-based individual and corporate income taxation of the federal government; and the greater independence from self-seeking local pressures in a state or national capital where to some extent the local interests find their power countervailed.

In spite of this substantial evolution, the states remain highly significant in a system that is still truly federal. How else can we explain (as foreigners so often question) the inability of our federal government to try, let alone punish, the apprehended murderers of civil rights workers, abducted and slain within the boundaries of a single state (and hence beyond any federal authority)? Such well-publicized cases underline the fact that in America it is the states alone which possess that most important power of government —the police power. And the police power goes far beyond mere criminal restraint, encompassing diverse areas, from control of land utilization to restrictions against false and misleading advertising.

It must be noted, moreover, that the powers of state government as well of local, far from diminishing over the past century and three-quarters, have in fact increased. From municipal police, fire, and water departments to state parks and recreation areas, these governments are today undertaking more and broader functions than ever before. Only the even more rapid expansion of federal power has made their growth seem slow or even retrograde in comparison. As we look to the future, it seems clear that our federal government will come to play a still greater role in the intergovernmental relationship. Meanwhile, however, there will also be significant new tasks as well as old chores of undiminished importance to be tackled by our state and local governments in action.

FREEDOM AND FEDERALISM
Peter H. Odegard

Peter H. Odegard is Professor of Political Science at the University of California, Berkeley. In 1961–62 he conducted the two-semester course in American Government seen over the National Broadcasting Company's "Continental Classroom." He has served as president of the American Political Science Association and is the author of numerous publications in his field.

It is an axiom of a free society that the individual shall have maximum freedom to choose his way of life. Subject only to the influences or conditions of his cultural environment, he ought to be free to choose his religion, his politics, his job, his school, his friends—even his wife.

And it is characteristic of a free, pluralistic society—as distinguished from a monolithic-authoritarian one—that the alternatives among which he is free

From *National Civic Review*, December 1962. Reprinted by permission.

to choose are many rather than few. A free society strives to encourage diversity, knowing that only a pluralistic culture is compatible with the manifold differences that distinguish individuals from one another. And knowing also that it is open-eyed diversity and not blind conformity that gives to a free society its dynamic quality.

It is in the competition of ideas, patterns of behavior, multiple power centers and value systems that that fugitive mistress, Truth, is most likely to be found. Indeed, the late Oliver Wendell Holmes went so far as to say that the best test of an idea is its capacity to win its way in a free market of ideas.

Holmes was but repeating what had been said by many wise men before him, from Socrates to Seneca and Justinian to Jefferson. John Milton put it most eloquently in his essay *Aereopagitica*:

> Though all the winds of doctrine were let loose to play upon the earth, so Truth be in the field, we do injuriously by licensing and prohibiting to misdoubt her strength. Let Her and Falsehood grapple: whoever knew Truth put to the worse, in a free and open encounter?

There are many Americans in these days of continuing crisis who seem to have forgotten this simple notion—that without diversity there is no choice and without choice, no freedom. To speak of safeguarding freedom by denying or impairing the individual's capacity to choose among different and even conflicting alternatives is, of course, a contradiction in terms.

You may well ask what all this has to do with the "Web of Government," the assigned theme for these meetings. Let me explain.

The basic goals of the American Republic are set forth in the Preamble to the Constitution: (1) "To form a more perfect union," (2) "establish justice," (3) "insure domestic tranquility," (4) "provide for the common defense," and (5) "secure the blessings of liberty to ourselves and our posterity."

All that follows in the Constitution concerning the structure and powers of government has no meaning apart from the goals outlined in the Preamble. The relation between the Preamble and Articles I through VII of the Constitution, including the 23 amendments, is a relation of means and ends. The structure and powers of Congress, the President and the courts, the outline of intergovernmental relations in Article II and Section 10 of Article I, the process of amendment described in Article II, the Bill of Rights and the other amendments have no purpose or meaning but to achieve the goals outlined in the Preamble.

The terms in which these goals are outlined are highly ambiguous. What is a more perfect union? What does it mean to establish justice or to promote the general welfare? To point to this ambiguity is to emphasize that these are political terms designed to unite people of highly diverse interests upon common goals, leaving to the political process—that complex interplay of personal, partisan and interest-group competition—to define them more precisely and to agree upon appropriate means for their realization.

The broader goals themselves are quite ambiguous, but they are not meaningless. On the contrary, they provide a basic consensus within which the political process of definition and discovery can go on without resort to violence. It is in this sense that the political process may be defined as a continuous exercise in the logic of ambiguity. Because they are ambiguous, value propositions admit of a variety of definitions as to particular ends and means at particular times and places. That is to say, they admit of various alternatives among which reasonable men may choose. And because they admit of choice, they admit of freedom to choose—and thus help to preserve the blessings of liberty to ourselves and our posterity.

Some of the choices to be made are within the span of control, as it were, of the individual; others are made by individuals as members of some private group or organization like the family, the corporation or the trade union. Still others are made by individuals as members of some political community, i.e., as citizens. In all these situations people make decisions affecting their way of life as it relates to the broad goals outlined in the Preamble to the Constitution. But it is as a citizen that the individual is most directly caught up in the web of government as it reaches from the town meeting to the Security Council of the United Nations.

Because the central purpose of a free society is to secure and promote the freedom and welfare of individuals it strives also to maintain the greatest possible measure of decentralization in the decision-making process.

Freedom, it can be argued, is more secure where each individual himself is able to make the basic decisions affecting his own life. And for those which are beyond his own span of control, a free society requires that the individual participate as directly as possible in the making of decisions for the community in which he lives. To the extent that these decisions are made by authorities remote from the individual, or by a process in which he cannot significantly participate, to that extent he is not free. By this test it is argued that human freedom is most secure when political decisions are made at the lowest possible level of the total web of government—presumably by that unit closest to the people concerned and in which they can most directly and effectively take part. Hence, if we value freedom, we must constantly strive to maintain in the highest possible degree a decentralized system for making political decisions.

Yet increasing centralization is one of the most obvious facts of our political life. Some measure of the trend may be seen in one statistic from President Eisenhower's Commission on Intergovernmental Relations. Whereas in 1929 state and local taxes represented approximately 75 per cent of all taxes collected as against about 25 per cent for the federal government, by 1955 these positions are almost exactly reversed—with state and local taxes comprising about 24 per cent of the total and federal taxes 76 per cent. As our society becomes more closely integrated, this trend will no doubt continue. Presidents deplore it, governors and congressmen view it with alarm; but specific proposals for reversing the trend seem never to get off the drawing-boards.

President Eisenhower's Commission on Intergovernmental Relations (the so-called Kestnbaum Commission), reporting in July 1955, made numerous recommendations for the improvement of federal-state relations and for an increase in state and local responsibility in a number of areas. But so little came of this effort that, in 1958, a subcommittee on Intergovernmental Relations was set up by the House Committee on Government Operations "to evaluate the recommendations of the Kestnbaum Commission and to ascertain what action is being and should be taken concerning them." And in 1959 a permanent Advisory Commission on Intergovernmental Relations was established.

Many of the proposals that have been made involve not merely a reallocation of functions and finances, not merely questions of organization and administration, but questions of policy, i.e., of politics. Consequently, discussion often proceeds on a high level of ambiguity. The following statement of the President's commission will serve to illustrate:

> Leave to private initiative all the functions *that citizens can perform privately,* use the *level of government closest to the community for all public functions it can handle,* utilize cooperative intergovernmental arrangements *where appropriate* to attain economical performances and popular approval, reserve national action for residual participation where state and local governments are not fully adequate and for the continuing responsibilities that only the national government can undertake.

Few people will quarrel with these basic objectives. Conflict ensues when we undertake to translate these ambiguous terms into specific proposals. Not many years ago most folks would have said that unemployment and poor relief and the support of the aged were matters more properly left to the family or to private charity. Today an important body of opinion believes that even medical care should be as much a public responsibility as unemployment insurance, poor relief and old age pensions now are. The expansion of the public sector of our economic and social life continues to be a subject of heated debate. For those who regard social security legislation, medical care for the aged or massive support for public education as avoidable, undesirable and even malicious, it makes little difference whether these new public responsibilities are assumed by local, state or national governments. States' rights, local self-government and other slogans used to resist federal action in these areas are often a kind of semantic screen to conceal campaigns of opposition not to centralization as such but to the substance of the particular policies proposed.

Businessmen who talk solemnly about the evils of big government are singularly complacent as they contemplate the growth of big business. The most strident plea to "restore the states to their rightful place in our federal union," by keeping the federal government out of such fields as education, health and welfare, housing or urban renewal, is rarely accompanied by opposition to monumental defense expenditures, highway programs or subsidies to business enterprise. The leaders of the fight against welfare legislation in Washington more often than not also lead the fight against welfare legislation at the state capitol and the city hall. Nevertheless, these conflicts over particular policies are not unrelated to our basic assumption that human freedom and welfare will be most secure under a system based on the greatest possible decentralization of decision-making. Political decisions, it is said, should really be made at the "lowest possible level." But the lowest possible level will vary not only with time and place but with the kind of decisions to be made. The lowest possible level at which decisions affecting police, fire protection, garbage disposal, water supply, stream pollution, reclamation, mass communication or transportation, national defense, war and peace, will vary from the town meeting to the city council, the metropolitan area, the state legislature, the regional council or authority, the Congress of the United States or a summit meeting in Geneva.

What is the lowest possible unit for making decisions concerning smog control, mass transportation and a dozen other problems that confront our great metropolitan areas—especially those that overlap state boundaries and include dozens of towns, cities, counties and special districts?

What is the lowest possible unit for making decisions concerning the regulation of oligopolies, with headquarters in New Jersey or Delaware but with branches reaching not only into nearly every state but into many foreign countries? To say that these decisions should be made by the cities, counties and states within which these giants operate is to set David against Goliath with the cards all stacked against David.

The fact is, of course, that under the impact of irresistible centripetal forces—population growth, density and mobility, technological developments reducing barriers of time and space, hot wars and cold wars, etc.—major political decisions will increasingly be made at higher and higher levels in the great web of government.

Does this centralization of decision-making necessarily imply a threat to freedom? Does centralized decision-making by great corporations under conditions of monopolistic competition threaten freedom and welfare or has large scale enterprise accelerated economic growth, increased our standard of living and expanded our freedom in our range of choice? When the Supreme Court decides that states are not free to enforce racial segregation in public schools, will not this decision, in spite of temporary setbacks, give to both Negroes and whites greater freedom in choosing the schools to which they may send their children? Is freedom jeopardized or restricted when Congress, through grants-in-aid, enables states and municipalities to undertake programs of education, housing and urban rehabilitation, public health, transportation and welfare that in the absence of such grants would be impossible? Do not these programs, in fact, expand the scope of individual freedom by multiplying the alternatives among which he may realistically choose?

But, it will be said, even if the centralization of political decision-making poses no serious threat to freedom, it may threaten our democratic institutions by making participation in the decision-making process more difficult and thus undermining our will and capacity for self-government. "Municipal institutions," said de Tocqueville, "constitute the strength of free nations. Town meetings are to liberty what primary schools are to science: they bring it within the people's reach, they teach men how to use and how to enjoy it." This model of democracy with its roots and its strength in local assemblies has much to commend it.

Unfortunately, de Tocqueville's model had a closer fit to the comparatively stable agrarian society of 1832 than to the highly integrated, mobile society of 1962. There was a singular vitality in local assemblies when the major problems of government were local and could be met by decisions made at the village, town or county level. But as the scope and complexity of the major problems increased, as it became clear that local units of government—even when endowed with home rule by the state—were unable to deal with them, the center of power and the focus of civic interest moved away from the town to the county, the state and the nation.

The fact is that, to thousands of our citizens, the state and even the federal government seem closer and more visible than the city or the county. Indifference and apathy characterize democracy at the grass roots and may, in time, as de Tocqueville said it would, undermine our will and capacity for self-government. A recent study of elections for governing boards of local special districts says that "voter turnout is low, it being quite common for only 1 per cent to 5 per cent of the voters to participate." If we are to do something about this more constructive than wringing our hands, we shall have to take some radical measures to restore power and vitality to local political institutions. For civic interest follows power. A few things we might consider include:

1. A reform in the structure of our state governments is needed. State constitutions are almost models of what constitutions ought not to be. State legislatures are unrepresentative of the most dynamic forces in society and attract at best but mediocre talents. Recent court decisions may help to make legislatures at least more representative. The size, organization and procedures of most state legislatures inhibit honest discussion and debate, obscure responsibility for policy decisions and invite excessive influence, if not domination, by special interests.

2. Part of the problem arises from the inability of the governor to assume leadership and responsibility for policy and administration. He is normally but one of several elected executive officers—a hydra-headed monster often going in different directions at the same time. Moreover, the long ballot which this system entails, made longer by direct legislation, makes the voters' task all but impossible.

3. Congress and the states might seriously explore establishment of more regional authorities on the order of the TVA, where decisions can be made in the region with closer and continuous ties to local communities rather than in Washington, thus achieving decentralization on terms compatible with demography and common sense. Some of these results can be attained under interstate regional compacts provided Congress is prepared to give the necessary financial assistance at the beginning.

4. The reorganization of government in our great metropolitan areas can do much to revitalize interest in local affairs. The application of the federal principle to the government of these areas might make possible a maximum of decentralization of truly local functions with areawide authority over others.

5. The consolidation of thousands of special district authorities with the county, city or metropolitan area government to which they are properly related might help to stop the progressive Balkanization of local governments.

6. Independent authorities for air pollution, transit, etc., now engaged in performing special services in metropolitan areas should be brought under an areawide government owing political responsibility to the citizens of the area.

7. Partisanship in state and metropolitan government should be restored and revitalized so that major issues of public policy can be debated by leaders responsible to effective political parties rather than to clandestine combines of pressure groups. There is, in fact, a Republican, Democratic or Socialist way to run a great city.

8. A continuous review by the permanent Advisory Commission on Intergovernmental Relations of state–federal–local fiscal relations can explore more equitable and realistic allocation of functions and sources of revenue.

These are but a few of the problems that confront the American web of government in the United States as it seeks to respond to the demands of a society in the midst of almost cataclysmic change. Part of this change is in the structure of the American economy and American society, part of it in the transformation of our federal system. For American federalism wears a new face and has a new orientation. The new orientation is toward closer and more cooperative relations between federal, state and local governments—through grants-in-aid, cooperative law enforcement, interstate compacts and regional authorities. This new orientation includes also a growing realization of the importance of the federal principle in the government of metropolitan areas.

The web of government in the United States, moreover, reflects a new and more affirmative relation between public and private power structures. The freedom which federalism was designed to conserve has come to mean not merely freedom from monolithic, arbitrary power but also freedom to take affirmative action to provide for the common defense, promote the general welfare and preserve the blessings of liberty to everyone regardless of race or class or creed. The new federalism, says Robert Hutchins, "tends to look upon law (not so much) as an invasion of freedom . . . (but) as a means of establishing, extending or confirming freedom."

If the decentralization of decision-making among federal, state and local governments is important to freedom and welfare, so too is the decentralization of decision-making in business and industry, the learned professions and labor, in education and other organized groups which compose the private power structure of our society. But centripetal forces are in the saddle, both in public and in private life, not because evil men have conspired to put them there but because a common market of continental and even world dimensions demands decision-making on a continental scale. The future of our federal system and of our freedom and welfare as individuals will depend upon our success in reconciling this fact with that degree of decentralization that will release in the greatest possible measure the creative initiative and energies of our people.

THE ROLE OF THE STATES
Mark O. Hatfield

Now United States Senator from Oregon, Mark Hatfield served as governor of that state from 1959 to 1966. He was formerly a state legislator, state senator, and secretary of state for Oregon. He was Professor of Political Science at Willamette University from 1949 until 1956, as well as dean of students from 1950 to 1956.

Twenty years ago Harold Laski declared that, "The epic of federalism is over." The obituary was premature, to say the least. Laski's indictment, however, has just enough truth to demand our attention. He declared that federalism "is insufficiently positive in character; it does not provide for sufficient rapidity of action; it inhibits the emergence of necessary standards of uniformity; it relies upon compact and compromise . . . ; its psychological results, especially in an age of crisis, are depressing to a democracy that needs the drama of positive achievement to retain its faith."

Two decades later the states are not on the governmental junk-heap. Indeed, there has been both increased interest and action directed toward strengthening our state governments. The President's Commission on Intergovernmental Relations, the American Assembly sessions on "the forty-eight states: their tasks as policy makers and administrators," and this meeting of the National Municipal League are among many evidences of the vitality of the nation's interest in the role of the states.

James Madison expected that in our federal system "the most natural

From *National Civic Review*, December 1959. Reprinted by permission.

attachment of the people would be to the governments of their respective states." But our current interest in state government reflects to some extent our agreement with John Stuart Mill that, "A government cannot have too much of the kind of activity which . . . aids and stimulates individual exertion and development. The mischief begins when . . . it makes them work in fetters or bids them stand aside." We are beginning to recognize that there are real disadvantages and not a little danger in the assumption that "big brother" government can provide better answers from the banks of the Potomac than we can reach on the banks of the Charles, the Hudson, the Delaware or the Willamette.

It is not my purpose to call for a return to another era. We must respond to the "Challenge of the Sixties" and I would like to suggest what I believe should be the role of the states in responding to that challenge. In doing so, it seems necessary, first, to appraise the present "state of the states"; second, to identify the political and structural prerequisites to a vigorous federal system; and, finally, to propose some goals for the decade ahead.

In 1830, Indiana called upon Congress to open the federal purse to "minister consolation to all whom casualty or misadventure may render dependent upon benevolent protection." The federal government has responded to the invitation to a degree that would have appalled John C. Calhoun—who found "something ominous in the expression, 'the secretary of the interior' "—or President Pierce—who vetoed a grant of land to the states for the benefit of the insane because he did not want to see "the dignity of the states . . . bow to dictation of Congress by conforming their legislation thereto."

We "have grown accustomed to the look" of federal programs and policies in performing local functions. With John W. Davis, we accept the fact that "so long as our Republic endures as a federal system there is likely to be no end to the change in the powers of nation and state. These powers will develop and grow . . . to satisfy the ever-changing requirements of the American people." This is not to say that we all approve the drift of policy decisions to Washington. Rather it is our affirmation that one of the enduring strengths of a federal system is the fact that the political vacuum created by inaction at one level does not long remain unfilled.

The growth of the scope and power of the national government is perhaps the most important single fact about the nature of our federal system today. If the states fumble or fail to perform, there is now always available the alternative of national action—whether we are concerned with such inescapably local problems as urban renewal or sewage disposal or with such traditionally—and properly—local problems as education or election administration.

This competition for political power in our federal system poses a real challenge to the states. They must perform in accord with the needs of the people or stand aside.

A second significant fact about "state government—1959" is its own size.

Oregon's budget this year is nearly twenty times that of only twenty years ago and 300 times that of fifty years ago. This experience is far from unique. Governor Lawrence of Pennsylvania, in an address to the National Institute of Municipal Law Officers in October, reminded us that in 1946 federal expenditures accounted for 82 per cent of all government expenditures. Now the states are responsible for 36 per cent of all government expenditure— double the percentage of thirteen years ago.

These facts suggest both a substantial increase in function—often in response to the prodding of the national government—and an equally significant increase in our financial problems. We should also note that the states, which until the 1930's spent roughly half as much as local governments, now spend approximately the same amount, partially accounted for by increases in state grants to local government.

A third major factor in any appraisal of state government is its infinite variety. Although we applaud the opportunities for experimentation provided by 50 state governments, we presently lack adequate means of achieving uniformity where uniformity is desirable. The Commissioners on Uniform State Laws, the Council of State Governments and the related organizations have helped reduce unnecessary diversity. But, while I believe in the desirability of bold experimentation, I would insist that our experiments should lead us to conclusions and that the conclusions should more quickly be put to general use than is now the case.

Finally, any appraisal of the "state of the states" must acknowledge a number of real but intangible assets. The continued usefulness of the states is a matter of geography, political power and tradition. The mass of public business to be transacted in a nation covering three-million square miles requires state government. The states are going concerns with a substantial degree of governmental authority. State political parties are the units through which national political battles are waged. And the states have the strength born of emotional ties that give us pride in local achievement. The eclipse of the Lone Star by the North Star has not noticeably diminished the pride of Texans in the accomplishments of what is now only the second largest state. We may be Tarheels, or Sooners, or 49-ers, we may come from Hoosierland or Hulaland, but we do identify ourselves with the states in which we live.

Let me turn now to the identification of the conditions that will permit the states to meet the needs of the nation. If the United States is to flourish as a *federal* system—as the overwhelming majority of the nation still believes it should—the role of the states will be effective only if we insist on action in accord with four briefly stated propositions:

First, it is logical and natural to assume that the national government should focus on world problems and the truly national problems. There is more than enough business here to occupy the attention of Congress.

Second, there is real danger in permitting governmental authority to be over-centralized. The very real strengths of our dual system would disappear should political paralysis afflict either the nation or the states. We can condone neither an excess of states' rights nor a long-continued drift toward increased national authority.

Third, there are positive advantages in local decisions on a great many public issues. The scope and quality of public welfare programs, some (now federally regulated) aspects of unemployment compensation, and the management of public education will be better defined and decided close to home than in Washington. And I would also stress that local government should be freed and strengthened to permit local decisions (now made in state capitals) to be made by local government.

Finally, we must assume that we can improve the capability of the states to cope with the "Challenge of the Sixties." The executive budget, the Council of State Governments, the work of the little Hoover Commissions are recent evidences of the existence of a real desire—and ability—on the part of the states to meet the new responsibilities confronting us all.

Building on these propositions, what are the goals that we should set for the states in the years ahead?

Elihu Root once declared that "the only way to maintain the power of the government is to govern." We sometimes observe the failure of state governments to recognize this simple truth. If the states are to merit continued existence, they must have the will to govern.

But there must also be a way.

The Congress has just established an advisory commission to concern itself with intergovernmental relations. It is to be hoped that this delicately balanced commission—sugar-coated with state, county and city representatives—may serve to improve intergovernmental coordination.

I certainly concur in the desirability of a free flow of information between levels of government. I have conferred with members of Oregon's congressional delegation both in my office and in Washington about our mutual concerns. Last month, in addressing the League of Oregon Cities, I called for closer collaboration between state and local government, to be facilitated by a Division of Intergovernmental Services.

But neither the deliberations of the new national commission nor these other devices for intergovernmental coordination should distract us from the urgent need for a nationwide re-thinking of the role of the states—not, I should hope, under the sponsorship or domination of the national government.

Through the voluntary instrument of state coordination, the Council of State Governments, I suggest that in the course of the next five years the states should develop an action program that would achieve:

1. A greater degree of organizational similarity among the states,
2. A reduction of self-defeating fiscal and economic competition among the states,
3. An increased ability to anticipate and plan the solution of state and local problems,

4. Wider development of interstate solutions to interstate problems.

Our efforts as states to coordinate—or even to compare—our programs are often unsuccessful because of differences in the way we do things. These differences in organization and procedure sometimes reflect differences in political philosophy but overwhelmingly they are the result of the fact that we have not adequately evaluated the thousands of years of cumulative experience with state government this nation has had while we have grown from thirteen colonies to 50 states over a period of 170 years. We should aggressively seek a kind of national consensus about the meaning of our experience.

Out of a crisis a generation ago, Oregon developed a system for coordination of our institutions of higher education that is widely envied but rarely emulated. The variations in the pattern of higher education are, in my judgment, less the result of adaptation to local conditions than the result of simple inertia. And this judgment is confirmed by what we find when we engage in the comparison of almost every other function of state government. We must break the shackles of tradition that leave state governments with organization and procedures that limit their ability to deal effectively with problems facing state government.

One of the strengths of our nation has been the fact that ours has been a *national* economy. Barriers to commerce among the states, competition in offering tax concessions to migrating industry, aggressive state-sponsored advertising campaigns have been increasingly evident as our states each seek their own advantage. Minnesota's Governor Freeman has proposed to solve one symptom of this malady by transferring some of the states' revenue-collecting function to the national government. Transferring the political burden of tax collection to the federal government is hardly likely to reduce taxes and even less likely to reduce competition among the states for new industry. We have to find a more workable method of averting the excesses of interstate economic competition that threaten to destroy our free and national economy.

In recent years, the Council of State Governments has produced a number of significant monographs on problems confronting the states. Unfortunately the resources of the council, while of high quality, are limited and the record of action by the states in dealing with these problems discloses a need for more effective devices in anticipating and solving state problems. The conferences held under the sponsorship of the council (governors, budget officers, the National Legislative Conference, etc.) are valuable, but most states—and these national organizations, too—need to do a better job of identifying the problems we face, in developing patterns of solution and in securing action. It is in securing action that we seem to be particularly inept.

One reason, of course, is that those of us in elective office are forced to devote a considerable time to the task of obtaining and retaining our positions of influence. In a democratic government, short-term contracts for policy-makers are inevitable. I trust the good judgment of the voters—up to now—but the fact remains that every defeated incumbent takes with him to political limbo a knowledge about government problems and opportunities that his successor can acquire only by arduous labor. In my inaugural message I recommended one small step to lessen this loss by suggesting that former governors have floor and speaking privileges in the State Senate. While this is a beginning, we need to do a great deal more to reduce the loss of governmental wisdom that accompanies political turnover.

The federal government, because it is a single entity, because turnover of personnel is slower and because it is a prime focus of public interest, suffers less from this weakness than do the states. Our cities, at least to the extent that we have professionalized city management, are also better off. Better planning and more effective action by state government will not be likely until we first eliminate the unduly artificial restraints on tenure—such as two-year terms and one-term limits.

A second step is to find ways of increasing professionalism in state government. Civil service is, of course, imperative for non-policy-making posts. But we need to increase career opportunities for those who share policy-making responsibility. The directors and commissioners of administration and legislative fiscal officers occupy crucial positions in any state government. The heads of some other departments also have a professional role to play. The states cannot afford their biennial or quadrennial loss, simply through the turn of the political wheel of fortune.

The effective development of river basin resources or of imaginative and constructive solutions of metropolitan problems have rarely come from the states. In such a circumstance, national action has been almost inevitable. But these—and other—problems are properly the object of state or regional solution. This is particularly important to me, coming from the basin of the Columbia River. The states in this basin can never achieve their full potential unless the river is fully harnessed to multiple use. A regional corporation is probably the best solution. The problems of river basins and metropolitan regions are not national problems—unless the states fail to act.

The states associated in the New York Port Authority have demonstrated their capacity to cope with complex and difficult interstate problems. In Oregon, where we have a state-sponsored Port of Portland Commission and a city-sponsored Portland Dock Commission, we need to improve Oregon's response to our ports' problems and also to associate with the state of Washington in assuring that our solutions are of mutual benefit to those who reside on both banks of the Columbia.

The states should move with increasing vigor to attack their regional problems—in many cases by use of the interstate compact. I would urge the federal government to endorse such a policy by providing general legislation for each of the various kinds of regional problems—legislation which would assent to compacts containing such provisions as are essential to the national interest.

If the states are going to be full partners in the federal system they must retain and improve their ability to deal effectively with the changing complex of problems that require governmental solution. The more surely the states can move in concert in solving state and local problems the more surely will they be called upon to widen their sphere of service. Without a conscious program of action to cope with state problems and opportunities, we can be sure that we will drift on a widening flood of federal centralization to the Dead Sea of national decisions for local problems.

To Laski's indictment, the states must plead: "Not guilty."

Our states *can* be sufficiently positive in character. We *can* move with rapidity and, where necessary, with uniformity. The positive achievements of our states give eloquent testimony to their continued capacity for this age of crises.

The epic of federalism is not over. Rather, we stand on the threshold of a thrilling chapter in that epic, if only we have the wit, the will and the wisdom to meet the "Challenge of the Sixties."

CITIES LOOK TO THE STATE
Frank C. Moore

Frank C. Moore, president of the Government Affairs Foundation, was formerly lieutenant governor and comptroller of New York State. He is chairman of the New York State Board of Equalization and Assessment and the Advisory Board of the New York State Office for Local Government.

There is increasing agreement in the nation today that the complex of difficulties of our metropolitan areas is its number one problem on the home front. The president has characterized these problems as both a challenge and an opportunity and called upon the states to take the lead in attacking them. No greater challenge confronts our states and their localities now and in the decade ahead.

The Council of State Governments, at the request of the Conference of Governors, prepared a report in 1956 pointing out the several alternative methods of approach by the states. Effective results obviously depend upon the actions of the individual states. They vary considerably in the distribution of the functions of government between the states and their local governments and among the several types of local governments. Local governments usually provide and largely finance most of the day-to-day services that mean so much to the comfort, safety, health and happiness of the people.

From *National Civic Review*, February 1960. Reprinted by permission.

But the municipalities and other subdivisions are creations of the state. They must look to their states for assistance in removing roadblocks to the solution of their difficulties and for the additional powers or the better distribution of existing powers required for effective local action.

Until recently students of the subject seemed to divide into two almost irreconcilable groups as to the solution of the governmental aspects of urban sprawl. On the one hand there are those who advocate creation of a single governmental agency with responsibility for the solution of all the area-wide difficulties of a metropolitan community. On the other hand, there are those who argue that the resulting gains in governmental effectiveness would not be worth their cost in local traditions and hometown pride, in decreased citizen interest, influence and participation in local governments.

Within recent months there have been encouraging efforts to compromise the differences between the two groups by political inventions such as the proposed "metropolitan council." Rather lengthy association with the local governments of New York State prompts my belief that in most areas greater progress may be made along some such route as this than by demanding the total abandonment of present forms and structures in favor of colossal new agencies of government still further removed from the citizenry.

Opportunities for state helpfulness to its localities are many and varied. It is not my purpose to inventory or even to summarize generally all the efforts under way to progress against these difficulties of growth and movement of population but rather to mention briefly some of them and then to discuss more fully the program initiated in my home state of New York.

In the constitution prepared for the new state of Alaska maximum freedom was given to define the structure and powers of local governments to fit the needs as they developed hereafter.

In Minnesota a State Commission on Municipal Annexation and Consolidation has recently reported to the legislature its proposal to completely recodify and revise the laws and procedures relating to municipal incorporation, annexation and other boundary changes in that state. It is my understanding, however, that the new statutes relating to the incorporation of municipalities are limited in their effect to the seven-county metropolitan region surrounding Minneapolis and St. Paul and other counties containing cities of the first and second class.

In North Carolina two legislative study commissions—the Municipal Government Study Commission and the Tax Study Commission—have successfully sponsored the enactment of new laws re-defining state and local responsibilities for urban growth so as to encourage joint planning; strengthening local powers in planning zoning and land subdivision; and providing a new system of periodic re-evaluation of real property and uniform assessments.

In a recent article in *Public Management* George H. Esser, Jr., assistant director of the Institute of Government at the University of North Carolina, says:

The new legislation is a framework rather than a blueprint for solving urban problems. Even "solving urban problems" may be an over-statement because North Carolina cities are still too young and too new to have the tough complicated problems typical of older urban areas. Perhaps it is more accurate to say that this legislation equips cities and counties to anticipate the problems generally resulting from rapid urban growth and to take constructive and preventive action.

In New York State we have adopted a somewhat different approach, the keystone of which is cooperation not only among the several levels of government—federal, state and local—but among the various types and many units of local government.

New York is probably unique among the states in the number of its municipal organizations and their individual strengths in leadership and members. For many years, however, these groups have followed policies of defense of the existing structures, administrative organization, procedures and practices of the agencies of local government they represent. Almost every proposal for the general strengthening and improvement of our system of local government has been reviewed with suspicion, and frequently objection, if it involved any compromise of traditional powers or autonomy.

Quite recently—perhaps coerced by their difficulties in meeting the upsurging demands of their people, the vigorous competition among all governments for a greater share of the taxpayer's dollar and a realization that the survival of our present system of local government may be threatened unless we demonstrate that we can do the job confronting us— we seem to have moved into a new era of willingness—if not eagerness— to explore the opportunities for cooperation among the local governments of our state in tackling common problems.

With vigorous and separate agencies representative of cities and villages, counties, towns, school districts and fire districts, to say nothing of additional organizations of individual officers, we have lacked, however, a medium or agency of government to encourage, develop and implement such cooperation.

Upon the recommendation of Governor Nelson A. Rockefeller, legislation was enacted at the 1959 session of the legislature establishing a new Office for Local Government in the Executive Department. It is headed by a director, with an Advisory Board of nine members including representation of both local and state governments. The board includes the executive secretary and also vice president of the State Conference of Mayors and other Municipal Officials, the executive director of the State Association of Counties, the former secretary of the Association of Towns and the executive secretary of the State Association of School Boards. New York City is represented by a former deputy mayor, and the president of the State Tax Commission and myself complete its membership with one vacancy.

The law assigns the following functions, powers and duties to the Office for Local Government:

1. To assist the governor in coordinating the activities of state departments and agencies to provide more effective services to local governments;

2. To inform the governor as to the problems of the localities to assist him in formulating policies and utilizing resources of the Executive Department for the benefit of the localities;

3. To serve as a clearing house of information relating to common problems and state and federal services available to assist in their solution;

4. When requested, to advise and assist localities in the solution of their particular problems;

5. To make studies and analyses of local government problems;

6. To encourage and assist cooperative efforts among the localities in developing solutions of common problems;

7. To encourage expansion and improvement of in-service training facilities.

After the bill establishing the Office for Local Government was introduced but before it was passed there was a sudden unexpected opportunity to test its workability.

Pending before the legislature was a bill to aid the financially distressed railroads of the state. Among other things it provided for a reduction of real property taxes to the railroads that qualified by loss of earnings. It was estimated that this feature would save the distressed railroads approximately $15 million annually and that the state would reimburse the localities for half their loss in real property taxes. In the closing days of the legislature there were signs of uncertainty as to the reaction of the localities to such legislation. A meeting of leaders of the several organizations of municipalities was called. After a two-hour session analyzing the bill, appraising its general effect, the meeting was adjourned for one day for consideration of some suggested amendments, which were quickly approved by the proponents of the legislation.

The small group met again the next day and agreed to offer no opposition to the enactment of the legislation. One of the participants in the discussion said: "This is the first time in my memory that the representatives of cities, villages, counties and towns have sat down together to consider their action on a common problem." The proposed legislation was enacted with a minimum of opposition from any locality.

In the spring of 1959 the governor appointed Robert Aex, city manager of Rochester, as director of the new office. In his own county of Monroe, important progress has been made in unravelling common governmental problems and progressing towards their solution through cooperation between the city of Rochester and its smaller municipal neighbors.

Subsequently Milton Alpert, a top ranking member of the attorney general's office with a splendid background of experience in the legal affairs of all types of local as well as state government, accepted appointment as counsel to the Office for Local Government.

Not long ago the governor referred to the Office for Local Government

25 bills which had been introduced in the last session of the legislature. These divided into three groups: some had failed of passage, some had been passed by the legislature but vetoed by the governor, others had been passed by the legislature but signed by the governor with statements of reservation.

Almost all these bills had a common denominator: There was sharp disagreement among the several types of local governments concerning either their objectives or the methods set forth for the accomplishment of such objectives. Some were old legislative chestnuts that had been brought up year after year in one form or another in the climate of disagreement, which led either to their defeat or unsatisfactory compromise.

After two meetings of the Advisory Board unanimous agreement was reached with respect to the objectives of sixteen of the bills. In the instance of five additional bills, which involved relationships between state departments and the localities, unanimous agreement was reached among the members of the Advisory Board but final action was withheld pending conferences with representatives of the respective state departments to obtain their viewpoints concerning the proposals. In the instance of the four remaining bills, it was agreed that there was a need for more study and consultation with others before any recommendations could be offered.

At an early meeting with the Advisory Board certain initial policies were adopted. It was agreed that the new office should not duplicate services being adequately performed by existing agencies.

It was noted that the authorizing legislation indicated that some of the services of the office were to be extended only upon request by the localities. It was agreed that such services would not be extended except upon the request of the appropriate offices of the municipality affected and that, in the instance of a problem involving more than one municipality, the request of all should be required.

As a matter of policy it was also agreed that, when requested, the Office for Local Government should inform the localities of the alternative solutions for their problem presently available, as well as the solutions adopted by other localities within and without the state for similar problems, but that the choice among such possible solutions should be made by the appropriate officials of the localities themselves.

Some have recognized for years the need in New York State for an agency such as the new Office for Local Government but it could not have been born in a more favorable climate of state action to meet the challenge of present and future needs of our local government.

Two years ago the legislature established the Hughes Committee to tackle the problems of urban growth. This committee has prepared a series of publications on municipal corporations, state-local relationships and an inventory of existing statutes authorizing the joint performance by municipalities of certain common functions.

At the November 1959 general election New York State voters approved an amendment eliminating constitutional obstacles to the joint performance and finance by two or more municipalities of any activity which they could perform separately. This opened splendid new opportunities for the accomplishment of better municipal services without the waste resulting from separate duplicating capital and operational expense.

At the general election of 1958 the voters approved the so-called county home rule amendment permitting reorganization of local government in any county to strengthen structure and effectiveness.

The amendment was implemented by the necessary legislation at the legislative session of 1959. As a first result a proposal for the reorganization of the government of Erie County—the largest upstate county—was overwhelmingly approved by separate referenda, both in the cities and in the towns, on November 3, 1959.

A Temporary State Commission on Governmental Operations of the City of New York has been established to recommend plans to improve and strengthen the city's governmental and fiscal structure and administrative management.

An interdepartmental committee has been assigned the task of undertaking a basic and comprehensive review of the entire state and local tax structure including the various formulae under which the state returns over $1 billion annually to the localities.

Another agency has been assigned responsibility for augmenting state assistance to the localities to improve building codes and for the testing of new materials and techniques for housing construction.

A new Office of Transportation has been established and an Interdepartmental Traffic and Safety Committee Study organized.

A survey of future recreational facilities has been initiated.

In November 1958, the voters of New York State authorized a fund of $25 million for state assistance to cities, towns and villages for urban renewal programs receiving federal aid. Implementing legislation was passed by the legislature of 1959.

A comprehensive study of the state's educational system and its needs is under way and will soon report its findings and recommendations.

Several new studies are under way to improve the economic climate of the state for the benefit of all its people, including not only business and labor but also local governments.

The Temporary Commission on the Revision and Simplification of the Constitution has issued the first report of a series on revision of the state constitution.

Two studies of the executive branch of state government have been initiated by Governor Rockefeller. One is a sweeping inventory of the work of all departments and agencies in the executive branch in an effort to hold down the growing cost of state government. The other is the first comprehensive review of the administrative structure of the executive branch since its reorganization under Governor Alfred E. Smith 35 years ago.

In passing it might be noted that almost all of the studies referred to have been initiated by the governor and that in most cases the membership of the study groups has been selected by the governor, resulting in a generous participation by outstanding citizens.

Never before in my memory has there been greater confidence in my home state that it can and will meet the challenges of the 1960's.

The American stereotype of state and local politics and pressure groups is essentially negative. The average citizen views the politician as a crude, unlettered and ruthless dealer in power; he sees the "great game" of politics as essentially rigged, the lobbyist as something less than respectable, the activity of pressure groups as subterranean, self-seeking, and contrary to the public good.

Reformers, taking their cues from this widely shared outlook, have sought to clean up the "dirty business" by eliminating parties and politicians, by substituting "non-partisan" elections, and by "taking politics out of administration." The interest groups have attempted to mold a better image for themselves without necessarily changing their activities. Distracted by these efforts, the average American has failed to appreciate the necessity of improving both parties and pressure groups as instruments of a more responsible, more responsive government. Political parties, on their part, have failed to see that the best politics lies in providing the best possible government; and the pressure groups have failed to understand that their long-run interest lies in promoting the public interest. Just as it has been said that the politician who would be a statesman must look to the next generation rather than to the next election, so the lobbyist who would become a public leader must look past the next contract to the next decade.

Pressure groups and political parties share many identifying elements—numbers, organization and a common purpose. Both seek to achieve similar goals in our political system: to elect friendly candidates and to initiate favorable policies. The features that separate them from each other are the party's willingness to accept formal responsibility for the conduct of government, and the pressure group's avoidance of visible control in favor of behind-the-scenes influence.

Parties and pressure groups share four major functions in the state and local arena. First, both are instruments of government—the party an overt, internal agent, the pressure group a covert, external force. Both strive to link the citizen to his government, both are part of the legislative, executive and judicial processes of state and local government. Both provide transregional bridges across the nation, and both are necessary to make such basically unworkable concepts as separation of powers function even tolerably well in practice.

Second, both seek to influence the election of candidates to public office. The party, indeed, accepts full responsibility for the nomination process. Whether there be a statewide convention or a direct primary, the party's closed-door caucus usually makes the actual decisions. In less visible fashion, the pressure group attempts to influence, with suggestions, money and support, both the caucus decision and the ultimate electoral outcome.

Third, both parties and pressure groups help to focus public attention on the issues of the day. The majority party attempts to muster support for its plan of action, the minority party may seek either to obstruct that action or to modify it with alternative suggestions. Each party hopes that its identification with the public good will simultaneously promote its own interests. Similarly, the pressure groups seize upon issues favorable to themselves for massive promotional campaigns, while strenuously opposing those policies inimical to their interests.

Finally, both parties and pressure groups may serve as instruments of public education and information. If they see support through public enlightenment, they may spare no expense in providing full data and details. Occasionally, however, both have been guilty of incomplete disclosure and even of *misinformation* where ignorance would seem to serve their ends.

In spite of these functional likenesses, the organization and operation of party and pressure group display many dissimilarities. In actual operation party organization bears little resemblance to the neat theoretical hierarchy sometimes portrayed. The pyramid of state and local structure—with registered voters at the base, elected committeemen, ward and town leaders, county committee, county chairman in ascending order above them, and state committee and state chairmen at the peak—turns out to be a phantom. Power resides, not at the base, nor even at the pinnacle of this imposing structure, but rather at the level of the county leaders. As governors and presidents alike can testify, the county chairmen are the real kingmakers of America. Only rarely and only through a most delicate wooing and forging of alliances have state leaders of either party been able to consolidate the power of these local overlords. Never has a national leader been able to harness them for longer than the fleeting weeks of a presidential campaign.

A second fact has been the twentieth-century decline of the urban machine. Deprived of its traditional stock in trade—its Christmas baskets, its winter coal, and summer boatrides—by a welfare state that has made such benefits impartially available to all, the machine has watched its regimented voters, with their committeeman drill sergeants, fade away. Only in the rural areas, where machine presence has been little noted, or in an occasional adaptive city, have the traditional party organizations survived unchanged.

The looseness of party bonds is another surprising phenomenon. Hardly the rigid closed-shop system sometimes sketched, local party participation may better be described as a series of loose concentric rings. At the outer fringes of the typical county system are the *enrollees* of a given party, generally less than half the registered voters in a two-party area, since many citizens remain independents. Within the ranks of these nominal affiliates are the much smaller numbers of party *regulars,* those who provide a steadfast support, including participation in primary elections. They may number as few as one in five of the total enrollees, according to some surveys. Among the regulars will be found the party *workers* and the campaign *contributors,* probably not more than three or four per election district. Among them will be perhaps one or two actual *decision participants* per ward or town. As one narrows down to the inner circle, there may be a dozen real *decision makers* surrounding a *leadership core* that consists of a single "boss" or several coleaders. At this heart of the party, a new type of leader has been steadily emerging—polished, professional and persuasive. Even where change has been superficial, the old-time politician has endeavored to replace the invidious designation of "boss" with the more dignified title of "leader."

Among the pressure groups, those best known on the state and local scene are economically-oriented. In every state, business is important, especially businesses subject to state regulation or seeking state contracts. Organized labor is powerful in most Northern states, farm groups are influential in the Midwest. Racial and ethnic groups are well organized in many areas, as are professional groups—doctors, lawyers, teachers, morticians, beauticians and others subject to state licensing.

Of the lesser-known pressure groups, government itself looms large. Associations of towns and local governments are often among the most powerful and influential. State departments and their administrators frequently possess a powerful voice in the legislative chambers. Associations of employees—firemen, policemen and teachers—are sometimes more stridently vocal, though not necessarily more effective, in the same arenas. Finally, there are religious groups and veterans' groups, good-government groups, cheap-government groups, and uncounted other groups.

The methods of personal operation involve far more than the term "lobbyist" would indicate. While some spokesmen do seek to influence the enactment (or prevention) of legislation, others attempt to control the execution of law by the departments and commissions, or to affect the interpretation and application of law by the courts. Still others may confine themselves to molding public opinion—attempting in hundreds of grass roots contacts with local community leaders, reporters and editors, preachers and teachers to create a positive image of their employers.

Pressure groups serve many positive functions. They provide a measure of functional representation for geographically defined districts. They constitute a rallying point for the particular views held by groups too small to influence the major parties directly. They provide valuable research assistance to overworked, understaffed state legislators. By resolving conflicts among the divergent opinions of their own members, they speak with a single voice, much more easily understood and evaluated by political leaders. And when the public interest coincides, their special pleadings may serve for its advancement.

With both party and pressure group, significant problems arise. In the case of the party there may be one-party domination, a lack of healthy bipartisan competition that is frequently reflected in inferior candidates and an evasion of issues. There may be irresponsibility, stemming from boss control and a lack of citizen participation. Obviously there is widespread need for improving the two-party system, increasing party responsibility, strengthening the minority where it is weak, stimulating the responsiveness of the majority where it dominates.

For the pressure group there is often a lack of countervailing power on state and local levels. Frequently there may be an advancement of the selfish interest at the expense of the public good. There may be little internal democracy within the interest groups; their views may reflect a narrow leadership clique rather than the rank and file. But, above all, there may be a community-wide distortion of the "one man, one vote" doctrine into a "one dollar, one vote" practice. The need exists for controls which, while protecting the valued constitutional right to petition, will nonetheless limit the most flagrant abuses, relying perhaps on the fresh wind of disclosure to sweep the stables clean.

The need for increased public participation in political parties and increased attention to pressure groups is clearly indicated. For both institutions are vital to our governmental processes; both are far more important than structure in determining the actual shape of our state and local government in action.

EXIT THE BOSS, ENTER THE LEADER
Warren Moscow

> Warren Moscow, long time Albany correspondent for the *New York Times*, is the author of *Politics in the Empire State*. He served from 1958 to 1965 as executive assistant to Mayor Robert F. Wagner of New York City, and before that as executive director of the New York City Housing Authority. He is now Editor-in-Chief of the *New York Law Journal*.

In less than a year, Frank Hague of Jersey City and Ed Kelly of Chicago, both of whom doubled in brass as Mayors and political bosses, have quit one or both of their jobs. In Kansas City, Jim Pendergast, son of the late Tom Pendergast, has pulled out by request and in Hoboken the McFeely brothers' edition of the Hague machine has crumpled like the only slightly older one-hoss shay.

Pendergast and McFeely got out because they had to. As to Kelly and Hague—two of the most powerful bosses of modern times—there is the well-grounded suspicion that they got out while the getting was good, before the electorate began kicking them around, too.

The luxury-loving Mr. Hague turned his Jersey City mayoralty over to his

From *The New York Times Magazine,* June 22, 1947. © 1947 by The New York Times Company. Reprinted by permission.

nephew in pretty much the way an eastern caliph would assign his household and perquisities to his favorite son; but it is still much too soon after the event to tell whether the old Hague machine will stand up long against a national trend which has been operating against the traditional big-city political machines.

In general, it is true, all around the country, that the city machines no longer control the vote the way they used to; and that they can no longer elect whom they please, when they please and how they please.

But that the machines are crumbling, that the old-fashioned boss can no longer proclaim and get away with an "I am the law" attitude, does not mean that political parties have become anachronisms. Just as the pot-bellied Alderman has been replaced by the pauchless Councilman, so is the boss being replaced by the "leader" and the machine by the "organization."

Political organizations, whether known as machines or organizations, will be around as long as we have a two-party system, with nominations for public office to be made by the party members. And there is pretty sure to be some dominant member or group to run the show. It was so in the days of the party caucus, held in the back room of McGillicuddy's saloon, and it is so today as the "boys"—and nobody else—go through the motions of picking candidates in legalized primary elections.

But the difference between organization and machine, between leader and boss, is more than a purely semantic one. It is a difference in methods—brought on by necessity—a difference in respectability, at least on the surface, demanded by changing times.

Because the boss was the product of the machine, even though he may have seemed both its progenitor and copyright owner, it is the change-over from machine to organization that has caused the mutation of boss to leader.

The old machine *controlled* the vote. It took immigrants, made them citizens, supplied them with jobs, bailed them out in Night Court, kissed their babies and took their adolescents on picnics. It fixed traffic tickets for business men and winked at the violations of building and sanitary codes. It took various racial groups and saw to it that their most aggressive leaders were supplied with reasonably lucrative sinecures on the public payroll. Then, on election day, it took their votes in exchange, the citizenry knowing that their day-to-day destinies—if not their zoning laws and sanitation problems—were in good hands.

Of course, if the citizenry did not respond with a normal vote, just because of some extraneous issue like the tariff or the collapse of the foundations of the new jail, the organization took the votes anyhow. The organization did the counting—sometimes only the weighing—of the vote.

Gradually, over the years, the machine lost its power to do most of these things. The tide of immigration was dammed and the machines had no new crop of rapidly created citizens to help. Government welfare services replaced the clubhouse handout. Probation officers took over from the leader or his deputy in reviewing for the court the background of a youthful offender. Business men, during the depression, became more conscious of the organization "cut," as reflected in the tax rate, than grateful for the favors of the past. And, with the increased use of voting machines and Federal supervision of any election in which a Federal office was voted upon, it became tougher and tougher to steal votes. Those who did, got caught, as witness the recent Kansas City vote scandal.

So the machine became obsolete and the "organization" slipped quietly in to take its place. The organization does not control the vote, it *influences* the vote. When it goes after racial and religious blocs—and both parties do—it does so by nominating a Negro to a higher office than ever before was offered to a member of his race, or an Italian for State-wide office, or a member of the Jewish faith for a post on the highest court of the State. It sees that its members in Congress vote "right"—for local rather than broad governmental reasons—on allocations of Federal aid abroad or on anti-lynching legislation. Similarly, it sees that its local legislative members petition Congress for action in support of the Vatican or a free Palestine.

It can no longer win the vote by the beer party and the free handout, but it can woo the laboring man by jacking up wage scales or it can increase unemployment insurance payments and prolong their duration.

Naturally the "boss" who sat out on the sidewalk, presiding in tireless and vestless grandeur over a very informal receiving line, has been displaced by the leader—serge-clad, neat and conscious of issues. His alliances may be with the community's entrenched respectability, rather than the underworld, but he is not necessarily more scrupulous—just more careful and much smoother. In most cases, the leader is personally "money honest." This, of course, is not necessarily a recent development. Many political bosses of the past refused to go along with George Washington Plunkitt's contention that there was such a thing as "honest graft."

But look at the difference in type today between the old boss and the new leader. The background is different to start with. In the old days a good ward boss, possibly restricted in education to grammar school or less, rose, nevertheless, to be a good city or county boss, and, if hard-bitten, tough, practical and ambitious enough, got to be a State boss whose name was known and whose word was law for miles around. Intrinsically, despite exceptions like Boies Penrose and Mark Hanna, the usual city or State boss was just the best of the ward bosses. He understood his colleagues and preserved most of their characteristics.

Today, the big bosses are not the men who come up as ward bosses or district leaders. They are business men, Governors, United States Senators. Harry F. Byrd's Virginia organization has been called the tightest and best organization in the country today. And Byrd, a Senator and member of an old family, is its active leader. In New York and Indiana, to take two States at random, there are powerful Republican organizations of which the active as well as the titular head is the Governor.

In Indiana, where they play politics for keeps, this writer saw Governor Gates run a recent State convention with an iron hand. The incumbent United States Senator was dropped as the party nominee because the Governor wanted the State chairman in the job. A judge of a high State court was dropped, local reporters said, because he had dared cast a lone dissenting vote in that court in a case in which the organization was interested.

In New York, Tom Dewey had been elected District Attorney of New York County and had made one unsuccessful though spectacuiar race for Governor when the Republican leaders of the Legislature—representing the party in the State as a whole—signed and published a solemn declaration that in matters of policy (State-wide politics) they would consult with Mr. Dewey and be guided by his judgment. That was in 1939, and in the intervening years he has consolidated his hold to the point where no one questions his one-man leadership of the party in the State today. Many a loyal Republican would be hard pressed to give the name and initials of the titular State chairman.

In near-by Nassau County, J. Russel Sprague, a popular, efficient county executive—the equivalent of Mayor under Nassau's special charter—is as powerful as Frank Hague was in Jersey City in his heyday. He and his organization make the law, but do not proclaim that they are the law.

How do they do it? In the old days there was a political axiom that a boss should not run for public office, but should put his men in office, should be the power behind the throne, able at all times to dictate who should hold what job, either elective or appointive. As the machines went slowly into the discard, the successful remaining bosses were those who paid no attention to the rule. Hague and Kelly, Crump in Memphis, held on longer than the others of their type because they began to dictate policy, too, from the administrative and policy-making public jobs they held.

The new leaders dictate policy and use the patronage whip to enforce their views. Many a balky legislator has given up his objections—founded on whim, prejudice or principle—after a series of phone calls. The Governor's office calls his home county chairman, tells him the legislator's vote is needed and asks if the county chairman will please see that the legislator changes his mind. If the county chairman can't control the legislator, maybe the county chairman is not the proper person to dispense patronage in his county. The chairman gets the idea and the legislator is notified of the trouble he is causing. Of course, if he is just going to be a persistent trouble-maker, interfering with the broad policies of the party in the State, maybe he'll have trouble in the next primary election. The legislator gets the idea.

In one case a legislator who declined to take persistent hints like that, found that his past had been raked into and some disagreeable incidents disclosed, and the next hint was that those might be disclosed to his constituency. This time he saw the light.

Job patronage can't win an election any more, with the extension of civil service, the increase in the size of the electorate and the general lack of interest on the part of the public in low-paying county, city, State and Federal jobs. But it remains extremely important for control of the party organization, indispensable for remaining in power.

So it is not surprising that a systematic, efficient, and comprehensive job-dispensing program exists wherever there is a strong organization in control. In one State, where the Governor was "leader," he had one special secretary whose job was patronage dispensing. To this secretary were referred all requests by county chairmen and city leaders. He would weigh the possibilities, with an eye to present and future policies, and pass the recommendation up higher—to the Governor, if the job was important enough either in salary or favor-dispensing potentialities. The recommendation also went to the State chairman. When both had approved, the applicant was appointed by the appropriate department head. And, to eliminate any possibility of error or later dispute, the Governor and the State chairman both signed the card of recommendation.

For lesser jobs there are certain to be, and in this case there were, local patronage dispensers, for an area in the State, who did the preliminary sifting of possible appointees and forwarded what amounted to final recommendations to the Capitol, even though there they went through an additional processing. The ramifications can best be realized when it is understood that appointees to staff an anti-racial discrimination commission were so selected.

Job patronage can be, and is, defended on the ground that those in sympathy with a governmental policy should be the ones appointed to administer it. But job patronage in policy making or administering posts is also important for the favors patronage it carries with it.

Doing favors has been the way of making friends for political organizations ever since they were started—the old machines or their more modern replacements. Priority on the liquor license list, assignment of a building application to an inspector who will look on it with friendly tolerance, passage of a bill through the Legislature which helps some particular group —such are reasonably frequent demonstrations of favor patronage; and if the man on top is to benefit, either through election support or party contributions, the deputy commissioners, the non-salaried board members, even the legislative leaders, must be men who recognize the paramount importance of the organization and the man who heads it.

They must owe their positions to him, and usually do, or feel that their continuance in those jobs is a matter he can control.

So the new leaders find public office, high public office, a good place from which to run an organization. Many an old-time leader who did take office contented himself with a non-policy-making sinecure which gave him a headquarters and a secretaryship in which he could place, at public expense, the most trusted of his aides.

Now it is the press secretaries and the ghost writers who, the leader makes sure, are in sufficient supply to do the job of influencing public opinion in order to influence votes and win elections.

Compare the photographs of Dewey, Gates, Byrd and Sprague with those of Croker, Taggart and Bill Barnes and you see the difference that a change in methods from machine to organization has made in the men who rule, the change from bosses to leaders.

Somehow the old-time, big-city machines were never able to achieve respectability, while the new organizations have it as a matter of course. Old Charles Francis Murphy, the Tammany leader who developed Al Smith, Jim Foley and Bob Wagner, as well as others, came closer in his declining years to achieving it for Tammany, but he never actually got there.

And Charles Murphy, knowing that, used to complain that if the Democrats did anything wrong the public cried, "Stop thief," but that "the Republicans can get away with murder in this town."

The difference, of course, was that the Democrats at one time or another had been caught at thieving, while the Republicans had never been caught at murder, or even at lesser crimes. The old-time machines did steal blatantly and openly. They had the Robin Hood attitude that it was okay to take things from the rich to give to the poor, with a percentage of the take for operating expenses and a good time for the boys.

Those days are gone, possibly forever. Modern improvements have brought big business methods to the field of politics.

JESSE UNRUH: "BIG DADDY" OF CALIFORNIA
Ed Cray

Ed Cray is a West Coast journalist who contributes regularly to national publications, chiefly on California political matters.

The inscription scrawled across the bottom of the picture reads, "To Jesse Unruh, with deep appreciation and warmest regards, John F. Kennedy." It is just one of many hints that the hulking Speaker of the California State Assembly is the Kennedy man in California—and could turn out to be the key Kennedy man in the nation when the 1964 Presidential campaign rolls around.

For, in all probability, the 1964 Presidential battle will center here, in the biggest state in the union. This will certainly be true if Rockefeller turns out to be the GOP nominee, in which case the Democrats will need California's huge electoral vote to compensate for the possible loss of New York. The loss of both states, coupled with unfavorable Democratic

From *The Nation*, March 9, 1963. Reprinted by permission.

prospects presented in heavily populated Pennsylvania, Ohio and Michigan (all three acquired Republican governors last year) could mean Kennedy's defeat.

So it could easily be that as California goes in 1964, Kennedy will go; and it is the ambition of Unruh, youthful (he's only forty), personally charming and intelligent, to see that as *he* goes, California will go. As a result of this driving ambition, Unruh has earned both the nickname "Big Daddy" and the undying enmity of California's celebrated volunteer political movement.

Unruh's Roman-candle political career could only have happened in the fireworks factory of California politics, where skyrockets and meteoric rises are commonplace. Discharged from the Navy at the end of World War II, he enrolled at the University of Southern California, soon became a prime mover in the campus veterans' organization, Trovets, and flirted with the political Left. His greatest success was to force the administration of the Methodist-founded school to remove the usual question about religion from the university's admission application. He gathered around him a group of friends, many of whom have since climbed in political status with him— and largely because of him. In 1948, he split off from the "extreme" Left when, as he puts it, he objected to the Communist-run campaign of the Independent Progressive Party and Henry Wallace. Unruh preferred to stay within the Democratic Party—his boyhood in Texas taught him that politics meant "Democrat." Moreover, he was busy running for state office, entering the Democratic primary. Poorly financed, he lost to a man generally considered to be more conservative.

In 1949, he was one of the founding members of the Democratic Guild, a local political club in southwest Los Angeles. Active in Helen Gahagan Douglas' campaign for the Senate, he was rewarded with a patronage appointment in the 1950 census count. (He suspects that he was far down on the list, but was the only candidate the Census Bureau would accept.) His stint as director of the census in southwest Los Angeles taught the journalism graduate the sociological minutiae which make for winning political campaigns.

Elected to the Los Angeles Democratic County Committee in 1950, Unruh was one of a group of reformers who attempted to breathe life into that stagnant body and to do battle as a "good government" group against "bossism." The reformers included a number of men who have since become opponents of Unruh, including Lt. Gov. Glenn Anderson, former State Senator Richard Richards and former chairman of the Los Angeles County Committee, Don Rose.

Part of the reform was to include the organization of volunteer clubs whose pre-primary endorsements could bring some order to the chaos of the cross-filed primary, which permitted a candidate, without party label, to enter both party primaries. (The Republican Assembly had been doing this since 1935.) In 1948, there were approximately twenty-five clubs in

Los Angeles County; four years later, there were a hundred clubs, but the vast volunteer enthusiasm ignited by Adlai Stevenson's campaign in 1952 had yet to be effectively organized.

Eisenhower took California in spite of volunteer enthusiasm and Unruh was beaten in his attempt to unseat a veteran Assemblyman who had the backing of Los Angeles' conservative labor unions. Two years later, Unruh had digested an important political lesson: volunteer efforts without labor's backing and, even worse, without money, weren't enough. With a war chest of $2,800 and the party label attached to his name due to a change in the state law, Unruh ran again. His opponent, who had beaten him two years before, chose to switch his registration from Democrat to Republican and then lost the labor support he had earlier enjoyed. Heavy contributions from lobbyists were not enough to beat Unruh's volunteers who, by then, had become an effective Assembly District organization.

Jesse Unruh went off to Sacramento in 1954 as a member of a liberal caucus within the Democratic minority in the State Assembly. Artie Samish, long the dominant force in state politics, had been convicted of income-tax evasion and sent off to a federal prison, leaving behind a power vacuum. Goodwin Knight was Governor now, replacing Warren who had moved up to the Supreme Court.

Unruh joined with Tom Rees, today State Senator from Los Angeles County (one-thirtieth of the population of the United States), William Munnell and two others to fight in vain against the tidelands oil "giveaway," the uniform sales tax and a bill exempting oil companies from state antitrust laws. Unruh's own bills, such as one to create a prototype Consumer Council, never came out of committee.

But the Republican flood was ebbing. In 1952, Democrats held only fifty of 162 partisan offices, despite a 4-3 edge in registration; they held seventy-four at the time Unruh was re-elected to the Assembly in 1956.

This resurgence—or more accurately, birth—of the Democratic Party in California was the result of a number of factors. While cross-filing was still in effect, party labels were now added after the names, thus permitting traditional party loyalties to offset the built-in advantages of the incumbent. Of equal importance, the volunteer political movement had crystallized into the California Democratic Council. The CDC in 1957 had more than 500 clubs affiliated and a membership of 40,000. Though feuding among themselves constantly on policy positions (a matter which was to grow more divisive as time passed) and largely untested in the political arena, the CDC represented the largest single body of dedicated campaign workers the country has ever seen. Unruh was then, and—to a degree which CDC leaders refuse to acknowledge—is still a CDC supporter. His own election was directly attributable to a Democratic Club and to volunteer activity. (In 1962, when he ran for re-election, the ant-labor of the campaign was handled by unpaid, middle-aged and elderly women from the district.)

The 1957 legislature was leaderless. The affable Goodie Knight's program was designed to alienate no one, since his political strength lay in the middle-of-the-road posture which Warren had studiously maintained and passed on. The lobbyists were still seeking a replacement for Samish, fighting among themselves for the first time in their unrecorded history.

Bill Munnell, today a Superior Court judge in Los Angeles, was elected minority leader, and two more members, Gordon Winton and Robert Crown, had joined the liberal caucus, which took over the balance of power in the legislature. Munnell's leadership came by virtue of his seniority and the chairmanship of the Finance and Taxation Committee; Unruh's came by virtue of his membership on that committee and his friendship with the chairman. The lobbyists sought out Unruh as a man close to the minority leader and one who might ease their bills through. In return, they offered campaign contributions. Unruh, however, had little need of a lavish war chest; he was in a safe Democratic district. But he knew of deserving Democrats who did need funds and he was glad to steer lobbyists accordingly. He handled no money himself, acting only as an adviser. (Unruh has never had direct personal control over campaign contributions or party funds. The CDC has sought in vain for proof of charges of "corrupt machine politics" which they would like to lay at Unruh's doorstep.)

Politically astute, a parliamentarian with a growing reputation as the fastest gavel in the West, a man to whom legislators owed a favor, Unruh was picked in October, 1957, by Fred Dutton to manage the Southern California gubernatorial campaign for the then Attorney-General Edmund G. "Pat" Brown. He went on the Brown payroll at $10,000 per year while continuing to serve in the legislature. First he had to overcome the objections of the party's big financial contributors, who felt he was too close to the maverick CDC; then he had to make his peace with the conservative unions that have long dominated the Los Angeles County Labor Council.

The gubernatorial campaign of 1958 was the best organized, and offered the Democrats' first united front, in the history of the state. "Pat" Brown was running against William F. Knowland, Oakland newspaper publisher, conservative Republican and a Chaing Kai-shek supporter in the U. S. Senate. The ideological lines were clearly drawn: Knowland supported a right-to-work measure on the ballot; Brown was advocating a liberal program of legislation which the state had long needed and never received. Labor, for the only time in the state's history, backed its claims of delivering the vote. The CDC, now grown to 100,000 members, had become a political veteran. Two unsuccessful Stevenson campaigns and a losing Senatorial race in 1956 (when Senator Kuchel defeated Richard Richards) had added professional skills to amateur enthusiasm.

In the maelstrom of precinct operations in California, there are no ward heelers, no patronage appointments, no jobs on the city rolls, no welfare handouts. In short, there is nothing to compel the voters' loyalty to the machine. Without party loyalty (and Democratic switching once ran as high as 30 per cent), the only solution is voter education. This the CDC handled with great skill. By 1958, many club members were walking precincts for the third time and had come to know the residents on a first-name basis. Months prior to the election, key precincts were combed, then worked again and again. Some precincts had workers make as many as three door-to-door sweeps, talking issues, explaining the Democratic platform, extolling the merits of the *entire* ticket.

Brown's campaign manager, Fred Dutton (now an Assistant Secretary of State for Congressional Affairs) and Don Bradley, campaign manager for Senatorial candidate Clair Engle, built a state-wide operation unprecedented in thoroughness and efficiency. Jesse Unruh learned a great deal about politics from these two while serving as Brown's Southern California chairman.

Brown beat Knowland by more than a million votes. Democrats elected six of seven state-wide candidates, reversed the Republican edge in the House delegation from 17-13 to 16-14, and gave Brown sizable majorities in both houses of the state legislature.

The legislature which convened in Sacramento in 1959 offered Brown's program little opposition, primarily because Jesse Unruh had political muscle and a willingness to use it. Unruh had some claim to high office in the Assembly as a reward for the Southern California campaign. The speakership—probably the second most important office in Sacramento—was open. Assemblyman Gus Hawkins, a twenty-four-year veteran who, for the first time in his career, was a member of the majority, was a front-runner for the office. Munnell was heir apparent to the majority leader's post. In one of the most politically important of his many moves, Unruh backed Assemblyman Ralph Brown for the Speaker's chair. To this end, he rounded up the support of Richfield Oil, pointing out to its lobbyist that Hawkins was heavily backed by Superior Oil Co.

The battle of the oil companies is another of California's unique and ubiquitous political problems. The oil industry here is divided into two large groups—"Big Oil" and "Little Oil." Aside from a common endorsement of the 27.5 per cent depletion allowance and an aversion to state gasoline taxes, the two have little in common. "Big Oil"—Standard, Shell, Signal, Tidewater, Union and Texaco—are huge companies which not only drill and refine oil, but maintain their own retail outlets. "Little Oil" constitutes such companies as Superior, Wilshire, Pauley and some others little known outside the state. Richfield shifts between the two groups, a maverick with a large retail operation but a dependence upon the major producers for a large share of its crude. With one person of every five in the state employed directly or indirectly in the service of the internal combustion engine, and with gasoline tax revenues of $357.6 million second only to the retail sales tax in state income, the state legislature figures heavily in the considerations of the various oil companies.

At work even before the legislature opened, Unruh lined up support for Ralph Brown. Many Assemblymen owed Unruh a favor for having steered campaign contributions their way. Brown was elected Speaker and Unruh's reward was chairmanship of the powerful Ways and Means Committee. For the first time he had an official position which made him the equal in prestige of his tutor, William Munnell. Additionally, Unruh was the funnel through which campaign contributions now poured. Assemblymen who had received assistance repaid their debts; Assemblymen who might need assistance —in both parties—listened to the powerful Unruh.

Around Unruh gathered a group of legislators who had once been the core of the liberal minority. On the Assembly floor, the group was dubbed the Praetorian Guard, the phalanx of the advocates for the Governor's program. Off the Assembly floor, a handful of convivial, though not necessarily well-heeled, lobbyists were added. The "Cub Scout Den," as it came to be called—Unruh was known familiarly as "the Den Mother"—became the source of Unruh's political strength.

"Pat" Brown's legislative program was long overdue. His principal spokesman, especially on matters of taxation, was Jesse Unruh. Cross-filing was repealed, a Fair Employment Practices Act was passed, state aid to education and unemployment compensation were increased, $75 million in workers' benefits were approved. The Governor was later to say that Unruh made his reputation on his, Brown's, program and that Brown made his on the strength of Unruh's ability to push it through.

There was one major failure. As part of an eight-point program to raise $245 million in taxes, Brown asked for an oil-severance tax which would have raised $23 million a year. Brown fought hard, but Unruh was not enthusiastic for the measure; neither were the various Assemblymen who had come to appreciate the value of Unruh-apportioned oil contributions. The proposal was defeated.

Unruh had waited through two fruitless sessions for the heavy Democratic majorities needed to pass the two bills of which he is the most proud. His Civil Rights Act flatly prohibits racial or religious discrimination in all business transactions in the state and has come to be the one item that confounds those who view the man as a conservative. (Naturally, the measure did nothing to hurt its author in the Negro precincts of his own district, while the lobbies it antagonized—real estate, for example—were already opposed to him.) The second act to which he put his name was brilliant in its Machiavellian design. The Retail Credit Act established interest rates and effectively stifled the loan sharks who had pillaged lower-class neighborhoods for years. In halting the politically powerless loan sharks and appearing as the friend of the little man, Unruh also set a 1.5 per cent per month (18 per cent per year) interest rate on revolving credit funds favored by the metropolitan department stores. The 18 per cent per year rate—which Unruh tacitly concedes may be high, "but we had no previous experience anywhere to draw on"—obtained for him the backing of James S. Sheppard, former president of the state bar, a conservative Democrat and counsel for most of Los Angeles' largest department stores. A member of Democratic Associates, the party's largest fund-raising source, Sheppard was also influential with the multi-million-dollar, Republican-owned firms he represented, and was thus able to tap conservatives of both parties. And Unruh had a claim upon him.

Unruh was planning ahead, knowing full well that John F. Kennedy did not like California's political climate, despite the considerable support from the California delegation he had received in his abortive bid for the Vice-Presidential nomination in 1956. In California, there was no machine to deal with, no party discipline, the Congressional delegation was a collection of "me-firsts" with local machines and little party loyalty. Worst of all, there was the CDC, that collection of wild-eyed liberals who took part in political campaigns for the fun of it or out of democratic (small "d") idealism without thought of political preference or monetary reward for themselves. Furthermore, the CDC strongly favored Adlai Stevenson and would have happily dragooned him into running a third time. (The massive Stevenson demonstrations at the Democratic National Convention in Los Angeles were staged and staffed almost entirely by CDC people with a happy disregard for the professional politicians.)

Late in 1959, Unruh met with Kennedy's two political tacticians, Lawrence O'Brien and Kenneth O'Donnell. The three saw eye-to-eye, pocketbook-to-pocketbook. Unruh had a growing appreciation of image-politics, thanks to his apprenticeship in California's cross-filing campaigns. At that meeting Unruh acquired the inside track to the White House because "Pat" Brown was simultaneously making a serious political mistake: he was picking the state's delegation to the Democratic convention in a democratic (small "d" again) fashion.

In 1950, as an early step to broaden the base of the Democratic Party, Glenn Anderson, then Los Angeles County Committeeman, worked out a scheme whereby the delegation to the Democratic National Convention would be picked literally from the grass roots. In addition to office holders and their petty-patronage appointees, one or two people were to be selected from each Congressional district after the district had caucused and presented a list of six or eight to the head of the delegation.

Ten years later, Brown followed this formula to the letter. He had problems which the Kennedys, in their machine-politics wisdom, could not and would not appreciate. If Brown was for Kennedy as he had said, then, dammit, he should appoint a delegation which, like those of the Eastern states, would stay in line. There was steady pressure on Brown from Unruh and others to do just that. But Brown had to run for re-election whether Kennedy won or not, and he needed the support of all elements in the party. (California's gubernatorial election does not fall in the same year as the Presidential; with no top-down support, the candidate in California must do it from the bottom up.)

California was badly split; the Stevenson contagion was as virulent as ever. Kennedy had major strength here, most of it from the party professionals, including both Brown and Unruh; but there was also support for both Lyndon Johnson and Symington. Brown put a finger into the wind, decided to double the size of the delegation (giving each member one-half vote), and began choosing. He had no control over the votes of the delegation (a matter which still leaves Eastern politicians shaking their heads) and had only the option of when he might release them.

Kennedy's strategy was for a quick, first-ballot victory at the convention; he needed every vote California could give him. The Kennedy camp, through Unruh, exerted as much pressure as it could to force Brown to release the delegation on the first ballot; the Stevenson, Johnson and Symington people on the delegation demanded that he hold the votes as a favorite son. Second-ballot defections, they all reasoned, would give *their* candidate a better chance. Brown wavered, and in that wavering he lost the confidence of Kennedy's professionals.

Unruh, who had filled a vacuum in Sacramento left when Samish was involuntarily retired, was there to fill another one. Brown now projected the image of a man of hair-trigger indecision and, in national party terms, was therefore unfit for the mantle of leadership. The National Committeeman was Attorney General Stanley Mosk. Mosk had been elected just prior to the Democratic National Convention to replace Paul Ziffren, an eight-year veteran who had made no bones of his dislike for Lyndon Johnson. The order to dump the liberal Ziffren came not from Kennedy, as has been whispered, but from Speaker of the House Sam Rayburn, who was promoting Lyndon Johnson's candidacy. Rayburn passed the word to the House delegation that Ziffren had to go or they might have trouble getting bills through.

The Kennedy campaign in California was hardly an unqualified success. Dutton had overall charge; Bradley was to handle the northern half of the state. Unruh, who again was the paid campaign manager in Southern California, ignored the CDC, partly out of a growing suspicion of volunteer politics and partly because the Kennedy men were running a different sort of campaign, one with a heavy reliance on television. The CDC, in turn, volunteered little; for many, the joy was gone from politics. Kennedy had bought the nomination (walkie-talkies on the convention floor rankled) and Stevenson had been finally deprived of the Presidency. Even the candidacy of Richard Nixon did little to stir their partisan juices. Then, too, the replacement of Ziffren, their much-admired defender, as National Committeeman, also smacked of big-city, Eastern bossism. If that was the way politics was, they weren't going to play.

Late in the campaign, with the Kennedy drive hardly a model of efficiency, Representative James Roosevelt and Manny Rohatiner, a field secretary for Los Angeles County Supervisor Ernest Debs, went to Unruh, suggesting that he install a get-out-the-vote drive on Election Day in addition to everything else that was planned. The result was a last-minute operation. The effort was focused in those lower-class, traditionally Democratic districts where the vote turnout is also traditionally poorest; its intent was to produce an extra 10 per cent of the registered Democrats who normally wouldn't come out to vote. According to Rohatiner, the effort turned a loss of 75,000 in Los Angeles County into a narrow 25,000 Kennedy victory. Nixon, however, won the state by 35,000 votes (of six million cast). Neither Dutton nor Unruh was charged by the White House with the loss; after all, Unruh had delivered Los Angeles County and its 40 per cent of the state-wide vote—at a cost of $313,000.

Kennedy safely in the White House, Unruh was involved in the apportionment of political favors. To provide regional balance in the Cabinet, the Postmaster General was to come from California. Governor Brown reportedly favored Hugo Fisher, the liberal State Senator from Republican-voting San Diego who had carried much of the Governor's program in the upper house. Unruh wanted someone less closely aligned with the party's "liberal" wing and the CDC. The new President named J. Edward Day, then chairman of Democratic Associates, former legal and legislative assistant to Adlai Stevenson in Illinois, and vice president of Prudential Insurance Co. CDC leaders grumbled privately.

Similarly, Unruh's suggestion that George E. O'Brien, head of the electricians' union and the dominant force in the Los Angeles Labor Council, would make an excellent U.S. Marshal was acted upon. O'Brien had provided many of the people for the get-out-the-vote drive, paying some of the unemployed union people from COPE funds.

In Sacramento, Unruh's power had grown substantially. His assistance to selected candidates to whom he also channeled money from the ever-eager lobbyists now was to be repaid. Meanwhile, the CDC was struggling with a host of problems.

In many areas, the volunteers had worked for local Assembly and Congressional candidates, but had ignored the top of the ticket. (Kennedy ran 200,000 votes behind the Los Angeles County Assembly candidates, one million behind the state's Democratic registration.) The volunteers reserved the right to refuse service to anyone. Although individual clubs were strong, weaknesses in the organization as a whole were painfully obvious. The CDC is a grass-roots organization, but it is some of the highest-price grass around. There are few clubs in areas of high minority-group registration. Labor, that huge bloc of lower-middle-class voters, is virtually unrepresented in it. Individually, and collectively as COPE, the unions have disdained the CDC as an organization unresponsive to labor's demands and far too cerebral. The CDC's greatest strength lies largely in those upper-middle and upper-class areas where Democrats have the slimmest chances of election. Individual clubs promote discussion of issues—some more than others—and these discussions cruise along at a university-seminar level, far above the rank and file's collective head. Formed to educate the voter, the CDC has served to educate precisely those people least in need of help.

The organization's leadership is well aware of these weaknesses and has taken steps to correct them. But a basic conflict remains.

Once elected, politicians become extremely cagey about taking public stands. Even more, they want to avoid having positions thrust upon them. Those in office before the CDC became a force in California politics have carefully avoided the organization. Representative James Roosevelt, liberal enough for the CDC, represents a district which is a hotbed of volunteer activity, but has never been a CDC supporter.

At its height during Brown's campaign in 1958, the volunteer movement numbered 100,000; just two years later, it had fallen to half that. Those remaining were the most dedicated; but, to the anger of the politicians; the dedication was not to the party, but to the issues which had led the volunteers to the party in the first place.

Unfortunately, the loyal troops were not as diligently backing their policy positions (e.g., abolish HUAC, admit Red China to the UN, repeal state loyalty oaths and reduce arms expenditures) with precinct work. In the 1958 primary, CDC candidates, including incumbents, took twenty-nine of thirty-one races. "Extreme" (in terms of the currently muted political debate) or not, the CDC could not be ignored when it produced such results. But the volunteers' enthusiasm flagged during the Kennedy campaign and has not returned. The correct cause-effect relationship will never be clear. Unruh and the professionals surrounding him insist they ignored the CDC because its enthusiasm for their candidate had waned. The CDC's defenders argue that their enthusiasm was dissipated precisely because Unruh and the Kennedys ignored the volunteer movement.

By the opening of the 1961 session of the state legislature, Jesse Marvin Unruh was running the Assembly. Presiding as chairman of Ways and Means (which, like its Washington namesake, is a kingpin committee), he helped the Speaker appoint committees, fought a running feud with the upper house, and perfected his ability to appraise each bill for its inherent worth, financial or otherwise, to the party. Three terms in the Assembly had given him the background he needed, and the keys to enough skeleton closets, to suggest in strong terms to lobbyists that this or that bill was worth this or that sum of money.

According to one lobbyist, Unruh views all bills as being one of three types: it will help only the lobby at the expense of the taxpayer; it will help the taxpayer at the expense of the lobby; or it will help one without harming the other. The first type does not move; Unruh's stock response is, "I don't think this is the year for your bill." Bills favoring the taxpayer at the expense of the lobbyist will pass the Assembly if the lobby is not particularly strong. The bills which hurt no one (although they usually mean that the lobbyist will benefit financially) acquire unspoken values—sometimes blocks of $25-a-plate dinner tickets, sometimes outright contributions to one campaign or another, sometimes the promise not to oppose a bill in which another group is interested. There are many rumors and few facts about this general weighing of legislation. One thing is clear: Unruh has become a past master at it.

During this 1961 session, Assemblyman Charles Wilson, long a CDC foe, introduced two bills in the legislature designed to curb the volunteer organization's power. The most important would have deprived the CDC of the right to make preprimary endorsements, thereby removing that group's dulled Sword of Damocles. Neither bill became law, although it was not Unruh's fault. Rammed through the Assembly by Unruh, one bill died in the upper house and the other was vetoed by the Governor at the request of Paul Ziffren, patron saint of the CDC. The Governor's veto was fulfillment of his promise to Ziffren that, as Governor, he would not permit any weakening of the CDC by the legislature now that Ziffren was no longer able to use the National Committeeman's office to protect his offspring. For his part, Ziffren was to do everything possible to keep the CDC united behind the Brown ticket.

Ralph Brown was still the Speaker, and though an important figure in getting the Governor's program through the legislature, he was more and more overshadowed by Unruh. Brown let it be known that he was interested in retiring from Sacramento—a District Court of Appeals judgeship would be adequate, he thought. Unruh was the heir apparent, although Speaker pro-tem Carlos Bee would automatically move up if Brown were to resign after the legislature ended its session in June. Late in April, Unruh announced that he had the necessary votes to be elected—seven weeks before the legislature was to adjourn and four months before Ralph Brown's judgeship would be available. Brown chose not to view this as an affront; he only wanted out. Unruh maneuvered to have an urgency clause written into the judgeship bill, but was thwarted by state law. (The urgency clause would have set the court up before September, permitted Brown to resign as soon as the post was available and set the stage for Unruh's immediate election before the session ended.)

Lower house members offered no opposition to the judgeship bill, fearing what Unruh might do in the upcoming reapportionment were they to vote against the bill. Moreover, Unruh suggested to those who might oppose him that pet legislation might not find its way out of his committee. The judgeship for Brown went through; Brown resigned from the legislature at the end of the session and Bee moved up temporarily. Flexing his political muscle, Unruh managed an unprecedented, between-sessions call of the Assembly at which he was elected Speaker.

He was now officially the second most powerful man in Sacramento, a role he had filled unofficially for almost three years.

The reapportionment was to be a satisfying personal victory.

California is not one of those states which refuse to reapportion its Congressional and lower-house seats every ten years. Republican-dominated legislatures have over the years gaily redistricted the state with a vengeance, coupling reapportionment to the cross-filing primary to insure GOP dominance in the Assembly and Congressional delegation. But from 1950 to 1960, the state's population had increased 5.2 million—after a 3.6 million increase during the previous decade. The new residents moved into districts which had once been considered safely Republican and they registered 4-3 Democratic (about the same percentage as the state's "old-timers"). The massive population increase brought the state eight new Congressional seats and had long since upset the neatly drawn lines of 1950. Ten years later, Democrats had majorities in both houses and in the Governor's chair. Unruh set to work with relish.

No reapportionment in the state's history was done with such attention to sociological and political detail. Unruh had one of his closest lieutenants, Assemblyman Robert Crown, as head of the committee in charge of the gerrymander, as it was jokingly called, and Unruh himself sat on the committee. Crown, says Unruh, was "purely and simply the architect, although he came to me on everything." Crown was fortified by political scientists paid by the party who offered advice, by special studies of Los Angeles voting behavior for which Unruh rounded up the money, and by the sure knowledge that the final bill would go through pretty much as proposed.

Unruh's intention was to make this reapportionment stick for the next ten years, by which time a new census would award even more seats to California. (The state is ballooning at the approximate rate of one new Congressional seat each year.)

Furthermore, the state was awarded eight new Congressional seats by the 1960 census—seats badly needed by the Kennedy Administration in the conservative-dominated House of Representatives. O'Donnell, O'Brien and Robert Kennedy watched closely as Crown drew lines which would guarantee that a minimum of twenty-four of the state's thirty-eight-man delegation would be Democrats. (At that time, the balance favored the Democrats 16-14.) And while they were at it, architect Crown ruined the chances of three Republican incumbents, including the houses's two members of the John Birth Society. (But for the untimely death of Rep. Clem Miller and the illness of Rep. Dalip Saund which prevented him from campaigning, the reapportionment would have netted twenty-six house seats for the Democrats. It now stands at 24-14 and the Democrats expect to reclaim both Miller's and Saund's seats.) Incumbent Congressmen, including Rep. Charles Gubser, a Republican, were given an opportunity to draw the lines as they wanted. Crown made some adjustments, but none that left any Democrats very unhappy.

The state's Assembly districts were completely redrawn. Crown had two considerations: pleasing the Democratic incumbents and winning support from a signficant number of Republicans so as to forestall the possibilities of a referendum which would upset the redistricting. The liberal Crown did much to draw districts which would favor liberals of both parties.

Once on the floor, Unruh used the reapportionment bill to cut up the already weak Republican minority. As the bill moved through the Assembly, Unruh openly traded good Republican districts to GOP Assemblymen in return for their votes. He had a Democratic majority in the legislature, and the Republicans voted for the bill, forestalling any GOP-backed referendum. Even more, Unruh had destroyed Republican unity, splitting the minority into small groups of feuding legislators and redistricting the GOP leadership in the Assembly out of office.

This was Unruh's political "muscle," fully flexed.

Invested now with both the power and the glory of the Speakership, Unruh began planning for "Pat" Brown's re-election campaign. As he had in 1958 and 1960, he would handle the south. Don Bradley, Brown's political pro, would be in charge of the state-wide organization. In addition, Unruh was to handle the coordination of both Assembly and Congressional races in Southern California.

On Jan. 12, 1962, 1,200 people, one-third of them Republicans, paid $50 to attend a testimonial dinner for the new Speaker. He frankly admitted that the money from the dinner would be spent on deserving Assembly candidates. Lobbyists were conspicuous by their presence.

The co-chairman of the dinner committee represented the power bloc that Unruh had put together by that time. All were from the south. Hugh Evans, chairman of the Democratic Associates, was a savings and loan executive. Howard Ahmanson owned the world's largest savings and loan (a firm with assets of more than $1.1 billion), a bank and the largest fire-underwriting insurance company in the state. William Bassett represented the Los Angeles Labor Council. John Canaday was a vice president of Lockheed Aircraft. Neil Curry was a leader in the California Horse Racing Association and owned a trucking line. Edwin Pauley, long-time Democratic fat cat, owned his own oil company. Leslie Shaw, a Negro, represented the minorities; he also was a vice president of a savings and loan. Louis Warschaw, like Pauley, was a fixture at these dinners. His money, and advice, figured in Democratic politics; his wife was a prominent party officeholder.

The smoldering fight between the CDC and Unruh erupted with the June primary. In Los Angeles' 31st Congressional District (Unruh's own), Assemblyman Charles Wilson (he of the anti-CDC bills) was facing the CDC-oriented liberal, Jerry Pacht. Unruh had promised Wilson a Congressional district to his liking; Unruh wanted to add much of the high Democratic registration in Wilson's Assembly district to his own, but to do so would leave Wilson out on a limb. So Wilson was to run for Congress.

Pacht's long identification with the CDC, his forthright liberalism and his backing by Californians for Liberal Representation, a peace-oriented, civil-liberties-advocating group, all combined to make the fight a "natural." It is doubtful if Unruh thought that Wilson was the most brilliant legislator the party had sent to Sacramento, or even if he was the best man for Congress. But if Unruh demanded party loyalty in the legislature, he returned it in the campaigns. Into the district poured troops and money.

Unruh told Pacht that he would do "everything possible" to beat him. "Everything possible" included Red-baiting (which Unruh may not have been responsible for, but made no effort to stop) and sending out a mailing to every Democrat in the district. The mailing, appearing as a telegram, bore the legend: "Kennedy Repudiates Pacht." The text was taken from a telegram sent at Unruh's request to Wilson by Larry O'Brien in the White House. Circled in red ink was the statement, "The President has neither by letter nor in any other way endorsed the candidacy of Mr. Pacht or. . . ." The heavy red circle blotted out the rest of the sentence: ". . . or any other candidates for the nomination." It was a professional job of misrepresentation only slightly mitigated by the fact that it had been prompted by the circulation of a letter sent to Pacht in 1960 by then-candidate Kennedy when the President-to-be endorsed Pacht's bid for Congress in another district. Although Pacht had reproduced the entire Kennedy letter, the date could easily be overlooked or discounted; the effect of the letter was to make it appear that Pacht had the President's support in the primary.

Wilson won by 5,000 votes of 57,000 cast, and Unruh had beaten the CDC in their first open battle.

The next month, Assemblyman Tom Bane, another of the "Cub Scout Den," and a slate of candidates representing both labor and the Negro and Mexican-American minorities, defeated a CDC slate for control of the Los Angeles County Committee. Even here Unruh's money approach to politics was apparent. The county committee had picked up ninety-nine new members (of 249) after COPE mailed to voters in Los Angeles slate cards naming Unruh supporters as endorsed candidates. In the virtual anonymity in which county-committee candidates run, the slate card was the voters' only aid.

The loss deprived the CDC of three important needs: the county committee's endorsement of candidates sympathetic to the CDC; a place to put to work its ideas of party reform and political education; and of equal importance, control of the chartering of the Democratic clubs.

Those who controlled the chartering could also influence the make-up of the clubs, refusing to recognize those clubs which might be too "liberal" (i.e., CDC-oriented). By extension, when these same clubs, plus whatever paper organizations Bane wished to charter, went to annual CDC conventions, they would favor those policy resolutions least likely to be "extreme" in the eyes of officeholders.

The following month Eugene Wyman, husband of Los Angeles City Councilwoman Rosalind Weiner Wyman, who had been a founding member of the Democratic Guild with Unruh thirteen years before, was elected chairman of the State Central Committee. Wyman had been appointed to the committee by the Governor only the year before with this express purpose in mind. A member of Democratic Associates, Wyman could be expected to see things as both the Governor and the Speaker saw them. The end result was to impress upon Congressional and Assembly candidates that the font of their good fortune was Unruh.

Brown's campaign for re-election was a great deal better than anyone has given the Governor credit for. First of all, he ran on his record of four years of progressive legislation, including the massive $1.75 billion Feather River project which would bring water to parched Southern California (Brown's administration will probably be best remembered for this project).

In great measure, this was a new "Pat" Brown, hardly the man whose image was one of indecisiveness, or that of a man manipulated by others. On orders from the White House, Unruh again installed a get-out-the-vote drive on Election Day (the Kennedys wanted a full-dress trial run for their operation in 1964). Unlike the 1960 drive, this one was to be staffed entirely by paid workers, each of whom was to receive $10 for his work. Unruh's operation recruited and briefed 13,000 people to man 4,000 precincts with high Democratic registration and loyalty records. Two-thirds of the estimated $150,000 spent on the operation in Los Angeles came from the Brown, Mosk and state-committee war chests. COPE paid 3,500 of the precinct workers who had been drawn from unemployment rolls. (This is probably the closest thing to precinct patronage in California; unfortunately, the work is intermittent and the pay too poor to make much of an impression.) The thoroughness of the Unruh operation was impressive; the county registrar of voters was led to remark, for example, on the unprecedented number of requests for absentee ballots in county hospitals.

To the volunteers, Unruh turned over the 8,000 precincts in which he had no operation going. Once again, the attempt was to bring out the extra 10 per cent of the Democratic vote which would normally sit it out.

Brown's re-election win over Nixon by 297,000 votes has been credited to everyone but Brown. Those who worked on the get-out-the-vote drive immediately issued victory statements; Unruh was characteristically more modest. He estimated that the get-out-the-vote drive garnered 100,000 votes for the top of the ticket. Even without those votes, Brown would have won. The CDC people, fearing that their efforts would be ignored, countered with claims of their own. Some 3,000 of the get-out-the-vote workers, paid or not, were CDC members. And in the precincts which Unruh had left untouched, even those with high Republican registrations, the Democratic turnout had been gratifying.

The CDC did contribute to the Brown victory, but the figures offered to support their claims to laurel wreaths are explained by something other than shoe-leather and persuasion. The highest voter turnouts were in districts worked by the CDC, but these districts are, by and large, the highest in income and socio-economic status. Democrats there would have turned out anyway.

The Unruh people claim a vote haul of 100,000—a figure which campaign strategists close to the Governor suspect might be more realistically pegged at 75,000. But the percentage of Democratic registration voting for Brown was lower in Los Angeles County (69.85 per cent) than in the two comparable counties in the San Francisco Bay Area (San Francisco, 74.69 per cent; Alameda, 73.5 per cent) and neither county had a paid operation going. In the only other county in the state with a registration over 250,000, Republican San Diego, the loyalty figure was 63.4 per cent, in spite of the fact that 200 of its 1,991 precincts were covered by the Unruh drive.

The man who, in successive elections, had beaten the two biggest Republicans in California, William Knowland and Richard Nixon, was given no credit for his victory. The image of the indecisive, good-natured, but bumbling "Pat" Brown, lingered longer in the minds of the party functionaries than it did in the minds of the voters.

The vote solidified Unruh's position of authority with the Assembly and Congressional delegations. As chairman in the Southern California area for these campaigns, Unruh aided with money, planning and advice a number of candidates. He argues that the total campaign in Southern California has been vindicated. In Los Angeles County, he points out, Democrats captured twenty-two out of thirty-one Assembly seats, eleven out of fifteen Congressional seats and the State Senator's seat, "all that we had a right to expect."

Unruh's power will grow even more should the CDC be unable to haul itself up by its bootstraps. Paul Ziffren, Unruh's most powerful opponent and the CDC's protector, speaks now of the necessity of reorganization of the grass-roots movement, making it broader in appeal. Ziffren would also lead CDC back to state issues, where it can have immediate influence, foregoing national issues where its voice counts for less. But paradoxically, any move to bring the group back to prosaic, more parochial matters will disaffect a substantial group of the liberals who have fought for both the right to take stands on international questions and to serve as the conscience of the party. For them, the problem of the admission of Red China to the UN is far more intriguing than reorganization of county government.

Unruh has made it clear that the CDC, in his opinion, must be either an endorsing body or a debating society; it cannot be both. If the group endorses and works for candidates, it should not issue policy resolutions which might embarrass those whom it endorses. If it chooses to discuss issues and pass resolutions, Unruh is more than willing to have it do so—as long as the group does not endorse. He can point to a great number of incumbent office-holders who believe the CDC endorsement a hindrance.

Ziffren believes the CDC can be both; it once was. The CDC conference, held in usually somnolent Bakersfield on the last weekend in March, will have serious consequences for the future of grass-roots politics in the United States. Whatever happens there, Jesse Unruh cannot be hurt; the CDC has no influence in the legislature.

The CDC's influence in Sacramento comes almost entirely from the Governor's office. A disagreement between Brown and Unruh on either the CDC or a major piece of legislation could trigger an open break between Brown's "center" and Unruh's "conservatives." (Only in California can a politician with a 100 per cent labor, 80 per cent American Friends Service Committee, pro-civil liberties voting record be a conservative.) Unruh is the Kennedy man in California, but Pat Brown is steadily reasserting his role as the head of the party. Neither man wants a power struggle which would lead inevitably to a north-south split and leave a shambles for Kennedy to pick his way through when he comes campaigning. But as Unruh's prestige increases with such honors as the Chubb fellowship to Yale, the unspoken challenge to Brown's leadership of the party also increases. A break could be thrust upon them.

The battle lines are shaping up. After Unruh had shown a lack of enthusiasm for a proposed anti-discriminatory housing bill, the CDC president, Tom Carvey, Jr., accused him of having invited the real-estate interests to attack the bill. Unruh dismissed the CDC spokesman as a "hilltop liberal." Governor Brown, asked to comment, said that "without disagreeing with the Speaker," he none the less intended to use the full powers of his office to see to it that good housing shall no longer be denied to any citizen because of the color of his skin or the kind of church he goes to.

Unruh's political future is a matter of some speculation. It is widely believed that he wants to succeed Brown as Governor; his denials are discounted as the politician's usual remarks in such a situation. If the Governor's Victorian mansion is Unruh's goal, the "bossism" image would prove to be the largest roadblock, a fact of which Unruh is well aware. There are other problems too. Unruh has one base of strength: the support, if not the undying devotion, of elected legislators. In Los Angeles, he also controls the county committee. But he has no popularity with the voters outside of his Assembly district and little contact with local politicians outside of Los Angeles County.

Unruh is a political animal. Being Governor of California is undoubtedly attractive to him, but there are others much closer to the party's nomination than he, including the CDC's first president, State Controller Alan Cranston, with whom Unruh is openly bickering.

The most likely spot for Unruh is somewhere on the national political scene, perhaps as Democratic National Chairman. There he can operate in a fashion which is most gratifying to him. He has mentioned leaving the speakership in four years, alluding to attractive business offers which would take him out of politics. Such a move is unlikely; Unruh likes politics and without a large personal fortune, or legislative office, he would be unable to maintaion his stature in California's affairs.

Whatever his future, he will be more and more a man of political influence on the national scene. The tides of migration will boost California's status as the number one state in the Union, the Congressional delegation will inevitably grow in size and seniority, the heavy defense spending will continue to shift the financial center of power to the West Coast. California's benevolent lordling will inevitably extend his horizons and domain.

BUSINESSMEN IN POLITICS
Thomas R. Reid

Thomas R. Reid is civic and governmental affairs director for the Ford Motor Company at Dearborn as well as consultant to the Office of Defense Mobilization. He is a member of the governing board of the Citizens Research Council of Michigan and other civic groups and was formerly executive vice-president of the U.S. Junior Chamber of Commerce and a member of the city council of Baltimore.

What happens in business today is determined more and more by what happened in government yesterday.

Government has an impact on business policy and planning at least as great as the impact of competition in the market place because government, to a large degree, determines the nature of the market place. In recent weeks, perhaps as never before, this fact has been brought home strikingly by certain extraordinary events. Yet, in spite of the clearest evidence, many businessmen who spend their leisure hours indignantly berating the actions of government are content, when they go to work, to take their place in a management structure that concerns itself 99 per cent with nongovernmental factors and at best one per cent with the impact of governments on business.

I suggest it is time that business—all business—admitted that governmental relations is a proper and essential management function. It is, in fact, a responsibility of management to advocate its business interests vigorously and effectively before courts, legislatures and administrative bodies. Some businessmen, I realize, wince when they hear this said straight out. They seem to feel that the relationships between business and government are somehow under-the-counter merchandise. Such relationships exist all right, they say, but let's not talk about them. People might become suspicious.

But why should any of us apologize for taking an active interest in all matters that affect our business, including governmental problems? There is no reason to conceal such interest or to act as if it didn't exist. Doing business with governments should be as forthright and straightforward as doing business with customers. The very fact that such action is an open and avowed expression of self-interest wins for it public acceptance.

The problem with public affairs activities of businessmen is not to conceal their existence or to apologize for them or to pretend that they are not essential both to business and government. The important point is to make sure that these activities are adequate, effective, open and aboveboard and conducted with impeccable taste and discretion.

This is the theme I should like to discuss.

From *National Civic Review,* September 1962. Reprinted by permission.

The first point is that businessmen in all areas of commerce and industry are doing an increasing amount of business with governments.

I am not thinking of ordinary commercial relations. What I do refer to is the dealings that all of us in business have with a whole array of governments, from local school districts up to the federal government in Washington. Zoning ordinances, air pollution controls, unemployment compensation laws, property taxes, excise taxes, corporate profits taxes, U.S. foreign trade policy—these and a host of other actions, policies, regulations and statutes of government at all levels are the basis for this relationship. Since they permeate every area of our businesses, we have a compelling need to recognize that big government is here to stay and that we are going to have to live with it and do business with it.

In all honesty we must admit that our complicated society demands big government. Short of resolving the Cold War, we are not likely to see any curtailment of its scope. Probably most businessmen recognize that fact. But the disquieting thing is that so many have not begun to act as though they have fully caught its implications. Perhaps they entertain the hope that, if they don't look, it will go away. But history offers no support for that view. Over the centuries, under almost every kind of government, there has been some measure of public supervision of business affairs.

In the United States the present pattern of the business-government relationship has been building since the depression—and even before. It was given great impetus and much of its formal structure by the New Deal. But it has survived and been further extended by both Republican and Democratic administrations. There is no evidence at all that government intervention in business will lessen. Rather, in Washington and state capitols alike, the question is: What are the outer limits of government's reach in business affairs? How far is too far?

The role that government has assumed in the economy is not something that wily administrators and lawmakers have slipped over on an unsuspecting and fundamentally disapproving public. There is every indication that the American public accepts and often demands a basically activist role for government—in Washington, in the state capitol, even in the city hall. With such encouragement, governments tend to make more and more of the decisions affecting people's freedom rather than allowing people to exercise these choices themselves.

We find it difficult to understand how any large part of the electorate could concur with this attitude, even though it may be both benevolent and sincere. We wonder why people fail to see that any significant interference with free market forces and the freedom of individuals to choose as they will can in the long run bring on more ills than it heals. We deplore their willingness to let governments attempt drastic cures on a vital and useful economic system that can stand only a limited amount of manhandling.

We may—and should—try to educate, persuade and convince the electorate of the fundamental value of our system. But at the same time we must realize that many, many people seem perfectly content that governments created at their direction intervene in the workings of the economy. Big government is not going to wither away for lack of popular approval.

Our job, then, is to learn how to do business with governments as they actually exist here and now. How do we go about this? The first thing we must do is to change some of our attitudes and put them in step with the political, governmental and business realities of our day. As a start I would make these suggestions.

First, it is not enough for businessmen to cry that government is anti-business unless they seriously ponder whether business may be anti-government.

Second, it is not enough for businessmen to moan that this or that problem is none of the government's business, unless they are willing to take a hand in resolving the problem through other means—and thereby make it unnecessary for government to step in.

Third, it is not enough for businessmen to decry the further centralization of government in Washington without doing something themselves to help strengthen the hand of state and local governments to deal with the things that Washington otherwise will have to handle.

Fourth, it is not enough for businessmen to lament the proliferating functions of government while they work only for the adoption of governmental actions or programs that will protect their own interests and meet their own business needs.

Too many people in business often act and talk as though government were their mortal enemy. The overall basis for this psychology is dubious—no matter what we may think of the wisdom of many things that government does. Beyond that it is an ineffectual attitude. We surely would accomplish more if we devoted more of our energy to the adoption of programs and policies that are sound and practical from the standpoint of the whole public.

Do not mistake me. I do not suggest we be any less vigilant toward government. Every service that is provided, every function that is performed by government must be justified in need and in sound and balanced public policy. We must get our money's worth for every dollar spent. Nor do I suggest that business people do an about-face and become the happy advocates of all that they have in their hearts and consciences been opposing.

What I do suggest is that the businessman's interest in the things he is for and the things he is against needs to be registered more effectively. And this means being ruthlessly efficient with ourselves. We have to get rid of attitudes and methods that do not fit our times and replace them with positive and practical new approaches—no matter how much it may hurt.

What does this imply in terms of concrete action?

In the first place every company must give full recognition to the fact that government relations is a management function to be handled as forthrightly as sales, production, personnel or any other activity.

This is essential. But before anything much will happen, certain specific things must be done:

1. A good understanding of the over-all objective and the basic principles to be followed must be conveyed up and down the management line.

2. Some measure of planning and organization must be introduced so that people will know their particular responsibilities and have a good grasp of "how-to-do-it" techniques.

3. Provision must be made for a continuing process of communication and decision-making.

At Ford Motor Company we have sought to train our management people how to do business with governments just as we train them how to sell cars or maintain quality standards. One of the methods we use is a management training film recently completed. It illustrates how one company is translating principle into action. We begin by citing three basic premises of the company's approach as stated in a formal policy letter:

First, "The company recognizes that a democratic form of government, a free enterprise system and a healthy and improving free society are essential to the accomplishment of its corporate objectives and that government actions and social and economic developments vitally affect the company's operations and interests."

Second, "The company also realizes that a basic premise of our democratic system is the acceptance by all citizens, individual and corporate alike, of a responsibility to participate in its functions."

Third, "The company believes, therefore, that it is essential to its own interests and to the proper discharge of its responsibilities as a corporate citizen to participate actively in maintaining a sound social, economic and political environment."

Building on these premises, we treat two closely related areas: civic affairs and governmental affairs.

As to civic affairs, "The company will maintain an active interest in the general welfare of our society and participate in programs and citizen efforts concerned with social and civic improvement. The company is particularly interested in the social, civic and physical betterment of the communities in which it operates."

As to governmental affairs, "The company will maintain an active interest in governmental affairs and will give effective expression of its position on public issues affecting its interests. Its position on such issues will be determined on the basis of an assessment of both its own legitimate interests and the requirements of sound public policy."

These, then, are the over-all purposes of Ford Motor Company in the civic and governmental field. But the company itself cannot exert civic leadership—or affect the adoption of legislation. To state a simple truth— the company, as such, has no voice. It speaks and acts only through its management representatives. They are the voice and the personification of the company. Only they can give substance to these aims.

Members of management are expected to maintain an active interest in public affairs and, as appropriate, to participate in the formulation and representation of company positions on issues affecting its interests. Management members are also expected to do their part in fulfilling the company's responsibilities as a corporate citizen and to consider participation in constructive civic and community activities on behalf of the company as part of their management responsibilities.

Our training film concludes with these words of Henry Ford II:

> The growing interest in public affairs among business people is one of the most significant and constructive developments in American industry in many years. But the job is too big to expect any one staff or office to do it all. The thing I most want to stress is that civic and governmental affairs *is every company manager's business*. It is as much a part of his job as if it were written into his job description.

Those excerpts will serve to illustrate the nature and purpose of our public affairs program. Many other companies have adopted similar programs in the past two or three years. Without describing our whole program in detail, I do want to point out what the film emphasizes—namely, the importance we at Ford attach to making government relations a line management responsibility supported by a specialized staff.

I suppose there is a tendency in every company to regard any activity not directly concerned with production or sales as expensive overhead or a frill. Let me assure you that company public affairs programs are no frill. A dollar added to the cost of a product or service by government action has just as much effect on profits as a dollar added by capital outlay or higher labor rates. Conversely, constructive or advantageous actions of government can cut costs just as much as a more efficient production method.

While the dollars-and-cents impact of governmental action, however, is the most tangible gauge we have of the effectiveness of a public affairs program, it is really the intangible element that may be most significant. That is the effect of governmental action, not as it relates to business costs, but to such matters as the freedom to manage and to principles that bear on the long-range health of our society.

Corporate public affairs programs are not merely an intensification of lobbying activity, important as that is. What is needed is a new dimension in lobbying. We must do more than just utilize the processes of government to represent our own interests and gain our own objectives. We must begin to participate actively and constructively in the process of free government. Let me illustrate what I mean.

Last year, Ford Motor Company supported constitutional amendments that were proposed in three states to increase the pay of state legislators. We reasoned that our company has an important stake in state governments wherever we have substantial operations. Since we believed that effective state government would be furthered by compensating legislators better, we felt it entirely appropriate to take a stand on this question.

Similarly, Ford—like hundreds of other companies—has designed programs to encourage its employees to participate fully in politics. Even though government in America is the product of a political process, American business has traditionally maintained a stiff-necked attitude toward politics and politicians. Politics was supposed to be controversial and not altogether respectable and therefore should be avoided.

If we want better government, then this thinking simply has to go. When we discourage people from political activity, we cut off the very lifeblood of good government. Whatever may be wrong with politics, the trouble is not so much with those who are in it as with those who are not. Because of its former attitude, business has to take the lead in encouraging more people to participate actively in their own political parties. One of the most heartening developments in the business world is that so many companies have recognized this fact and are creating a climate that encourages free and full political participation by all employees.

Again, a commission named by the President recently recommended, among other matters, that individual political contributions be made tax deductible within certain limits. A bill including this provision has now been recommended to Congress by the administration. I have advocated such action on many occasions. Inasmuch as it assists our democratic processes, it is healthy. Supporting it is a constructive action that any businessman can take.

I do not suggest that we make busybodies of ourselves by poking our noses into every possible kind of question. But I do say that it is foolhardy to take too constricted a view of our proper area of interest with governments.

The course of free government reflects a rough approximation of a wavering and shadowy consensus that emerges from the insistent needs, demands and considerations that impinge on it from all the interests in our society. It is fundamental that all interests be properly represented. Business views and needs will be well represented to the extent our underlying attitude toward government is sound and our practical planning and organization are effective.

Recently I asked a businessman associated with a rather large organization what action his company would take about a federal government decision that directly affected it. He said they would do nothing. And his reason was that the company had other matters at stake with the government that were so important that the company did not want to antagonize anyone in government.

Multiply this attitude many times. What would happen if, for fear of reprisals, all business retreated to the relative safety of doing nothing and saying nothing? What would happen to the great plans and ideas that expand the economy and create new jobs? Where would our growth come from? How far would our living standards decline? Where would we develop the muscle to meet the challenge of world competition? Isn't it likely that, by meekly trying to hold on to what we have, we might lose even that?

The answer is not for businessmen to retreat into a sullen, fearful silence. It is rather for them to be active and articulate in working for the kind of government under which our free enterprise can grow and prosper. It is for them to be as imaginative and efficient in doing business with government as they are in doing business with their customers.

Finally, it is for them to recall the advice given by Thomas Jefferson when he said, "I know of no safe depository of the ultimate powers of society but the people themselves; and if we think them not enlightened enough to exercise their control with a wholesome discretion, the remedy is not to take it from them, but to inform their discretion by education."

It is time for all businessmen to inform their own discretion and to act on what they know.

13 GOVERNING THE FIFTY STATES

Knock on the door of the gubernatorial mansion in any major state and it is likely to be answered by a presidential aspirant—either an active contender or, at the least, a hopeful. In this century, the preferred route to the White House has been through a state house. Nearly half of the nominees of both major parties, and far more of the serious contenders, have been governors of the larger states. Even in the smaller states, the chief executives are frequently singled out as potential vice-presidential nominees. As a result, public interest has made all of our state governors subject to automatic press coverage and national prominence.

Also responsible for this personal prominence is the role a governor plays in national politics—supporting or rejecting other presidential aspirants, consulting with the president if they are of the same party, shaping the national policy of the opposition, as in the Republican Governors' Conference. And, within his own state, a governor—as leader of the people, initiator of governmental programs, target for the opposition party—attracts the bulk of local news coverage. In short, a governor occupies a highly visible post. Naturally, the average citizen tends to be more aware of his governor than of any other official this side of Washington.

But how well is the gubernatorial office understood by the man in the street? Is it really the best training ground for the presidency, as commonly claimed? What are the powers possessed by the state's leading executive? What are the limitations upon his exercise of those powers?

Our governors are charged with four duties that make the governorship a "little presidency," lacking only foreign policy responsibilities. First, the governor must be the chief executive and principal administrator of state government. As chief executive he has the authority to initiate studies, to set forth his program, and to lead the citizens in support of this program. As principal administrator, he usually controls the state's budget—a multi-billion dollar operation in the larger states—he supervises thousands of state employees, he appoints key administrators, and he is responsible for the not inconsequential administrative organization and machinery of the state. Even in those states where he must share the ballot with other elective officials, his name always heads the ticket.

Second, on the legislative front, the Governor must be leader or principal negotiator, depending on whether his party controls a majority within the co-equal branch. His voice sets forth legislative programs, virtually dictates state spending programs, and keeps the legislators informed as to popular and administrative needs. The constitutional incapacity of legislative bodies to lead, so noticeable on the national level, becomes even more pronounced within the chambers of State Senate and Assembly. A governor in the position of the Democratic governors of New York State, faced with what the late Alfred E. Smith used to call the "constitutional Republican majority" of the state legislature, finds that he must be an astute "horse trader" in coping with the majority as well as the leader of his own minority forces—offering one concession for another enactment, threatening to veto some key majority measure if a desired minority bill is not enacted.

Third, the governor must be leader of his party lest the task go by default to someone behind the scenes, or be endlessly fought over by contesting county chairmen. In this political role, the governor may generate great power if he chooses to build an organization (his opponents would say "machine") as indicated by the New York examples of Dewey and Smith, the Wisconsin and Louisiana instances of La Follette and Long. Given the support of key county leaders, the governor can extend his domain over the lesser districts, and by skilled distribution of rewards and punishments, come to exercise a personal domination. In some states, he may be aided by the power to appoint friends and supporters to state office—"patronage" in the generally accepted sense. Appointment patronage, however, is far from the solitary building block of the partisan edifice that the public sometimes believes it to be. Thanks to civil service reform in most states, it is only in Pennsylvania that a modern governor can find an estimated 115,000 patronage posts to fill upon his election. Today's political favoritism commonly resides in more divergent—and more lucrative—areas such as contract awards, monopoly grants, and protective legislation.

Finally, in his role of public leader, the governor of even the smaller states occupies an unchallenged position. Though his fame may not have spread beyond the state's borders, he nonetheless finds little challenge from such potential contenders for state power as the House Speaker and Senate Majority Leader. Neither runs on a state-wide ticket or represents a state-wide constituency, and neither is likely to be known to the public at large. The governor is also chief lobbyist and spokesman for his state—urging upon the Congress of the United States programs that will benefit the state's economy and well-being; working out with federal administrators the application of these programs; seeking to attract new industries or additional tourists; subtly countering the similar blandishments of other states' governors.

Having noted a general pattern of fourfold gubernatorial responsibility, we must add that there are fifty varieties of governorship in practice. Historically there has existed a wide range of mastery and incompetence, of strength or weakness, among those holding the post. Like the presidency, the governorship, subject to constitutional and political restraints, has tended to be pretty much what the incumbent makes of it.

The range in gubernatorial powers is broad; some states still adhere to Revolutionary precedents of a weak governorship, while others have "modernized" to create a strong one. States that wish to keep their chief executive weak often forbid him to succeed himself; only an unusually distinguished few, like Pinchot of Pennsylvania, have subsequently gained non-consecutive reelection. Other states surround their governors with a host of competing elective officials, who may represent conflicting factions even though nominally of the same party, or who may, if of the opposition, deliberately hamper the governor. Elsewhere the governor must deal with departments headed by multi-membered boards responsible, if at all, only to the legislature that appointed them. And in many of the more populous states the governor, in spite of his own popular majority at the polls, has had to contend with a state legislature (at least until the recent court-ordered reapportionment) controlled by an outnumbered rural constituency.

More progressive states have armed their chief executive with an impressive array of powers. The short ballot system—eliminating a multiplicity of elective offices in favor of executive appointment—has given him the authority to select those erstwhile rivals for administrative power. Unlimited terms of office, which leave to the voters the decision on rewards for performance, provide him with both incentive and political authority. Key fiscal powers, including the executive budget and item veto, keep his hand firmly on the purse strings. Additional staff assistance and greater controls over personnel (including those under merit system protection) enable him to surround himself with sympathetic yet competent administrators. In some states, such as New York, the potent investigatory power, normally reserved to the legislature, has been assigned to the governor. In New York and elsewhere the governor also possesses the highly significant power to remove incapable or corrupt local officials and to replace inadequate district attorneys, giving him practical working control over local governments.

Significant limitations and restrictions exist, however, in even the most powerful governorships. The same publicity which lends him power serves simultaneously as his principal restraint. Personal shortcomings and weaknesses may be portrayed by the press just as unerringly as strengths and accomplishments. A governor who is a serious contender for national office must be particularly careful of his "image"; even if his ambitions have narrower state limits, he must constantly be concerned with electoral prospects— either his own reelection or the choice of a successor. On the administrative scene he is all too likely to be thwarted by the inertia of bureaucracy, the resistance to programmatic change on the part of established agencies staffed by career civil servants sometimes deaf to the policy importunings of a transient executive only nominally their chief. Finally, the power of local political leaders will operate as a constant reminder to the governor to "keep his fences mended," to keep the county custodians of his renomination in his camp.

Despite the many limitations, however, the governor emerges as the one man with sufficient power, the one man with adequate political support to provide the necessary leadership for a modern state government in action.

THE DEVELOPMENT OF THE GOVERNORSHIP
William H. Young

William H. Young is Professor of Political Science and Chairman of the Department at the University of Wisconsin.

The American governorship was conceived in mistrust and born in a strait jacket, the creature of revolutionary assemblies. Most of the colonial Governors were executive agents of British dominion, and the Revolution was fought, in part at least, to be rid of them. "He (the King) has forbidden his Governors to pass laws of immediate and pressing importance," says the first indictment of the Declaration of Independence. The revolutionists were determined that no home-grown "Monarchs" would obstruct the will of the legislatures. The Colonial assemblies, centers of revolutionary zeal, established their own separate state governments on the basis of legislative supremacy. The Governors provided in the first state constitutions were assigned short terms, in many cases were selected by the legislatures, and were authorized neither veto nor appointive powers.

The shortcomings of legislative dominance of the thirteen young republics were soon apparent: the legislatures were unable to provide vigorous leadership themselves and refused to allow anyone else to provide it. To the critics, the answer lay in a strong national government equipped to overcome the parochialism of the regional legislatures and to deal firmly with commercial rivalries, debtor-dominated money policies, military weakness, and the ambitions of European statesmen. Hamilton, Madison, Washington, Jay looked not to strong state executives but to strong national leadership to steady the ship of state. The Constitution of 1787, drafted by critics of the state legislature, provided the foundation upon which has subsequently been erected the towering structure of our modern central government. This decision relieved only temporarily, however, the need for powerful and effective direction at the state capitals.

NINETEENTH CENTURY CONCEPTIONS

Throughout much of the nineteenth century the conceptions that government should do as little as possible, and that little as close to home as convenient, made the principal regional foci of governmental power the city hall and the county courthouse. An irresistible demand for strong and effective leadership in Albany, Harrisburg, Richmond, Trenton, or Columbus arose only when the lives of our people were importantly and intimately affected by decisions made in the state capitals.

Our first Governors were concerned primarily with military questions as

From *State Government,* Summer 1958. Reprinted by permission.

they sought to support the War of Independence, the never-ending struggles with the Indians, the renewed battles with Great Britain in 1812, the war with Mexico, and finally the catastrophic upheaval of 1861. Recruitment of militiamen, training of recruits, procurement of supplies, appointment of officers, these were major state executive functions before 1870. State military formations were swallowed up in a national army in the twentieth century, and ceased to be of any great importance long before that as the Indians were pushed steadily westward.

IN JACKSON'S ERA

Meantime, the demand for internal improvements in the Jacksonian era had provided a real challenge to state enterprise and wisdom and produced one of the first great state executives, Dewitt Clinton of New York. Under Clinton's skillful management, the construction of the Erie Canal gave Albany and New York City a great forward push to commercial supremacy. In most of the state capitals, however, canal-turnpike programs produced only bankruptcy, scandal, and disappointment. The decentralization of control of the credit system of the United States accompanying the destruction by Jackson of the Bank of the United States found most states unable or unwilling to meet the challenge. Legislative control of banking resulted only in wildcatting, debased currency, fraud, and general mismanagement.

During this era, the tide of popular government swept over the new nation and, by broadening the suffrage and providing for the popular election of the Governor and other state officials, paved the way for the state executive ultimately to develop, like the President, as a tribune of the people. With popular election came also the veto of legislative proposals. Democracy of the Jacksonian style, moreover, introduced the spoils system, the use of the state executive branch to support the party apparatus. This in turn meant the domination of the state service by the party leaders rather than by the elected officials. It also introduced the hope, largely futile as it turned out, of frustrating caucus and party oligarchy by relying on direct, popular election. One administrative office after another was placed on the ballot. At the end of this particular reforming era it was hard to find what was left of the constitutional injunctions—borrowed in most cases from the national document—that the state executive power was entrusted to a Governor and that he was to take care that the laws be faithfully executed.

One final aspect of the Jacksonian era deserves notice. This was an age of prison reform, and state after state assumed the responsibility for the correction of the worst offenders in maximum security penitentiaries, where solitary confinement and hard labor were expected to produce penitence and spiritual rebirth. Thus was one of the enduring state programs introduced and thus was begun the movement of functions and responsibilities from county seat to state capital which has characterized regional government in the United States ever since.

By 1865, the typical state Governor was elected for a two-year term, was equipped with a veto over legislative actions, and was authorized to appoint a few deputies in the state service. The New York experience, more or less, typifies the stages by which this came about. In 1821, the New York Governor was made elective, given a two-year term (untypically, his term had been three years), and equipped with the veto. Power to appoint administrative officers was, however, lodged in the legislature until 1846 when most of them were made elective.

AS INDUSTRY BURGEONED

What little public confidence in the state governments remained after the bank scandals and the turnpike fiascos of the 1840's was completely undermined by the rapid spread of industrial capitalism in the Grant-Hayes-Arthur epoch. Party oligarchies, supported by patronage and leagued with corporate giants, bought and browbeat Governors, legislators and administrative officers as the great public utilities, essential to urban industrialism, were established. Railroads, traction companies, gas suppliers, electricity distributors needed and got state privilege and state protection. City hall and state capital became the resort of lobbyists, grafters, and influence-peddlers. Power fell into the hands of the "invisible government." Elihu Root stated the case exactly to the New York State constitutional convention in 1915. Of the late decades of the nineteenth century he said: "For I don't remember how many years, Mr. Conkling was the supreme ruler in this state; the Governor did not count, the legislatures did not count. . . . Then Mr. Platt ruled the state. . . . It was not the Governor; it was not the legislature; it was not any elected officers; it was Mr. Platt."

It did not at first occur to the critics of boodle that the answer might lie in creating a vigorous and popular executive. Governors, too, were under the thumb of the oligarchy. Government must be rendered powerless to do evil, demanded the reformers. A new wave of state constitution writing fixed one shackle after another on the state legislature: no special enactments; short sessions; no railroad passes; no special charters. New agencies equipped to regulate utility rates and services, to promote and foster agriculture, to regulate banks and insurance companies, and in other ways to try to bring these new and rampaging forces of industrialism under control were established. All of them, however, were placed out of the reach of gubernatorial influence and were garbed in the robes of judicial independence.

Out of this era, however, came one tool of executive power which turned out to have a high degree of survival value: the item veto. Borrowed from the Constitution of the Confederacy, the item veto of appropriation bills was awarded to one Governor after another in an effort to mitigate the fiscal irresponsibility of state legislatures and to keep tax burdens from becoming onerous.

Urban industrialism brought also some new concepts of state service. Despite the failures of legislatures and Governors in dealing with the railroads and the urban utilities, there were some successes in meeting the challenges of the new order. The discovery by Pasteur of the germ causation of communicable disease led to the inauguration of new state health programs to supplement local efforts. Hand-in-hand with the national government, a broad program of education, demonstration and research in aid of a sagging agriculture was inaugurated in state capitals and state colleges. New concepts of state care for the mentally ill and defective in huge state asylums were introduced, and state support of and supervision over the far-flung public school system took on new depth and scope. Gradually, too, the old locally-assessed and locally-elected property taxes were abandoned as a main source of support by one state after another. New corporate and excise taxes were introduced, requiring state assessment and collection of state revenues.

MUCH FORM, LITTLE SUBSTANCE

For every new program of service or control, however, the sponsors sought administration by agencies freed, it was hoped, from the domination of the party rulers, the spoils appointees, and the elected officials of the government. In most cases, the result was to insure irresponsibility and to frustrate genuinely popular control.

Thus by 1910, the state government of one of our large industrial states consisted of a legislature hemmed about with restrictions on its authority, limited in the time or energy it could bestow on state problems, and organized to inhibit the influence of the growing population and wealth of the industrial and commercial cities. The Governor occupied a post in the executive branch which was all form and little substance. On paper it might appear that he presided over an agency of perhaps seventy or eighty separate and distinct units employing several thousand persons and expending millions of dollars annually. In fact, he presided over a few personal aides, shared some power of patronage distribution with legislators and party chiefs, and for the rest pleaded, wheedled or threatened his way into whatever influence he could obtain over state policy by these tactics. Most of the programs of the state touching the lives of the citizen were under boards, commissions, or secretaries elected directly by the voters or appointed for long and overlapping terms by the Governor and the Senate. On many of these boards the Governor could sit as an *ex-officio* member, but powers of command he had none. The original constitutional mandates requiring him to enforce the laws were still empty of meaning or utility.

STRONG GOVERNORS EMERGE

Towards the end of the last century, however, a new type of Governor began to appear. One with a program, a following, and a spirit of dedication to positive governmental exertions in behalf of the people. Grover Cleveland was such a one and he showed by example that the doors of the White House might be opened to a Governor who governed. As the new century dawned, Hughes and Roosevelt of New York, La Follette of Wisconsin, Wilson of New Jersey all demonstrated that the Governor's office, rightly conceived, provided unparalleled opportunities for leadership and for realizing the deep-seated wishes of the masses. The voters also responded with enthusiasm and insisted that legislators and party leaders respond also.

The emergence of the new type of political leader in the Governor's chair probably was the prerequisite to the reconstruction of the office which has occurred in the past forty years. The opportunity to achieve the presidency drew the very best efforts from the Governors of the great pivotal states. Prior to 1880, the path to the White House did not lead directly from the Governor's chair. While one-third of the Presidents had been Governors, most of these had been members of Congress immediately preceding their successful bids. Since 1880 more than half of the Presidents arrived at this high office almost directly from the state capitals.

Accompanying the appearance of the new popular executive was also continued growth and expansion in state services. Beginning in the early twentieth century, the states moved with mounting zest into highway construction and maintenance. This movement became a veritable flood in the 20's and 30's. Then came law enforcement programs, and uniformed state police began to appear, first to combat unions but later to regulate traffic and to stop the spread of gangsterism into the hinterlands. Vocational education appeared in the second decade and new programs of child welfare in the 20's. Efforts to mitigate the harshness of the industrial struggle led to wage and hour laws, workmen's compensation insurance, factory inspection. The depression brought new concepts of poor relief, unemployment insurance, old-age pensions. New discoveries in medicine broadened demands for better programs for tuberculosis and mental illness. Accompanying most of these new programs, however, were new definitions of national responsibility and the inauguration of an ever-growing system of federal grants-in-aid. In many cases, the pioneer efforts in these new fields came from the Governors of those states where the office was being reconstructed. In many cases, too, ineptness or incapacity in the state house contributed to the demand for national action. Despite the growth of national responsibility, the need for effective and vigorous state leadership was scarcely diminished as program followed program, involving the states ever more deeply in the lives of their citizens.

THE OFFICE ADVANCES

The major remaining stages in the emergence of the modern Governor may be listed as: (1) the change to a four-year term; (2) reorganization of the executive branch into a few major executive departments headed by subordinates of the Governor; (3) the development of the executive budget, accompanied by further restriction of the legislative power of initiative in the field of finance; (4) the establishment of administrative management agencies in the Governors' office; (5) the centralization of publicity in the Governor's office.

To lengthen the Governor's term from two years to four—and this has now occurred in a majority of states—may seem like a little change, but it is really a very big one. The paths to executive leadership in both legislation and administration are not clearly marked out for all to see. They must be learned. Two years is not long enough to learn them well before one is swept up in a new campaign. In many states, two-year terms will include only one budget and one legislative session, and both of these before the new Governor is well settled in his chair. Fiscal policy cannot be made in the midst of a campaign or in a state of exhaustion when it has just ended. New leaders cannot be found for major agencies in so short a time. They, too, must learn their jobs.

The story of how Frank Lowden of Illinois reorganized the executive branch of that great state into a few single-headed departments and set a pattern for virtually all subsequent efforts of this type needs no retelling here. Successive epidemics of state administrative reorganization have occurred in the 20's, 30's and 50's, and there is much yet to be done. Administrative reorganization designed to achieve responsible, effective, co-ordinated, efficient, and competent government is never finished. Agencies grow, programs change, legislators constantly intervene, and public interest in this subject is rarely high. The single-headed, partisan-directed executive agency of the Illinois, New York and Pennsylvania pattern has not commended itself to every state. The debate on this subject continues to wax and wane, but the tools of modern management—central procurement, specialized engineering and architectural services, machine methods, space allocation, etc.—have in most cases remained permanent features of executive departments.

BUDGET AND MANAGEMENT

More important to executive leadership than departmental reorganization or the abilities of the board or commission as directing agency is the executive budget system. The New York Bureau of Municipal Research was probably the architect of the modern executive budget system, and Governor Smith of New York was its best known exponent. As adopted by the voters of New York in 1927, the gubernatorial budget program included: (1) the assignment to the Governor of the power to present to the legislature each year a consolidated request for appropriations in behalf of all of the agencies of the state government; (2) the limitation of legislative power in appropriation to that of reducing or striking out items in the Governor's budget—new expenditures, outside the budget, were required to be proposed each in a separate item and thus subjected to the Governor's item veto. The effect of this system is completely to reverse the traditional fiscal roles of the two branches. The Governor becomes the initiator; the legislature has only the veto. Many states have since installed the executive budget without the added restraints on the legislature. Through the budget, whatever the legislative power may be, the Governor receives his greatest single opportunity to review and to influence the programs, policies and procedures of the executive agencies. Whether state agencies are directed by career civil servants, lay boards, independently elected secretaries or gubernatorial appointees, if they have to go through the Governor to get the money they require from the legislature, they are likely to heed his directions and to respect his wishes.

Governor Stassen of Minnesota probably deserves the credit for gathering under the Governor's sight many of the specialized agencies of modern public management and placing them under a full-time manager who becomes virtually an assistant governor. Departments or bureaus of administration or management have been appearing for over a decade now in one Governor's office after another. Sometimes the budget office is simply enlarged to accommodate the other services—procurement, space assignment, building maintenance, for example. This reform aims at securing for the state some of the advantages of the widely popular city-manager system without sacrificing policy leadership or political responsibility. The growth of managerial services under the Governor's immediate direction is one solution to the growing problem of bringing usable assistance to the Governor in support of his administrative responsibilities and closely parallels the growth of the White House Office in Washington.

OTHER SOURCES OF STRENGTH

The Governor's office, like the White House, is easy to see and to write about. Legislative procedures are intricate, baffling, and hard to describe. The modern media of mass communication tend to concentrate at the state level on the Governor's office. With the help of skilled public relations assistants, state executives are finding unprecedented opportunities to publicize themselves and their programs. In dealing with the legislature especially, the Governors are greatly aided by the relative ease with which they can get the ear of the public. Legislators ordinarily are not nearly as able to get attention. Press conferences and frequent radio and television reports are becoming standard features in the repertoire of our most skillful state Governors.

From detested minion of Royal power, to stepson of legislative domination, to popular figurehead, to effective executive is the story of the American Governor.

A GOVERNOR'S JOB AS SEEN BY A GOVERNOR
Chester Bowles

> Now, for the second time in his career ambassador to India, Chester Bowles was once Democratic governor of "Republican" Connecticut. He was the wartime head of the Office of Price Administration, and served a term as representative in Congress from Connecticut's 2nd District. He is the author of *Tomorrow Without Fear*.

Last November, somewhat to the surprise of my party, the pollsters and myself, I became Governor of Connecticut. I won by the second slimmest margin in the modern history of Connecticut elections—2,225 votes.

The Republican party even demanded a recount. In fact, not until four hours after the time set by tradition for my inaugural on January 5 did the Republican-controlled House of Representatives agree to accept me as Governor.

I can understand their reluctance. Connecticut is "a land of steady habits" and there had been only eleven Democratic Governors in the last hundred years. Connecticut Republicans, moreover, like those across the country, had been serenely confident. A Democratic victory was a bitter blow. I had run for Governor, in fact, not because I thought that any Democrat had a chance in 1948—least of all in Connecticut—but for several reasons which seemed to be, at least, very important.

Connecticut, like most other states, faced some serious problems. There was a critical shortage of schools and teachers which our towns couldn't solve unaided. Our Connecticut housing shortage was even more acute than that of other states—and we have more than our share of slums. There was pressing need for modern mental hospitals to replace antiquated fire traps built two generations or more ago. There was need for broadened labor legislation to meet growing unemployment, and need for increased old age assistance.

I felt that such problems could and should be solved by *state* action. I happen to believe that too great centralization of government in Washington can be unhealthy—and even dangerous. Yet, if a state government fails to house its people properly, or give good education to its children, or take care of its aged, the Federal Government must eventually step in, either of necessity or by default.

I could see no reason why a prosperous, intelligent state like Connecticut should, by shirking its clear responsibilities, put further concentration of power in Federal hands.

I believed that one extremely important way to prevent too great centralization of government in Washington was to improve the effectiveness of

From *The New York Times Magazine,* July 24, 1949. © 1949 by The New York Times Company. Reprinted by permission.

our state governments. From what I knew of state governments generally, and certainly here in Connecticut, administrative standards are nowhere near as high as they should be, or as high as those of the Federal Government itself.

It was my real hope, then, that if Connecticut and other states could set high enough standards of responsibility and efficiency in handling their problems, there would be less need to turn to Washington.

When the shock of my election wore off, and I took a clear look ahead, I saw two immediate jobs. First, I had to prepare a legislative program to carry out the platform on which I had been elected. And, second, I had to prepare a state budget.

I expected rough sledding on both jobs. For while the Connecticut Senate had a comfortable Democratic majority, the House of Representatives was overwhelmingly Republican.

Aside from these two responsibilities, I knew simply that it was my job to administer the state government as competently as I could and—the Legislature permitting—make whatever organizational changes would permit improved administrative efficiency. The last six months, however, have taught me that a Governor's life involves many other duties, responsibilities, headaches—and satisfactions.

One of the most rewarding—if time-consuming—phases of a Governor's job is to see a constant flow of people from all over the state. A Governor's office, in fact, looks like—and very often sounds like—a non-stop New England town meeting.

It is this part of a Governor's job which has convinced me even more thoroughly that state government fills a place no Washington agency could take. In a state like Connecticut, you live and work in close contact with those whose attitudes eventually decide public policies. When they think you are right—and especially when they think you are wrong—they manage to get their views to you very quickly. It is direct-action democracy—straight to the point and no holds barred.

My weekly list of visitors is a cross-section of the interests, professions and income levels of Connecticut. I see leaders of veterans' groups, of women's organizations, business groups, hospital and prison heads. I see mothers pleading for treatment for their children in a tuberculosis sanatorium already overcrowded.

I talk to people who want (or don't want) a new highway through their town; to labor leaders worried about unemployment; to school teachers concerned about the impact of our growing birth rate on our outdated school facilities.

In addition, I function as head of my political party—as every Governor must, I must be accessible at all times to my party's legislators, and my party's town chairmen and other state and local party officials, and help make political decisions.

Some cocktail lounge liberals, as well as some of our conservative friends, have a "touch-me-not" attitude toward politics that simply does not make sense. They want the world remade overnight with others handling the details, while they sit aloof and unsullied.

Politics is the science of government. Every great American President, Senator or Governor has been an able politician. If he hadn't been we never would have heard his name. Every man in public office is a politician of sorts. If he weren't, he never would have been elected—or even nominated.

I discovered that a Governor during the legislative session is forced to become also something of a legislative expert. Every morning that the Legislature convened I saw its Democratic leaders, and discussed with them their legislative strategy for the day. (The Republicans were invited, too, but they appeared only on rare occasions.) At any moment during the session my door would be—and was—thrown open by committee chairmen with a fresh legislative crisis on labor, education, housing or other bills to which they needed a quick answer.

All of these extra and special gubernatorial duties are absorbing, fascinating, and necessary. They do, however, pile up a tremendous load when added to a Governor's basic jobs.

According to our statutes, I was to prepare the state's budget for presentation on Feb. 1—just three weeks after the legislature convened.

I decided to put the state's complete financial story for the first time under one cover, and make it intelligible not only to financial experts, but to the general public as well, by means of illustrative charts. This is now commonly done by progressive business corporations. Oddly enough, it is a radical idea for state governments.

Luckily, I didn't know what I was up against. I found there were 108 budgeted agencies, whose myriad—and overlapping and often unnecessary—functions I had to understand thoroughly before making budget recommendations.

To make matters worse, almost all the actual work on the budget had to be done *before* I took office—in other words, while I was still an outsider looking into a state government completely controlled by the opposition party. It is small wonder that when we had finished the state's first coordinated budget, at 5:15 A.M. on Jan. 30, we felt we had captured Iwo Jima.

The job of efficient administration I knew from the start would not be easy. Connecticut's 108 agencies result in an administrative machine that would startle even Rube Goldberg. There are over 800 agency heads or commissioners theoretically directly responsible to me. If I should have the courage to call a "cabinet meeting," all 800 presumably would have to be present. Many of these agencies have "just growed," like Topsy. Some are frank political creations.

Many a Connecticut citizen interested in good government—Republican as well as Democrat—has tried to straighten out this costly, incredible state machinery. Governor Wilbur Cross attempted it in the Thirties and made a little headway. I decided to try again.

One of my first acts was to ask the legislature for government reorganization via a local "Hoover Committee." It consented, with a proper degree of reluctance and with some helpful prodding not only from Democrats but from Republicans and taxpayer groups concerned with government economy. Recommendations are to be made by that committee early next year. If we are lucky, Connecticut's government will have a new streamlined look by 1951.

Another curious administration handicap was to find that my sixteen chief commissioners were all Republicans, appointed by Republicans, and in some cases very frankly committed against my general program and policies. While many of them are able men, I sometimes feel that this is rather like trying to run General Motors with a board of directors provided by Chrysler.

My biggest—certainly my thorniest—job was to develop and see through a legislative program. In my inaugural message, I laid down a program on which I had been working with a capable staff almost since Election Day.

The Democratic Senate—and the Democratic party—was firmly behind the program. And so were many strong independent groups of citizens. With our Democratic majority in the Senate I knew we could count on legislative approval there. But the Republican-controlled House was another matter.

I should explain how and why the Connecticut House of Representatives has managed to remain Republican since the Civil War, regardless of Democratic tides, floods or landslides.

The reason lies in what is called here—by progressive Republicans as well as Democrats—the "rotten borough system." Under this system, every town, however small, which was incorporated before 1850, can send two representatives to the House. Since in Connecticut almost all the small towns have been overwhelmingly Republican since the Civil War, and since they vastly outnumber the cities, the House always has a guaranteed Republican majority.

Let me give you a few of the results. Although the Republicans have two-thirds of the representatives in the House, these legislators represent only one-third of the people. The Democratic minority in the House, numbering only one-third of the total House membership, on the other hand, represents two-thirds of the people.

Here's another example: Connecticut's five biggest cities have roughly 35 per cent of our population. But instead of electing 35 per cent of our representatives to the Lower House, they elect less than 3 per cent.

The ten representatives of these five largest cities, with a combined population of 656,000, moreover, can be outvoted (and usually are) by the twelve representatives of our six smallest towns, with a total population of 2,523 men, women and children.

The two representatives from Hartford, which has a population of around 170,000, can be outvoted two to one (and usually are) by the two Republican representatives from Union, which has a population of 290, plus the two representatives from Colebrook, with a population of 620.

George Conway, the Republican Majority Leader of the House, received 1,398 votes from Guilford in last fall's election; John Cotter, the Democratic Minority Leader, received 48,905 from Hartford.

Now I am very fond of small towns. In fact, I live in the small town of Essex, with a population of only 3,100. I believe that small towns should be well represented and well spoken for in any legislature. But obviously the representatives of these towns cannot be expected fully to understand the problems of the cities, regardless of their politics. And certainly there is no valid reason why they should be given the veto power over the wishes of the great majority of the people who live in the cities.

This situation does not make for imaginative, responsible leadership. Regardless of what he may say or do during the legislative sessions, no Republican legislative leader in the Connecticut House of Representatives is ever forced to consider even the remote possibility of being beaten at the polls.

When the Republican party loses a Connecticut state election, its leaders know in advance that they can retreat into their fortress in the House of Representatives and fight harassing guerrilla warfare from this impregnable position.

I am glad to say, however, that in spite of our split Assembly we managed to get agreement on some very important legislation—a $95 million public housing program; an act providing that race segregation should be banned once and for all in the Connecticut National Guard; a strong eviction law; broadening of our old age assistance program; a $15 million appropriation to make badly needed changes in our antiquated mental hospitals; and the commission to study the reorganization of our state government.

On the negative side of the ledger, however, are some critically important omissions—the urgent needs of our educational system were virtually ignored; not a single important step was taken to bring our workmen's compensation and unemployment compensation programs in line with those of the more progressive states; and I was left with a state budget which, by the most optimistic estimates, is several million dollars out of balance.

There is time now for sober reflection on the place of our state governments in our over-all democratic process. As I said earlier, I have already developed some strong convictions on this subject, and my first six months as Governor reinforce those beliefs.

This is the way it looks to me. Our world is growing steadily more complex; unemployment and depression, lack of security, poor education or ignorance affect not only individuals but the state, the nation—and the world. As a result, our government, whether we like it or not, is likely to take on increasingly broad functions.

Many liberals, however, will agree that the present necessity of looking to Washington for the solution of our governmental problems can, over a period of time, result in a dangerous over-centralization of governmental power.

Critics of liberal government use this argument as a means of killing off progressive proposals, such as social security and public housing. The fact that they fight such proposals just as hard on the state as on the federal level makes me suspect that their real objection is not to centralized federal power but to liberal legislation wherever it may be proposed.

Obviously we can't accept the suggestions of the conservatives that we solve this dilemma by the simple expedient of ignoring the problems themselves. If we are to assume that public problems must be met by one means or another, there is a strong case for meeting as many as possible through our states.

Clearly, that gives state governments a very important opportunity. But I believe that the states may be unable to meet their problems adequately unless they receive a careful overhauling at the hands of an earnest and vigilant citizenry, and unless their democratic machinery is geared to represent accurately the will and intent of the citizenry.

There are many encouraging signs that our states will successfully meet this exacting and critical test. Among the most impressive signs are the tens of thousands of young, able, serious-minded men and women who are now taking a new interest in the affairs of their government, and who are obviously agreed that shoddy, inefficient governmental standards, once satisfactory to past generations, are woefully inadequate today.

In any event, we have a big job cut out for us in the Nutmeg State. It is a fascinating and immensely rewarding job. It is also a job that requires patience, and the understanding that clean, competent, liberal government cannot be achieved overnight in Connecticut or anywhere else.

THE NEED FOR STRENGTH
Sherrill D. Luke

Sherrill D. Luke has served as Secretary for Urban Affairs in the office of the governor of California.

California's growth is the fastest in the nation at a rate of 1,600 persons a day, 600,000 per year. By July 1, 1980, a population of 27 and a half million is expected.

Some of the challenges of this mercurial growth are that California will have to build classrooms for 200,000 new youngsters every year; provide jobs for 200,000 new workers every year; construct freeways, highways, and streets to handle 250,000 new cars every year; and build 300,000 new homes every year.

From *National Civic Review,* March 1964. Reprinted by permission.

Needless to say, meeting these and other challenges will require bold and imaginative leadership from the governor. He will have to use all of his powers as chief executive to meet the needs of a burgeoning population. He will have to find new solutions to complex problems always weighing desirable goals against what is possible.

What are the requisites of a strong governor faced with challenges of this magnitude?

First: *constitutional authority*. It goes without saying that, in spite of the leadership abilities of the individual, a strong governor must have constitutional powers commensurate with his grave responsibilities.

In California, the constitution—adopted in 1849 and revised in 1879—vests "supreme executive power" in the governor. He is required to see that all legislative enactments and constitutional provisions are faithfully executed.

Although there are other constitutional officers independently elected and deriving their powers from the same source—the governor may require them to report to him from time to time on matters within their respective jurisdiction. Of course, there is the possibility for conflict, especially where one or two of the incumbents are of a different party. But as a practical matter this has been minimized and there has been little public clamor to make any of the other elective offices appointive except in the case of the superintendent of public instruction where the suggestion came up recently.

In the legislative field, the governor has the all-important veto power, including the item veto with respect to appropriation bills. He also has the sole power to call the legislature into special session and to limit the subjects of the call to those specified in his proclamation convening the session.

Second: *adequate personal staff*. To assist him in managing the affairs of state, a governor needs a personal staff of secretaries who are loyal to him, dedicated to the public service and experienced in the area of their staff specialties.

Governor Brown has ten such staff assistants. They include his executive secretary, legislative secretary, press secretary, cabinet secretary, extradition and clemency secretary, urban affairs secretary, research secretary, appointments secretary, travel secretary and private secretary.

They are "exempt" or non-civil service appointees who serve at the pleasure of the governor. Their salaries are paid out of the budget approved by the legislature for operation of the governor's office. Collectively, they relieve the governor of a myriad of administrative detail, freeing him to concentrate on matters of policy, ceremonial functions and executive leadership.

Third: *competent department directors*. A governor should also surround himself with a group of departmental directors carefully selected on the basis of their loyalty, administrative skills and determination to carry out his and the legislature's policies and programs.

In California, the governor has the power to make approximately 40 such "pleasure" appointments. In addition, he appoints the members of some 300 boards and commissions which determine the policies under which various state agencies should be run.

But the bulk of the state's work force consists of more than 100,000 civil service employees. The governor's patronage appointments are limited to roughly two-tenths of one per cent of the total number employed.

Some have argued that the patronage positions should extend farther down the administrative hierarchy than the top level jobs. But California has actually moved in the other direction by creating a new class of "career executives" at the last session of the legislature.

Fourth: *modernized administrative organization.* For maximum efficiency and economy, a governor must see to it that archaic forms of state organization are continuously streamlined.

Prior to 1961, California's more than 40 departments and 300 boards and commissions were autonomous entities whose heads reported directly to the governor. There had not been a major reorganization of state government since 1929, in spite of the fact that the state's population had almost tripled, its budget had grown from $125 million to $2.5 billion, and its employees had increased from 17,500 to over 100,000.

Under Governor Brown's reorganization plan, the state's major departments and boards and commissions were grouped into eight agencies. Four of them were created by legislative enactment and the other four by executive order. Administrators were appointed to coordinate the activities of departments within each agency. Together these agency heads comprise the governor's cabinet.

This plan brought the governor's span of control within reasonable limits and also improved the lines of communication from the governor's office down the chain of command. In the first year of operation, it produced savings of $174,000 from abolished positions and other operating economies.

Greater efficiency was achieved this year by creating a new General Services Department. This was accomplished by separating the "housekeeping" functions of the Department of Finance from its fiscal, planning and program responsibilities.

Fifth: *fiscal responsibility.* The key to a successful governor's administration is, of course, his ability to see that the state's income matches its expenditures, that its financial solvency is maintained, that a healthy business climate prevails.

To do these things, a governor must have control over the budget process. In California, that control is assured because under the state constitution the responsibility for preparing and administering the budget rests with the Department of Finance under the direction of a director appointed by the governor. After review and modification, the governor submits the budget as his own document to the legislature for adoption, which requires a two-thirds vote of both houses.

The importance of such control is illustrated by the fact that when Governor Brown first took office in 1959 he inherited an accumulated deficit of $68 million and was faced with the prospect of a $268 million deficit by the end of the first fiscal year. Through a broad tax adjustment program and efficient fiscal management, he eliminated that deficit in the first year and provided balanced budgets in every succeeding year.

As a result of tax reforms adopted this year, it is estimated that California can maintain its present level of services without new taxes through June 30, 1965.

Sixth: *legislative majority*. Nothing is more important to the success of a governor's legislative program than to have a working majority of his own party in both houses of the legislature.

In California's bicameral legislature, 52 of the 80 members of the lower house or Assembly are Democrats—two short of the two-thirds majority needed to pass the budget. On the other side, 27 of the 40 members of the upper house or Senate are Democrats—the exact number required for a two-thirds majority.

Assuming they are all healthy and all on the floor at all times and all in complete sympathy with all of the governor's program, he would have no trouble getting his program through. Needless to say, this is wishful thinking.

Not only do our Democratic legislators exercise a large measure of independence, but when the Republicans vote in a bloc—as they did on the budget last session—bills requiring a two-thirds vote are in serious jeopardy unless and until the deadlock is broken.

Seventh: *party control*. This, too, is a highly desirable ingredient in the formula for a strong governor.

It is a luxury which former California governors have seldom enjoyed because of the institution of cross-filing which was finally abolished in 1959. Since that time, the structure of both major parties has been greatly revitalized. And party responsibility has become something more than a cliche to which some pay lip service.

The dominant force in Democratic party politics is the California State Central Committee. It supplies the leadership, the platform and most of the campaign contributions. But its influence is being challenged by the California Democratic Council—a coalition of clubs having 70,000 volunteer members—which has become increasingly active in issue determination, fund raising and precinct work.

Since appointments to the State Central Committee are made by state legislators, the governor's control over that party organization depends on the election and perpetuation in office of assemblymen and senators who are friendly to him and his program.

Eighth: *good press relations*. A governor's lifeline is tied to this requisite, for it determines his ability to be heard, his chances for achieving a public consensus in support of his plans and programs.

The techniques used in California are no different from those employed by governors of other states. They include weekly press conferences, television coverage, press releases, radio tapings, speeches, personal appearances, television panels, newsletters, letters to editors and photographs with people promoting good causes.

Ninth: *planning program*. A strong governor is acutely aware of the need for an effective program to guide the future growth and development of his state.

In California, the principal vehicle is the State Planning Office which was established in 1959 in the Department of Finance. In June of 1962, that office received a "701" grant of $376,000 from the federal government to expedite the preparation of a state development plan. This plan will provide the governor and the legislature with a set of reliable alternatives for meeting the growth needs of the state.

It will assist the state's decision-makers in planning the highways needed to accommodate thousands of new cars; the rapid transit systems needed to alleviate traffic congestion and smog conditions in metropolitan areas; the recreational facilities needed to satisfy our leisure-time interests; the dams, reservoirs, aqueducts and pumping stations needed to supply water for domestic, industrial and agricultural use; the educational institutions needed to prepare our youth for careers in business and industry; and the homes needed to house our teeming masses.

Tenth: *economic development program*. This is closely related to physical development and hence should be considered an essential part of any governor's planning program.

The core of California's development plan is a series of population and economic studies designed to indicate the direction that our growth and development will take over the next fifteen to twenty years. From this data we are developing a "growth model" or economic forecasting device which will enable us to predict the level and composition of the state's economy in terms of jobs and income, and to test in advance the effect of possible changes in such critical factors as defense spending.

Electronic data processing techniques are being used to "feed in" proposed economic changes for evaluation and preparation of new estimates within moments. They will also be used for continuously "updating" data at periodic intervals. In other words, we will have an "early warning" system for compensatory state action in the economic field.

These vital statistics will be useful not only for public investment purposes; they will also be made available to private investors. They will have a marked effect on the joint efforts of our Economic Development Agency and State Chamber of Commerce to attract new industry to California.

Eleventh: *social consciousness*. In economic and other areas, a strong governor must demonstrate an awareness of the social implications of state action, especially as it affects the needs of persons disadvantaged by race, income or educational deficiencies.

In California this includes approximately one million Negro citizens and one and a half million Mexican-Americans. They make up a disproportionate share of the semi-skilled and the unskilled, and the unemployment rate among them is twice or three times as high as that of the general population.

Under the leadership of Governor Brown, California is taking affirmative action to get at the root of the problem of minority unemployment which is the beginning of a vicious cycle of frustration and despair.

Among other things, the state is trying to increase training opportunities for the unemployed or marginal worker; it is working with private industry in an effort to involve more of their number in apprenticeship and on-the-job training programs; it is studying the re-training problems of those displaced by automation and technological change; it has established a pilot project to encourage culturally deprived children to stay in school, to develop job skills and careers, to become self-supporting and self-respecting.

Solving the unemployment problem will go a long way toward solving the problems of ghetto housing, de facto segregated schools, discrimination in public accommodations and other legitimate concerns of minority groups determined to take their rightful place in the mainstream of life in California and every other state.

States' rights carry with them the responsibility of looking out for the general welfare of all the people. This includes securing and protecting the human rights guaranteed by the federal constitution and reinforced by federal statutes.

As the chief executive, a governor has an imposing obligation to use all of the resources at his disposal to achieve the American ideal. If he lives up to his responsibility, he need not be fearful that federal programs will infringe on his state's perogatives or diminish the prestige of his high office.

California governors have lived by this rule. As a result, many have gained national prominence while the state stands out as a living symbol of the strength of American democracy.

Until recent years, the question "What is the public image of our state legislature?" might have merited the not entirely flippant response, "What image? There isn't enough public knowledge or awareness for existence of an image." Today, however, thanks to the recent attention devoted to these legislative chambers by the United States Supreme Court, there is likely to be a broader range of response. At one extreme, there may be a less-than-reasoned defense of the state legislature as the "last outpost" of states' rights and state sovereignty against "federal encroachment." At the other extreme there may be an equally emotional outburst against the same state legislatures for their "complete disregard of the public interest" in voting the newest tax increase or the most recent public spending program.

Criticism has been directed also to the legislators and their staff members alike. State senators and representatives have been publicly labeled "mediocrities," and described as "pressure-dominated," or as "rubber stamps for the governor." Professional staff employees have been charged with representing the "last vestiges of the spoils system." In one instance an upstate New York reporter described a group of regularly-paid committee researchers as having been so infrequently on the job as to be "unable to find their way to the committee room without a seeing-eye dog."

What may we appropriately expect of our state legislatures and legislators? A few questions may suggest standards for judging. First, is the legislature representative of the people—not just in the "push-button" sense of responding completely and instantly to pressures from constituents, but in terms of providing leadership as well? Second, do legislative deliberations inform and educate the general public (granted, of course, the necessary degree of cooperation from the press)? Third, does the legislative procedure preserve and protect minority dissent, thus guaranteeing in practice a voice for the opposition? Finally, does the legislative system provide an adequate check upon the executive branch—the governor and his administration—to help keep them responsible to the electorate?

In considering these criteria, it is essential to note the changed and changing functions of the state legislatures in the latter half of the twentieth century. Faced in most states with an institutional incapacity to initiate policy, the legislature has become the "revisionist branch"—accepting or rejecting, revising or amending programs that increasingly originate with the governor and his departments. Even in such long-established domains as fiscal control, the modern state legislature has found it impossibe to provide more than a cursory examination of a budget whose formulation and execution are under executive control.

The greater concern of the average newspaper with doings either in

Washington or at City Hall has left a void at the state level and hampered the legislature's role as public forum.

The legislature's vital task of representing the legitimate interests of constituents in a state bureaucracy grown increasingly (and necessarily) large has been much maligned by those who see in this essential function only an undue representation of the interests of the few.

Inquiry and investigatory powers vary from state to state. In New York, they have been distinctly subordinate to those of the governor; in California they have seemed scarcely less restrained than those of the United States Congress in the McCarthy heyday of the 1950s. Nowhere have they developed into a careful systematic scrutiny of executive conduct that might compensate for the loss of legislative and fiscal initiative to the chief executive.

The legislatures of all our states save one, Nebraska, have adopted a bicameral structure (a fact which explains the chapter title). In this they have followed a colonial precedent which was not so much emulation of the British as it was response to the needs of direct lower house representation against the designs of royal governors and their upper-house senatorial advisers. Since then, the public support of state legislatures has steadily declined, first in the decades of scandalous road, canal and railway building which produced strict constitutional limits upon legislative powers; more recently due to unequal representation and the seeming impotence of legislatures in the face of demands for state action. The result has been an increasing concentration of authority in gubernatorial hands.

In the early 1960s the hallowed electoral arrangements, by which the ever-smaller rural minorities preserved their power over increasing urban and suburban majorities, finally gave way in a series of decisions of the United States Supreme Court. In *Baker v. Carr,* the Court finally entered what one justice called the "political thicket" of reapportionment, invoking the Fourteenth Amendment's "equal protection of the laws" clause to require state redistricting. The next year, it went still further in the Georgia county unit case, *Sanders v. Gray* to establish the principle of "one man, one vote." And finally, in a series of cases headed by *Reynolds v. Sims,* the Court required the legislatures of Alabama, New York and four other states to abandon not only the dual geographical representation which had emerged in practice but also the "little federal" principle of one geographically-based, one popularly-based house, theoretically required by most of their constitutions. Said the Court in unmistakable terms, "Both Houses of the state legislature must be based upon the principle of one man, one vote." There is no "little federal" analogy, since state government has never been based upon a concept of county, town, city, or village sovereignty. Thus, with judicial intervention, the problem of state "Houses of Mis-representation" seemed well on the way to solution—barring any successful effort on the part of conservative forces to ram through a constitutional amendment which would validate earlier practice.

The legislatures of the fifty states have been markedly similar in organization, with personal leadership the key to the major differences among them. In virtually every state legislature the speaker of the lower house and the majority leader of the upper house have been at the heart of legislative power. In nearly every instance, the theoretical second-in-command, the lieutenant governor, has been relegated to a position of obscurity. The new Alaskan Constitution has eliminated the post completely.

Legislative committees, though still significant on the state scene, have tended to be much less powerful than their Congressional counterparts. Partisan politics, on the other hand, has been much less gentlemanly and refined than on the national level, in part because of the absence in most state houses of the regular two-party rotation in the Nation's Capitol. In those states where the minority has the role of a perpetual and frequently futile "loyal opposition," the majority parties have all too often assumed an overriding arrogance. Party discipline, too, has been much stronger in many of the state legislatures than in Congress, particularly where a powerful governor has worked closely with the county leaders responsible for the nomination and reelection of his state legislative henchmen.

Many states lack the balance of economic forces that so frequently provides federal legislators with both sides of the picture. Consequently, lobbying in the state capital has often been more effective, and occasionally less scrupulous than in Washington. Finally, press attention to the state legislature has been sporadic at best. All too often, not a single paper supports the minority party; not a single reporter essays the critical role of a Drew Pearson or a David Lawrence.

Most of the suggestions advanced to alleviate the problems and shortcomings of state legislatures have tended to be mechanistic—the split session aimed at eliminating the closing session rush (but unsuccessful); electric voting machines to speed up the voting process (even though simple procedural devices are available, such as the New York state assembly's "short roll call" which satisfies in 15 or 20 seconds the mandate for a roll call of 150 members on every measure*); and Proportional Representation (a carefully contrived system which produced in practice not only a mathematically-precise representation of voter strength, but also an unanticipated and disproportionate legislative power for fringe groups). Even more importantly "PR" has led, where adopted, to a significant diminution of party responsibility and a weakening of the two-party system. The ultimate improvement of our state legislatures lies with an electorate which, for the first time in nearly a century, is about to attain representation in accordance with its numbers. Out of the court-mandated reapportionment there may emerge that two-party competition best calculated to produce a reinvigorated legislative system—one able to meet more adequately the demands on our state government in action.

* In the "short roll call", only the first and last names on the roll are called, plus those of the majority and minority leaders. A member who disagrees with his party leader raises his hand to record his contrary vote.

HAMSTRUNG LEGISLATURES
James Nathan Miller

James Nathan Miller has an extensive background in the field of
public relations. He is a contributor to *Harper's, Reader's Digest,*
and other national magazines.

Though visitors to the Massachusetts State House on the Boston Common
invariably come away impressed by the beauty of this fine piece of Bul-
finch architecture, the more observant among them also make note of a
strange and significant architectural omission: In the building's 170 years
of existence—from the cornerstone-laying by Governor Samuel Adams,
assisted by Paul Revere, through the five subsequent additions that make
the building today over ten times its original size—nobody thought to provide offices for the 280 legislators who are its major tenants.

With the exception of a few rooms for legislative leaders, the lawmakers'
only "offices" are their mahogany desks in the Senate and Assembly chambers, which during legislative sessions rapidly disappear under piles of
documents.

As a result, working conditions for the law-makers—who are supposed
to act as efficient overseers of a $750 million annual budget and the opera-
tions of 50,000 state employees—are squalid in the extreme. The secretarial
pool for the 240-man Assembly consists of five stenographers. Their message center is a honeycomb of little alphabetical pigeonholes reminiscent
of a fraternity house mailbox. Their private discussions are held on green-
leather couches in the public corridors. "My real office is a telephone
booth," says Thomas McGee, representative from Lynn—and sometimes he
has to wait in line fifteen minutes to reach this office during a recess.

Conditions such as these, duplicated in state capitols from coast to coast,
are merely visible symptoms of a deep and dangerous paralysis that is
sapping the strength of state legislatures—and in the process weakening
the very basis of state government in the United States today. For though
one hears much about the federal government's push to take over state
functions, there is also a tremendous pull: the mechanical inability of state
legislatures to keep up with the racing demands of the twentieth century.

Recently, I toured the country from Massachusetts to Oregon to watch
legislatures in action. I visited a cross-section sample of a dozen of them,
running from the best to the worst, from the most honest and efficient to
the most corrupt and incompetent. I read a foot-high stack of reports on
suggested reform, talked to scores of legislators, students of government,

From *National Civic Review,* April, 1965. Condensed in *Reader's Digest,* May 1965 legislative clerks and secretaries, lobbyists, and members of taxpayer groups.

In Washington, Charles S. Rhyne, a close observer of state government, summed up the size of the problem. Rhyne, a past president of the American Bar Association, has long been involved in efforts to modernize state laws. It was he who argued the historic *Baker* v. *Carr* case before the Supreme Court, bringing the "one man, one vote" decision that is revolutionizing the makeup of legislatures. I asked him whether this revolution would make them more effective. *"Baker* v. *Carr,"* he said, "affects only the way we select our law-makers. Internally, the legislatures remain as archaic as before. They continue to try to solve jet-age problems with horse-and-buggy methods and, in their failure to do it, they're digging their own graves and inviting federal intervention."

These horse-and-buggy methods are clearly identifiable and can be remedied. Ironically, the remedy involves divorcing ourselves from the theories of one of our greatest political philosophers, Thomas Jefferson. For it is Jefferson's dream of a simple agrarian society that today haunts operations of state legislatures. Jesse Unruh, speaker of the California Assembly and a leading legislative reformer, describes it thus: "Jefferson's model American would till the fields by day, improve his mind by study and learned discourse in the evening, and, for a few weeks during the winter when it was too cold to plow, he would travel to the seat of government, there to meet with his peers from other parts and enact just laws."

After 150 years, it is incredible how closely legislatures are still modeled after this image. For one thing, it is the reason they nearly all convene right after New Year's Day, in the dead of winter. But far deeper, it is the reason for their worst internal mechanical inefficiencies. To appreciate how serious these inefficiencies are, first observe the massiveness of the demands that modern society puts on state law-makers.

In size alone these responsibilities have been transformed in just the last generation. In voting on California's projected $4-billion 1965-1966 budget, its 120 legislators are responsible for more money than was spent by all 48 states in 1938. New York's current budget is larger than Australia's. Even tiny Maryland, which spent $67 million in 1946, has budgeted some $800 million for the coming year. Indeed, this year, for the first time in our history, states may spend more for goods and services (an estimated $70 billion) than the federal government.

One sees the signs of this growth all over the country. Twenty years ago, Louisiana had about 25 state agencies; now it has 240. In 1954, Illinois built a ten-story office building in Springfield to provide office space for its employees; since then, they have spilled out and are now once again housed in temporary quarters all over town. Says Thomas Graham, speaker of the Missouri House, "When I came to the legislature in 1951, the state university had one campus; now it has four."

But the problems are not only far bigger; they are also incredibly more complex. William Nelson, director of research for the Missouri legislature, explains: "When I was elected a representative in 1943, the legislature had no interest in the mentally retarded, in civil rights, in the growth problems of the cities, in air or river pollution. Pesticides were relatively harmless and atomic energy wasn't even heard of; our only concern about radiation control was with X-ray machines in dentists' offices."

Industrial safety laws used to involve simple problems like provision of fire escapes and installation of safety guards on machines. Now (as was the case recently in Bodega Bay, California) legislators must weigh the problem of whether a whole community may be endangered by an atomic plant. Conservation problems used to be as simple as cops and robbers: how to curb predatory interests that were destroying the wilderness. Now, increasingly, we the people have become the predatory interests as we blanket the land with houses and lace it with highways—while at the same time demanding more green space in which to enjoy increasing leisure time.

Hugh Sandlin, a representative in the Oklahoma legislature, sums it up: "I'm supposed to be an expert on everything."

Yet the basic fact is that most of our legislators are not experts. For, while we have become a complicated and urban society, legislatures remain geared to face the problems of Jefferson's simple agrarian day. There are three key areas in which their failure to make adjustment is causing basic damage to state government.

1. *Not enough pay.* The very basis of Jefferson's citizen-legislator concept was that a law-maker should not earn his living making laws. Edward Staples, executive director of the Missouri Public Expenditure Survey, is an exponent of the modern version of this view: "You don't want to develop a staff of professional governmentalists; you want the broad viewpoint of the farmers, the lawyers, the teachers, the doctors, the businessmen. A good farmer gives the flavor of the general citizenry to the legislature. Raise the pay too high and someone who values the job for the salary alone will run against him. It would be a sorry day."

Agrees Carl Dodge, a senator in the Nevada legislature: "We don't want to attract a lot of bums."

The voters, too, seem to concur. For years, in state after state, blueribbon commissions have been recommending more pay; when it has been put to the voters, however, in more cases than not, raises have been refused. The result is simple: By conservative estimate, at least 75 per cent of our population that would otherwise be qualified to serve cannot possibly afford to.

How many people, for instance, do you know who could afford to devote most of their weekends and evenings to campaigning and sitting at the phone "servicing the electorate," quit their jobs for an average of two to four months a year, support themselves during these months in a hotel in the capital city, spending anywhere from $1,000 to $15,000 every couple of years for campaign expenses—and do all this on a salary and expense allowance of $4,000 or $5,000 a year? This is what state legislators, whose annual pay ranges from a high of $10,000 in New York to a low of $100 in New Hampshire, must do.

The result? Take Connecticut, for instance. Says Rhyne, "Perhaps the most shocking and unbelievable discovery for me was the fact that, to augment their salaries, some Connecticut legislators have collected unemployment compensation insurance during the regular session of the Assembly."

In every state I visited, I asked the following question of a wide range of legislative observers: Have you lost any good men recently because of the low salary scale? Invariably the answer was the same—a ticking off of a half-dozen names that had dropped out in the last few sessions.

Jerome Waldie, majority leader of the California Assembly, cited a typical case: "Bill Biddick from San Joaquin County was as able a legislator as California ever had. He served two terms in the Assembly and rose to chairman of the Judiciary Committee. But, after the 1959-1960 session, the money problem caught up with him. He was in his late 30s, had five kids, didn't have the kind of law practice that would permit long absences in Sacramento and he just couldn't keep it up on a salary of $6,000. So he left and now he's a judge in a county court earning $24,000—when we need him badly here to do the really important work of California. It's a tragic loss to the people of the state."

Who can afford to run? Study the makeup of any legislature and you'll find it to be mainly three groups: retired people, men with independent incomes and professional people. The last group is the largest—lawyers, insurance men, real estate agents, well-to-do farmers, all of them with partners or families back home to keep the business running while they are gone. Many of them are fine people (in fact, the level of integrity and industriousness in our state capitols is far higher than the public appreciates), but they represent a very thin slice of America. Says John Driscoll, director of legislative relations for the Massachusetts Federation of Taxpayers Associations, Inc., "What the legislature doesn't get is the 35-to 40-year-old family man; we're short on the backbone of the community."

Agrees William Swackhamer, a well-to-do businessman who is speaker of the Nevada House: "There are many fine people operating one-man ranches and one-man law firms in the cow counties who'd like to run but can't afford to." In Oklahoma, Representative Sandlin says his tax man figures that his income drops by $3,000 to $5,000 every year the legislature is in session. He adds, "If I didn't have a law partner, I couldn't afford to serve."

The solution is obvious. Pay must be raised to the point where it will not cost a man money to serve in the legislature. The amount might vary from state to state—since the amount of legislative activity required would tend to be bigger in the big industrial states—but common-sense reasons for it are the same in all states: First, we want good men. Second, good men can earn good money in their own businesses. Third, though they should not get rich making laws, neither should they have to pay for the privilege.

What about the danger of creating "professional legislators?" Says Robert Crown, chairman of California's Assembly Ways and Means Committee, "Look. This is the twentieth century. The California legislature is the board of directors for a $4-billion corporation. The average assemblyman services an electorate of 200,000 people. Serving and getting elected is a full-time job. We need professionals. In fact, I like to think I am a professional. Yet I'm paid less than my secretary." He might have added that he is also paid less than a member of California's Board of Barber Examiners—which is a part-time job, at that.

2. *Not enough time.* In simple agrarian days, the idea of requiring the part-time legislator to get on his horse and travel to the state capitol every year seemed absurd. Problems didn't change that fast. Every other year was plenty.

Moreover, in order to guarantee that the legislatures would get work done expeditiously, various constitutional or statutory requirements placed strict limits on the time they could stay in session. In Louisiana, for instance, the constitution forbids sessions longer than 60 calendar days; in Alabama, no longer than 36 legislative days. The Texas legislature can meet for as long as it wants but it collects no pay after 75 days; in Nevada, pay ceases after 60 days.

Today, in most states, regular legislative sessions, still held every other year, consist of three to six months of short Monday-through-Thursday workweeks that give lawmakers long weekends for handling their personal affairs back home. Though a stopgap patchwork of offyear "special" and "fiscal" sessions has developed in an attempt to handle growing business volume, the overwhelming bulk of the work—from 500 bills to upwards of 17,000 —is still concentrated at the alternate-year regular sessions. This attempt to meet twentieth-century needs on a nineteenth-century timetable results in pure chaos.

In many states, legislators vote literally thousands of times during the brief session. In California, Waldie estimates he averages 30 to 40 floor votes daily, plus many more in committee.

The result? A Louisiana lawmaker cites a typical instance: "Not long ago an ex-legislator complained to me that he'd been arrested for speeding and had his license taken away because he couldn't post a bond. He was mad as hell. Said anyone who'd voted for a law like that must have been nuts. When I told him he voted for it, he swore I must be nuts. So we looked it up and, sure enough, he had."

In West Virginia, a lobbyist cited his rule of thumb for gauging the quality of a legislature: "If they understand 20 per cent of the bills they vote on, they're a damn fine bunch."

To see what all this adds up to in legislative conduct, listen to Rhyne's account of the 1963 spasm of the Connecticut legislature. It met for five months. At the end of the first two months, only five bills had been passed. Then they began to come through in increasing numbers—4,000 of them in all, droning through so fast and furiously during the final few days that many members had no idea what they were voting on, and the legislature actually adjourned while forgetting to pass an essential $6.4 million education bill. A special session had to be called to remedy the oversight. Said the *New Haven Register* of this comic-opera performance, the legislature "seemed to make more errors than the New York Mets do on one of their worst days."

The solution, again, is simple: Legislatures should meet every year and stay in session for as long as is necessary to get the work done. This requirement goes hand-in-hand with the need for higher salaries.

3. *Not enough help.* At each Oregon legislator's desk are two chairs, one a swivel chair for the lawmaker, the other a straight-backed model for his secretary. As in Massachusetts, Oregon law-makers have no offices, no privacy. "It can be extremely embarrassing," says Daniel Thiel, president *pro tempore* of the Oregon Senate, "to have to discuss private matters with a constituent—a drunken driving conviction, say, or a veteran's loan—and to know that a couple of other legislators at their desks a few feet away can hear every word. Sometimes I have to scribble a note telling the man to talk softer."

The same shortage applies to space for official deliberations. With 37 legislative committees, the Oregon legislature has only eighteen committee rooms and often a hearing must be cut short to make way for another committee. "It's like a bunch of people sharing the same bed in shifts," says a Senate official.

But it goes much deeper than mere shortage of space. In fact, probably the sickest aspect of our sick legislatures is their failure to provide themselves with adequate staffs and facilities to keep themselves informed. For, though laws can be no better than the information on which they are based ("We're really a great big jury," says Thiel), most legislatures are miserably equipped to gather information. Though most of them have permanent staffs of so-called "legislative councils" that are supposed to dig up facts, in all but a few states these are woefully understaffed and provide little help beyond the actual technical drafting of bills.

In Massachusetts, for instance, which has one of the country's largest insurance businesses, the House Committee on Insurance has neither secretary nor researcher. No transcripts are kept of committee meetings. How does the committee function? Says John F. Donovan, Jr., representative from Chelsea, "For each legislative session, we elect one of our members as clerk but we all take notes."

(In fact, probably 90 per cent of the debate and discussion in legislatures is never recorded, and one result is that courts have no so-called "legislative history" of state laws. Says Nelson in Missouri, "I get calls about once a month from attorneys asking for transcripts of committee hearings that would show legislative intent, but I have none.")

So woefully understaffed is the Massachusetts legislature that the Republican and Democratic clubs of Harvard Law School operate a kind of charity program of volunteer research assistance for the law-makers. Similarly, in Oregon, the state bar association provides 21 volunteer lawyers in two-week stints to help out with bill-drafting.

Says Bryce Baggett, an Oklahoma senator, "I'd rather have a research assistant than a raise."

This lack of research leads directly to the two worst weaknesses of our state legislatures. First is their domination by the governor and the huge machinery of his executive departments. In Oklahoma, a legislator put it this way: "The governor of this state has people working for him who are experts in anything you can name and we legislators are the people who are supposed to be checking on them for the taxpayer. But much of the time we don't even know what questions to ask them." Agrees Waldie in California, "Bureaucrats don't like to admit their mistakes and they can run rings around an uninformed legislature."

"It's a perfect example," says Unruh, "of the old truism that knowledge is power."

Where can the legislature go? "We are forced to depend primarily upon the lobbyists for necessary information," says Thomas Graham, speaker of the Missouri House. This leads into their second weakness: domination by lobbies and pressure groups.

Winton Hunt, chief clerk of the Oregon House and a former legislator, cites a typical example: "When I was in the legislature, a highway was being built through my district, and I started getting complaints from farmers that they weren't being adequately paid for damage to their land. To get a law correcting the situation, I first needed a lot more evidence but I had no way of getting it myself. So I asked the Farm Bureau, a lobby group, to go out and interview farmers along the route. It came up with a fine report and the law got passed, but I never did feel comfortable about having to depend on a farmers' lobby for the facts in this kind of bill."

In the last session of the Oregon legislature, one lobbyist contributed several days to interviewing highway department officials in order to help the Senate Highway Committee evaluate the merits of concrete versus asphalt. Some years ago, in an investigation of the alleged misuse of road money in Oklahoma, the Senate investigating committee's entire staff consisted of a researcher loaned to it by the Oklahoma Public Expenditures Council, a lobby group.

Such help is perfectly legitimate. Indeed, most lobbyists work publicly and straightforwardly, the way a lawyer presents his case. "Of course, a lobbyist gives you a prejudiced point of view," says F. F. Montgomery, speaker of the Oregon House. "You wouldn't respect him if he didn't."

For a legislature equipped to evaluate these prejudices, the lobbyist's role is honorable and constructive. But few legislatures are so equipped. As a result, in a majority of states the lobbyist—well paid, well staffed, well informed and working at his job full time—has become the tail that wags the dog of the under-paid, overworked, under-informed, parttime legislator. The lobbyists' collective title—"the third house"—is no fiction.

In the *New York Times* last year, reporter Charles Grutzner cited an incident that gave a revealing insight into third-house power: At two o'clock one morning, after an evening of nightclubbing, a lobbyist told a companion that he wanted to show him proof of popular opposition to a bill that was then being opposed by a lobby group. Thereupon the lobbyist drove with his companion to the deserted capitol building, produced a key that admitted them to an important senator's office and handed his companion a report. He then went on to boast that he had written the report, had the keys to nine other law-makers' offices and had earned the right to such access by providing facts and research assistance to these law-makers.

Senate Majority Leader Walter Mahoney's outrage over the incident was equally revealing. "I condemn the slime of the lobbyist," he thundered, "who in his boastful way would tell what he did to the reporter."

Report-writing is just the first step in the exercise of third-house power. Recently, a person very close to the workings of a state legislature described an example of the next step: law-writing. In the last legislative session, when a bill was put into the hopper that would have transferred the weighing of trucks from the Highway Department to the Department of Public Safety, a labor lobbyist recognized that it would cost the jobs of a number of union weighers. Investigating, he found that the bill was the creature of the truck lobby, which felt the fines on overloaded trucks would be lower under Public Safety than under Highways. The bill would also mean, however, that local townships would lose their share of the fines. So the labor lobbyist contacted the one for townships, and with the truck lobbyist they worked out a compromise that kept the weighers under the Highway Department but reduced fines. The compromise bill was passed.

In West Virginia, a lobbyist, after giving me his version of how the legislature really worked, added: "If you're going to use any of this stuff, don't quote me. These bozos [the legislators] like to think they make the law."

This subservience to outside forces can be licked. California's legislature —a dozen years ago infamous for its domination by lobbies—shows how. During the 1950s, following a national magazine exposé of lobby influence, the legislature intensified its fight for independence, using as a major weapon the development of its own fact-gathering facilities.

Today, it is superbly staffed and informed. Every legislator has his own office and secretary, plus an office and administrative assistant in his home district. A six-man reference service headed by a former political science instructor digs into questions submitted by individual assemblymen. A legislative counsel bureau of some twenty attorneys drafts all bills. All important committees are staffed with full-time researchers, who spend months gathering background on important bills. For special studies the legislature raids universities for experts, sometimes hires outside consulting firms.

The result is that rarest and most essential of legislative qualities: intellectual independence. For a recent legislative study on the care of mentally retarded children, for instance, committee researcher Arthur Bolton spent a year investigating Californian hospitals, interviewing hundreds of professionals in the field, as well as parents of children. Says Waldie, who headed the committee: "Bolton was able to do what no legislator would have had the time to do: become a true expert and ask truly penetrating questions. Just one part of his investigation—preparation of a 40-page questionnaire that was submitted to the hospital directors—would have been far too much to expect of any of the committee members. On the basis of Bolton's investigation, the committee is recommending a total change of direction in the program, something we could never have had the confidence to do without this kind of research behind us."

The result is that, though lobbyists have by no means died on the California vine (there are over 500 of them, outnumbering legislators four to one), their power has distinctly shrunk. Bert Clinkston, political editor of the *Sacramento Union,* calls the legislature's research facilities "the fourth house"; one lobbyist commented to me, only half jokingly, that the fourth house was some day going to cost him his job.

The vicious circle. The failure of legislatures to reform themselves works 'round and 'round in a self-perpetuating cycle. It goes like this.

First, underpaid legislators begin to find it easy to accept entertainment and minor favors—office space, secretarial help, etc.—from lobbyists. No specific favors are asked in return and it seems innocent enough. Even more elaborate favors—use of an oil company's private plane by a legislative official in California, a Caribbean cruise for New York legislators paid for by a savings bank association—can be explained away as deserved perquisites for overworked and underpaid officials.

Last winter I got to feel how nice these perquisites can be when I was guest at a party given by Harrah's Lake Tahoe gambling casino to welcome the Nevada legislature into session. I was treated—along with about 250 legislators, their wives, secretaries and secretaries' boyfriends—to an all-expenses-paid evening on the house, complete with dinner, champagne and entertainment by Robert Goulet. Nobody seemed to question the extending of such hospitality by a regulated industry to its regulators. Indeed, another such affair was scheduled for the following evening at The Nugget in Carson City. Said a member of the legislature's staff: "I'm just a flunky around here and I can't possibly do any favors for these gamblers. But if I ever go into a casino and they know where I work, I have to fight with the headwaiter to pay the bill."

Second, such relatively minor favors blend imperceptibly into the vast, grey area known as conflict of interest. Though every year brings to light a few cases of outright bribery, by far the most pervasive method of "getting to" a law-maker is far subtler and less easily combated. Bryce Baggett in Oklahoma, himself scrupulously honest, describes what happens: "You start getting indirect approaches—offers to retain you as a lawyer, hints that the members of a trade association would like to place their insurance through your firm. Nothing criminal, nothing you can really put your finger on. It's there but I'd hate to be the district attorney who had to prove any bribery was involved."

For some, it is easy to rationalize such offers as being totally divorced from legislative activities. In a recent article in *Harper's Magazine,* Illinois State Senator Paul Simon estimated that a third of the Illinois legislators accepted payoffs in the form of legal fees, public relations retainers or campaign contributions.

In Massachusetts, a commonly accepted method of helping a lawmaker make ends meet is to "run a time" for him: throw a party at which local interests—the electronics plant, teachers' association, railroad brotherhoods —kick in for "campaign expenses." Says a Massachusetts legislator, "on $5,200 a year, how else can I possibly support a family decently? Sure it means my vote gets tied down in some areas, but . . ."—and here comes the rationalization—"after all, these are legitimate local-interest groups."

The only cure lies in the honor and integrity of the men we select. Which brings us back to the vicious circle. For, while it is undoubtedly true that in most states the great majority of legislators are honest, a constant cloud of suspicion created by continual conflict-of-interest revelations colors them all in the public mind. Thus the circle is complete: low salaries and poor facilities, causing low standards and poor performance, causing public disgust, causing refusal by the public to raise salaries and improve facilities—and around and around.

"Mediocrity," said the *New Republic* recently of state legislatures, "attracts mediocrity."

Enter, the federal government. Thus state legislatures, slow-moving and bewildered in a world they never made, create a vacuum that pulls hard at the federal government. The *Baker* v. *Carr* reapportionment decision is a case in point. In the words of William J. D. Boyd of the National Municipal League, "The state legislatures brought it on themselves." At the time the case was argued, twenty legislatures were violating their own state constitutions by refusing to reapportion. Tennessee, where the case was brought, had not reapportioned for 61 years. Yet, sixteen years before *Baker* v. *Carr,* the Supreme Court had said it did not want to get involved in the "political thicket" of reapportionment. If legislators had done the job themselves, it would never have had to change its mind.

The real tragedy of this premature senility of state governments is the contrast it provides with the bright promise of their youth. Wrote Supreme Court Justice Louis Brandeis in 1932: "It is one of the happy incidents of the federal system that a single courageous state may . . . serve as a laboratory and try novel social and economic experiments without risk to the rest of the country."

In the last century and the beginning of this one, it was the states that pioneered in such legislative fields as child labor, railroad and utility regulation, unemployment and old age compensation, and factory inspection. Fifteen states, starting with Wyoming in 1869, had voted female suffrage before the federal government got around to it in 1920.

But, today, states have become the citadels of status quo and the federal government, the laboratory of change. (There are a few honorable exceptions—such as California in higher education, New York in state support of the arts, Wisconsin in conservation—but they merely prove the rule.) Why, for instance, is President Johnson now requesting a federal law to clean the junkyards from our highways? For the simple reason that the states, which could have long since abolished them, have allowed them to fester and grow. Why does the Interstate Highway Act contain a bonus provision to reward states that ban billboards from the interstate system? It is presented as a carrot to state legislatures to get them to stand up to the billboard lobbies.

Indeed, why is the federal government moving in across the board—in air and stream pollution, education, housing, mass transportation for cities, etc.? Though there can be honest disagreement about the rights and wrongs of this move, there is no question that a major cause is the failure of the states to do what needs doing.

In the words of Governor George Romney of Michigan, "People have needs and if state and local governments are unwilling or unable to meet those needs, we have only ourselves to blame."

That, in its simplest form, is why we must drag our state legislatures out of the age of Jefferson and into the twentieth century.

BREAKING THE RURAL STRANGLEHOLD
Will Maslow

Will Maslow is general counsel for the American Jewish Congress.

The momentous decision of the U. S. Supreme Court in *Baker v. Carr,* the Tennessee reapportionment case, and the thirty-odd state and federal decisions which it evoked, indicate that we are on the threshold of a development that may vastly improve our legislative bodies. More than fifty suits have been started in thirty-eight different states in the twelve months that have elapsed since the Supreme Court ruled that "invidious discrimination" in the apportionment or districting of a state legislature violated the Fourteenth Amendment. Although none of these suits has yet resulted in the permanent and equitable "remap" of a state legislature, enough has already been accomplished to quicken hope that the rural strangle hold of our state legislatures may soon be broken. There has been more action on reapportionment in this last year than in the prior twenty-five years. However, no equivalent attack has yet been mounted on the gerrymandering of Congressional seats.

The decision in *Baker v. Carr* was handed down on March 26, 1962.

From *The Nation,* April 6, 1963. Reprinted by permission.

Heroic efforts were at once made by disfranchised urban voters to enjoin the 1962 primaries to compel reapportionment of the state legislatures to be chosen in the general elections. But while fifteen state and federal district courts moved with unprecedented speed to find that existing legislative apportionments denied certain voters equal protection of the laws, they were not prepared, in the summer of 1962, to fashion judicial remedies until this year's state legislatures had an opportunity to correct glaring discrepancies in voting power. However, federal courts in Alabama, Florida, Georgia and Tennessee, and the state courts in Maryland, prodded state legislatures into special session, and temporary arrangements were hurriedly devised which increased urban representation in one or both chambers.

Forty-seven of the state legislatures will be in session this year. Even those that have not been warned by the courts are on notice that failure to reapportion equitably may result in judicial remedies for malapportionment.

Perhaps the greatest gains from last year's litigation were achieved in Georgia. The infamous "county unit" plan—whereby candidates for state offices and Congressional districts were required to obtain not a popular majority, but only a majority of the units assigned to counties and districts —was invalidated. On March 18, the Supreme Court not only sustained this decision, but went further: by a vote of 8 to 1, it outlawed any voting system in which votes were weighted. The Court stated that our "conception of equality . . . can mean only one thing—one person, one vote." The opinion, of course, does not affect apportionment of state legislators, but the overtones are unmistakable.

Another law suit in Georgia led to a reapportionment of the state senate hastily enacted by a special legislative session. Metropolitan Atlanta and other urban areas were assigned twenty-three of the fifty-four senate seats. In one senatorial district in Atlanta, with a heavy Negro concentration, two Negroes ran against each other in the general elections and Leroy Johnson, the Democratic candidate, was elected—the first Negro to serve in the Georgia legislature since Reconstruction.

In Tennessee, the legislature was called into special session even before the Supreme Court had remanded Baker v. Carr to the Federal District Court. The legislature enacted measures increasing the representation of the state's four metropolitan counties from about one-half to three-quarters of the number to which they would have been entitled on population standards. The federal court held, however, that the remap was still inadequate, and decided that the legislature to be elected in 1962 on the basis of the improved apportionment should have until June, this year, to revise the apportionment. The Court stated that "at least one house [of the legislature] should be based fully on population."

There have been surprisingly few setbacks in the coast-to-coast effort to overcome districting frozen for a generation. (Twenty-seven states have not reapportioned their state legislatures in twenty-five years; in eight states in more than fifty years.) A three-man federal district court upheld the apportionment in New York State fixed by its 1894 constitution; and appeal to the Supreme Court is now pending. New Hampshire's singular arrangement, whereby senate seats are divided according to direct taxes paid, was ruled constitutional. (The plan, though odd, is probably equivalent to representation based on population.) Suits in South Dakota and Wyoming were dismissed on technical grounds and efforts to challenge the reapportionment of Congressional seats in Florida, Georgia and Texas failed.

The federal and state courts that were suddenly confronted with reapportionment issues had little guidance from the Supreme Court. *Baker v. Carr* laid down no guide lines, substantive or procedural, and deliberately refused to indicate the extent of discrimination that would render an apportionment plan unconstitutional. After its decision in the Tennessee case, the Supreme Court reversed the decision of the Michigan Supreme Court and of a district court in New York, remanding both cases for further consideration in the light of *Baker v. Carr,* but giving no further clarification. Whether the Court can continue to avoid coming to grips with the thorny problems involved remains to be seen. On its fall docket are no less than ten reapportionment cases from Alabama, Georgia, Maryland, Michigan, New York, Oklahoma and Virginia.

Many questions must be decided. Must a state apportion both houses of its legislature on a population basis, or is a "federal plan" (with representation in one house based on geography or political subdivisions) sufficient? May a federal court set aside an inequitable distribution that was approved originally by popular vote? Must a federal court refrain from judicial intervention if a state allows its voters by initiative and referendum to by-pass the state legislature and place an apportionment plan on the ballot? Are federal courts limited to situations, like Tennessee, where apportionment plans violate state constitutions, or may they strike down discriminatory plans required by such constitutions? May an apportionment originally valid become unconstitutional by reason of the passage of time or changed circumstances? Is an apportionment constitutional because it is rational, i.e., based on some plan or principle, such as geography, even though it is obviously inequitable and discriminatory? And, finally, and perhaps most difficult: How discriminatory must a system be to violate the Fourteenth Amendment?

Some courts have been beguiled into sanctioning the so-called federal plan under which one house of a state legislature is apportioned on the basis of geography, not population. Others have explicitly rejected the federal analogy, pointing out that while a sovereign state may be entitled to equality of representation in the U.S. Senate, a political subdivision, like a county, is not. After all, small states gained equality in the original Constitution because, without such representation, there would have been no union. But our notions of voting equality have advanced since the eighteenth century and no such sacrifice of principle is required now.

Apart from the sixteen states which sanction the federal plan, there are twenty-five others in which the population basis of apportionment is qualified, usually by the requirement that each county, no matter how small, is entitled to at least one representative in one or both houses. The inevitable result of such qualifications is rural over-representation.

Some lower courts have struggled to find a numerical formula for voting inequality. A federal district court in Georgia indicated that it would sanction discrepancies in voting power provided the ensuing discrimination did not exceed the disparity that exists against any state in the Electoral College. But Alaska has one vote in the Electoral College for each bloc of 75,000 persons, whereas California has one elector for each 393,000. Thus the Electoral College analogy would sanction districts having a five-to-one advantage over others. On the other hand, a three-man federal court in New York found no constitutional discrimination in the 1894 apportionment under which it was alleged that state senate districts varied in population from 146,000 to 344,000 and assembly districts from 14,000 to 115,000.

Congressional districting presents simpler problems. The apportionment of seats in the House of Representatives among the states is done automatically each decade in accordance with census figures. But each state legislature is then free to draw its own Congressional district lines, dividing the seats allotted to it. Rurally dominated legislatures then proceed to gerrymander, diluting the value of urban and Negro votes. In Michigan, Congressional districts range in population from 177,000 to 802,000; in Texas, from 216,000 to 951,000; in Georgia from 272,000 to 823,000. In Florida, the state supreme court last October found nothing improper in a system whereby Congressional districts varied from 237,000 to 660,000.

Wherever there are large blocs of Negro voters, they are concentrated in one Congressional district instead of being dispersed among several which they might control or carry. According to a study published in *Ebony* magazine, Negroes constitute 17.8 per cent of the population of our thirty largest cities, yet there will be only five Negro Congressmen in the 88th Congress.

But Congress has the power not only to require "compact and contiguous" districts, but to forbid large population variances. Congressman Celler's bill, which will undoubtedly be pushed in 1963, forbids any Congressional district to vary from a state-wide average by more than 20 per cent, a minimum range enjoyed today in only a dozen states.

Perhaps the best way of appreciating the speed and forthrightness of the courts in coping with these unprecedented problems is to describe some of the most striking cases. On April 14, 1962, a three-judge federal district court, having before it an application for a temporary injunction to prevent the holding in Alabama of the state primary elections of May, 1962, and the general elections of November, 1962, did not wait for the introduction of evidence. It quoted the Alabama constitution requiring that "representation in the legislature shall be based upon population" and revised decennially, and took judicial notice of an Alabama state court decision that there had been no reapportionment based on population changes since 1901. It then postponed the suit until July 16, 1962, to give the Alabama legislature opportunity to comply with the state constitutional mandate.

The Alabama legislature was called into special session on June 5 and on July 12, four days before the judicial deadline, approved a proposed constitutional amendment (subject to popular ratification) reapportioning the state senate and lower chamber. It also adopted a stand-by statute, apportioning each chamber on a different basis to become effective if the constitutional amendment were rejected by the federal court or the people.

On July 21, the federal district court found that both the constitutional amendment and the stand-by measure were inacceptable and voided both. It then promulgated a temporary reapportionment plan solely to elect the 1963 legislature, incorporating the house apportionment of the constitutional amendment and the senate apportionment of the stand-by measure, choosing for each house the plan closest to true equality of representation. The court specifically rejected a "federal plan" which, indeed, would have been worse than the existing malapportionment. This was the first time a federal court had ever actually reapportioned a state legislature and was the first reapportionment in Alabama since 1901. Two days later, Gov. John Patterson (who has earned national notoriety for his intransigence on Negro suffrage and desegregation) accepted the order of the federal court. An effort to obtain a stay of the order from Supreme Court Justice Hugo Black proved unsuccessful and a second primary election was held in August, 1962.

The representation of urban areas has been increased in the new legislature, the Birmingham delegation being enlarged from seven to seventeen and that from Mobile County from three to eighteen. Nevertheless, 27.6 per cent of the people of Alabama still elect a majority of the Alabama senate.

The district court has meanwhile retained jurisdiction of the case (*Sims v. Frink*) in order to give this year's Alabama legislature an opportunity to provide for a true reapportionment of both houses and to break what the court called "the strangle hold." But the court warned that if the 1963 legislature failed to act, it would exercise its "solemn duty" to prevent a denial of the equal protection of the law.

Not all courts have been as forceful in seeking to achieve equality of representation. On July 23, 1962, a federal district court invalidated Florida's 1961 reapportionment and ordered a new plan to be promulgated for the 1962 elections, warning that if it were not done, the court would itself "fashion a remedy of judicial apportionment by judicial decree." The legislature met in special session in August, 1962, and drew up a new plan, which the court approved on September 6.

The apportionment plan was, however, rejected by the voters, the opposition being greatest in the more populous counties and cities. The Florida legislature was again called into special session to draft a new apportionment, but after twenty days of deadlock it adjourned without any action, leaving the matter once more in the hands of the federal court.

State courts were no less forceful than federal courts. On April 23, 1962, the U. S. Supreme Court, in a one-sentence opinion, reinstated a complaint in an apportionment suit brought by August Scholle, head of the Michigan State Federation of Labor, which the Michigan supreme court had dismissed (by a 5-to-3 vote) in 1960. On July 18, 1962, Michigan's highest court invalidated (by a 4-to-3 vote) the apportionment for the state senate which had been frozen into the constitution and approved by the voters in 1952. It also enjoined the primary election only three weeks off. The court "respectfully advised" that a new apportionment was urgently required, but warned that if it were not forthcoming, state senators would be chosen at large in a state-wide primary to be held on September 11.

The majority of the court found the largest senate district contained twelve times as many people as the smallest, and that 53 per cent of the state's population chose only 29 per cent of the senate. It ruled that such a discrepancy violated the Fourteenth Amendment.

At this juncture, Supreme Court Justice Potter Stewart stayed the Michigan court's ruling pending an appeal to the U. S. Supreme Court, thus reinstating the August primaries and making impossible any revision of Michigan apportionment until 1963. If the Supreme Court now agrees to hear *Scholle v. Hare,* it will have to decide whether one house of a state legislature may be chosen on the basis of geography, not population.

The litigation in Maryland demonstrates that rural domination of a state's legislature can only be broken by a court or the threat of court action. The Maryland constitution allots one senator to each county and six to Baltimore City, and also apportions the 123 members of the House of Delegates. The state legislature is given no express power to apportion. As a result, Baltimore and its four suburban counties, which contain 76 per cent of the state's population, elected only 34 per cent of the senate and 49 per cent of the house. Bills to call a constitutional convention have repeatedly failed because of rural opposition, even after proposals for such a convention had been approved by the voters.

On April 25, 1962, after reciting the above facts, the Maryland supreme court directed a lower court to receive evidence whether unconstitutional discrimination existed in the apportionment of either Maryland house. On May 24, 1962. Chancellor Duckett ruled that the Maryland senate might properly be chosen on the basis of geographical areas, but that the house apportionment was illegal. On May 24, the Maryland General Assembly met and reapportioned the Maryland house by creating nineteen new seats, which for the first time gave Baltimore and its four suburban counties control of that chamber. On July 23, the Maryland supreme court approved the house reapportionment, but ruled that the senate did not have to be chosen on a population basis. An appeal has been taken to the U. S. Supreme Court.

The litigation I have described above and the other cases for which a detailed description is impossible because of space limitation demonstrate that all of Justice Frankfurter's gloomy prophecies in his *Baker v. Carr* dissent have been disproved. The state legislatures have not played "ducks and drakes with the judiciary." The same courts which acquiesced in the patent circumvention of the Supreme Court's mandate in the school-segregation cases were quick to see and forceful to reject counterfeit reapportionment. The legislatures have heeded the courts' "admonitions." The courts have not been sunk in a "mathematical quagmire" because of the lack of judicial standards on voting inequality. There has been no flouting of any court's decision. And most important, there has been no weakening of the popular will in exclusive reliance on the judiciary. On the contrary, the litigation has revealed the extent of urban disfranchisement and released pent-up resentment.

Legislative redistricting referenda were on the ballot in twelve states in the last elections. In seven states, the voters approved easier procedures for future apportionments or defeated plans unfair to urban voters. In five others, however, including California, voters either rejected plans to give urban areas more representation or else approved plans unfair by population standards.

A great debate is now developing and political scientists and good-government groups can testify that more hard thinking is being done about legislative apportionment than the country has witnessed in decades. "One man, one vote" is becoming a rallying cry. Voter apathy is being replaced by voter determination and the courts are playing a catalytic role in stimulating legislation, shaping popular attitudes and preserving the fundamental principle of our democracy: the equality of man under the rule of law.

Much remains to be done. A recent study by the National Municipal League shows that less than 30 per cent of the population is able to elect a majority of the lower house in thirteen state legislatures and a majority of the upper house in twenty states.

This year's state legislative sessions—if they heed the responsibilities imposed on them by the courts and the Fourteenth Amendment—must address themselves to the ultimate goal: A system of legislative apportionment that is as automatic and mechanical as possible, in which rural domination of our state and federal legislatures is broken and in which the needs of the people, by now primarily urban, are filled by a legislature that is responsible, and responsive, to them.

REAPPORTIONMENT:
WHAT THE COURT DIDN'T DO
Robert G. Dixon, Jr.

Robert G. Dixon, Jr. is Professor of Law at the George Washington University Law School, Washington, D.C.

The Supreme Court's recent reapportionment decisions on the structure of state legislatures are a major event in America's long romance with the principle of egalitarianism. There is no doubt that much change was overdue in some states, and at least some change was overdue in most states. We are a democratic people and our institutions presuppose according population a dominant role in formulas of representation.

The court ruled that the members in both houses of state legislatures must be elected from districts of approximately equal population. At the same time, by its intensive focus on numbers, the court may have transformed one of the most intricate, fascinating, and elusive problems of democracy into a simple exercise of applying elementary arithmetic to census data.

Like so many of the Constitutional issues that have split the Supreme Court, the reapportionment decisions lend themselves to superficial characterization in simple, moral terms, but are devilishly difficult to assess in terms of political realism, political philosophy, and long-run implications. Chief Justice Warren's majority opinions in the reapportionment decisions find support in the oral argument, which the states, frankly, botched rather badly. But his opinions, and particularly the far-reaching opinion in the Colorado case, have not found universal support among legal writers. Among the general commentators there were many who hailed the decisions as a new charter of liberty, signaling a new majoritarianism that could yield fresh political force for more effective approaches to urbanism, civil rights, social welfare, and even international relations. They heard the death knell on a rule of rural virtue rooted in the mystique of the settler tradition, the log cabin, and the family farm. Several of the more perceptive columnists, however, such as Walter Lippmann and Max Freedman, have been sober and restrained in their praise, hesitating not so much over the need for reapportionment as the sweep of the decisions. As Anthony Lewis reported in the New York *Times* a few days after the decision, "even some liberal-minded persons, admirers of the modern Supreme Court, found themselves stunned by last Monday."

From *The Reporter,* October 8, 1964. Copyright 1964 by The Reporter Magazine Company.

IDEALS AND REALITY

The difficulty lies not so much in the results of these cases as in the court's absolutistic approach. None of the apportionment opinions, except Justice Stewart's, showed an adequate awareness of the complexity of representative government in a pluralistic society. This complexity involves trying to achieve fair representation of the many interests and groupings and shades of opinion in a multimembered body chosen from geographic districts. In any election in any district system, there is a minority that is weighted at zero and a majority that elects its man or its slate and so is weighted, at least until the next election, at one hundred per cent. Some vote weighting necessarily is involved in any election system of a multimembered body from separate districts. To talk of "equal votes" in this context simply is not responsive to the issue. The important thing, in assessing the Constitutional fairness of the system, is how these "equal votes" producing one hundred per cent majorities and zero minorities add up across a state.

Actual examples of this complexity and the insufficiency of a simple "equal-population" formula are not hard to find. For example, a few days after the equal-population rule was announced for Congressional districts last February, in a Supreme Court case that preceded and foreshadowed the reapportionment decisions, Maryland's old-line legislative leaders demonstrated their resilience. They unveiled a plan for new arithmetically equal districts which actually would have worsened the position of the underrepresented suburbs that had brought the redistricting suit. The gerrymandering plan, which was narrowly defeated in the final days of the session, would have carved and regrouped the populous counties without regard to community of interest to yield equal-population districts that preserved the traditional power structure.

A second cause of the inequities even under an equal-population standard is the familiar balance-of-power factor. Significant interest-group overrepresentation can occur whenever a minority group—religious, racial, or other—holds the balance of power in a series of districts. The prohibitionists proved this by actually obtaining a Constitutional amendment. Fear of this balance-of-power factor may be one explanation for the outcome of the Colorado referendum that selected the apportionment plan subsequently nullified by the Supreme Court.

The Colorado case had attracted special attention and was thought to raise deeper philosophic issues than any others in the group of fifteen apportionment cases on the Supreme Court's calendar. It presented an apportionment plan placing the lower house on a straight population basis and the upper house on a modified population basis. This plan had been approved by every county in Colorado in a referendum. In the same state-wide referendum, an alternative plan placing both houses on a straight population basis had been resoundingly rejected. Although Justices Clark and Stewart had given limited concurrence to Chief Justice Warren's basic opinion for the court in the Alabama case, they joined Justice Harlan in dissent in this case.

A third potential cause of gross inequities even under an equal-population standard is the possible operation of multimember districts. The South provides interesting examples of this in regard to two minorities in the populous urban-suburban centers: the Republicans and the Negroes. If single-member districts are used, the housing patterns in some populous areas will produce some Republican seats and some Negro seats. But if the legislators are chosen in large plural-member districts, the Negroes and the Republicans will be swamped, despite their substantial numbers.

In short, numbers are easy to play with so long as they remain mere numbers. If, as Aristotle said, "Law is reason unaffected by desire," the reapportionment opinions of Chief Justice Warren show up well as an ideal prescription for a theoretical society. But if what the Founding Fathers called "factionalism" rears its ugly head, and if, as Justice Holmes said, "The life of the law has not been logic; it has been experience," then the Warren opinions are inadequate. The basic difficulty seems to be that the court views all these cases as being simply civil-rights cases involving the personalized right of the individual voter to cast a vote that theoretically will have "equal weight" with the votes of all other voters. In one sense, of course, these cases do involve voting. But this simple characterization by the court misses the crucial point that in apportionment cases the personal civil right of the voter is intertwined with large, overriding questions concerning representation.

UNRESOLVED ISSUES

Perhaps the first need is to perceive what these cases are all about, and the effect the court order unavoidably will have. In reapportionment, courts sit in judgment on the structure of political power, even effect a judicial transfer of political power. To speak thus in terms of distribution of political power is to talk not of legislative acts, and not of judicial acts in the previously accepted concept of judicial review, but of constitutive acts. Reapportionment restructures government at the core.

Although the judiciary is deeply immersed in reapportionment litigation that the various measures before Congress will not be able to halt, there is not nearly enough information available for intelligent decision. One recent study of the House of Representatives, in which congressmen's votes on four issues were weighted by the population of their districts and recomputed, rather surprisingly suggests that the liberals benefit from such Congressional maldistricting as now exists. A similar recomputation of twenty-two roll-call votes in two sessions of the Texas legislature indicates that the outcome would have differed on only one measure. This is an area where political science, unfortunately, has let us down rather badly. We are just beginning to compile studies of the actual operation of legislatures and the relationships between legislators and their constituencies.

Another critically important aspect, the matter of standards, will need perpetual refinement as legislators develop new patterns of apportionment under which some identifiable group has disproportionate representation. It is a problem of putting real meaning into Chief Justice Warren's admonition that "fair and effective representation for all citizens is concededly the basic aim of legislative apportionment."

To achieve this goal, the court will have to move forward in two directions beyond the equal-population principle. It will have to join Justice Stewart in his concern for "ultimate effective majority rule." And it will have to be disposed to act against gerrymandering devices whereby a minority political party spreads its voters over enough districts in a state to control a majority of seats. Conversely, it should be disposed also to act against gross and continued underrepresentation of a minority party or group which finds itself so distributed and "locked into" a district system that its votes, though substantial, always achieve zero representation.

On the latter point, two lower Federal courts already have suggested that the equal-protection clause, on which the reapportionment decisions rest, may require breaking up multimember districts into single-member districts. Under a statute voided by a lower Federal court in Georgia last March, some voters had their own state senator in a single-member district. Other voters in populous counties having more than one senator were under a system whereby each senator was chosen at large in the county even though assigned for representation purposes to a subdistrict in the county, where he also had to reside. The court found unconstitutional discrimination between the single-member-district voters who "owned their man," so to speak, and the voters in the subdistricts in the plural-member counties who might be represented by a man elected at large but not favored by the very subdistrict he represented. It does not take much imagination to see that this system could operate, and perhaps was designed to operate, to overcome subdistrict majorities that were contrary to the county-wide majority.

In Pennsylvania a lower Federal court last April held that both political philosophy and Constitutional law prohibited the use of multimember districts along with single-member districts. "One man, one vote" means, the court said, that each voter must vote for the same number of legislators. Otherwise, some voters would have only one legislator looking out for their interests; others would have two, three, or four, although of course their districts might be two, three, or four times larger. The court added the more respectable rationale that "minority groups living in particular localities may well be submerged in elections at large but can often make their voting power much more effective in the smaller single-member district in which they may live." Both of these cases may be on the Supreme Court docket in the term starting this month.

In devising remedies for malapportionment, the courts also should guard against undue haste. How anomalous is the contrast between the "hell-bent for election" speed with which some courts approach reapportionment and the lengthy delay and procrastination in desegregation of public education! Desegregation is conceptually far more simple than legislative apportionment, and is a moral issue as well. It is almost exclusively a matter of vindicating a personalized civil right. And yet in desegregation we have had "all deliberate speed" over a ten-year period, whereas in reapportionment we have been treated to the spectacle of courts pressuring and threatening legislators and fixing exact deadlines measured in months or even weeks.

The "political thicket" that Justice Frankfurter warned the courts not to enter is no less political because the courts are in it. But the highest commitment is to the viability of the system and to maintenance of popular faith in it. With political avenues for redress of malapportionment blocked in many states, with protests mounting, the court has concluded that some judicial participation in the politics is a precondition to there being any effective politics.

Unfortunately, there are no simple formulas for making power just, and politics clean. An equal-population-district system will be no exception to the tendency of all district systems to exaggerate the strength of the dominant party, and may even heighten the tendency. As courts go forward in this new era of "one man, one vote," the task will be to assure both majority rule and equitable minority representation.

A motorist arraigned on a minor traffic charge in some dingy rural kitchen before an unkempt, unlettered Justice of the Peace may well develop a negative opinion of justice on the local and state levels. Throughout the nation, such JP courts have been justifiably criticized for both their procedures and their personnel. At the other extreme, the citizen attending a session of his state's highest tribunal, its Supreme Court or Court of Appeals, may have formed an opposite opinion of high and lofty justice dispensed by a professionally qualified bench dealing in superb fashion with a Law above and beyond all human manipulation. A more accurate image of our state court systems is probably somewhere between the two extremes.

In order to gauge accurately the performance of the state judicial systems, it is necessary first to reject the notion that law and the courts are too complex and specialized for examination and evaluation by the layman. Indeed, to paraphrase the old saying about war and generals, it may be claimed with some validity that law and justice are too important to be left to the judges and lawyers. However, if judges are to be judged, it is necessary to establish objective criteria.

What are some of the juridical goals shared by knowledgeable Americans? Most are concerned with the state court's role in *protecting the individual* against other individuals and, if need be, against officials and the very state itself. Second, they expect *impartiality* from judges, courts, and juries that are free from undue political, economic, racial, and religious pressures. Moreover they expect impartiality in the court procedures—public hearings, full presentation of testimony, and, in criminal cases, the opportunity to know the charges and to confront one's accusers. Third, there should be a high degree of both *certainty and predictability,* that the guilty can expect conviction and, even more importantly, the innocent can anticipate acquittal. It is essential also that the individual be afforded full opportunity for advance knowledge of the law. Another desirable goal for state jurisprudential systems is *accessibility,* that is, the opportunity for a trial close to home, at reasonable cost and without undue delays. In addition if justice is to triumph in the long run, it must be the concern of the entire community and not of the courts alone.

Before proceeding, two points should be noted regarding the state court systems in America. In theory, just as on the national level, the state courts are independent, co-equal partners of the executive and legislative branches, In practice, however, both separation and independence on the state level may be limited by outside pressure, informal influence, and the political selection of judges. In addition, the state courts have been increasingly subordinated to the Federal judiciary. Acting under the supremacy clause of the national Constitution, the Supreme Court of the United States has filled out the scope of its jurisdiction so that today it decides many cases once wholly within the police power of the states. In the nineteenth century it invoked the "due process" clause of the Fourteenth Amendment to nullify numerous state attempts at business regulation. In recent years it has employed a newer interpretation of the same clause to protect the individual against state infringement of rights guaranteed in the Bill of Rights. Thus the court has assured freedom of religion (as well as freedom *from* religion) in the North and has done much to combat racial segregation in the South.

What then are the major problems facing our state courts? Considerable attention has been devoted in recent years to the need for structural and jurisdictional reorganization. The judicial systems of New Jersey and Missouri have undergone sweeping revisions, while the new Alaskan and Hawaiian constitutions have embodied many reform ideas. In 1962, New York State introduced extensive changes in its New York City bench and minor modifications upstate. Yet even in these modernized systems, problems remain which go far beyond structure and jurisdiction. In many states, undue reliance continues to be placed upon a rigid, unyielding and inequitable legalism in court decisions. Unsolved administrative problems are vexing, yet they seem susceptible to rational treatment. One of the most widespread problems has been undue delay in court decisions, the result, primarily, of dockets clogged with automobile negligence actions.

Inadequacies in personnel exist not only in the Justice of the Peace courts noted above, but even in the higher ranks where legal training is a prerequisite to service. In many instances, judicial nominations have been decided on the basis of petty politics. In almost every case there has been a lack of public understanding of the importance of electing capable rather than merely "popular" judges. Often justice has suffered under a fluctuating rule of law; accused murderers, in the face of overwhelming evidence of guilt, have been acquitted by color-blinded juries; police brutality and "legal lynchings" have been publicly condoned on the grounds that the defendants "had it coming to them" regardless of legal niceties.

These, then, are some of the considerations to be borne in mind in examining and analyzing the judicial branch of our state and local government in action.

THE CRISIS IN THE COURTS
Louis Banks

Career journalist Louis Banks has served as national affairs editor
of *Time* since 1955.

The palsied hand of an obsolete court system had all but smothered the
workings of justice in Great Britain in 1827, and the *Edinburgh Review* knew
just why court reform was the most urgent of a host of national concerns.
The heart of everything that government sought to build and defend lay in
a promise of justice. A citizen's security was as much in danger from courts
mired in delay and irrelevant details as if Napoleon's legions had suddenly
reappeared astride Europe. Across the Atlantic, in that noisy new house of
Anglo-Saxon law, Daniel Webster voiced the same kind of reverence for the
courts at about the same time. "Justice," said he in his eulogy of Justice
Joseph Story, "is the great interest of man on earth."

Today the U.S. has urgent reason to be concerned about the condition of
justice. In recent years a small band of worried judges and lawyers have
been warning with increasing urgency that the composite picture of the
American courts is a sorry one. The thousands of federal, state, county, and
city courts obviously include many that are as good as the civics books say
they should be. But a layman's hard look at the condition of the courts
today results in the conclusion that the reformers are not alarmists; in fact,
the trouble with the administration of justice today is graver than they have
indicated. In state after state too many courts founder in mismanagement,
ineptitude, and archaic organization.

The most visible and most talked-about distress sign is the pile-up of
civil cases by the hundreds of thousands, year upon year, awaiting jury
trial in the civil courts. The mountainous statistics of delay are discouraging
enough in their own right, but the more important and less understood fact
is that delay is often a symptom of a deeper trouble in the quality of justice.
In the metropolitan areas state courts run an average of 22.6 months behind.
In Los Angeles County, among the best of the big-city court systems, civil
jury cases are stacked up for an average of seventeen months; in Cook
County (Chicago), the worst, the average case waits more than five years
before coming to trial. The federal courts do better, with a range of averages
from one to three years in their busiest districts. Under the circumstances,
writes Judges Irving R. Kaufman of the U.S. Court of Appeals, "it is not
surprising that most businessmen try to avoid litigation . . . Indeed, it is
surprising that the majority of our citizens still look to the courts to redress
their civil wrongs." Congestion of court calendars, said Justice William J.
Brennan Jr. of the U.S. Supreme Court to the Wharton School of Finance

and Commerce in Philadelphia, "is a problem of such gravity at some places as to threaten an actual breakdown in the administration of justice itself." And Chief Justice Earl Warren, raising a danger flag as high as it has ever flown atop the U.S. Supreme Court, warned as far back as 1958: "Interminable and unjustified delays in our courts are compromising the basic legal rights of countless thousands of Americans and, imperceptibly, corroding the very foundations of constitutional government."

The warning could hardly be more basic or the situation more urgent. The one American message that totalitarians can never match is the message of liberty under law, yet in cold-war terms the message is seriously compromised if American justice staggers when it comes down to cases. And stagger may yet turn out to be a mild word. The courts are deep in trouble just trying to keep up with problems that have been around for a long time —corporations, labor unions, civil rights, and, most notably, the automobile. They have hardly felt the impact of the onrushing developments of science and technology, the increasing scope and complexity of government activity, the new magnitude of international business operations, and a host of developments of the here and now—let alone the new realm opened up by, say, the joint corporate operation of a communication satellite in space. So the pile-up on court calendars means much more than a disturbing delay in disposing of old claims. It means that a system of justice which is not fit to handle yesterday's demands until today will not be able to handle tomorrow's demands at all.

DOWNHILL WITH ANDY JACKSON

Of all the major nations that live by Anglo-Saxon law, the U.S. stands alone in its plodding administration of justice. The reasons most commonly cited are external to the courts themselves—e.g., population growth and the number of automobile accidents. But such external reasons, though valid do not fully explain why the courts lack the vitality to adjust to new demands. Some students of the law dig back nearly a century for the beginnings of the answer. The popular election of state judges, an American invention of the Jacksonian era, stripped the court of the dignities of the robe and put the judge on the campaign platform with every shirtsleeved politician. New Jersey's great court reformer, the late Chief Justice Arthur T. Vanderbilt, believed that the bar and bench of the Jacksonian era lost the battle by default. In his *Challenge of Law Reform,* published in 1955, he accuses his nineteenth-century brethren of failing "both the profession and the public miserably." The long-standing result, he writes with some relevance to today, "was a lowering of judicial and professional standards, a lessening of respect for the courts and the law, and the failure of the law to keep pace with economic and social changes."

The election of judges is seen today in its worst form in the states where political machines control judicial appointments. Political judges do not command the respect of the lawyers that appear before them. On the other hand, many lawyers have come to develop a vested interest in complex procedure and slow motion. For nearly every group of reformers in the bar there is a special-interest group that uses its political influence to keep laws and court procedures from being modernized to fit the times. The public and the newspapers have tended to take the trial courts as a local necessary evil. Only now are outsiders beginning to understand what a few dedicated reformers have been trying to say—that the situation is both general and critical.

Some judges, along with public-spirited members of the bar, are taking a brisk lead in reform. Exemplary courts in such states as New Jersey, Michigan and California are blazing paths into new procedures and administrative techniques. More heroic, a few capable judges and bar leaders in the poorest of court systems—notably New York and Illinois—are battling from within for reform. The Chief Justice of the U.S. himself is working daringly and effectively behind the scenes to speed the work of the federal courts, and the presidential appointment of 115 new federal judges this year will help considerably. Committees of the American Bar Association, working with federal and state judges, are hammering at various aspects of improvement. But the best of the reformers' efforts show no sign of keeping up with the growing new demands on the courts. There are, in fact, sound grounds for wondering whether anything short of a general rehabilitation and rejuvenation of bench, bar, and law will achieve all that urgently needs doing.

SHUFFLING JUSTICE

Before describing the efforts at reform it is necessary to take a look at courts at their worst. Two of the largest cities in the land, Chicago and New York, offer striking examples not found in civics books.

The reporter who wanders through the ancient, dingy Cook County courthouse in Chicago is likely to find trials droning along over accidents that took place from six to eight years ago. Recently a Chicago jury was pondering the case of ten-year-old Nancy Vernola who was hit by an automobile while riding a bicycle. By trial time Nancy was a young mother of nineteen and brought her six-week-old baby to court with her. (She got a $250 judgment.) "Searching for the reasons for court congestion in Illinois," reports a *Fortune* correspondent in Chicago, "one is confronted by a court system that is bad almost beyond belief. One feels like a doctor who is examining a patient who complains of a cold but who, in fact, has cancer."

Or it could be just hardening of the arteries. The Illinois court system has not been revamped for ninety-one years, and it shows every minute of its age. Chicago has circuit and superior courts that handle approximately the same kinds of cases—with a passionately jealous rivalry. It also has a county court, a probate court, and a conglomeration of county and municipal courts whose civil jurisdictions differ only slightly. There is no master calendar to control the cases filed in the various courts. Lawyers can kill endless amounts of time by arguing whether a case is being brought in the right court, then take time to appeal the ruling if delay serves their purpose. Each court has its own costly system of juries, clerks, bailiffs, stenographers, and reporters. Judges guard their courtrooms like children with toys; time after time cases will be delayed in one court because there is no courtroom, while courtrooms are standing empty in a rival court.

Judges in Cook County are hand-picked by the Republican bosses. The organization candidate is rarely challenged and almost never beaten. Once elected, a judge serves his six-year term and, unless he has disgraced or defied the machine, is generally reslated until he dies. Occasionally lawyers will feel certain that a judge has been "talked to" about a case, but in general the problem is incompetence rather than actual corruption. The average age of fifty Cook County judges on the two principal courts is 65.8 years. Fourteen judges are over seventy. Seven judges have been severely slowed by age or illness. Five others are generally considered to be not pulling their weight; two or three others are rated so incompetent that lawyers go to any extreme to duck them.

Illinois has been talking about reforming its courts since the 1920's and the state and Chicago bar associations began to get worried in the late 1940's, when the jury-case backlog swelled to two years. After some preliminaries the bar associations came up with a plan to bring every court in the state into a sense-making, unified court system, with judges nominated on the endorsement of bar and civic leaders. The State General Assembly, Republican controlled and responsive to pressure from every outlying justice of the peace, turned reform down twice, finally approved it for referendum —after dropping the provision for nonpolitical appointment of judges. The 1958 referendum got enough votes to carry, but about 100,000 improperly wrote "yes" on the ballot instead of marking the prescribed X. (The bar associations clearly needed a lawyer; their costly reform campaign had been built on the slogan, "Vote YES for the Judicial Article.") the State Supreme Court finally ruled, six to one, that the "yes" votes were not valid and reform died again. It will be up for another vote next year.

THE BOSSES' LAST REFUGE

In New York City, the day after Mayor Robert Wagner won an overwhelming primary victory over the Tammany candidate last September, the newspapers crowed that the machine was flat on its back. Within the week the bosses and Wagner tested each other again when lawyer-politicians gathered for that strange political rite, the judicial nominating convention. With little trouble the bosses defeated two of Wagner's candidates for the state bench and nominated their own—one a lawyer for Tammany Hall.

The court systems—state, county, and municipal—are the last refuge of the machines, because they offer just about the last major area of attractive and sought-for patronage. The New York Supreme Court, the state's trial court of general jurisdiction, pays the nation's highest trial-court salary, $34,500 a year in the metropolitan area, and a machine candidate is supposed to kick back more than that to cover the cost of getting him elected to his fourteen-year term. Not all New York judges are machine candidates. But so much are the judgeships considered a proprietary right of the machine that in political circles they are tagged with the name of the district leader who wangles them from the boss. Thus if a district leader named Max Murdock manages to get a choice supreme-court designation for attorney Joe Smith, it would thereafter be known as "Maxie's job."

Few judges are suspected of actually "taking a contract" (vernacular for dismissing or throwing cases), for this means crossing that misty line between "honest graft" and dishonesty. A lot of honest graft derives from the power of the state courts to appoint lawyers to the lush jobs of receivers and referees. The surrogates appoint special guardians and trustees. One Brooklyn judge, sitting on an estate case, picked up the document that listed a Manhattan bank as trustee, scratched out the name of the Manhattan bank, and wrote in the name of a Brooklyn trust company in its place.

New York lawyers generally rate the local federal bench as much better than the state trial bench (although they have great regard for the Appeals Court). An old hand in one leading Manhattan law firm believes that more than half of the state judges lack the legal background or the judicial temperament that the job calls for.

SO PEACEFUL IN THE COUNTRY

Not all the horror stories are in the big cities. In American folklore the law is supposedly most at home in the old South. Yet many southern states have an archaic collection of overlapping courts, in which every court is a kingdom unto itself and every judge is a king. There is no official supervision, no concept of a court system as unified even as New York's. North Carolina, which woos industry on the strength of the state's popular enlightenment, once roundly defeated an attempt to reform its courts, but will try again on a half-loaf reform next year. A 1946 drive for reform in Arkansas died on the floor of the state bar convention to the cry that "the people's courts should not be taken from the people." Old-timers recall that one of the opposition floor leaders, now deceased, was a lawyer who held control of a weak judge and the jury system of a rural Arkansas county.

Most southern states (and many northern as well) still police the countryside with that literal hangover from horse-and-buggy days, the nonlawyer justice of the peace who lives by his fines and fees. A *Fortune* correspondent recently found Archie Woodward Speck, eighty, lame, white-haired, and one of Arkansas' 2,150 J.P.'s rocking on the front porch of his tiny weatherbeaten frame house just a half-hour's drive from the courts of Little Rock. Judge Speck, once "one of the best farmers in Grant County" tries some

200 cases a year on the strength of his seventh-grade education and a single copy of *Arkansas Statutes,* 1947 official edition. Says he: "I don't ever remember having one who wasn't guilty. If the sheriff picks up a man for violating the law, he's guilty or he wouldn't bring him in here. And anyway I don't get anything out of it if they aren't guilty."

THE HIGHLY VISIBLE SIGNAL

Though the court systems of the countryside and the big-city areas share many of the same creaking weaknesses, the metropolitan courts are beginning to come under heavy fire while the small-town courts jog along relatively uncriticized. The big difference is delay in the trial of cases. The phenomenal increase in the number of cases filed (up more than 60 per cent in the last ten years) hits hardest where people are packed closest—in the metropolitan areas. The way a court responds to delay is a visible measure of its vitality. Since the courts that are worst in quality also tend to be the most inefficient in dealing with the quantity of cases, they inevitably rise toward the top of the delay list. In fact, if delay is not the ruination of the courts it may turn out to be their salvation. Thanks to a new, painstaking gathering of court statistics by many agencies, the cold facts of delay in the courts are highly visible signal of trouble that any League of Women Voters can plainly see.

The Price Waterhouse of court auditors is the New York University Law School's Institute of Judicial Administration, founded by dint of Justice Vanderbilt's all-pervasive energy. Under the cool eye of its director, Shelden D. Elliott, the institute puts out an annual listing that ranks the nation's leading courts according to the length of delay.

Ninety per cent of the backlogged cases are of one kind: personal-injury cases, usually growing out of automobile accidents and awaiting jury trial. If both sides would take their chances before a judge without a jury, they could have court judgment within a reasonable time. (Most judges think that a reasonable time in the average personal-injury case is something short of a year.) In some areas, notably New York, other business has a special calendar and does not have to line up behind personal-injury cases for jury trial. In most federal courts and in other key areas this priority system is not available, so nearly all types of civil jury cases get caught in the personal-injury log jam. In either situation delay sets the tone of the courts and the pattern of justice—or injustice. In accident cases witnesses die, memories fog, and judgment hangs largely on a lawyer's skill in handling juries. Many personal-injury plaintiffs, living close to their incomes and menaced by bill collectors, accept inadequate out-of-court settlements. Businessmen make unsound deals to avoid the courts because one side or both cannot afford delay. Inevitably, a cynicism about justice comes to shape the pattern of the nation's business and personal relationships. Says Chief Justice John Biggs of the U.S. Court of Appeals: "The really dangerous thing is that delay comes to be expected, and we get used to it."

HIGH STAKES FOR LAWYERS

The lawyer's lack of interest in reforming the courts is as ancient as the problem itself. During Great Britain's reform struggle in the early nineteenth century, the *Edinburgh Review* reported that there is "scarcely a moment of delay which is not contrived to minister either to the ease or the profit of lawyers, if not to both." If "contrived" is a little harsh on the profession today, certainly no one rests more comfortably or more profitably in the net of delay than lawyers. A lawyer in an accident case has plenty of excuse for taking his time in rounding up witnesses, investigating, serving papers, and waiting for injuries to develop new symptoms. But busy lawyers often let simple cases slide seven to eight months before filing their suits. If a client complains, they foist the blame on the slowness of the courts. In five out of nine cases selected at random in Allegheny County (Pittsburgh), one or both of the attorneys caused an extra year of delay by tardiness in filing papers, report A. Leo Levin and Edward Wolley in a University of Pennsylvania Law School survey of Pennsylvania courts, *Dispatch and Delay*. Once the case is called for trial, adversary lawyers will cheerfully accommodate each other with as many continuances as the judge allows, even though client and witnesses may be in court and ready to go to trial. Every judge knows that successful lawyers attempt to handle too many cases, and each time a lawyer pleads for a continuance because of prior engagement he is adding to delay. Insurance-company lawyers are the worst offenders in this respect. But plaintiffs' lawyers love that comfortable feeling of having cases coming due with the regularity of government bonds. A Los Angeles firm estimates that 150 to 200 cases—involving from $80,000 to $100,000 in claims—must be "in process" at one time in order to operate a nine-lawyer office with an overhead of $20,000 a month. Patrick E. Gibbons, counsel for a New York City insurance company, grouses that "plaintiffs' lawyers stack up suits like airplanes and bring them in when they're clear."

Most plaintiffs' lawyers work on contingent fees, picking up from 25 to 50 per cent of their clients' awards or settlements. This system is defended on the ground that it provides counsel for the most impoverished accident victims. Its vices are more glaring: the contingent-fee system clogs the calendars with thousands of small, weak suits that should never have been brought; juries, knowing that the plaintiff's lawyer will get a third or more of the award, inflate their verdicts far beyond actual damages; naturally, this tendency has the effect of increasing premiums for liability insurance. A few plaintiff lawyers in nearly every big city solicit likely cases against "target defendants" (rich ones) and, in flat violation of professional ethics, advance funds to support clients until trial time. In California a special bar commission reported some contingent fees "unreasonable and unconscionable," but the state bar membership refused to set maximum limits of 33⅓ per cent of the first $20,000 and 20 per cent above that. The New

York Supreme Court's Appellate Division in Manhattan and the Bronx limits fees to 33⅓ per cent with exceptions for special cases. In New York City alone accident awards run $220 million a year to 160,000 people; no less than 75 million of that amount goes to lawyers. The American Judicature Society, hard core of the court-reform movement, estimates that contingent fees in the U.S. may run as high as $700 million annually. The senior partner of a Pittsburgh law firm, Ella Graubart, figures that a good plaintiffs' lawyer can count on fees of more than $250,000 a year.

Such high stakes, contingent on plenty of litigation and plenty of confusion, inspire special-interest legal groups to a performance that would raise the curls on a British barrister's wig. Some lawyers' lobbies use their considerable influence with state legislatures and city councils to kill changes in the law that might cut into the volume of legal business. For example, New York City is virtually defenseless against personal-injury suits blamed on defective sidewalks. The city pays out some $4 million a year in claims filed months after the alleged accident and on the strength of nothing but the testimony of a corroborating witness and a doctor's report of injury. A simple change in the law that would bring New York in line with most other cities and would save millions of dollars, was defeated by a lobby of plaintiffs' lawyers.

A WHISTLE FOR SPORTING JUSTICE

The legions of more respectable lawyers frown on the excesses of the contingent-fee brigade, but do very little about them. Lawyers have an enormous professional tolerance for each other's vagaries. And as a group— with notable individual exceptions—they have an approach to the courts that, if carried over into medicine, would result in considerable reverence for treatment by leech and mustard plaster.

With the public looking the other way and with most lawyers looking for business, a heavy responsibility falls upon the judges to provide the leadership for restoring order in the courts. A half century ago Roscoe Pound, now the venerable dean emeritus of the Harvard Law School, prophetically called for just such leadership. In his landmark 1906 speech in the American Bar Association he warned that "delay and expense . . . have created a deep-seated desire to keep out of court, right or wrong, on the part of every sensible businessman in the community." He shocked his listeners by denouncing the "sporting theory of justice"—the view that somehow justice triumphs when opposing lawyers have at each other with all the tricks of oratory, surprise, and cross examination, while the judge does little but keep order. Pound demanded more efficient court systems, and judges clearly in charge of courtrooms, counsel, and cases. Progress along this line has been painfully slow since Dean Pound's warning, but in recent years the hard facts of delayed justice have driven responsible judges to rethink their procedures and search avidly for better ways of getting justice done.

The search has led down two promising roads, one headed toward modernization of methods and procedure inside the courtroom, and the other toward more efficient management of court systems. In 1929 the late Chief Judge Ira W. Jayne of the Wayne County Circuit Court, Detroit, was looking for ways to clear up a docket of mechanics' lien cases. He took to having lawyers come by his chambers about a month before going to trial, found that frequently he could bring them together in settlement without any trial at all —or, failing that, he could shorten trial time by stripping the cases to their essential issues. Judge Jayne's informal chats have blossomed into a definite, formal procedure called pre-trial, the most important innovation in Anglo-Saxon justice in a century. Pre-trial conferences of judges and counsel are now compulsory in New Jersey and California, and commonly used in other areas with big case loads. Pre-trial shows to best advantage in the federal courts, where cases tend to be more complicated. Judge Irving Kaufman, in 1955, paced a three-judge pre-trial task force through 7,229 cases in the southern district of New York (Manhattan) in nine months, settled 5,429 of them without trial—equivalent to eight years of court time. Chief Judge William Campbell of the U.S. District Court in Chicago spent one hundred hours in chambers with lawyers in a gargantuan milk antitrust case, disposing of dozens of issues by agreement. As a result, trial time for the case was cut from a predicted eight months to one and a half days.

MANAGEMENT IN ROBES

The road to the second reform—efficient management of the courts—was pioneered for state systems by the late Chief Justice Vanderbilt in New Jersey. By dint of tireless campaigning, political persuasion, and pamphleteering, he got New Jersey to overturn a corrupt and antiquated court system by constitutional amendment in 1947. In its place was set up a simplified court structure with judges under the control of, and responsible to, the Chief Justice. Vanderbilt's efficiently managed system was the forerunner of a court on the other side of the U.S. that has combined modern procedure, efficient administration, and compassionate imagination to become the showcase trial court in the country—the Superior Court of Los Angeles County.

The Los Angeles Superior Court begins with a California superlative. It is the nation's largest court of general jurisdiction under one management (and in the world second only to the district court in Tokyo). It serves a population of 6,500,000, operates eleven detached branch courts including a psychiatric court in the General Hospital. It is staffed by 120 judges, all of fairly high caliber, since the governor of California clears his judicial appointments with bar-association committees and the judges then run—usually unchallenged—against their records.

In the mid-1940's the court was plowing along in headless fashion just like any other, trying to keep up with its mounting case load by adding more branches and more judges. Then, in 1947, *the judges themselves* took a step that was ultimately to lead to big changes. By a one-vote margin they decided to abandon their practice of rotating the job of presiding judge on a seniority basis for a one-year prestige term. Instead, they tried to bring some executive staying power to the job by electing the judge that the majority of judges thought best qualified. In 1957, a group of determined internal reformers carried the cause of Louis Burke, a Lincolnesque six-footer in his early fifties, with a warm heart for people and the law, and a cold, cold eye for red tape and time wasting. He was re-elected to an unprecedented four terms before he was appointed chief judge of a new division of the state court of appeals last September.

Burke's organizational talents had come to the attention of his colleagues in an unusual way. After a freshman's term on the divorce court, he volunteered for the unpopular job of running the Conciliation Court. Troubled by California's soaring divorce rate, he yearned to see if the law could not somehow serve to repair, or at least mitigate, the misery of broken families. The upshot was that the Conciliation Court was reorganized and staffed with trained counselors and commissioners, and today is rated as the best of its kind. Burke's special contribution to family peace in Los Angeles was a legal device no social-service worker would ever have dreamed of: a written contract of conciliation worked out with the man and wife, laying out the problems of the particular marriage, ranging from spending money to sexual intercourse, and the general responsibilities of each party in fulfilling the contract. It seemed to fulfill that ancient legal function of bringing order into chaos. And three out of four who sign a contract stick it out.

A CALENDAR'S NEW LEAF

When he was elected presiding judge, Burke moved fast to bring other kinds of order to the court. He prevailed on the court to hire a $19,500-a-year executive officer, Edward C. Gallas, an experienced management consultant and—notably—a nonlawyer. Gallas tiptoed diplomatically around ancient judges' ancient foibles to take over the hiring and firing of court personnel, budget making, and all the other administrative chores that steal time away from judicial duties. Calendar call was moved up to 8:45 a.m. and judges were required to be ready for business at 9 o'clock. Each judge gets a vacation of only twenty-one workdays a year, and the Superior Court runs all summer (thus inspiring the local federal courts to sit all summer, too, because the community and the bar now expect it). Burke assigned judges to their jobs at the end of each year, kept up with their performance through a steady flow of reports. The judge who spent what Burke deemed overmuch time researching preliminary motions was moved out of the law-and-motions department with little ceremony. Another who groused about the pressure for dispatch suddenly found himself dealing primarily with dull traffic cases.

Like every metropolitan court, Los Angeles thinks it needs more judges. Its jury-trial backlog has inched back to a seventeen-month average, from fourteen months a year ago. Burke hopes that the eighteen new judges (he asked for twenty-four) commissioned this fall will cut the backlog. He and his colleagues believe that a modern metropolitan area must figure on one judge for every 50,000 people, which would raise the county's 120 to 130, with a prospect of another new judge every four months at the present rate of expansion. Fast-growing Florida has provided by constitutional amendment for an automatic 1-to-50,000 ratio.

A COURT GROWS IN BROOKLYN

Of all the courts in the land, the federal-court system has the richest opportunity to lead administrative justice out of the wilderness. Its eleven appeals courts and ninety-one district courts reach into every state and territory. Its important cases are the leading edge of great social and economic change. Lower courts look to it for moral support as they fight their own reform battles. Chief Justice Warren, the keenest student of administration to grace the topmost chair since William Howard Taft, is well aware of the challenge and the opportunity, but has no powers other than his own influence to work the needed changes throughout the federal system. His problem, happily, has nothing to do with machine control or the election of judges. On the contrary, it stems from the fact that federal judges are appointed for life, and some of the old breed (forty-six active U.S. district and appeals-court judges are over seventy) scoff at the new need for efficiency, timesaving procedures, and statistics.

In 1959 a group of reform-minded federal judges decided that the time had come for dramatic action. The statistics had long pointed to the eastern district of New York, the six-judge court in Brooklyn, as the slowest federal court in the land. Its backlog was running more than 2,000 cases, with the average case taking forty-three months to get to jury trial. Two of the judges were in their eighties and only two judges sat all day on the bench. The Brooklyn court spurned pre-trial and other new methods; in the words of a Senate appropriations-subcommittee investigator, the situation was "shocking," and "a prime example of a court where the bar had almost gotten out of hand." The Chief Justice was well aware of the situation, thanks largely to his fact-finding arm, the Administrative Office of the U.S. Courts—headed by his California protege, Warren Olney III, assistant attorney general for criminal affairs in the Eisenhower Administration. Olney and the reform-minded judges got permission from the chief judge in Brooklyn to send in outside help. Then they organized a task force of the brightest judges in the federal system to straighten out the Brooklyn mess. They hand-picked as boss of the operation William Francis Smith, then chief judge of the U.S. Court for the District of New Jersey.

Bill Smith's arrival in Brooklyn must have rivaled, in somewhat lower key, Gary Cooper's walk down Main Street in *High Noon*. Smith and his first five visiting judges set up a separate court in the new state Supreme Court Building, across Johnson Street from the regular federal courtrooms in the old Post Office Building. Smith and colleagues took the oldest cases, while the regular court went ahead with the regular docket. Smith's court began work punctually at 9:30 a.m. and ran until 4:30 p.m., the regular federal court across the street kept its regular hours of 10:30 to 4:00. Tension ran high in Brooklyn's clannish bar when the Smith court's first blunt pre-trial notices began raining down out of the mails. (*Take notice . . . the attorneys for the respective parties are hereby directed to . . .*) Over the weeks the Brooklyn lawyers got to know and respect a new kind of judge. Heavyset, blunt Bill Smith was a businesslike judge who ran his pre-trial conferences with shirtsleeve impartiality, chain-smoked his way through session after session, day after day, with no apparent weariness. He and his fellow judges obviously had worked long hours to know as much about the cases as the lawyers did. At the end of Smith's special two-month term, the record for his court stood at 1,050 old cases processed, 681 settled prior to trial, 325 scheduled for subsequent trial, and forty-four cases dropped. On the average, civil-case delay had been whittled down by five months to three years and two months, and the Brooklyn court—soon strengthened with younger blood—did adopt some of the new procedures. More important, the velvet-gloved hands that gently guide the destinies of the federal courts had made it clear to all that this was the way they wanted business done. Last September, Bill Smith, archetype of the new breed ("If a judge doesn't control his courtroom the lawyers will") was promoted to the U.S. Court of Appeals.

NEW HOPE IN NEW STRENGTH

With so much hanging on individual judicial performance, judges and bar leaders anxiously watch while President Kennedy fills the largest number of federal vacancies that ever confronted a President. Congressional approval of sixty-three new district and ten appeals-court judgeships, plus the existing forty-two vacancies, gives the Kennedy Administration power to name one-fourth of the federal bench. Federal judgeships have traditionally been considered prime senatorial patronage, although in his last months Harry Truman began the custom of submitting the names of the Senate's favorite candidates to the American Bar Association's Committee on the Judiciary in advance of public announcement. Presidents Eisenhower and Kennedy have followed suit. In the present period of pressure, the U.S. owes more than it knows to a gutty Philadelphia corporation lawyer, Bernard G. Segal, who is chairman of the A.B.A. watchdog committee on judicial appointments. Segal's committee has won the complete confidence of judges, lawyers, and law schools in scrutiny of nominees' records. With a member in each of the eleven circuits, it frequently gets tipped to a candidate's weakness by the very individuals who have written effusive letters recommending appointment. The committee grades each candidate as EWQ (exceptionally well qualified), WQ, Q or NQ, and while Attorney General Robert Kennedy does not promise to be bound by A.B.A. ratings, he pays close heed to Segal & Co. Of the sixty new judges nominated and confirmed by the Senate when Congress adjourned, two were rated NQ by Segal's committee, largely for lack of trial experience. Three more NQ's have been nominated but as yet not confirmed.

Generally the men most earnestly concerned with the quality of the federal bench are well pleased with most of the nominees they have seen, but they will keep their fingers crossed until the last confirmation at the next session of Congress. From the heart of one of the nation's busiest federal district courts, a chief judge breathed a prayer as he shuffled papers at eight o'clock one recent night: "Please, God, don't let them send us any political hacks. We're just too busy. If there's anything worse than venality on the court it's stupidity."

THE AUTHENTIC IDIOM

The 25 per cent increase in federal judgeships, plus the drive for better administration and procedure, head an imposing list of new beginnings of U.S. court improvement. In fact, Administrator Olney, speaking the Chief Justice's mind, has bluntly put it to federal judges that the new help robs them of the last excuse for failure to clear up old cases. The new federal judges are getting a better indoctrination in such specialties as the use of pre-trial and criminal sentencing than their predecessors ever did. Advancing on another front, bench and bar have organized a new Joint Committee for Effective Administration of Justice, chaired by Justice Tom Clark of the U.S. Supreme Court, which has already begun profitable seminars for state judges and lawyers in several parts of the country. Early last month New York voters approved a reform amendment that simplifies the state court structure and administration (but leaves untouched the political appointment of judges).

These and other exemplary efforts in the state and federal courts will be important and valuable only if they are recognized for what they are—just beginnings. For the court blight is serious and reforms are long overdue. Law is the authentic idiom of the American people in the struggle for the world, carrying within its wisdom much of the morality, the charity, the restraint and experience in the nation's heritage—all waiting for application to specific, new cases. The great task is to bend and fashion the workings of justice to fit the nation's—and the world's—newest needs. But when the handling of cases is tardy and tawdry in so many courts, the cases themselves begin to seem irrelevant. If the trial courts become little more than claims agents and if lawyers come to think more of exploiting and avoiding the courts than of revising codes to fit modern needs, then the U.S. will come to have very little to say on the subject where its example should be the most important aspect of its presence in the world.

Yet a nation with the habit of justice, founded on lawyers' documents, is obviously hungry for the leadership of law. And it is the strength of the law that this can begin any place, any day, any time—in Los Angeles or Brooklyn, Chicago or Manhattan. The chosen are the judges, who begin when they reassert control of their courts, whether from lawyers or politicians or plain old mismanagement. Off the bench good judges spread their influence by working with lawyers to perfect new methods, to draft and push new codes and lobby for changes in procedures and statutes that are obsolete or unworkable. Law schools help when they restore courses in legal ethics and put more emphasis on the responsibilities of the profession and less on overspecialized bread-and-butter courses. A general rejuvenation and rededication of the bar would have an incalculable effect in raising the level of all public life, for lawyers keep the consciences of unions and corporations; they dominate legislatures and influence nearly every public-minded group in society.

The American courts must move fast if they would purge themselves of their present low esteem. If they do, they can be the principal institution that gives point to American national development. If they do not, there will not be much point to the development.

SOMETHING'S WRONG WITH OUR JURY SYSTEM
Jerome Frank

The late Jerome Frank was one of America's most outstanding Federal jurists. He was the author of *Courts on Trial, Fate and Freedom, If Men Were Angels, Law and the Modern Mind* and many other publications.

If a surgeon were to call in 12 men untrained in surgery, give them an hour's talk on the instruments used in appendectomies, and then let them remove a patient's appendix, we would be appalled. Yet similar operations on men's legal rights are performed every day by juries, amateurs entrusted with the use of legal rules which lawyers and judges understand only after long special training.

From *Collier's,* December 9, 1950. © 1950 by Crowell-Collier Publishing Co. Reprinted by permission of Mrs. Jerome Frank.

No sensible business outfit would decide on the competence and honesty of a prospective executive by seeking the judgment of 12 men and women, taken from a group selected almost at random—and from which all those had been weeded out who might have special qualifications for deciding the question. Yet juries chosen in this way are given the job of ascertaining facts on which depend a man's property, his reputation, his very life.

That man may be you, for no one is immune from lawsuits. Your land-lord may sue you on your lease. Someone may assert in court that you broke your contract to sell him your house. The driver whose car you bumped one Sunday afternoon may bring an action against you for a broken leg. You may be charged with falsifying your income-tax return or violating the antitrust laws. If any such case is tried before a jury, the decision will depend on that jury's verdict. The way jury trials are conducted is, then pretty serious business for everyone of us.

Thomas Jefferson described juries as "the best of all safeguards for the person, the property and the reputation of every individual." His words have been so often repeated that the man in the street regards it as gospel that no better form of trial could be imagined. Many of our lawyers and judges feel the same way.

Increasingly, however, in recent years, eminent members of the bench and bar have expressed a contrary opinion. One of our wisest judges Learned Hand of the United States Court of Appeals, said he was "by no means enamored of jury trials, at least in civil cases." He also said of such trials: "As a litigant, I should dread a lawsuit beyond almost anything short of sick-ness and death." The late Supreme Court Justice Oliver Wendell Holmes said he had "not found juries especially inspired for the discovery of truth," and the late Chief Justice William Howard Taft believed that civil-jury trials should be abolished.

A well-known jurist warned me that if I publicized such views I would expose myself to severe criticism. But I think those views are justified and that the public should learn that the jury system is by no means all it's cracked up to be.

This conclusion stems from reflection on the methods jurors often use to arrive at their verdicts. For there is a world of difference between the theory and practice of jury trials.

At the beginning of a trial every juror takes an oath, as a public official, that he will "well and truly try the matters in issue and a true verdict render according to the law and the evidence." After the evidence and the lawyers' arguments have been heard, the judge addresses—or "charges"—the jurors. He describes the "law"—the legal rules—which, he says, must govern their verdict. He instructs them that it is their sworn duty to apply those legal rules, whether or not they like them, to the fact they "find"; that their "finding" of the facts must be based entirely on the evidence they have heard during the trial, and not on any personal knowledge; and that they must dismiss from their minds all bias for or against either party to the suit, and act fairly and impartially.

INSIDE STORY OF VERDICT ISN'T TOLD

The jurors then retire to the jury room for secret deliberations. If they agree on the result, they come back to the courtroom and report their verdict. They are not required to, nor do they, give any explanation whatever of their verdict. What went on in their secret session, whether they acted in accordance with their oaths and with the judge's instructions—this the judge very seldom learns.

But it is known, through late interviews with jurors, that juries frequently pay no heed to what the judge tells them to do. In many a civil trial the jurors decided for one side or another on the flip of a coin. In one instance the jurors agreed to draw a number between 1 and 100, the decision to be that of the juror whose age came closest to the number he drew. Then too, there are cases in which one of the jurors who disagreed with the others surrendered his honest judgment because he mistakenly thought he had to go along with the majority, or because the other jurors threatened him, or because he was anxious to go home.

Of course not all juries behave this way. But there is reason to believe that if full reports were made on all jury deliberations, public confidence in jury trials would be badly shaken.

In his 1932 book, *Convicting The Innocent,* Edwin Borchard, Yale law professor, revealed an alarming number of cases in which innocent men were convicted in jury trials—several of them for murdering persons who were later found to be still alive. He noted that when a sensational crime occurs the jury often succumbs to the public demand for a scapegoat.

Since Borchard's book there have been many other such demonstrated tragedies. In 1938, a New York jury found Bertram Campbell guilty of passing forged checks. In 1946, after Campbell had spent eight years in jail, another man confessed to the crime. The court then vacated Campbell's conviction. The state of New York awarded him $155,000 for the wrong it had done him. But he died three months later. In Colorado, Loren Hanby, after serving six years of a life sentence for murder, was found innocent and pardoned in 1946. Only last June, in New Jersey, Clifford T. Shephard received the governor's pardon as an innocent man after he had already completed his sentence of 18 months for forgery.

If there have been such mistaken verdicts in criminal cases, it is most unlikely that similar mistakes have not often happened in civil cases. A wrong decision in a civil case may also spell tragedy. When, through a jury's mistake, a man loses his savings, his business or his job, then his life may also be ruined.

In some criminal cases, like Campbell's, the mistakes were subsequently uncovered, and the innocent victims released from jail. But we can by no means be sure that all such blunders have been uncovered and rectified. Maybe—although I doubt it—all those mistakes would have been made just the same by judges deciding in jury-less cases. Maybe they were made by jurors who acted conscientiously. But no one knows. Some of these tragedies may well have resulted from dicebox verdicts or from other irrational and improper methods used by jurors. On the other hand, similar cases may have led to the acquittal of many guilty men.

You may ask: Won't judges do their best to discover whether the jurors have decided by lot or flipping a coin, or by otherwise disregarding the trial evidence or the legal rules? Won't most such verdicts be overturned? The answer, unfortunately, is no.

WHAT COURTS PREFER NOT TO KNOW

For the truth is that, in general, the courts don't want to know, and won't permit themselves to learn, how juries reach their verdicts. Most courts have this amazing rule: After a jury has reported its verdict and been discharged, the judge is ordinarily not allowed to listen to jurors who offer to swear that in the jury room the members of the panel had not complied with their oaths—although usually only by such testimony can jury-room misconduct be learned. In one typical case, after a Negro had been convicted of a crime, a Negro juror wanted to testify that he had voted for conviction because the 11 white jurors had intimidated him. The court said that, were this true, of course the conviction would be vacated. But it also said that this fact could not be proved by his testimony—the only method of proof available.

The courts give this reason for this rule: If a judge were allowed to consider such revelations by jurors after a case was over, then jurors might be subjected to improper pressures by the losing party to upset the verdict— and, under those pressures, the jurors might lie about what had occurred during their deliberations. That is an unconvincing reason: Jurors are not more likely than other men to testify falsely.

Some judges have given a different reason. If, said Judge Learned Hand, the courts were actually to apply the test "that every juror has been entirely without bias, and has based his vote solely upon evidence he has heard in court," it "is doubtful whether more than one in a hundred verdicts would stand such a test." No one knows, of course, whether that percentage is precisely correct. But it does seem that many courts are unwilling to inquire closely into this skeleton in our legal closet because of an apprehension that the disclosures would cause the collapse of the jury system—as it now operates.

We ought, however, not to blame jurors if they do not always behave as they are supposed to, since the duties imposed upon them are often impossible to discharge. For one thing, jurors are supposed to discard all sympathy, passion or prejudice. But do trial lawyers generally aim to pick jurors capable of acting impartially? Look at any one of a large number of books by reputable trial lawyers, books designed to be read by other lawyers, not non-lawyers. There you will find the lawyer advised that in many types of cases, he should seek the sort of juror who "will most naturally respond to an emotional appeal," and that, as the jurors' "judgment is more easily deceived" when their "passions are aroused," the lawyer has an obligation to make the best use of the weakness in his client's interest.

LAWYERS MISUSE ACTING TALENT

Prominent trial lawyers boast of "hypnotizing" juries. They regard themselves as master actors before audiences of 12 each. Since such are the acknowledged aims and beliefs of lawyers who daily deal with juries, it is folly to think that most jurors will be able to decide solely on the basis of the evidence. The jury lawyers, however, should not be censured for the methods they use. Most of those methods are the natural accompaniments of trial by jury.

Some lawyers maintain that since jurymen, in their own daily out-of-court affairs, reach many decisions about facts after listening to other persons, they are admirably equipped similarly to find facts in the courtroom. That is a slimsy argument. Not only are the issues of fact in some trials of an unusually complicated character—involving intricate details of engineering, chemistry, physics, medicine or accounting—but the surroundings in any jury trial differ greatly from those in which the jurors conduct their own affairs.

No juror is able to withdraw to his own room or office for individual reflection. After the judge instructs them, the jurors are cooped up in the jury room and urged to come to a joint decision in a few hours—scarcely a good atmosphere for conscientious deliberation. It is well known that sheer fatigue often plays its part in coercing a reluctant minority, or the desire to escape bickering and to get home. Even 12 able judges, conferring together in such circumstances, could not function effectively.

Another large obstacle with which jurors have to contend takes the form of "exclusionary" rules of evidence. Those rules bar the jury from hearing an immense amount of important testimony without which, often, no one—no matter how competent—could possibly get near the true facts of the case.

One such rule is that which, in jury trials excludes "hearsay"—so-called "secondhand" evidence, based not on a witness' own direct observation but on what someone else saw and told him.

Hearsay, to be sure, should always be cautiously used. But on its use depends 90 per cent of the world's work out of court. Much of the data utilized in making decisions by business men, government officials, legislatures and commanders of armies consist of such secondhand evidence. Yet we cut juries off from it—because we don't trust them to handle it wisely. And since, frequently, hearsay constitutes the sole available evidence of a crucial fact, the hearsay rule may leave a litigant without any proof of that fact.

A third well-nigh impossible task we ask of jurors is to perform prodigious feats of memory. Often the judge and the lawyers, trained listeners, forget just what a witness had said on the stand a day or two earlier; and when a judge tries a long non-jury case, before rendering his decision, he reads over a typewritten record of the testimony he has heard. But we pretend that jurors, given no transcript, and usually not allowed to take notes, will recall the evidence even in a trial lasting several weeks.

To make matters worse, not until all the evidence has been heard does the judge (by his instructions) let the jurors know the issues; that is, just what facts they are to look for.

In a trial there are many dull but significant stretches, with little lively interest for the jury. With no training in listening to testimony, the jurors' minds wander. I've often seen jurors actually sleep when some important witness was testifying. All lawyers know that a witness' demeanor—his tone of voice, gestures, use of his eyes—may furnish the most valuable clues to the reliability of his testimony. An inattentive juror will miss many such clues.

The legal rules with which jurors are entrusted as they go into their jury-room deliberations are yet another factor in making a juror's lot a difficult one. Do we or don't we want jurors to apply these rules which the judge's instructions and the jurors' oaths say they must apply? Some legal minds say yes, others no.

A BAR ASSOCIATION REPORT

Even a committee of the American Bar Association took a yes-and-no attitude on the issue. In a 1946 report it argued on the one hand that jurors should be told that, as "sworn officers of a court" they must "let the law prevail" without regard to their "likes or dislikes." Yet that same committee report also said that "the jury often stands as a bulwark between an individual . . . and an unreasonable law." Many distinguished lawyers have proclaimed it the glory of the jury system that, thanks to jury-room secrecy, juries can and do defy any law they deem undesirable and instead, apply secret laws the jurors choose to make. Yet you can't possibly square this notion of juries as secret lawmakers with the idea that, in the courts, a law should not mean one thing for one man on one day and something wholly different for another man the next. If each jury may apply different rules from those on the books, then each jury is a small, ephemeral legislature which may make an unpublished law for each particular case—surely a most undemocratic method of lawmaking.

In truth, jurors often fail to apply a rule enunciated by the judge not because they dislike it but because they pay no attention to it. They don't dislike the rule, which may be an excellent one. They dislike the defendant's lawyer, or they are sorry for the plaintiff—a poor widow or a beautiful brunette with soulful eyes. Or they are prejudiced against the defendant's chief witness, an old man who speaks broken English. I know of one case where a woman juror voted for the plaintiff because his lawyer kept his papers in a "nice neat stack."

Even more often, a jury disregards a legal rule because it just can't understand its niceties. For most legal rules contain legal words and phrases that through decades have acquired subtle shades of meaning. Even the relatively uncomplicated rules include such terms as "proximate cause," "willfully," "malicious," "good faith"—and about the legal significance of those, and other legal terms, hundreds of lawyers' treatises and court opinions have been written.

THE JUDGE'S LAW LECTURE

Since, as law-school examinations show, many second-year law students cannot fully comprehend the legal subtleties, it is ridiculous to suppose that they will be intelligible to jurors through the judge's brief law lecture to them. So the judge's charge to the jury about those rules is frequently a futile ritual.

The rise and fall of the jury's reputation is an interesting story. England was the home of the modern jury trial. Thence it was imported into the American colonies. With the colonists, juries became immensely popular because they resisted the Royalist judges who were regarded as oppressors. As a result, our state constitutions required jury trials in all cases which had been so tried at English common law.

From England, jury trials in criminal cases spread to almost all civilized countries. But in the twentieth century the jury's popularity markedly declined. Pre-Hitler Germany gave it up; so did some Swiss cantons; France grew increasingly critical. Most significant, England—before the advent of the . . . Socialist regime—virtually abandoned the jury except in major criminal suits, and of such suits relatively few are now tried by jury. More and more English litigants, dissatisfied with the incompetence of juries, came to prefer trials by judges. Canada has seen much the same development.

Since in none of the democracies, other than ours, today the jury is held in high esteem, it cannot be considered as an essential part of democratic government.

Every year in our own country thousands of civil cases are tried in which trial by jury is neither required nor permitted. For example, if John Doe sues a private company because he was injured by one of the firm's trucks, he may have a jury trial. But he may not have one if the truck was owned and operated by the United States government. So, also, there can be no jury trials in many suits in admiralty (as, for instances, suits for heavy property losses when ships collide), and in many other types of cases, such as those seeking accountings by trustees, or injunctions, or usually when the suit is against the estate of a dead man or a bankrupt.

If the jury is an indispensable bulwark of legal rights, as its admirers claim it is, then surely it is absurd and unjust to deny such a trial in the above-mentioned cases, for ordinarily they are fully as important as—often more important than—the civil cases where a jury can be demanded. Nevertheless, even the most devout jury worshipers do not suggest that we should cut out most of these judge trials; and they never explain why the judges should be trusted in those cases and not in all others.

Any visitor to the courts can see for himself the striking difference between a jury trial and a judge trial. A trial by jury is full of melodrama. The lawyers put on an act. In a juryless trial, the histrionics, the stagy tensions, the constant appeals to the emotions and the aroma of the prize ring vanish. The judge and the lawyers speak the same language; the judge, unlike the jury, is accustomed to courtroom ways.

Any able, well-trained trial judge understands the legal rules better than the wisest juror; he also has far more experience and skill in getting at the facts, in seeing through the lawyers' tricks of the trade, in detecting the lies of a "coached" witness, and in perceiving that an honest but timid witness, heckled by a lawyer, may give the appearance of speaking falsely.

Judges are human, therefore, fallible. No trial judge will ever be perfect. A skilled judge, however, has learned to discount and control his worst prejudices.

A few judges may perhaps be biased, bigoted or stupid; a very few may be, alas, corrupt. Indeed, I think that escape from decisions by unfit trial judges is the only good reason for trial by jury. But making all allowances for unfit judges, still no one would think of saying of decisions in judge trials the equivalent of what Judge Learned Hand said of jury verdicts—that probably not more than one per cent would stand up if tested by whether the jurors fully discharged their supposed duties.

Moreover, reformation of the bench is possible. We can get rid of the very few dishonest judges, and we can see to it that virtually all trial judges have a high degree of competence—by special training for trial judging and by providing that no lawyer may be eligible for the post of trial judge who has not passed stiff oral and written examinations. Nothing can be done to provide jurors possessed of anything like the same competence. For jurors are amateurs, and adequate judging is a job for professionals.

An increasing number of American lawyers and judges wish that we would abandon all jury trials in civil cases. If we do, it might be well to have suits tried before a bench of three judges, so the possible biases of each judge will tend to be modified.

Because of our traditions, almost no American lawyer would deprive a man accused of a crime—particularly a major crime—of the right to be tried by a jury if he so wished. Some lawyers, however—I am one of them —do not share the belief that a jury will invariably be more merciful than a judge to a defendant in such a plight.

At any rate, the accused should be told that, if he so desires, he need not go to trial before a jury, but may "waive" the right, as he is permitted to do in many states. He should always know—as today he often does not know because ordinarily his lawyer doesn't tell him—what he may be up against if he chooses a jury trial: that the jury may ignore the evidence, may be dominated by passion, or may decide the case by drawing lots.

TWO STATES LEAD THE WAY

In the federal courts the country over, juries still try more than 50 per cent of criminal cases; much the same is true in many states. But in Maryland, for more than 30 years, criminal trials by jury very often have been waived; in 1949, only 118 out of a total of 7,754 criminal cases in Baltimore were tried by jury. The story in Connecticut is much the same. Apparently in those states the lawyers and their clients have come to trust their judges. Perhaps before long the rest of the country will catch up with Maryland and Connecticut.

In civil suits, everywhere in America, "waiver" of jury trials is on the increase. But many such suits are still jury-tried (in the federal courts, about one third). And inasmuch as our constitutions require such trials, if requested in certain types of cases, and since many years will certainly elapse before those constitutional provisions could be wiped out by amendments, we must count on the continued use of juries for a long period. We ought, therefore to consider reforms of the jury system to purge it of its gravest evils; the worst of these evils stems from verdicts which cover up what the jurors did and found. Sometimes, however, some courts use another less opaque "special verdict": The judge requires the jury merely to report for instance whether Jones phoned Smith on June 5, 1948, or whether the signature on Brown's deed to his house is genuine. To facts thus specifically found the judge, not the jury, then applies the appropriate legal rules; the jurors need neither understand nor apply them. And because the jury may be unable to figure out whether its answers will favor one side or the other, the appeal to the jurors' prejudices sometimes may be far less effective. But the special verdict, at best, is no panacea, for it still leaves to the jury the difficult task of getting at the facts.

Whether or not the judge uses a special verdict, he ought to be obliged at the trial's opening to give the jurors a tentative rough ouline of the issues, so that, while listening to the evidence, they may know what facts to look for. There also is every reason why, to aid their memory, the jurors should be permitted to take with them into the jury room a written transcript of the evidence and of the judge's charge.

One helpful device is now too rarely employed: When some of the facts of a case are complex, the judge refers them to an expert; the expert's report is presented to the jury—although they are not obliged to accept it.

At one time, in England and in some of our own states, jurors were selected because of their peculiar knowledge of the customs of a particular trade in which the parties to the suit were engaged. "Special juries" of that kind, often far more skillful in finding facts than the usual jury, might well again be employed.

Reforms in selection of prospective jurors have thus far been rather feeble. Certainly, we should test each juror's eyesight and hearing before he enters the jury box. In some cities no one can obtain a license to drive a car who hasn't passed a psychiatric test; because deciding court cases is at least as serious as driving through traffic, we ought similarly to screen prospective jurymen.

APTITUDE TESTS FOR JURORS

In a widely approved statement, the late Merrill Otis, federal district judge in Missouri, said a few years ago that serious injustices are bound to happen unless all jurors have the "capacity quickly to comprehend the applicable law and intelligently to apply it." He also said that no more than one man in ten possesses that capacity. To restrict juries to such unusual men, he proposed this method: Enact some very generally worded high standards for jury service, and take care of choosing the officials who select those citizens eligible to become jurors. Some states have adopted that method and have obtained somewhat more competent juries. But it's unbelievable that any such simple expedient will give us jurymen able quickly to understand and to apply complicated legal rules. A Los Angeles practice has more merit: A prospective juror must meet oral and written aptitude tests.

But those tests can hit the high spots only. A more helpful proposal is that of barring from jury service any person who has not attended and passed a detailed course, to be given in the public high schools, on the function of the jury and the nature of jury trials. (I won't guarantee the constitutionality of such a plan.) With better equipped jurors, we could well afford to eliminate most of the "exclusionary" evidence rules, especially the rule which bars "hearsay."

Everyone knows it's wrong for an outsider to talk to a juror about a case while it is on trial. Yet, during an important criminal trial, newsmen and radio commentators in effect insinuate themselves into each juror's home to comment on the defendant's guilt or innocence.

ANOTHER SOURCE OF PREJUDICE

Since it is all but impossible to suppose that jurors won't read the papers and listen to the radio, such discussions, which may gravely prejudice the jury for or against the defendant, add seriously to the difficulties of trial by jury, as United States Supreme Court Justice Robert Jackson said in a speech some months ago. The English courts forbid and punish such publications. (The English press did not comment on the . . . case of Klaus Fuchs, the atomic-secrets spy, until it ended.)

The United States Supreme Court has held that almost no such publications during a judge trial may be published, but has left open the question as it applies to jury trials. Some lawyers, who think that a judge should know how to and have the courage to withstand press-pressures, hope the Supreme Court will recognize that jurors are more susceptible. Perhaps, as an alternative, our editors and news commentators, if made aware of the gravity of the problem, will exercise self-restraint.

To sum up, here are the reforms I think would improve our jury system: (1) Use "special" or "fact" verdicts in most cases. (2) Have the judge, at the trial's beginning, roughly outline the issues for the jurors. (3) Let the jurors take with them to the jury room a transcript of the evidence and of the judge's charge. (4) Supply the jury with an expert's report of complicated facts. (5) Employ, in many cases, "special juries" composed of jurors having knowledge of the customs of the trade involved. (6) Strictly enforce the ban against jurors who have defective hearing or eyesight or who are physically or mentally ill. (7) Require all prospective jurors to take a detailed course of study dealing with the function of juries. (8) Eliminate many of the "exclusionary" evidence rules. (9) Discourage publication, in the press or on the air, of anything but straight reporting of the courtroom evidence in a jury trial, until the case ends.

Although trial by jury can be improved, in my opinion it will remain the weakest spot in our judicial system—reform it as we may. But the judges (like me) who want to see the civil jury abolished and the use of the criminal jury limited, will of course, as long as the jury system endures, comply with their oaths of office and strive to make the jury system work as best it can.

THE ESSENTIALS OF A SOUND JUDICIAL SYSTEM
Arthur T. Vanderbilt

The late Arthur T. Vanderbilt, Chief Justice of New Jersey's highest court, was one of the best-known jurists in the United States. He devoted a lifetime to judicial reform, finally achieving for his own state a judiciary acclaimed as second to none. He was the author of *Judges and Jurors: Their Functions, Qualifications and Selection; Men and Measures in the Law; Studying Law;* and other publications.

Men inevitably have disputes, and it is one of the great functions of the courts to adjudicate them according to law. This is termed the administration of civil justice. Men also commit offenses against the laws provided for the protection of all of us, and at the suit of the state the courts pass on the question of their guilt and enforce the law against any wrongdoers in an effort to protect society. This we call the administration of criminal justice Of the two, although most people, including many lawyers who should know better, do not seem to realize it, the administration of criminal law is by far the more important. Of what value is a civil right under a contract or to a piece of property, or even the right to life itself, if its owner cannot enjoy it because of some breakdown in the enforcement of the criminal law? Going a step further and looking at both the civil and criminal law, of what real worth are the fundamental rights guaranteed by our federal and state constitutions if they cannot be enforced in a fair trial? In the last analysis, then, the right to a fair trial is the most fundamental of all rights, for without it all other rights are mere words, empty and meaningless.

From this point of view the judiciary, though the weakest of the three great departments of government—"It has no influence over either the sword or the purse," to quote the *Federalist*—is the most important of all to the citizen in distress and looking for a fair trial, either civil or criminal. Everything that is necessary to accord him a fair trial is an essential of a sound judicial system. Here at least is one point where there is no conflict between the needs of the individual and of the public.

Fortunately for us all the essentials of a sound judicial system are relatively few in number and are well known to the legal profession from centuries of experience (both good and bad, I hasten to add). All we have to do to attain a sound judicial establishment is to overcome our professional inertia and selfishness and adopt the standards of judicial administration that every intelligent and public-spirited lawyer (my adjectives, you will note, limit the class considerably) knows should long since have been adopted . . . Nothing else . . . would contribute so much to restoring the faith in government and the respect for law so essential to the preservation of democratic, representative government.

From *Northwestern University Law Review,* March-April, 1953. Reprinted by permission.

Let me enumerate and comment briefly on the several essentials of a sound judicial system as I see them:

1. The first essential of a sound judicial establishment is a simple system of courts, for the work of the best bench and bar may be greatly handicapped by a multiplicity of courts with overlapping jurisdictions. Lord Coke lists 74 courts in his *Fourth Institute,* but three are all that are needed in a modern judicial establishment: (1) a local court of limited civil and criminal jurisdiction, (2) a trial court of general statewide jurisdiction, and (3) an appellate court or courts, depending on the needs of the particular state. Although only three courts are called for, instead of the many courts with special jurisdictions as we now have in many states, there may well be—indeed there should be—considerable specialization by judges in the trial courts. Without limiting the general jurisdiction of each trial judge, he should be assigned to a division of his court specializing in the kind of work for which he is best qualified—criminal, civil (generally with a jury), equity, probate, juvenile, traffic, and the like. Some very good equity judges shrink from jury work and some very good law judges dislike equity. For sound judicial administration, therefore, someone should have the power to assign the judges where they are needed and to the work for which they are best fitted. Because this power of assignment is a delicate one to be exercised only on mature reflection for the best interest of the judicial establishment as a whole, it may best be committed to the chief judicial officer in the state and he, in turn, would do well to seek the advice of his colleagues, even though the ultimate responsibility for assignments must be solely his.

2. The second essential of a sound judicial system is, of course, a corps of judges, each of them utterly independent and beholden only to the law and to the Constitution, thoroughly grounded in his knowledge of the law and of human nature, including its political manifestations, experienced at the bar in either trial or appellate work and preferably in both, of such a temperament that he can hear both sides of a case before making up his mind, devoted to the law and justice, industrious, and, above all, honest and believed to be honest. These standards necessarily exclude all judges who are not members of the bar and all part-time judges who are judges one minute and practicing lawyers the next. Relatively few judges have all these qualifications and yet are there any of them that you would dare to term superfluous? Of course, some good judges have learned their law after ascending the bench, and more have acquired courtroom experience as judges rather than as lawyers, but either process is an expensive and unsatisfactory one both for the litigants and the public and would not be tolerated in business. Some may question my insistence on a knowledge of man as a political animal, but politics plays so large a part in American life that a judge to be competent must know what it is all about. Understanding politics, however, is one thing; playing politics from the bench is something far different. It is utterly reprehensible.

How are we to recruit judges such as I have been describing? There is, it must be frankly admitted, no entirely foolproof way of selecting judges. The practice of executive appointment from among the leaders of the trial and appellate bar, pursued in all common-law countries except our own, produces the best results, but even so, every now and then a distinguished barrister proves to be a mediocre judge. No system of selection could be worse, however, than popular elections on party tickets along with a host of other national, state, and local party candidates running for a wide variety of offices . . . .

The plain truth is that popular, partisan judicial elections would have failed long since were it not for the fact that in state after state about one-third of the judges in office die or resign giving the governor an opportunity to make ad interim appointments. . . .

There is much to be said for requiring . . . the appointment of all judges on a bipartisan basis. Justice, on principle, should be bipartisan. . . . Its administration should not be vested in a single party. Bipartisan appointments are the best way of proving to the public that one party does not control the courts and that the courts are not in politics. The matter is of especial importance in the decision of highly controversial political issues. If all the judges in a bipartisan court, regardless of party affiliations, concur in the decision of such an issue, as they frequently do, their decision carries a weight with the public that an opinion from a partisan bench could not possibly do. I am speaking from experience because in New Jersey, without any constitutional or statutory requirement, we have had a bipartisan judiciary for nearly a hundred years.

3. Honest and intelligent juries, representing a cross-section of the honest and intelligent citizenry of a county, are as essential to the administration of justice as upright and learned judges. It is a mockery of justice to go through the form of a trial with a dishonest or unintelligent juror in the jury box. The jury is an integral part of the administration of justice and the selection of the panel from which juries are drawn should therefore be entrusted to the court or to commissioners appointed by the courts. This has been done in thirty-three states, but in the remaining fifteen the selection of the jury panel is in political hands, with the inevitable resultant dangers to the administration of justice.

4. In addition to good judges and good jurors, we must have honorable, well educated lawyers and an effective organization of the bar. It is too much to expect that the work of judges or of juries will often rise much above the level of the work of the lawyers appearing in the cases the judges and juries decide. . . .

The complexities of our age call for more than individually good lawyers. We need a good organized bar. And how may we recognize a good bar? Without attempting a definition, I venture to say that a good bar will feel a very real sense of responsibility for the administration of justice, for the selection of judges and jurors, for legal education both before and after admission, for unauthorized practice of the law, for improving the substantive law, and for encouraging good government. A large order, you will say, but what may we omit without loss to both the profession and the public?

5. A simple court structure, good judges, jurors, and lawyers—what more do we need? We must have competent court clerks, stenographic reporters, and bailiffs, but above all we need an administrative judge and his *alter ego,* an administrative director of the courts working under him, to supervise the judicial system and to see that it functions effectively as a business organization. The Constitution of New Jersey was the first to declare that "The Chief Justice of the Supreme Court shall be the administrative head of all the courts in the state" and that "He shall appoint an administrative director of the courts to serve at his pleasure." I have found that my administrative work takes from a third to half of my time and all the time, of course, of the administrative directors and his staff. What other state-wide business do you know of that attempts to operate without management, without supervision, without operating statistics, without periodic conferences of its key personnel, or without administrative rules? When you think of the lack of all these factors in most of our court systems, the wonder is that the judicial branch of our government has worked as well as it has.

With the right kind of courts, judges, jurors, lawyers, court officers, and administrative organization available, what else is needed for a sound judicial system suited to the needs of these troublesome times? Manifestly the next thing that is needed is a realization by all concerned of the defects of the judicial establishment, especially those defects which are so obvious that the people are complaining of them. These defects may be grouped under three heads: inexcusable delays, the lack of a fair trial on the merits of each case, and bad judicial manners. I will next discuss these defects in the order named.

6. Subordinate only to the complaint against dishonest judges is the popular resentment of the law's delays. The grievance is an ancient one. We find it mentioned in Magna Carta. Hamlet comments on it. Every step in the process of litigation, of course, takes time, but that is not what the public is complaining of. What the people object to is unnecessary delays. Often delays that are attributed to the courts should really be ascribed to the lawyers. I know of one New England state where the judges are unusually prompt in their decisions, but in which cases are often delayed by the bad habits of lawyers. The judges there owe the public and themselves the duty of placing the blame where it belongs.

Most of the delays of which complaint is made are quite avoidable. They fall into three classes:

First of all, litigants, witnesses, and jurors alike get very much annoyed when the judge fails to open court at the appointed hour. No single judicial fault, save lack of integrity, can do so much to create a bad impression. The failure of a judge to appear in court on time indicates to laymen his lack of interest in his judicial work and his unwillingness to conform to the rules of court, while insisting that others conform, as well as a failure to appreciate the value of others' time. It irritates the laymen's sense of equality, for with all their respect for the law and for judicial office as symbolizing the law, people regard a judge as a man. They have been taught, have they not, that all men are equal, and a judge should be wise enough to recognize their teaching. I have discovered that this bad judicial habit could be cured only by a positive rule requiring the opening of court at a fixed hour throughout the state. Here again a strong example has proved helpful; if the seven justices of our supreme court can get to the state house from all over the state in time to open court at ten o'clock, surely any judge can manage to get to his nearby county seat by the same hour. To some of you this may seem a small matter and unworthy even of mention here, but in actual practice it is an essential rule of judicial administration.

The second cause of complaint about the law's delays is the failure to get on to trial after all the necessary preliminaries of pleading and pretrial procedures have been disposed of. Here let me observe that a judge can never do his best work when he is asked to tackle a task which he knows is impossible of accomplishment, when he sees that for every case he tries two are being added to his list. Where arrearages have accumulated, the number of judges must be increased, either temporarily or permanently. It is a curious but nevertheless demonstrable judicial fact that two judges working on the same calendar can dispose of twice as many cases as they could working separately in different courthouses. The extent to which this principle may be applied depends upon the number of available courtrooms, the number of available trial judges, and the number of available trial lawyers. But subject to these limitations, an increase in the number of judges, either permanently or temporarily, at the congested spot is the first step in eliminating delays in bringing cases on to trial. This requires giving to someone, preferably to the chief justice, the power to assign the trial judges to those counties where they are most needed. Whatever success we have had in New Jersey in clearing our calendars—some cases in Chancery as much as ten or twenty years old—I think must be attributed in large measure to the power given by our Constitution to the chief justice to assign judges. In Chancery matters we cleared the decks within six months. On the law side within two years we disposed of all arrearages in sixteen of our twenty-one counties so that cases could be tried within three or four months after they were started, and in the remaining five counties we obtained a similar state of currency within the third court year—a striking contrast to the delays of the old system, in which one not infrequently had to wait two or three years for a jury trial.

In the work of clearing the dockets compulsory pretrial conferences, in all court cases except divorce cases, have also played a large part, for we have discovered that in county after county numerous cases have been settled before trial as a result of what has developed at the pretrial conference. The pretrial conference is an invaluable feature of adequate judicial administration and I shall refer to it again in dealing with trials on the merits where I deem it even more important. . . . The final cause of delay is the failure of the judge to promptly decide a case after he has heard the testimony, read the briefs (in advance of the arguments, of course), and heard the arguments of counsel. These delays in deciding matters are largely a matter of bad judicial habit. A judge can only decide one case at a time. No judge, moreover, will ever know more about a given case than he does when the testimony is fresh in his mind and while the arguments of counsel are still ringing in his ears. We in New Jersey have suffered much in the past from this bad judicial habit of delaying decisions. Some of our vice-chancellors were truly judicial descendants of Lord Eldon. For them to delay a decision six, eight, ten, or even twelve years was not unknown. Four years ago when our new system started I had to assign three judges to work for several weeks on the arrears of one distinguished vice-chancellor who had retired leaving a large number of cases undecided, some dating back more than six years. This bad habit of delaying decisions is not an easy one to break, but our administrative rule requiring all motions to be decided as a matter of routine within ten days, all cases to be disposed of within four weeks after trial, and all motions and cases heard but undecided to be reported in the judge's weekly report has completely eliminated the public's justifiable criticism of this phase of the law's delays. Most judges would rather decide a case than report it as undecided. The judge's weekly report is therefore an indispensable aid to sound judicial administration, and I shall have more to say of it in another connection.

7. The next great popular grievance against the courts is a failure in too many cases to get a decision on the merits. All too often the tendency is for a trial to become a battle between opposing counsel rather than an orderly, rational search for the truth on the merits of the controversy. There can be no doubt of the justice of this complaint. It is a complaint that is more difficult to overcome than the dishonesty—or the reputation therefore —of some judges or the law's delays. Three factors in particular contribute to this great evil. The first is the popular notion that a trial, and especially a criminal trial, is a sporting event rather than an orderly search for truth with justice as its great objective. In all too many communities counsel are still rated primarily for their histrionic ability. Secondly, this improper attitude toward litigation has been heightened by the fact that in the second quarter of the nineteenth century in many of the states the chief powers of the common-law trial judge were taken away from him by legislation as part of the equalitarian and antiprofessional revolt that culminated in the triumph of Jacksonian democracy. In many states the trial judge was deprived of the right to put questions to the witnesses even when they were necessary to bring out the truth. He was stripped of the right to organize the evidence into a systematic whole in his charge to the jury and to comment in his charge on the testimony of the witnesses. He was even shorn of his right to charge the jury in his own language, being obliged to charge in the technical language of the requests to charge submitted to him by counsel. Moreover, his charge so-called but really his selection between the plaintiff's or the defendant's requests to charge, came before the summation to the jury by the

defendant's and the plaintiff's counsel, so that whatever the judge said was quite forgotten by the jury after it had listened to the lawyers' barrage and counterbarrage of eloquence. The third cause of difficulty in the trial courts is the fact that the rules of pleading practice, and procedure were prescribed by the legislature and in many states became increasingly complicated as a result of continuous legislative tinkering, with the result that the trial judge was often forced by statute to do things in the course of the trial that were obviously unjust and contrary to common sense. The trial judge was thus reduced to the position of an umpire all but gagged and blindfolded.

The situation I am portraying is by no means fanciful. In this age of scientific inquiry, there are still twenty states in which the judge is not allowed to sum up the evidence, thirty-six states in which he is not allowed to comment on the evidence, twenty states where the instructions precede the final argument of counsel, and three states in which, believe it or not, the court must instruct the jury that his statements of the law are purely advisory and that it has the right in criminal cases to find the law as well as the facts! And yet with these odd notions of trial procedure we still expect judges and juries to do justice.

The first step in remedying the situation is, of course, to restore to the trial judge his common law power to preside effectively at the trial. This is easier said than done. Many counsel cling tenaciously to their prerogative of surprise in the courtroom, to their concept of a trial as a battle of wits between two lawyers rather than a search for the truth, to the notion that the judge should be seen but not heard. Until these false notions are banished, justice will often be but a sham and a mockery.

The next step is to give the rule-making power to the highest court in each state. After what has been accomplished in the federal courts through the judicial exercise of the rule-making power, there should be no need of any argument to establish its advantage over legislative codes. The results of judicial rule-making speak for themselves. I doubt very much that strict judicial rule-making—and by that I mean the making of rules by the judges alone—would have been a great improvement on codes and statutes had not the methods pursued by the United States Supreme Court in drafting the Rules of Civil and Criminal Procedure insured the workability of its rules. Not only were the rules drafted by advisory committees of experts appointed by the court, but they were submitted and resubmitted to the criticism of the bench and bar throughout the country. After ten years of use the Civil Rules have again been reworked by the same process and over half of them have been amended. This method gives the court the benefit of the experience of both trial judges and practicing lawyers. The process of rule-making should be continuous. Judicial conferences or judicial councils in the several states should annually call for suggestions from the bench and bar and these suggestions shoud be carefully debated each year for the benefit of the supreme court in its rule-making capacity. Through such a continuous process, and through this process only, may we hope for a system of procedure that will be at all times adapted to its purpose and that will be at all times subordinate to establishing the substantive rights of the litigants.

A third step in obtaining a trial on the merits rather than a theatrical performance is the full use of modern pretrial procedures, such as interrogatories, depositions, examinations before trial, inspections and the like, culminating in a pretrial conference at which the pleadings are reviewed to see how they can be simplified and the issues are restated as preliminaries to seeing what facts may be stipulated and what documents may be admitted so as to shorten the trial. The pretrial conference gives counsel an opportunity, if they so desire, to canvass the possibilities of settlement, but the judge, of course, must never attempt to force a settlement. The most important aspect of pretrial conferences is not that many cases are customarily settled as a result of each party facing the facts on both sides for the first time under expert guidance, nor is it that the trial time of each case is greatly reduced. The great advantage of pretrial conferences is that the judge has a preview of what will be coming at the trial, and he can, if he thinks it necessary in an unusual case, direct the filing of briefs in advance of the trial. No longer does he have to fumble through the pleadings to find out what the case is all about, while endeavoring to listen to the opening statements of counsel. No longer need he guess the answer to novel questions of law. He has a complete outline of the trial before him in the form of the pretrial conference order and he is master of the situation from the outset.

8. The third significant cause of public discontent with the courts springs from an occasional exhibition of judicial bad manners. There is less of it in the appellate courts than in the trial courts for the reason, among others, that the process of legal argument does not so often lead to the clashes that characterize the presentation of testimony. Judging from the number of complaints that come my way, judicial discourtesy is very much more prevalent in the criminal courts of limited jurisdiction than in either the general trial courts or the local civil courts. This may be accounted for in part by the fact that a large number of municipal magistrates are still laymen, in part by the difference in the mental attitude of the attorneys appearing in the local criminal courts, and in part by the volume of work in some of these courts. But whatever the cause there can be no excuse whatsoever for judicial discourtesy. A judge's bad manners can only serve to bring the administration of justice into disrepute. Establishing conditions under which a judge may work honestly and keep his self-respect will go a long way toward reducing complaints on this score. A judge who is not beholden to anyone and who is up to date with his work is less likely to be irritable than one who is under obligations and fears that others know it, or who is behind with his work. But whatever the cause, an irritable judge cannot be justified or tolerated in view of the disrespect for law which he inevitably creates. Requiring a judge, even of a local court, to wear a judicial robe has a marked tendency to increase decorum in the courtroom. It helps to keep court officers in their place. Every witness should stand and everyone in the

room should remain silent while the oath is being administered to the witness by the judge himself. Applying to the local criminal courts the same rules of conduct as are applied in other courts is equally essential. But the affirmative way of meeting any charges of discourtesy in the local criminal courts is for the judge to take the necessary minute or two to explain to each defendant just why he is being found guilty and why the particular sentence is being imposed on him. This can be done in a friendly manner so as to make clear the purpose of the sentence, whether it be intended as punishment for a violation of the law or as a deterrent for the purpose of saving life and limb. I know of one judge who by doing just this had eighty per cent of his "customers" thank him publicly for his courtesy, while at the same time he had increased the amount of his fines over sixty per cent. There is much to be said for the practice of the English chancellor who, when asked his formula for selecting judges, replied, "I pick a gentleman and if he knows a little law so much the better." We need gentlemen in our local courts quite as much as in our courts of general jurisdiction.

While we are awaiting the judicial millennium, perhaps the most effective way of counselling courtesy is for the chief justice to bring to the attention of the individual judge every charge of discourtesy by sending him a copy of any complaint against him and asking for his version of the facts. Sometimes the judicial alibis are so thin as to be almost transparent and they are often accompanied by a considerable show of indignation, but it is noticeable that following such correspondence complaints cease to come from the particular community again. Moreover, the news of such correspondence travels fast throughout a county by what is commonly known as "the grapevine" and serves as a deterrent to other judges. From my experience I arrive at another principle of judicial administration. Every complaint should promptly receive the chief justice's personal attention and should be pursued to a conclusion both with the complainant and with the judge against whom the complaint is made. . . .

9. Judges as well as litigants have their complaints. A principle of judicial administration, rarely discussed publicly but never out of the minds of the judges is the fair division of work. Some judges are much more effective in their work than others; some judges are reversed less than others; some judges give more satisfaction to the bar and to the public than others; and some judges are more conscientious, more devoted to their work than others. These individual differences cannot be changed administratively, but there should be equality in the number of hours each judge of the same court spends in the courtroom. This may be accomplished by having each judge make a weekly report of the number of hours he has spent on the bench each court day, the number of cases and motions he has heard and disposed of, and the number of cases and motions he has heard but has not disposed of, with the reasons therefor. With this information available in summarized form the chief justice is in a position not only to make assignment of the judges to meet emergencies at the time they arise without waiting until a heavy list has been allowed to accumulate in a particular county, but also

to prevent inequalities in work. You may ask, how will the making of a weekly report make an indolent judge work. The chief justice and his administrative director cannot hope to make a lazy judge work, and neither of them should be expected to be a policeman, but if summaries of these weekly reports are circularized among the judges in each court, it is truly remarkable how the relatively few laggards will mend their ways rather than incur the silent or occasionally vocal censure of their brother judges.

10. Statistics from the judges' weekly reports and from other data supplied by the court clerks are compiled in weekly and monthly reports by the administrative director, and these in turn are combined into quarterly and annual reports. In these reports there are comparative summaries of the work of the individual judges which disclose to every judge and to the public whether his record is above or below the average for his court. In the relatively few states where any judicial statistics at all are gathered, they have all too generally been compiled long after the event. I call these "dead" or historical statistics because for the most part they are useless in affecting the work of the judicial establishment currently. After working with "live" statistics for four years, I am so impressed with their importance that I do not see how a judicial system can function effectively without them any more than a business could be run without current reports from its accounting department. By using "live" statistics and by assigning our judges on the basis of such statistics where they were most needed and to the kind of work they could best do, we not only increased the output of our general trial courts ninety-eight per cent in the first year and an additional twenty per cent in the second year—with twenty per cent fewer judges—but we have also improved the judges' working conditions and the quality of their work immeasurably. I am therefore rather emphatic in asserting that "live" statistics assembled into weekly, monthly, quarterly, and annual reports, both for the use of the chief justice and the judges themselves and for information of the public, are an essential of orderly judicial administration.

The examination of these weekly, monthly, quarterly and annual reports, the assignment of judges and the general supervision of their work, the investigation of complaints from individuals or bar associations, conferences with individual judges concerning their work, attendance every few months at informal meetings of the judges of each court and each division thereof (I would list such meetings, which generally are dinner meetings with their friendly personal contacts, as indispensable to sound judicial administration) all put a heavy burden on the chief justice of a state who is given broad powers of administration, even though he has the aid of a competent administrative director of the courts and staff. I am convinced from my experience, however, that all of these things are as indispensable to the functioning of an effective judicial establishment as they are to a business organization. Yet strangely enough those powers are rarely granted. Indeed, in twelve states the chief justice shifts every year or so and in two of these states, believe it or not, every six months. It is not without political significance that these short terms are so arranged that the title goes to a judge who is about to run for reelection. Clearly, it is essential for the proper administration of justice that there be a chief justice with a substantial term of office and with the power to call for reports, to collect "live" statistics, to assign the judges, to supervise the work of all the courts including the local criminal courts, to hold informal conferences with the judges, and to call judicial conferences in which the bar and the public are liberally represented to discuss the work of the judicial establishment.

The burden of this work necessitates giving the chief justice an administrative director of the courts to act as his *alter ego* in attending to the multitudinous details of running a great statewide business with branches in every county and in every community of the state. Time will not permit me to detail the wide variety of his activities. Such an officer must not only be a good lawyer and a diplomat versed in the ways of judges, but he must have executive ability and be skilled in the dispatch of business. Such an administrative director is, it goes without saying, a *sine qua non* of successful judicial administration.

The final essential of a sound judicial system is an abiding conviction, consistently acted upon by everyone in the judicial establishment, that the law and the courts exist not for the benefit of judges or lawyers or court officers who are merely the servants of the law, but for the benefit of the litigants and of the state.

There is nothing esoteric about these essentials of a sound judicial system! They are all quite obvious. They are not difficult to put into effect once there is the will to do so. They must be achieved in every state if we are to have an administration of justice worthy of the name. There can be no doubt as to the importance to us all of attaining such a goal if our kind of government is to function as it should. The only question is whether the judges and lawyers in each state will take the leadership in fulfilling the foremost obligation of the profession to society or whether they will abdicate to laymen. Once we become convinced of this self-evident truth, the law becomes our mission in the sense so eloquently described by Holmes:

> Law is the business to which my life is devoted, and I should show less than devotion if I did not do what in me lies to improve it, and, when I perceive what seems to me the ideal of its future, if I hesitated to point it out and to press toward it with all my heart.

Local government in America poses both paradoxes and problems in abundance. Despite its being "closest to the people," it is an area of public indifference, apathy and ignorance. The public's lack of knowledge of the legislative and administrative arrangements of its home towns is profound. The general lack of interest is shown by the small participation in local elections—"off-year elections," as they are labeled in tribute to their "insignificance." Yet local America is an area of ever-increasing demands for governmental services—for water supply, sewage disposal, police and fire protection—all provided little more than a century ago by private enterprise. The earlier self-sufficiency is impossible in a modern urban society whose population now expects full metropolitan services throughout the countryside.

In local government the predominant twentieth century public concern has been with form and structure, as attested by the successive zeal for commission plans, or for council-manager arrangements, as alternatives to the mayoral system. Yet in spite of these concerns, one of our major unsolved problems is faulty structure, demonstrated in the proliferation of special districts, in the retention of hundreds of tiny government units.

In local government there has been increasing centralization, along with ever-stronger insistence on a theory of *de*centralization. The inadequacies of local leadership, deficiencies of local tax base, and the shortsighted pressures of provincial interest groups have caused citizens to turn first to the state and then increasingly to the federal government for solution to local problems. At the same time, demands for greater "local self-reliance" have become more vociferous. In short, in local government "more home rule" has been widely touted as the answer to the many metropolitan problems, even as local demands have increasingly necessitated a regional solution and hence, in all likelihood, *less* home rule.

Local government possesses a democratic potential as yet unrealized. In spite of all its demonstrated shortcomings and past failures, it continues to offer an arena for decentralized, locally-adapted administration, to afford a laboratory for experiments in government, and to provide a school for citizenship, a training ground for participation in government. If the potential is to be realized, however, better public understanding is necessary.

The basic structure of local government in all our states save the newest two (Alaska and Hawaii) is incredibly complex. Across America there exist multiple layers below the federal and state systems. The average suburbanite may live under six and sometimes as many as nine or ten separate governmental units; only the dweller in a large city is likely to be subject to as few as two. There are geographical subdivisions, the counties and towns;

there are incorporated entities, the cities and villages; and there are thousands of special districts with varying functions and varying degrees of independence.

Counties exist as subdivisions of every state of the union save two—Connecticut, where they were only recently abolished, and Alaska where the *borough* is a close counterpart. (In Louisiana similar subdivisions are called *parishes.*) County-level government is relatively unimportant in the New England states; elsewhere, it is highly significant, providing such major services as public welfare, and highway construction and maintenance (except in North Carolina).

Towns (or townships as they are designated in some states) are geographical subdivisions of the counties. They exist only north of the Mason-Dixon line, and as far west as the Great Plains. In New England, they dominate the counties, in New York and Pennsylvania they share their importance; but across the Midwest they become increasingly subordinate.

Among the *special districts,* education districts are nearly universal and the most powerful. Governed for the most part by independently elected boards, they generally possess their own power of taxation. Other varieties of district (sometimes called *ad hoc*) exist for a multitude of purposes ranging from the collection of duck waste (on Long Island) to suburban planning. Water supply, sewage disposal, fire and police protection are among the most common. While education districts tend to be larger and to cover the entire area of the state, *ad hoc* districts are limited to those localities where the residents have agreed upon their formation. Frequently their existence is disguised by the town's issuance of consolidated tax bills, in which the levy of each district constitutes a separate item. Nonetheless they are separate and distinct units of local government.

The core problems of local government are both political and structural. Irresponsibility, compounded by a low order of visibility, is perhaps the most serious of the political problems. In areas of one-party dominance (far more widespread than sometimes recognized), the lack of an effective opposition may permit a majority party to rule in perpetuity, sometimes with callous disregard for the public interest. In other one-sided districts, the minority may have become the "captive" of the majority—either "bought off," or perhaps merely persuaded that its own best interests lie in quiet, restrained commentary. Elsewhere the personal dictates of a powerful boss may shape the entire policy outlook of a complaisant, well-fed following.

Press and public indifference frequently contribute to these problems. It is difficult for local government to be visible if adequate press coverage or vigorous critical commentary is lacking. Even with a vigilant press, the public may respond with a "what's the use?" attitude of despair or accept a passive philosophy that fails to hold accountable the trustees of its own will.

Often the lack of public interest is blended with a lack of public understanding. The prevalent "something-for-nothing" philosophy has repeatedly undermined the cause of good government. The expectation that high-level urban services can be provided with low-level rural taxes is one evidence of this philosophy. Another is the widespread resistance to scientific reassessment of real property, based on the mistaken notion that below-market appraisal automatically means a lesser share of the tax burden. Another difficulty is the feeling that the shortcomings of government can be readily solved by some structural reform—hiring a city manager, perhaps, or consolidating a few departments, or some electoral innovation—the direct primary, the initiative, or the recall.

Structural defects constitute a second major problem area, even though experience has demonstrated that while structural reform may be necessary, it alone is never sufficient to produce good government. The atomization of government, the attempt to use fractional jurisdictions and piecemeal administration to provide vast, interrelated services will obviously doom even the best political efforts. The most competent and well-intentioned local officials frequently balk at cooperation with neighboring governments in the face of constituent opposition. Local voters all too often have exhibited the attitude voiced by one such group, "Our houses are on top of the hill. Why should we join in a drainage district that will benefit only those at the bottom?"

Not all local officials are competent and qualified for the demands of modern service-oriented administration. Since many of them are part-time or retired amateurs, professional tasks such as assessment and tax collection are often bungled. With county governments almost invariably lacking in any single administrative or executive head, it is not surprising that the performance of subordinates goes unrewarded or uncriticized and that tenure is determined primarily by political affiliation.

The situation in American local government is admittedly grim in terms of the problems that must be faced. Nonetheless, the past and present accomplishments of a few communities give hope for the future. Certain needs are already apparent, such as the need for consolidation of governmental structure. And yet, as the experience of cities as widely separate as Philadelphia and Honolulu has demonstrated, the existence of a streamlined, unified county–city government headed by a newly strengthened mayor aided by an appointive chief administrative officer or managing director does not guarantee a solution for problems which are principally political. Only greater visibility, better accountability *to* the public and an acceptance of much more responsibility *by* the public seem likely to improve the level of local government in action.

A HOME RULE PUZZLE
Kenneth C. Tollenaar

Kenneth C. Tollenaar is executive secretary of the Association of Oregon Counties. He was formerly assistant director of the Bureau of Municipal Research and Service of the University of Oregon, in charge of its Portland Office, and executive secretary of Oregon's Legislative Interim Committee on Local Government.

Perhaps it was reasonable in 1916 for Howard Lee McBain to describe the city as "a natural economic and sociological unit" and "a perfectly logical governmental unit." By the time of Joseph D. McGoldrick's follow-up home rule study in 1933, however, it was difficult to make such generalizations. "We are concerned," said McGoldrick, "with the development of a municipal home rule broad enough to include not merely the skyscraper that surmounts our modern city but the slums in its shadow and the homes of all those who daily come to work in it."

In a contemporary restatement of the same theme, the Kestnbaum commission observed: "Self-determination in one isolated unit of a large community often restricts the opportunity for genuine home rule in the whole community."

If home rule is to be developed and applied at the metropolitan level, then careful consideration must be given to the present distribution of home rule powers among municipalities and to adjustments in the theory and practice of municipal home rule which will be needed to accommodate the new concept. Not all can rule the home. It may be possible, however, to divide the total package of home rule powers between counties or other area-wide units and the local municipalities in such a way that all will benefit.

Home rule—like "states' rights"—is a difficult doctrine to define. This may be due partly to the fact that, historically, home rule is a negative concept. Its historical purpose was to terminate and prevent legislative involvement in such politically pregnant processes as the control of local police forces, construction of local public works, grant of utility franchises and use of the city payroll as an outlet for party patronage.

A few state constitutions, notably Colorado's, attempt to spell out the scope of municipal home rule powers, but the preferred approach has been to leave the constitutional language broad and general except when dealing with the adjectival process of charter adoption. Thus the job of defining home rule has been left largely to the courts and what has been held to be a home rule power in a given state at a given time may be held a state prerogative in another state or at another time. That it should be otherwise in a rapidly changing society is not to be expected.

From *National Civic Review,* September 1961. Reprinted by permission.

One useful statement of the general subjects to which home rule might extend is that developed by Jefferson B. Fordham in his analysis of the American Municipal Association's *Model Constitutional Provisions for Municipal Home Rule.* Fordham analyzed home rule in three main contexts —substantive powers, governmental organization and administration, and the geographical reach of governmental authority. These categories are convenient to employ in evaluating the present status of home rule in metropolitan areas and in re-thinking the concept for the future.

SUBSTANTIVE POWERS

Even in the simplest governmental structure a municipality does not enjoy full self-determination of its substantive powers. A city "must live in a world in which there are numerous other governments—local, state and national—with which it continually rubs elbows. The powers of each of these governments must necessarily be relative to the powers of the others."

In the complex governmental environment of metropolitan areas effective municipal home rule is even more narrowly circumscribed. Limitations exist with respect to metropolitan relationships between governmental units which do not overlap the same geographic area as well as between those that do.

Non-overlapping units. Neighboring municipalities in the same metropolitan area cannot be said to enjoy full control over their substantive powers, even though equally endowed with legal home rule authority. The efforts of one suburban city to zone in furtherance of a sound development pattern may be undermined if its neighboring cities fail to do likewise. An ordinance to regulate business operations must take into consideration possible competitive disadvantages to which local firms would be subjected and similar considerations will overshadow the city's self-determination of taxation and revenue sources. Efforts by one municipality to prevent stream pollution may be thwarted by indifference of a sister city and each may be frustrated by the other in any attempt to secure domestic water supplies from wells tapping the same ground sources.

Illustrations of the point could be continued indefinitely. It is clear, however, that a metropolitan municipality will find its range of choice under home rule restricted because it controls fewer of the factors which influence its destiny than it would if it were the only municipality in the area.

Overlapping units. A city overlapped by a metropolitan park or transit district cannot really be said to enjoy home rule with reference to those functions, even though in the legal sense its powers are unrestricted. Exercise of the home rule power in such a situation is not unknown. Portland, Oregon, has a Commission of Public Docks, created by charter amendment, the powers of which overlap those of the Port of Portland, a metropolitan district created by a special legislative act. But the relationship between the two agencies is an uneasy one and there are efforts from time to time to consolidate them.

Considerably more unsettling is the prospect of conflict between home rule cities and the county or counties of the metropolitan area, or between the municipalities and general metropolitan governments, particularly when the latter are themselves vested with home rule powers. How can duplication and confusion be avoided when two equally sovereign units proceed to exercise home rule rights to determine their own substantive powers?

The Dade County (Miami, Florida) charter meets this issue of home rule head on. Although it reserves to the voters of the municipalities the sole right to abolish the municipality, it permits the county to set minimum standards for the performance of any service or function and to "take over and perform" a service within any municipality which fails to meet the standards. Clearly, the Dade charter reduces drastically the amount of legal municipal home rule authority in the area of substantive powers.

Efforts of municipalities to continue their self-determination of substantive powers despite the terms of the Dade County charter have helped to keep the "metro" pot boiling for four years and no one can yet say what the outcome will be. Those contending for the home rule rights of the municipalities as against the home rule rights of Dade County have carried their fight into the political arena after failing in efforts either to gain voter approval of charter amendments or to win their cases in the courts. The board of Dade County commissioners is now about equally split between those who represent the municipal point of view and those with a county-wide outlook. A change in the county's top management has been made. The voters will go to the polls again this fall to decide on a proposal to repeal the charter.

Except for the Dade County plan, resolution of the conflict between overlapping home rule jurisdictions has been sought in two main ways—division of territory and multiple vote procedures.

The idea that county home rule powers operate only outside city limits has been assumed as the basis of urban county operations in California. Extensions of county services inside city limits by the Lakewood plan in Los Angeles County rests on voluntary contracts which do not violate the home rule theory. But the fact that California counties can and do provide many services outside cities which are not extended inside city boundaries has produced some prolonged and bitter battles. It may be questioned, moreover, whether confining the metropolitan county to the role of a suburban government fully realizes the county's potential as a device for reducing metropolitan chaos.

Multiple vote procedures, requiring separate approval by some or all of the existing governmental units affected by any change in substantive powers, are common in proposals for county home rule and metropolitan government. They are, in fact, effective devices for preserving the autonomy of home rule municipalities as against the creation of an area-wide government. The Ohio and Texas constitutional county home rule amendments require charter approval by separate majorities in various combinations of central cities, suburban municipalities and unincorporated areas. Most proposals for metropolitan government (with the notable exceptions of the successful Dade County and Baton Rouge plans) have required concurrent approval by the voters of at least the central city and the outside areas.

Both division of territory and multiple vote procedures beg the question of permanently resolving the conflict between overlapping units of equal sovereignty in the self-determination of substantive powers. The Dade County charter clearly subordinates the home rule powers of the municipalities to those of the county. In doing so it steps firmly on the toes of the municipalities but, in the long run, it may avoid resort to even more remote levels of government to meet the inadequacies of unregulated municipal home rule in the metropolis.

GOVERNMENTAL STRUCTURE AND ADMINISTRATION

Metropolitan municipalities exercise the home rule power to determine their own organization and procedures with little apparent difficulty. One city may adopt the manager plan, for example, without regard to the form of government utilized by its neighbor or by the county. It may adopt a performance budget, abolish civil service or revise its administrative code without impairing the rights of the local units.

Nor does the exercise of home rule over structure and administration at the metropolitan level limit or restrict the enjoyment of equivalent authority by the municipalities. The Ohio constitution illustrates this principle by permitting county charter adoption in the larger counties by county-wide vote if only organizational or administrative changes are made but requiring approval by separate majorities in the central cities and the area outside if exclusive exercise of powers is assigned to the county.

The worst that can be said about the exercise of home rule in this context is that it results in a lack of uniformity as between the municipalities in the same metropolitan area. There are those, of course, who find virtue in such uniformity, apparently for its own sake.

The possible convenience of uniformity must be evaluated against the possible merits of experimentation in governmental structure and administration. Such experimentation in metropolitan areas may actually be facilitated by such characteristics as area-wide communications media, civic and fraternal organizations, population mobility and the informal contacts between officials and personnel in the same geographical area.

GOVERNMENTAL AREAS

The act of incorporating a municipality may itself be regarded as an exercise of home rule power to determine the geographic reach of governmental authority. Some state constitutions expressly prohibit the legislature from enacting a municipal charter.

Home rule, moreover, involves protection of existing municipal boundaries as against an attempt by the state legislature to change them by special act. It also involves, at least by implication, the insularity of such boundaries against annexation by another home rule municipality.

Whether home rule should also include the power to extend municipal boundaries by unilateral action is a controversial question. Although McBain himself regarded this idea as "little short of ridiculous," such a doctrine is receiving much attention today, and has been specifically recognized in Texas.

In the metropolitan area situation, this concept would be severely restricted in any event by its inapplicability to territory already incorporated in another home rule municipality, even though one such municipality may be only a small fraction of the size of the other.

In a modification of this idea, North Carolina and other states have provided for self-determination of boundaries when certain specific statutory standards are met. Again, however, the metropolitan situation impedes full enjoyment of this home rule right, since two or more neighboring municipalities may meet the requirements for annexation of the same area and one or more must forego its expansion in favor of the other.

It goes almost without saying that the adjustment of county boundaries in a metropolitan area is identical to the problem of adjusting the boundaries of contiguous home rule municipalities. In neither case is it possible to exercise a home rule privilege of self-determination.

It is conceivable that a greater degree of over-all home rule as to municipal boundaries could be made available to the citizens of a metropolitan area if there were an area-wide governmental entity to receive and exercise them. The Florida constitution makes such a grant of home rule powers possible by authorizing Dade County to adopt a charter which would permit the county to "change the boundaries of, merge, consolidate and abolish . . . all municipal corporations." The charter actually adopted in 1957, however, did not avail the county of the full scope of this authority, making boundary changes subject to "the approval of the municipal governing bodies concerned."

This analysis suggests that the doctrine of municipal home rule has some characteristics of a myth when it is applied to governmental units in metropolitan areas. Metropolitan conditions tend to limit significantly the amount of true municipal autonomy in the determination of substantive powers and governmental areas.

This is not to deny that home rule in its traditional application—i.e., in the relation between cities and the state—has made, and is still making, a valuable contribution to the quality of local government in the United States. The point is merely that the proper limits of home rule in metropolitan areas need to be understood and that, if possible, constitutional provisions and statutes should so qualify home rule powers that they do not impede or prevent area-wide solutions to area-wide problems.

In the one instant attempt to do this directly and forthrightly—the Dade County charter—it is evident that the myth of municipal home rule dies hard even when it is assailed by clear legal authority, the electorate and the courts. It is probable that the officials of metropolitan municipalities will be among the last to acknowledge the need for modifications in the municipal home rule theory.

The persistence of the myth will prove troublesome even in metropolitan devices which fall far short of unified metropolitan government.

For example, the hypothesis that annexation can solve urban area problems becomes more academic each time a new suburban municipality is incorporated. Indeed, many such incorporations are conceived and carried out with the express purpose of attaining "home rule" protection for municipal boundaries as against the annexation plans of a neighboring municipality. If annexation is to be used at all in efforts to integrate the government of metropolitan areas, restrictions will have to be placed on the "home rule" right to incorporate. Yet this will not solve the problem as to municipalities which already exist and it is difficult to conceive of any workable scheme whereby the annexation powers of some municipalities could be ranked as superior to those of others.

Voluntary cooperation itself is not immune to the disruptive effects of metropolitan municipal home rule. The effectiveness of a joint study, agency or facility often depends on participation by all municipalities affected, or by certain municipalities which are in a geographically or financially strategic position. The regional councils organized in San Francisco, Detroit, Washington, D.C., New York and Salem, Oregon, might find it profitable to explore the possibility of substituting "majority rule" for "home rule" in their efforts to achieve functional consolidation.

To modify the doctrine of municipal home rule, which many states have embedded securely in constitutional provisions and supreme court decisions would be a task of mammoth proportions. If real progress is to be made toward a solution of metropolitan governmental problems, however, the effort should be made.

GOVERNMENTS GALORE
Norman Beckman and Marjorie Cahn Brazer

Norman Beckman is assistant director (metropolitan areas) of the Advisory Commission on Intergovernmental Relations. He formerly served with the U.S. Bureau of the Budget where he dealt with federal organization for urban development and housing.

Marjorie Cahn Brazer is a staff member of the Advisory Commission on Intergovernmental Relations whose area of concern involves the economics of metropolitan areas.

From *National Civic Review,* March 1963. Reprinted by permission.

The first volume of the *1962 Census of Governments,* "Governmental Organization," confirms the view of many Cassandras that local government structure continues to grow more fragmented and complex. The controversial special district dominates this process, showing a 15 per cent increase between 1957 and 1962. Municipalities contribute substantially to the proliferation of local governments, having added almost 5 per cent to their number over the same period. Counties have remained stable in number if not in function.

Only school district enumeration offers encouragement to those who wish to see the pattern of local government simplified and coordinated. These units continue to decrease dramatically—by almost one-third since the 1957 census was taken, about one-half since 1952 and by over two-thirds since 1942.

There are lessons in the report for each level of government. It reveals some of the past sins of commission—federal encouragement to creation of autonomous special districts such as housing authorities and conservation districts—and sins of omission—lack of state regulation of municipal incorporation and local resistance to multipurpose urban service corporations. On the other hand, state efforts at school district consolidation have been widely effective.

The census document makes no value judgments about governmental structure. Rather, its classification and enumeration of local units represent the most comprehensive body of benchmark data ever assembled for state and local governments. Just as the report of the President's Commission on Intergovernmental Relations, the "Kestnbaum Report," was termed the million-dollar textbook, the *1962 Census of Governments* might now be termed a million-dollar source book.

The companion volumes on taxable property values, government employment and government finances, to be published during the next fifteen months, will provide the flesh and sinew for the skeletal structure defined in the first volume. Together they will permit an up-to-date interpretation of the role and impact of local government in American life. Volume II will provide data on assessed values for all types of taxable property by state and county as well as on the relationship between assessed and market value of taxable realty. Volume III will offer detailed data on the number of employees and related payrolls of state and local governments. Volume IV, on governmental financing, the most detailed of the reports, will provide fiscal year data on taxes and other revenue, expenditures by object and function, indebtedness and financial assets of state and local units of government, including publicly operated utility and retirement systems.

The completed *1962 Census of Governments* will provide grist for the research mills of public officials, civic and taxpayer organizations, and students of public finance and political science. With some caution, meaningful comparative studies of communities, metropolitan areas, regions and states will be possible. The promoters of governmental reorganization, the advocates of accommodation and the defenders of *status quo* will all be able to argue their respective positions with new facts. Researchers will have a statistical universe of definitive information on each local government in the United States, including the 212 standard metropolitan statistical areas. It is to be hoped that this wealth of data will stimulate fresh research effort into such relatively neglected subjects as federalism and state-local relations.

For census enumeration purposes, "A government is an organized entity which, in addition to having governmental character, has sufficient discretion in the management of its own affairs to distinguish it as separate from the administrative structure of any other governmental unit." The problem of definition is certain to grow more complex in the future as attempts are made to solve metropolitan problems through new governmental forms. "Contract" cities, dependent for their services on other jurisdictions, regional planning agencies with review and approval powers, and metropolitan councils of locally elected officials with operating budgets are some of the new species appearing in the laboratory of politics.

The initial groundwork on enumeration and analysis of governments, from which the current census program has evolved, was completed by William Anderson in 1942. He laid out a "rationalized scheme of local government units for the United States" to include a total of 17,800 units or an average of 370 per state. The actual total in 1962 was 91,236, an average of 1,825 per state. Anderson's model called for the abolition of all independent school districts (state supervised schools would be administered by general local governments) and elimination of almost all special districts (counties and cities concerned could establish assessment districts). Townships in most of the midwest and several middle Atlantic states would become administrative districts, and the number of rural counties would be reduced. A single layer of local government would serve over three-quarters of the nation's people.

Type of government	1962	1957a	1952a	1942
Total	91,236	102,392	116,807	155,116
U.S. Government	1	1	1	1
States	50	50	50	48
Local governments	91,185	102,341	116,756	155,067
Counties	3,043	3,050	3,052	3,050
Municipalities	17,997	17,215	16,807	16,220
Townships	17,144	17,198	17,202	18,919
School districts	34,678	50,454	67,355	108,579
Special districts	18,323	14,424	12,340	8,299

a Adjusted to include units in Alaska and Hawaii, which were reported separately prior to adoption of statehood for these areas in 1959.

The table above indicates what has actually happened in the intervening years for each of the major types of local governments. What are some of the significant findings that emerge from these data?

URBAN AND RURAL COUNTIES

In many sections the county is evolving from its traditional position as an administrative subdivision of the state to a more independent role in the provision of municipal services throughout all or the unincorporated parts of its jurisdiction. This development is occurring as a direct result of the rapid pace of urbanization over the last twenty years. Shifts in population have enlarged the dichotomy between relatively urbanized counties and the more numerous rural counties. The number of county governments serving 50,000 people or more has increased by 19 per cent to 560, while 818 counties, 7 per cent more than in 1950, are now below the 10,000 population level. Promising efforts are being made to strengthen the predominately urban county as a general unit of government. The viability of the depopulated rural county as a unit of government deserves similar attention.

The number of governments located within counties ranges from three per county-type area in Alaska and Virginia to 93 in Pennsylvania, averaging 29 over the country as a whole. This average represents a reduction of 12 per cent since 1957, 24 per cent since 1952. One-third of all counties contain fewer than ten units each, 115 contain 100 units or more. In Los Angeles County, the number of units rose from 212 to 234 between 1957 and 1962, and in Cook County (Chicago) from 446 to 460.

TOWNSHIPS STATIC

Little change has taken place in the last decade in the number of townships. Although the 17,000 townships are limited by and large to twenty northeastern and north central states, there are virtually as many of these units as there are municipalities or special districts. Most townships, particularly in north central states, are primarily rural and perform few administrative functions. In New England and certain other states, however, townships (or towns) perform municipal functions and it has been state policy to keep them relatively strong by preventing the rise of counties as a competing unit. On the other hand, in New York, New Jersey and Pennsylvania, townships operate alongside a vigorous system of county government. As farm population declines and transportation improves township governments in rural areas may cease to exist as important governing and administrative jurisdictions.

MUNICIPALITIES INCREASE

Almost 18,000 municipalities were reported in the 1962 census, 4.5 per cent more than in 1957. The addition of 782 was nearly twice the increase of the 1952-1957 period. The geographic distribution of population, traditions of local self-government, the strength of demand for urban services, the financial ability to provide these services and, most important, state standards for incorporation, are the primary factors determining the rate and extent of municipal incorporation.

Although 116 million people in the United States live in municipally governed areas, three-quarters of all municipalities serve a population of less than 2,500. Indeed, the majority (54 per cent) have fewer than a thousand inhabitants each, and serve only 3.5 per cent of the nation's residents living in municipalities. This preponderance of small units raises questions about the ability of such communities to provide essential urban services. At the other extreme 44 per cent of the population served by municipalities resides in the 130 cities of 100,000 or more.

SCHOOL DISTRICTS—GOING, GOING

The marked decline in independent school districts was the brightest finding in the 1962 census for those concerned with reducing the present multiplicity of units, lessening competition for tax funds and improving school services. These were the only units to decline in substantial numbers —by nearly 16,000 or 30 per cent—during the last five years.

The greatest decrease since 1957 has occurred in school districts serving fewer than 50 children. Although over 11,000 of them remain, this represents almost a 50 per cent reduction in five years. Furthermore, about one-third of the 9,000 non-operating school districts existing in 1957 were eliminated by 1962. While all school districts with fewer than 600 pupils declined in number, those above this enrollment level increased.

School districts still constitute the most numerous units, totaling 34,678, but the trend toward consolidation is certain to continue. Almost half the remaining districts operate schools for fewer than 150 pupils. Another 17 per cent operate no schools at all but reimburse adjacent districts to provide schooling. Many states have been and are continuing to wage a vigorous campaign to consolidate small districts in order to raise educational standards through broadening the scope of the curriculum and achieve operating economies. The techniques they have employed may provide lessons for reducing the number of special districts and other overlapping units in both rural and urban areas.

SPECIAL DISTRICTS—UP, UP

The most notable phenomenon reported in the 1962 census has been the proliferation of local public authorities and special districts created to provide a single governmental service. Between 1957 and 1962 their number increased by 15 per cent to 18,323. Three-fifths of all special districts are accounted for by ten states with 700 or more such units each. This concentration emphasizes the extent to which state enabling legislation affects the organization and the structural pattern of local government.

One-third of all special districts is engaged in natural resources activities such as soil conservation, drainage and irrigation. The next largest group consists of fire protection districts, which comprise 18 per cent of the total. The remaining units are divided among numerous other primarily urban categories, water supply and housing contributing 8 and 6 per cent, respectively. Multipurpose districts, one of the promising approaches to reducing the number of autonomous districts and meeting areawide problems, account for only 2 per cent. Moreover, many are likely to be dual-purpose rather than truly multipurpose.

"Special districts are particularly fascinating," comments John C. Bollens, "because some of their characteristics are very much out of the usual governmental pattern and because they seemingly offer clues and insights into a better understanding of other parts of our governmental system."

What accounts for the apparently irresistible tendency to create special districts and what is the cause for anxiety about their expanded use? In most states they are easy to establish. Moreover, the alternative to special districts in many cases might be governmental reorganization, which would threaten the status of some existing local units. Supporters of a particular governmental service seek to "cut red tape," take the function "out of politics" or, most significantly, evade debt and tax limitations. On the other hand, the creation of special districts constitutes a piecemeal approach to meeting area problems. If carried to its ultimate conclusion, local general government is reduced to a hollow shell. The continuing increase in autonomous special districts is especially disturbing in light of the need for closely coordinated decisions regarding all urban development activities (highways, schools, housing, sewage treatment, open space, etc.), if individual program objectives are to be met and if sound and orderly growth in urban areas is to be achieved.

METROPOLITAN MAZE

Two-thirds of the people now live in metropolitan areas and this proportion is rapidly increasing. The pattern of local government structure in these areas is, therefore, of great significance.

Only 20 per cent of all local governments are located in metropolitan areas, but the average number per standard metropolitan statistical area is 87. This average covers a wide range, from 24 for SMSAs of less than 100,000 population up to 301 for SMSAs of a million or more; the Chicago metropolitan area leads the nation with 1,060 local governments. The residents of metropolitan areas are typically served by more layers of overlapping local governments than are the residents of non-metropolitan areas. Yet it is in the more densely populated metropolitan communities that the need is greatest for coordinating services and fixing clear lines of responsibility.

Contrary to the national trend, the total number of local governments in SMSAs has increased by 3 per cent since 1957. This indicates that metropolitan areas are leading the nation in municipal incorporations and establishment of special districts, and lagging in reduction of school districts.

The number of municipalities in metropolitan areas increased by 8 per cent between 1957 and 1962, compared with 4.5 per cent for the country as a whole. This relationship results from the more rapid growth of population in SMSAs and the construction of whole new settlements in suburban areas.

Metropolitan areas, with 23 per cent of the nation's municipalities, contain all cities of 50,000 or more and over half of those with 25,000-50,000 population. Yet half the municipalities within SMSAs serve fewer than 2,500 people each and 25 per cent of SMSA populations live outside municipalities.

Because the *1962 Census of Governments* reclassified special districts it is not possible to determine precisely how much of the dramatic national increase in these units occurred in SMSAs. Metropolitan areas account for 30 per cent of all special districts, but they contain 51 per cent of water supply districts and 61 per cent of sewerage districts.

The reduction in school districts has been taking place at a slower rate in metropolitan areas than in the rest of the country—20 per cent since 1957 as compared to 31 per cent in the nation. This lag reflects the fact that all the reduction took place in districts which enrolled fewer than 600 pupils. Metropolitan areas contain only a small proportion of these, but they include a much larger fraction of school districts with high enrollments than do non-metropolitan areas. The latter group increased substantially in number both nationwide and in SMSAs. By far the largest increase in school districts, 81 per cent over 1957, is found in the 12,000-25,000 pupil class, and virtually all these are located in metropolitan areas. Of the 6,000 school systems in SMSAs, however, 26 per cent enroll fewer than 300 pupils and 14 per cent are nonoperating. Metropolitan areas have as long a way to go toward eliminating small and inefficient school districts as do many rural areas.

REGIONAL PATTERNS

A regional pattern of local governments emerges clearly from the census data. Historically, in the south the county was the basic unit of government; in the north the city and township were the basic units, supplemented by the special district. As settlement pushed horizontally west, the new settlers took their concepts of local government with them. In the south and in certain western states, the number of local units and the levels of government affecting the average citizen are few. In the states from Connecticut west to North Dakota, and south to Kansas, governmental structure became and remains to this day more complex.

Our newest states, Alaska and Hawaii, are conspicuous for the relative simplicity of their governmental structures—few or no counties, no townships, relatively few municipalities, state schools systems and relatively few special districts. The older states of the northeast and upper midwest, however, are characterized by complex local organization—a high average (40 or more) of local units per county and numerous small townships and school districts which overlap with municipalities. Six states in the upper midwest, plus Missouri, accounted for over two-thirds of the decrease in school districts since 1957. Although it lacks townships, California rivals numerous midwestern states in number of separate governmental units, with an average of 69 per county.

CONCLUSIONS

The *1962 Census of Governments* presents a picture of numerous local governments overlapping unnecessarily and of rapidly increasing autonomous single purpose districts. There are too many local units in too many parts of the country. Concern for simplification and streamlining must be translated into action at all three levels of government.

There is a need for federal programs to be coordinated with one another and to be more sensitive to their impact on the organization and development of communities. For example, at the inception of the public housing and urban renewal programs, the federal government directly advocated and supported creation of autonomous local authorities, among other reasons to avoid local tax and debt limits. Some of the local financial limitations have disappeared but the autonomous units remain. Creation of additional independent authorities may be encouraged by recent federal open space legislation which provides a financial bonus if grants are administered by an agency authorized to acquire open space land for all or a substantial portion of an urban area.

At the state and local level incentives to creation of special districts can be eliminated by removal of restrictions on the structure and functions of local general government and on local borrowing and taxing powers. Restricting the authority by which local units may incorporate and independent agencies may be created, while liberalizing municipal annexation powers, will help reverse the trend of proliferating units. Metropolitan and regional planning to coordinate individual governmental decisions needs to be strengthened. These and other permissive powers must be made available and used if our units of local government are to retain responsibility and authority to meet effectively the needs of their citizens.

THE CHANGING ROLE OF COUNTY GOVERNMENT
Edward W. Weidner

Edward W. Weidner is a political scientist who heads the Center for Developmental Change at the University of Kentucky. Formerly vice chancellor of the East-West Center at the University of Hawaii, he is the co-author (with William Anderson) of *American City Government* as well as *State and Local Government*. He also served as director of the Michigan State University Program for training Vietnamese officials in public administration.

If the structure of county government is to be reorganized intelligently, consideration must be given to the changing role of the county. There is much disagreement as to what its role is. There have been those during the last fifteen years who have been proclaiming its death. The process of centralization, it is asserted, is making counties outmoded units of government. Evidence is submitted to prove that states now perform functions these localities once did.

It is true that most counties have inadequate areas for maximum efficiency and economy. It is likewise true that states are now performing some of the functions that counties performed fifteen years ago. These facts alone, however, do not justify the conclusion that county government is on the decline, much less that it is doomed.

Far from becoming less important, judged on the basis of the number of functions performed and the amount of money expended, counties today are a more vital part of our governmental system than ever before . . .

The list of functions added to county responsibilities in the last fifteen years is much longer than the list of functions taken away. In an occasional state such as North Carolina complete state control over a former county service such as highways is now the case. More frequently a state now performs part of a function which previously was almost entirely under county control, such as the increased mileage of state highways and enlarged welfare activities. In contrast a listing of the various functions added to county government jurisdiction would consume at least a page. For the most part such functions fall in two groups—those which the national government has promoted and those of a local as compared with a state-delegated character.

Examples of the latter include a broadening of the police power, rural as well as urban planning and zoning, recreation and local publicity. County participation in rural housing, the categorical aid program, defense councils, agriculture and natural resources protection, full-time health de-

From *The American County: Patchwork of Boards* (New York: National Municipal League, 1946). Reprinted by permission.

partments and electric utility ownership has been promoted by the national government.

GROWTH OF COUNTIES

The extent to which counties in all parts of the United States have made use of their new powers is impressive. Of 3,050 counties, full-time health departments increased from 762 in 1935 to 1,577 in 1941 and since that time many other states have authorized such units. Over twenty counties have been reported as establishing county planning boards or agencies in the last three years, and the actual number is undoubtedly well in excess of this figure. Hardly a month goes by that several counties are not reported as building hospitals.

While the reporting of activities of particular counties is poor, we do have an accurate count of state legislative enactments which vest more powers in counties. From 1941 to 1944, for instance, two states authorized full-time health units for counties, three recreation activities, four conservation function, three expenditures for advertising counties and twelve planning or zoning agencies.

The conclusions for county government reorganization are unmistakable. First of all, counties are not on their way to extinction. They are performing more and more services that are demanded by the electorate under modern conditions. Many changes in our society have taken place in the last fifteen years, and it is only natural that some readjustments of functions as between levels of government was required. Reflecting a more positive philosophy of government, counties have acquired many more new functions than they have given up to the states or the nation.

Secondly, it is obvious that it is no longer adequate to describe counties as merely administrative and judicial subdivisons of the state. They are that, but they also are real local units of government and have an important relationship to the nation and the national economy. We are in a period which stresses the need for intergovernmental cooperation, and every level of government has its effect upon and is affected by other levels of government.

In a political system where counties are intimately affected by national and state governments, it is useless to view the problem of structural reorganization from a purely local standpoint. Some of the most important alterations in county structure in the last fifteen years have been the direct or indirect result of national government activity. The Social Security Act of 1935 has revolutionized county welfare and health administration. The categorical aid program consumes a fifth of county expenditures. Sixty per cent of the states require all their counties to have welfare boards for this program.

The same act of Congress has been the chief factor in the organization of full-time county health departments, with the result that in several states there are two sets of laws, one providing for a board of health for full-time activities. Noticeable too, are the many inter-county and city-county boards of health authorized by state laws and reflecting the program developed by the United States Public Health Service.

One of the oldest and most important services of counties, agricultural extension work, was established largely as a result of national government action. Under the . . . Highway Act of 1944 Washington . . . [has] more influence over county roads, but so far this influence has been confined largely to administrative standards and not extended greatly to government structure.

If counties are to be reorganized on modern lines, some agency of the national government should be given the power to advise the national functional agencies of the effects of encouraging establishment of county special function boards and commissions and even independent units of government such as soil conservation districts. If counties are to remain vital units of local government, it follows that coordination of policy and administration on a county level is necessary. So long as state and national functional agencies view counties as essentially administrative districts, this remains an impossible goal.

State officials have been just as guilty on this score as national officials. Each state department—highways, welfare, health, education and agriculture—considers the corresponding county officers or boards as responsible mainly to it. While national-state-local cooperation is desirable and necessary, as long as some local discretion in policy and administration is to be preserved there should be some opportunity given to counties to coordinate the various local programs.

Almost all county reorganization proposals involve the idea of a unified county executive. Whether such an executive is to be a manager appointed by the governing body or an elected executive, clerk, auditor, or judge, certain prerequisites are necessary before the executive can be effective.

First of all, control over the functions performed is essential. In many cases today not even the county governing body has control of independently elected officers and special function boards.

Secondly, a halt must be made to the splintering of locally-performed functions. Too many independent units of local government are being established for particular purposes such as soil conservation and irrigation. Unified county control will not mean much if local government functions are not vested in the counties.

Finally, a county-wide viewpoint must become more prevalent not only within the county but also in the minds of state and national officials. On this score county officers and the electorate are primarily at fault, however.

ELECTORATE APATHETIC

In most counties the chief characteristic of the electorate's attitude toward county government seems to be one of apathy. At least so far as improvement is concerned, county electorates seem, on the whole, to defend the status quo by inaction. . . .

The apathetic attitude of the electorate has led some people to say that, at least in rural counties, a county executive is out of place because the people like to elect their friends to public office, and administration is carried out in an easy, personal, friendly manner. According to this view, it is inconceivable that rural electorates will ever give up their right to elect many administrative officers or demand strict economy by way of such things as centralized purchasing.

The answer lies in seeing the picture in broad perspective. There are at least two rather widespread trends in counties today. It has already been pointed out that the people are demanding more services from their county governments. Equally significant, although it takes a determined movement to bring it out, there is a trend toward improvement of county structure along the lines of providing a unified executive. That is to say, the awakening of the citizens, while difficult, is not an impossible task.

The situation has been well summarized in the field of road administration in a recent paper by C. M. Nelson, editor of *Better Roads:*

> There is a large southern state in which county road administration jogs along at a kind of lazy trot. Suppose that we call it the state of Montezuma. In about five-sixths of the counties in Montezuma there is nothing even slightly resembling engineering direction of county road work. The individual county commissioners are the road bosses of their own precincts. The prevailing spirit is the spirit of inertia. But here and there we find a Montezuma county where county road administration has really grown up. There have been some gratifying—even electrifying—changes within the past year or so.
>
> Now there are some people on the sidelines down in Montezuma who none the less condemn county road administration on the record of the average county; occasionally it is even proposed that the counties retire from the highway business. I think that we ought to be more patient than that—so long as we can see hopeful signs. We ought to chastise the backward officials and carry some light to the citizens who sit in darkness. We ought to give local administration a chance to grow up.

The cry of "informal" government is not enough. Today, people want an active government and services performed adequately. If their counties fail to do this, eventually the citizens demand efficiency.

It is significant that the reform of county government structure parallels the growth in importance of county functions. Since 1930 nine states—California, Montana, Virginia, Texas, Ohio, New York, North Dakota, Oregon and Missouri—have acted to remove barriers to structural improvement. Although only eighteen of the 3,050 counties have county manager or executive plans, fourteen of the eighteen adopted their new systems since 1930. More important, interest in these plans is more intense than it has ever been. . . .

As counties continue to perform more and more functions, including those of a purely local character, it is reasonable to expect that their governmental structures will come to approximate more closely those of the cities which long have been vital units of local government. The county electorates have given ample indication that they are ready to begin to make the transition.

COUNTY GOVERNING BODIES

Assuming that the manager plan is the best solution to the structural weaknesses of counties—and as counties become more like cities there is every reason to suppose that it is—one of the first lines of attack by the reformers should be county governing bodies. The effectiveness of the manager plan depends in part upon the manager's ability to coordinate and supervise all activities of the county from a county-wide viewpoint. When the governing body is constituted so that it represents various district viewpoints and not a county-wide one, it defeats a prime objective of coordinated administration.

The present status of county governing bodies is clear. Less than 20 per cent of them have all their members elected at large. The district or township system is widely entrenched. Even worse, several hundred counties have a rotten borough system of representation. The twin objectives of the manager system, efficiency and economy, are hardly encouraged by such a practice, where each representative has his own way in matters affecting his district.

There are at least three other ways in which county governing bodies, as organized at present, hamper the development of a manager system. The manager plan is founded on the basis of the differentiation of powers—a belief that one body should not perform policy-making, administrative and judicial functions, and that specialization in their performance is desirable. County governing bodies frequently perform all three of these functions, and in a few hundred counties the members of the body are individually also town or township officers.

It is time that we stopped expecting our county governing body members to be experts in all governmental activities. It is impossible for them to represent adequately the electorate in all these ways at the same time. Judicial and town or township functions should be severed from their jurisdiction, and the appointment of a manager would give them the administrative expertness so necessary in modern times.

The fact that 1500 counties have three or less members on their governing bodies poses another problem. A board this small is likely to find it difficult to leave administrative matters to the manager. Indeed, the chief explanation for the smallness of these bodies is that they have been considered administrative and judicial instrumentalities of the state. A minimum of five members, as suggested by *Principles of a Model County, County Government* of the National Municipal League, would seem desirable. As a matter of fact, enlarging very small county governing bodies would be an excellent way to give more people in the rural communities a chance to participate in their government; it would compensate in part for the loss of directly elected administrative officials.

Finally, the failure of state legislatures and administrative officials to vest more power over policy matters in the general governing bodies of the counties works against the manager principle. Such power is now dispersed; the governing body, state legislature, state administrative officials, special function boards and commissions, special fiscal bodies and independently elected officers all have a share in it. A manager would find it impossible to please so many "bosses." Simple and direct lines of responsibility are essential for effective management.

As a practical matter it should be kept in mind that even if the manager system were beyond political feasibility, a step in the right direction would be the reorganization of county governing bodies. If they were given adequate control and proper organization, they might well help lead the movement for more effective over-all management.

SPECIAL FUNCTION BOARDS

The growth in number of special function boards and commissions on a county level is a reflection of four somewhat diverse factors. First, a distrust of the present county government structure as adequate to perform new activities is evident. The distrust is justified in many cases, but the long-run solution to a problem is hardly that of ignoring it or of making it worse. Second, the failure of counties with inadequate areas and population to consolidate has led to numerous intercounty boards and commissions. Certainly such boards and commissions are to be encouraged if consolidation, which is a more difficult problem to solve, seems impossible of achievement. Yet the problem should be recognized by both local and state officials and an ultimate solution reached.

Third, many state officials feel that their particular function should be separated from the regular county governing body, and that a special board is the best for this purpose. This argument was analyzed at an earlier point and found wanting.

Finally, there is a genuine belief in many quarters that a board is a better administrative device than a single officer. Authorities in public administration, however, usually suggest that if a board is to be used it be placed in a purely advisory role. One of the noticeable results of a recent study of authorized special functions boards and commissions is the general lack of provision for advisory boards. Most boards are of a policy-determining type and many of an administrative type as well. Boards are usually defended on one of two grounds: (1) That they are necessary because policy matters are involved—to which might be replied, for what are county general governing bodies; (2) that the advice of experts or of a cross-section of the community is needed—to which might be replied, why not create an advisory body?

The manager principle is founded on administrative centralization and policy-forming centralization. To the extent that county special function boards and commissions are not advisory, they violate these tenets.

CONCLUSION

The changing role of county government is a phenomenon for the times. Twentieth century liberalism is replacing nineteenth century liberalism. That this twentieth century movement should have its effect on city, state and national governments somewhat before its full weight was felt on the county level is understandable, since political problems were more acute in the former cases. Once the problem of the future of county government is recognized in these terms, the solution in terms of structural reorganization along the lines of a county manager system is more understandable.

The full implications of the manager system for counties in this interdependent world should not be underestimated. It involves changing the viewpoints of state and national officials, arousing the electorate to action, amending state constitutions and statutes, reorganizing county governing bodies, and for the most part eliminating special function boards and commissions and independently elected officers. That is a task of no small proportions. But it can be, and is being done.

The realm of local government leadership, the world of managers and mayors, has been dominated by the common American belief that what is needed is "more business in government, less government in business," and a tendency to rely on gimmicks and structural changes to cure the alleged evils of "politics" and "bossism." This business-oriented approach has often placed an overwhelming emphasis upon efficiency and economy, and failed to distinguish between the profit and the service motives. Stemming from this anti-governmental attitude have been the beliefs that restraint of local government is the primary need and that elimination of partisan politics is both possible and desirable. Complex systems of separation of powers and checks and balances have been devised on the assumption that government inevitably tends to corruption and that its practitioners must be tightly controlled. This philosophy has been further reflected in the practices of keeping mayoral terms of office short, initially one or two years; of requiring legislative concurrence for the chief executive to appoint, and even to remove his administrative subordinates; of denying executive control over city finances. Distrust on the county level has led to the even more anarchic absence of *any* chief executive and the diffusion of executive power among a profusion of lesser elected officials and legislative committees.

Before examining the logic of these approaches, we might first ask ourselves: "What do we expect of a mayor or a manager?" What are his appropriate functions in this latter third of the twentieth century?

(1) Whether elected or appointed, he must be both chief executive and chief administrator. If there are to be municipal plans and policies, he must be responsible for them. He must supervise enforcement of the law and protection of the public safety. The chief executive must regularly oversee such staff functions as purchasing and personnel administration in addition to regular line operations from water supply to street construction and maintenance. In all except the largest cities, he will probably serve as his own principal fiscal officer, handling or closely supervising the multitudinous details of budget preparation. He should be prepared to do battle with his city council over its sometimes provincial interests, vetoing, if necessary, those ward-oriented authorizations and appropriations which, in his view, fail to promote the general good. Finally he must supervise the ultimate expenditure of the budget funds involved.

(2) In addition to his administrative role, the mayor or manager must also function as chief legislator. Here his informal authority as initiator will be even more important than his formal power as presiding officer of the city council. Proposing new legislation, submitting new ordinances and resolutions, reporting studies and findings to the councilmen, exercising the veto power—all these activities reflect his role as chief councilman. He is far better equipped than any part-time council member to understand the legisla-

tive programs necessary to achieve community goals. He is the specialist, the professional on the job each day, receiving complaints, examining problems, handling the details of city management. Consequently, if there is a default of leadership by the chief executive, be he manager or mayor, there is likely to be *no* effective leadership.

(3) Scarcely less important than his executive and legislative functions is the role of the chief executive as political leader. While not every mayor will actually head the political party which carried him into office, and while an occasional incumbent may stand accused of being only a "front man for the machine," the chief executive, nonetheless, is looked to by the man in the street as political head of the city. If he fails in this, a power vacuum inevitably results. Indeed, the lack of an institutionalized political chief in council-manager cities has sometimes forced the theoretically nonpartisan city manager not only to provide policy guidance but to assume political leadership, even engaging in campaigning for the candidates of the party which appointed him. Elsewhere, an occasional manager has sought to build a personal basis of political support—his own individual machine. Conversely, the manager who has held himself completely above all political involvement has seldom proved effective.

(4)   Closely related to the political role of the urban chief executive is his role as popular leader and spokesman for the city's interests. In ceremonial capacity, he becomes the focal point for public attention, cutting ribbons, presiding over supermarket openings, and welcoming both school-children and distinguished visitors to city hall. As the city's leading spokesman, he may be required to serve as its chief lobbyist, representing its interests to both state and federal administrators, pleading its cause in both state and national capitols, seeking to guard its citizens against any possible legislative or executive "shortchanging." In addition, he has such lesser functions as performing marriage ceremonies and heading civilian defense. It is truly a complex and exacting office, with its varied and unceasing demands.

What are the fundamental problems that emerge from this complexity? That first stems from the multiple role required of a chief executive—the simultaneous demands upon him as executive, administrator, legislator, politician, and popular leader. The qualifications for each of these important tasks are obviously widely varied. Those traits best calculated to arouse electoral fervor are not necessarily the same ones requisite to the day-to-day conduct of city government. In addition, the incumbent executive must also possess demonstrable skill in the "engineering of consent." Without this talent, his best conceived plans may seldom progress beyond a discussion stage. To fulfill his demanding role, he will need other basic qualities —integrity, vision and foresight, statesmanlike zeal, and many more.

He must also face up to the complexity of responsibility and accountability in a democracy. The local executive must operate with many eyes peering intently over his shoulder. For his is a multiple responsibility—to the public at large, to the political forces which brought him to office, and to his administrative profession. He must also accept the need for visibility of his actions, quite proper in a democracy, but nonetheless frustrating on those occasions when delicate negotiations may well be slowed because they must be conducted in a goldfish bowl. Then, too, the chief executive constantly faces the aptly-titled "inertia of bureaucracy." He finds that, if he is to execute his program, he must go far beyond issuing orders. He finds his nominally subordinate municipal civil servants possess independent sources of political and economic support; he realizes they know that they will be back after the next election and that he may not. Then, too, the chief executive must face up to the nature of his personal accountability—he must devote himself to the day-in, day-out chores of public relations, of image building and preservation, if he is to withstand the periodic and ultimate test of the election campaign.

All these factors, taken together, suggest the sweeping challenge facing the local chief executive. They suggest the necessity for a careful examination if we are to understand better the role of our mayors and our managers in the vital processes of our local government in action.

THE CITY MANAGER: ADMINISTRATIVE THEORY AND POLITICAL POWER
Duane Lockard

Duane Lockard, Associate Professor of Political Science at Princeton University, once served in the Connecticut State Senate. He is the author of *The Politics of State and Local Government, New England State Politics,* and other publications.

Although the formal structure of the city-manager government has not changed much since the system originated half a century ago, its theory and practice have changed considerably. That the operational patterns and theoretical conceptions of manager government should change is no occasion for surprise—no institution with a dynamic role to play could fail to change in such times. The rise of the metropolis, the development of suburbs, the growth of planning, the initiation of urban renewal, and many other factors have had their impact on the manager system as on other institutions of local government. Also, significant developments in administrative theory have contributed to the revision of manager theory in interesting ways. Summarily stated, the theory of absolute separation of policy and administration, once a key idea of protagonists of the manager system, has

Reprinted with permission from the *Political Science Quarterly,* Vol. 77, No. 2, June 1962, pp. 224-236.

been abandoned by nearly all administrative theorists, and even the leading spokesmen of the manager profession have joined in the abandonment. In essence, changes in administrative theory have eroded away much of the theoretical foundation on which the manager system was originally erected.

This changed conception of the place of the manager in the political life of a community cannot be dismissed as unimportant on the ground that theoretical constructions are matters apart from the day to day operations of officials in a city-manager government struggling with immediate problems and not given to cogitation on administrative or other abstractions. On the contrary, the behavior of all agents in the local political process is conditioned by their conception of appropriate roles for themselves and others and by their respect or contempt for the principles underlying any governmental system. Behavior follows belief and belief reflects theory, however vague or profound the comprehension of the theory may be. Doctrinal shifts filter down slowly from learned journals and the exchanges of theoreticians, but in the end they have an effect. The theoretical principles of the city-manager system may have sunk to the cliché level by the time they reach some of the practitioners who are influenced by them, but the effect is not less important. Changes in theoretical conception of the managerial role inevitably affect what an actual manager will feel it is his duty to do (or not do), for he, like every human faced with dilemmas of decision, seeks a rationalization to explain and justify his actions to himself and to others. (There is a "feed-back" process, too, as the ensuing pages suggest: that is, observations and reports from "the field" condition theory which then guides future actions.)

Herbert Kaufman a few years ago traced three lines of development of administrative theory and speculated on some of the "emerging conflicts" that these diverging lines of thought and action were producing. His categories were broad, but they fit perfectly the shifts of doctrine concerning the manager system in the past half-century. Kaufman identified three separate "quests" that had motivated theorists and practitioners alike in the history of American government, emphasizing separate quests for representativeness, neutral competence, and executive leadership. Each theme, he noted, has been dominant at various times, although never to the absolute exclusion of the others. Early emphasis on representativeness (as seen in the long ballot, for example) gave way to a drive for neutral competence (for example, the demand for civil service careers and training for administrators). Governmental fragmentation and irresponsibility later produced a new theme: the demand for concentration of power in the hands of the chief executive (for example, the plea for integration of administration under a strong executive).

THE MANAGER AND "NEUTRAL COMPETENCE" THEORY

The manager plan, dedicated to competence and "objectivity" in management, is the apotheosis of the quest for neutral competence. Believers in the separation of politics and administration (and this included most of the great names of political science in the years when the manager system was emerging) took readily to the manager plan; it seemed an ideal way of proving that it was possible to remove "politics" from administration. This was after all an age of emerging emphasis on specialization and expertise, and it must therefore have seemed that trained technician-managers, independent of the "political" council in matters of administration, would produce "nonpolitical" government. Leonard White, writing when the manager movement was young, said:

> It ought to be possible in this country to separate politics from administration. Sound administration can develop and continue only if this separation can be achieved. For a century they have been confused, with evil results beyond measure . . . (City) managers have an unparalleled opportunity and a deep obligation to teach the American people by their precept and conduct that their job is to administer the affairs of the city with integrity and efficiency and loyalty to the council, without participating in or allowing their work to be affected by contending programs or partisans.

Faith in the doctrine of separation died hard among reformers and the more traditionally oriented managers, and indeed some cling to the doctrine yet. In 1940 when Stone, Price and Stone turned out their detailed comparative study of the manager system, they adhered to the separation idea, notwithstanding the fact that the book otherwise reflected a political realism unusual in the literature on the subject. They admitted that not all cities had achieved a proper separation but reserved kind adjectives for cities that had come closest. It is revealing to note that they slip into description of the character of the *electoral* process rather than of the decision-making process when they seek to demonstrate the separation of politics and administration. They speak of a "complete distinction between politics and administration" that developed in cities which "conducted their political campaigns entirely without reference to the city manager or the administration. . ." Under these conditions, "the city manager and his relations with the council never became a political issue." This, it scarcely needs be said, is no evidence that the conduct of the government in these cities left administration and politics in separate categories. It merely says that the manager did not become involved in open controversy, which is not the same thing as saying that the manager had nothing to do with the formulation of policy or that the administrative decisions of the city did not involve the significant use of influence among competitors for the prizes at stake in a city—to use the language of Sayre and Kaufman's *Governing New York City*.

In order to go on believing that administration and policy were separate entities, it was helpful, perhaps necessary, to think in rigidly structural terms. Early students of the manager plan, and even more so the reformers promoting it, tended to see the system in static terms, emphasizing formal relations between manager and council rather than viewing the government in more dynamic terms. Thus Stone, Price and Stone say that it "seems obvious that in the last analysis the city manager has absolutely no independence and exercises his authority only at the pleasure of the council, for the council may discharge him at its discretion, and he has no legal recourse." It does not seem obvious at all. A city manager with long tenure and support among influential community leaders has a considerable base of power from which to act. He may not be independent in the sense that he can ignore the council (few executives in democratic systems can for that matter), but to cite the fact that the manager has no "legal recourse" is to miss the political essence of the relationship. The many case studies in city manager government of recent years (for example, Frank Abbott's telling study of the Cambridge City Manager) demonstrate beyond doubt that a manager is an actor in the politics of a city. It is hard to imagine a council that would move against a manager without taking account of the resources for counter-attack at the disposal of the manager. Whether this is independence in the legal sense of the term is the least of the matter; the calculation of the power resources is the significant factor. It is always possible, subtly or otherwise, to convert an attack on a manager into an attack on the manager system—or at least to convince a good many manager-system supporters that it is less the manager than the manager system that is under attack. And this, as candid councillors will admit, can be a political force of considerable moment. The legally prescribed remedy, removal by majority vote, gives no hint of the political difficulties that dissuade councillors from taking that step.

As the hortatory and formalistic approach to local government has slowly been replaced by analysis concentrating more on operational realities and decision-making processes, the theory of separation has inevitably suffered. The changed method of inquiry as well as the jettisoning of the normative element (*promoting* separation, as well as looking for evidence of it) doomed the theory.

Notwithstanding the acceptance of the doctrine among early managers, the system had not long been in operation before managers began to debate the principles of separation. Having tested the precepts in practice, they debated among themselves as to the appropriate role of the manager, and particularly they questioned the extent to which a manager should allow himself to become involved in open contests over public policy. At first a conventional line consistent with the separation doctrine, prevailed—although over the complaints of a minority who disliked so neutral a role. The prevailing doctrine, enunciated in the first "Code of Ethics," was that the manager should remain apart from political controversy: "No manager should take an active part in politics."

Each annual convention of the International City Managers Association produced a new round of discussion on the point, however. It was agreed that the manager should stay out of partisan politics and election campaigns for the council. But there was far less agreement on whether the manager should influence the choice of community policy goals and actively promote them. Public speech making and open support of policies agreed upon by the council became common practice and were supported in the professional manager journals. Some managers right from the start had been active promoters, but many in the early days (no doubt most of them, in fact, since the majority of managers were trained as engineers) did little to promote policies but instead served as expert-caretaker-administrators. The advocates of a freer role for the manager won out in the redrawing of the Code of Ethics in 1938 and added considerably stronger language to describe the managerial responsibility for leadership:

> The City Manager is in no sense a political leader. In order that policy may be intelligent and effective, he provides the council with information and advice, but he encourages positive decisions on policy by the council instead of passive acceptance of his recommendations . . . The City Manager keeps the community informed on municipal affairs but keeps himself in the back-ground by emphasizing the importance of the facts.

The negative tone of the denial that the manager is a political leader is deleted in the 1952 version of the code; instead there is an affirmation that the manager is a "community leader" who "submits policy proposals to the council and provides the council with facts and advice on matters of policy to give the council a basis for making decisions on community goals . . ." At another point in the code the following is added: "The city manager keeps the community informed on municipal affairs. He emphasizes friendly and courteous service to the public. He recognizes that the chief function of local government . . . is to serve the best interests of all the people on a nonpartisan basis."

CITY MANAGERS ON CONTEMPORARY MANAGER THEORY

The very fact that the Code has been revised twice suggests that the managers themselves have derived from their practice some notions on theory and have made their own contributions to its evolution. Indeed some managers have now denied the validity of some of the first precepts of the system. Thus in 1959, two city managers said:

> When modern political scientists state that administration is part of the political process and that administrative agencies are engaged in politics, they mean that administrative officials and their staffs are inescapably a part of the total process of government which includes the determination of policy. The new definition seems to the city manager perfectly evident and arguments to the contrary uninformed.

This should not be taken to mean that the managerial profession now embraces open political participation, nor even that the idea of the political content of administration is widely accepted. Thus another manager comments:

> We have passed from the clear and definitive separation of policy and administration . . . [to the idea] that the two are but aspects of a whole approach, commingling in the heady wine of practice. Be that as it may, the council-manager plan's unique contribution is the establishment of a formal polarity by which general policy matters flow to the consideration of the elected representatives and administrative details gather themselves together at the desks of the appointed officials.

In short, by emphasizing the distinctions between the more political and the more administrative elements of the governmental process (and the evident tendency in manager government is to emphasize these distinctions) the concept of separation subtly re-enters. The case is made for "polarity" of aspects of government rather than for absolute distinctions. Yet in terms of the dilemmas of power—the contests over desired prizes that bring political influence into the situation—the polarity has little meaning. Budget-making is a matter of both policy and administration. The desk on which the duty of budget-drafting lands does not classify the subject according to its essential quality, as a vigorous fight over teachers' salaries well illustrates. The problem is that the manager's desk is *both* administrative and political; in cases where it matters most, the polarity argument has little bearing.

Still another manager illustrates the problems of managerial leadership with a finesse that would have charmed the great Florentine master of political strategy. Dismissing two types of manager-leaders as ineffectual (one, "who leads with his neck" and has the facts but is sometimes "statistically right and politically wrong"; the other, who really doesn't lead at all but passively waits the bidding of the council), he then describes his ideal manager. The ideal type should be a good "salesman" and should have the "ability to set goals, that is, to determine the final objectives which underlie any successful program." He should keep in harmony with the council, for

> With the manager playing a large role in developing policy, decisions must be sound because the council in the end will be judged by the public on its over-all policy decisions. *Indeed, in a sense, the success or failure of a city council is a definite responsibility of the manager.* It is difficult for a city council to stand up and defend a city policy when it is not 'saleable'. . . .
>
> A manager should stay in the background—should push and lead through the council and the staff. *The council is elected for leadership.* Things should be accomplished through others, avoiding differences whenever possible. It is practically axiomatic that in most council-manager differences, the manager generally comes out second and goes out first. When the manager is right, few people remember; when wrong, no one forgets . . .

Recognizing that brickbats come to the adventurous and unsuccessful policy promoter, Leonard White urged a diametrically opposite course of action for managers. To supplant the council as leader may be a sore temptation when the council fails, but to take this course, White said,

> will sound the death knell of the manager plan as now conceived, for a manager who undertakes civic leadership stakes his position on the acceptance of his program by the voters. If his program is rejected, and no man can supply effective leadership without openly courting the possibility of rejection, he sacrifices his position as manager.

City manager Matthews, quoted above on the manager's responsibility to develop policy, openly (and some others more covertly) suggests a way around the dilemma posed by White, suggesting that the manager push policies by strongly endorsing points raised by his staff or by council members. Charles Adrian, in his intensive five-year study of three operating manager systems, found a consistent pattern of managerial promotion of policy through others. He observes that there

> appeared to be a psychological advantage to the manager if he could place himself in the position of defending a policy developed by [administrators, advisory groups, or private groups]. He would take a strong stand, but could use the protective coloration of saying, 'professional planners tell me . . .' He would, in other words, take a public position of *leadership* in policy matters, but preferred to attribute policy innovation to technical experts or citizens groups.

Although many contemporary managers speak of their duty of "seizing the initiative," of "taking the government to the people and . . . presenting it in symbols they know and understand," and of being "human" so as to win public popularity and support, the case histories of managers who have gone too far out on the limb of policy innovation without substantial backing apparently has convinced managers of the need for due caution before venturing forth.

"NEUTRAL COMPETENCE" *vs.* "EXECUTIVE LEADERSHIP"

Are there implicit difficulties in the effort to achieve simultaneously neutral competence, so much at the heart of the system in theory, and executive leadership, so universal a quest in modern government? Are the two quests incompatible in that the maintenance of neutrality forbids the development of vigorous leadership? Executive leadership certainly appears to be a "need" in modern society where bureaucracy rises in importance and the legislative branch declines and where pluralism seems to vest all with some power, rendering the more significant the degree of centrality of power that a strong executive leader can muster. To curb and occasionally stimulate the bureaucracy, to persuade warring factions that concessions are necessary, to rise enough above the fray to acquire visibility convertible into political influence, may well be the one thing the chief executive can supply that no other political agent can. A "neutral" avoider of initiative cannot be chief executive in this sense, a point well illustrated by colorless mayors who do not exploit their potential.

There is an obvious temptation for a manager to assume a leadership role when other elements of the political system fail to provide it. Thus a manager recently said, in an off-the-record session with some students, that "when the carpet-bagging housing developers come in and begin to spoil your town, you don't fuss about what's policy and what's administration, you do something to stop them." If the manager more openly becomes the "politician" that Karl Bosworth rightly asserts he is in reality, then can he retain the aura of neutrality that affords him the opportunity to make the most of his managerial expertise?

Perhaps the more appropriate way to put the question is this: Under what circumstances can the manager contribute enough leadership to cope with the existing problems and yet not get into difficulty by alienating elements in the community so as to spoil his effectiveness as an expert in management? The answer at least in major part would appear to be this: The difficult task of carrying off both these roles will be hardest where (1) the social divisions in the community are deepest and (2) the gravity (and therefore the divisiveness) of the issues are most serious. This is, of course, no new discovery. The difficulty of the manager system in getting a foothold in larger cities is in part a reflection of this fact, as well as a result of the blocking actions of city political machines. Moreover, the higher rate of abandonment of the manager system in large cities suggests of the same conclusion: the deeper the social schisms the tougher the leadership role.

Meyerson and Banfield claim that the efficiency-low cost-businesslike government themes of manager government are popular in "communities where middle and upper class people have an overwhelming preponderance of political power" and not so acceptable to the citizens of more unbanized and polyglot cities. Possibly the distinction between the types of cities reflects more the social divisions that make leadership so difficult in the larger cities than the appeal of the middle-class slogans and goals, but the point is moot since obviously both factors are involved.

The interesting question for the future of the manager plan is whether the trends of population migration will produce more homogeneous communities as a result of the splashing of population outward along the lines of transportation radiating from the metropolitan centers. If the homogeneity factor increases then perhaps manager government may grow even more rapidly than in the past and the strain posed by the neutrality-leadership conflict may not be the deterrent that in theory it appears to be. Surely the main tendency of suburbanization has so far been to produce greater homogeneity if for no other reason than that the poorest elements cannot afford to commute and the few Negroes who can afford it are systematically excluded. On the other hand, the arrival of southern Negroes and hill country whites and Puerto Ricans in northern cities, both large and small (Newburgh, New York, is a city of 31,000 and one of the smoldering fires in its welfare controversy is the animus toward incoming Negroes and Puerto Ricans) will surely work in the other direction. That is, communities will be caught on the rack of social tensions in the next generation as they have not been since the years when an earlier wave of migrants primarily from eastern and southern Europe produced social conflict and long lasting resentments with deep political consequences. The evidence of Newburgh's city manager leadership in its welfare fight is hardly valid since it is atypical behavior, and yet the divisions in that community, partly due to the racial factor, have apparently become serious.

The homogeneity factor can hardly be predicted with certainty. One may be reasonably sure, however, that there will be many communities with placid politics which will not often present the manager with fundamental choices that will bring one element or another of the community out for his scalp. But when other communities, both urban and suburban, face up to the problems of adjusting to life within a metropolitan area (for instance, rapid population growth and diminution of water supply), and begin also to feel the need to rebuild the slums that generations of unplanned expansion have endowed them with, will they respond to the siren call of strong "executive leadership" or not? Will manager cities, when faced with major and divisive problems, respond as other kinds of American government have increasingly done in this century, by turning toward the chief executive as a *representative, policy-initiating, policy-promoting* center of power? Diffusion of leadership is an endemic problem in manager cities, for the council commonly lacks a basis of power from which to lead and rarely do manager-city mayors succeed in establishing the leadership base that, for example, Cincinnati mayors have set for themselves. Will this fact of the common pattern of manager-system operation further encourage the manager to feel justified in becoming a stronger leader since he feels the "need" for policy innovation and "justification" in modern manager theory and current executive leadership trends elsewhere in American government? Quite apart from the customary question which comes alike from friend and foe of the manager system—whether the system is "democratic" when the manager's power grows—is it possible that currents in community development and changes in the internal political characteristics of the system now endanger its effectiveness?

The answer to such questions can only be speculative. One can be reasonably sure that the *logic* of the situation will not be the decisive influence, or else the system would have foundered long ago on the rocks of erroneous assumptions about the separation of politics and administration. But traditions and beliefs do affect the way a governmental system works. In formulating tentative answers to the operational problems of the system for the future it would be well to keep in mind these beliefs and common tendencies: (1) the favorable reputation that the manager system undeniably has for efficiency and honesty, and which will sustain managers when they are hard-pressed; (2) the increasing deference to expertise and experts in matters of economics, industry, personal life and in government as well; (3) the patently strong trend toward emphasizing executive leadership over legislative power, reserving to the former the initiative and to the latter a veto role; and, (4) the significant traditional attachment of the American people to the elective process as a means to popular control over leaders. In any given community the dynamics of its political system (interests, personalities, particular problems, local traditions) will define the limits of leadership effectiveness, and yet these local factors will operate within the context of changing conceptions of the manager system and the currents of popular belief about government and politics.

THE GENERAL MANAGER
IDEA FOR LARGE CITIES
Wallace S. Sayre

Wallace S. Sayre, Edison Professor of Public Administration at Columbia University, has been a member of the Mayor's Advisory Council in New York City since 1954. He is the author (with Herbert Kaufman) of *Governing New York City,* and many other volumes.

A new managerial idea is taking hold in the large cities of the United States. This idea is that the administration of large city governments requires general managerial direction and that this requirement can best be met by establishing under the mayor a general manager who will, in greater or less degree, be the city government's second-in-administrative-command. The general manager plan thus builds upon the strong-mayor tradition as the most widespread form of city government in the United States. By marrying the manager idea with the idea of the elected chief executive, the general manager plan preserves the office of mayor as the center of political leadership and responsibility. In large cities this center is widely regarded as indispensable to effective government.

The general manager plan may be regarded either as a competitor of the council manager idea or as a more mature form of the manager idea, reflecting the judgment in the larger cities that the council manager plan represents an unnecessary surrender of the values of leadership and accountability found in the institution of the elected chief executive. The general manager or mayor manager plan, its proponents emphasize, captures the advantages of the council manager plan without the risks of abandoning the elected

Reprinted from the *Public Administration Review,* journal of the American Society for Public Administration. Vol. XIV, No. 4, Autumn 1954, pp. 253-258, by permission of the publisher.

chief executive. An effective manager, they believe, is no less likely to be chosen by a mayor than by a city council.

The council manager plan has not found acceptance in the large cities of the United States. Cincinnati, the largest city using the plan, has a population of a half million. Of the seventeen other cities having a population of a half million or more, only one city—Cleveland—has ever adopted the plan, and it was abandoned there more than twenty years ago. In the last decade (perhaps even longer), no large city has given serious consideration to the adoption of the council manager plan.

The literature of the council manager movement does not provide an answer to the question: why has the plan failed to find support in large cities? In fact, the literature does not tell us much about the ecology of the council manager plan in adoptions and operations. Why, for example, are half of all the council manager cities to be found in six states (California, Florida, Maine, Michigan, Texas, and Virginia)? Does the council manager plan find acceptance primarily in particular social, economic, and political environments? Does it, for example, find greatest acceptance and operate most successfully in one-party or in "non-partisan" constituencies? Is the affinity between the council manager plan and small and middle-sized cities the result of the plan's suitability for the management of the particular governmental problems to be found in cities of such size? Is the council manager plan particularly attractive to cities which are growing rapidly in size or to those which are declining in population and resources? To these and other questions about the council manager plan we do not yet have the answers.

THE LARGE CITIES TURN TOWARD THE MAYOR MANAGER PLAN

Eight large cities (Boston, Los Angeles, Louisville, Newark, New Orleans, New York City, Philadelphia, and San Francisco) have now established some kind of general managerial assistance for the mayor. In two others (Chicago and Detroit) proposals for such general managerial arrangements have been made.

This new managerial trend in large cities has not resulted from an organized effort by municipal reformers with a symmetrical design for the improvement of city government. In fact, this new form of the manager idea in city government has not yet acquired a distinctive label. Some observers call it the mayor manager plan, to emphasize its contrast with the council manager plan; others call it the mayor administrator plan; and still others name it the general manager plan.

The general manager idea for cities began its governmental history in San Francisco in 1932, when charter revision movement established the office of chief administrative officer. This office represented a compromise solution between those who urged a council manager form and those who supported the retention of the strong mayor form. The plan was not widely noticed, but it has prevailed to the general satisfaction of the electorate. In 1934 New York City's new charter established the office of deputy mayor, an office which developed more as a center of legislative and political assistance to the mayor than as a center of managerial aid. In 1941, Lent D. Upson proposed a general manager under the mayor for the city of Detroit, but the proposal was not accepted. In 1948, Louisville began a related experiment with the appointment of a city consultant-administrator who serves as general managerial assistant to the mayor. In 1951, Los Angeles established a city administrative officer. In the same year, Philadelphia's new charter took a long step forward in developing the general manager idea by establishing the office of managing director with substantial powers. In 1953, New Orleans adopted a new charter which established the office of chief administrative officer, with powers similar to but greater than those of Philadelphia's managing director. In the same year, Boston established a director of administrative services and Newark adopted a new charter which established the office of business administrator under the mayor, the option under the New Jersey statutes closest to the general manager idea. In 1954, New York City established the office of city administrator, with Luther Gulick the first incumbent. And in September, 1954, the staff report to the Chicago Charter Revision Commission recommended the adoption of the general manager plan for that city.

Thus the experiment begun in San Francisco over twenty years ago has captured civic interest and has led to official action in an impressive portion of the large cities. Why has this happened? Several explanations may be suggested:

1. The council manager plan had proved to be unacceptable in large city environments, but the values of the managerial idea were still sought in some more attractive structural form.

2. The office of mayor—an elected chief executive who is the center of energy and of public leadership and the focus of responsibility for policy and performance—had become too important an asset in large cities to be exchanged for the speculative values of legislative supremacy and a city manager as represented in the council manager plan.

3. The mayor manager plan fits comfortably and easily into the American political system: it preserves the elected chief executive; it keeps the mayoralty as the focus of the party battle; it emphasizes the values of integration, hierarchy, and professional management, all made familiar doctrine by a half-century of administrative reorganizations in national, state, and municipal governments and by the doctrine of the council manager movement itself.

EMERGING ELEMENTS
OF THE GENERAL MANAGER IDEA

The idea of a general manager serving under the mayor has not been a pre-packaged solution developed as finished doctrine by municipal reformers. Rather, its evolution has been experimental, each application being worked out in relation to local experience and governmental conditions, and varying with the boldness or caution of local leadership. There are several discernible trends in the successive adoptions, however. These can be briefly stated as follows:

1. The general manager is increasingly made more clearly the managerial agent of the mayor, "the mayor's man." In San Francisco in 1932 the manager was made virtually irremovable, but under 1953-54 provisions in New Orleans and New York City the manager holds office at the pleasure of the mayor.

2. As the manager is more responsible to the mayor, he tends to be given more power—to approach more nearly the status of second in administrative command. In New Orleans and Philadelphia, the cities which represent the most full-bodied application of the general manager idea, the manager is given, for example, the power to appoint and remove the heads of most of the city departments with the approval of the mayor.

3. There is a continued ambivalence in deciding whether the general manager's authority and responsibility should center upon the "staff" or upon the "line" agencies and activities of the city government.

In almost every instance the manager is given primary responsibility for administrative planning and for other organization and methods work. In Los Angeles and New Orleans he has responsibility for budget preparation and execution; in Philadelphia and New York these activities are not under the manager's jurisdiction. In no city does the manager directly supervise the personnel agency. In New Orleans, New York, and Philadelphia the "line" agencies are the manager's major responsibility. The two extremes are represented by Los Angeles, where the manager's responsibilities are focused upon the management functions (except personnel), and by Philadelphia, where the manager's powers are centered upon the "line" agencies.

4. There is some tendency to create a new and smaller cabinet institution under the mayor, consisting of the general manager and the heads of the "staff" agencies. This is particularly the case in Philadelphia and New York. The heads of the "line" agencies, when they function as a cabinet (as they do in Philadelphia), do so in a meeting presided over by the manager.

VARIATIONS IN THE OFFICE AND POWERS OF THE GENERAL MANAGER IN FIVE LARGE CITIES

The variety as well as the trends in the development of the general manager idea in the large cities of the United States may perhaps best be seen through a more specific description of the office and the powers conferred upon it in Los Angeles, New Orleans, New York City, Philadelphia, and San Francisco.

Titles: In San Francisco and New Orleans the manager is called chief administrative officer; in Philadelphia, managing director; in New York, city administrator.

Appointment: In every instance, the manager is appointed by the mayor. Only in Los Angeles is council approval required.

Term: In San Francisco, Los Angeles, New Orleans, and New York, no term is specified. In Philadelphia the term of the manager is four years, corresponding to the term of the mayor appointing him.

Removal: In New Orleans and New York the mayor may remove the manager. In Los Angeles, the mayor may remove the manager, but the approval of the council is required. In Philadelphia the mayor must prefer charges; the manager may appeal his removal to the Civil Service Commission which may award him compensation but may not restore him. In San Francisco the mayor may not remove; the manager is subject to recall in an election, or the legislative body may remove him by a two-thirds vote. In Los Angeles and New Orleans the council may also remove the manager— in Los Angeles by a two-thirds vote and in New Orleans by a majority vote of all members.

Powers of the manager: The powers of the managers may be described in three categories: (1) the power to appoint and remove heads of city agencies; (2) the power to supervise city administrative operations; (3) the power to provide general advice and assistance to the mayor.

1. *To appoint and remove heads of agencies:* In Philadelphia, New Orleans, and San Francisco, the managers appoint and remove the heads of specified city departments and agencies. In San Francisco the manager does not need the mayor's approval for such appointments or removals; in Philadelphia and New Orleans the mayor's approval is required. In New Orleans the manager's power to appoint and remove extends to the heads of all but two city departments (law and civil service); in Philadelphia it includes all but finance, law, and personnel. In neither of these two cities does the power to appoint and remove include members of boards or commissions. In San Francisco, the power extends to departments specified by name in the charter; such departments constitute about half of the city agencies.

In neither Los Angeles nor New York does the manager have the power to appoint or remove heads of departments.

2. *To supervise city administration operations:* In San Francisco the power of the manager to supervise is confined to the departments specifically assigned to him by the charter. In Los Angeles the manager's opportunities for supervision flow solely from his role as city budget officer. In Philadelphia the manager's power to supervise is largely confined to the departments whose heads he appoints, but some more general supervision flows from his powers to perform the administrative analysis function in all city agencies.

In New Orleans the manager has more general supervisory authority. He supervises not only his own subordinate agencies (which include most of the city agencies), but he also gives "general oversight" to law, civil service, and the City Planning Commission (which are outside his appointing and removal authority), prescribes standards of administrative practice to be followed by all agencies and boards, prepares and supervises the operating and capital budgets, surveys the organization and procedures of all agencies and boards, and may require reports from any or all of them.

In New York City the city administrator, although lacking any power to appoint or remove, has a broad supervisory assignment. Under the direction of the mayor, he "shall supervise and coordinate the work of all agencies under the jurisdiction of the mayor" except law, investigation, budget, the construction coordinator, and boards, commissions (which include personnel), and authorities. He may convene heads of agencies singly or collectively, procure information and reports, require the keeping of management records, conduct work studies, and establish management standards for most, if not all city agencies.

3. *The power to provide general advice and assistance to the mayor:* In Philadelphia and New York the manager is under a special obligation to serve as general management adviser to the mayor. In Philadelphia the managing director is required to report periodically to the mayor concerning the affairs of the city government (not merely the affairs of his own departments), and he is authorized to make recommendations on matters concerning the affairs of the whole city government. In New York the city administrator is required to "prepare annual and all such other reports as the mayor shall require," and to "analyze and report to the mayor concerning impending policy decisions affecting the management of the city and the agencies." He is also directed to "maintain liaison with civic and community groups on matters of governmental management."

In both Philadelphia and New York the manager derives special status from cabinet arrangements, established by the charter in Philadelphia and by the mayor's action in New York. In each city there is a small top-level cabinet group meeting weekly with the mayor, in which the manager plays a central role.

The managers in the other three cities have no explicit responsibility to serve as the general adviser to the mayor on management matters. In these cities, the manager's role in this respect is implicit, if it exists at all. In San Francisco it would seem difficult to join such a role with that of an almost autonomous manager. In New Orleans it would seem to be a logical and natural development. In Los Angeles, it would appear to be a more confined but possible development.

THE FUTURE COURSE OF THE MAYOR MANAGER PLAN

The invention and recent growth of the general manager idea in large cities is a product of many influences. Some of these influences would seem to be of reasonably permanent rather than transient character. The larger cities of the United States have developed complex administrative establishments which require strengthened central managerial leadership, direction, and coordination. These cities have also, almost without exception, developed an increasing reliance upon the elected chief executive—a mayor with extensive powers to appoint, to remove, and to direct the heads of administrative agencies—as the main institution of governmental leadership and accountability. The electoral contest for this office has been the primary instrument of popular control of the city government and the main occasion for public education and participation in city affairs. The office of mayor in large cities has, in addition, become more important as a prize in the party battle, its possession one of the significant keys to state and even national party power. It would seem unlikely that any large city would abandon such a governmental and political asset.

But if the institution of the "strong" mayor in large cities has come to stay, then it would also seem that such mayors, no less than the President, need managerial help. The mayor manager idea is a response to this felt need in the large cities. In this sense, the mayor manager plan is in the mainstream of the administrative doctrine heralded by the President's Committee on Administrative Management in 1937, and reaffirmed by the Hoover Commission's later studies of the national government. The central idea of these studies, and dozens of their counterparts in the states, has been to strengthen the position of the elected chief executive in his political and administrative leadership.

The mayor manager plan is likely to dominate the course of large city administrative reorganizations for the next several years. The council manager plan is not likely to break into the large city league, because this plan does not represent an accommodation to either the political or the managerial requirements of the large cities. The emergence of the mayor manager plan has breached the monopolistic claim of the council manager plan to the managerial virtues by presenting the new and strong competition of an alternative manager plan.

Not only is the mayor manager plan likely to hold its own and to extend its scope to most of the largest cities, but it is also probable that it will become an attractive solution for many (perhaps most) of the one hundred and five cities with 100,000 population or more. In contrast with the council manager plan, the mayor manager plan is elastic in its formal arrangements, and it can thus respond more easily to local priorities, customs, and personalities. To the strong mayor cities, it offers an evolutionary transition, buttressing rather than discarding the values which have been built up around the leadership of the elected chief executive. To these cities, the mayor manager plan offers the same managerial gains as does the council manager plan, but at much less risk. The strategic and tactical advantages of such an offer in the political world can hardly be exaggerated.

The mayor manager plan will, as it evolves toward its own institutionalization, be confronted with dilemmas which can now be only partially anticipated. The plan may ultimately acquire its own protective guild of practitioners and advocates, transforming it into an inelastic plan unresponsive to the changing needs of the cities. It may be drowned in a few dramatic "failures."

The mayor manager idea will probably encounter its severest test in the effort to give the manager sufficient power to provide him with adequate leverage to infuse the values of professional management into the administration of a large city government. Philadelphia and New Orleans have made the clearest and strongest effort to insure this result. The Devereux Josephs Commission, in the most complete formulation of the mayor manager plan (*Four Steps to Better Government of New York City,* 1953-54), proposed still greater strength for the manager while making him also more clearly the mayor's administrative agent. The range of variation in managerial power is wide among the cities using the mayor manager idea. The trend in official action and civic opinion—particularly on the manager's appointing power—is not conclusive, but it seems to run toward the grant of greater managerial leverage.

The mayor manager plan will also encounter, perhaps early in its development, the politics-administration dilemma which increasingly bedevils the council manager plan in operation. Can the general manager be at once both a professional administrator and the mayor's second in administrative command? That is, can he be (with the mayor) the effective maker and protagonist of policy proposals which are certain to be controversial without sacrificing his professional managerial status? This dilemma plagues the council manager plan even more deeply (because council manager doctrine emphasizes council monopoly over policy while practice underscores the necessity for policy leadership by the manager), but this fact provides merely an advantage rather than a solution for the mayor manager advocates. The trend in mayor manager cities is not yet clear, but the general manager in a large city seems at this stage no more likely to become a career manager in that city than has the city manager in this.

Some observers profess to see in the mayor manager plan merely a compromise stop toward the council manager plan. The reverse would seem to be the more likely development, if any such transference is to occur. The essential ingredient of the mayor manager plan is the appointment and removal of the manager by the mayor as the elected chief executive. The distinctive contrasting feature of the council manager plan—the selection of the chief administrator by the city council—was not only something of an historical accident in the United States; it was also a striking anomaly in a country in which the most distinctive political institution is the elected chief executive as the keystone of political, governmental, and managerial progress. The mayor manager idea has the great and lasting value that it brings the reorganization of our city governments back into a familiar focus, consistent with our efforts in the national and state governments. In this respect it is an indigenous political idea.

THE ETHICAL PROBLEMS OF AN ELECTED POLITICAL EXECUTIVE
Stephen K. Bailey

> Stephen K. Bailey is dean of the Maxwell Graduate School of Citizenship and Public Affairs, Syracuse University. Formerly a professor of political science, he is the author of *Roosevelt and His New Deal, Congress Makes a Law,* and several textbooks on American government. He has had an active political career of his own, including a term as mayor of Middletown, Connecticut.

Any attempt to construct what John Buchan once called "an essay in recollection" is fraught with ethical puzzles. When such an essay is addressed, upon commission, to the moral dilemmas of a political experience of some years ago, ethical issues are piled crazily one on top of the other. And they are nudged into further disarray by the tricks which rationalization and memory play upon all autobiographers. In view of the number of friends whose good names must be protected against my possibly accurate reporting of their (and my) occasional moral lapses; in view of the impossibility, six to eight years after events, of my recapturing the precise pattern of considerations which shaped the matrix within which decisions were made; and in view of the inscrutability of many of the ethical issues with which I, as mayor of a city of 30,000 had to deal, it is clear that this essay must be content with the perennially probable rather than the historically precise.

Insofar as I refer specifically to experiences in Middletown, Connecticut, during the years when I was mayor of that city, I hope that friends there will show me the same charity that Huckleberry Finn showed Mark Twain. Referring to *The Adventures of Tom Sawyer,* Huck commented, "That book was made by Mr. Mark Twain, and he told the truth, mainly. There was things which he stretched, but mainly he told the truth. That is nothing. I never seen anybody but lied one time or another, without it was Aunt Polly . . ." And Huck Finn was perceptive in spotting the moral flaw in Aunt Polly and in her old maid sister, Miss Watson: a flaw of self-righteousness so hideous that when Huck learned that Miss Watson was living "so as to go to the good place," Huck could "see no advantage in going where she was going," so he made up his mind he wouldn't try for it.

I have worried far more about the ethical consequences of my decisions as mayor since leaving office than I ever did as an incumbent. And perhaps this is the first point to be made. Most elected executives find that there is an ethics of action which is normally far more compelling than the urge to

From *Ethics and Bigness,* edited by Harlan Cleveland and Harold D. Lasswell. © 1962 by The Conference on Science, Philosophy and Religion in Their Relation to the Democratic Way of Life, Inc. Reprinted by permission of Harper & Row, Publishers.

balance with precision the ethical niceties of pressing pubilc issues. There are times when the good of the community demands firmness and decision at the expense of marginal injustice. Those who would make justice the sole criterion of the good society are not only, in my judgment, myopic in their ethical vision, they establish an impossible operating norm for administrators. Justice, in the sense of "just desserts," presumes omnipotence and omniscience. An elected mayor in a "weak-mayor" form of government, alas, has neither. He may desire to be just, but occasions arise when justice is not the highest ethical priority. If a local hospital, which has run a county-wide ambulance service for years, suddenly decides for budgetary reasons to disown this responsibility, it may be unjust to make the tax-payers of a single city in the county pick up the check for keeping the county-wide ambulance service going on an emergency basis. But, here, what is necessary overrides what is just.

And emergency actions by an authorized executive have meaning and value quite apart from the justice or injustice of any decision taken by the executive under his emergency authority. The justification for the emergency powers of the public executive are, I believe, not only in the necessities of organization under stress; there is a most significant social therapy in the public's sense that "somebody is in charge." The sight of Winston Churchill making his way through the rubble of blitzed London and barking orders to subordinates had the effect of strengthening resolve and dissolving fear among the affected public. Even lowly political executives at times perform this valuable emergency role.

But even when an emergency does not exist, there are frequently statutory deadlines or political deadlines—budgets, elections, schedules of compliance established by a higher level of government—which precipitate executive decisions largely uncomplicated by labored ethical considerations. Deadlines are great strengtheners of the resolve to choose. Those who would build theories of decision-making removed from the context of the clock and the calendar know nothing of the inner life of a political executive. And, even then, no executive in public life is free from having his life arbitrarily and often whimsically scheduled by real or fancied immediacies which are superimposed upon the clock and calendar, no matter how carefully the latter have been anticipated.

In brief, although almost every issue with which an elected executive must deal is charged with ethical dilemmas, it is rare that the executive has either the time, the context, or the liver for constructing balanced ethical judgments. He does what he must. Ethically, elected executives tend, like successful fighter pilots, to "fly by the seat of their pants." Speed is the enemy of deliberation, and in administration, speed—in the sense of dispatch—is often the condition of maintainng a tolerable if ineffable balance among those interests, obligations, and necessities which crowd the world of the elected executive.

All of this is not meant to suggest that ethical considerations are somehow peripheral to an elected executive's life. It is only to say that ethical issues are rarely trotted out for leisurely inspection and deliberate choice. This may be unfortunate, but my guess is that if ethical considerations were always carefully and honestly articulated in decision-making, the ensuing chaos—moral and administrative—would be impressive.

If we are talking about the real world, then, we are talking in large measure about the inarticulate moral premises of the office holder—the ethical sign-posts which a harried political executive catches out of the corner of his eye.

With this statement, of course, the essay could well end. Any attempt to list all of the precepts, proverbs, fables (and their rationalized versions) which conscience picks to guide or to justify actions, would lead to an endless and formless recitation of the obvious and the inscrutable. And ultimately such a recitation would tell us nothing about conscience itself; that ego-tempered temperer of egos; that culture-bound transcender of culture; that ultimate sorter of ethical ambiguities. It gets us nowhere to suggest that all of the Philosophy 1-2 classroom stumpers are present in political life—as they are in all life. Should a cancer specialist be honest or kind? Ultimately, is it more honest to be kind or more kind to be honest? Is a half-truth a worse enemy of the truth than a falsehood? Should promises be kept if the situation changes (and when doesn't it change)? Should friends be reported if you know them to be mostly good and you know that they probably will not do it again? Should you subject someone to the consequences of wrong-doing if you are reasonably sure that the penalty is sufficiently harsh and inelastic as to be inequitable?

To pretend that there are clear religious, moral, or legal answers to such questions is to fly in the face of all sensitive moral inquiry.

How difficult the means-ends questions of living really are is known by every parent who ponders such matters. After a generation of permissiveness in raising children, we are finally returning to a belief that metes and bounds backed by sanctions are ultimately kinder to the growing child and the society than uninhibited license. But how many sanctions? How extensive the metes and bounds? Someone once commented that the Lord had left the two most difficult and important jobs in the world to amateurs: citizenship and parenthood. Elected political executives, at least most of them, are also amateurs, and their jobs may be no less difficult or important than the others mentioned. What is common to the life of all of these amateurs is that the value questions are extraordinarily complex, and the chances of adequate time for deliberation are slim.

But are there not peculiar ethical risks run by elected political executives? Surely, most people are not faced frequently with questions of bribery, spoils, corruption, favoritism. The difficulty is, neither are elected political executives; and even when venality raises its head, it rarely looks to the responsible political executive as ugly as it appears in newspaper cartoons or Sunday sermons. Venality, like virtue, is rarely unambiguous. G.D. Chesterton wrote perceptively when he suggested that the error of Diogenes "lay in the fact that he omitted to notice that every man is both an honest and a dishonest man. Diogenes looked for his honest man inside every crypt and cavern, but he never thought of looking inside the thief. And that is where the Founder of Christianity found the honest man. He found him on a gibbet and promised him paradise."

When the nicest people have rationalized their selfishness with a tactical deference to the public interest, elected political executives are often grateful that they are too preoccupied to be ethically astute. Even where venality seems clearest, as in the rare case of an attempt at straight bribery ("Mayor, here's a thousand dollars in five-dollar bills if you get that easement through the council,"—the political version of "payola"), the ethical issues may not be self-evident. Let us make some assumptions: suppose that the mayor knows that the easement will go through "on its merits" (begging what that slippery phrase means). Suppose further that the mayor knows that the party needs money not only to run the forthcoming election but to pay debts on a past election. Suppose the mayor knows further that the voting public has not responded favorably and positively to the appeal of the American Heritage Foundation for everyone to give to the party of his choice. Suppose finally that the mayor believes that a working two-party system is the nation's and the community's greatest safeguard of democracy and freedom. If it could be proved to the mayor's satisfaction that the lack of $1,000 at the moment could do irreparable damage to the two-party system in the area, would it be a higher principle in a naughty world for the mayor to accept the money on behalf of the party, or to refuse the money?

Stated that way, the issue is still not very complex for most people. "They've known what's right and wrong since they've been ten." You do not accept bribes, period; and you most certainly do not compound evil, by cheating the briber. This is all very clear. But is it, really? There are ways of playing slight variations on this theme which would remove from the sternest Presbyterian moralist any burden of guilt. The briber has made a number of contributions to the party over the years. The latest thousand is simply another indication of his belief in the great principles of the party. On the easement question, every party member on the council, including the mayor, attempts to examine the issue on its merit. But a "will to believe" has set in—a subtle coloration of the problem. Good old Joe is a friend who provided all the favors for the party picnic. Isn't it fortunate that the merits of the easement case are on his side?

And bribery can take so many forms: money, favors, flattery, help in time of trouble, influence in building status. To pretend that bribery is a simple and easily spotted phenomenon is naive. To pretend it takes place only in politics is silly. I have seen the egos of older university professors successfully bribed by astute and ambitious instructors; I have seen great institutions bribe men into conformity with promises of promotions or de-motions. I have seen them kill, spiritually, those who resisted. I have received threats that unless such-and-such happened, I'd be voted out of office at the next election. Is this not attempted bribery? Is money any more a thing of value than power or status or re-election? If there are clear moral distinctions here, they escape me, even though our cultural inheritance sanctions certain kinds of bribery and frowns on others.

I once asked a municipal judge in Middletown to tell me what pressures were most constant in trying to influence his impartial administration of justice. He thought a minute and then said, laughingly, "The university deans and the town clergy." But why should he have laughed? Certainly few would question the motives of deans and clergy in attempting to save the reputations of individuals known to them, and under their keep, who have been accused of wrong-doing. But what of the wrong-doer who has no "friend in court"? Anyone who has ever watched a municipal court in action over a period of time knows that "political influence" is frequently a corrective for the partial justice that results from the rich litigant's capacity to purchase superior legal talent. Middleclass justice is not always equitable to the poor. This is not to condone political influence in courts of law, it is to suggest that without political influence certain inequities might be greater than they are, and that those inequities need as much attention as overt or covert political influence.

I was never asked to fix a traffic or parking ticket in Middletown; but I cannot swear that tickets were not occasionally fixed while I was mayor. And I am not sure that under certain circumstances (e.g., a hectic woman delayed in buying her six children school clothes) I would not have paid the dollar fine myself rather than penalize her for something beyond her effective control. Nothing is more unjust than unexceptional law except law that is all exceptions. Surely, one of the most difficult ethical problems in all governance is the drawing of lines between rules and exceptions. That the lines, to be moral, must be drawn near the rules end of the spectrum I do not question. But that exceptions are never warranted seems to me the most callous of all moral judgments.

To the moralist, words like bribery, favoritism, spoils, patronage, graft, are as clear and as evil as though bottled and marked with skull and cross-bones. To those with political responsibility, on the other hands, it occasionally seems clear that poison can be therapeutic. The fact that poison is labelled with a skull and crossbones and placed back on a high shelf of the medicine closet may not mean that it is never to be used; only that it is to be used with care and in small doses. It is possible that if an elected executive had infinite time he might be able to discern ways to achieve his goals without using morally uncomfortable means—although the question of where rationalizations begin and end with this sort of game plays hob with moral certainty. But if an unskilled city job to a not-incompetent nationality-group representative might make the difference between winning or losing on an urban renewal referendum of vast benefit to the entire city for years to come, I know few elected executives who would boggle over making such an appointment even if the executive was convinced that someone else might do the unskilled job better.

George Bernard Shaw once wrote what many politicians must at times have felt. Shaw learned that a Labour candidate named Joseph Burgess had refused to compromise on some issue and had thereby lost his seat in Parliament. Shaw commented bitterly:

> When I think of my own unfortunate character, smirched with com-
> promise, rotted with opportunism, mildewed by expediency—dragged
> through the mud of borough council and Battersea elections, stretched
> out of shape with wire-pulling, putrified by permeation, worn out by
> twenty-five years pushing to gain an inch here, or straining to stem a
> backrush, I do think Joe might have put up with just a speck or two on
> those white robes of his for the sake of the millions of poor devils who
> cannot afford any character at all because they have no friend in parlia-
> ment. Oh, these moral dandies, these spiritual toffs, these superior per-
> sons. Who is Joe, anyhow, that he should not risk his soul occasionally
> like the rest of us?

I was once confronted with a possible kick-back on a fire truck purchase. The party representative reminded me that it cost money to run elections; that generosity from fire-truck manufacturers to those who had the insight to see the need for public safety in their communities was rather standard; and that no one would really suffer. The gift would come as a preordained slice of the salesman's commission, who would give of his own income because "he believed in the principles of the Democratic Party." I drew myself up to my maximum height, stared at my good friend, and said in what I am sure must have been the most patronizing of tones, "If the party needs four or five hundred dollars, I shall be happy to try to raise the money personally; but I shall not do it *that* way." I then went a step further. I called the poor fire truck salesman into the office and made him add about $400 worth of extra equipment to the fire truck at the bid price he had quoted. In a swift double blow I had proved my moral worth and defended the taxpayer's interest. I had proved that at least in one American community "public office is a public trust."

I had also proved that it is easy to be moral when the pressure is not really on. Suppose the party coffers *had* been empty? Suppose my confident bluff to raise "four or five hundred dollars" for the party had been called? Suppose the alternative to a Democratic re-election was the election of a rather disreputable Republican gang who would have practiced "boodle" with more frequency and with infinitely less flair than the Democrats? What then? And why should we refuse to accept money for the imperative cause of political party machinery, almost regardless of source, when the so-called "good" people of the community would not be caught dead giving to their political party—to the system of options which does far more than the Constitution to guarantee freedom and democracy?

I could not be a partner to a kick-back, not because I had carefully weighed the moral issues, but because my moral viscera told me it was wrong. Unfortunately, my moral viscera are not always right. If they were right in this particular case, they were right for reasons removed from the issue at hand. They were right because, without sufficient time and eloquence, I could not have explained any contrary action—if forced to by the local newspaper or an official inquiry—to the satisfaction of the adult public whose moral viscera are quite as dogmatic as mine. I thereby would have undercut the public's faith in my honesty, and would have damaged that most priceless of all public executive resources, the public's confidence. There would then have been an unhappy and unproductive feedback into everything else I did or tried to do as an elected official. The moral dilemma remains however: for I am confident that if I had had the insight to have taken the kick-back and the time and eloquence to have explained to the public why I had done it—describing to them the impossible position they put politicians into by their not assuming disinterested responsibility for financing party campaigns—they would have seen the point and respected me for my action. They even might have taken the lesson to heart and decided to give to their party as frequently and as richly as they give to other causes they value—such as community chests and churches.

The only serious ethical struggle I had with party leaders in Middletown dealt with a request for a zoning exception. Here I was firm, morally aroused, and dogmatic, and would be to this day. The story is quickly told. A contractor, who had contributed liberally to both political parties locally, hired a leading Democratic lawyer to plead for a commercial spot zone in a strictly residential area. The people of the area were almost solidly opposed to the change. Even if they had not been, nothing can ruin the orderly and aesthetic development of a growing city like politically-inspired spot zoning in contravention of a general plan. The members of the zoning committee, to their credit, said to me, "Mayor, there's a lot we'll do for the party, but we won't do this." The final showdown on this case took place in the lawyer's office with all major party leaders present. I walked in swinging. I made it quite clear that if the plumbing broke down in city hall, I would hire a licensed Democratic plumber over a licensed Republican plumber any day of the week; that if the law did not force us to go to bid, I would buy insurance from a Democratic rather than a Republican insurance agent; but that when it came to what Edmund Burke once called "the permanent forces" in the community, I was ready to do battle. I suggested that although there was much in politics that one rendered to Caesar, almost without qualms, city planning was rendered only to God. A few party leaders were upset; but most of them were understanding; and the lawyer in question, who over the years has been one of the most brilliant as well as constructive forces in the community and state, had the grace to accept my position without rancor.

But I have already dwelt far too long on such matters. In my two years as mayor, these kinds of party issues could not have represented more than one-fiftieth of my working time. Contrary to what many people seem to believe, the hard ethical issues of public life rarely concern party politics. Party decisions tend to roll according to pre-set patterns. Every elected executive works out a few obvious bench-marks for relationships with political leaders, (for example, "consult party leaders on all appointments, but solicit their help in trading little appointments to the party for big appointment to you"). In any case, to suggest that most party officials are frequently ethical "problems" is to distort their normal role beyond recognition. For every occasion when a party leader asked me for a favor that disturbed my conscience, I can think of a dozen times when *that very same party leader* helped me defend the public interest against the importunities of non-party pressure groups.

Upon reflection, it is my firm belief that insofar as party politics interferes with the pursuit of the public interest, it is largely a result of the necessities of campaign finance. Most venality in public life could be abolished or reduced to insignificance if the public would assume responsibility for broadly-based campaign financing and would insist upon the public auditing and disclosure of all campaign gifts and expenditures. This would not eliminate corruption entirely, for wherever power and money converge some venality will be found. But our present method of financing political campaigns is, in my estimation, the single most corrupting factor in our political life—local, national, and especially, state.

If what has been discussed so far are not the major ethical issues of the elected executive, what are? To the man who is ethically sensitive, the hair-turning issues are those which involve impossible choices among contending interpretations of the public interest. Again, the necessity of dispatch is psychologically therapeutic; but the drain on energy and conscience is substantial nonetheless. Take ten or a dozen problems which faced me as mayor, and which are typical of perhaps a hundred which I faced in two years as an elected executive.

(1) A peacock farm on the edge of town kept neighbors awake for a month or so a year during the peacock mating season. The City was asked by the neighbors to see to it that the birds were quieted. Ethical question: is a temporary irritation—including loss of sleep—for ten families worth the destruction of a hobby and a partial livelihood for one person?

(2) A leading department store on Main Street said it had to have a rear access service garage on Broad Street or it would be forced to leave town. Broad Street was zoned residential. Ethical question: would the loss of the department store be a greater loss than a break in the city's zoning pattern?

(3) The best detective on the chronically-underpaid police force is suspected of taking protection money from some local two-bit gamblers. The evidence is too vague and unsubstantial to stand in court. Ethical question: is the *possibility* of the evidence being correct important enough to warrant

a substantial investigation, with a consequent probable loss in efficiency and morale in the police department during and long after the investigation, a certain loss in public confidence in the whole force, and the ever present possibility that the rumor was planted by a crank? And out of the many pressing issues coming across the mayor's desk, how much time and effort does such an investigation warrant from the mayor himself?

(4) The whole scheme of volunteer fire departments is looked upon by the chief of the city's only paid department as wasteful, inefficient, and dangerous to the public safety. The volunteers claim that their fire-fighting record is top-notch, that they save the taxpayers money. Ethical question: if neither side can be proved incorrect, how does one weigh the values of volunteer community endeavors against marginal inefficiencies in operation of a vital service?

(5) Many years ago, one department store was far-sighted enough to have bought up some land for off-street parking. This off-street parking gave the store quite a competitive advantage. The city, in a new municipal parking program, needed a portion of the private parking lot assembled by the department store years before. When established, the municipal lot might destroy the store's competitive advantage. Ethical question: at what point does the public interest demand that private far-sightedness be penalized?

(6) Two mayors in four years happened to have lived on Wyllys Avenue. Wyllys Avenue desperately needed repaving. But so did some other streets in the city. Ethical question: should Wyllys Avenue be paved, granted a heavy presumption that many citizens would claim that the mayor had "taken care of himself"?

(7) A federal grand-in-aid cut in half the city's welfare load, making a sinecure out of one of the two city welfare positions. The holder of the sinecure was a negro appointed by the opposition party. Ethical question: should work somehow be "made" for the negro, or should he be dropped? (For anyone who knows the problems of status, morale, and upward mobility among negroes in a largely white community, the political questions posed by this case are easy compared to the long-range ethical questions.)

(8) The virulent opposition of a local printer-publicist might be tamed on a few key issues with the proper placing of a few city printing contracts. Ethical question: obvious.

(9) Buying of tires in wholesale lots would save the taxpayers $300 a year—about one cent per citizen per annum. A score of little Middletown tire merchants would lose ten dollars or more in income. Ethical question: how does one balance one cent each for 30,000 people vs. ten dollars each for twenty merchants?

(10) Parents concerned with the safety of their children on the way to and from school are constantly demanding increased police protection and more sidewalks. A more legitimate demand would be hard to imagine. But there are limits. Ethical question: granted that *total* safety never can be

assured, what grounds beyond obvious necessity and "the squeaky wheel gets the grease" can be found for awarding or denying protection?

(11) A health officer is technically qualified and conscientious, but egregiously officious. Ethical question: is the damage done to the city government's relations with its citizens by the meticulous and unfeeling enforcement of ordinances likely to be sufficiently serious to warrant the health officer's dismissal?

(12) There is a likelihood that one of the major industries in town will have to close down a sizeable slice of its operations. This may mean 2,000 unemployed. A steel company is looking for a New England site for a steel mill. It finds an "ideal" location in Middletown. That "ideal" location is a stretch of the Connecticut River which is unspoiled and is deeply treasured by small boat owners and by nature lovers. Ethical question: is the provision of employment for 2,000 people worth the destruction forever of natural beauty?

These are samples of the tough ones. And in most cases, the ethical values are sufficiently balanced so that no matter which side the mayor takes, half the concerned citizens in the community will charge him—and with considerable justification in their own minds—with having sold out. This is one of the reasons for the low image of politicians in our society: the fact that the losing cause in public policy generally has substantial merit on its side, with the consequence that the loser can see nothing but venality or partiality in the elected official's decision. People get sore at politicians for the same reason they throw pop-bottles at umpires: the disagreements always come on the close ones. If only citizens could pause on occasion to realize that the issues really are complex; that most elected officials do the best they can to be fair; that the peaceful resolution of conflict is a vast service to humankind, and is a most difficult art; that Solomon himself was perplexed by some of the issues posed by communities of men.

If I should be asked today how I resolved, in my own mind, the ethical dilemmas posed on the preceding pages, I should not know how to answer. Most of the dilemmas were not mine to resolve alone. Other people shared official power with me, and many citizens without official power assumed substantial unofficial responsibility for community decisions. There is not the loneliness and, perhaps, terror in executive decision-making at the local level which I assume there must often be at higher executive levels in American government. Consequences of errors in judgment are far less apocalyptic.

But insofar as I had to make up my mind by myself, or felt that my judgment might be determining in the minds of others, I did repair to two or three very general propositions for ethical guidance. In practice, the propositions were never articulated, but in retrospect, I know that they were there. All of them had been woven into my life by parental, religious and academic influences—in most cases by all three. My father, although never a minister, was a Professor of Religion and a firm believer in the Social Gospel. My studies at Oxford had brought me close to Immanuel Kant and Jean Jacques Rousseau. Ideas like "the categorical imperative" and "the general will" were connected in my mind with such Biblical injunctions as "Let justice roll down as waters; and righteousness as a mighty stream." I had nothing in my system that told me what was right; but I did have something in my system that told me to search for what was right. The most helpful single question I could ask myself seemed to be, "What do you want Middletown to be like ten years from now?" Against this many things fell into place. I wanted more beauty, fewer slums, less bigotry, more recreation, more community spirit, a more sustained sense of public responsibility, a more dynamic and prosperous economy, better education, a stronger and more truly competitive two-party system, and a heightened sense of personal dignity for all. These were some of the bench marks against which specific ethical issues were measured or rationalized. They were not my marks. They were the marks of the civilization of which I was a miniscule and clouded reflection. As Carl Becker once wrote:

> To have faith in the dignity and worth of the individual man as an end in himself; to believe that it is better to be governed by persuasion than by coercion; to believe that fraternal goodwill is more worthy than a selfish and contentious spirit; to believe that in the long run all values are inseparable from the love of truth and the disinterested search for it; to believe that knowledge and the power it confers should be used to promote the welfare and happiness of all men rather than to serve the interests of those individuals and classes whom fortune and intelligence endow with temporary advantage—these are the values which are affirmed by the traditional democratic ideology. . . . They are the values which since the time of Buddha and Confucius, Solomon and Zoroaster, Plato and Aristotle, Socrates and Jesus, men have commonly employed to measure the advance or decline of civilization, the values they have celebrated in the saints and sages whom they have agreed to canonize. They are the values which readily lend themselves to rational justification, yet need no justification.

There are, perhaps, two other matters which ought to be touched upon in an essay of this nature. The first has to do with the effect of power upon personality. Acton is quite explicit that "All power corrupts and absolute power corrupts absolutely." This I cannot gainsay. I remember one evening when I was returning with political friends from a television performance. For a half-hour they told me what a brilliant performance mine had been. By the end of the half-hour I was aware only that a new political star had been born on the horizon; namely me, and that I could not long deny the people of the state of Connecticut the chance to vote for me either for governor or at the very least for United States senator. It was not until I got home that my wife—with that wonderful sixth sense of a level-headed and thoughtful woman—reminded me that my performance, had, in fact, been a little on the mediocre side—but that she was sure I had just had an off night. The most devastating traps of public office are the ones set to catch the ego. It is so easy to forget that the tribute is to the office, not to the person. Even a mayor stands out a little: fathers bring up their daughters to "shake the mayor's hand"; the mayor sits at head tables; he officiates; he is often the central figure in ceremony. All this inflates the sense of personal worth and waters the thirsty garden of vanity. The consequences are often pathetic, often silly, sometimes dangerous. But Acton was wrong in suggesting that the only flowers in the garden of vanity are the weeds of corruption. Power may corrupt, but it also can ennoble. The sense that you, and the office you hold, are widely valued often creates a heightened sense of responsibility, a desire to live close to the public expectation, a wish to become a kind of community example. Too few people appreciate the ennobling effect of public office. I have seen men utterly transformed by a judgeship. A politician—an old pro in western Connecticut—once confided to me that he hated all judges. "What are they but some hack lawyers who happened to know a politician?" And he went on, "After you've made 'em, what do they do? They turn around and kick you in the teeth! They draw their robes around them as though they were Solon or something! You can't touch them! Who the hell do they think they are?" The fact is that they think they *are* Solon; they suddenly realized that instead of petty politicians they are an essential part of the fabric of civilization—a fabric which can last only so long as there is wide-spread public belief that judges in courts of law will try to be just. And what is true of judges is equally true of elected executives.

The ennobling effect of public office is one of its greatest psychic dividends. Those who believe that men seek to hold public office only because it gives them power and status do not appreciate the importance to many men of simple feeling that the job they hold makes them better members of the human race. The heightened capacity for doing good in the world is one of the key attractions of political power, and from my limited observations is a far more fundamental factor in determining the direction of men's ambitions than the baubles and tinsel of temporary status and deference.

This brings me to my final point. All ethical questions ultimately revert to propositions about the nature of man. The underlying complexity of ethical questions stems from the fact that man is morally ambiguous and teleologically inscrutable. Perched precariously on a whirling planet, blind to his origins, blind to his reasons for being, beset by the terrors of nature and of his own creation, man wobbles drunkenly between a certainty that he is nothing and an occasional, blinding revelation that he has a transcendent dignity and perhaps destiny. When man feels alienated from his universe, he may huddle in fear with his fellow men; but he cannot reach them with the fullness of feeling, that intenseness of identity, which is suggested by the Christian concept of love, or by the civil concept of community. I am not a mystical person, but I sense strongly that my best moments as mayor came when I felt—in an almost religious way—that what we were attempting to do in Middletown had meaning beyond itself. I remember Fred Smith, the editor of the local paper, once writing me an intimate note when I was particularly discouraged about the public response to some issue. "Never," he wrote, "lose faith in your neighbors." And he went on to explain, not that they were perfect, but that he had known them for a long time, and that they would ultimately respond to the good if they could be shown the good.

Surely this is the ultimate ethical postulate in a democracy: not that man is good, but that he is capable of good; not that he is wise, but that he is capable of valuing wisdom; not that he is free from corruption, but that he is desperately sick of it; not that he has fashioned the good society, but that he has caught an unforgettable glimpse of it. Ultimately the ethical problems of the elected executive are what they are for all human beings; the struggle to discover ends and means which heighten man's sense of individual worth in an ever more meaningful, extensive, and inclusive community.

18 NATIONAL, STATE, AND LOCAL GOVERNMENT— THE FUTURE

"That government governs best which governs least." Perhaps better than any other brief statement, this oft-quoted remark of Thomas Jefferson reflects the basic belief of the American people about government's proper role. Yet Big Government has grown up all around us. Indeed, a careful examination of the Jeffersonian philosophy in practice suggests that Jefferson himself would be among the first to reject an agrarian-oriented government for one more closely attuned to modern industrial society.

Despite the cries of "unconstitutional usurpation of power," despite the protests against "bureaucrats taking away our freedoms" by taking governance away from those jurisdictions reputedly "closest to the people," government has grown not only larger but stronger and more centralized over the past 180 years. Indeed, the process seems unlikely to lessen, let along halt, in the foreseeable future.

Before turning to an examination of the complex functions of government in a modern society and an assessment of the levels at which services should be provided, we might well consider the desirability of these trends toward more government and more centralized government. Perhaps the best criterion by which to judge these developments is found in Abraham Lincoln's comment that government must do for the people those things they cannot do at all for themselves or cannot do so well. This practical approach may also suggest a response to a related question: which level of government, local, state or federal, should undertake the tasks. A rejection of irrational ideology, of states' rights and laissez-faire dogma alike, suggests that the services should be performed by that jurisdiction most capable of undertaking them.

The history of government's ever-expanding role shows that Americans have, by and large, followed both the Lincolnian suggestion and a pragmatic intergovernmental assignment of tasks. The rise of Big Government can be traced to responses to needs arising out of critical situations (wars and depressions in particular) for which traditional approaches proved inadequate. In area after area, government regulation proved necessary to counter the abuse of public privilege by groups which had successfully pleaded their identity with the public interest. More often than not, initial controls were attempted at the state or local level; it was only after these attempts failed that federal action was demanded.

From this pragmatic approach, our national government has emerged in the final third of the twentieth century with three clearly defined functions—a *negative* and a *positive* function, and a third which may be termed *conciliatory-representative*. The negative functions of government—the traditional preservation of law and order, and protection against invasion—have been vastly expanded in recent years to include protection of the public health, defense against fraudulent practices, and suppression of public nuisance sometimes arising from an overly free use of private property. The positive functions—long with us in the form of a postal service, a protective tariff, and in the grant of corporate privilege—have similarly been amplified in the present century to include social security, unemployment insurance, workmen's compensation, school-lunch programs, and the beginnings of medical care for the aged—in short, the "welfare state."

The third function of the national government has stemmed from the twentieth-century rise of those "great aggregates of socioeconomic power," the pressure groups. These groups have made their presence known not only in their demands and counter-demands for service to themselves and regulation for others. When their opposing forces have clashed head on, or at times joined in conspiratorial agreement, they have made inevitable a government intervention to protect the public interest; moreover, since the power of these pressure groups is not always countervailed, particularly at state and local levels, the central government must speak for the unorganized, and represent the consumer and the non-union worker.

As for the states, they, with Mark Twain, might well observe that the reports of their death are greatly exaggerated, since they exercise the police power—that most vital of all governmental powers which, in our system, has been reserved to them. Assignment to the states of this broad-ranging mandate, involving protection of individual freedoms and regulation of corporate activities as well as the better-known restraint of personal transgressions, has proved a mixed blessing. While we have never had to face the threat of an all-encompassing scrutiny of political beliefs and activities by a national police force, we have had to resort to the commerce clause to establish an interstate jurisdiction that would permit the FBI to apprehend kidnappers (who transported their victims across state lines) and to break up stolen-car rings (whose operations were similarly interstate). In recent years we have turned to federal intervention to establish for minority groups those rights presumably protected, but so frequently violated, by state exercise of the police power.

A second significant function, somewhat neglected in recent years, is also available to the states: conducting explorations and experiments in democratic self-government. We do not have to await a nationwide decision and an elaborate, costly full-scale testing of new ideas. We have in our separate state capitals fifty arenas for trying out new proposals under actual working conditions. Indeed, many significant innovations have stemmed from state initiative: minimum-wage and maximum-hours legislation, use of the executive budget, bank-deposit insurance (in Minnesota), and the more recent Consumer Counsel in New York and California. Similarly there have been the widespread constitutional reforms of Wisconsin, Alaska, and Hawaii.

A third function, likely to become increasingly important for state governments, is providing a framework for the decentralized administration of nationally determined policies. Here the states offer an unequaled opportunity for the flexible adaptation of Washington-based programs to the specific demands of varying regional requirements.

To perform these functions as well as many others, however, the states must strive for a greater efficiency of operation and a better balanced representation of interests than has thus far been attained. The reluctance of so many legislatures to adopt a progressive income tax because of internal state pressures is only one instance. The practice of offering unhealthy tax concessions to woo industry away from other states represents another. In the face of an increasingly mobile population, the unwillingness to cooperate in setting uniform state standards in areas ranging from motor vehicle regulation to marriage and divorce laws reflects another facet of state provincialism.

Inadvertently, the U.S. Supreme Court's reapportionment decisions may have aided the states in overcoming the most important single obstacle to solution of the most pressing problems facing them—those of the metropolitan areas. Nonetheless, some states continue temporizing and evasion in the face of court-ordered reapportionment. Will the states look ahead to their new role and modernized functions? Or will they battle their way backwards into a political thicket of their own making, wherein they must certainly wither away?

Finally, what of the local governments, which nearly a century ago earned the comment of the distinguished British visitor Lord Bryce, that they constituted American democracy's "most conspicuous failure"? The proliferation of governments, local public apathy, inadequate services, faulty administration, and other evidence substantiate the continuing validity of this harsh appraisal. Before assessing future prospects, we must note that many problems of local government have been increasingly passed on up to state capitals for solution, just as state problems have been passed on to Washington. Yet our local governments have regularly enjoyed a preferred position with the people, close to their hearts if not always present in their minds. Notwithstanding the increasing importance of national and state governments, Americans have looked first to their own communities for the rational conduct of nationwide and statewide programs as well as for meeting urgent and immediate local needs. They have viewed local government as more understandable, more tractable, more accessible, more their own.

The problems of local government may be conveniently grouped under three broad headings: fundamental, functional and structural. The fundamental problems include politically irresponsible government—government which, despite its claims of being "closest to the people," is often invisible government dominated by a few in the interests of a few. One-party rule, bossism and the lack of responsible opposition are but a few symptoms of the underlying malaise. The failure of traditional geographical-political boundaries to coincide with modern socioeconomic regions constitutes another fundamental weakness, one which is reflected in the piecemeal approach to government functions, and the inability to provide governmental services on a coherent, unified basis throughout the areas requiring those services.

Structural problems are reflected in the existence of too many governments —governments too small to meet functional demands on an efficient scale, too small to hire full-time professional administrators and expert technicians, too small to utilize efficiently the costly equipment and machinery of modern government, from computers to tax maps and rotary snowplows. On the county level, structural problems are reflected in the widespread lack of executive leadership; there is no single official responsible for county performance. In the legislative arena, inadequate representation for city and suburb, gerrymandering, and the continued overrepresentation of depopulated rural "rotten boroughs" offer further evidence of the difficulties.

Finally, the sheer ugliness of urban and suburban America (except for a handful of cities and "new towns") offers mute but unrelenting testimony to the unsolved esthetic problems of planning and urban development. Chronic water shortages, persistent air and water pollution, regular despoliation of the land add their all-too-tangible evidence of failure.

What of the future? The structural approach has been tried and found wanting, because it was directed to surface symptoms rather than underlying political causes. Structural reforms may well prove useful in the years ahead, but only in conjunction with more fundamental political reforms. Many of the physical problems are already amenable to technological solution. Our engineers can provide effective remedies for smog-filled skies and sewage-laden streams. They stand on the verge of scientific breakthroughs likely to offer even desert cities abundant, inexpensive fresh water from the sea. But this is not enough.

To one looking at America as a whole, viewing national, state and local governments together, the solution of our many problems remains far from certain. The dubious prognosis reflects unanswered political questions about the extent of commitment, the degree of concern on the part of the American public. This is a nation blessed with a wealth of material resources, a nation that is the proud possessor of an institutional and technical know-how second to none. And yet, even in such an affluent nation, democracy, like water, cannot rise above its sources. The sources of democracy are the people themselves; only the people can make the necessary decisions, exert the necessary will, provide the on-going commitment that will bring to fruition the long-promised potential of American government in action.

TO STRENGTHEN OUR FEDERAL SYSTEM
Meyer Kestnbaum

The late Meyer Kestnbaum, who was president of Hart, Shaffner and Marx, had a long-standing interest in the improvement of government. Chairman of the influential Committee for Economic Development from 1953 to 1955, he served as special assistant to President Dwight D. Eisenhower from 1955 to 1961. The present article presents his summary of the report prepared by the Commission on Intergovernmental Relations under his chairmanship.

After 168 years the American federal system is still one of the most impressive experiments in the art of government ever undertaken. The central problem remains the same today as in 1787: how to combine national strength with local freedom and initiative. The continuing element of experiment lies in the necessity of adapting the system to the constantly changing conditions of the modern world.

It may be the pragmatic genius of the American people that enabled us to come to the mid-twentieth century without having felt the need for an overall reappraisal of the system. In any event, the Commission on Intergovernmental Relations, appointed in 1953, is the first official body to make an intensive study of the central feature of federalism: the relations between the National Government and the States and their political subdivisions.

There were two basic motivations for the establishment of the Commission. One was the feeling that our system might be growing top-heavy as a result of the concentration of too much responsibility for government at the national level. The other was the conviction of public administrators and others professionally interested in government, that the haphazard complex of intergovernmental relationships might be rendered more manageable after a thorough checkup.

The inevitable effect of technical and economic change has been to focus increasing attention and responsibility on central government. Two world wars and an intervening depression within a thirty-year period had forced upon the national government the exercise of powers and the raising and spending of money on such a scale as to have altered greatly the historic balance between states and nation. However, the fact that the state and local governments reacted by strengthening their own operations and by seeking a reconsideration of national trends is proof of their continuing vitality. It is significant that much of the impetus for establishment of the Commission on Intergovernmental Relations came from Governors' Conferences and other bodies concerned with the state and local levels of government.

None of these organizations has done more to develop an understanding of the growing importance of intergovernmental relationships than the Coun-

From *State Government,* Summer 1955. Reprinted by permission.

cil of State Governments. The Commission has benefited greatly from its publications and reports and from the active cooperation of officers and staff. As Chairman, I can testify also to the immense value of the contributions made by the Commission members with experience as Governors or in other state and local offices, to say nothing of the many others who served on the Commission's ten Study and Advisory Committees.

The Commission was directed "to study the proper role of the Federal Government in relation to the States and their political subdivisions" with a view to recommending proper allocations of responsibilities in the light of the fiscal and other capacities of the several levels of government. In order to carry out this mandate, the Commission found it necessary to direct certain suggestions and recommendations to the national government and others to state and local governments. It recognized that the responsibility for maintaining a sound federal system must be shared by all elements in the system, including the people, who are the ultimate sovereign.

In brief, the Commission urged upon the national government the need for greater restraint in entering new fields or in expanding activities in areas traditionally within the scope of state and local governments. Partly for this purpose and partly to increase the efficiency of interlevel relationships, the Commission recommended the establishment in the Executive Office of the President of a modest staff agency directed to pay continuing attention to problems in this field. It also recommended that, in dealing with states and their subdivisions, the national government should minimize controls or other arrangements that tend to curtail their autonomy or freedom of action and should act affirmatively to enhance their role.

On the other hand, the Commission found an urgent need for action on the part of the states to increase their own capacity for meeting the needs of modern government. Specifically, it found a widespread need for modernization of state constitutions, better apportionment of state legislatures, more efficient organization of state administrations, better balanced state and local tax structures, and extension of a greater amount of home rule to properly organized county and municipal governments.

The Commission made some suggestions for immediate or early withdrawal or curtailment of certain national activities and expressed the conviction that further action of this sort should be possible as the states and national government progressed in carrying out some of its basic recommendations.

The membership of the Commission, composed of United States Senators and Representatives, officials in the executive branch of the national government, present and former state and local officials, and private citizens, brought to its deliberations a variety of backgrounds that helped every member enlarge his concept of American federalism in action. Many members of the Commission testified that their outlook on important controversial issues had gradually been altered by the exchange of ideas and experience around the meeting table. The final report of the Commission represents more substantial agreement, both on general principles and specific issues, than anyone would have thought possible at the outset.

The Commissioner's objective was to produce a balanced report that would recognize the importance, capacities, and responsibilities of government at each of the several levels. All of the members were mindful of the paramount importance of maintaining a strong and effective national government able to sustain our position of leadership in the free world. All recognized that the national government must concern itself with the soundness of the national economy, and with the demonstration of our basic concepts of liberty and the value of the individual. At the same time the Commission recognized the importance of enhancing the citizen participation which has been nurtured by self-assertive, semi-autonomous state and local institutions.

The original deadline of March, 1954 for the Commission report was patently unrealistic. Even as the Commission approached its postponed deadline of June 30, 1955, it realized that its task could well have continued indefinitely. The legitimate demands upon government and the conditions for meeting them change continually. Consequently, there can never be a final study of intergovernmental relations. There can only be periodic or continuing stock-taking followed by purposeful readjustments. The Commission's report was prepared with this in mind.

The report is divided into two distinct parts. In Part I, the Commission sought to assess the basic forces and principles that have influenced the development of our federal system since 1787 and to establish some guidelines for the future course of intergovernmental relations. In Part II, the Commission reviewed intergovernmental relationships in each of twelve broad fields, such as Agriculture, Health, Welfare, Education, and Employment Security, in which grants-in-aid play an important role.

While application of the principles developed in Part I enabled the members of the Commission to reach agreement on most of their recommendations for grant programs, there were naturally more dissents and qualifying views expressed in Part II. Different interpretations of the facts as well as different philosophical attitudes necessarily led to different conclusions about such matters as federal aid to education and the methods of financing highway construction.

The Commission's recommendations on the future course of intergovernmental relations flow logically from its study of the history of the division of powers between the nation and the states. The Commission found confirmation for the belief that despite great changes in the world, our federal system is sound and flexible enough to serve the country indefinitely. The problem is one of understanding and adaptation. All members of the Commission recognized that federalism must be dynamic. It cannot be maintained by dividing responsibilities neatly and permanently between the national and state governments. As the Commission observed in the Introduction: "The

National Government and the States should be regarded not as competitors for authority but as two levels of government cooperating with or complementing each other in meeting the growing demands on both."

The importance of state and local government was underscored by the fact that the normal peacetime activities of these governments have been expanding more rapidly than those of the national government. This is particularly reassuring in view of Supreme Court decisions that tend more and more to let the policy-making authorities of the national government fix the boundaries of national action. Relaxation of judicial controls impelled several members of the Commission to express their concern in footnotes. All the members of the Commission joined in expressing the view that this development makes it more necessary than ever for citizens and officials alike to assume more responsibility for maintaining the integrity and soundness of constitutional government. In the words of the report: "The preservation and strengthening of our federal system depend in the last analysis on the self-restraint and responsibility, as well as the wisdom, of our actions as citizens."

The members of the Commission completed their work firmly convinced that the advantages of this system so far outweigh those of a highly centralized government that we are warranted in making "every effort to preserve and strengthen its existence." The flexibility of our system enhances its ability to deal with crises and new conditions, while its inherent decentralization helps to maintain the principle of consent and to facilitate citizen participation.

The future of the federal system rests where in truth it has always rested, in the hands of the people and their officials at the several levels of government. That future depends mainly on the way in which the people and their agents discharge their responsibilities from year to year.

The report points out that the federal principle may be undermined or lost either by overuse or misuse of national authority or by nonuse of state and local authority. Overuse or misuse of national authority can be avoided by exercising restraint and wisdom. Nonuse and consequent erosion of state and local authority can best be avoided by making state and local governments so effective that they are able to respond to needs at least as promptly as the national government.

The Commission became convinced that Washington's share in domestic government will be measured largely by how much the state and local governments do themselves and how much they leave to Washington by default. Members of the Commission, including those with gubernatorial experience, pointed out that the possibility of returning certain functions to the states or of strengthening others at the state and local levels depends mainly upon the readiness of the states to perform them. The Commission concluded that, at least to a considerable extent, it is within the power of the states themselves to determine whether their future role shall expand or diminish.

Looking for specific ways in which state and local governments can qualify for larger responsibilities, the Commission found much that was encouraging in the work of the Council of State Governments and in the record already made in many states and communities. There is, therefore, nothing essentially new in the Commission's suggestion for an agenda for strengthening the states, but the Commission did feel that this agenda was more urgent than many people had supposed. It observed that "many good citizens and well-intentioned groups that respond readily to an appeal to improve the efficiency of the National Government have not shown an equal interest in similar proposals for improving and strengthening State government." Consequently the Commission suggested that it may be time to concentrate on a nationwide, state-by-state examination of state constitutions, state legislatures and administrations, state tax systems, interstate cooperation, and the network of local governments through which many of the responsibilities of the states are discharged.

The Commission did not attempt to review all of the possible elements in a program for strengthening the States that might emerge from such an examination. It did, however, highlight a number of matters.

It appeared from the Commission's studies that some weaknesses at the state level result from failure to apply fundamental principles of our American system of government: (1) all constitutions ought, like the Constitution of the United States, to deal with fundamentals and not with the details of governmental organization and power; (2) legislative bodies should be fairly representative of the people as a whole so that every important segment of the community can be heard in the making of public policy; (3) the executive branch should be so organized that the Chief Executive can be held responsible for the way the laws are executed and services performed; and (4) so far as possible, self-government should be extended to the people in their local communities.

Most Americans would doubtless accept these principles in theory. But in practice they are seldom applied consistently by our state governments. In a real sense, therefore, what is required to make the state governments more nearly adequate to modern needs is to make them conform more closely to these first principles.

Whereas the United States Constitution was deliberately designed to facilitate action by a strong national government, most of the state constitutions, by successive revisions and amendments, have become compendiums of self-imposed constitutional limitations that make it unnecessarily difficult for the state and local governments to meet the modern needs of their citizens. Again and again in its study of federal programs in fields that might be considered appropriate for state and local action, the Commission was confronted by the plea that federal intervention was necessary because of limitations imposed upon the states by their own constitutions. The Commission, therefore, found "a very real and pressing need for the States to improve their constitutions."

The Commission was particularly concerned over the results of widespread under-representation of urban communities in State legislatures. It concluded that legislative neglect of these communities has been an important factor in leading "more and more people to look to Washington for more and more of the services and controls they desire." There is reason to believe that this trend will continue until many states take energetic action to readjust legislative representation to the current distribution of population. The Commission pointed out that "the same shift of population which has resulted in State legislatures becoming less representative of urban areas has had the effect of making the United States Senate more representative of these areas, because Senators, elected at large, must depend heavily upon urban voters, even in predominantly rural States."

The Commission found that the effectiveness of state government was impaired not only by unduly limited and poorly representative legislatures but also by constitutionally weak and uncoordinated state administrations. Effects of weakness in a state's executive branch seem to be accentuated by certain aspects of federal-state relations. Complaints came from a number of states that grant-aided programs tended to be conducted without proper regard to over-all fiscal and administrative policies of the state governments. A tendency was noted for "groups of professional administrators in a single, specialized field, working at National, State and local levels, to become a more or less independent government of their own, organized vertically and substantially independent of other State agencies." It was noteworthy that there were few complaints from states with fairly strong gubernatorial powers, and modern budget and other staff services.

The Commission found that it could not appraise federal-state relations and the feasibility of increased state responsibility without looking rather carefully at State-local relations and the structure of local government. Many of the important responsibilities that are constitutionally vested in the states are, or can best be, discharged by local governments. Many of the complexities in intergovernmental relationships stem from the fact that many of the 109,000 separate, local governmental units in the United States have neither the size, the resources, nor the legal powers needed for effective self-government. Some of the more pressing demands for federal aid can be traced to the inability of many existing units of local government to conduct or finance important services without outside direction and assistance —which they are not obtaining from their own states. This is especially true in metropolitan areas, described by the Commission's Advisory Committee on Local Government as "the most important focal points for intergovernmental relations."

The Commission could not undertake to tell the states how to deal with their local governments. It did point out, as had the Committee on State-Local Relations of the Council of State Governments some years ago, that there was a need for vigorous state leadership to achieve genuine home rule for a smaller number of better organized local governments.

As for the special problems of metropolitan areas, the Commission observed: "The time is long overdue for an intensive nationwide study of governmental areas with special attention to metropolitan communities. The study should engage the cooperation of National, State and local governments, as well as universities, private foundations, and civic agencies. Political invention in this field is greatly needed."

The Commission's studies of civil defense and urban vulnerability and of housing and urban renewal revealed the urgent need for better planning and more effective coordination of governmental activities in metropolitan areas. The Commission specifically recommended "that States and municipalities give increased attention to unifying their community services through the creation of metropolitan planning authorities to deal with problems related to urban affairs" and urged the states to provide financial and technical assistance wherever necessary. More effective metropolitan area planning backed up by better organization of governments in metropolitan areas would simplify federal-state-local relations and cooperative arrangements in many fields.

The Commission noted a revival of county government and an increasing recognition of its importance, both in rural and in metropolitan areas. It pointed out that the county is commonly used as a basis for administering a number of important federal programs. At the same time, municipal-type functions are being transferred to many counties from municipalities with inadequate area and resources. The conclusion was reached that modernization and strengthening of county government would advance the cause of local self-government and "take some of the load off State administration and simplify the task of administering National programs based upon the counties."

A great deal of study was devoted to the problem of financing the several levels of government. The Commission recognized that the power to govern is heavily dependent upon the power to obtain adequate revenues and that under modern economic conditions the national government has a distinct advantage in its ability to levy on the total resources of the nation. Any strategy for maintaining the vigor of the state and local elements must consider what can be done to strengthen their financial base.

It would be comforting to say we could divide up tax sources so that each level could pay its way with little or no overlapping taxation. A hardheaded analysis indicates, however, that while greater separation of tax sources is a goal worth working toward, anything approaching complete separation would be impracticable and positively harmful. The Commission pointed out that some overlapping of tax sources enables the governments at different levels to maintain "more balanced and stable tax structures than would be possible if each level were limited to fewer types of taxes." On the other hand, full tax separation would tend to leave the ultimate determination of tax policy for the whole country to the federal government and thus deny the states the right to determine their own tax structures. Moreover, the Commission found that disadvantages of overlapping can be subsantially miti-gated by more cooperative arrangements between governments and by vari-ous arrangements for greater tax coordination.

The Commission recognized the inevitably depressing effect of the current high level of federal taxation upon the fiscal capacities of state and local governments. Substantial reduction in the level of federal taxation and expenditures could do more for the fiscal capacity of state and local govern-ments than anything else. And in such a reduction lies the best chance of reducing tax overlapping, since it would then be possible to consider the full repeal of certain taxes.

One of the Commission's most detailed studies was made by the Study Committee on Payments in Lieu of Taxes and Shared Revenues. The Com-mission recognized that tax immunity of federal property has weakened many local governments. The Study Committee's report was offered as a basis upon which Congress may "build a sound program of payments in lieu of taxes on federal properties and make such adjustments in shared revenue arrangements as may be needed." At the same time, the Commission called attention to the need for comparable state payments-in-lieu for the benefit of municipalities and counties.

Fortunately, the states generally do not need to wait for action in Washing-ton to strengthen their own fiscal position and that of their local units. The Commission's studies make it clear that most states could, if they would, tap substantial unused revenue sources. The fiscal problems of many state and local governments are compounded by self-imposed constitutional and statu-tory limitations. These governments have limited their taxing and borrowing powers and earmarked revenues for specific purposes in ways that defeat fiscal flexibility and deprive legislatures and executives of budgetary control.

Inhibitions on full employment of the fiscal potentiality of state and local governments have complicated the issues in such controversies as that over federal aid for education. The truth is that the actual economic capacity of states and localities can never be determined until many of them unlock their own legal shackles.

The Commission, therefore, expressed the opinion "that each State should undertake a searching reappraisal of its fiscal policies, including the constitu-tional and statutory limitations on its taxation and borrowing activities, the limitations on the fiscal powers of local governments, the system of property tax administration, and the financial aids it is providing its subdivisions."

Believing in the durability and improvability, if not the perfectibility, of state and local governments, the Commission devoted much of its attention to methods of enhancing their substantive role. After a careful review of the history of the system, the Commission unanimously accepted this general statement on the principles that should be observed in allocating governmental activities and responsibilities: "Assuming efficient and responsible govern-ment at all levels—National, State, and local—we should seek to divide our civic responsibilities so that we—

"Leave to private initiative all the functions that citizens can perform privately; use the level of government closest to the community for all public functions it can handle; utilize cooperative intergovernmental arrangements where appropriate to attain economical performance and popular approval; reserve National action for residual participation where State and local governments are not fully adequate, and for the continuing responsibilities that only the National Government can undertake."

The meaning of this broad declaration of faith in state, local, and private activity is spelled out in the Commission's report with standards for testing proposals affecting the division of governmental responsibilities. The first and most obvious rule is one stated earlier: that the national government should exercise self-restraint in determining whether or not to act where state or local governments may have some competence. A corollary is that if national action is desirable it should take the form that will least infringe on the area of state and local action. In general, therefore, the Commission expressed a preference for joint action over direct, exclusive, national performance of a given function when there is a reasonable choice between the two. Although recognizing that "there is a risk that State participation in joint schemes, while bolstering the States as going organizations, may induce habits of subordination and deference to external initiative and guidance," the Commission concluded that "In the long run this risk is less serious for the States than the effects of being bypassed."

These principles apply, although in somewhat different ways, both to regulatory and to service activities. In regulation, they lead to the conclusion that national laws should not be assumed to preempt any field against state action unless the intent is clearly stated, and that exercise of national power should not "bar State action on the same subject unless there is positive inconsistency." These principles also call for various forms of administrative cooperation between national and state regulatory agencies under parallel or related national and state laws. The Commission believes there is room for considerbly expanded use of such devices as joint boards representing agencies on two levels, joint hearings, joint action in drafting regulations under national law, joint inspections, and inter-level exchanges of personnel and information. These arrangements can have several beneficial effects. They give the states an opportunity to influence the administration of national policies in which the states have some direct interest. They tend to invigorate administrative agencies of the state governments while reducing administrative burdens on the national government. And they facilitate automatic coordination of national and state regulatory action and thus minimize inconvenience to private interests being regulated by two levels of government.

The Commission was impressed by the virtually universal approbation accorded to the great variety of services-in-aid, including much technical and professional assistance, that pass between the national government and state and local governments. Many of these services are incidental to the cooperative relationships described above. This aspect of cooperative federalism has helped States, counties, and municipalities to do better and more effective jobs in law enforcement, milk inspection, building codes, personnel training, and scores of other activities. The mere assembling of certain kinds of information in a central place can be a very valuable service to all levels of government. As an example, the Commission noted the work of the Governments Division of the Census Bureau. It agreed with its Advisory Committee on Local Government that more emphasis should be put on many of these services-in-aid.

Although grants-in-aid bear some resemblances to services-in-aid they differ from them in important ways and raise important policy questions to which the Commission devoted a great deal of attention. There is an unfortunate tendency to think of federal-state relations in terms primarily of grants-in-aid. These grants have, of course, become an important feature of American government. What has already been said, however, indicates that they are only one of many aspects of the cooperative system of federal-state-local relationships that has grown up under our Constitution. The Commission, therefore, studied the grant-in-aid system not in isolation but in relation to these other forms of interlevel dealings.

The grant-in-aid is sometimes spoken of as if it were essentially a centralizing device by which the national government "invades" the proper sphere of state and local government. There is no denying the centralizing potentialities in the use of federal money to induce state and local governments to carry out particular programs in particular ways. However, the grant-in-aid system can be and is an effective method of achieving decentralization when it is used to enable state and local governments to perform services that would otherwise be performed directly by the national government.

The Commission studied grants-in-aid to see how they can be limited to legitimate national objectives and handled so as to strengthen rather than weaken state and local government. With these purposes in mind it considered such drastic proposals as substitution of so-called block grants for the traditional conditional grants for carefully specified purposes. It also considered the possible merits of a system of subsidies designed to equalize the capacity of the poorer states to provide governmental services. The Commission concluded that the recent trend toward including equalizing factors in grant formulas can well be extended, but it would not be good business for the federal government, nor would it meet the ultimate need for strengthening state and local institutions, to depart radically from specific conditional grants. The Commission did agree that in some instances both national objectives and state autonomy would be better served by less narrow definition of program objectives, by greater flexibility in the permissible use of funds, and by less rigid legal and administrative controls.

In determining whether or not a grant-in-aid is the best approach to a given objective, it is necessary to compare it with direct national action on the one hand and with any other possible form of national-state cooperation on the other. While there are situations where direct national action is to be preferred, the Commission tended to favor the grant-in-aid over "a direct National program which would give the States no role whatsoever."

In reviewing the well established grants-in-aid, the Commission applied its criteria for the allocation of responsibilities among the levels of government somewhat less rigidly than it would for a proposed new grant. But it identified some grants that could be dropped or tapered off and pointed out that old programs should be kept under constant scrutiny to conform to sound principle and good practice. It insisted that all proposals for future programs should be analyzed to determine their probable effect on the federal system.

The Commission felt that a common failure to give proper attention to the intergovernmental implications of policy and administrative decisions has led to many of the past mistakes in the handling not only of grants-in-aid but also of other matters. This failure results naturally from the preoccupation of policy makers and administrators with specific functions rather than with the machinery of government. No single device will guarantee that due consideration will be given hereafter to these matters, but the Commission came to the conclusion that it would help if the importance of interlevel relationships were given more explicit recognition in the organization of the executive branch of the national government.

It made a number of suggestions to this end, the most important of which is that there should be a Special Assistant in the Executive Office of the President, with a small staff and an Advisory Board on Intergovernmental Relations, to serve as a permanent center for over-all attention to national-state-local relations. It suggested that the Advisory Board be appointed by the President "after such consultation as he deemed appropriate with associations that represent various levels."

The primary responsibility of this staff agency "would be to advance a strategic sense of federal relations in the formulative stages of many types of legislation and administrative action." It is hoped that this arrangement would help the national government exercise that greater restraint with respect to undertakings affecting states and localities which the Commission feels is important to the survival of a genuine federal system. While giving assistance to policy makers facing immediate decisions, the agency should be in a position to carry out or stimulate further studies on subjects that this Commission was able barely to open up. It might, for example, "facilitate the further development of the kind of guidelines for determining the conditions and circumstances justifying National action" that are outlined in the report. It should also cooperate with other agencies, private and public, that may be studying such specific problems as those found in metropolitan areas.

Limitations of space make it impossible to cover in any detail the suggestions and recommendations in the twelve chapters dealing with the major grant-in-aid programs. The general tenor of the recommendations in these chapters is summarized about as succinctly as possible in the following paragraph from the report: "The Commission's approach was not calculated to, and in fact did not, produce findings and recommendations pointing uniformly in any one direction. In some areas, for example in welfare and in certain phases of agriculture, its recommendations call for a relative increase in State and local responsibilities. In other fields, notably civil defense, the direction is toward increased National responsibility. In still others, including civil aviation and housing, the Commission's findings generally support the existing division of responsiblities, at least for the immediate future."

The Commission hopes the Congress will find that the recommendations regarding specific grant programs are helpful as legislation affecting them is considered. The Commission is conscious, however, that the breadth and variety of the subjects it was required to study made it impossible to go into the facts of every functional field. While its members could not agree unanimously on all its conclusions, there was general agreement that the method of approach to grants-in-aid was sound. In the long run the value of the work of the Commission will depend less upon the extent to which its recommendations on grants are carried out than upon the extent to which citizens and policy makers and administrators at all levels of government apply the basic principles enunciated in the report and use the standards, guidelines, and procedures suggested for the future management of intergovernmental relationships.

A CALL FOR PLAIN TALK
Thomas H. Reed

Thomas H. Reed, government consultant and expert on metropolitan problems, was one of the authors of the National Municipal League's pioneer study, *The Government of Metropolitan Areas* (1930). Among his metropolitan surveys have been those for Allegheny County, Pennsylvania; St. Louis, Missouri; and Atlanta and Fulton County, Georgia. Among the many charters he has drafted has been that for the consolidated city of Baton Rouge and East Baton Rouge Parish, Louisiana.

For almost ten years since Toronto's "metro" burst on a startled academic world there has poured from the pens or typewriters of scholars, statisticians and newsmen a veritable flood of facts and observations concerning the portentously rapid urbanization of the formerly rural areas around our larger cities, and the awful consequences if adequate arrangements are not made to control this growth and to provide the inhabitants of suburbia with essential public services. Eminent free-lance scholars and strongly-manned study

From *National Civic Review*, March 1962. Reprinted by permission.

commissions have warned repeatedly that no other problem relating to the structure of government in the United States calls so loudly for solution.

Alas, however, in spite of all this to-do, almost nothing actually has been done about it. In consequence many of the younger scholars who have been most active recently in the discussion of the problem have lost faith in the prospect for any thoroughgoing reorganization of local government in metropolitan areas.

They must have been aware all along that an earlier generation of reformers had vigorously advocated integrated government for metropolitan areas and that bitter but mostly fruitless battles had been waged in its behalf on the Alameda shore of San Francisco Bay and in areas centering in Pittsburgh, St. Louis, Birmingham and other cities. They knew, too, that from the final coalition of Denver and a portion of Arapahoe County in 1916 to the approval of the "Plan of Government" for Baton Rouge and East Baton Rouge Parish in 1947 not a single victory had been scored by the advocates of integrated metropolitan government.

When in 1953, however, reports of Toronto's "metro" broke unexpectedly on their ears, they suddenly felt sure that a new day had dawned for the metropolis. Ignoring the fact that the Toronto metro had been ordained by the Ontario legislature without the formality of a referendum of any kind, they saw "metros" of their own conception rising right and left from the turgid sea of metropolitan politics. As a further boost to optimism they discovered that the coffers of the great foundations would open generously for studies of every phase of the metropolitan problem—a governmental researcher's dream come true.

Unhappily the new era has produced no more concrete results than its predecessor. Only one more comprehensive metropolitan government—that of Dade County in 1957—has been established. Consequently many "experts" in the field have renounced as futile the promotion of metropolitan government on the Toronto, Baton Rouge, Dade County or similar models. They are advocating measures primarily calculated to meet the immediate service needs of the suburban population, such as voluntary cooperation among the units of a metropolitan area leading to interunit contracts and joint enterprises or to the voluntary transfer of functions between units; the setting up of limited-purpose special districts or "authorities"; and the creation of metropolitan planning agencies.

Its friends call this the "functional" and its critics the "piecemeal" approach to the metropolitan problem. It has been given added weight by the recent report of the Advisory Commission on Intergovernmental Relations which recommended to the states not a workable form or forms of metropolitan government but "an arsenal of remedial weapons" to be used in meeting critical service needs as they arise. In other words, this approach emphasizes the immediate satisfaction of needs such as roads, schools or sanitary facilities rather than the achievement of a well-rounded system of local government as the source of such services.

All countries, even despotic ones, find it necessary to have a system of local units which are allowed some degree of autonomy in purely local matters. Complete centralization would mean, in Lamennais' famous phrase, "apoplexy at the center and paralysis at the extremities." Fortunately our complicated federal system was erected on the broad base of an exceptionally vigorous set of local institutions. The abiding self-confidence of the American people in their ability to look out for themselves in their home communities enabled us to develop national and state governments on a vast scale without losing our essentially democratic spirit. In recent years the increasing difficulty of financing local government, especially under the strain of depression, has weakened its independence and elasticity.

To leave unsolved the growing problems caused by the suburban surge of the last half century is unthinkable. To turn these problems over to the states or the nation, simply because we have not adapted the organization of local government to metropolitan conditions, would give us a long start down the road to paralyzing centralization. To preserve to their fullest extent our democratic traditions we must not only solve the metropolitan problem but must solve it in the right way by devising and enacting adequate forms of metropolitan self-government. Important as it may seem that every part of every metropolitan area have its complement of roads, schools and what-have-you, it is far more important that each state have its own pattern of local government adapted to current population trends and socio-economic conditions.

From the time of the first English settlements in what is now the United States early in the seventeenth century until somewhat past the beginning of the twentieth, the colonies and the states which succeeded them had systems of local government, imperfect in many ways but which adjusted themselves reasonably well to the growth and change incident to the peopling of a continent. It is safe to say that throughout that long period the widely different and in some respects conflicting needs of urban and rural communities were met by local governments specifically geared to their respective requirements. This was possible for two obvious reasons.

First, politically, because there was a consistent demand for more and more units of both types—more towns in compactly settled New England, more counties in the broad expanses of the west, more cities everywhere. There has never been any invincible objection by politicians to the creation of new units of government, even where it involves the division of old ones. More city halls and more courthouses mean more jobs and more money to be spent, things intrinsically agreeable to the political mind.

Second, in the horse-and-buggy era, before science and invention had made modern domestic conveniences possible in a rural setting, families which could not find room in a city were prone to build their homes close to the city line and to welcome the city's proposals to annex them.

When, however, in the early 1900's, the popularization of the automobile and the possibility of modern bathrooms independent of city water and sewer systems synchronized with an unprecedented farm-to-city migration, all this changed almost overnight. Annexation sank to a relative trickle and the pattern of local government was frozen in its then existing form, except that many states, not knowing how else to meet suburban service needs, kept on incorporating new municipalities in metropolitan areas, thus constantly adding further complication to the already overcomplicated situation we call the metropolitan problem.

That problem municipal reformers have been trying to solve for half a century with, as we have seen, small success. Their goal has been and remains the development in each normal metropolitan area of an areawide agency capable of handling effectively, on a self-governing basis, areawide affairs, and the establishment of a workable relationship between that agency and the municipalities and other units necessary to a complete system of local government. It is impracticable to define their objectives more precisely in relation to past events or future activities.

The three metropolitan governments actually in successful operation— those of Toronto, East Baton Rouge Parish and Dade County—are of radically different types. It is natural to assume that, where a metropolitan area, as defined by the Bureau of the Census, is confined to a single county, as a majority of them are, the government of the county, with suitable modifications, should become the desired areawide agency. Beyond that it would only hamper future progress to lay down any hard-and-fast rule by which the territorial limits of metropolitan areas for governmental purposes should be determined.

All such questions, especially when they have to do with great metropolitan complexes such as that centering on New York City, should be settled on the basis of thorough study of all the circumstances of the specific situation. Dedicated men and women will have to press forward as they have done, blunderingly perhaps but persistently, along the wide and varied front presented by the metropolitan problem.

It is obvious that formidable obstacles stand in the way of their success. That knowledge was beaten into many of us years ago by bitter experience. There was, and still is, the natural objection of officeholders and political leaders, whose power, prestige and pelf depend on the continuance of the status quo, to giving up the least bit of their present advantage. There was, and still is, the sentimental attachment of the rank and file citizenry to the "Home Town" as it is, which predisposes them to back the judgment of the office-holders and politicians.

There was, and still is, that strange perversion of the principle of home rule which makes of every incorporated city, village or borough, no matter how young or insignificant, an impregnable fortress within which opposition to integrated metropolitan government can entrench itself. "Home rule" is a term, made popular by municipal reformers, descriptive of the right of the people of a municipality to govern themselves with a minimum of legislative interference. The people of home rule municipalities have the right to frame their own charters and through their elected representatives to manage their local affairs.

In this sense home rule enjoys general public approval. It cannot be extended properly to confer immortality on a municipality, with unaltered boundaries and powers, except as its people may vote to give them up. To do so is to give the people of even the tiniest municipality a practical veto power not only over annexation proposals but also over establishment of any integrated form of metropolitan government. It is to deprive the state of its power to alter in the public interest the pattern of local government as required by population movements and changing social and economic conditions. To deny the states this power is to leave the whole matter of readjustment of the system of local government to be fought out by rival municipalities on the basis of their selfish interests and, what is worse, that of their officials and political leaders.

Annexation has proved effective in forestalling the rise of the metropolitan problem in a few states with liberal annexation laws. It might be an effective remedy for existing metropolitan ills in many other areas, especially the smaller ones, if it could be adopted but, barring a change in the law or in popular thinking in the suburbs, it is still slated for almost certain defeat. At the same time, the high cost of servicing annexed areas and the fear that an annexation may change the balance of party strength in the core city make some core city officials loath to propose annexation.

The two-level system characteristic of the Dade County charter, which preserves a measure of independence to the pre-existing municipalities, seems to offer a better chance of adoption than outright consolidation. Experience there, however, plainly indicates that the division of authority between "metro" and the municipalities provides ample occasion for resistance on the part of the municipalities and their leadership.

There can be no difference of opinion among competent students of metropolitan phenomena that establishing in such areas a pattern of local government adapted to present needs is a tough assignment. It does not follow, however, that its advocates should give up trying. In the first place, the alternative suggested by the advocates of the piecemeal approach offers nothing better than some amelioration of the evils from which metropolitan areas now suffer.

The idea of voluntary cooperation between neighboring units of local government is by no means novel. Taking the country as a whole, there are numerous examples of interunit contracts and joint enterprises, some of them dealing with matters of real importance. There have never been enough of them in any one metropolitan area, however, even if properly coordinated, to approximate faintly a workable system of government for the area. Cooperation undoubtedly can help to make life in a metropolitan area somewhat more tolerable—as when a core city sells water at double the regular city rate to its suburbs—but, far from leading to the establishment of a strong areawide government, it may delay indefinitely the attainment of that goal by diminishing the popular demand for it.

The most vigorous use of the interunit contract has been made in Los Angeles County where under the so-called Lakewood Plan cities may contract with the county to perform all their administrative functions. So far at least that plan has proved attractive chiefly to newly created municipalities in which no traditions of local patriotism have developed and where no one has become habituated to the enjoyment of power. The fact remains that the Los Angeles area still presents a picture of extraordinary governmental complexity.

It must be borne in mind, moreover, that while an interunit contract can stabilize for the term of the contract the relations of two or more units with regard to the character and cost of any specified service, a unit of local government cannot by contract acquire or cast off any of the so-called police or regulatory powers. As to such vitally important matters in metropolitan areas as master plans, zoning ordinances, building codes and traffic regulations, any arrangement between units has no more binding force than any other gentleman's agreement.

Another device for providing an essential service in a metropolitan area as an alternative to seemingly impossible "metro" is the metropolitan special district or "authority." It has proved relatively easy to unite public opinion behind such districts to supply a single highly necessary service or group of related services. Some such procedure is practically the only recourse where the metropolitan area lies in two or more states, and a considerable number are in operation in both one- and two-state areas. Some of them have made impressive records and, since they add to rather than subtract from the number of governmental agencies and consequently payrolls, they rate highly with the politicians.

On the other hand, experience indicates that the creation of one such agency does not lead either to broadening its functions or to the creation of other agencies. Rather than leading to a solution of the metropolitan problem in general, in many instances it has had exactly the opposite effect. The solution of one areawide problem in which the public is deeply interested, like the lack of sewer or water facilities, naturally reduces the intensity of public demand for further action concerning metropolitan affairs in general.

For example, when in 1929 six towns surrounding Hartford, Connecticut, joined with that city in ratifying a law creating a metropolitan district which assured them of an adequate water supply and sewer system, largely at Hartford's expense, they gave up—as time has shown—any thought of real metro government.

In 1889 the Massachusetts legislature, rejecting the example of the Administrative County of London offered it the previous year by the British Parliament, decided to entrust the sewering of Boston and neighboring towns to a state-appointed commission. It followed with a park commission in 1893 and a water commission in 1895, and combined them in the present Metropolitan District Commission in 1919, but a genuine Greater Boston is as far away as ever.

The creation of a special district with sufficient functions to make grave impact on the metropolitan problem obviously is confronted by the same elements of opposition as any other drastic change in the distribution of political power. It has occurred to some people, however, that such a district once established might gradually accumulate additional functions if machinery were provided for so doing.

One state—Washington—set up by general law in 1957 procedures by which "metropolitan municipal corporations" may be established by local initiative and may be entrusted with any or all of the following functions: water supply, sewage disposal, garbage disposal, public transportation, parks and parkways, and comprehensive planning. The proposal to establish such a corporation, with a statement of the functions to be performed, must be ratified by the people of the principal city of the area and the remainder of the population separately. Additional functions from the list may be assumed with the approval of the people of the area as a whole.

This plan is recommended by the Advisory Commission on Intergovernmental Relations for general adoption by the states. Whether it will work as the commission hopes is an open question. The Washington experience offers as yet no definitive evidence one way or the other. It is significant, however, that in the Seattle area, from which the demand for the legislation chiefly came, a proposed three-purpose "corporation" was defeated by the suburban vote and one limited to sewage disposal was adopted subsequently.

The creation of metropolitan planning agencies is now going on rapidly throughout the country. Such agencies should definitely be a feature of all metropolitan governments and no valid objection can be found to creating them ahead of the metro governments to which they belong. It should be done, however, with eyes open to the fact that a planning agency not associated with a government with authority to execute plans as they are made is often futile. A strong planning commission with an adequate staff can supply the basic material for sound policies even in advance of metro. It can serve a worthwhile purpose in helping to coordinate local, state and federal activities in the area. Finally it can prepare the way for advanced thinking on the subject of metro government itself. A weak planning commission with an incompetent and underpaid staff, however, is worse than useless.

Whatever the difficulty of selling integrated government for metropolitan areas, the piecemeal approach, except for the last item, is plainly futile. There are, of course, circumstances in which, a whole loaf being unattainable, it is the part of wisdom to take what crumbs one can get, but it should be with full knowledge that the prospects of accumulating enough crumbs to form a loaf are practically nil.

On the other hand, the modification of the existing system of local government to conform to current population trends and socio-economic conditions, while difficult, is by no means impossible if the right strategy and tactics are employed. Do not forget that two genuine metro governments—in East Baton Rouge Parish and Dade County—have been adopted and maintained against vigorous opposition, and that these were the only two instances in which the new form of government was submitted for ratification to the people of the area as a whole.

To be successful the movement for integrated metropolitan government —to begin with at any rate—must be directed primarily at the state legislatures with a view to removing the legal roadblocks arising from misapplication of the home rule principle, and to securing workable machinery for the formulation and adoption of plans of metropolitan government by the people affected. This course is recommended in substance by the Advisory Commission on Intergovernmental Relations. It is based on the simple fact that the states alone have consitutional authority to make or authorize the making of changes in the pattern of local government. Their failure to recognize the significance to local government of the population movement of the last 50 years is largely responsible for the sorry jungles of governmental agencies which bedevil metropolitan areas today. This unhappy record certainly imposes a high moral obligation on the states to do something about the metropolitan problem now.

There are three major measures which should be urged upon the state legislatures.

One of them relates to annexation which could be an effective means of dealing with the problems of some areas, especially the smaller ones, if its use were not so generally blocked by the veto power of the voters in the territory to be annexed. Annexation elections are not decided on the basis of fair and careful examination of the facts but as the result of appeals to prejudice, passion and narrowly conceived self-interest. Legislation should be adopted or constitutional changes proposed in all states, conferring on an administrative board (as in the province of Ontario) or on the courts (as in Virginia) the power to hear and determine proposals for annexation of incorporated places as well as unincorporated territory, in accordance with criteria set forth in the statute.

The second measure to be sought has to do with the creation of two-level systems of government in which existing municipalities retain their identity and many of their present powers and duties while matters of concern to the metropolitan area as a whole are entrusted to an areawide agency. The legislature should be urged to provide by statute, or if necessary by the initiation of a constitutional amendment, for creation in an area of a metropolitan study commission on petition of a fixed percentage of its qualified electors. The members of the commission should be chosen in a manner to make it truly representative of the people of the area. It should have power to study the needs of the area and to frame a plan of government suitable to those needs. This plan should become effective only when approved by a majority of those voting on the proposition in the *metropolitan area as a whole*.

The third measure is aimed at the indiscriminate incorporation of small suburban communities by some states, which constantly increases the difficulty of finding a solution to the metropolitan problem at the same time that it unduly increases the cost of local government. The states should be asked to set up, by statute or constitutional amendment, high standards of area, population and economic resources which any community within the limits of a metropolitan area must possess before it could apply for incorporation.

So much for grand strategy. Of equal importance is the constant education of the public if legislatures are to be induced to remove the legal obstacles to metropolitan integration and the people of such areas are to be moved to action. The American people are capable of distinguishing right from wrong and wisdom from folly if they can be reached with the facts. They are equally capable of acting with great vigor when convinced of the necessity. We live, however, in a time when so many issues clamor for public attention that the claims of the metropolitan problem for notice require peculiarly effective presentation. It is somewhat disconcerting therefore to be told by some specialists in metropolitan affairs that no interest in the problem can be aroused except among the intellectual elite and that to the general public "metro" is just a "bad" word.

The reason for this is clear enough. The movement for integrated metropolitan government so far has been chiefly a scholars' movement. It is true that in the relatively few instances in which the question of adopting metro has been taken to the polls such diverse elements as chambers of commerce, women's clubs and the press have played an active part. The background for all such recent efforts and most earlier ones has been provided by an elaborate professional study which has set the tone of the whole enterprise.

Still more significant is the number of planners, political scientists, economists, sociologists and other academicians who, on their own account or on behalf of official commissions or interested foundations, have produced in the last few years a veritable library of plans, reports and treatises. Some have dealt with specific situations, others with the broadest aspects of the metropolitan problem. On the whole their quality has been high and they have been eagerly read in academic circles. They have had little or no impact, however, on the general public. The average citizen, who reads very little anyway except his daily paper, does not read this kind of highbrow literature at all and the more of it there is forced on his attention the more negative his reaction is likely to become. This vast supply of material on the metropolitan problem has remained, as far as promoting integrated metropolitan government is concerned, largely useless because for the most part it has never been translated into the vernacular.

The only portion of the scholarly output which has been widely publicized by the press and other publicity media in a manner to catch the eyes and ears of the run-of-the-mind of humanity consists of its alarming prophecies as to such things as the growth of suburbs and their rapid deterioration, the strangulation of traffic and the imminent decay of core cities. These prophecies were for the most part sound but, like Cassandra's best efforts, with one exception they have fallen largely on deaf ears. The unwisely located and badly planned suburb, which in the eyes of the professional planner is no better than a potential slum, to most of its inhabitants is a better place to live than they have ever enjoyed before. The public services may be below the standards of the best municipalities but most suburbanites actally have from a combination of public and private sources all the services and facilities essential to their health and safety. Were that not so the suburban surge would long ago have been self-terminating.

Even on the crowded highway with its annoying traffic jams Mr. Suburbanite's small car gets him daily to his job and back more quickly and more comfortably than any other means of transportation in his experience. The average American cannot be frightened by cries of alarm, which have no relation to his own experience, into building a fallout shelter or a new concept of metropolitan government. The success of the vivid accounts the metro experts have given of encroaching decay in the downtown sections of core cities—something the citizen can see for himself as well as hear about —is the exception proving the rule.

The question naturally is asked, "Why, since state legislative action lies at the basis of progress toward effective metropolitan government, have not the able studies of so many scholars already convinced our legislators of the need for action?" It is not because state legislators as a class are incapable of reading and understanding such works. In fact, it is a fair presumption that legislative leaders have been reading and absorbing at least some of these studies. The insistence of President Kennedy on the creation of a department of urban affairs is a plain indication of the extent to which awareness of the metropolitan problem has penetrated the upper strata of politics. Legislative leaders, however, rarely undertake to champion reforms in the structure of government except in response to public demand. It is perhaps a little unreasonable to expect our elected representatives to promote structural changes in local government of an almost revolutionary character without the assurance of public support.

The adoption of a rational form of metropolitan government, geared to the movement of population and to other socio-economic conditions of today, is a great and worthy enterprise. There is ample justification for a national movement in its behalf, in the necessity of supporting constructively the principle of local self-government in units, adapted to twentieth century conditions. It must be remembered, however, that this is a very large country and that an almost infinite variety of conditions are to be found from one state and one metropolitan area to another.

If we are to stop bombarding the people with scholarly phrases and talk to them in terms they can understand about conditions they are familiar with, there must be local centers of educational activity in each state and area. This is a large order but, with the slogan "Self-government for Metropolitan Areas" and a bit of the spirit which actuated the municipal reform movement of an earlier day, real headway may be made in solving the metropolitan problem within a reasonable time.

That does not mean tomorrow. It takes time in these United States to bring about a change like this. We have had but one Revolution in our history and it left untouched the underlying system of local government. It is only in the last 50 years that professional planners and political scientists discovered that there was a metropolitan problem. It is only in the last decade that there has been anything like general interest in the subject even among the elite. It may well be another twenty years before genuine reform measures are widely adopted. But anyone who writes off sound metropolitan government as an impossibility because the somewhat stepped-up publicity triggered by Toronto experience has been seemingly without result is lacking in historical perspective.

INSTRUMENT OF FREEDOM
Brooks Hays

Brooks Hays, a member of the Tennessee Valley Authority's board of directors, was a member of the U.S. House of Representatives from Arkansas for eight terms. In Congress, he served on the Banking and Currency and the Foreign Affairs Committees and was also a member of the President's Commission on Intergovernmental Relations.

There is no more puzzling and controversial section of our constitution than the clause in its preamble dealing with promoting "the general welfare." Even though it is puzzling and contentious, this provision has paradoxically been one of the most useful in enabling our governmental system to adapt to the changing needs of the times.

That which the federal government should do in the interests of "the general welfare"—the apportionment, that is, of powers and responsibilities between the state and local units and the federal government—is a decision which each generation of Americans has made for itself. Some decisions have been made out of necessity, some out of expediency. Some have been wise, others questionable. Some we would agree with today, others we would dispute. But the fact that these decisions were made, and had to be made, is evidence of the need to adapt to changing conditions.

What governments should or should not do for the general welfare cannot

From *National Civic Review,* January 1961. Reprinted by permission.

be decided once and set for all time. The guidance even of our constitutional forefathers is valid only for the times in which they lived. We can offer them our gratitude, however, for not placing us in a constitutional strait jacket; for giving us, in fact, the flexibility of government to enable us to adapt as the need requires. Much of this flexibility is in the general welfare clause.

Change is forced upon us not so much by the will of man as by the course of history. It is not the abstract thought of the political theoretician that persuades us to mold our institutions but the facts of our times, the problems we confront, and the need to meet them head on. When wise men saw that private toll roads and ferries were no longer adequate for the growing volume of our national commerce, they offered as a solution a national system of highways, bridges and canals. A great national debate arose over the constitutionality of these "internal improvements." Presidential candidates were elected and defeated on the issue. In the end, the right and duty of the federal government to enter this important field of national communications was sustained by the courts and by the electorate.

Scientific progress brings changes in our way of living which are reflected in our governmental processes. With the invention of steam locomotion came the railroads and the opportunity to unite our eastern and western states with rapid communication. Land grants from the federal domain helped make possible our transcontinental rail network. As railroading grew, competition between lines also grew. Freight rates became important economic factors in many sections of the country—too important, in fact, to leave entirely in private hands. Thus the Interstate Commerce Commission came into being to regulate both destructive competition and unwarranted freight charges.

With the coming of electricity another new industry was born toward which the people soon developed a great common concern. Inherently monopolistic in nature, this industry was left to the states to regulate in the federal interest. State regulation failed in the late 1920's and early 1930's and the federal government stepped in to promote the general welfare with the Public Utility Holding Company Act and other measures. The Tennessee Valley Authority was created to provide, among other things, a demonstration of how an electric power system can be operated efficiently and profitably in the public interest.

Resource development similarly became an important part of the general welfare. Great interstate rivers overflowed their banks creating flood disasters of national proportions and requiring national remedies. As electricity became more significant in the economy, great natural hydro-electric power sites remained undeveloped. Engineering science made available the multipurpose dam with which floods could be controlled, power generated, rivers made navigable and thousands of acres irrigated. The very size of the task of mastering these great streams made it obvious that the national government had to take a strong hand in development.

National and world events have forced changes in our concept of the role of government in relation to "the general welfare." The great depression convinced all America that the federal government can never again stand idly by while business cycles make people jobless and hungry. Federal action to counteract both inflation and deflation is now accepted national policy, regardless of party politics.

The current trend of world events offers prospects of federal action beyond our imagination: atomic research with its infinite potential; rockets and satellites bring us to the horizon of space travel and revolutionary new communications methods. The importance of these sciences to national defense is so critical and urgent, and their cost so titanic, that only the federal government can undertake them. So we have a whole new realm of federal responsibility destined to radiate into every corner of our lives and penetrate our society to an extent we cannot foretell.

The prospect leads to the question every one of us is asking: Is this trend to federal power inexorable? Are we facing the demise of strong state and local governments? Or is there a way we can adapt our institutions so that the strong federal power so necessary to our national existence can be employed to make stronger state and local governments? I am convinced there is such a way. My formula has two parts:

1. Federal programs of the present and of the future must be so organized and so established as to assure a large measure of local participation.

I base this tenet on the conviction that decisions affecting primarily local interests should be made primarily by local people through the governmental institutions responsible to them at the local level.

It is often said that the federal government should do only what the states cannot do. I think this is a tale which falls by its own oversimplicity. For example, the federal government has not only an interest but also a responsibility for getting done jobs that states can do but won't. The efforts made by the individual states are often uneven in matters such as housing for example, or highways or health or education. Some states make great efforts, others exert the bare minimum. Federal action becomes necessary because state and local governments either fail or refuse to act.

There are also instances in which state action is less preferable than federal action because it would be actually harmful to other states. This can be true in the regulation of the river. A single state may set out to develop the stream to its own advantage but in so doing it may deny to other states the water and water rights to which they are entitled and which they need. The kind of controversy and bitterness which can result from such situations is all too well known. Yet the federal government can develop an entire watershed to serve many needs in the total region.

2. The second half of my formula for preserving a balanced federal-state-local framework holds that state and local governments must be equipped, organized and staffed to take decisive action in solving the problems of their

people. Another one of those rules which we too often accept without thinking is that "the least government is the best government." It is as simple as a fairy tale and has about as much validity. Failure to govern, or refusal to govern, is the closest thing to anarchy; and anarchy cannot be tolerated.

One of the facts we must face, though our wishes may be to the contrary, is that our society is a complex one and our interrelationships are extremely close. The interests of the farm are linked with those of the city, labor with business, national defense with civil rights, and resource development with housing and education, with wages and profits. Where the federal government refrains from action, state and local governments cannot refuse or neglect to assert their authority. They must be perceptive of the problems about them. They must be active and intelligent, fair and impartial, and above all imbued with a sense of the public interest. The initiative they show will have much to do with the ultimate answer to the question of the balanced growth of state and federal power.

I am confident this formula will work because I have seen it work in the Tennessee Valley. Let me quote from a speech by Barrett Shelton, editor of the *Decatur Daily* of Decatur, Alabama. Mr. Shelton has lived the life of the Tennessee Valley since before TVA. He saw the erosion of the soil and felt its consequences in his business and in the welfare of his community. He, with his neighbors, experienced the despair of what seemed to be a hopeless future; and the arrival of TVA seemed to them the coming of the alien force of federalism to reshape their lives whether they liked it or not. Said Mr. Shelton:

> Into this dismal, perplexed economic setting one late midwinter afternoon came David Lilienthal, then a member of the Board of Directors of the Tennessee Valley Authority. Four of our citizens, who had long been hopeful of improving conditions generally, met him in conference. We were almost frankly hostile for he represented to us another way of thought and another way of life. And our conversation might be summarized in this fashion, "All right, you're here. You were not invited, but you're here. You are in command, now what are you going to do?"
>
> Dave leaned his chair back against the wall and the twinkle of a smile came into his eyes, as he said gently and firmly, "I'm not going to do anything. You're going to do it."
>
> He went on to tell us something we never knew before. He went on to say that TVA would provide the tools of opportunity—flood control, malaria control, navigation on the river, low-cost power, test-demonstration farming to show how our soils could be returned to fertility, a fertility lost through land erosion, another wayward child of a one-crop system. He told us the river would no longer defeat man but would become the servant of man. "What you do with these tools," he said, "is up to you."
>
> Dave Lilienthal had passed the task right back to us, right back to local control. He let us know that simple economics could be applied in the Tennessee Valley and that the faith, determination and sweat of the people would bring about the result we had eagerly sought for so many years.

Mr. Shelton went on to relate that this counsel from an administrative head of this great new federal agency actually was the signal to the local people to roll up their sleeves and get to work. They undertook to create new farm processing plants. They persuaded the local ice company to put in a packing plant. They pooled local capital in order to establish a milk processing center. The object was to create a steady payroll for both the community and the farmers. Soon the Tennessee River became navigable to Decatur's doorstep and flour millers began importing midwest grain for distribution in the south. A cooperative established a fertilizer mixing plant. Soon this organization saw the possibility of selling seed commercially and put in a seed cleaning plant. An alfalfa drying plant was set up.

This was a small beginning for Decatur, Alabama, but it was like the beginning of a giant snowball. Decatur today is a prosperous, growing community. It is a service center for the surrounding agricultural area and its waterfront on the Tennessee River now includes industrial plants from among the "who's who" of American industry.

The story of Decatur is an example of the result of the operation of the TVA formula—resource development brought to successful fruition through local initiative.

In 1933 TVA was given the huge synthetic nitrate facilities built by the government at Muscle Shoals, Alabama, during the First World War. It was told by Congress to use these facilities in the interests of agriculture, principally for the production of chemical fertilizer. TVA might have set up an entirely federal organization to do this work. Instead, it enlisted the cooperation of the state agricultural colleges. Their experiment stations through the years have been the chief testing grounds for the new experimental fertilizers turned out by TVA scientists. The college extension services have been the principal media for adult education among the farmers in the modern use of improved fertilizers. Decisions as to the best cropping practices to be encouraged in the interests of the state economy thus are local decisions, not federal, made by state employees and state officials acting in the state interests.

This form of cooperation—TVA and the agricultural colleges—extends into two thirds of the states, and the methods and the results are similar. The colleges are stronger. They serve the people better.

The TVA power program also is a cooperative venture with local interests. TVA is the producer and wholesaler of electricity. Retail distribution is performed by local distribution systems owned by the cities in urban areas and by farmer cooperatives in the rural areas. These distribution systems are locally managed and financed independently of TVA. The tremendous growth in the use of electricity in the valley is due in large part to the vigorous initiative of these local institutions.

The private sector of the Valley's economy has been similarly strengthened by the investment of public funds in TVA facilities and without damage—

indeed, with positive benefit—to other regions. Federal funds invested in New York harbor increase the business volume of that port but do not detract from the commerce of New Orleans or San Francisco. Federal funds invested in the Columbia River basin development provide greater opportunity for industry in the Pacific northwest but do not detract from the potential of California or Pennsylvania.

Just so, funds invested in the natural resources of the Tennessee Valley have provided new opportunities for commercial and industrial growth in the Tennessee Valley without taking away from any other section of the country. For example, over $800 million have been invested in new or expanded industrial plants along the Tennessee waterway since 1933. This is private enterprise using new "tools of opportunity"—flood-free sites, water transportation, precious water itself for processing, as well as low-cost electricity.

These are not acts of industry piracy of which TVA has been so often accused. Nor are they even a luring of industry. The industrial development of the Tennessee Valley has been the natural result of industries using resources to the best advantage for themselves, their consumers and the nation. The federal government provided the tools. State and local governments and private interests have made the basic decisions as to how the tools should be used.

The other half of this picture—this struggle to maintain state and local institutions in their rightful place in our governmental structure—is the necessity on the part of state and local governments to organize themselves and staff themselves so they can take over responsibilities that belong to them.

Now this is not an automatic process. It means attracting trained and perceptive people into state and municipal governments. To attract them, you will have to pay them well. You will have to give them assurance that politics and the spoils system will not endanger their working security and that of their staff; they will have to have some assurance that acts of political expediency will not undermine the results of their labors. You will have to support their decisions and recommendations against the frustrating attrition of special interests.

Vigorous state and local governments require the existence of an administrative organization within governments able to anticipate problems, analyze them and make the necessary decisions. Planning bodies, therefore, are an integral part of the decision-making process at both the state and local level.

The task of government today is not to oppose federalization. Nor is it its task to aggrandize state's rights. Neither is it to compromise principles of democratic government. This is no time for a doctrinaire approach by which we denominate all federal action as bad and all state and local action—or even inaction—as good.

We must face facts. We must look honestly at our problems. If we do, we will recognize the tremendous events taking place in the world which affect us personally and locally and yet demand our national attention. We will recognize that people can be inventive in their governmental operations. They can rise above special interest and adapt their governmental machinery to new conditions. State and local governments can be honorable and capable and responsible to the electorate and at the same time work closely and effectively with the federal government to accomplish their goals and solve their problems.

Democratic government is the instrument of freedom. Freedom encourages thought and invention and everlasting change in our society. Democratic government must keep pace with the change that democracy itself makes possible. Ingenuity is as important in government as in science or business or farming. We have seen a merging of federal and state efforts in the Tennessee Valley with results that have surpassed our hopes. I am convinced it is a pattern which can be adapted to other valleys, to other regions and to many current problems of government.